Term	Symbol	Abbreviation	Term	Symbol	Abbreviation
Effective power	W		Collector-to-ground voltage	V_C	
Input power	P_i		Collector-to-base voltage	V_{CB}	
Output power	P_o		Collector supply voltage	V_{CC}	
Reactive power	VAR	var	Collector-to-emitter voltage	V_{CE}	
Power factor		PF	Emitter-to-ground voltage	V_E	
Push-pull		pp	Emitter supply voltage	V_{EE}	
Quality	Q		Tuned radio frequency		trf
Radius	R, r	rad	Turns ratio		TR
Reactance	X		Vacuum tube		VT
Capacitive reactance	X_C		Plate	P	
Inductive reactance	X_L		Plate current	I_p	
Resistance	R		Plate resistance	R_p	
Root mean square		rms	Plate voltage	E_p	
Revolutions per minute		rpm	Screen current	I_s	
Second	T	s	Volt	E	V
Microsecond		μs	Kilovolt		kV
Sigma	Σ		Millivolt		mV
Sine		sin	Microvolt		μV
Specific resistance	K		Voltage	E	
Tangent		tan	Average value	E_{av}	
Television		TV	Effective value	E	
Time	T		Instantaneous value	e	
Transistor	Q		Maximum value	E_{max}	
Dc base current	I_B		Volt-ampere	VA	VA
Dc collector current	I_C		Kilovolt-ampere	KVA	kVA
Dc emitter current	I_E		Voltage ratio	VR	
Alpha—the ratio of ΔI_C to ΔI_E	α		Watt (unit of electrical power)	P	W
Beta—the ratio of ΔI_C to ΔI_B	β		Kilowatt		kW
Base bias resistor	R_B		Kilowatthour		kWh
Collector-to-base resistance	R_{CB}		Milliwatt		mW
Resistance in the collector leg; the load resistor	R_L		Microwatt		μW
Base-to-ground voltage	V_B		Watthour		Wh
Base supply voltage	V_{BB}		Wavelength	λ	
Base-to-emitter voltage drop	V_{BE}				

BASIC MATHEMATICS FOR ELECTRICITY AND ELECTRONICS

BASIC MATHEMATICS
FOR ELECTRICITY
AND ELECTRONICS

BERTRAND B. SINGER
Samuel Gompers Vocational
and Technical High School

THIRD EDITION

McGraw-Hill Book Company
New York   St. Louis   San Francisco
Düsseldorf   Johannesburg   Kuala Lumpur
London   Mexico   Montreal
New Delhi   Panama   Rio de Janeiro
Singapore   Sydney   Toronto

This book was set in Garamond by Black Dot, Inc., printed by The Murray Printing Company, and bound by The Book Press Company. The designer was Edward Zytko; the drawings were done by John Cordes, J. & R. Technical Services, Inc. The editors were Bob Flowers and Cynthia Newby. Robert R. Laffler supervised production.

**BASIC MATHEMATICS
FOR ELECTRICITY
AND ELECTRONICS**

Library of Congress Catalog Card Number 77-170866

07-057467-7

7 8 9 0 MUBP 7 9 8 7 6

CONTENTS

8

KIRCHHOFF'S LAWS   274

9

APPLICATIONS OF SERIES AND PARALLEL CIRCUITS   330

10

EFFICIENCY   389

11

ELECTRICAL ENERGY   407

12

RESISTANCE OF WIRE   414

13

SIZE OF WIRING   445

14

TRIGONOMETRY FOR ALTERNATING-CURRENT ELECTRICITY   457

15

INTRODUCTION TO AC ELECTRICITY   476

20

ALTERNATING-CURRENT POWER   649

PREFACE

The success of the first and second editions of this book has been credited to the presentation of the principles of mathematics as the direct result of a need encountered in the development of the electrical theory. This objective has been emphasized to an even greater degree in this third edition.

As before, very little is taken for granted. Whenever a new mathematical operation is needed—no matter how simple—a checkup and brushup on the operation is provided. Each checkup is a mathematical diagnostic test and motivation for the following job. The problems are electrical in nature but can be solved purely on the basis of the mathematical principle involved without any knowledge of the electrical theory to follow. Each brushup reviews the mathematical concepts immediately necessary for the continuance of the electrical development and application. For example, Jobs 2-6 and 2-7 (Checkup and Brushup on Formulas) immediately precede the algebraic manipulation of the Ohm's law formula to find the current or resistance.

The theory is developed in slow, simple stages and is directly and immediately applied to the solution of actual practical problems in electrical installation and electronic equipment servicing. The number and scope of these problems have been increased for each job.

Each new concept, electrical or mathematical, is developed from fundamental principles and then applied to a variety of situations. This is accomplished by breaking each chapter down into a set of short "jobs" that concentrate on a small portion of the large concept involved in the chapter. Each job develops either a new mathematical operation or a new electrical concept and is illustrated by a series of examples that increase in both arithmetical difficulty and electrical scope. The many users of this book have indicated that this illustration method makes the book particularly suitable for individuals in the trade as well as for students in basic courses in electricity and electronics.

The illustration method has been further enhanced by programming the last example of each job and the summaries and reviews. These self-test examples serve as a final check on the student's understanding, forcing him to stop, think, and check *each* step of the problem, thus reenforcing the concepts learned in the previous illustrations. A tremendous advantage of these self-tests is that the student has a chance to reach his own conclusions *before* he gets the answer. Each self-test becomes a diagnostic test to pinpoint the precise error in the student's thinking before he tackles the problems of the job.

The problems in each job are very carefully graded, starting with simple whole numbers through fractions and decimals to provide answers that are first whole numbers, then fractions, and finally decimals. Answers to the odd-numbered problems are provided to augment the self-help features of the book. Continued review and drill in both mathematical and electrical concepts are obtained by extending the electrical theory and application.

In response to many requests, the following jobs have been added to enhance the practical value of this edition and to serve as an enrichment of the basic course. (1) Powers of Ten, (2) The Potentiometer Rule, (3) Equivalent Delta and Star Circuits, (4) Thevenin's Theorem, (5) Transistor Circuits and their Dc Equivalent Circuits, (6) Attenuator Circuits, and (7) Series-parallel Ac Circuits. Also, many out-dated vacuum-tube circuits have been removed and replaced with modern transistor circuits.

Diagrams (many in color) are still used extensively, with particular attention being paid to the process of changing the words of a problem into a simple sketch, properly labeled with all the information given and to be found. A programmed summary and set of review problems as well as many tests are included in each chapter. The review jobs attempt to attack the problems in the chapter from a slightly different point of view to round up any loose ends in the student's mind. Modern standards as recommended by the Institute of Electrical and Electronics Engineers have been used throughout this book.

The author wishes to thank Mr. Stanley Egelberg and Mr. Harold Tofallos of the electronics staff of the Samuel Gompers Technical High School for their many constructive criticisms and contributions. He also wishes to acknowledge his indebtedness to the many users of this book for their valuable suggestions for this revision.

BERTRAND B. SINGER

BASIC MATHEMATICS FOR ELECTRICITY AND ELECTRONICS

1

INTRODUCTION TO ELECTRICITY

JOB 1-1 BASIC THEORY OF ELECTRICITY

We shall start our study of electricity with an examination of the materials from which electrical energy is produced.

Elements. Science has discovered more than 100 different kinds of material called elements. These cannot be made from other materials and cannot be broken up to form other materials by ordinary methods. Gold, iron, copper, oxygen, and carbon are some examples of elements.

Atoms. An atom is the smallest amount of an element which has all the properties of the element. An atom may be broken down into smaller pieces, but these pieces have none of the properties of the element. It is now believed that all material is electrical in nature. All matter is made of combinations of elements, which, in turn, are made of atoms. The atoms themselves are merely combinations of different kinds of electrical energy. The theory presently accepted is that an atom, because it is electrically neutral, is made of positive charges of electricity called *protons* and an equal number of negative charges called *electrons*. There are also a number of electrically neutral particles called *neutrons*. Similarly charged particles will repel each other, while particles of opposite charge will attract each other. For example, two electrons will repel each other, and two protons will repel each other, but an electron will be attracted to a proton as shown in Fig. 1-1.

Structure of the atom. An atom is believed to resemble our solar

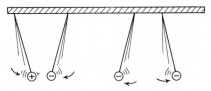

FIGURE 1-1
Opposite charges attract; like charges repel each other.

1

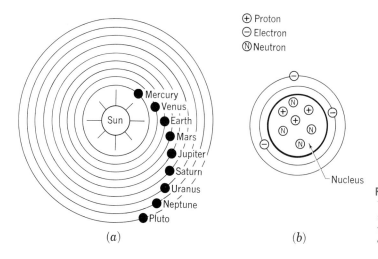

⊕ Proton
⊖ Electron
Ⓝ Neutron

(a)

(b)

Nucleus

FIGURE 1-2

The resemblance between the solar system (a) and the theoretical diagram of an atom of lithium (b).

system with the sun at the center and the planets revolving around it, as shown in Fig. 1-2a. An atom consists of electrons revolving around a nucleus, which contains the protons and neutrons, as shown in Fig. 1-2b. The number of revolving, or *planetary,* electrons is equal to the number of positively charged protons in the nucleus.

Free electrons. The electrons farthest from the nucleus are called *free electrons* because they are bound very loosely to the nucleus. The word "electricity" comes from *elektron,* the Greek word for amber. Thales, a Greek philosopher, observed that if amber was rubbed, it would attract small objects. You can observe the same effect by running a hard-rubber comb through your hair or by rubbing the comb on your coat sleeve. The comb will then attract small pieces of paper. As the comb is rubbed on the sleeve, some of the free electrons are rubbed off the cloth and deposited on the comb. The comb is now considered to be *negatively charged* because it has accumulated an *excess* of electrons. On the other hand, the coat sleeve is *positively charged* because of the *shortage* of electrons. A small bit of paper will now be attracted and held by the charged comb. A similar transfer of electrons occurs if you shuffle your feet over a rug on a dry day. Electrons are rubbed off the rug and are accumulated on your body. Touching a metal doorknob or some other conductor will produce a slight shock as the electrons *flow* through your body to the ground.

Electron flow. Notice that no shock will be experienced while the body is accumulating the electrons. The shock will occur only when the electrons *flow* through your body in one concerted surge. This directed flow, or movement, of the electrons is one of the most important ideas in electricity. In order to understand this better, let us compare the particles of matter with a brick wall, as in Fig. 1-3. A brick in a wall is like an atom, since it is the smallest part of the wall that has the characteristics

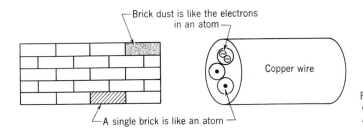

Brick dust is like the electrons in an atom

Copper wire

A single brick is like an atom

FIGURE 1-3
Comparison of brick dust with electrons.

of the wall. If an individual brick were to be powdered into dust, we could compare a single grain of dust with an electron. The grains of brick cannot do any useful work by themselves, but if a powerful pressure like a blast of compressed air were allowed to hit the particles as would occur in a sandblasting machine, then enormous energies would be available.

We can also consider the drops of water in a stream to be like the electrons in a piece of matter. If the drops of water move aimlessly, as in a water sprinkler, then their energy is small. But if all the drops are forced to move in the *same direction,* as in a high-pressure fire hose, then their energy is large. We can see, then, that if electrons are to do useful work, they most be *moving under pressure,* as do the grains of sand or drops of water.

Electrical pressure: voltage. In order to move the drops of water or the grains of sand, a mechanical pressure supplied by a water pump or an air compressor is required. Similarly, an electron pressure is required to move the electrons along a wire. This electrical pressure is called the *voltage* and is measured in units of *volts* (V). This unit of measurement was named after Count Alessandro Volta, an Italian physicist (1745–1827).

Producing electrical pressures. A working pressure is considered to exist when there is a *difference* in energies. Water in a high tank will exert a pressure because of the *difference* in the height of the water levels, as shown in Fig. 1-4. Elements differ not only in the number of elec-

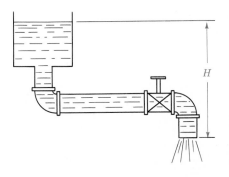

H

FIGURE 1-4
The difference in height between the water levels causes pressure.

trons that make up their individual "solar systems" but also in the energies of their electrons. Therefore, if two different materials are brought together under suitable conditions, there will be a *difference* of electron energies. This difference produces the electrical pressure that we call the voltage.

Different combinations of materials will produce different voltages. A dry cell of carbon and zinc produces 1.5 V, a lead and sulfuric acid cell produces 2.1 V, and an Edison storage cell of nickel and iron produces 1.2 V. These combinations are called *batteries*. A voltage pressure may be produced in several other ways, which we shall learn about later. For example, the 110 to 120 V supplied by an ordinary house outlet is produced by a machine called a generator. An automobile spark coil delivers about 1,500 V. The purpose of all voltages, however produced, is to provide a force to *move* the electrons. It is appropriately termed an electron-moving, or *electromotive, force,* which is abbreviated as emf. Very often the simple symbol E is used to indicate voltage.

Quantity of electricity. The amount of electricity represented by a single electron is very small—much too small to be used as a measure of quantity in practical electrical work. The electron has already been compared with a drop of water. It is obviously ridiculous to measure quantities of water by the number of drops. Instead, we use quantities like a gallon or a quart, each of which represents a certain number of drops. Similarly, the practical unit of electrical quantity represents a certain number of electrons and is called a *coulomb*. This unit was named after C. A. Coulomb, a French physicist (1736–1806). The coulomb is equal to about 6 billion billion electrons (6,000,000,000,000,-000,000). The symbol for the coulomb is Q, since it represents a definite quantity of electrons.

Current. When a voltage is applied across the ends of a conductor, the electrons, which up to now have been moving in many different directions (Fig. 1-5a), are forced to move in the *same direction* along the wire (Fig. 1-5b). Individual electrons all along the path are forced to leave the atoms to which they are attached. They travel only a short distance until they find an atom that needs an electron. This motion is transmitted along the path from atom to atom, as motion in a whip is transmitted from one end to the other. This *flow* of electrons is called an *electric current* (Fig. 1-6). The speed of this flow is very nearly equal to the speed of light, which is about 186,000 miles per second (mi/s). The actual

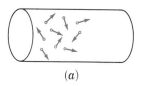

(a)

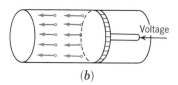

(b)

FIGURE 1-5

(a) The electrons in the wire move in many different directions. (b) When a voltage pushes the electrons, they all move in the same direction and make an electric current.

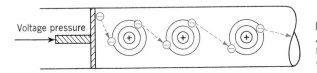

FIGURE 1-6

An electric current is produced by billions of electrons *moving* through a wire.

speed of the individual electrons is much slower, but the effect of a pressure at one end of a wire is felt almost instantaneously at the other end.

The flow of water is measured as the number of gallons per minute, barrels per hour, etc. Similarly, the flow of electricity is measured by the number of electrons that pass a point in a wire in 1 s. We do not have special names for the flow of water, but we do have a special name for the flow of electrons. This name is *ampere* (A) of current. A current of 1 A represents a flow of 1 coulomb of electricity (6 billion billion electrons) past a point in a wire in 1 s.

The symbol for current is I. The ampere was named after André Marie Ampère, a French physicist and chemist (1775–1836). Since an electron is so small (about 25 trillion to an inch) and since there are so many of them, it is impossible actually to count them as they go by. However, when electrons are moving as an electric current, they can do useful work, such as lighting lamps, running motors, producing heat, and plating metals. We can make use of this last ability of an electric current to measure and define it accurately. An international commission has thus defined an ampere as the number of electrons that can deposit a definite amount of silver [0.001118 gram (g)] from a silver solution in 1 s. A 100-W 110-V lamp uses about 1 A. A 600-W 110-V electric iron uses about 5.5 A, and the current required by a radio or television tube may be as low as 0.001 A.

Resistance. We have learned that "free" electrons may be forced to move from atom to atom when a voltage pressure is applied. Different materials vary in their number of free electrons and in the ease with which electrons may be transferred between atoms. A *conductor* (Fig. 1-7a) is a material through which electrons may travel freely. Most metals are good conductors. An *insulator* (Fig. 1-7b) is a material that

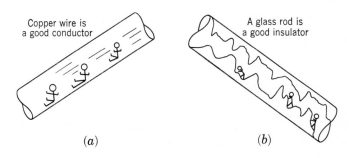

Copper wire is a good conductor

A glass rod is a good insulator

(a)   *(b)*

FIGURE 1-7

(*a*) Electrons travel freely through conductors. (*b*) Insulators prevent electrons from flowing freely.

prevents the electrons from traveling through it easily. Nonmetallic materials like glass, mica, porcelain, rubber, and textiles are good insulators. No material is a perfect insulator or a perfect conductor.

The ability of a material to resist the flow of electrons is called its *resistance* and is measured in units called *ohms* (Ω). This unit of measurement was named after Georg Simon Ohm, a German physicist (1787–1854). The symbol for resistance is R. An international agreement defines the ohm as the resistance offered by a column of mercury of uniform cross section, 106.3 cm long (about 41.8 in), and weighing 14.45 g (about ½ oz). For example, 1,000 ft of No. 10 copper wire has a resistance of almost exactly 1 Ω, the resistance of a 40-W electric light is 300 Ω when hot, and a 150-V voltmeter has a resistance of 15,000 Ω.

There are many electrical devices which make use of the fact that materials offer resistance to the flow of an electric current. Soldering irons, electric heaters, and electric-light bulbs contain conductors which have a high resistance compared with the resistance of the connecting wires. Radio and television circuits contain many resistance elements, called *resistors*. They are not always made of special resistance wire. Carbon and mixtures of carbon and insulating materials are molded to form resistors.

JOB 1-2   ELECTRICAL MEASUREMENTS AND CIRCUITS

The voltage, current, and resistance of an electtical circuit are measured with special instruments. An *ammeter* measures the current I in units of amperes. A *voltmeter* measures the voltage E in units of volts. An *ohmmeter* measures the resistance R in units of ohms.

How to use the ammeter. In order to measure the flow of water in a pipe, a flowmeter is inserted into the pipe, as shown in Fig. 1-8*a*. The pump supplies the pressure to force the water through the pipe and flowmeter against the resistance of the faucet valve. Since all the water in the system must flow through the flowmeter, it must indicate the number of gallons per minute that flow through the pipe. In the same way, in order to measure the flow of current in a wire, an ammeter must be

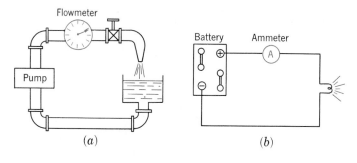

(a)   (b)

FIGURE 1-8
(a) A flowmeter is inserted in the line of flow of the water.
(b) An ammeter is inserted in the line of flow of the electrons.

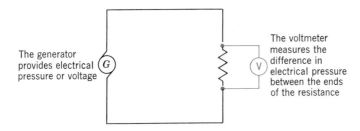

The generator provides electrical pressure or voltage

The voltmeter measures the difference in electrical pressure between the ends of the resistance

FIGURE 1-9

A voltmeter is always connected across the ends of a part when the voltage across it is being measured.

inserted *directly into the circuit* so that all the electrons will be forced through it. The ammeter has a very low resistance and thus does not stop the flow of current. When large currents are measured, certain adjustments must be made in order to prevent the ammeter from burning out (Job 9-6). In Fig. 1-8*b*, the battery supplies the electrical pressure that forces the electrons through the lamp against the resistance of the lamp. Since all the electrons in the circuit must pass through the ammeter, it will indicate the number of electrons per second, or amperes, passing through it.

How to use the voltmeter. As we have already learned, the amount of water that will flow in a pipe depends on the *difference* in the pressure between any two points. In the same way, the electric current that will flow through a resistance depends on the *difference* in electrical pressure (voltage) between the two ends, or terminals, of the resistance. In order to measure this difference, a voltmeter must be connected across the ends of the resistance, as in Fig. 1-9. Note that the current that flows through the resistance does *not* flow through the voltmeter. Since a voltmeter is designed to measure the electrical pressure, it should be placed in the circuit so that the pressure across the resistance is also across the voltmeter. An ammeter, on the other hand, is inserted *into* the circuit and receives the full current of the circuit. A voltmeter is merely attached to the ends of the part across which the voltage is to be measured.

How to use the ohmmeter. An ohmmeter is really an ammeter whose dial has been marked to read the resistance in ohms instead of the current in amperes according to a very simple relationship called *Ohm's law*, which we shall study soon. An ohmmeter will measure the resistance of the individual parts of a circuit by connecting the leads of the instrument across the ends of the part, as is done with a voltmeter.

Electrical circuits. A *circuit* is simply a *complete* path along which the electrons can move. A complete circuit must have an *unbroken* path, as shown in Fig. 1-10*a*, with the source of energy acting as an electron pump to force the electrons through the conductor (usually a copper wire) against the resistance of the device to be operated. When the switch is opened as in Fig. 1-10*b*, the electrons cannot leave one side of the switch

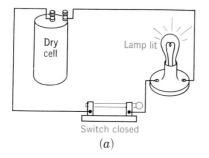 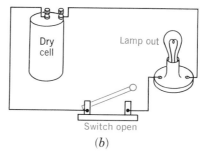

FIGURE 1-10

(a) With the switch closed, current flows through this complete circuit. (b) With the switch open, no current flows through this broken or open circuit.

to enter the other side and so return to their source because of the very high resistance of the air gap. This is an *open circuit,* and no current will flow.

Fuses. One of the effects of the passage of an electric current is the production of heat. The larger the current, the more heat produced. In order to prevent large currents from accidentally flowing through our expensive apparatus and burning it up, a device called a *fuse* is placed directly into the circuit, as in Fig. 1-11, so as to form a part of the circuit through which all the electrons must flow. To protect a circuit, a fuse must be a device which will *open* the circuit whenever a dangerously large current starts to flow. Accordingly, a fuse conpletes a circuit with a piece of special metal designed to melt quickly when heated excessively, as would occur when a large current flows. The fuse will permit currents smaller than the fuse value to flow but will melt and therefore break the circuit if a larger, dangerous current ever appears. A dangerously large current will flow, for instance, when a "short circuit" occurs. A short circuit is usually caused by an accidental connection between two points in a circuit which offer very little resistance to the flow of the electrons. If the resistance is small, there will be nothing to stop the flow of the electrons and the current will increase enormously. The resulting heat generated might cause a fire. However, if the circuit is protected by a fuse, the heat caused by the short-circuit current will melt the fuse wire, thus breaking the circuit and reducing the current to zero.

Fuse ratings. Fuses are rated by the number of amperes of current

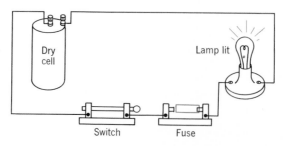

FIGURE 1-11

A fuse completes an electrical circuit and protects it against the flow of dangerously large currents.

that can flow through them before they melt and break the circuit. Thus we have 10-, 15-, 30-A, etc., fuses. We must be careful that any fuse inserted in a circuit be rated low enough to melt, or "blow," before the apparatus is damaged. For example, in a house wired to carry a current of 15 A it is best to use a fuse no larger than 15 A so that a current larger than 15 A could never flow.

Delayed fuses. In ordinary house wiring, a 15-A fuse is used to protect the line wires from overheating and producing a fire hazard. However, if a current larger than 15 A were to flow for only a few seconds, it would not harm the wires. There are many times when a wire must carry a current larger than it was designed to carry—but only for a short time. For example, a normal 5 A may be flowing in a line. If the motor of a washing machine is suddenly turned on, the current drawn may go up to 35 A for a few seconds but then drop to a normal 10 A after the motor is running. The ordinary fuse would blow, since the current is larger than the rated 15 A. However, since there is no danger, as the current drops again very quickly, we would like a fuse that could carry larger currents for a short time. This type of fuse is called a *time-delay* fuse. It is designed to carry about twice its rated current for 20 to 30 s but to blow if the rated current is exceeded for 1 min. The net effect is that the fuse will hold for *temporary* overloads but will blow on continuous, small overloads or short circuits.

Symbols. Most of our diagrams up to this point have used pictures of the various electrical devices. However, everybody cannot draw pictures quickly and accurately, and so we shall substitute special simple diagrams to illustrate the various parts of any circuit. Each circuit element is represented by a simple diagram called the *symbol* for the part. The standard symbols for the commonly used electrical and electronic components are given in Fig. 1-12.

Circuit diagrams. Every electrical circuit must contain the following:

1 A source of electrical pressure or voltage E, measured in volts.
2 An unbroken conductor through which the electrons may flow easily. The amount of electron flow per unit of time is the current I, measured in amperes.
3 A load, or resistance R to this flow of current, measured in ohms.

EXAMPLE 1-1 Draw a circuit containing two battery cells, an ammeter, a fuse, a single-pole switch, a resistor, and a lamp. Label each part, using E for voltage, R for resistance, and I for current.

SOLUTION
See Fig. 1-13.

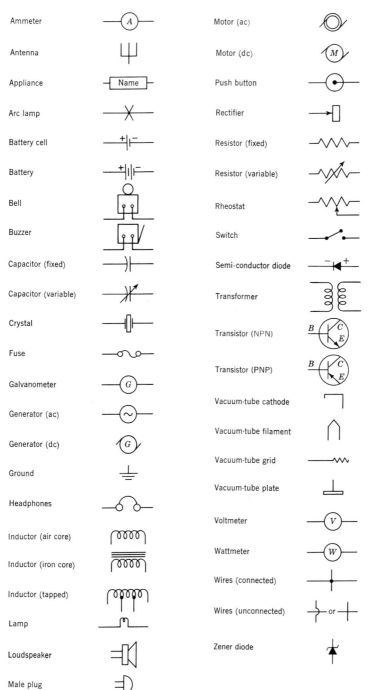

Ammeter

Antenna

Appliance

Arc lamp

Battery cell

Battery

Bell

Buzzer

Capacitor (fixed)

Capacitor (variable)

Crystal

Fuse

Galvanometer

Generator (ac)

Generator (dc)

Ground

Headphones

Inductor (air core)

Inductor (iron core)

Inductor (tapped)

Lamp

Loudspeaker

Male plug

Motor (ac)

Motor (dc)

Push button

Rectifier

Resistor (fixed)

Resistor (variable)

Rheostat

Switch

Semi-conductor diode

Transformer

Transistor (NPN)

Transistor (PNP)

Vacuum-tube cathode

Vacuum-tube filament

Vacuum-tube grid

Vacuum-tube plate

Voltmeter

Wattmeter

Wires (connected)

Wires (unconnected)

Zener diode

FIGURE 1-12
Standard circuit symbols.

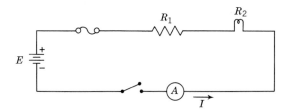

FIGURE 1-13

Note: The numbers 1 and 2 under the letter R are a convenient way to indicate the first resistance R_1 and the second resistance R_2.

PROBLEMS

Using the circuit symbols shown in Fig. 1-12, draw a circuit for each problem to include the elements indicated. Label the diagram completely, using the subscripts 1, 2, 3, etc., to indicate the parts of the circuit.

1. A battery of two cells, a fuse, and two resistors.
2. An ac generator, a switch, an ammeter, a bell, and a buzzer.
3. A battery, a switch, an ammeter, two resistors, and a lamp with a voltmeter across it.
4. A battery, a switch, and four vacuum-tube filaments.
5. A dc generator, a switch, a rheostat, and a dc motor.
6. A dc generator, a switch, a fuse, an arc lamp, and a resistor.
7. A male plug, an electric iron, a rheostat, and a switch.
8. A male plug, four vacuum-tube filaments, a switch, and a resistor.
9. Complete the circuit shown in Fig. 1-14 with a PNP transistor using a one-cell battery in the base circuit and a two-cell battery in the collector circuit. Label the ammeters with the proper current symbols. (See list of symbols and abbreviations.)

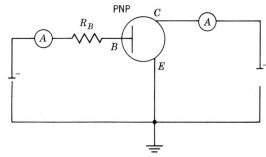

FIGURE 1-14
A common-emitter transistor circuit.

SELF-HELP FEATURES

The summaries and the various steps in some of the illustrative problems that follow are incomplete. The correct answers will be found at the right side of the page. To achieve the maximum benefit from this type of instruction, please follow these instructions carefully.

1 Place the response shield over the answers at the right of the page.

2 Read the statement on the left side of the page, noting the blank space where you are to respond.

3 Write the correct response in the blank space.

4 Slide the response shield down to uncover the correct answer.

5 If you have responded correctly, continue to the next line.

6 If your response is incorrect, *stop!* Review the preceding material to discover the reason for your error.

7 When you are satisfied that you understand, draw a line through the incorrect answer and write the correct answer above it.

8 Repeat steps 2 to 5 above.

SUMMARY

1 All material is made of _____ charges.

electrical

2 Negative charges are called _____.

electrons

3 Positive charges are called _____.

protons

4 Similar charges _____ each other, and _____ charges attract each other.

repel   opposite

5 A _____ represents a quantity of 6 billion billion electrons.

coulomb

6 An *ampere* is a current of 1 ___/s. The symbol for current is ___.

coulomb I

7 Current is measured by an _____, which is always inserted directly into the circuit and reads _____.

ammeter
amperes

8 Electrons move because of the pressure of an electromotive force, or _____. The symbol for voltage is ___.

voltage E

9 Voltage is measured by a _____, which is always connected across the _____ of the circuit element and reads _____.

voltmeter
ends (or terminals)   volts

10 The resistance of a circuit is the resistance offered by the circuit to the flow of _____. The symbol for resistance is ___.

electrons R

11 Resistance is measured by an _____, which is always connected across the _____ of the circuit element and reads _____.

ohmmeter
ends (or terminals)   ohms

12 A *conductor* is a material that allows _____ to flow.

current (or electrons)

13 An _____ is a material that prevents current from flowing easily.

insulator

14 A fuse is a thin strip of easily _____ material. It protects a circuit from large currents by melting quickly and thereby _____ the circuit.

melted
breaking

SIMPLE ELECTRICAL CIRCUITS

JOB 2-1 CHECKUP ON FRACTIONS (DIAGNOSTIC TEST)

Before we go any further into our study of electrical circuits, let's stop to check up on our knowledge of the multiplication of fractions. The following are some problems often met by electricians and electronic technicians in their daily work. They are all solved by multiplying the numbers involved in the problem. If you have difficulty solving any of these problems, see Job 2-2, which follows.

PROBLEMS

1. What length of two-conductor BX cable is needed to obtain six pieces each $4\frac{1}{4}$ ft long?
2. What is the total horsepower delivered by five $\frac{3}{4}$-hp motors?
3. A voltage divider develops an emf of $\frac{1}{20}$ V for each ohm of resistance. What voltage would be measured across 1,800 Ω of resistance?
4. If the resistance of one turn of a variable wire-wound resistor is $2\frac{1}{3}$ Ω, what is the resistance of three turns?
5. What is the cost of $2\frac{1}{4}$ lb of magnet wire at 30 cents/lb?
6. An industrial shop uses $9\frac{1}{2}$ kWh of electricity per day. How many kilowatthours are used in a month of 24 working days?
7. How many hours of work were spent on an electrical installation if five men each worked $7\frac{1}{2}$ hours (h)?
8. A neon electric sign uses $4\frac{1}{2}$ W of power per foot of tubing. How many watts are used for a sign which uses 21 ft of tubing?
9. Number 9191 Fiberduct conduit adapters weigh $1\frac{1}{2}$ lb each. Find the weight of 24 such fittings.
10. How many feet of antenna wire are there in a $1\frac{1}{8}$-lb coil if the wire runs 18 ft to the pound?

11. $2\frac{1}{2} \times 3\frac{1}{5}$ 12. $\frac{2}{5} \times 20$ 13. $\frac{22}{7} \times 21$ 14. $\frac{1}{2} \times \frac{1}{3}$

13

15. $20 \times \frac{1}{1,000}$ **16.** $\frac{2}{3} \times \frac{3}{4}$ **17.** $\frac{3}{8} \times \frac{1}{4}$ **18.** $\frac{1}{10} \times 25$
19. $5\frac{1}{3} \times 8\frac{1}{2}$ **20.** $3\frac{1}{7} \times 5\frac{1}{11}$

JOB 2-2   BRUSHUP ON FRACTIONS

Meaning of a fraction. A fraction is a shorthand way of describing some part of a total amount. Figure 2-1*a* shows a whole pie. If the pie is cut into four equal pieces, as shown in Fig. 2-1*b*, then each piece is just

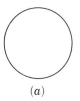  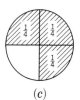 

(a)   (b)   (c)   (d)

FIGURE 2-1
Fractional parts of a pie.

one part out of the total of four parts. This is written as the *fraction* $\frac{1}{4}$ and means 1 part out of 4 equal parts. The fraction $\frac{3}{4}$, as shown by the shaded portion in Fig. 2-1*c*, says that a whole was divided into 4 equal parts and that 3 of these parts were used. The fraction $\frac{1}{8}$, as shown in Fig. 2-1*d*, says that a whole was divided into 8 equal parts and that 1 of these parts was used. It is evident that we can divide the pie into any number of equal parts. Each part will be 1 part out of the total number of parts. In Fig. 2-2*a* the pie is cut into 8 equal parts. Each part is $\frac{1}{8}$ of the pie. The shaded portion is 3 of these, or $\frac{3}{8}$ of the pie. In Fig. 2-2*b* the pie is cut into 5 equal parts. Each part is $\frac{1}{5}$ of the pie. The shaded portion is 2 of these, or $\frac{2}{5}$ of the pie. In Fig. 2-2*c* the pie is again cut into 8 equal parts. Each part is $\frac{1}{8}$ of the pie. The shaded portion is 2 of these, or $\frac{2}{8}$ of the pie. If the pie were cut into 4 equal parts, our shaded portion would then be $\frac{1}{4}$. Thus, $\frac{2}{8} = \frac{1}{4}$.

  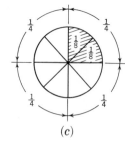

(a)   (b)   (c)   FIGURE 2-2

Simplifying fractions. We have seen that a portion of a total may be expressed in two different ways. That is, $\frac{1}{4}$ is the same as $\frac{2}{8}$. The fraction $\frac{1}{4}$ is called the *simplified,* or *reduced,* form of $\frac{2}{8}$. To simplify a fraction means to change it into another equivalent fraction. When the numerator and denominator of a fraction have no common divisor except 1, the fraction is said to be simplified, or reduced, to lowest terms.

RULE	To simplify a fraction, divide the numerator (top number) and the denominator (bottom number) by the largest number that divides evenly into both of them.

EXAMPLE 2-1   Express $^4/_{12}$ in lowest terms.

SOLUTION
Select a number that will divide evenly into both the numerator and the denominator. Try 4.

$$\frac{4 \div 4}{12 \div 4} = \frac{1}{3} \qquad Ans.$$

EXAMPLE 2-2   Express $^{24}/_{96}$ in lowest terms.

SOLUTION
We can divide both the 24 and the 96 by 24 to get $^1/_4$ in one step.

$$\frac{24 \div 24}{96 \div 24} = \frac{1}{4} \qquad Ans.$$

Or we can simplify in several steps. Dividing by 8 will give

$$\frac{24 \div 8}{96 \div 8} = \frac{3}{12}$$

and then dividing by 3 will give

$$\frac{3 \div 3}{12 \div 3} = \frac{1}{4} \qquad Ans.$$

The next example is a self-test type. Please cover the right side of the page with your response card.

SELF-TEST 2-3   The turns ratio of the step-up transformer shown in Fig. 2-3 is $\dfrac{36}{60}$. Express the ratio in lowest terms.

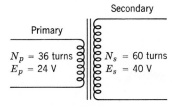

FIGURE 2-3
A step-up transformer.

SOLUTION

To simplify a fraction, we must __(multiply/divide)__ both the numerator and the denominator of the fraction by the _____ number. The numbers that will divide exactly into both 36 and 60 are 2, 3, ___, ___, and ___. Suppose that we divide the 36 and the 60 by 6. Then,

$$\frac{36 \div 6}{60 \div 6} = \frac{6}{?}$$

Now, to simplify further, divide both the 6 and the 10 by ___.

$$\frac{6 \div 2}{10 \div 2} = \frac{?}{?}$$

Can the fraction $^3/_5$ be simplified any further?   __(yes/no)__
The answer is ___.

SELF-TEST 2-4

The voltage ratio of the step-up transformer shown in Fig. 2-3 is the comparison, by division, of the primary voltage E_p to the secondary voltage E_s. By substituting the values given, we get the fraction _____. Express the fraction $\frac{24}{40}$ in lowest terms.

SOLUTION

The largest number that will divide exactly into both 24 and 40 is ___.

$$\frac{24 \div 8}{40 \div 8} = \frac{?}{?}   Ans.$$

divide
same
4   6   12
10
2
$\frac{3}{5}$
no
$^3/_5$
$\frac{24}{40}$
8
$\frac{3}{5}$

PROBLEMS

Express the following fractions in lowest terms:

1. $^4/_8$ 2. $^3/_9$ 3. $^4/_{16}$ 4. $^4/_{80}$
5. $^{12}/_{16}$ 6. $^{20}/_{32}$ 7. $^5/_{20}$ 8. $^3/_{12}$
9. $^{24}/_{72}$ 10. $^{12}/_{36}$ 11. $^{30}/_{1,000}$ 12. $^{12}/_{48}$
13. $^{24}/_{64}$ 14. $^{40}/_{100}$ 15. $^{14}/_{32}$ 16. $^{15}/_{60}$
17. $^{15}/_{45}$ 18. $^{15}/_{75}$ 19. $^{60}/_{100}$ 20. $^{42}/_{72}$

21.   The ratio of the diameter (in mils) of No. 6 wire compared with No. 12 wire is about $^{162}/_{81}$. Express in lowest terms.

22.   The resistance of iron wire compared with nichrome wire is $^{90}/_{600}$. Express in lowest terms.

23.   The current gain of a transistor β is the ratio of the change in the output current compared with the change in the input current. If $\beta = {}^{196}/_4$, express in lowest terms.

24.   The turns ratio of a step-up transformer is $^6/_{120}$. Express in lowest terms.

25.   The current in a certain parallel circuit divides in the ratio of $^{12}/_{30}$. Express in lowest terms.

Reducing mixed numbers to improper fractions. In a *proper fraction* the top number (the numerator) is always *smaller* than the bottom number (the denominator). Some examples of proper fractions are $\frac{1}{2}$, $\frac{3}{4}$, and $\frac{8}{11}$. A *mixed number* is made of two numbers—a whole number and a proper fraction. Some examples are $2\frac{1}{2}$, $3\frac{1}{4}$, and $5\frac{3}{16}$. In an *improper fraction* the top number is always *larger* than the bottom number. Some examples are $\frac{5}{3}$, $\frac{8}{5}$, and $\frac{22}{7}$.

EXAMPLE 2-5   Change $3\frac{3}{4}$ to an improper fraction.

SOLUTION
The improper fraction will be a certain number of fourths. Each whole equals $\frac{4}{4}$. In the number 3, there are 3×4, or 12, fourths—or $\frac{12}{4}$. But in addition to the 3 wholes, we have $\frac{3}{4}$ more. Therefore,

$$3\frac{3}{4} = \frac{12}{4} + \frac{3}{4} = \frac{15}{4} \quad Ans.$$

RULE	To change a mixed number to an improper fraction, multiply the denominator of the fraction by the whole number and add the numerator of the fraction. Place this answer over the denominator to make the improper fraction.

EXAMPLE 2-6   Change $2\frac{3}{8}$ to an improper fraction.

SOLUTION
The numerator is equal to 2×8, or 16, plus the 3, which equals 19. Placing this 19 over the denominator 8 gives

$$\frac{19}{8} \quad Ans.$$

PROBLEMS

Change each of the following mixed numbers to improper fractions:

1. $2\frac{1}{4}$	2. $3\frac{3}{8}$	3. $2\frac{2}{9}$	4. $5\frac{3}{8}$
5. $1\frac{3}{10}$	6. $4\frac{3}{4}$	7. $4\frac{1}{6}$	8. $3\frac{7}{10}$
9. $4\frac{5}{8}$	10. $10\frac{1}{2}$	11. $3\frac{1}{3}$	12. $2\frac{1}{12}$

CHANGING IMPROPER FRACTIONS TO MIXED NUMBERS

EXAMPLE 2-7   Change $\frac{15}{2}$ to a mixed number.

SOLUTION
$\frac{15}{2}$ means 15 divided by 2, or $15 \div 2$. This means that 2 is contained in 15 only 7 times, which is 14, leaving a remainder of 1. This is written as

$$\frac{15}{2} = 7\frac{1}{2} \quad Ans.$$

RULE	To change an improper fraction into a mixed number, divide the numerator by the denominator. Any remainder is placed over the denominator. The resulting whole number and proper fraction form the required mixed number.

EXAMPLE 2-8   Change $^{25}/_{10}$ to a mixed number.

SOLUTION
$25 \div 10 = 2$ with a remainder of 5, or $2^5/_{10}$. Any remaining fraction like $^5/_{10}$ should be reduced to lowest terms. Therefore,

$$2^5/_{10} = 2^1/_2 \quad Ans.$$

PROBLEMS

Change the following improper fractions to mixed numbers or whole numbers:

1. $^7/_4$	2. $^9/_2$	3. $^{13}/_3$	4. $^8/_3$	5. $^{15}/_4$
6. $^{23}/_5$	7. $^8/_5$	8. $^{23}/_4$	9. $^{33}/_{10}$	10. $^{14}/_5$
11. $^{20}/_2$	12. $^{43}/_{10}$	13. $^{29}/_3$	14. $^{26}/_8$	15. $^{64}/_4$
16. $^{16}/_9$	17. $^{18}/_5$	18. $^{52}/_4$	19. $^{96}/_8$	20. $^{31}/_4$
21. $^{70}/_{10}$	22. $^{38}/_3$	23. $^{17}/_{10}$	24. $^{59}/_8$	25. $^{47}/_9$
26. $^{19}/_6$	27. $^{108}/_9$	28. $^{47}/_{11}$	29. $^{147}/_{12}$	30. $^{66}/_{10}$

MULTIPLICATION OF FRACTIONS

RULE	To multiply fractions, place the multiplication of the numerators over the multiplication of the denominators and reduce to lowest terms.

EXAMPLE 2-9   Multiply $^1/_2 \times ^3/_4$

SOLUTION
$^1/_2 \times ^3/_4$ means

$$\frac{1 \times 3}{2 \times 4} = \frac{3}{8} \quad Ans.$$

EXAMPLE 2-10   Multiply $^1/_2 \times 5$.

SOLUTION

$$\frac{1}{2} \times 5 = \frac{1}{2} \times \frac{5}{1} = \frac{1 \times 5}{2 \times 1} = \frac{5}{2} = 2\frac{1}{2} \quad Ans.$$

Cancellation. To cancel numerators and denominators means to divide both a numerator and a denominator by the same number.

EXAMPLE 2-11   Multiply $\frac{3}{8} \times \frac{4}{9}$.

SOLUTION
Notice that the 3 on the top and the 9 on the bottom can both be divided by 3. Cross out the 3 and write 1 above it. Cross out the 9 and write 3 under it. Also, the 4 on the top and the 8 on the bottom can both be divided by 4. Cross out the 4 on the top and write 1 above it. Cross out the 8 and write 2 under it as shown below.

$$\frac{3}{8} \times \frac{4}{9} = \frac{\overset{1}{\cancel{3}}}{\underset{2}{\cancel{8}}} \times \frac{\overset{1}{\cancel{4}}}{\underset{3}{\cancel{9}}} = \frac{1 \times 1}{2 \times 3} = \frac{1}{6} \qquad Ans.$$

SELF-TEST 2-12   Multiply

$$\frac{7}{15} \times \frac{25}{14}$$

SOLUTION
The numerator 7 and the denominator ___ may both be divided by ___. Cross out the 7 and write 1 above it. Cross out the 14 and write ___ under it. The numerator 25 and the denominator ___ may be divided by ___. Cross out the 25 and write ___ above it. Cross out the 15 and write ___ under it.

$$\frac{\overset{1}{\cancel{7}}}{\underset{3}{\cancel{15}}} \times \frac{\overset{5}{\cancel{25}}}{\underset{2}{\cancel{14}}} = \frac{1 \times 5}{3 \times 2} = \frac{?}{?} \qquad Ans.$$

14	7
2	
15	5
5	3
$\frac{5}{6}$	

PROBLEMS

Multiply the following fractions and reduce to lowest terms:

1. $8 \times \frac{1}{2}$ 2. $\frac{2}{5} \times \frac{1}{3}$ 3. $\frac{1}{10} \times 3$
4. $\frac{1}{4} \times 3$ 5. $5 \times \frac{1}{2}$ 6. $\frac{1}{4} \times 7$
7. $\frac{1}{3} \times \frac{1}{5}$ 8. $\frac{3}{8} \times 4$ 9. $\frac{3}{8} \times 16$

10. A 40-W lamp uses about $\frac{3}{8}$ A. How many amperes would four lamps use when connected in parallel?
11. A motor delivers only seven-eighths of the power it receives. Find the power delivered if it receives 6 hp.
12. What is the total thickness of three $\frac{1}{8}$-in-thick washers?
13. The actual value of the resistance of many radio resistors may be off as much as one-fifth of the rated value. What would be the error in a 230-Ω resistor of this type?

14.   What total horsepower is required for the operation of three $\frac{1}{6}$-hp single-phase capacitor motors?

15.   About two-fifths of the electrolyte in a storage battery is acid. If the battery contains 5 oz of electrolyte, how many ounces of acid are in the cells of the battery?

16.   Only four-fifths of the wattage of an electric range is used in computing the size of entrance wires. Find the wattage to use if the range is rated at 4,000 W.

17.   What is the cost of $\frac{3}{4}$ lb of magnet wire at 28 cents/lb?

18.   In transmitting 2 hp by belts, one-twentieth of the energy is lost in slippage. How much horsepower is lost?

19.   What is the total thickness of three insulating plates if each plate is $\frac{5}{64}$ in thick?

20.   A capacitor charges to about two-thirds the applied voltage in one time constant. If the applied voltage is 10 V, what is the voltage after one time constant?

21. $\frac{2}{3} \times \frac{1}{2}$	22. $\frac{7}{10} \times \frac{5}{14}$	23. $\frac{1}{7} \times 5$	24. $\frac{3}{5} \times \frac{5}{9}$
25. $\frac{3}{5} \times \frac{4}{5}$	26. $\frac{4}{5} \times \frac{1}{16}$	27. $\frac{3}{4} \times \frac{2}{15}$	28. $\frac{2}{9} \times 11$
29. $\frac{7}{8} \times \frac{3}{5}$	30. $\frac{3}{4} \times \frac{3}{5}$	31. $\frac{3}{16} \times \frac{2}{3}$	32. $\frac{5}{8} \times 17$

MULTIPLICATION OF MIXED NUMBERS

EXAMPLE 2-13   Multiply $2\frac{1}{4} \times 10$.

SOLUTION
Before we can multiply, we must change all mixed numbers into improper fractions.

$$2\frac{1}{4} \times 10 = \frac{9}{4} \times 10$$

$$= \frac{9}{\underset{2}{\cancel{4}}} \times \frac{\overset{5}{\cancel{10}}}{1} = \frac{45}{2} = 22\frac{1}{2} \qquad Ans.$$

EXAMPLE 2-14   Multiply $1\frac{7}{8} \times 3\frac{1}{3}$.

SOLUTION

$$1\frac{7}{8} \times 3\frac{1}{3} = \frac{15}{8} \times \frac{10}{3}$$

$$= \frac{\overset{5}{\cancel{15}}}{\underset{4}{\cancel{8}}} \times \frac{\overset{5}{\cancel{10}}}{\underset{1}{\cancel{3}}} = \frac{5 \times 5}{4 \times 1} = \frac{25}{4} = 6\frac{1}{4} \qquad Ans.$$

SELF-TEST 2-15   A gallon of water weighs $8\frac{1}{3}$ lb. Find the weight of six-tenths of a gallon.

SOLUTION

The total weight equals $8\frac{1}{3} \times \frac{6}{10}$. $8\frac{1}{3}$ may be written as the improper fraction
____. The multiplication may now be written as $\frac{25}{3} \times \frac{6}{10}$. The numerator 25
and the denominator ____ may both be divided by ____. Cross out the 25 and
write ____ above it. Cross out the 10 and write ____ under it. The numerator 6
and the denominator ____ may both be divided by ____. Cross out the 6 and
write ____ above it. Cross out the 3 and write ____ under it.

$\frac{25}{3}$	
10	5
5	2
3	3
2	1

$$\frac{\overset{5}{\cancel{25}}}{\underset{1}{\cancel{3}}} \times \frac{\overset{2}{\cancel{6}}}{\underset{2}{\cancel{10}}}$$

Now cancel the two 2s by dividing them both by ____. By multiplying the numerators and denominators separately, we get $\frac{5}{1}$, or the final answer ____.

2
5

PROBLEMS

Multiply the following fractions and mixed numbers. Express the answer in lowest terms.

1. $1\frac{7}{9} \times \frac{3}{8}$
2. $\frac{1}{5} \times 4\frac{3}{8}$
3. $3\frac{1}{6} \times 3$
4. $1\frac{1}{4} \times 3\frac{2}{5}$
5. $2\frac{1}{3} \times \frac{1}{7}$
6. $3\frac{1}{3} \times 1\frac{1}{5}$
7. $1\frac{1}{3} \times 3\frac{3}{4}$
8. $2\frac{1}{4} \times 3\frac{3}{5}$
9. $\frac{1}{5} \times 3\frac{1}{3}$

10. A neon electric sign uses $4\frac{1}{2}$ W of power per foot of tubing. How many watts are used for a sign which uses 20 ft of tubing?
11. Find the total voltage supplied by three $1\frac{1}{2}$-V dry cells connected in series.
12. Number 70G77 G-E autotransformers weigh $1\frac{6}{10}$ lb each. How much does a dozen weigh?
13. The distance across the corners of a square (the diagonal) is almost $1\frac{5}{12}$ times the length of one side. Find the diagonal when one side is (a) 18 in, (b) 36 in, (c) 108 ft.
14. UTC power transformers are given a surge test for insulation break-down of $2\frac{1}{2}$ times the normally developed voltage. What is the test voltage for a transformer which delivers 510 V?
15. A drill-press operator requires $1\frac{5}{8}$ min to drill through 1 in of steel. How long will it take him to drill through $\frac{4}{5}$ in of the same steel?
16. If one-twentieth of the energy put into a motor is lost by friction, copper, and iron losses, how many kilowatts are lost if the motor receives $\frac{2}{5}$ kW?
17. Deltabeston aircraft cable AN-22 weighs $5\frac{7}{10}$ lb/1,000 ft. What is the weight of 500 ft?

18. If one electrical outlet requires 13½ ft of flexible conduit, how many feet of conduit are required for five such outlets?
19. What is the total resistance of three 7¼-Ω resistors in series?
20. A capacitor should be checked for dielectric breakdown at 1½ times its rated working voltage. If the capacitor to be tested has a working voltage of 600 V, what test voltage should be applied?
21. On a certain electrical installation, six men worked 3½ h each. The job was then completed by eight men, each working for 2¾ h. Find the total number of manhours.
22. A factory uses four ¾-hp motors and five ¼-hp motors. What is the total horsepower used when all motors are operating?
23. How long a piece of brass rod will be needed to make 24 pieces each 3 in long, if ¹⁄₁₆ in is allowed for each saw cut?
24. An electrician gets time and one-half for overtime. If he worked 4¾ h overtime, for how many hours will he be paid for this overtime?

SUMMARY

1   A fraction is made of two parts, a _____ and a _____ .

numerator   denominator

2   The _____ is the top portion of the fraction.

numerator

3   The _____ is the bottom portion of the fraction.

denominator

4   A fraction is a mathematical way to describe some _____ of a total amount.

part

5   If you divide the numerator and denominator of the fraction ¹⁰/₁₅ by 5, the form of the fraction will be different but the _____ of the fraction will not be changed.

value

6   Consider the fraction ¹²/₁₈. The largest whole number which divides evenly into both parts of the fraction is ___ .

6

7   When this number is divided into both parts of the fraction ¹²/₁₈, the value of the fraction will not change, and the new fraction will be ___ .

²/₃

8   Can you divide the parts of ²/₃ evenly by any other number except 1? (yes/no)

no

9   When you write ¹²/₁₈ = ²/₃, you have expressed the fraction in _____ terms.

lowest

10   To express a fraction in lowest terms, we must (multiply/divide) both the numerator and the denominator by the largest number that divides _____ into both of them.

divide
evenly

11   An improper fraction is one in which the numerator is (larger/smaller) than the denominator.

larger

12   Mixed numbers should be changed into _____ fractions before multiplying.

improper

13   To change a mixed number into an improper fraction, multiply the _____ of the fraction by the whole number and add the numerator of the fraction. Place this answer over the _____ to form the improper fraction.

denominator
denominator

14   To change an improper fraction into a mixed number, _(multiply/divide)_ the numerator by the denominator.   Any remainder is placed over the _____.

15   To multiply fractions, place the _(product/quotient)_ of the numerators over the _(product/quotient)_ of the denominators and express in _____ terms.

16   To cancel means to _____ _any_ one of the numerators and _any_ one of the denominators by the _____ number.

divide

denominator
product
product   lowest

divide
same

TEST—FRACTIONS

1. Express in lowest terms (_a_) $^{10}/_{16}$, (_b_) $^{8}/_{20}$, (_c_) $^{20}/_{64}$, (_d_) $^{30}/_{45}$, and (_e_) $^{40}/_{1,000}$.
2. Change to improper fractions (_a_) $1^{3}/_{8}$, (_b_) $3^{1}/_{4}$, (_c_) $5^{1}/_{2}$, (_d_) $2^{7}/_{10}$, and (_e_) $4^{1}/_{3}$.
3. Change to mixed numbers (_a_) $^{9}/_{4}$, (_b_) $^{23}/_{3}$, (_c_) $^{19}/_{5}$, (_d_) $^{42}/_{5}$, and (_e_) $^{61}/_{8}$.
4. Multiply and express in lowest terms (_a_) $^{22}/_{7} \times 28$, (_b_) $^{3}/_{2} \times ^{11}/_{3}$, (_c_) $^{15}/_{4} \times ^{20}/_{3}$, and (_d_) $^{5}/_{3} \times ^{21}/_{5}$.
5. Multiply and express in lowest terms (_a_) $4^{1}/_{2} \times ^{3}/_{16}$, (_b_) $^{3}/_{32} \times 5^{1}/_{3}$, (_c_) $3^{1}/_{4} \times 4^{1}/_{2}$, and (_d_) $5^{1}/_{16} \times ^{3}/_{32}$.

JOB 2-3   OHM'S LAW

In Job 1-2 we learned that the following three factors must be present in every electrical circuit:

1   The _electromotive force E_ expressed in _volts,_ which causes the current to flow.
2   The _resistance_ of the circuit _R_ expressed in _ohms,_ which attempts to stop the flow of current.
3   The _current I_ expressed in _amperes,_ which flows as a result of the voltage pressure exceeding the resistance.

A definite relationship exists among these three factors, which is known as _Ohm's law._   This relationship is very important, since it is the basis for most of the calculations in electrical and electronic work.   In the three circuits shown in Fig. 2-4, the voltage _E_ of the battery is mea-

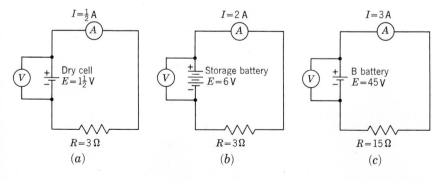

FIGURE 2-4
The voltage equals the current multiplied by the resistance in a simple circuit.

sured by a voltmeter. The current *I* that flows is measured by an ammeter. The resistance *R* of the resistor is indicated by the manufacturer by distinctive markings on the resistor. Let us put the information from Fig. 2-4 into a table (see Table 2-1).

TABLE 2-1

FIGURE	*E*	*I*	*R*	*I* × *R*
a	1½	½	3	½ × 3 = 1½
b	6	2	3	2 × 3 = 6
c	45	3	15	3 × 15 = 45

In the last column of Table 2-1 we have multiplied the current *I* by the resistance *R* for each circuit. Evidently, the result of this multiplication is always equal to the voltage *E* of the circuit. This is true for all circuits and was first discovered by George S. Ohm. This simple relationship is called *Ohm's law.*

RULE	Voltage equals current multiplied by resistance.

FORMULA

$$E = I \times R$$

2-1

In this formula,

E must always be expressed in volts (V).
I must always be expressed in amperes (A).
R must always be expressed in ohms (Ω).

SOLVING PROBLEMS

1 Read the problem carefully.

2 Draw a simple diagram of the circuit.

3 Record the given information directly on the diagram. Indicate the values to be found by question marks.

4 Write the formula.

5 Substitute the given numbers for the letters in the formula. If the number for the letter is unknown, merely write the letter again. Be sure to include all mathematical signs like × or =.

6 Do the indicated arithmetic at the side so as not to interrupt the continued progress of the solution.

7 In the answer, indicate the letter, its numerical value, and the units of measurement.

EXAMPLE 2-16 A doorbell requires ¼ A in order to ring. The resistance of the coils in the bell is 24 Ω. What voltage must be supplied in order to ring the bell?

SOLUTION

The diagram for the circuit is shown in Fig. 2-5.

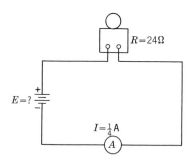

$R = 24\,\Omega$

$E = ?$

$I = \frac{1}{4}\,\text{A}$

FIGURE 2-5

1 Write the formula.

$$E = I \times R$$

2 Substitute numbers.

$$E = \frac{1}{4} \times 24$$

3 Multiply the numbers.

$$E = 6\,\text{V} \qquad Ans.$$

EXAMPLE 2-17   A relay used to control the large current to a motor is rated at 28 Ω resistance. What voltage is required to operate the relay if it requires a current of 0.05 A?

SOLUTION

The diagram for the circuit is shown in Fig. 2-6.

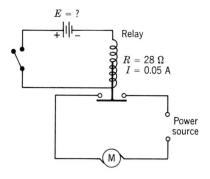

$E = ?$

Relay

$R = 28\,\Omega$
$I = 0.05\,\text{A}$

Power
source

FIGURE 2-6

A relay controls the large
current drawn by the motor.

1 Write the formula.

$$E = I \times R$$

2 Substitute numbers.

$$E = 0.05 \times 28$$

3   Multiply the numbers.

$$E = 1.4 \text{ V} \quad Ans.$$

SELF-TEST 2-18   An automobile battery supplies a current of 7.5 A
to a headlamp with a resistance of 0.84 Ω. Find the voltage delivered
by the battery.

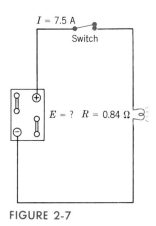

SOLUTION
The diagram for the circuit is shown in Fig. 2-7.

1   Write the formula.

$$E = \underline{\quad} \times \underline{\quad}$$

	I	R

2   Substitute numbers.

$$E = \underline{\quad} \times 0.84$$

7.5

3   Multiply the numbers.

$$E = \underline{\quad} \text{ V} \quad Ans.$$

6.3

FIGURE 2-7

PROBLEMS

1.   What voltage is needed to light a lamp if the current required is
2 A and the resistance of the lamp is 55 Ω?
2.   A 20-Ω heating-element resistor draws 3 A from a line. Find the
voltage across the resistor.
3.   If the total resistance (impedance) of a radio receiver is 240 Ω and
it draws ½ A, what voltage is needed?
4.   A certain television tube takes 0.15 A. Its resistance is 80 Ω. What
voltage does it need?
5.   An arc lamp with a hot resistance of 9 Ω draws 6.2 A. What voltage
is required?
6.   What voltage is required to operate a 5,500-Ω electric clock which
draws 0.02 A?
7.   A 52-Ω electric toaster uses 2¼ A. Find the required voltage.
8.   A 180-Ω line cord resistor carries 0.15 A. Find the voltage drop
in the resistor.
9.   What voltage is needed to energize the field coil of a loudspeaker
if its resistance is 1,100 Ω and it uses 0.04 A?
10.   The coils of a washing-machine motor have a resistance of 21 Ω.
What voltage does it require if the motor draws 5.3 A?
11.   What voltage is registered by a voltmeter with an internal resistance of 150,000 Ω when 0.001 A flows through it?
12.   What voltage is required for an electroplating tank with a resistance
of 0.35 Ω that requires a current of 80 A?
13.   The line from an automobile battery to a distant transmitter must
not develop more than 0.25 V when the transmitter is operating.

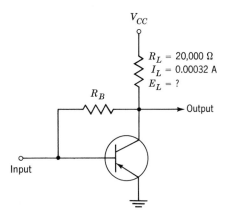

FIGURE 2-8
A self-bias transistor circuit.

If the current from the battery is 18 A, will a 0.015-Ω line be satisfactory?

14. The winding of a transformer has a resistance of 63 Ω. What is the voltage drop in the winding when it carries a current of 0.059 A?

15. A neon electric sign draws 1.07 A. If its resistance is 98 Ω, find the voltage needed.

16. An electric bell has a resistance of 25 Ω and will not operate on a current of less than 0.25 A. What is the smallest voltage that will ring the bell?

17. The resistance of a telephone receiver is 1,000 Ω. If the current is 0.032 A, what is the voltage across the receiver?

18. What voltage is supplied to a 0.015-Ω dc arc welder drawing 650 A?

19. A 125-Ω relay coil needs 0.15 A to operate. What is the lowest voltage needed to operate the relay?

20. In the self-bias transistor circuit shown in Fig. 2-8, the load resistor $R_L = 20,000$ Ω and carries a current $I_L = 0.00032$ A. Find the voltage drop across the load.

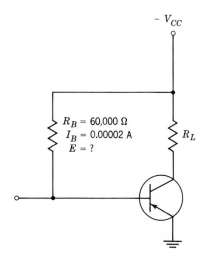

FIGURE 2-9
A fixed-bias transistor circuit.

21. What is the voltage across the shunt of an ammeter if the shunt has a resistance of 0.005 Ω and carries 9.99 A?

22. A 250,000-Ω resistor in the plate circuit of a 6CL6 video amplifier tube draws 0.0003 A. Find the voltage across the resistor.

23. In the fixed-bias transistor circuit shown in Fig. 2-9, the base resistor $R_B = 60,000$ Ω and the base current $I_B = 0.00002$ A. Find the voltage drop across the base resistor.

24. In the voltage divider circuit shown in Fig. 2-10, find the voltage across the resistors R_1, R_2, and R_3.

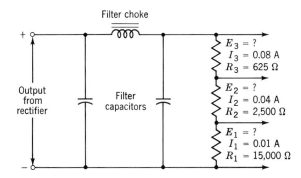

FIGURE 2-10
A voltage divider provides different voltages from a single source.

JOB 2-4   CHECKUP ON DECIMALS (DIAGNOSTIC TEST)

Did you have any difficulty with the decimals in the last job? The following problems occur in the everyday work of the electrician and electronic technician. They all involve decimals and will help you to check up on their use. If you have difficulty with any of these problems, see Job 2-5 which follows.

PROBLEMS

1. Find the total current drawn by the following appliances by adding the currents: electric iron, 4.12 A; electric clock, 0.02 A; 100-W lamp, 0.91 A; and radio, 0.5 A.

2. Find, by addition, the total series voltage required by a five-tube heater string using tubes rated at 12.6, 12.6, 12.6, 50, and 35 V.

3. Find the total capacitance of a parallel group of capacitors by adding these values: 0.00025, 0.01, and 0.005 μF (microfarad).

4. How much larger in diameter is No. 10 copper wire (0.1019 in) than No. 14 wire (0.0641 in)?

5. The current drawn by a motor is 1.21 A at no load and 1.56 A at full load. What is the increase in the current?

6. A motor receives only 117.4 V when connected to a distant generator delivering 120 V. Find the voltage lost in the line wires.

7. The laminated core of a power transformer is made of 15 sheets of steel each 0.079 in thick. Find the total thickness of the core.

8. The maximum value of an ac voltage wave is 1.414 times its ac

meter reading of 46.5 V. Find the maximum value of the voltage wave.

9. If 65 ft of BX cable costs $14.95, what is the cost of 1 ft of this cable?

10. The resistance of 24.5 ft of No. 16 copper wire is 0.0982 Ω. Find the resistance of 1 ft of this wire.

11. Add 7.05, 2, 3.5.

12. Subtract: 6.75 − 3.

13. Which current is larger: 0.4 or 0.25 A?

14. Write the following decimals in words: (*a*) 4.3, (*b*) 0.359, and (*c*) 0.41.

15. Multiply $3/10$ by 0.05.

16. Write as a decimal (*a*) $1/4$, (*b*) $4/7$, (*c*) $5/8$, and (*d*) $1/16$.

17. Subtract 12 from 18.24.

18. Arrange the following numbers starting with the largest: 0.050, 0.30, 0.0070, 1.1.

19. Find the difference between three-tenths and twenty-five hundredths.

20. What is the excess of 5 over 2.75?

JOB 2-5   BRUSHUP ON DECIMAL FRACTIONS

Meaning of a decimal fraction. A decimal fraction is a fraction with the denominator not written but the value indicated by the position of a decimal point (.) in the numerator. The denominator of a decimal fraction is always a number like 10, 100, 1,000, et cetera.

To write the fraction $3/10$ as a decimal fraction, the decimal point must be placed in the numerator so that there is only *one* digit following the decimal point. Thus,

$3/10$ = 0.3, which is read as three-tenths.

$9/10$ = 0.9, which is read as nine-tenths.

To write the fraction $23/100$ as a decimal fraction, the decimal point must be placed in the numerator so that there will be *two* digits following the decimal point. Thus,

$23/100$ = 0.23, which is read as twenty-three hundredths.

$47/100$ = 0.47, which is read as forty-seven hundredths.

Now, if we wish to write $3/100$ as a decimal fraction, the decimal point must still be placed so that there will be two digits following the decimal point. In order to make up these two digits, we must place a zero between the decimal point and the number 3. The zero will now push the 3 into the second place, which means hundredths. Thus,

$3/100$ = 0.03, which is read as three-hundredths.

$7/100$ = 0.07, which is read as seven-hundredths.

When the denominator is 1,000 (meaning thousandths), the decimal point is placed in the numerator so that there will be *three* digits following the decimal point. Thus,

$123/_{1,000}$ is 0.123   and $457/_{1,000}$ is 0.457

If we wish to write $43/_{1,000}$ as a decimal, the point must be placed so that there will still be *three* digits after the decimal point. Therefore, to make up the three digits, a zero must be placed between the point and the digits 43.

Thus,

$43/_{1,000}$ is written as 0.043

$87/_{1,000}$ is written as 0.087

If we wish to write $7/_{1,000}$ as a decimal, we must insert zeros so that the 7 will be in the *third* place following the decimal because we need *three* places to indicate thousandths. Thus,

$7/_{1,000}$ is written as 0.007

$3/_{1,000}$ is written as 0.003

Following this procedure, *ten-thousandths* require four places, *one hundred thousandths* require five places, and so on.

This may all be summed up as follows.

The first digit after the decimal point means tenths.
The second digit after the decimal point means hundredths.
The third digit after the decimal point means thousandths.
The fourth digit after the decimal point means ten-thousandths.
The fifth digit after the decimal point means hundred-thousandths.
The sixth digit after the decimal point means millionths, etc.

Note: Zeros placed at the *end* of a decimal do *not* change the value of the decimal but merely describe the decimal in another way. For example, 0.5 (five-tenths) = 0.50 (fifty-hundredths) = 0.500 (five hundred-thousandths).

Equal fractions

TABLE 2-2

WORDS	FRACTION	DECIMAL
Seven-tenths	$7/_{10}$	0.7
Twenty-three hundredths	$23/_{100}$	0.23
Seventy-hundredths	$70/_{100}$	0.70
Three-hundredths	$3/_{100}$	0.03
Three-thousandths	$3/_{1,000}$	0.003
Fifteen-thousandths	$15/_{1,000}$	0.015
One hundred and forty-nine thousandths	$149/_{1,000}$	0.149
Seven hundred thousandths	$700/_{1,000}$	0.700

Comparing the value of decimals. When comparing the value of various decimal fractions, we must first be certain that they have the same denominators. This means that the decimals must be written so that they have the same number of decimal places.

EXAMPLE 2-19   Which is larger: 0.3 or 0.25?

SOLUTION
Since 0.3 has only one decimal place and 0.25 has two decimal places, we must change 0.3 into a two-place decimal by adding a zero. This does *not* change the value but merely expresses it differently. Therefore, 0.3 or 0.30 (thirty hundredths) is larger than 0.25 (twenty-five hundredths). *Ans.*

PROBLEMS

Write the following fractions as decimal fractions:

1. $7/10$	2. $29/100$	3. $114/1,000$	4. $3/10$
5. $6/100$	6. $9/1,000$	7. $18/1,000$	8. $3/1,000$
9. $11/100$	10. $4/10$	11. $13/1,000$	12. $74/100$
13. $45/1,000$	14. $316/1,000$	15. $6/10$	16. $23/100$

Arrange the following decimals in order starting with the largest:

17. 0.007, 0.16, 0.4   18. 0.2, 0.107, 0.28   19. 0.8, 0.06, 0.040
20. 0.496, 0.8, 0.02   21. 0.5, 0.051, 0.18   22. 0.90, 0.018, 0.06
23. 0.1228, 0.236, 0.4   24. 0.006, 0.05, 0.3   25. 0.19, 0.004, 0.08
26. 0.060, 0.40, 0.0080   27. 0.02, 0.004, 0.14   28. 0.0026, 0.092, 0.125

Changing mixed numbers to decimals. When a mixed number is read as a decimal, the word "and" appears as a decimal point. For example, $2 7/10$ is read as two *and* seven-tenths and is written as 2.7. A whole number may be written as a decimal if a decimal point is placed at the *end* of the number. For example, the number 4 means 4.0 or 4.00 or 4.000.

PROBLEMS

Change the following mixed numbers to decimals:

1. $2 3/10$	2. $18 5/100$	3. $3 144/1,000$	4. $1 17/100$
5. $2 25/1,000$	6. $7 35/100$	7. $2 20/1,000$	8. $3 9/100$
9. $1 2/1,000$	10. $62 90/100$	11. $9 145/1,000$	12. $3 27/1,000$

Changing fractions to decimals. We shall discover that many of the answers to our electrical problems will be fractions like $1/8$ A, $7/40$ μF, and $3/13$ Ω. These will be perfectly correct mathematical answers, but they will be completely worthless to a practical electrician or television mechanic. Electrical measuring instruments give values expressed as decimals and *not* as fractions. In addition, the manufacturers of electrical components give the values of the parts in terms of decimals.

Suppose that we worked out a problem and found that the current in the circuit should be ⅛ A. Then, using an ammeter, we tested the circuit and found that 0.125 A flowed. Is our circuit correct? How would we know? How can we compare ⅛ and 0.125? The easiest way is to change the fraction ⅛ into its equivalent decimal and then to compare the decimals.

RULE	To change a fraction into a decimal, divide the numerator by the denominator.

EXAMPLE 2-20 Change ⅛ into an equivalent decimal.

SOLUTION

⅛ means 1 ÷ 8. To write this as a long-division example, place the numerator inside the long-division sign and the denominator outside the sign as shown below.

$$8 \overline{)1}$$

We can't divide 8 into 1; but remember that every whole number may be written with a decimal point at the end of the number. As many zeros may be added as we desire without changing the value. Our problem now looks like this:

$$8 \overline{)1.000}$$

1 Put the decimal point in the answer directly above its position in 1.000.

$$8 \overline{)1.000}^{\quad .}$$

2 Try to divide the 8 into the first digit. 8 does not divide into 1. Then try to divide the 8 into the first two digits. 8 divides into 10 one time. Place this number 1 in the answer directly above the last digit of the number into which the 8 was divided.

$$8 \overline{)1.000}^{\;0.1}$$

3 Multiply this 1 by the divisor 8 and place as shown below. Draw a line and subtract.

$$\begin{array}{r} 0.1 \\ 8 \overline{)1.000} \\ \underline{8} \\ 2 \end{array}$$

4 Bring down the next digit 0 and divide this new number 20 by the 8. The 8 will divide into 20 two times.

$$\begin{array}{r} 0.1 \\ 8\overline{)\,1.000} \\ \underline{8} \\ 20 \end{array}$$

5   Place this 2 in the answer directly above the last digit brought down.

$$\begin{array}{r} 0.12 \\ 8\overline{)\,1.000} \\ \underline{8} \\ 20 \end{array}$$

6   Multiply the 2 by the divisor 8, and continue steps 3 to 5. The answer comes out even as 0.125. This means that $1/8 = 0.125$ *Ans.*

$$\begin{array}{r} 0.125 \\ 8\overline{)\,1.000} \\ \underline{8} \\ 20 \\ \underline{16} \\ 40 \\ \underline{40} \\ 0 \end{array}$$

EXAMPLE 2-21   Change $7/40$ into an equivalent decimal.

SOLUTION

$$7/40 = 40\overline{)\,7.000}\quad Ans. \\ \begin{array}{r} 0.175 \\ \underline{4\,0} \\ 3\,00 \\ \underline{2\,80} \\ 200 \\ \underline{200} \\ 0 \end{array}$$

EXAMPLE 2-22   Change $6/13$ into an equivalent decimal.

SOLUTION
The answer does not come out evenly:

$$6/13 = 13\overline{)\,6.000} \\ \begin{array}{r} 0.461 \\ \underline{5\,2} \\ 80 \\ \underline{78} \\ 20 \\ \underline{13} \\ 7 \end{array}$$

We see that there is a remainder. If the remainder is more than half the divisor, we drop it and add an extra unit to the last place of the answer. Since 7 is more than half of 13,

$$0.461^{7}/_{13} \text{ becomes } 0.461$$
$$\frac{+1}{0.462} \quad Ans.$$

If any remainder is less than half the divisor, drop it completely and leave the answer unchanged. For example,

$$0.236^{5}/_{12} = 0.236 \quad \text{(since 5 is less than half of 12)}$$
$$0.483^{1}/_{4} = 0.483 \quad \text{(since 1 is less than half of 4)}$$

A big question may have occurred to you by now: "If it doesn't come out even, how long should I continue to divide?" The answer to this depends on the use to which the answer is to be put. Some jobs require five or six decimal places, while others need only one place or none at all. For example, the value of a grid leak capacitor should be worked out to an answer like 0.00025 μF; a grid bias resistor of 203.4 Ω is just as well written as 203 Ω or even 200 Ω.

Degree of accuracy. A very general rule for the number of decimal places required in an answer is given in Table 2-3.

TABLE 2-3

ANSWER	NO. OF DECIMAL PLACES	EXAMPLE
Less than 1	3	0.132, 0.008
From 1 to 10	2	3.48, 6.07
From 10 to 100	1	28.3, 52.9
From 100 up	None	425, 659

PROBLEMS

Change the following fractions to equivalent decimals:

1.	$1/4$	2.	$3/8$	3.	$5/8$	4.	$1/3$	5.	$2/5$
6.	$3/10$	7.	$3/20$	8.	$2/7$	9.	$7/8$	10.	$3/16$
11.	$4/9$	12.	$13/15$	13.	$3/32$	14.	$21/25$	15.	$25/40$
16.	$9/16$	17.	$1/50$	18.	$1/200$	19.	$5/26$	20.	$9/64$

Using the decimal equivalent chart. There are some fractions that are used very often. These are the fractions which represent the parts of an inch on a ruler, like $1/16$, $3/8$, $5/32$, $9/64$, etc. Since they are so widely used, a table of decimal equivalents has been prepared. In order to find the decimal equivalent of a fraction of this type, refer to Table 2-4.

Addition of decimals. When adding decimals, be sure to write the numbers so that the decimal points will be kept in a straight vertical line.

EXAMPLE 2-23   Add $2.52 + 0.007 + 13.03 + 0.7 + 26$.

SOLUTION

$$
\begin{array}{r}
2.52 \\
0.007 \\
13.03 \quad \text{or} \\
0.7 \\
26. \\
\hline
\end{array}
\qquad
\begin{array}{r}
2.520 \\
0.007 \\
13.030 \\
0.700 \\
26.000 \\
\hline
42.257 \quad \textit{Ans.}
\end{array}
$$

← Lined up decimal points

The empty spaces are filled in with zeros as shown in the column at the right in order to aid in keeping the numbers in the correct column.

TABLE 2-4
TABLE OF DECIMAL EQUIVALENTS

FRACTION	$\frac{1}{32}$DS	$\frac{1}{64}$THS	DECIMAL	FRACTION	$\frac{1}{32}$DS	$\frac{1}{64}$THS	DECIMAL
		1	0.015625			33	0.515625
	1	2	0.03125		17	34	0.53125
		3	0.046875			35	0.546875
$\frac{1}{16}$	2	4	0.0625	$\frac{9}{16}$	18	36	0.5625
		5	0.078125			37	0.578125
	3	6	0.09375		19	38	0.59375
		7	0.109375			39	0.609375
$\frac{1}{8}$	4	8	0.125	$\frac{5}{8}$	20	40	0.625
		9	0.140625			41	0.640625
	5	10	0.15625		21	42	0.65625
		11	0.171875			43	0.671875
$\frac{3}{16}$	6	12	0.1875	$\frac{11}{16}$	22	44	0.6875
		13	0.203125			45	0.703125
	7	14	0.21875		23	46	0.71875
		15	0.234375			47	0.734375
$\frac{1}{4}$	8	16	0.25	$\frac{3}{4}$	24	48	0.75
		17	0.265625			49	0.765625
	9	18	0.28125		25	50	0.78125
		19	0.296875			51	0.796875
$\frac{5}{16}$	10	20	0.3125	$\frac{13}{16}$	26	52	0.8125
		21	0.328125			53	0.828125
	11	22	0.34375		27	54	0.84375
		23	0.359375			55	0.859375
$\frac{3}{8}$	12	24	0.375	$\frac{7}{8}$	28	56	0.875
		25	0.390625			57	0.890625
	13	26	0.40625		29	58	0.90625
		27	0.421875			59	0.921875
$\frac{7}{16}$	14	28	0.4375	$\frac{15}{16}$	30	60	0.9375
		29	0.453125			61	0.953125
	15	30	0.46875		31	62	0.96875
		31	0.484375			63	0.984375
$\frac{1}{2}$	16	32	0.5		32	64	1.

PROBLEMS

Add the following decimals:

1. $3.28 + 9.5 + 0.634 + 0.078$
2. $56.09 + 14 + 4.876 + 49.007$
3. $13 + 3.072 + 0.7 + 6.06$
4. $54 + 0.033 + 0.713 + 8.05$
5. $0.087 + 6.18 + 4 + 1.7$
6. What is the cost to rewind a motor if the following materials and labor were used: top sticks at \$0.11, No. 17 wire at \$1.05, No. 26 wire at \$0.58, armature lacquer at \$0.42, and labor at \$6.25?
7. Find the total drop in voltage in a distribution system if the voltage drops across each section are 1.06, 36.4, and 8 V.
8. Find the total thickness of insulation on shielded radio wire covered with resin (0.022 in), lacquered cotton braid (0.018 in), and copper shielding (0.03 in).
9. Find the total thickness of three shims with individual thicknesses of 0.125 in, 0.0625 in, and 0.250 in.
10. The three sides of a triangle are 3.65 in, 4.87 in, and 5.06 in long. Find the perimeter of the triangle by adding the three sides.
11. The diameter of a motor shaft bearing is 0.0025 in larger than the shaft of the motor. What is the diameter of the bearing if the shaft has a diameter of 2.25 in?
12. Find the total resistance of the leads of an installation if the resistances are 0.054, 1.004, 1.2, and 1.2 Ω.
13. The emitter current of a transistor is always equal to the sum of the collector current and the base current. Find the emitter current if the collector current is 0.03 A and the base current is 0.0015 A.
14. What is the cost to repair three electrical outlets if each outlet requires one loom box at \$0.082, one toggle switch at \$0.29, one hickey at \$0.09, and 1 h of labor at \$3.25?
15. In Fig. 2-11, find the outside diameter of the pipe if the inside diameter is 2.025 in and the pipe is made of iron $\frac{3}{16}$ in thick.

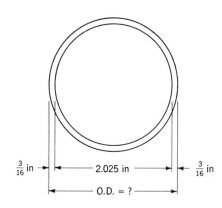

$\frac{3}{16}$ in → |←——— 2.025 in ———→| ←| $\frac{3}{16}$ in

|←——— O.D. = ? ———→|

FIGURE 2-11

Subtracting decimals. When subtracting decimals, write the numbers in columns as for addition, lining up the decimal points in a straight vertical column.

EXAMPLE 2-24   Subtract 2.36 from 4.79.

SOLUTION
The number *after* the word "from" is written on top. The number *after* the word "subtract" is written underneath.

$$\begin{array}{r} 4.79 \\ -2.36 \\ \hline 2.43 \end{array} \quad \textit{Ans.}$$

EXAMPLE 2-25   Subtract 1.04 from 3.

SOLUTION
The number 3 is written as 3.00 to locate the decimal point correctly.

$$\begin{array}{r} 3.00 \\ -1.04 \\ \hline 1.96 \end{array} \quad \textit{Ans.}$$

EXAMPLE 2-26 $2^{1}/_{2} - 1.32$.

SOLUTION
Since $2^{1}/_{2} = 2.5$ or 2.50, we have

$$\begin{array}{r} 2.50 \\ -1.32 \\ \hline 1.18 \end{array} \quad \textit{Ans.}$$

PROBLEMS

1. $0.26 - 0.03$	2. $1.36 - 0.18$	3. $0.4 - 0.06$
4. $0.05 - 0.004$	5. $18.92 - 11.36$	6. $^{5}/_{8} - 0.002$
7. $0.627 - 0.31$	8. $0.827 - 0.31$	9. $3 - 0.08$
10. $0.5 - 0.02$	11. $6 - 0.1$	12. $0.83 - ^{1}/_{2}$
13. $2.89 - 0.5$	14. $12.6 - 7$	15. $0.316 - 0.054$
16. $14 - 8.06$	17. $5^{1}/_{4} - 2.63$	18. $3.125 - ^{1}/_{8}$

19. Subtract $^{1}/_{4}$ from 0.765.
20. Find the difference between 110 and 54.9.
21. Find the difference between (*a*) 0.316 and 0.012, (*b*) 3.006 and 1.9, (*c*) 0.5 and 0.11, (*d*) 7.07 and 1.32, and (*e*) 2 and 0.02.
22. Subtract (*a*) 0.008 from 0.80 and (*b*) 0.216 from 2.16.
23. From 2.004 subtract 1.09.
24. What is the difference in the diameters of No. 1 wire (0.2893 in) and No. 7 wire (0.1447 in)?

25. The electric-meter readings on successive months were 70.08 and 76.49. Find the difference.

26. A tapered pin has a small-end diameter of 2.125 in and a large-end diameter of 2.2675 in. Find the difference in the diameters.

27. In Fig. 2-12, if the total resistance required is 60 Ω, how many ohms of resistance must be added to the circuit to make up the required 60 Ω?

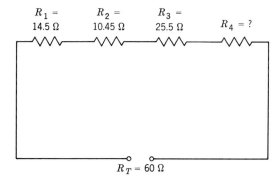

FIGURE 2-12

28. A circuit in a television receiver calls for a 0.0005-μF capacitor. A capacitor valued at 0.00035 μF is available. How much extra capacitance is needed if connected in parallel?

29. A 6GM6 tube used as an IF amplifier in a television receiver draws current from the 250-V tap of the power supply. If the voltage loss in the plate load is 118.6 V, what voltage is available at the plate of the tube?

30. The intermediate frequency at the output of a converter stage is found by obtaining the difference between the oscillator frequency and the radio frequency. If the radio frequency is 1.1 MHz (megahertz) and the oscillator frequency is 1.555 MHz, what will be the intermediate frequency?

Note: The International Electrotechnical Commission (IEC) has adopted the name hertz (Hz) as the unit of frequency. Thus:

1 Hz (hertz) = 1 c/s (cycle/second)

1 kHz (kilohertz) = 1 kilocycle/s

1 MHz (megahertz) = 1 megacycle/s

Multiplication of decimals. Decimals are multiplied in exactly the same way that ordinary numbers are multiplied. However, in addition to the normal multiplication, the decimal point must be correctly set in the answer.

RULE	The number of decimal places in a product is equal to the sum of the number of decimal places in the numbers being multiplied.

EXAMPLE 2-27   Multiply 0.62 by 0.3.

SOLUTION

> 0.62 (multiplicand, 2 places)
> ×0.3 (multiplier, 1 place)
> 0.186 (product, 2 + 1 = 3 places)   *Ans.*

EXAMPLE 2-28   Multiply 0.35 by 0.004

SOLUTION

> 0.35 (multiplicand, 2 places)
> ×0.004 (multiplier, 3 places)
> 0.00140 (product, 2 + 3 = 5 places)   *Ans.*

In this problem, extra zeros must be inserted between the decimal point and the digits of the answer to make up the required number of decimal places.

SELF-TEST 2-29   What is the total material cost for a job that uses 1,475 ft of two-conductor BX cable at $0.035/ft and 32 boxes at $0.082 each?

SOLUTION

The price of $0.035/ft means that the cable costs $0.035 for __(how many)__ ft?	1
For 2 ft of this cable, the cost is ___ × $0.035. For 5 ft of this cable, the cost is	2
5 × ___. For 1,475 ft of this cable, the cost is 1,475 × ___.	$0.035 $0.035
When 1,475 is multiplied by 0.035, the number of digits after the decimal	
point is ___. If 1,475 × 0.035 = 51,625, then the decimal point should be placed	3
after the digit ___. The answer $51.625 should be rounded off to _____.	1 $51.63
The cost for 32 boxes at $0.082 each means that the total cost for the boxes is	
32 × _____. 32 × 0.082 = _____. Since this represents dollars, $2.624	$0.082 2.624
should be rounded off to $_____. The total material cost is obtained by adding	2.62
$51.63 and _____.	$2.62
When adding decimals, we must remember to keep the decimal points in a	
_____ line.	straight, or vertical

> $51.63
> +$ 2.62
> $_.__   *Ans.*
> ⌐— Lined up decimal points

$54.25

PROBLEMS

Find the product of

1.   0.005 × 82   2.   1.732 × 40   3.   1.13 × 0.41
4.   0.9 × 0.09   5.   0.866 × 35   6.   44.6 × 805
7.   7.63 × 0.029   8.   0.354 × 0.008   9.   6.2 × 0.003

10. 0.033×0.0025 11. 106×0.045 12. 73.8×1.09

13.   If a 100-W lamp uses 0.91 A, how much current would be used by five such lamps in parallel?

14.   If BX cable costs \$0.235/ft, what would be the cost of 52.5 ft?

15.   Figure 2-13 shows a bolt with a countersunk head. The distance A is 1.85 times the diameter D. If the diameter is 0.375 in, find the distance A.

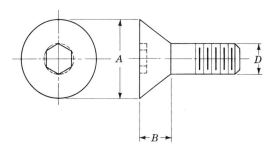

FIGURE 2-13

16.   In Fig. 2-13, the distance B is 0.424 times the diameter. If the diameter is 0.5 in, find the distance B.

17.   If a battery is made of 45 small 1.5-V dry cells in series, find the total voltage of the battery.

18.   The number of milliamperes is found by multiplying the number of amperes by 1,000. Find the number of milliamperes equal to (a) 0.25 A, (b) 0.025 A, and (c) 2.5 A.

19.   The screw thread in a micrometer advances 0.025 in in one complete turn. How far will it advance in 11 complete turns?

20.   An electrician worked 1.5 h to install a junction box. If his rate of pay is \$4.25/h, how much did he earn?

21.   Number 8 (B. & S.) gage sheet metal is 0.1285 in thick. Find the thickness of a pile of 32 of these sheets.

22.   The standard unit of resistance is measured by the resistance of a column of mercury 106.3 cm high. If 1 cm equals 0.3937 in, what is the height of the mercury column correct to the nearest thousandth of an inch?

23.   The inductive reactance of a coil is found by multiplying the constant 6.28 by the frequency and the inductance. Find the inductive reactance of a coil if the frequency is 60 Hz and the inductance is 0.15 H (henry).

24.   What is the capacity of a battery (expressed in ampere-hours) if it discharges at the rate of 9.6 A for 7.25 h?

25.   If a steel tape expands 0.00012 in for each inch of its length when heat-treated, how much will a tape 20 ft long expand?

Division of decimals

EXAMPLE 2-30   Divide 4.788 by 14.

SOLUTION

The division is accomplished in the same manner as in changing fractions
to decimals. See Examples 2-20 to 2-22.

$$
\begin{array}{r}
0.342 \quad \textit{Ans.} \\
14\overline{)4.788} \\
\underline{4\,2} \\
58 \\
\underline{56} \\
28 \\
\underline{28} \\
0
\end{array}
$$

EXAMPLE 2-31   Divide 1.38 by 0.06.

SOLUTION

When dividing by a decimal, it is best to move the decimal point all the
way over to the right so as to bring it to the end of the divisor.

$$
.06.\overline{)1.38}
$$

If this is done, the decimal point in the dividend must also be moved to
the right *for the same number of places*. Then we can divide as before.

$$
\begin{array}{r}
23. \quad \textit{Ans.} \\
.06.\overline{)1.38.} \\
\underline{1\ \ 2} \\
18 \\
\underline{18} \\
0
\end{array}
$$

EXAMPLE 2-32   Divide 3.6 by 0.08.

SOLUTION

A zero must be added after the 6 to provide the two places that the decimal point must be moved to the right.

$$
\begin{array}{r}
45. \quad \textit{Ans.} \\
.08.\overline{)3.60.} \\
\underline{3\ \ 2} \\
40 \\
\underline{40} \\
0
\end{array}
$$

EXAMPLE 2-33   Divide 0.0007 by 0.125.

SOLUTION

$$
\begin{array}{r}
0.0056 \quad \textit{Ans.} \\
0125.\overline{)\,0000.7000} \\
\underline{625} \\
750 \\
\underline{750} \\
0
\end{array}
$$

SELF-TEST 2-34   In qualifying for the "Indy 500," a racing car covered 200 m (miles) in 1.47 h. Find its average speed correct to the nearest hundredth of a mile.

SOLUTION

The average speed is obtained by dividing the _____ by the _____. In our problem, the distance (200) divided by the time (1.47) may be written as

$$200 \div 1.47 \quad \text{or} \quad \frac{200}{1.47} \quad \text{or} \quad 1.47\overline{)\,200}$$

The decimal point in the number 200 is placed so that it appears as _____.
Before we divide, the decimal point in 1.47 must be moved ____ places to the
_____. Then the decimal point in 200.00 must also be moved ____ places to the
right. The problem will now appear as

$$
\begin{array}{r}
136.05 \\
147\,\overline{)\,20000.00} \\
\underline{147}\text{xx xx} \\
530 \\
\underline{44}1 \\
890 \\
\underline{882} \\
8\,00 \\
\underline{7\,35} \\
65
\end{array}
$$

The remainder (65) is _more/less_ than half of 147. The final answer is _____ m/h.

distance	time
200.00	
two	
right	two
less	136.05

PROBLEMS

1. $3.9 \div 0.3$	**2.** $12.56 \div 0.4$	**3.** $80.5 \div 0.5$
4. $51 \div 0.06$	**5.** $38.54 \div 8.2$	**6.** $1{,}591 \div 0.43$
7. $2.8296 \div 0.0036$	**8.** $140.7 \div 0.021$	**9.** $9.1408 \div 3.94$

10.   Using the formula $I = E/R$, find I if $E = 79.5$ V and $R = 265$ Ω.

11.   Shielded rubber-jacketed microphone cable weighs 0.075 lb/ft.
      How many feet of cable are there in a coil weighing 15 lb?
12.   What is the smallest number of insulators, each rated at 12,000 V,
      that should be used to safeguard a 220,000-V transmission line?
13.   The Q, or "quality," of a coil is a measure of its worth in a tuned
      circuit.   It is found by dividing the reactance of the coil by its
      effective resistance (see Job 16-4).   Find the Q of a coil if its react-
      ance is 1,820 Ω and its effective resistance is 30 Ω.
14.   A 50-ft-long wire has a resistance of 10.35 Ω.   What is the resist-
      ance of 1 ft of this wire?
15.   Forty complete turns of the screw thread in a micrometer will ad-
      vance it 1.000 in.   How far will one complete turn advance the
      screw?
16.   The current-amplifying ability of a transistor (β) is obtained by
      dividing the collector current I_C by the base current I_B.   Find β if
      $I_C = 0.0004$ A and $I_B = 0.00001$ A.

Multiplication of fractions and decimals

EXAMPLE 2-35   Multiply $\frac{1}{5}$ by 2.5.

SOLUTION

$$\frac{1}{5} \times 2.5 = \frac{1}{5} \times \frac{2.5}{1} = \frac{2.5}{5} = 0.5 \qquad Ans.$$

EXAMPLE 2-36   Multiply $\frac{3}{10}$ by 0.5.

SOLUTION

$$\frac{3}{10} \times 0.5 = \frac{3}{10} \times \frac{0.5}{1} = \frac{1.5}{10} = 0.15 \qquad Ans.$$

EXAMPLE 2-37   Multiply $\frac{2}{3}$ by 0.19.

SOLUTION

$$\frac{2}{3} \times 0.19 = \frac{2}{3} \times \frac{0.19}{1} = \frac{0.38}{3} = 0.127 \qquad Ans.$$

EXAMPLE 2-38   Multiply $2\frac{1}{4}$ by 0.35.

SOLUTION
If the fraction is one that can be easily changed to a decimal, do so and
multiply the resulting decimals.   Since $2\frac{1}{4}$ is equal to 2.25 (from the
decimal equivalent chart),

$$2\frac{1}{4} \times 0.35 = 2.25 \times 0.35 = 0.788 \qquad Ans.$$

PROBLEMS

1. $\frac{1}{5} \times 3.5$	2. $\frac{2}{5} \times 0.25$	3. $\frac{1}{5} \times 0.05$	4. $\frac{1}{2} \times 2.4$
5. $\frac{1}{10} \times 0.5$	6. $\frac{1}{10} \times 0.01$	7. $\frac{1}{3} \times 0.27$	8. $\frac{1}{5} \times 30.5$
9. $\frac{1}{8} \times 12.6$	10. $\frac{1}{10} \times 2.5$	11. $1\frac{1}{2} \times 0.3$	12. $\frac{2}{5} \times 0.1$
13. $\frac{1}{8} \times 0.13$	14. $\frac{3}{5} \times 2.7$	15. $\frac{1}{6} \times 4.9$	16. $\frac{2}{7} \times 3.12$
17. $5\frac{3}{4} \times 0.192$	18. $1\frac{1}{3} \times 0.23$	19. $0.056 \times 3\frac{1}{2}$	20. $0.91 \times 2\frac{1}{5}$

SUMMARY—WORKING WITH DECIMALS

1   Decimal fractions are fractions whose _____ are numbers like 10, ____, 1,000, et cetera.

2   The denominator is shown by the number of digits to the _____ of the decimal point. Thus, 0.6 represents six-_____.

0.57 represents fifty-seven _____.
0.123 represents one hundred-twenty-three _____.
3.09 represents three and nine-_____.

3   Decimals can be compared only when they have the _____ number of decimal places.

4   The word "and" in a mixed number such as five and three-hundredths is written as a _____ point. This number would be written as ____.

5   Fractions are changed to decimals by _____ the _____ by the _____.

6   A whole number always has a decimal point understood to be at the (beginning/end) of the number.

7   When dividing decimals, if a remainder is more than _____ of the divisor, drop it and add a full unit to the last _____ of the answer. If the remainder is _____ than half, drop it completely.

8   When adding or subtracting decimals, line up the decimal points in a _____ column.

9   The product of two decimals has as many decimal places as the ____ of the places in the numbers being multiplied.

10   When you divide decimals, move the decimal point in the divisor to the _____ as many places as is necessary to bring the point behind the last digit. Then move the point in the dividend to the right for the _____ number of places.

denominators
100
right
tenths

hundredths
thousandths
hundredths

same

decimal   5.03
dividing   numerator
denominator

end
half
digit
less

vertical
sum

right
same

TEST—DECIMALS

1.   Add two and seventy-three thousandths, four and one-hundred-five thousandths, seven, and sixty-seven hundredths.
2.   Add $5.04 + 8 + 19.243 + 62.7$.
3.   Arrange in order of size starting with the largest: (a) 0.05, 0.2, 0.0035; (b) 0.0061, 0.063, 0.62.

4. Subtract fifty-one and fifty-eight thousandths from seventy-nine and ninety-nine hundredths.
5. From 16½ subtract 10.359.
6. Change ³⁄₇ to a three-place decimal.
7. Change ²⁄₃ to a three-place decimal.
8. Multiply 14.32 × 0.035.
9. Divide 4.092 by 0.31.
10. Multiply 2½ × 0.66.

JOB 2-6 CHECKUP ON FORMULAS IN ELECTRICAL WORK (DIAGNOSTIC TEST)

In Job 2-3 we used our first *formula*. When Ohm's law is written using only the letters which represent the words of Ohm's law it is called a *formula*. As we continue with our study of electricity, we shall meet many new formulas. Some are simple like Ohm's law, but others are more complicated. Let us check up on our knowledge of how to use formulas. The following problems involve the use of formulas. The electrician and the electronic technician find it necessary to solve problems like these in their daily work. If you have any difficulty with these problems, see Job 2-7 which follows.

PROBLEMS

1. Using Ohm's law ($E = I \times R$), find the current I drawn by a 10-Ω automobile horn R from a 6-V battery E.
2. Using Ohm's law, find the number of ohms of resistance R needed to obtain a bias voltage E of 6 V if the current I is 0.02 A.
3. Using the formula for electrical power, $P = E \times I$, find the voltage E necessary to operate a 500-W electric percolator P if it draws a current I of 4.5 A.
4. Using the formula $P = E \times I$, find the current I drawn by a 440-W vacuum cleaner P from a 110-V line E.
5. Write the formula for the following rule: Kilowatts (kW) equals current I multiplied by voltage E and divided by 1,000.
6. Using the series-circuit formula $I = E/(R_1 + R_2)$, find I if $E = 100$ V, $R_1 = 20$ Ω, and $R_2 = 30$ Ω.
7. Using the ac formula $I = E/Z$, find the impedance Z of an ac circuit if the voltage E is 50 V and the current I is 2 A.
8. Using the formula mA = A × 1,000, find the number of amperes which is the equivalent of 125 mA (milliamperes).
9. $I_T = I_1 + I_2 + I_3$ is the formula for the total current in a parallel circuit. Find the total current I_T if $I_1 = 2$ A, $I_2 = 5$A, and $I_3 = 4$A.
10. The formula for the number of coulombs of electricity which can be placed on the plates of a capacitor is $Q = C \times E$. Find the voltage

E which is necessary to place a charge Q of 0.0000002 coulomb on the plates of a capacitor whose capacitance C is 0.000000002 F (farad).

JOB 2-7   BRUSHUP ON FORMULAS

Meaning. A formula is a convenient shorthand method for expressing and writing a rule or relationship among several quantities.

Signs of operation. The quantities involved in any simple relationship are held together by one or more of the following operations:

1   Multiplication ($\times$).
2   Division ($\div$).
3   Addition ($+$).
4   Subtraction ($-$).
5   Equality ($=$).

Each of these operations may be written in several ways.

Multiplication. The multiplication of two quantities is often expressed as the "product of" the two quantities. This may be written as follows:

1   Using a multiplication sign ($\times$) between the numbers or letters.
2   Using a dot ($\cdot$) between the numbers or letters.
3   Writing nothing at all between the numbers or letters.

For example, the product of 3 and 4 may be written as (1) 3×4 or (2) $3 \cdot 4$. The third method cannot be used when only numbers are involved because the meaning would not be clear. For example, 34 would mean the number thirty-four and *not* 3×4. This method of indicating multiplication by omitting all signs between the quantities can be used only for combinations of numbers and letters or combinations of letters.
The product of 6 and R may be written as (1) $6 \times R$, (2) $6 \cdot R$, or (3) $6R$. All three forms indicate that 6 is to be multiplied by the quantity called R.
The product of P, R, and T may be written as (1) $P \times R \times T$, (2) $P \cdot R \cdot T$, or (3) PRT. All three forms indicate that the quantity P is to be multiplied by the quantity R and then multiplied by the quantity T.

Division. The division of two quantities is often expressed as the "quotient of" the two quantities. This may be written as follows:

1   Using a division sign ($\div$) between the numbers or letters.
2   Using a fraction bar to indicate division.

For example, the quotient of 8 divided by 2 may be written as (1) $8 \div 2$ or (2) $\frac{8}{2}$.

The quotient of 12 divided by I may be written as (1) $12 \div I$ or (2) $12/I$.

The quotient of E divided by R may be written as (1) $E \div R$ or (2) E/R.

Addition. The addition of two or more quantities is often expressed as the "sum of" the quantities and is indicated by a plus sign (+) between the quantities. For example,

The sum of 6 and 4 is written as $6 + 4$.

The sum of 3 and R is written as $3 + R$.

The sum of E_1 and E_2 is written as $E_1 + E_2$.

Subtraction. The subtraction of two quantities is often expressed as the "difference between" the quantities and is indicated by a minus sign (−) between them. For example,

The difference between 9 and 4 is written as $9 - 4$. This is read as (1) 9 minus 4 or (2) 4 subtracted from 9.

The difference between 20 and R is written as $20 - R$. This is read as (1) 20 minus R or (2) R subtracted from 20.

The difference between E_T and E_1 is written as $E_T - E_1$. This is read as (1) E_T minus E_1 or (2) E_1 subtracted from E_T.

Equality. An equality sign (=) is used to indicate that the combination of numbers and letters on one side of the equality sign has the same value as the combination of numbers and letters on the other side. For example,

$$3 \times 4 = 12$$
$$a \cdot b = ab$$
$$2R = 10$$

Changing rules into formulas. To change a rule into a formula

1 Replace each quantity with a convenient letter.

2 Rewrite the rule. Substitute these letters for the words of the rule. Include the symbols for the signs of operation.

Note: The letters used to replace the words are usually the first letter of the word representing the quantity. However, any letter may be used. For example, if a letter has already been used to represent some quantity, it cannot be used again in the same formula to represent another quantity. In this event, a letter which is *not* the first letter of the word would be used.

EXAMPLE 2-39 Change the following rule into a formula. The area of a rectangle is equal to its length multiplied by its width.

SOLUTION

The length is replaced by the letter L.

The width is replaced by the letter W.

The area is replaced by the letter A.

The area is equal to the length multiplied by the width.

$$A \qquad = \qquad L \qquad \times \qquad W$$

Thus,

$$A = L \times W \qquad \text{or} \qquad A = L \cdot W \qquad \text{or} \qquad A = LW \qquad Ans.$$

EXAMPLE 2-40   Change the following rule into a formula. The voltage is equal to the current multiplied by the resistance.

SOLUTION

The voltage is replaced by the letter E.

The current is replaced by the letter I.

The resistance is replaced by the letter R.

The voltage is equal to the current multiplied by the resistance.

$$E \qquad = \qquad I \qquad \times \qquad R$$

Thus,

$$E = I \times R \qquad \text{or} \qquad E = I \cdot R \qquad \text{or} \qquad E = IR \qquad Ans.$$

EXAMPLE 2-41   Change the following rule into a formula. The voltage E of a series circuit of two resistors is equal to the current I multiplied by the sum of the resistances R_1 and R_2.

SOLUTION

The word "sum" is indicated by a plus sign. This sum is actually a *single* quantity obtained by adding R_1 and R_2. This must be shown by enclosing R_1 and R_2 in a pair of parentheses. The current I will then be multiplied by the parentheses. Thus,

$$E = I \times (R_1 + R_2) \qquad \text{or} \qquad E = I(R_1 + R_2) \qquad Ans.$$

SELF-TEST 2-42   Change the following rule into a formula. The total resistance R_T of two resistors in parallel is equal to the product of the resistances R_1 and R_2 divided by the sum of the resistances.

SOLUTION

The diagram for the circuit is shown in Fig. 2-14.

1   The word "product" means to   (add/multiply/divide) .

2   The product of R_1 and R_2 is written as R_1 ___ R_2.

3   The word "sum" means to   (add/subtract) .

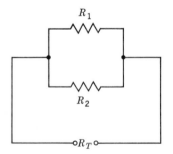

FIGURE 2-14
Resistances in parallel.

multiply

$\times$

add

4   The sum of R_1 and R_2 is written as $R_1 \underline{\hspace{1cm}} R_2$.

5   The division in our formula may be written as a fraction. The numerator of the fraction will be the __(sum/product)__ of the resistances.

6   The denominator will be the __(sum/product)__ of the resistances.

7   The formula will read as:

$$R_T = \frac{R_1 \ ? \ R_2}{R_1 \ ? \ R_2} \qquad Ans.$$

+

product

sum

×

+

PROBLEMS

Write the formula for each of the rules given. Use the italic letters and abbreviations in parentheses to indicate each word.

1.   The electrical power P is equal to the current I multiplied by the voltage E.

2.   The effective voltage E of an ac voltage wave is equal to 0.707 times the maximum value E_{max}.

3.   The efficiency (Eff) of a motor is equal to the power output P_o divided by the power input P_i.

4.   The total resistance R_T of a series circuit is equal to the sum of the individual resistances R_1, R_2, and R_3.

5.   The capacitive reactance X_C of a capacitor is equal to 159,000 divided by the product of the frequency f and the capacitance C.

6.   The power factor (PF) of an ac circuit is equal to the total resistance R_T divided by the impedance Z.

7.   The diagonal D of a square is equal to 1.414 times the side S of the square.

8.   The net price N of an article is equal to the list price L minus the discount D.

9.   The minor diameter d of a screw thread is equal to the major diameter D minus twice the depth of the thread h.

10.   The circumference C of a circle (the distance around the circle) is equal to 3.14 times the diameter D.

11.   The area of a triangle A is equal to ½ times the base B times the height H.

12.   The interest on an investment I is equal to the product of the principal P, the rate of interest R, and the time T.

13.   The perimeter P of a rectangle is equal to the sum of twice the length L and twice the width W.

14.   The resistance R_s of an ammeter shunt is equal to the product of the meter current I_m and the meter resistance R_m divided by the shunt current I_s.

15.   The current I_m in an ammeter is the difference between the line current I and the shunt current I_s.

16.   The total current I_T in a series circuit of two resistors is equal to the total voltage E_T divided by the sum of the resistances R_1 and R_2.

17. The resistance R_s of an ammeter shunt is equal to the meter resistance R_m divided by 1 less than the multiplying factor N.
18. A man's salary S is the sum of his basic salary B plus 1.5 times the number of hours of overtime H times his hourly rate R.

Changing formulas into rules

EXAMPLE 2-43   Express the formula $P = EI$ as a rule if P is the number of watts of power used, E is the voltage, and I is the current.

SOLUTION
The number of watts of power used is equal to the voltage multiplied by the current in the circuit.   *Ans.*

PROBLEMS

Express the formula in each problem as a rule.

1. $P = EI$
   where P = number of watts of power consumed
   E = voltage across the circuit
   I = current through the circuit

2. $R = \dfrac{e}{I}$
   where R = internal resistance of a dry cell
   e = voltage delivered by the cell
   I = current delivered by the cell

3. $\lambda = 300{,}000/\text{kHz}$
   where λ = wavelength of a radio wave
   kHz = frequency measured in kilohertz

4. $I_T = I_1 + I_2 + I_3$
   where I_T = total current in a parallel circuit
   I_1, I_2, and I_3 = current in the individual branches

5. $R = \dfrac{KL}{A}$
   where R = resistance of a wire, Ω
   K = specific resistance
   L = length of the wire, ft
   A = area of the wire, cmil (circular mils)

6. $X_L = 6.28\,fL$
   where X_L = inductive reactance of a coil, Ω
   f = frequency, Hz
   L = inductance, H

Substitution in formulas. As we have learned, we can change a rule into a formula by substituting letters for words. Since each word or letter actually represents some number in a specific problem, we can go one step further and substitute specific numbers for the letters in any formula or expression. This is called *substitution in a formula*. The numbers are then combined according to the signs of operation shown by the formula.

EXAMPLE 2-44   Using the formula $P = EI$, find the power P necessary to operate an incandescent lamp using a voltage E of 110 V and a current I of 2 A.

SOLUTION
The diagram for the circuit is shown in Fig. 2-15.

1   Write the formula.

$$P = EI$$

2   Substitute numbers.

$$P = 110 \times 2$$

3   Multiply the numbers.

$$P = 220 \text{ W} \qquad Ans.$$

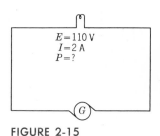

FIGURE 2-15

EXAMPLE 2-45   In the NPN transistor circuit shown in Fig. 2-16, the formula for the emitter current is $I_E = I_B + I_C$. Find the emitter current if the base current is 0.000004 A and the collector current is 0.0002 A.

SOLUTION
The diagram for the circuit is shown in Fig. 2-16.

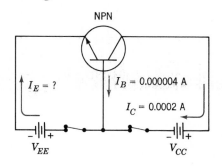

FIGURE 2-16
The total emitter current is equal to the sum of I_B and I_C.

1   Write the formula.

$$I_E = I_B + I_C$$

2   Substitute numbers.

$$I_E = 0.000004 + 0.0002$$

3   Add the numbers.

$$I_E = 0.000204 \text{ A} \qquad Ans.$$

EXAMPLE 2-46   Using the formula $I_m = I - I_s$, find the current I_m in an ammeter if the line current I is 50 A and the shunt current I_s is 49 A.

SOLUTION
The diagram for the circuit is shown in Fig. 2-17.

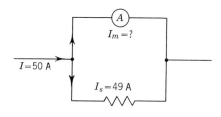

$I = 50$ A

$I_m = ?$

$I_s = 49$ A

FIGURE 2-17

1   Write the formula.

$$I_m = I - I_s$$

2   Substitute numbers.

$$I_m = 50 - 49$$

3   Subtract the numbers.

$$I_m = 1 \text{ A} \qquad Ans.$$

SELF-TEST 2-47   Using the formula $E_T = I(R_1 + R_2)$, find the total voltage E_T in the series circuit shown in Fig. 2-18.

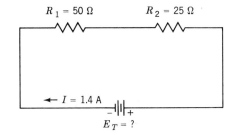

$R_1 = 50 \ \Omega$ $R_2 = 25 \ \Omega$

$\leftarrow I = 1.4$ A

$E_T = ?$

FIGURE 2-18

SOLUTION

1   Write the formula.

$$E_T = I(R_1 + R_2)$$

2   Substitute numbers.

$$E_T = 1.4(50 + \underline{\quad})$$

| 25

3   Find the value of the parentheses first.

$$E_T = 1.4(\underline{\quad})$$

| 75

4   Multiply.

$$E_T = \underline{\quad} \text{ V} \qquad Ans.$$

| 105

PROBLEMS

Solve the following problems using the formulas that are given in each problem. If there is no diagram that applies to the problem, set down the given information in the space ordinarily used for the diagram.

1. Using the formula $A = LW$, find the number of square feet of area A in a rectangle if the length L is 15 ft and the width W is 9 ft.
2. Using the formula $I = E/Z$, find the number of amperes I if E is 110 V and Z is 22 Ω.
3. Using the formula $I_T = I_1 + I_2 + I_3$, find the total number of amperes I_T if $I_1 = 2$ A, $I_2 = 3$ A, and $I_3 = 5$ A.
4. Using the formula kW $= EI/1,000$, find the kilowatts (kW) of power if the voltage E is 200 V and the current I is 2 A.
5. Using the formula for the distance F across the flats of a hexagonal bolt head, $F = 1.732\ S$, find F if $S = 0.5$ in.

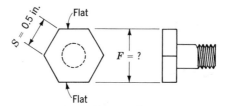

FIGURE 2-19

6. Using the formula $D = (N + 2)/P$, find the diameter of a gear blank D to cut a 32-tooth gear N if the pitch $P = 6$.
7. Using the formula $R_T = R_1 + R_2 + R_3$, find the total resistance R_T of a series circuit if R_1 is 18.2 Ω, R_2 is 45.8 Ω, and R_3 is 76.4 Ω.
8. The formula for the shunt current in an ammeter hookup is $I_s = I - I_m$. Find the current I_s through the shunt if the line current I is 0.045 A and the meter current I_m is 0.009 A.
9. Using the formula $d = D - 2h$, find the minor diameter d of a screw thread if the major diameter $D = 1.5$ in and the depth of the thread $h = 0.081$ in.
10. The formula for the perimeter P of a rectangle is $P = 2L + 2W$. Find the perimeter P of a rectangle if the length $L = 20$ in and the width $W = 8.5$ in.
11. Using the formula $R_T = (R_1 \times R_2)/(R_1 + R_2)$, find the total resistance R_T of a parallel circuit if R_1 is 30 Ω and R_2 is 60 Ω.
12. Using the formula $X_L = 6.28fL$, find the inductive reactance X_L of a coil to a frequency f of 60 Hz if the coil has an inductance L of 0.15 H.
13. Using the series-circuit formula $I = E/(R + r)$, find the current I if $E = 6$, $R = 16$, and $r = 8$.
14. In Fig. 2-20, the taper per foot T may be found by using the formula $T = \dfrac{12(D - d)}{L}$. Find T.

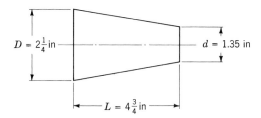

FIGURE 2-20

A tapered pin decreases in diameter.

15. Using the formula to change Centigrade temperature to Fahrenheit temperature, $F = \frac{9}{5}C + 32$, find F if $C = 20°$.

16. Using the formula $S = a + d(n - 1)$, find S if $a = 5$, $d = 2$, and $n = 7$.

17. Using the formula for a differential pulley,

$$F = \frac{W(R - r)}{2R}$$

find the force F needed to lift a weight $W = 960$ lb if $R = 8$ in and $r = 7$ in.

18. Using the formula for the current delivered by a number of battery cells in series, $I = nE/(R + nr)$, find I if the number of cells $n = 8$, the voltage of each cell $E = 1.5$, the load $R = 9.6\ \Omega$, and the internal resistance of each cell $r = 0.05\ \Omega$.

19. Using the formula for the effect of temperature on resistance, $R_t = R_o(1 + 0.0042t)$, find the resistance R_t at a temperature $t = 50°$, if the resistance at $0°C$ (R_o) is $60\ \Omega$.

20. Using the formula

$$I = \frac{C(E_1 - E_2)}{t}$$

find the current I that flows during the discharge of a capacitor if $C = 0.000015$, $E_1 = 250$, $E_2 = 150$, and $t = 0.03$ s.

JOB 2-8 SOLVING THE OHM'S LAW FORMULA FOR CURRENT OR RESISTANCE

Formulas are equations. As you may have noticed, every formula contains the sign of equality. The statement that a combination of quantities is *equal* to another combination of quantities is called an *equation*. In this sense, every formula is an equation. Examples of some equations are

$$3 \times 4 = 12$$

$$2 \times I = 10$$

$$12 = 3 \times R$$

$$E = IR$$

In order that a statement be termed an equation, it is necessary only that the value on the left side of the equality sign be *truly equal* to the value on the right side.

Working with equations. Many mathematical operations may be performed on an equation. Whatever is done, however, the basic equality of the statements on each side of the equality sign must not be destroyed. This equality must be maintained if the equation is to remain an equation. This is accomplished by applying the following basic principle.

BASIC PRINCIPLE	Any mathematical operation performed on one side of an equality sign must also be performed on the other side.

For example, let us subject the equation $3 \times 4 = 12$ to different mathematical operations.

RULE 1	The same number may be added to both sides of an equality sign without destroying the equality.

1 Write the equation.

$$3 \times 4 = 12$$

2 Add 3 to both sides.

$$(3 \times 4) + 3 = 12 + 3$$

3 Do the arithmetic.

$$12 + 3 = 12 + 3$$

$$\text{or } 15 = 15$$

which is a true equation, since the left side is still equal to the right side.

RULE 2	The same number may be subtracted from both sides of an equality sign without destroying the equality.

1 Write the equation.

$$3 \times 4 = 12$$

2 Subtract 3 from both sides.

$$(3 \times 4) - 3 = 12 - 3$$

3   Do the arithmetic.

$$12 - 3 = 12 - 3$$

$$\text{or } 9 = 9$$

which is a true equation, since the left side is still equal to the right side.

RULE 3	Both sides of an equality sign may be multiplied by the same number without destroying the equality.

1   Write the equation.

$$3 \times 4 = 12$$

2   Multiply both sides by 3.

$$(3 \times 4) \times 3 = 12 \times 3$$

3   Do the arithmetic.

$$12 \times 3 = 12 \times 3$$

$$\text{or } 36 = 36$$

which is a true equation, since the left side is still equal to the right side.

RULE 4	Both sides of an equality sign may be divided by the same number without destroying the equality.

1   Write the equation.

$$3 \times 4 = 12$$

2   Divide both sides by 3.

$$\frac{3 \times 4}{3} = \frac{12}{3}$$

3   Do the arithmetic.

$$\frac{12}{3} = \frac{12}{3}$$

$$\text{or } 4 = 4$$

which is a true equation, since the left side is still equal to the right side.

Solving equations.   Consider the equation $2R = 10$. To solve this equation means to find the value of the unknown letter R in the equation. This value is found *when the letter stands all alone on one side of the equality* *sign.* When this occurs, the equation has the form

$$R = \text{some number}$$

This number will obviously be the value of the letter R, and the equation will be solved.

How do we get the letter all alone? In the equation $2R = 10$, the letter will be alone on the left side of the equality sign if we can somehow eliminate the number 2 on that side. The number 2 will actually be eliminated if we can change it to a 1, since $1R$ means the same as R. This can be done by applying Rule 4 above. In order to eliminate the 2, we shall *divide both sides* of the equation *by that same number.*

1 Write the equation.

$$2R = 10$$

2 Divide both sides by 2.

$$\frac{2R}{2} = \frac{10}{2}$$

3 Simplify each side separately.

$$\frac{\overset{1}{\cancel{2}}R}{\underset{1}{\cancel{2}}} = \frac{\overset{5}{\cancel{10}}}{\underset{1}{\cancel{2}}}$$

or $1R = 5$

or $R = 5$

Suppose the unknown letter appears on the right side of the equality sign as in the equation $12 = 3R$. In this situation, we proceed exactly as before. To solve the equation means to get the letter R *all alone* on one side of the equality sign. We can do this by changing the $3R$ to $1R$ by *dividing both sides* of the equation by 3.

1 Write the equation.

$$12 = 3R$$

2 Divide both sides by 3.

$$\frac{12}{3} = \frac{3R}{3}$$

3 Simplify each side separately.

$$\frac{\overset{4}{\cancel{12}}}{\underset{1}{\cancel{3}}} = \frac{\overset{1}{\cancel{3}}R}{\underset{1}{\cancel{3}}}$$

or $4 = 1R$

$$\text{or } 4 = R$$

$$\text{or } R = 4$$

Notice that the number that is multiplied by the unknown letter will be canceled out *only* if we divide both sides of the equality sign *by that same number*. Dividing both sides by any other number will *not* eliminate this number.

RULE 5	To eliminate the number which is multiplied by the unknown letter, divide both sides of the equality sign by the multiplier of the letter.

EXAMPLE 2-48   Solve the following equations for the values of the unknown letters.

SOLUTION

1   Write the equations.

$$2R = 10 \qquad\qquad 14 = 7E$$

2   Divide both sides of each equation by the multiplier of the letter.

$$\frac{2R}{2} = \frac{10}{2} \qquad\qquad \frac{14}{7} = \frac{7E}{7}$$

3   Cancel out the multiplier of the letters.

$$R = \frac{10}{2} \qquad\qquad \frac{14}{7} = E$$

Dividing,

$$R = 5 \quad Ans. \qquad 2 = E \quad Ans.$$

We are now in a position to shorten our work. Notice that in each example, the effect of dividing both sides of the equality sign by the multiplier of the letter has been to *move* the multiplier *across the equality sign* into the position shown in step 3. Since this will always occur, we can eliminate step 2 and proceed as shown in Example 2-49.

EXAMPLE 2-49   Solve the following equations for the values of the unknown letters:

SOLUTION

1   Write the equations.

$$2R = 10 \qquad\qquad 14 = 7E$$

2   Divide the quantity all alone on one side of the equality sign by the multiplier of the letter.

$$R = \frac{10}{2} \qquad\qquad \frac{14}{7} = E$$

3 Dividing,

$$R = 5 \quad Ans. \qquad 2 = E \quad Ans.$$

RULE 6	To solve a simple equation of the form "a number multiplied by a letter equals a number," divide the number all alone on one side of the equality sign by the multiplier of the letter.

EXAMPLE 2-50   Solve the equation $4I = 23$ for the value of I.

SOLUTION

$$4I = 23$$
$$I = \frac{23}{4}$$
$$I = 5\tfrac{3}{4} \quad Ans.$$

EXAMPLE 2-51   Solve the equation $18 = 0.3Z$ for the value of Z.

SOLUTION

$$18 = 0.3Z$$
$$\frac{18}{0.3} = Z$$
$$60 = Z$$
$$\text{or } Z = 60 \quad Ans.$$

SELF-TEST 2-52   In a common-emitter transistor circuit, the relationship between the base current I_B and the collector current I_C is given as $\beta I_B = I_C$. Find the value of I_B if $\beta = 50$, and $I_C = 0.002$ A.

SOLUTION

1 Write the formula.

$$\beta I_B = I_C$$

2 Substitute numbers.

$$50 I_B = \underline{\qquad}$$

0.002

3 Solve for I_B.

$$I_B = \frac{?}{?}$$

$$\frac{0.002}{50}$$

4 Divide the numbers.

$$I_B = \underline{\qquad} \text{ A} \quad Ans.$$

0.00004

PROBLEMS

Solve the following equations for the value of the unknown letter:

1. $3I = 15$	2. $5R = 20$	3. $2E = 12$
4. $48 = 8R$	5. $7I = 63$	6. $4L = 21$
7. $3R = 41$	8. $16R = 4$	9. $20I = 117$
10. $19 = 2E$	11. $\frac{1}{2}W = 20$	12. $20 = 100R$
13. $0.3R = 120$	14. $0.04Z = 60$	15. $40 = 0.2Z$
16. $8 = 0.4Z$	17. $0.15R = 120$	18. $0.003R = 78$
19. $117 = 0.3Z$	20. $\frac{3}{5}T = 12$	21. $8E = \frac{1}{2}$

Solving the formula for Ohm's law. The formula for Ohm's law is actually an equation. By applying Rule 6, we can solve Ohm's law for any unknown value of current or resistance.

EXAMPLE 2-53   The total resistance of a relay coil is 50 Ω. What current will it draw from a 20-V source?

SOLUTION
The diagram for the circuit is shown in Fig. 2-21.

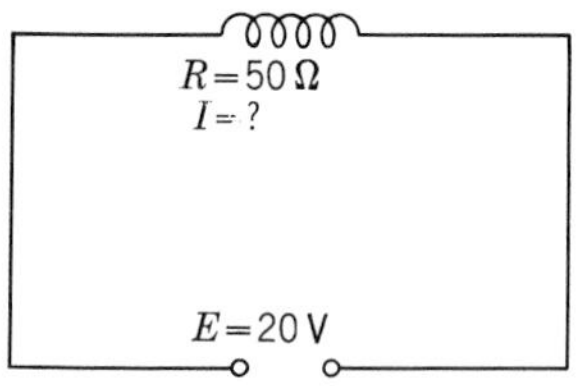

1   Write the formula.

$$E = IR$$

2   Substitute numbers.

$$20 = I \times 50$$

3   Solve for I.

$$\frac{20}{50} = I$$

4   Divide the numbers.

$$0.4 = I$$

or $I = 0.4$ A   *Ans.*

$R = 50\ \Omega$
$I = ?$

$E = 20$ V

FIGURE 2-21

EXAMPLE 2-54   Find the total resistance of a telegraph coil if it draws 0.015 A from a 6.6-V source.

SOLUTION
The diagram for the circuit is shown in Fig. 2-22.

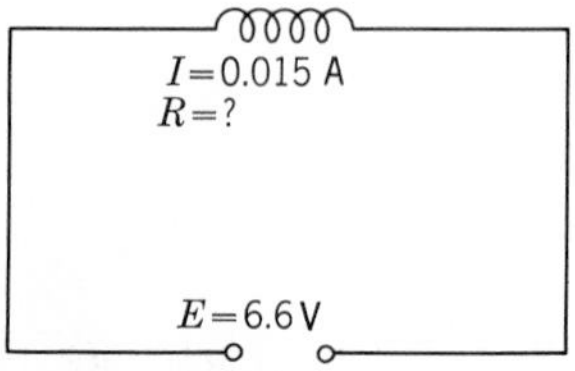

1   Write the formula.

$$E = IR$$

2   Substitute numbers.

$$6.6 = 0.015 \times R$$

$I = 0.015$ A
$R = ?$

$E = 6.6$ V

FIGURE 2-22

3   Solve for R.

$$\frac{6.6}{0.015} = R$$

4   Divide the numbers.

$$440 = R$$

$$\text{or } R = 440 \ \Omega \qquad Ans.$$

SELF-TEST 2-55   Find the current through the emitter resistor R_E in the common-base amplifier circuit shown in Fig. 2-23.

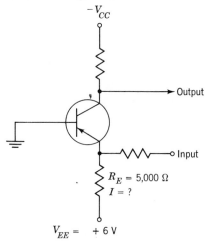

$-V_{CC}$

→ Output

○ Input

$R_E = 5{,}000 \ \Omega$
$I = ?$

$V_{EE} = \ +6 \ V$

FIGURE 2-23

A common-base amplifier circuit.

SOLUTION

1   Write the formula.

$$E = I \times \underline{} \qquad\qquad R$$

2   Substitute numbers.

$$\underline{} = I \times 5{,}000 \qquad\qquad 6$$

3   Solve for I.

$$\frac{6}{?} = I \qquad\qquad 5{,}000$$

4   Divide the numbers.

$$\underline{} = I \qquad\qquad 0.0012$$

$$\text{or } I = \underline{} \ A \qquad Ans. \qquad\qquad 0.0012$$

PROBLEMS

1.   What is the hot resistance of an arc lamp if it draws 15 A from a 30-V line?

2. The resistance of the motor windings of an electric vacuum cleaner is 20 Ω. If the voltage is 120 V, find the current drawn.

3. An electric enameling kiln draws 9 A from a 117-V line. Find the resistance of the coils.

4. The field magnet of a loudspeaker carries 0.04 A when connected to a 40-V supply. Find its resistance.

5. How much current is drawn from a 12-V battery when operating an automobile horn of 8 Ω resistance?

6. What is the hot resistance of a tungsten lamp if it draws 0.25 A from a 110-V line?

7. What current would flow in a 0.3-Ω short circuit of a 6-V automobile ignition system?

8. A 2N525 transistor is used as a transistor switch to control a 20-V source across a 100-Ω load. Find the current that flows when the switch is conducting.

9. In the circuit shown in Fig. 2-23, find the emitter resistance R_E if the emitter current $I_E = 0.002$ A and the emitter supply voltage $V_{EE} = 10$ V.

10. A dry cell indicates a terminal voltage of 1.2 V when a wire of 0.2 Ω resistance is connected across it. What current flows in the wire?

11. Find the resistance of an automobile starting motor if it draws 90 A from the 12-V battery.

12. A meter registers 0.0002 A when the voltage across it is 3 V. Find the total resistance of the meter circuit.

13. What is the resistance of a telephone receiver if there is a voltage drop of 24 V across it when the current is 0.02 A?

14. What current is drawn by a 5,000-Ω electric clock when operated from a 110-V line?

15. Find the current drawn by a 52-Ω toaster from a 117-V line.

16. Find the resistance of an electric furnace drawing 41 A from a 230-V line.

17. The resistance of the field coils of a shunt motor is 60 Ω. What is the field current when the voltage across the coils is 220 V?

18. The resistance of a common Christmas-tree lamp is about 50 Ω. What is the current through it if the voltage across the lamp is 14 V?

19. The large copper leads on switchboards are called bus bars. What is the resistance of a bus bar carrying 400 A if the voltage across its ends is 0.6 V?

20. If a radio receiver draws 0.85 A from a 110-V line, what is the total resistance (impedance) of the receiver?

21. A 32-candlepower lamp in a truck headlight draws 3.4 A from the 6-V battery. What is the resistance of the lamp?

22. If the resistance of the air gap in an automobile spark plug is 2,500 Ω, what voltage is needed to force 0.16 A through it?

23. A voltage of 5 V appears across the 2,500-Ω load resistor in a self-biased transistor circuit. Find the current in the resistor.
24. What current flows through an automobile headlight lamp of 1.2 Ω resistance if it is operated from the 6-V battery?
25. What is the resistance of a buzzer if it draws 0.14 A from a 3-V source?
26. Find the resistance of an iron if it draws 3.8 A from a 110-V line.
27. A 160-Ω telegraph relay coil operates on a voltage of 9.6 V. What is the current drawn by the relay?

JOB 2-9   REVIEW OF OHM'S LAW

In any electrical circuit,

1 The voltage forces the _____ through a conductor against its resistance.

2 The _____ tries to stop the current from flowing.

3 The current that flows in a circuit depends on the _____ and the resistance.

current

resistance

voltage

The relationship among these three quantities is described by Ohm's law. Ohm's law applies to an entire circuit or to any component part of a circuit.

FORMULA

$$E = IR \qquad \boxed{2\text{-}1}$$

where E = voltage, V
       I = current, A
       R = resistance, Ω

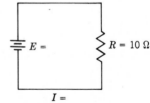

The formula for Ohm's law may be used to find the value of any one of the quantities in the formula. It is of equal importance that the student be able to determine the relative values of each quantity as one of the other quantities is changed in amount.

In Fig. 2-24, if the resistance $R = 10$ Ω remains unchanged,

FIGURE 2-24
When the resistance remains constant, the larger the voltage, the larger the current.

When the voltage $E = 10$ V, the current $I =$ ____.
When the voltage $E = 20$ V, the current $I =$ ____.
When the voltage $E = 50$ V, the current $I =$ ____.
When the voltage $E = 100$ V, the current $I =$ _____.

1 A

2 A

5 A

10 A

As you can see, when the resistance remains constant,

The larger the voltage, the larger the current.
The smaller the voltage, the _____ the current.

smaller

In Fig. 2-25, if the voltage $E = 100$ V remains unchanged,

When the resistance $R = 1$ Ω, the current $I = $_____.   100 A

When the resistance $R = 10$ Ω, the current $I = $_____.   10 A

When the resistance $R = 50$ Ω, the current $I = $____.   2 A

When the resistance $R = 100$ Ω, the current $I = $____.   1 A

As you can see, when the voltage remains constant,

The larger the resistance, the smaller the current.

The smaller the resistance, the _____ the current.   larger

Formulas in electrical work. A formula is a shorthand method for writing a rule. Each letter in a formula represents a number which may be substituted for it. The signs of operation tells us what to do with these numbers.

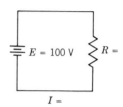

$I =$

FIGURE 2-25
When the voltage remains constant, the larger the resistance the smaller the current.

Steps in solving problems

1   Read the problem carefully.

2   Draw a simple diagram of the circuit.

3   Record the given information directly on the diagram. Indicate the values to be found by question marks.

4   Write the formula.

5   Substitute the given numbers for the letters in the formula. If the number for the letter is unknown, merely write the letter again. Include all mathematical signs.

6   Do the indicated arithmetic.

   a If after substitution the unknown letter is multiplied by some number, divide the number all alone on one side of the equality sign by the multiplier of the unknown letter.

7   In the answer, indicate the letter, its numerical value, and the units of measurement.

EXAMPLE 2-56   Solve the equation $6.3 = 0.3R$ for the letter R.

SOLUTION

1   Write the equation.

$$6.3 = 0.3R$$

2   Solve for R.

$$\frac{6.3}{0.3} = R$$

3   Divide the numbers.

$$21 = R$$

$$\text{or } R = 21 \quad Ans.$$

SELF-TEST 2-57   In Fig. 2-26, the bleeder resistance draws 0.004 A from the 300-V power supply when no loads are connected to the various voltage divider terminals. Find the total bleeder resistance.

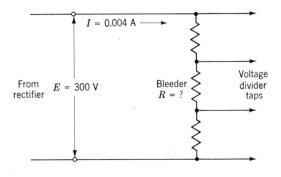

FIGURE 2-26
The bleeder resistor is made of three resistors in series.

SOLUTION

1   The diagram for the circuit is shown in Fig. 2-26.

2   Write the formula.

$$E = I \times \underline{\hspace{1cm}}$$ R

3   Substitute numbers.

$$300 = \underline{\hspace{1cm}} \times R$$ 0.004

4   Solve the equation.

$$\frac{300}{?} = R$$ 0.004

5   Divide the numbers.

$$\underline{\hspace{1cm}} = R$$ 75,000

$$\text{or } R = 75,000 \underline{\hspace{0.5cm}} \quad Ans.$$ Ω

PROBLEMS

1.   The resistance of an electric percolator is 22 Ω. If it draws 5 A, what is the operating voltage?

2.   An electric heater whose coil is wound with No. 18 iron wire is connected across 110 V. If it draws a current of 10 A, what is the value of its resistance?

3.   According to the National Electrical Code, No. 14 asbestos-covered type A wire should never carry more than 32 A. Is this wire safe to use to carry power to a 10-Ω 230-V motor?

4.   A washing-machine motor has a total resistance of 39 Ω and operates on 117 V. Find the current taken by the motor.

5.   What is the voltage drop across an Allied model BK relay of 12,000 Ω resistance if it carries 0.0015 A?

6. What is the resistance of a cathode bias resistor which causes a drop of 20 V when 0.05 A flows through it?

7. What is the voltage across a telephone receiver of 800 Ω resistance if the current flowing is 0.03 A?

8. A spot welder delivers 7,000 A when the voltage is 4.9 V. What is the resistance of the piece being welded?

9. A 600-W soldering iron is used on a 120-V line and has a resistance of 24 Ω. Find the current drawn.

10. A volume control similar to that used in the Panasonic RF 738 transistor radio is shown in Fig. 2-27. How many ohms of resistance are engaged in the potentiometer if the voltage drop is 7 V and it passes a current of 0.0007 A?

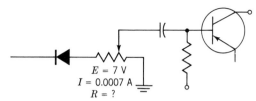

$E = 7 V$
$I = 0.0007 A$
$R = ?$

FIGURE 2-27

A volume control in a simple transistor radio.

11. If the full-scale reading of an ammeter is 10 A, what is its resistance if this current causes a voltage drop of 0.05 V?

12. What is the resistance of a bus bar carrying 300 A if the voltage drop across it is 1.2 V?

13. A sensitive dc meter takes 0.009 A from a line when the voltage is 108 V. What is the resistance of the meter?

14. An electromagnet draws 5 A from a 110-V line. What current will it draw from a 220-V line?

15. The resistance of the series field coils of a compound motor is 0.24 Ω, and they carry a current of 72 A. Find the voltage drop across these coils.

16. A power pack delivers 42 A to a flash lamp through a cord with a resistance of 0.65 Ω. Find the voltage drop along the cord.

17. A 5,000-Ω resistor in a voltage divider reduces the voltage across it by 150 V. What current flows through the resistor?

18. A series resistor is used to reduce the voltage to a motor by 45 V. What must be the resistance of the resistor if the motor draws 0.52 A?

19. If a 0.6-Ω rail connector accidentally shorted the 12-V system of a model railroad, what current would flow?

20. An automobile dashboard ammeter shows 5.5 A of current flowing when the headlights are lit. If the current is drawn from the 6-V storage battery, what is the resistance of the headlights?

21. A voltmeter has a resistance of 27,000 Ω. What current will flow through the meter when it is placed across a 220-V line?

22. A 110-V line is protected with a 15-A fuse. Will the fuse "carry" a 5.5-Ω load?

23. A voltage of 28.8 V is required to send 7.2 A of current through a wire 5 mi long. What is the resistance of the wire? What is the resistance per mile of wire?

24. What bias voltage is developed across a grid leak resistor of 2,000,000 Ω resistance if the current through it is 0.0000002 A?

25. A series of insulators leak 0.00003 A at 9,000 V. Find the resistance of the insulator string.

TEST—OHM'S LAW

Draw a diagram for each problem, and label it completely. Write the formula, substitute, and show all steps necessary for the solution of the problem. Show all arithmetical calculations at the side.

1. A neon electric sign draws 1¼ A. If its resistance is 92 Ω, find the voltage needed.

2. What current is drawn by a 6,000-Ω electric clock when operated from a 110-V line?

3. What is the resistance of a motor if it draws 5 A from a 110-V line?

4. The resistance of a telephone receiver is 425 Ω. If the current is 0.06 A, what voltage is required?

5. Find the current used by a bell of 8.5 Ω resistance when used on a 12.6-V circuit.

6. What is the resistance of a truck windshield-wiper motor if it draws ¾ A from the 6-V battery?

7. A 24-Ω soldering iron requires 5 A for proper operation. What voltage is necessary?

8. An arc lamp with a resistance of 2½ Ω operates on a 70-V line. What current does it draw?

9. What is the voltage across a voltmeter of 24,000 Ω resistance if it carries 0.0015 A?

10. Neglecting the very small base-emitter resistance, find R_B in the common-emitter transistor circuit shown in Fig. 2-28.

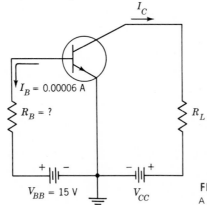

FIGURE 2-28

A common-emitter circuit.

SERIES CIRCUITS

JOB 3-1 VOLTAGE, CURRENT, AND RESISTANCE IN SERIES CIRCUITS

Wiring a series circuit. A series circuit is one in which all the component parts are connected in succession from plus (+) to minus (−), as shown in Fig. 3-1. In a series circuit there is *only one path* through which the electrons may flow. The flow of current in a series circuit may be compared with the flow of water in a series-connected water system. In Fig. 3-2*a*, the pump forces the water through the three valves in succession. In Fig. 3-2*b*, the electron-moving pump—the battery—forces the electrons through the three resistors in succession. In both series circuits there is *only one path* that the water or the electrons may travel. If the water circuit is broken at any point, by either closing a valve or breaking a pipe, the flow of water around the system will stop. If the electrical series circuit is broken at any point, no energy will be available to any part of the circuit, since there will be no return path for the electrons to follow. For example, in Fig. 3-3, a push button is usually placed in series with the bell it controls. As long as the button is held up by the force of the spring inside it, the circuit is broken. Since no current can flow in a broken, or "open," circuit, the bell will not ring. When the button is depressed, the wires make contact, completing the circuit. The current then flows through the bell and the bell rings.

Symbols for series circuits. Numbers or letters written underneath other numbers or letters are called *subscripts*. Numbers like 1, 2, or 3

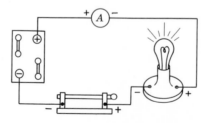

FIGURE 3-1
A simple series circuit. The parts are connected so that the current can flow in only one path.

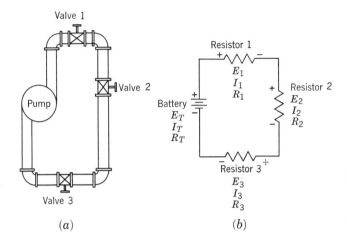

FIGURE 3-2

(a) Valves in series in a water-supply system. (b) Resistors in series in an electrical circuit.

are written under the letters $E, I,$ or R to indicate these quantities in the first, second, or third part of the circuit. For example, in Fig. 3-2b,

E_1 represents the voltage across the first resistor.

I_2 represents the current through the second resistor.

R_3 represents the resistance of the third resistor.

E_T represents the total voltage in the circuit.

I_T represents the total current in the circuit.

R_T represents the total resistance in the circuit.

Total current in a series circuit. In Fig. 3-2a, the water was forced through each valve in turn because it had no other place to go. Whatever quantity of water flowed through the first valve had to flow through the second and third valve also. In Fig. 3-2b, the electrons that were forced through the first resistor R_1 also had to flow through the second resistor R_2 and through the third resistor R_3 because there was no other place for them to go. If follows, then, that any current entering the circuit must flow *unchanged* through all the other parts of the circuit.

RULE	The total current in a series circuit is equal to the current in any other part of the circuit.

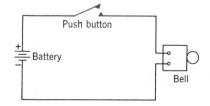

FIGURE 3-3

A push button in series controls the flow of current from the battery to the bell by opening or closing the circuit.

FORMULA

$$I_T = I_1 = I_2 = I_3 = \cdots \text{ etc.} \qquad \boxed{3\text{-}1}$$

where I_T = total current
I_1 = current in first part
I_2 = current in second part
I_3 = current in third part, etc.

Total voltage in a series circuit. In Fig. 3-4*a*, the total force required to lift the weights must be equal to the *sum* of the forces required to lift the individual weights. In Fig. 3-4*b*, the total electrical pressure supplied by the battery must be equal to the *sum* of the pressures required by each lamp.

RULE	The total voltage in a series circuit is equal to the sum of the voltages across all the parts of the circuit.

FORMULA

$$E_T = E_1 + E_2 + E_3 + \cdots \text{ etc.} \qquad \boxed{3\text{-}2}$$

where E_T = total voltage
E_1 = voltage across first part
E_2 = voltage across second part
E_3 = voltage across third part, etc.

Total resistance in a series circuit. In Fig. 3-4*a*, the resistance that must be overcome by the body is equal to the *sum* of the weights. In Fig. 3-4*b*, the total electrical resistance of the circuit is equal to the *sum* of the resistances of all the lamps.

RULE	The total resistance of a series circuit is equal to the sum of the resistances of all the parts of the circuit.

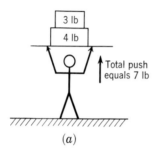

(a)

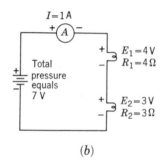

(b)

FIGURE 3-4

Similarity between (a) a force system and (b) an electrical circuit.

FORMULA

$$R_T = R_1 + R_2 + R_3 + \cdots \text{etc.}$$

3-3

where R_T = total resistance
$\quad R_1$ = resistance of first part
$\quad R_2$ = resistance of second part
$\quad R_3$ = resistance of third part, etc.

EXAMPLE 3-1   A 45- and a 90-V battery are connected in series as shown in Fig. 3-5. What is the total voltage available?

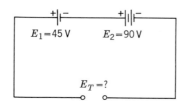

$E_1 = 45$ V $E_2 = 90$ V

$E_T = ?$

FIGURE 3-5

SOLUTION

1 Write the formula.

$$E_T = E_1 + E_2 \tag{3-2}$$

2 Substitute numbers.

$$E_T = 45 + 90$$

3 Add the numbers.

$$E_T = 135 \text{ V} \qquad Ans.$$

EXAMPLE 3-2   A 6-V 20-Ω filament and a 12-V 40-Ω filament are connected in series with a 20-Ω limiting resistor using 6 V and 0.3 A. Find (*a*) the total voltage, (*b*) the total current, and (*c*) the total resistance.

SOLUTION
Draw the circuit diagram as shown in Fig. 3-6.

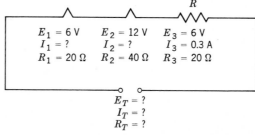

R

$E_1 = 6$ V	$E_2 = 12$ V	$E_3 = 6$ V
$I_1 = ?$	$I_2 = ?$	$I_3 = 0.3$ A
$R_1 = 20\ \Omega$	$R_2 = 40\ \Omega$	$R_3 = 20\ \Omega$

$E_T = ?$
$I_T = ?$
$R_T = ?$

FIGURE 3-6

a Find the total voltage.

1 Write the formula.

$$E_T = E_1 + E_2 + E_3 \tag{3-2}$$

2   Substitute numbers.

$$E_T = 6 + 12 + 6$$

3   Add the numbers.

$$E_T = 24 \text{ V} \quad Ans.$$

b   Find the total current.

1   Write the formula.

$$I_T = I_1 = I_2 = I_3 \tag{3-1}$$

2   Substitute numbers.

$$I_T = I_1 = I_2 = 0.3$$

3   Total current is

$$I_T = 0.3 \text{ A} \quad Ans.$$

c   Find the total resistance.

1   Write the formula.

$$R_T = R_1 + R_2 + R_3 \tag{3-3}$$

2   Substitute numbers.

$$R_T = 20 + 40 + 20$$

3   Add the numbers.

$$R_T = 80 \ \Omega \quad Ans.$$

SELF-TEST 3-3   In the voltage divider circuit shown in Fig. 3-7, find (a) the total voltage, (b) the total bleeder current, and (c) the total resistance of the load resistance.

SOLUTION
The diagram for the circuit is shown in Fig. 3-7.

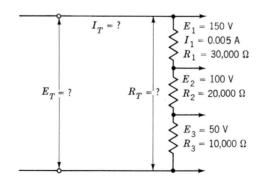

FIGURE 3-7
Various taps provide different voltages from a voltage divider.

a Find the total voltage.

1 Write the formula.

$$E_T = \underline{\hspace{3cm}} \qquad (3\text{-}2) \qquad E_1 + E_2 + E_3$$

2 Substitute numbers.

$$E_T = 150 + \underline{\hspace{1cm}} + \underline{\hspace{1cm}} \qquad\qquad 100 \qquad 50$$

3 Add the numbers.

$$E_T = \underline{\hspace{1cm}} \text{ V} \quad Ans. \qquad\qquad 300$$

b Find the total current.

1 Write the formula.

$$I_T = I_1 \overset{?}{=} I_2 \overset{?}{=} I_3 \qquad (3\text{-}1) \qquad = \qquad =$$

2 Substitute numbers.

$$I_T = \underline{\hspace{1cm}} = I_2 = I_3 \qquad\qquad 0.005$$

3 The total current is

$$I_T = \underline{\hspace{1cm}} \text{ A} \quad Ans. \qquad\qquad 0.005$$

c Find the total resistance.

1 Write the formula.

$$R_T = R_1 \overset{?}{=} R_2 \overset{?}{=} R_3 \qquad (3\text{-}3) \qquad + \qquad +$$

2 Substitute numbers.

$$R_T = 30{,}000 + 20{,}000 + \underline{\hspace{2cm}} \qquad\qquad 10{,}000$$

3 Add the numbers.

$$R_T = \underline{\hspace{1.5cm}} \ \Omega \quad Ans. \qquad\qquad 60{,}000$$

PROBLEMS

1. In the circuit shown in Fig. 3-8, find (*a*) the total voltage, (*b*) the total current, and (*c*) the total resistance.

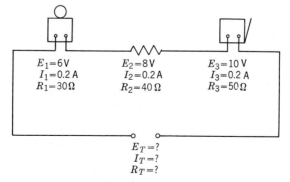

$$E_1 = 6\,\text{V} \qquad E_2 = 8\,\text{V} \qquad E_3 = 10\,\text{V}$$
$$I_1 = 0.2\,\text{A} \qquad I_2 = 0.2\,\text{A} \qquad I_3 = 0.2\,\text{A}$$
$$R_1 = 30\,\Omega \qquad R_2 = 40\,\Omega \qquad R_3 = 50\,\Omega$$

$$E_T = ?$$
$$I_T = ?$$
$$R_T = ?$$

FIGURE 3-8

2. In an antique car, a 3-V 1.5-Ω dash light and a 3-V 1.5-Ω taillight are connected in series to a battery delivering 2 A as shown in Fig. 3-9. Find (*a*) the total voltage and (*b*) the total resistance.
3. Three resistances are connected in series. $E_1 = 6.3$ V, $I_1 = 0.3$ A, $R_1 = 21$ Ω, $E_2 = 12.6$ V, $R_2 = 42$ Ω, $E_3 = 24$ V, and $R_3 = 80$ Ω. Find (*a*) the total voltage, (*b*) the total current, and (*c*) the total resistance.
4. The receiver, transmitter, and line coil of a telephone circuit are connected in series. For the receiver: $E = 2.5$ V, $I = ?$, and $R = 12.5$ Ω. For the transmitter: $E = 18.6$ V, $I = 0.2$ A, and $R = 93$ Ω. For the line coil: $E = 6.7$ V, $I = ?$, and $R = 33.5$ Ω. Find (*a*) the total voltage, (*b*) the total current, and (*c*) the total resistance.

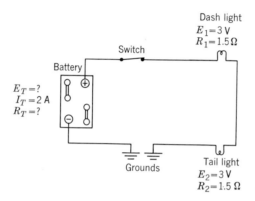

FIGURE 3-9
Series-connected automobile
dash and taillight for Prob. 2.

JOB 3-2   USING OHM'S LAW IN SERIES CIRCUITS

Ohm's law may be used for the individual parts of a series circuit. When it is used on a particular part of a circuit, great care must be taken to use *only* the voltage, current, and resistance of that particular part. That is, the *voltage of a part* is equal to the *current in that part* multiplied by the *resistance of that part*. This may be easily remembered by using the correct subscripts when writing the Ohm's law formula for a particular part.

For the first part:

$$E_1 = I_1 \times R_1 \qquad \boxed{3\text{-}4}$$

For the second part:

$$E_2 = I_2 \times R_2 \qquad \boxed{3\text{-}5}$$

For the third part:

$$E_3 = I_3 \times R_3 \qquad \boxed{3\text{-}6}$$

EXAMPLE 3-4   Solve the circuit shown in Fig. 3-10 for all missing values of (*a*) current, (*b*) voltage, and (*c*) resistance.

SOLUTION
We can find the total values by the following formulas:

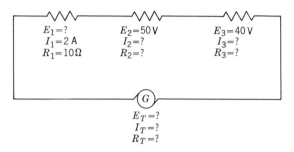

$E_1 = ?$
$I_1 = 2\text{ A}$
$R_1 = 10\,\Omega$

$E_2 = 50\text{ V}$
$I_2 = ?$
$R_2 = ?$

$E_3 = 40\text{ V}$
$I_3 = ?$
$R_3 = ?$

$E_T = ?$
$I_T = ?$
$R_T = ?$

FIGURE 3-10

$$I_T = I_1 = I_2 = I_3 \tag{3-1}$$

$$E_T = E_1 + E_2 + E_3 \tag{3-2}$$

$$R_T = R_1 + R_2 + R_3 \tag{3-3}$$

However, in order to use these formulas, we must know the individual values for each part of the circuit. These values may be found by using the Ohm's law formulas for each part.

$$E_1 = I_1 \times R_1 \tag{3-4}$$

$$E_2 = I_2 \times R_2 \tag{3-5}$$

$$E_3 = I_3 \times R_3 \tag{3-6}$$

a   Since the current has the same value at every point in a series circuit, it is easiest to find the current first.

1   Write the formula.

$$I_T = I_1 = I_2 = I_3 \tag{3-1}$$

2   Substitute numbers.

$$I_T = 2 = I_2 = I_3$$

3   The current value is

$$I_T = I_1 = I_2 = I_3 = 2\text{ A} \qquad Ans.$$

b   Find E_1. Use $I_1 = 2$ A from step *a*.

1   Write the formula.

$$E_1 = I_1 \times R_1 \tag{3-4}$$

2   Substitute numbers.

$$E_1 = 2 \times 10$$

3   Multiply numbers.

$$E_1 = 20\text{ V} \qquad Ans.$$

Find E_T. Use $E_1 = 20$ V from step *b*.

1   Write the formula.

$$E_T = E_1 + E_2 + E_3 \tag{3-2}$$

2   Substitute numbers.

$$E_T = 20 + 50 + 40$$

3   Add the numbers.

$$E_T = 110 \text{ V} \qquad Ans.$$

c   Find R_2 and R_3. Use $I_2 = I_3 = 2$ A from step a.

1   Write the formula.

$$E_2 = I_2 \times R_2 \qquad (3\text{-}5) \qquad\qquad E_3 = I_3 \times R_3 \qquad (3\text{-}6)$$

2   Substitute the numbers.

$$50 = 2 \times R_2 \qquad\qquad\qquad 40 = 2 \times R_3$$

3   Solve.

$$\frac{50}{2} = R_2 \qquad\qquad\qquad\qquad \frac{40}{2} = R_3$$

$$R_2 = 25 \ \Omega \qquad Ans. \qquad\qquad R_3 = 20 \ \Omega \qquad Ans.$$

Find R_T. Use $R_2 = 25 \ \Omega$ and $R_3 = 20 \ \Omega$ from step c.

1   Write the formula.

$$R_T = R_1 + R_2 + R_3 \qquad (3\text{-}3)$$

2   Substitute numbers.

$$R_T = 10 + 25 + 20$$

3   Add the numbers.

$$R_T = 55 \ \Omega \qquad Ans.$$

SELF-TEST 3-5   Part of the first stage of a two-stage transistorized amplifier is shown in Fig. 3-11. Solve the circuit for all missing values of (a) current, (b) voltage, and (c) resistance.

SOLUTION

a   Find the total current.

1   Write the formula.

$$I_{AB} = I_1 = \underline{\qquad} \qquad (3\text{-}1) \qquad\qquad I_2$$

2   Substitute numbers.

$$I_{AB} = \underline{\ \ ?\ \ } = I_2 = 0.00008 \qquad\qquad I_1$$

3   The current is

$$I_{AB} = I_1 = I_2 = \underline{\qquad\qquad} \text{ A} \qquad Ans. \qquad\qquad 0.00008$$

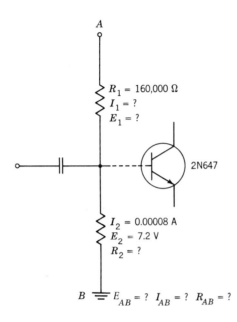

FIGURE 3-11

The base circuit of a transistor amplifier.

Values shown in figure:

A

$R_1 = 160,000\ \Omega$
$I_1 = ?$
$E_1 = ?$

2N647

$I_2 = 0.00008\ A$
$E_2 = 7.2\ V$
$R_2 = ?$

B $E_{AB} = ?$ $I_{AB} = ?$ $R_{AB} = ?$

b Find the voltages.

   Find E_1. Use $I_1 = $ _____ A from step *a*.   0.00008

   1 Write the formula.

$$E_1 = I_1 \times \underline{\quad}\qquad\qquad (3\text{-}4)$$ R_1

   2 Substitute numbers.

$$E_1 = 0.00008 \times \underline{\qquad}$$ 160,000

   3 Multiply numbers.

$$E_1 = \underline{\quad}\ V \qquad Ans.$$ 12.8

   Find E_{AB}. Use $E_1 = 12.8$ V from step *b*.

   1 Write the formula.

$$E_{AB} = E_1 + \underline{\quad}\qquad\qquad (3\text{-}2)$$ E_2

   2 Substitute numbers.

$$E_{AB} = 12.8 + \underline{\quad}$$ 7.2

   3 Add the numbers.

$$E_{AB} = \underline{\quad}\ V \qquad Ans.$$ 20

c Find the resistances.

   Find R_2. Use $I_2 = $ _____ A   0.00008

   1 Write the formula.

$$E_2 = \underline{\quad} \times R_2\qquad\qquad (3\text{-}5)$$ I_2

2 Substitute numbers.

$$7.2 = \underline{\hspace{1.5cm}} \times R_2$$ | 0.00008

3 Solve.

$$\frac{7.2}{?} = R_2$$ | 0.00008

$$R_2 = \underline{\hspace{1cm}} \Omega \quad Ans.$$ | 90,000

Find R_{AB}. Use $R_2 = \underline{\hspace{1cm}} \Omega$ from step c. | 90,000

1 Write the formula.

$$R_{AB} = R_1 + \underline{\hspace{0.8cm}} \qquad (3\text{-}3)$$ | R_2

2 Substitute numbers.

$$R_{AB} = \underline{\hspace{1cm}} + 90,000$$ | 160,000

3 Add the numbers.

$$R_{AB} = \underline{\hspace{1cm}} \Omega \quad Ans.$$ | 250,000

PROBLEMS

1. A lamp using 10 V, a 10-Ω resistor drawing 4 A, and a 24-V motor are connected in series. Find (*a*) the total current, (*b*) the total voltage, and (*c*) the total resistance.

2. A small arc lamp designed to operate on a current of 6 A has a resistance of 14 Ω. It is used in series with a limiting resistor of 6 Ω. Find (*a*) the total current, (*b*) the total voltage, and (*c*) the total resistance.

3. A series-connected automobile dash- and taillight circuit similar to that shown in Fig. 3-9 operates from a 6-V battery. The dash operates on 2 V and 0.8 A. The taillight requires 4 V. Find (*a*) the resistance of each light, (*b*) the total resistance, and (*c*) the total current.

4. A lamp, a resistor, and a soldering iron are connected in series. The lamp has a voltage across it of 16 V. The voltage across the resistor is 12.8 V. The iron has a resistance of 6 Ω and carries a current of

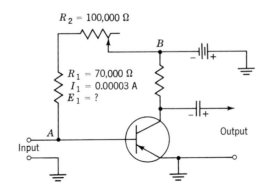

FIGURE 3-12
A class A audio amplifier.

3.2 A. Find (*a*) the total current, (*b*) the total voltage, and (*c*) the total resistance.

5. A 17,000-Ω 150-V scale voltmeter is combined in series with a 51,000-Ω resistor in order to increase the range of the meter to read 600 V. Find the current in the meter when it reads 600 V.

6. Using the circuit shown in Fig. 3-12, find the total voltage between the points *A* and *B*.

7. The first video IF amplifier in the RCA TV chassis KCS 176 uses a base circuit similar to that shown in Fig. 3-13. Find (*a*) E_1, (*b*) E_2, and (*c*) E_T.

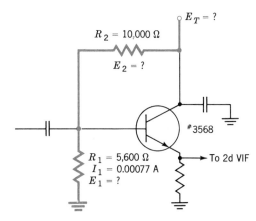

FIGURE 3-13

A 1st video amplifier circuit in a modern TV chassis.

8. The Magnavox color TV chassis T940 uses a high-voltage regulator circuit essentially the same as that shown in Fig. 3-14. Find all missing values of (*a*) current, (*b*) voltage, and (*c*) resistance.

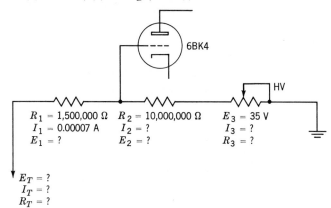

FIGURE 3-14

A high-voltage regulator circuit in a color television receiver.

TEST—OHM'S LAW IN SERIES CIRCUITS

1. Find (*a*) the total voltage, (*b*) the total current, and (*c*) the total resistance for the circuit shown in Fig. 3-15.

2. A 100-V 25-Ω motor and a 15-V rheostat are in series with a dc

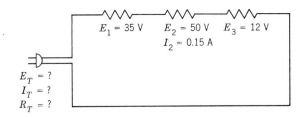

$E_1 = 35$ V $E_2 = 50$ V $E_3 = 12$ V
$I_2 = 0.15$ A

$E_T = ?$
$I_T = ?$
$R_T = ?$

FIGURE 3-15

source delivering 4 A. Find (*a*) the total current, (*b*) the total voltage, and (*c*) the total resistance.

3. In a circuit similar to that shown in Fig. 3-12, $R_1 = 20,000$ Ω, $R_2 = 80,000$ Ω, and $I_1 = 0.00012$ A. Find the voltage between points *A* and *B*.

4. Three resistors are in series. The first resistance is 100 Ω and the second resistance is 20 Ω. The third resistor uses 0.5 A and has a voltage drop of 30 V across it. Find (*a*) the total current, (*b*) the total voltage, and (*c*) the total resistance.

5. In a circuit similar to that shown in Fig. 3-11, $E_1 = 2$ V, $I_1 = 0.00002$ A, and $R_2 = 400,000$ Ω. Find all missing values of (*a*) current, (*b*) voltage, and (*c*) resistance.

JOB 3-3 USING OHM'S LAW FOR TOTAL VALUES IN SERIES CIRCUITS

Ohm's law was used in the last job to find the voltage, current, and resistance of the individual parts of a series circuit. Ohm's law may also be used to find the *total values* of voltage, current, and resistance in a series circuit.

RULE	In a series circuit, the total voltage is equal to the total current multiplied by the total resistance.

FORMULA

$$E_T = I_T \times R_T \qquad \boxed{3\text{-}7}$$

where E_T = total voltage, V
I_T = total current, A
R_T = total resistance, Ω

FINDING THE TOTAL VOLTAGE

EXAMPLE 3-6   A resistor of 45 Ω, a bell of 60 Ω, and a buzzer of 50 Ω are connected in series as shown in Fig. 3-16. The current in each is 0.2 A. What is the total voltage?

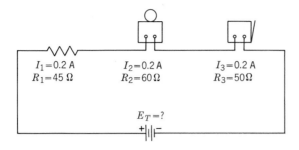

FIGURE 3-16

SOLUTION

In order to use Ohm's law to find the total voltage, we must first obtain the values for the total current and the total resistance. These values may be found by the following formulas:

$$I_T = I_1 = I_2 = I_3 \qquad (3\text{-}1)$$

$$R_T = R_1 + R_2 + R_3 \qquad (3\text{-}3)$$

1   Find the total current.

$$I_T = I_1 = I_2 = I_3 = 0.2 \text{ A} \qquad Ans. \qquad (3\text{-}1)$$

2   Find the total resistance.

$$R_T = R_1 + R_2 + R_3 \qquad (3\text{-}3)$$

$$R_T = 45 + 60 + 50$$

$$R_T = 155 \ \Omega \qquad Ans.$$

3   Find the total voltage.

$$E_T = I_T \times R_T \qquad (3\text{-}7)$$

$$E_T = 0.2 \times 155$$

$$E_T = 31 \text{ V} \qquad Ans.$$

FINDING THE TOTAL CURRENT

EXAMPLE 3-7   A portable spotlight of 3 Ω resistance is connected to a 6-V power pack with two wires, each of 0.4 Ω resistance. Find the total current drawn from the power pack.

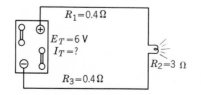

FIGURE 3-17

SOLUTION

The diagram for the circuit is shown in Fig. 3-17. In order to use Ohm's law to find the total current, we must first obtain the values for the total voltage and the total resistance. These values may be found by the following formulas:

$$E_T = E_1 + E_2 + E_3 \qquad\qquad (3\text{-}2)$$

$$R_T = R_1 + R_2 + R_3 \qquad\qquad (3\text{-}3)$$

1   The total voltage is known: $E_T = 6$ V.
2   Find the total resistance.

$$R_T = R_1 + R_2 + R_3 \qquad\qquad (3\text{-}3)$$

$$R_T = 0.4 + 3 + 0.4$$

$$R_T = 3.8 \ \Omega \qquad Ans.$$

3   Find the total current.

$$E_T = I_T \times R_T \qquad\qquad (3\text{-}7)$$

$$6 = I_T \times 3.8$$

$$\frac{6}{3.8} = I_T$$

or $I_T = 1.58$ A $Ans.$

EXAMPLE 3-8   Fig. 3-18 illustrates a simple computer AND circuit. Find the total current.

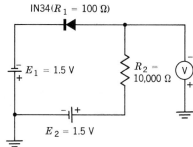

IN34$(R_1 = 100 \ \Omega)$

$E_1 = 1.5$ V

$R_2 = 10,000 \ \Omega$

$E_2 = 1.5$ V

FIGURE 3-18
A simple computer AND circuit.

SOLUTION
In order to use Ohm's law to find the total current, we must first obtain the values for the total voltage and the total resistance.

1   Find the total voltage.

$$E_T = E_1 + E_2 \qquad\qquad (3\text{-}2)$$

$$E_T = 1.5 + 1.5$$

$$E_T = 3 \ V \qquad Ans.$$

2   Find the total resistance.

$$R_T = R_1 + R_2 \qquad\qquad (3\text{-}3)$$

$$R_T = 100 + 10,000$$

$$R_T = 10,100 \ \Omega \qquad Ans.$$

3   Find the total current.

$$E_T = I_T \times R_T \qquad\qquad (3\text{-}7)$$

$$3 = I_T \times 10{,}100$$

$$\frac{3}{10{,}100} = I_T$$

$$\text{or } I_T = 0.000297 \text{ A} \qquad Ans.$$

FINDING THE TOTAL RESISTANCE

EXAMPLE 3-9   A motor, a lamp, and a rheostat are connected in series. The motor uses 80 V, the lamp takes 10 V and 2 A, and the rheostat uses 30 V. Find the total resistance of the circuit.

SOLUTION
The diagram for the circuit is shown in Fig. 3-19. In order to use Ohm's law to find the total resistance, we must first obtain the values for the total voltage and the total current.

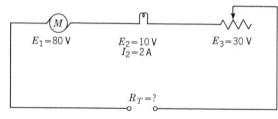

$E_1 = 80 \text{ V}$ $E_2 = 10 \text{ V}$ $E_3 = 30 \text{ V}$
$I_2 = 2 \text{ A}$

$R_T = ?$

FIGURE 3-19

1   Find the total voltage.

$$E_T = E_1 + E_2 + E_3 \qquad\qquad (3\text{-}2)$$

$$E_T = 80 + 10 + 30$$

$$E_T = 120 \text{ V} \qquad Ans.$$

2   Find the total current.

$$I_T = I_1 = I_2 = I_3 = 2 \text{ A} \qquad Ans. \qquad (3\text{-}1)$$

3   Find the total resistance.

$$E_T = I_T \times R_T \qquad\qquad (3\text{-}7)$$

$$120 = 2 \times R_T$$

$$\frac{120}{2} = R_T$$

$$\text{or } R_T = 60 \ \Omega \qquad Ans.$$

SELF-TEST 3-10   A Philco-Ford TV chassis 20L23 uses a brightness-control circuit similar to that shown in Fig. 3-20. Find the total voltage between ground and point B.

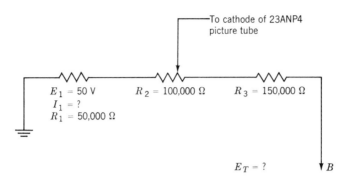

FIGURE 3-20

A brightness-control circuit in a television receiver.

SOLUTION

In order to use Ohm's law to find the total voltage, we must first obtain the values for the total _____ and the total _____.

current   resistance

1   Find the total current.

We can find the total current if we can find the current in any resistance. The only resistor about which there is sufficient information is ____.

R_1

Find I_1.

$$E_1 = \underline{\quad} \times R_1 \qquad (3\text{-}4)$$

I_1

$$50 = I_1 \times \underline{\qquad}$$

50,000

$$\frac{50}{?} = I_1$$

50,000

$$I_1 = \underline{\qquad} \text{ A}$$

0.001

Now, in a series circuit,

$$I_T = I_1 = I_2 = I_3 = \underline{\qquad} \text{ A} \qquad Ans. \qquad (3\text{-}1)$$

0.001

2   Find the total resistance.

$$R_T = R_1 + R_2 + \underline{\quad} \qquad (3\text{-}3)$$

R_3

$$R_T = 50{,}000 + \underline{\qquad} + 150{,}000$$

100,000

$$R_T = \underline{\qquad} \ \Omega \qquad Ans.$$

300,000

3   Find the total voltage.

$$E_T = I_T \times \underline{\quad} \qquad (3\text{-}7)$$

R_T

$$E_T = \underline{\qquad} \times 300{,}000$$

0.001

$$E_T = \underline{\quad} \text{ V} \qquad Ans.$$

300

PROBLEMS

1.   Five lamps are connected in series for use in a subway lamp bank. Each lamp has a resistance of 110 Ω. What is the subway circuit total voltage if the total current drawn is 1 A?

2. A railroad signal lamp and the coil of a semaphore are connected in series. The resistance of the lamp is 16 Ω, and that of the coil is 5 Ω. The current is 2 A. What is the total voltage?

3. In a telephone circuit, the receiver, transmitter, and line coil are connected in series. The receiver resistance is 2.2 Ω; the transmitter resistance is 6.2 Ω; the coil resistance is 1.2 Ω. If the current in the receiver is 0.5 A, what is the total voltage of the circuit?

4. A motor, a lamp, and a rheostat are connected in series. The voltage across the motor is 96 V, across the lamp 24 V, and across the rheostat 40 V. If the current in the motor is 2 A, find (*a*) the total current, (*b*) the total voltage, and (*c*) the total resistance.

5. A current of 0.003 A flows through a resistor that is connected to a 1.5-V dry cell. If three additional 1.5-V cells were connected in series to the first cell, find the current now flowing through the resistor.

6. A series circuit consists of a heating coil, an ultraviolet lamp, and a motor for an electric clothes drier. The current in the motor is 5 A. The voltages are 50 V for the lamp, 80 V for the motor, and 100 V for the heating coil. Find (*a*) the total current, (*b*) the total voltage, and (*c*) the total resistance.

7. Figure 3-21*a* illustrates a dual-supply universal transistor circuit. Its dc equivalent circuit is shown in Fig. 3-21*b*. Find (*a*) the total current, (*b*) the total resistance, and (*c*) the total voltage between points *A* and *B*.

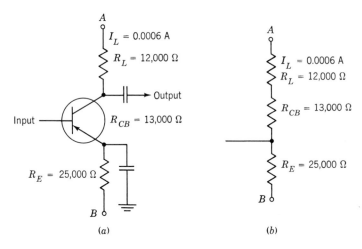

FIGURE 3-21
(a) A dual-supply universal transistor circuit. (b) The dc equivalent circuit.

8. Four lamps are wired in series. The resistance of each lamp is 0.5 Ω. The voltage across each lamp is 0.4 V. Find (*a*) the total current, (*b*) the total voltage, and (*c*) the total resistance.

9. Three arc lights are connected in series with a resistance of 21 Ω. The resistance of each arc light when hot is 10 Ω. The voltage across each arc light is 40 V, and the voltage across the resistance

is 84 V. Find (*a*) the total voltage, (*b*) the total current, and (*c*) the total resistance.

10. A voltage divider in a television receiver consists of a 6,000-, a 3,000-, and a 1,500-Ω resistor in series. If the total current is 0.015 A, find the total voltage drop.

JOB 3-4 INTERMEDIATE REVIEW OF SERIES CIRCUITS

A series circuit is one in which the electrons may flow in only ____ path. | one

Finding the total voltage. The total voltage in a series circuit may be found by use of the following formulas:

$$E_T = E_1 + E_2 + \underline{\quad} \qquad \boxed{3\text{-}2} \qquad E_3$$

$$E_T = \underline{\quad} \times R_T \qquad \boxed{3\text{-}7} \qquad I_T$$

Finding the total resistance. The total resistance in a series circuit may be found by use of the following formulas:

$$R_T = R_1 + R_2 + \underline{\quad} \qquad \boxed{3\text{-}3} \qquad R_3$$

$$E_T = I_T \times \underline{\quad} \qquad \boxed{3\text{-}7} \qquad R_T$$

Finding the total current. The total current in a series circuit may be found by use of the following formulas:

$$I_T = I_1 = \underline{\quad} = I_3 \qquad \boxed{3\text{-}1} \qquad I_2$$

$$\underline{\quad} = I_T \times R_T \qquad \boxed{3\text{-}7} \qquad E_T$$

EXAMPLE 3-11   Find the total resistance of the circuit shown in Fig. 3-22.

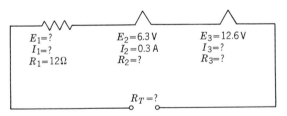

$$E_1=? \qquad E_2=6.3\,V \qquad E_3=12.6\,V$$
$$I_1=? \qquad I_2=0.3\,A \qquad I_3=?$$
$$R_1=12\,\Omega \qquad R_2=? \qquad R_3=?$$

$$R_T=?$$

FIGURE 3-22

SOLUTION
In order to use the formula $E_T = I_T \times R_T$ to find the total resistance, we must know the value of E_T and I_T. If the individual voltages are unknown, we must find them in order to get E_T.

1   Find the currents in the circuit.

$$I_T = I_1 = I_2 = I_3 \qquad (3\text{-}1)$$

$$I_T = I_1 = I_2 = I_3 = 0.3\,A \qquad Ans.$$

2 Find E_1.

$$E_1 = I_1 \times R_1 \qquad\qquad (3\text{-}4)$$

$$E_1 = 0.3 \times 12$$

$$E_1 = 3.6 \text{ V} \qquad Ans.$$

3 Find E_T.

$$E_T = E_1 + E_2 + E_3 \qquad\qquad (3\text{-}2)$$

$$E_T = 3.6 + 6.3 + 12.6$$

$$E_T = 22.5 \text{ V} \qquad Ans.$$

4 Find R_T.

$$E_T = I_T \times R_T \qquad\qquad (3\text{-}7)$$

$$22.5 = 0.3 \times R_T$$

$$\frac{22.5}{0.3} = R_T$$

or $R_T = 75 \ \Omega \qquad Ans.$

SELF-TEST 3-12   A 12-Ω spot light in a theater is connected in series with a dimming resistor of 31 Ω. If the voltage drop across the light is 31.2 V, find (*a*) the current in the light, (*b*) the current in the dimmer, (*c*) the total current, (*d*) the voltage drop across the dimmer, and (*e*) the total voltage and total resistance.

SOLUTION
The diagram for the circuit is shown in Fig. 3-23.

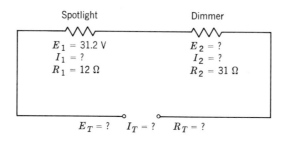

Spotlight   Dimmer

$E_1 = 31.2$ V $E_2 = ?$
$I_1 = ?$ $I_2 = ?$
$R_1 = 12 \ \Omega$ $R_2 = 31 \ \Omega$

$E_T = ? \quad I_T = ? \quad R_T = ?$ FIGURE 3-23

a Find the light current.

$$E_1 = I_1 \times \underline{\quad} \qquad\qquad (3\text{-}4) \qquad\qquad R_1$$

$$31.2 = \underline{\quad} \times 12 \qquad\qquad\qquad\qquad I_1$$

$$\frac{31.2}{?} = I_1 \qquad\qquad\qquad\qquad\qquad 12$$

$$I_1 = \underline{\quad} \text{ A} \qquad Ans. \qquad\qquad\qquad 2.6$$

b Find the current in the dimmer.

$$I_T = I_1 = \underline{\quad} \qquad\qquad (3\text{-}1) \qquad\qquad I_2$$

$$I_T = \underline{\quad} = I_2 \qquad\qquad\qquad\qquad\qquad 2.6$$

$$I_2 = \underline{\quad} \text{ A} \qquad Ans. \qquad\qquad\qquad\qquad 2.6$$

c   The total current $= I_T = \underline{\quad}$ A $Ans.$ $\qquad\qquad$ 2.6

d   Find the voltage drop across the dimmer.

$$E_2 = \underline{\quad} \times R_2 \qquad\qquad (3\text{-}5) \qquad\qquad I_2$$

$$E_2 = \underline{\quad} \times 31 \qquad\qquad\qquad\qquad\qquad 2.6$$

$$E_2 = \underline{\quad} \text{ V} \qquad Ans. \qquad\qquad\qquad\qquad 80.6$$

e   Find the total voltage.

$$E_T = E_1 + \underline{\quad} \qquad\qquad (3\text{-}2) \qquad\qquad E_2$$

$$E_T = \underline{\quad} + 80.6 \qquad\qquad\qquad\qquad\qquad 31.2$$

$$E_T = \underline{\quad} \text{ V} \qquad Ans. \qquad\qquad\qquad\qquad 111.8$$

Find the total resistance.

$$R_T = R_1 + \underline{\quad} \qquad\qquad (3\text{-}3) \qquad\qquad R_2$$

$$R_T = \underline{\quad} + 31 \qquad\qquad\qquad\qquad\qquad 12$$

$$R_T = \underline{\quad} \ \Omega \qquad Ans. \qquad\qquad\qquad\qquad 43$$

Check: If we have been correct in our calculations, our values for the total voltage, total current, and total resistance should satisfy the Ohm's law formula for total values.

$$E_T = \underline{\quad} \times R_T \qquad\qquad (3\text{-}7) \qquad\qquad I_T$$

$$\underline{\quad} = 2.6 \times 43 \qquad\qquad\qquad\qquad\qquad 111.8$$

$$111.8 = \underline{\quad} \qquad\qquad\qquad\qquad\qquad\qquad 111.8$$

The equation __(does/does not)__ check. $\qquad\qquad\qquad\qquad$ does

PROBLEMS

1.   Three resistors are connected in series. R_1 has a resistance of 40 Ω. The second resistor causes a 6-V drop, and the third resistor has a resistance of 120 Ω. Find the total voltage across the circuit if the series current is 0.3 A.

2.   A 40-Ω resistor is in series with a 25-Ω resistor. Find the total voltage if the series current is 0.5 A.

3.   Three resistors are in series. $I_1 = 0.5$ A, $R_1 = 2\ \Omega$, $R_2 = 3\ \Omega$, and $E_3 = 3.5$ V. Find the total voltage.

4.   Two resistors and a motor are connected in series. The motor current is 3 A, and its resistance is 25 Ω. The voltage across each resistor is 37.5 V. Find (*a*) the total current, (*b*) the total voltage, and (*c*) the total resistance.

5. A voltage divider consists of a 3,000-, a 5,000-, and a 10,000-Ω resistor in series. The series current is 0.015 A. Find (a) the voltage drop across each resistance, (b) the total voltage, and (c) the total resistance.

6. A lamp and two bells are connected in series in a burglar-alarm circuit. The lamp draws a current of 0.25 A and has a resistance of 160 Ω. Each bell uses 35 V. Find (a) the total current, (b) the total voltage, and (c) the total resistance.

7. Three resistors are in series: $E_1 = 31.2$ V, $E_2 = 48$ V, $I_2 = 1.2$ A, and $R_3 = 44$ Ω. Find (a) the total current, (b) the total voltage, and (c) the total resistance of the circuit.

8. In a series circuit, $I_1 = 0.5$ A, $R_1 = 35$ Ω, $E_2 = 91$ V, $R_3 = 23$ Ω, and $E_4 = 40$ V. Find the total voltage.

9. Three resistances are in series. They use 8, 10, and 14 V, respectively. The total resistance of the circuit is 80 Ω. Find all missing values of current, voltage, and resistance including the total values.

10. Three resistances of 30, 40, and 50 Ω are in series. The total voltage impressed across the circuit is 24 V. Find all missing values of current, voltage, and resistance, including the total values.

TEST—SERIES CIRCUITS

1. Four lamps are in series. The first two lamps take $1\frac{1}{2}$ V each. The third lamp draws 0.5 A and has a resistance of 2 Ω. The fourth lamp has a resistance of 4 Ω. Find the total voltage required by the circuit.

2. A 12BY7A video amplifier whose heater requires 12.6 V and 0.3 A is in series with a limiting resistor using 104.4 V. Find (a) the total current, (b) the total voltage, and (c) the total resistance.

3. Three resistors are connected in series. $E_1 = 20$ V, $E_2 = 40$ V, $I_2 = 1.5$ A, and $R_3 = 60$ Ω. Find (a) the total current, (b) the total voltage, and (c) the total resistance.

4. Find all missing values of current, voltage, and resistance in the circuit shown in Fig. 3-24.

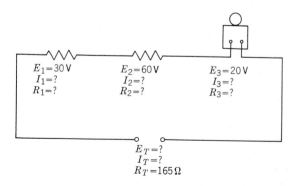

$E_1 = 30$ V
$I_1 = ?$
$R_1 = ?$

$E_2 = 60$ V
$I_2 = ?$
$R_2 = ?$

$E_3 = 20$ V
$I_3 = ?$
$R_3 = ?$

$E_T = ?$
$I_T = ?$
$R_T = 165$ Ω

FIGURE 3-24

5. A 10,000-Ω voltmeter draws a current of 0.01 A. If a multiplying resistor of 5,000 Ω is connected in series with the voltmeter, find the voltage drop across the combination.

JOB 3-5   CHECKUP ON FORMULAS INVOLVING ADDITION AND SUBTRACTION (DIAGNOSTIC TEST)

In our next electrical job we shall be required to solve some formulas which are slightly different from any we have solved up to this point. The following 10 problems are of this type. If you have any difficulty with them, see Job 3-6 which follows.

PROBLEMS

1. Using the formula $E_T = E_1 + E_2 + E_3$, find E_2 if $E_T = 78$, $E_1 = 17$, and $E_3 = 32$.
2. Using the formula $P = 2L + 2W$, find L if $P = 80$ and $W = 14$.
3. Using the formula $I_T = I_1 + I_2 + I_3$, find I_3 if $I_T = 5$ A, $I_1 = 1.6$ A, and $I_2 = 2.3$ A.
4. Find R in the equation $7 + R = 5.4 + 19$.
5. Find E in the equation $3E + 8 = 29$.
6. Find I in the equation $I - 5 = 40$.
7. Find I in the equation $3I - 4 = 32$.
8. Find R in the formula $R + r = E/I$ if $E = 60$, $I = 5$, $r = 9$.
9. What resistance must be placed in series with six 15-V Christmas-tree lights in order to operate them on a 110-V circuit? Each light requires 0.8 A.
10. What series resistor is necessary to operate a circuit requiring 79 V at 0.3 A if it is to be operated from a 110-V line?

JOB 3-6   BRUSHUP ON FORMULAS INVOLVING ADDITION AND SUBTRACTION

Solving a formula means to find the value of the unknown letter in the formula. In Job 2-8, after substituting the numbers for the letters, we obtained statements of equality such as $2 \times R = 10$ or $12 = 3 \times R$. In each instance, a number *multiplied* by a letter was equal to another number. We obtained the value of the unknown letter by eliminating the number multiplied by it. This was accomplished by *dividing both sides* of the equality sign by that *same* number. In general, to solve *any* formula or equation, we must eliminate all numbers and letters which appear on the same side of the equality sign as the *unknown* letter. This is done by applying the basic principle given in Job. 2-8.

BASIC PRINCIPLE	Any mathematical operation performed on one side of an equality sign must also be performed on the other side.

In simple language this says, "whatever we do to one side of an equality sign must also be done to the other side."

FORMULAS INVOLVING ADDITION

Is the statement "$5 + 3 = 8$" a true equation? ___(yes/no)___ Suppose that we subtract 3 from each side of the equation. It would look like this:

$$
\begin{array}{rr}
5 + 3 = & 8 \\
- 3 & - 3 \\
\hline
5 + 0 = & 5 \\
\text{or } 5 = & 5
\end{array}
$$

yes

Is the equation still true? ___(yes/no)___ Suppose that we subtract 5 from each side of the equation. It would look like this:

$$
\begin{array}{rr}
5 + 3 = & 8 \\
-5 & -5 \\
\hline
? + 3 = & 3 \\
\text{or } 3 = & 3
\end{array}
$$

yes

0

Is the equation still true? ___(yes/no)___ Suppose that we subtract 6 from each side of this equation.

$$4 + 6 = 10$$

yes

It would look like this:

$$
\begin{array}{rr}
4 + 6 = & 10 \\
- 6 & -6 \\
\hline
4 + 0 = & ? \\
\text{or } 4 = & 4
\end{array}
$$

4

Is the equation still true? ___(yes/no)___ This gives us the following rule.

yes

RULE	The same number may be subtracted from both sides of an equality sign without destroying the equality.

SELF-TEST 3-13 Solve the equation

$$x + 3 = 7$$

SOLUTION

Solving an equation means to get the letter all alone on one side of the equality sign, with its value on the other side. Therefore, all we have to do to solve the equation is to get the x alone. This will be accomplished if we can get rid of the number ____. We can do this by _____ 3 from both sides.

$$\begin{array}{rr} x + 3 = & 7 \\ -3 & -3 \\ \hline x + 0 = & ? \\ x = & 4 \quad Ans. \end{array}$$

SELF-TEST 3-14   Solve the equation

$$y + 4 = 9$$

SOLUTION
We can get y alone on one side of the equality sign if we just subtract __ from each side.

$$\begin{array}{rr} y + 4 = & 9 \\ -4 & -4 \\ \hline y + ? = & 5 \\ y = & \_ \quad Ans. \end{array}$$

EXAMPLE 3-15   In an antique car a 6-V battery supplies a 2-V dash light and a taillight in series. What is the voltage available at the taillight?

SOLUTION
The diagram for the circuit is shown in Fig. 3-25.

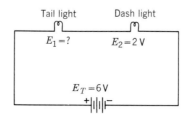

FIGURE 3-25

1   Write the formula.

$$E_T = E_1 + E_2 \qquad\qquad (3\text{-}2)$$

2   Substitute numbers.

$$6 = E_1 + 2$$

Step 2 asks the question, "2 plus what number equals 6?" We can find E_1 if we can eliminate the number 2. This may easily be done by *subtracting 2 from both sides* of the equality sign.

3   Subtract 2 from both sides.

$$\begin{array}{rr} 6 = & E_1 + 2 \\ -2 & -2 \\ \hline \end{array}$$

+3   subtracting

4

4

0

5

4   Subtract.

$$4 = E_1 + 0$$

5   The voltage is

$$E_1 = 4 \text{ V} \qquad Ans.$$

EXAMPLE 3-16   Using the formula $R_T = R_1 + R_2 + R_3$, find the resistance R_3 if $R_T = 100$, $R_1 = 20$, and $R_2 = 40$.

SOLUTION

1   Write the formula.

$$R_T = R_1 + R_2 + R_3$$

2   Substitute numbers.

$$100 = 20 + 40 + R_3$$

3   Simplify (add 20 + 40).

$$100 = 60 + R_3$$

Step 3 asks the question, "60 plus what number equals 100?" We can find R_3 if we can eliminate the number 60. This may easily be done by *subtracting* 60 *from both sides* of the equality sign.

4   Subtract 60 from both sides.

$$\begin{array}{r} 100 = 60 + R_3 \\ -60 - 60 \\ \hline \end{array}$$

5   Subtract.

$$40 = 0 + R_3$$

6   Resistance is

$$R_3 = 40 \qquad Ans.$$

SELF-TEST 3-17   In the base-bias voltage divider circuit shown in Fig. 3-26, find the value of R_1 if the normal voltage developed across $R_1 = 7.7$ V.

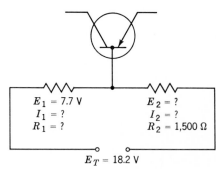

$E_1 = 7.7$ V
$I_1 = ?$
$R_1 = ?$

$E_2 = ?$
$I_2 = ?$
$R_2 = 1,500 \ \Omega$

$E_T = 18.2$ V

FIGURE 3-26

SOLUTION

We can find R_1 if we know the value of I_1.

We can find I_1 if we know the value of I_2.

We can find I_2 if we know the value of ____. E_2

We can find E_2 by using the formula for the total voltage in a series circuit.

1   Write the formula.

$$E_T = E_1 + E_2 \qquad\qquad (3\text{-}2)$$

2   Substitute numbers.

$$\underline{\quad ? \quad} = 7.7 + E_2 \qquad\qquad\qquad\qquad 18.2$$

Step 2 asks the question, "7.7 plus what number equals 18.2 ?" We can find E_2

if we can eliminate the number ____ from the right side of the equality sign.   7.7

This may be done by subtracting ____ from both sides of the equality sign.   7.7

3   Subtract 7.7 from both sides.

$$
\begin{array}{rl}
18.2 = & 7.7 + E_2 \\
\underline{-7.7} & \underline{-\ 7.7} \\
? = & 0\ + E_2
\end{array}
\qquad\qquad 10.5
$$

or $10.5 = E_2$

Now that we know E_2, we can find I_2.

1   Write the formula.

$$E_2 = I_2 \times \underline{\quad} \qquad\qquad (3\text{-}5) \qquad R_2$$

2   Substitute numbers.

$$10.5 = I_2 \times \underline{\qquad} \qquad\qquad\qquad 1{,}500$$

3   Solve.

$$\frac{10.5}{?} = I_2 \qquad\qquad\qquad 1{,}500$$

4   Divide.

$$\underline{\qquad} = I_2 \qquad\qquad\qquad 0.007$$

Now that we know I_2, we can find I_1.

1   Write the formula.

$$I_T = I_1 = \underline{\quad} \qquad\qquad (3\text{-}1) \qquad I_2$$

2   Substitute numbers.

$$I_T = I_1 = \underline{\qquad} \qquad\qquad\qquad 0.007$$

$$I_1 = 0.007 \text{ A}$$

Now that we know I_1, we can find R_1.

1   Write the formula.

$$E_1 = I_1 \times \underline{\hspace{1cm}} \qquad (3\text{-}4) \qquad\qquad R_1$$

2   Substitute numbers.

$$\underline{\hspace{1cm}} = 0.007 \times R_1 \qquad\qquad\qquad 7.7$$

3   Solve.

$$\frac{7.7}{?} = R_1 \qquad\qquad\qquad 0.007$$

4   Divide.

$$\underline{\hspace{1.5cm}} = R_1 \qquad\qquad\qquad 1{,}100$$

$$\text{or } R_1 = \underline{\hspace{1cm}} \ \Omega \qquad Ans. \qquad\qquad 1{,}100$$

PROBLEMS

Solve each of the following equations for the value of the unknown letter:

1. $E + 3 = 9$ 2. $2 + R = 10$
3. $10 + P = 80$ 4. $110 = E + 60$
5. $E + 18 = 70$ 6. $I + 2\frac{1}{2} = 3\frac{1}{2}$
7. $E + 40 + 30 + 25 = 120$ 8. $I + \frac{1}{2} = 5$
9. $I + 3.5 = 10.8$ 10. $20 + 10 + E = 110$
11. $E + 6.8 = 35$ 12. $I + 2\frac{1}{2} = 15\frac{1}{2}$
13. $R + \frac{3}{4} = 6$ 14. $E + 12.9 = 75.6$
15. $I + 0.2 + 1.3 = 7.6$ 16. $12.6 + 6.3 + E = 120$
17. $110 = 35 + 12.6 + 6.3 + E$ 18. $I + 2\frac{1}{2} = 8.4$

19.   Using the formula $R_T = R_1 + R_2 + R_3$, find the resistance R_1 if $R_T = 175$, $R_2 = 40$, and $R_3 = 15$.
20.   Using the formula $P_T = P_1 + P_2 + P_3$, find the power P_3 if $P_T = 1{,}100$, $P_1 = 300$, and $P_2 = 275$.
21.   Using the formula $I_T = I_1 + I_2$, find the current I_2 if $I_T = 99$ and $I_1 = 26$.
22.   Using the formula $I_s + I_m = I$, find the shunt current I_s if the line current $I = 1.64$ and the meter current $I_m = 0.014$.
23.   Using the formula $C_1 + C_2 + C_3 = C_T$, find C_1 if $C_T = 0.00025$, $C_2 = 0.00012$, and $C_3 = 0.00005$.
24.   Using the formula $E_1 + (I_2 \times R_2) = E_T$, find E_1 if $I_2 = 2$, $R_2 = 25$, and $E_T = 117$.
25.   Using the formula $I_T = I_1 + (E_2/R_2)$, find I_1 if $I_T = 1.5$, $E_2 = 6.3$, and $R_2 = 126$.

FORMULAS INVOLVING SUBTRACTION

Is the statement "$8 - 5 = 3$" a true equation?   <u>(yes/no)</u>   Suppose   yes
that we add 5 to each side of the equation. It would look like this.

$$8 - 5 = \quad 3$$
$$\underline{+5 \quad +5}$$
$$8 + 0 = \quad 8$$

or $8 = \quad 8$

Is the equation still true? $\underline{\quad(yes/no)\quad}$ yes
   Suppose that we add 6 to each side of this equation:

$$9 - 6 = 3$$

It would look like this.

$$9 - 6 = \quad 3$$
$$\underline{+6 \quad +6}$$
$$9 + \underline{?} = \quad 9$$ 0

or $9 = \quad 9$

Is the equation still true? $\underline{\quad(yes/no)\quad}$ yes
This gives us the following rule.

RULE	The same number may be added to both sides of an equality sign without destroying the equality.

SELF-TEST 3-18   Solve the equation

$$x - 3 = 7$$

SOLUTION
Solving an equation means to get the letter all alone on one side of the equality
sign. We can get x alone on the left side of the equality sign if we can get rid
of the number ____. We can do this by _____ 3 to both sides of the equality -3 adding
sign.

$$x - \quad 3 \ = \quad 7$$
$$\underline{+ \quad 3 \quad + \quad 3}$$
$$x + \underline{?} \ = \quad 10$$ 0

$$x \ = \ \underline{\quad} \quad Ans.$$ 10

EXAMPLE 3-19   Using the formula $C = S - P$, find the selling price
S if the cost C is \$10 and the profit P is \$2.

SOLUTION

1 Write the formula.

$$C = S - P$$

2 Substitute numbers.

$$10 = S - 2$$

Step 2 asks the question, "what number may 2 be subtracted from in order to give 10?" We can find the S if we can eliminate the -2 from the right side of the equality sign. This may easily be done by *adding 2 to both sides* of the equality sign.

3 Add 2 to both sides.

$$10 = S - 2$$
$$\underline{+\,2 \qquad +\,2}$$

4 Add

$$12 = S + 0$$

5 Selling price is

$$S = \$12 \qquad Ans.$$

SELF-TEST 3-20   Using the series-circuit formula $E - Ir = IR$, find the voltage E in the circuit shown in Fig. 3-27.

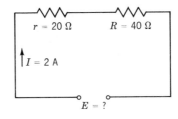

$r = 20\ \Omega \qquad R = 40\ \Omega$

$I = 2\ A$

$E = ?$

FIGURE 3-27

SOLUTION

1 Write the formula.

$$E - Ir = IR$$

2 Substitute numbers.

$$E - 2 \times 20 = 2 \times \underline{\quad} \qquad\qquad 40$$

3 Multiply numbers.

$$E - \underline{\quad} = 80 \qquad\qquad 40$$

Step 3 asks the question, "what number may 40 be subtracted from in order to give 80?" We can find E if we can eliminate the $\underline{\quad}$ from the left side of the equality sign. This may easily be done by $\underline{\qquad}$ 40 to both sides of the equality sign.

$\qquad -40$

adding

4 Add 40 to both sides.

$$E - 40 = \quad 80$$
$$\underline{+\,40 \quad +\,40}$$

5 Add.

$$E + \ 0 = \underline{\quad} \qquad\qquad 120$$

6 The voltage is

$$E = \underline{\quad}\ V \qquad Ans. \qquad\qquad 120$$

PROBLEMS

Solve each of the following equations for the value of the unknown letter:

1. $R - 5 = 12$
2. $12 = E - 3$
3. $I - 4 = 18$
4. $30 + R - 10 = 50$
5. $I - \frac{1}{2} = 4\frac{1}{2}$
6. $P - 3.2 = 8.3$
7. $9 = I - 3.5$
8. $E - 2.2 = 6.3$
9. $E - 17 = 62$
10. $82 = R - 14$
11. $I - 7\frac{3}{4} = 3$
12. $I - 1\frac{1}{2} = 6\frac{3}{4}$
13. $12 = R - 3\frac{1}{4}$
14. $72\frac{1}{2} = R - 5\frac{1}{4}$
15. $120 = R + 70 - 30$
16. $I - 0.045 = 0.85$
17. $C - 0.08 = 0.019$
18. $0.00025 = C - 0.00005$

19. Using the formula $C = S - P$, find S if $C = \$18.23$ and $P = \$3.60$.
20. Using the formula $I_1 = I_T - I_2$, find I_T if $I_1 = 8$ and $I_2 = 6$.
21. Using the formula $E_T - E_h = E_R$, find E_T if $E_R = 110$ and $E_h = 62$.
22. Using the formula $E_T - (I_1 \times R_1) = E_2$, find E_T if $I_1 = 2$, $R_1 = 30$, and $E_2 = 57$.
23. Using the formula $S - 5L = A$, find S if $L = 3.2$ and $A = 1.05$.
24. Using the formula $E - R = RM$, find E if $R = 8$ and $M = 2.5$.
25. Using the formula $R_1 = R_2 - \dfrac{E}{I}$, find R_2 if $R_1 = 9$, $E = 2.5$, and $I = 0.025$.

Transposition. The method of eliminating a number from one side of an equality sign by adding or subtracting the same number may be shortened by the method known as *transposition.* Let us investigate the following four examples in an effort to determine the rule for the transposition of quantities.

EXAMPLE 3-21   Find R in the equation $R + 2 = 10$.

SOLUTION

1 Write the equation.

$$R + 2 = 10$$

2 Subtract 2 from both sides.

$$R + 2 - 2 = 10 - 2$$

3 Subtract.

$$R + 0 = 10 - 2$$
$$R = 8 \quad Ans.$$

EXAMPLE 3-22   Find E in the equation $8 = E + 3$.

SOLUTION

1   Write the equation.

$$8 = E + 3$$

2   Subtract 3 from both sides.

$$8 - 3 = E + 3 - 3$$

3   Subtract.

$$8 - 3 = E + 0$$

$$5 = E$$

$$\text{or } E = 5 \qquad Ans.$$

EXAMPLE 3-23   Find S in the equation $S - 4 = 10$.

SOLUTION

1   Write the equation.

$$S - 4 = 10$$

2   Add 4 to both sides.

$$S - 4 + 4 = 10 + 4$$

3   Add.

$$S + 0 = 10 + 4$$

$$S = 14 \qquad Ans.$$

EXAMPLE 3-24   Find I in the equation $9 = I - 5$.

SOLUTION

1   Write the equation

$$9 = I - 5$$

2   Add 5 to both sides.

$$9 + 5 = I - 5 + 5$$

3   Add.

$$9 + 5 = I + 0$$

$$14 = I$$

$$\text{or } I = 14 \qquad Ans.$$

Notice that in each of the last four examples, the number to be eliminated—the number in color —seems to have *moved* from one side of the equality sign to the *other side*. Also, the sign in front of the number changed from (+) to (−) or from (−) to (+). This gives us the following rule for transposing.

RULE	Plus or minus quantities may be moved from one side of an equality sign to the other if the sign of the quantity is changed from (+) to (−) or from (−) to (+).

EXAMPLE 3-25   Find E in the equation $E + 8 = 12$.

SOLUTION

1   Write the equation.

$$E + 8 = 12$$

2   Transpose the 8.

$$E = 12 - 8$$

3   Subtract.

$$E = 4 \quad Ans.$$

EXAMPLE 3-26   Find R in the equation $9 = R + 3$.

SOLUTION

1   Write the equation.

$$9 = R + 3$$

2   Transpose the 3.

$$9 - 3 = R$$

3   Subtract.

$$6 = R$$

$$\text{or } R = 6 \quad Ans.$$

EXAMPLE 3-27   Find S in the equation $S - 5 = 16$.

SOLUTION

1   Write the equation.

$$S - 5 = 16$$

2   Transpose the 5.

$$S = 16 + 5$$

3   Add.

$$S = 21 \quad Ans.$$

EXAMPLE 3-28   Find I in the equation $4 = I - 9$.

SOLUTION

1   Write the equation.

$$4 = I - 9$$

2   Transpose the 9.

$$4 + 9 = I$$

3   Add.

$$13 = I$$

$$\text{or } I = 13 \quad \textit{Ans.}$$

SELF-TEST 3-29   Using the series-circuit formula $R + r = \dfrac{E}{I}$, find the resistance r in the circuit shown in Fig. 3-28.

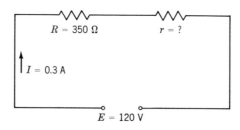

$$R = 350 \ \Omega \qquad r = ?$$

$$I = 0.3 \ A$$

$$E = 120 \ V$$ **FIGURE 3-28**

SOLUTION

1   Write the formula.

$$R + r = \frac{E}{I}$$

2   Substitute numbers.

$$350 + \underline{\quad} = \frac{120}{0.3}$$ r

3   Divide numbers.

$$350 + r = \underline{\quad}$$ 400

Step 3 asks the question, "what number r added to 350 equals 400?" We can get r all alone on the left side of the equality sign by just _____ the 350 to the right side.   transposing

4   Transpose the 350. (A + sign is understood to be present in front of the 350.)

$$r = \underline{\quad} - 350$$ 400

5   Subtract.

$$r = \underline{\quad} \ \Omega \quad \textit{Ans.}$$ 50

PROBLEMS

Solve the following equations by transposition:

1. $E + 3 = 14$
2. $16 = E + 3$
3. $2 + R = 8$
4. $13 = I + 2$
5. $6 + 4 + E = 20$
6. $3 + R + 2 = 15$
7. $21 = 4 + 5 + I$
8. $6 + I = 15$
9. $P - 2 = 6$
10. $14 = R - 4$
11. $0.06 + I = 1.6$
12. $20 = E - 2$
13. $18 - 3 + R = 25$
14. $16 = R - 4 - 5$
15. $R + 6.7 = 18.2$
16. $I + 0.045 = 0.09$
17. $0.025 = C + 0.004$
18. $X + 2.6 + 1.05 + 3.0 = 9.4$
19. $R + 7 - 2.40 + 3.60 = 19.68$
20. $I + 0.07 = 3.4$
21. $X + 3\frac{1}{2} = 5$
22. $I + 0.03 = 6.3$

23. Using the formula $P_T = P_1 + P_2 + P_3$, find P_1 if $P_T = 600$, $P_2 = 120$, and $P_3 = 300$.
24. Using the formula $I_1 = I_T - I_2$, find I_T if $I_1 = 8$ and $I_2 = 3$.
25. Using the formula $E_T = E_1 + E_2 + E_3$, find E_3 if $E_T = 110$, $E_1 = 30$, and $E_2 = 50$.
26. Using the formula $R_T = R_1 + R_2 + R_3$, find R_2 if $R_T = 245$, $R_1 = 85$, and $R_3 = 90$.
27. Using the formula $I_s = I_L - I_m$, find I_L if $I_s = 75$ and $I_m = 1.5$.
28. Using the formula $E_T - E_h = E_R$, find E_T if $E_R = 97.2$ and $E_h = 6.3$.
29. For $C_T = C_1 + C_2$, find C_1 if $C_T = 0.00035$ and $C_2 = 0.0001$.
30. For $C_T = C_1 + C_2$, find C_2 if $C_T = 0.004$ and $C_1 = 0.00015$.

JOB 3-7 CONTROL OF CURRENT IN A SERIES CIRCUIT

In Job 2-9 we learned that resistance affected the current in an electrical circuit. The greater the resistance, the smaller the current; the smaller the resistance, the greater the current. There are many instances where a certain current must be maintained in a circuit. We can accomplish this by adjusting the resistance of the circuit so as to obtain any required current.

EXAMPLE 3-30   How much resistance must be added to the circuit shown in Fig. 3-29 in order to allow only the rated current of 2 A to flow?

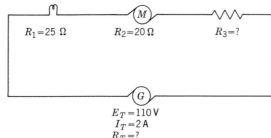

$E_T = 110$ V
$I_T = 2$ A
$R_T = ?$

FIGURE 3-29

SOLUTION

The diagram for the circuit is shown in Fig. 3-29. If we can find the total resistance required to limit the current to 2 A, then we can use formula (3-3) to find the missing extra resistance.

Find R_T.

1   Write the formula.

$$E_T = I_T \times R_T \qquad\qquad (3\text{-}7)$$

2   Substitute numbers.

$$110 = 2 \times R_T$$

3   Solve for R_T.

$$\frac{110}{2} = R_T$$

4   Divide.

$$R_T = 55\ \Omega \qquad Ans.$$

Find R_3, the resistance to be added.

1   Write the formula.

$$R_T = R_1 + R_2 + R_3 \qquad\qquad (3\text{-}3)$$

2   Substitute numbers.

$$55 = 25 + 20 + R_3$$

3   Simplify (add $25 + 20$).

$$55 = 45 + R_3$$

4   Transpose the 45.

$$55 - 45 = R_3$$

5   Subtract.

$$10 = R_3$$

$$\text{or } R_3 = 10\ \Omega \qquad Ans.$$

EXAMPLE 3-31   What resistance must be added in series with a lamp rated at 12 V and 0.3 A in order to operate it from a 24-V source?

SOLUTION

The diagram for the circuit is shown in Fig. 3-30. If we can discover how many volts are available in excess of that required by the lamp, then we can find the resistance which will use up that extra voltage at the rated 0.3 A.

Find the extra voltage supplied E_x.

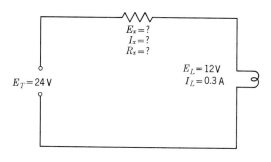

FIGURE 3-30

1 Write the formula.

$$E_T = E_x + E_L \qquad (3\text{-}2)$$

2 Substitute numbers.

$$24 = E_x + 12$$

3 Transpose the 12.

$$24 - 12 = E_x$$

4 Subtract.

$$12 = E_x$$

$$\text{or } E_x = 12 \text{ V} \qquad Ans.$$

Find the current I_x in the unknown resistor.

1 Write the formula.

$$I_T = I_x = I_L \qquad (3\text{-}1)$$

2 Substitute numbers.

$$I_T = I_x = 0.3$$

$$I_x = 0.3 \text{ A} \qquad Ans.$$

Find the resistance R_x which will use up the extra 12 V.

1 Write the formula.

$$E_x = I_x \times R_x \qquad (2\text{-}1)$$

2 Substitute numbers.

$$12 = 0.3 \times R_x$$

3 Solve for R_x.

$$\frac{12}{0.3} = R_x$$

4 Divide.

$$40 = R_x$$

$$\text{or } R_x = 40 \ \Omega \qquad Ans.$$

EXAMPLE 3-32   A 200,000-Ω resistor is connected in series with the 6-V base supply voltage and the base-to-emitter junction of a transistor. If the base-to-emitter current is thereby limited to 0.000027 A, (*a*) what is the voltage drop in the resistor and (*b*) what is the voltage V_{BE} at the base-emitter junction?

SOLUTION

The diagram for the circuit is shown in Fig. 3-31.

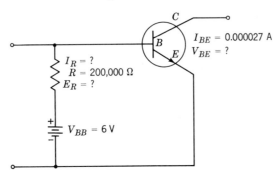

FIGURE 3-31

a   Find I_R.

   1   Write the formula.

$$I_T = I_R = I_{BE} \tag{3-1}$$

   2   Substitute numbers.

$$I_T = I_R = 0.000027$$

   3   Answer.

$$I_R = 0.000027 \text{ A} \qquad Ans.$$

Find E_R.

   1   Write the formula.

$$E_R = I_R \times R_R \tag{2-1}$$

   2   Substitute numbers.

$$E_R = 0.000027 \times 200,000$$

   3   Multiply.

$$E_R = 5.4 \text{ V} \qquad Ans.$$

b   Find the voltage V_{BE} at the base-emitter junction.

   1   Write the formula.

$$E_T = E_R + E_{BE}{}^* \tag{3-2}$$

   2   Substitute numbers.

$$6 = 5.4 + E_{BE}$$

3   Transpose the 5.4.

$$6 - 5.4 = E_{BE}$$

4   Subtract.

$$0.6 = E_{BE}$$

*5   Since E_{BE} is written as V_{BE} in transistor nomenclature,

$$V_{BE} = 0.6 \text{ V} \qquad Ans.$$

SELF-TEST 3-33   In the voltage divider circuit shown in Fig. 3-32, the total load resistance between points A and B also serves to "bleed off" any charge on the filter capacitors after the rectifier is turned off. If the bleeder current I_b is to be limited to 0.015 A, find the resistance of R_1.

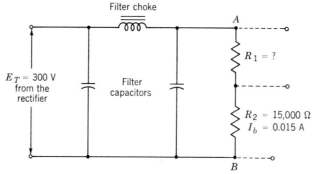

FIGURE 3-32

A voltage divider with no loads attached.

SOLUTION

If we can find the total resistance of the load which will limit the bleeder current to 0.015 A, then we can use the formula for total _____ to find R_1.   resistance

Find R_T.

1   Write the formula.

$$E_T = \underline{\quad} \times R_T \qquad (3\text{-}7)$$ I_T

2   Substitute numbers.

$$\underline{\quad} = 0.015 \times R_T$$ 300

3   Solve for R_T.

$$\frac{300}{?} = R_T$$ 0.015

4   Divide.

$$R_T = \underline{\qquad} \ \Omega \qquad Ans.$$ 20,000

Find R_1, the resistance to be added to R_2 to make a total of _____ Ω.   20,000

1   Write the formula.

$$R_T = R_1 + R_2 \qquad (3\text{-}3)$$

2   Substitute numbers.

$$20,000 = R_1 + \underline{\qquad}$$ 15,000

3   Transpose the 15,000.

$$20,000 - 15,000 = \underline{\quad}$$ R_1

4   Subtract.

$$\underline{\qquad} = R_1$$ 5,000

$$\text{or } R_1 = \underline{\qquad} \ \Omega \qquad Ans.$$ 5,000

PROBLEMS

1. How much resistance must be connected in series with a 30-Ω lamp rated at 2 A if it is to be used on a 110-V line?
2. A 10-Ω lamp rated at 5 A is to be operated from a 120-V line. How much resistance must be added in series to reduce the current to the desired value?
3. A motor of 22 Ω resistance and a signal lamp of 25 Ω resistance are connected in series across 110 V. Find the series resistor that must be added to limit the current to 2 A.
4. A boy wants to illuminate five houses on his model railroad, using five 20-Ω lamps in series. What resistance must be connected in series in order to limit the current to the 0.5 A needed by the lamps if the circuit is to be operated from the ordinary 110-V house line?
5. What resistance must be placed in series with a 12-Ω bell if it is to draw exactly $\frac{1}{4}$ A from a 24-V source?
6. Five ordinary 0.90-A 110-V lamps must be used in series when operated from the 550-V subway system. If only one of these lamps were used, what resistance must be placed in series with it to operate it from the 550-V line?
7. If a vacuum tube rated at $\frac{1}{4}$ A and 5 V is to be operated from a 6-V battery, what series resistor is needed?
8. In a circuit similar to that shown in Fig. 3-31, $V_{BE} = 0.5$ V, $I_{BE} = 0.00009$ A, and $V_{BB} = 5$ V. Find the value of R.
9. A 3-V airplane instrument lamp is to be operated from the 12-V electrical system. What resistance should be inserted in series so that the lamp will receive its rated current of 0.1 A?
10. The Panasonic AM-FM RE 7329 receiver uses an output stage similar to that shown in Fig. 3-33. If the effective $R = 100$ Ω, the collector current $I_C = 0.005$ A, and the collector supply voltage $V_{CC} = 9$ V, find the collector voltage V_C.
11. An 80-A motor is connected to a 250-V generator through leads which have a resistance of 0.3 Ω for each lead. What is the voltage available at the motor?
12. The wiring in a house has a resistance of 0.4 Ω. What is the volt-

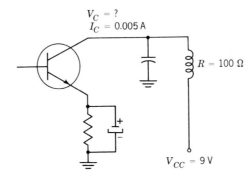

$V_C = ?$
$I_C = 0.005\ A$

$R = 100\ \Omega$

$V_{CC} = 9\ V$

FIGURE 3-33

The output stage of a transistor radio.

age available at an electric range using 12 A if the voltage at the meter is 117 V?

13. A flood lamp of 10 Ω resistance is connected in series with a variable dimming resistor of 0 to 45 Ω and is operated from a 110-V line. What is the maximum and minimum current that may be supplied to the lamp?

14. The voltage drop in the line cord of a portable transmitter must not exceed 0.25 V. If the transmitter draws 20 A from a 12-V battery, find the resistance of the line cord.

15. A portable transmitter of 0.575 Ω resistance is to operate at 11.5 V. What is the maximum resistance of the line cord connecting the transmitter to a 12-V battery?

JOB 3-8   REVIEW OF SERIES CIRCUITS

Definition. A series circuit is a circuit in which the electrons can flow in only one path.

RULE 1	The total current is equal to the current in any part of the circuit.
	$$I_T = I_1 = I_2 = I_3 \qquad \boxed{3\text{-}1}$$
RULE 2	The total voltage is equal to the sum of the voltages across all the parts of the circuit.
	$$E_T = E_1 + E_2 + E_3 \qquad \boxed{3\text{-}2}$$
RULE 3	The total resistance is equal to the sum of the resistances of all the parts of the circuit.

$$R_T = R_1 + R_2 + R_3 \qquad \boxed{3\text{-}3}$$

RULE 4	Ohm's law may be used for any part of a series circuit.

$$E_1 = I_1 \times R_1 \qquad \boxed{3\text{-}4}$$

$$E_2 = I_2 \times R_2 \qquad \boxed{3\text{-}5}$$

$$E_3 = I_3 \times R_3 \qquad \boxed{3\text{-}6}$$

RULE 5	Ohm's law may be used for total values in a series circuit.

$$E_T = I_T \times R_T \qquad \boxed{3\text{-}7}$$

SELF-TEST 3-34   In Fig. 3-34, the type 2N247 transistor has a collector current I_C of 0.01 A and a collector voltage V_C of 9.2 V. Find the total supply voltage V_{CC}.

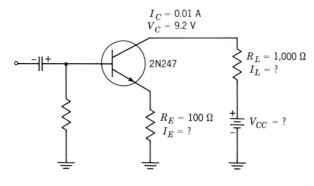

FIGURE 3-34
The total supply voltage is equal to the sum of the voltages around the circuit.

SOLUTION
Since the electrons complete the circuit flowing from the emitter to the collector of the transistor, it is a __(series/parallel)__ circuit.   series
  Find the current in each part of the circuit.

$$I_T = I_E = \underline{\quad} = I_L \qquad (3\text{-}1) \qquad I_C$$

$$I_T = I_E = 0.01 = I_L$$

$$I_T = \underline{\quad}\ \text{A} \qquad\qquad 0.01$$

$$I_E = \underline{\quad}\ \text{A} \qquad\qquad 0.01$$

$$I_L = \underline{\quad}\ \text{A} \qquad\qquad 0.01$$

Find the voltage across each part of the circuit.

$$E_{RE} = I_E \times \underline{\quad} \qquad (3\text{-}4) \qquad R_E$$

$$E_{RE} = 0.01 \times \underline{\hspace{1cm}}$$ | 100

$$E_{RE} = \underline{\hspace{0.5cm}} \text{ V}$$ | 1

$$E_L = \underline{\hspace{1cm}} \times R_L \qquad\qquad (3\text{-}5)$$ | I_L

$$E_L = 0.01 \times \underline{\hspace{1cm}}$$ | 1,000

$$E_L = \underline{\hspace{0.5cm}} \text{ V}$$ | 10

Find the total supply voltage V_{CC}.

$$V_{CC} = E_{RE} + V_C + \underline{\hspace{1cm}} \qquad\qquad (3\text{-}2)$$ | E_L

$$V_{CC} = \underline{\hspace{0.5cm}} + 9.2 + 10$$ | 1

$$V_{CC} = \underline{\hspace{0.5cm}} \text{ V} \qquad Ans.$$ | 20.2

PROBLEMS

1. Three resistors are connected in series. $E_1 = 24$ V, $I_2 = 2$ A, $R_2 = 30$ Ω, and $R_3 = 13$ Ω. Find all missing values of voltage, current, and resistance, including the total values.

2. The two field coils of a generator have a resistance of 55 Ω each and are connected in series across the brushes, which deliver 110 V. What is the current in the field coils?

3. An electric heater whose resistance is 10 Ω is to be used on a 220-V line. The maximum current permitted through it is 10 A. What resistance must be added in series with the heater in order to hold the current to 10 A?

4. In the universal transistor circuit shown in Fig. 3-35, the resistances between points A and B are in series. Find (a) the total current and (b) the voltage drop across each resistance.

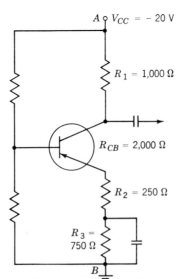

FIGURE 3-35

A universal transistor circuit.

5. The field coils of a motor draw 4 A from a 112-V line. What is the resistance of the coils? If a 14-Ω resistor is added in series with the coils, find the current in the coils and the voltage across the coils.

6. What value of resistance must be placed in series with two 50-Ω lamps, each taking 50 V, if they are to be operated from a 220-V line?

7. Three resistors are connected in series across 220 V. $R_1 = 15 \ \Omega$, $R_2 = 25 \ \Omega$, and $R_3 = 60 \ \Omega$. (a) Find the total current. (b) If the maximum permissible current is 2 A, how much resistance must be added in series to keep the current at this value?

8. In order to dim a bank of stage lights, a rheostat may be connected in series with the lights to reduce the current and therefore the brightness of the lights. What value of resistance must be connected in series with a lamp bank drawing 20 A from a 120-V line in order to reduce the total current drawn to 5 A?

9. Two 25-V 25-Ω incandescent lamps are connected in series with a demonstration motor requiring 30 V at 1 A. What extra resistance should be added in series in order to draw the required current from a 110-V line?

10. When a voltmeter indicates its maximum rated voltage of 150 V, it is drawing a current of 0.01 A. What value of resistance is in series with the moving coil of the voltmeter if its resistance is 20 Ω?

11. In a circuit similar to that shown in Fig. 3-34, $V_C = 8.5$ V, $I_C = 0.015$ A, $E_{RE} = 3$ V, and $R_L = 1,500 \ \Omega$. Find the emitter resistance R_E and the total supply voltage V_{CC}.

12. In the Zenith TV chassis 14Z21, the picture control circuit is essentially the same as that shown in Fig. 3-36. Find the voltage that is applied to the grid of the tube between (a) ground and point A, and (b) ground and point B.

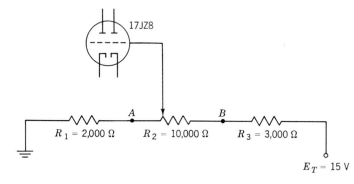

FIGURE 3-36
Different voltages may be applied to the grid of the tube by varying the position of the potentiometer arm.

TEST—SERIES CIRCUITS

1. A lamp, a coil, and a resistor are in series. The voltage across the lamp is 16 V and across the resistor 44 V. The coil has a resistance of 30 Ω and carries a current of 2 A. Find all missing values of current, voltage, and resistance, including the total values.

2. Three resistances are connected in series. $E_1 = 30$ V, $R_1 = 60$ Ω, $E_2 = 50$ V, and $R_3 = 76$ Ω. Find all missing values of current, voltage, and resistance, including the total values.

3. Three resistances are in series. $E_1 = 50$ V, $I_1 = 0.4$ A, $E_3 = 40$ V, and $E_T = 110$ V. Find all missing values of voltage, current, and resistance, including the total values.

4. What resistance must be placed in series with a 48-Ω bell if it is to draw exactly 0.25 A from a 20-V source?

5. A buzzer is designed to operate at 0.15 A and 2.5 V. What resistance must be placed in series with the buzzer in order to operate it from a 10-V source?

PARALLEL CIRCUITS

JOB 4-1 TOTAL VOLTAGE, TOTAL CURRENT, AND TOTAL RESISTANCE IN PARALLEL CIRCUITS

Recognizing a parallel circuit. A parallel circuit is a circuit connected in such a manner that the current flowing into it may *divide* and flow in *more than one path*. In the parallel circuit shown in Fig. 4-1, the current divides at point *A*, part of the current flowing through the lamp in path 1 and the rest of the current flowing through the motor in path 2.

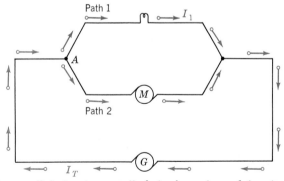

FIGURE 4-1
The current in a parallel circuit flows in more than one path.

The various paths of a parallel circuit are called the branches of the circuit. Notice how different this is from a series circuit shown in Fig. 4-2, in which the current can flow in *only one path*.

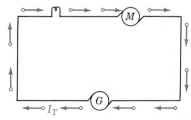

FIGURE 4-2
The current in a series circuit can flow in only one path.

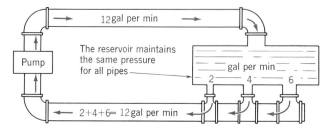

FIGURE 4-3
A water-distribution system in "parallel."

Total voltage in a parallel circuit. Figure 4-3 shows a water-distribution system which might be called a parallel system because the water can flow in more than one pipe. A similar electrical system is shown in Fig. 4-4. In this circuit, the 110-V outlet acts as an electrical pump and supplies an equal pressure to all the branches in parallel.

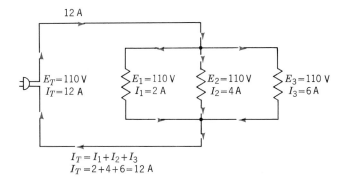

FIGURE 4-4
Three resistors in parallel. The voltages across all the branches are equal.

RULE	The voltage across any branch in parallel is equal to the voltage across any other branch and is also equal to the total voltage.

FORMULA

$$E_T = E_1 = E_2 = E_3 = \cdots \text{etc.} \qquad \boxed{4\text{-}1}$$

Total current in a parallel circuit. In Fig. 4-3, we can see that the total number of gallons per minute flowing in the main pipe equals the number of gallons per minute discharged by all the pipes together, or 12 gal/min. In the same way, the total current that flows in the circuit of Fig. 4-4 is equal to $2 + 4 + 6 = 12$ A.

RULE	The total current in a parallel circuit is equal to the sum of the currents in all the branches of the circuit.

FORMULA

$$I_T = I_1 + I_2 + I_3 + \cdots \text{etc.} \qquad \boxed{4\text{-}2}$$

Distribution of current in parallel. The current in a parallel circuit might be distributed as shown in Fig. 4-5. A total of 12 A is drawn from the line. At A, 2 A is drawn off through R_1, leaving only 10 A to flow along to point B. At B, 4 A is drawn off through R_2, leaving 6 A to flow through the rest of the circuit R_3 around to C. At C, this 6 A combines with the 4 A from R_2 to give 10 A, which flows along to D. Here it combines with the 2 A from R_1 to make up the total of 12 A available originally.

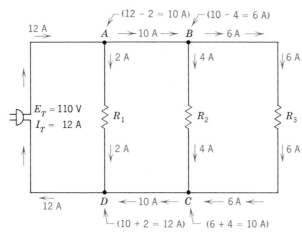

FIGURE 4-5

Distribution of current in a simple parallel circuit.

Line drop. The distribution of the current as indicated above is based on the assumption that the connecting wires have no resistance, which is never true. In most instances, however, the resistance of the connecting wires is so small that we may neglect it completely. If the line wires are so long that their resistance is large, its effect must be included. This case will be taken up later in Job 5-4 under Line Drop.

TOTAL RESISTANCE IN A PARALLEL CIRCUIT

RULE	The total resistance in a parallel circuit is found by applying Ohm's law to the total values of the circuit.

FORMULA

$$E_T = I_T \times R_T \qquad\qquad (3\text{-}7)$$

EXAMPLE 4-1   A toaster, a waffle iron, and a hot plate are connected in parallel across a house line delivering 110 V. The current through the toaster is 2 A, through the waffle iron 6 A, and through the hot plate 3 A. Find (*a*) the total current drawn from the line, (*b*) the voltage across each device, and (*c*) the total resistance of the circuit.

SOLUTION
The diagram for the circuit is shown in Fig. 4-6.

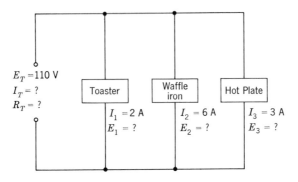

FIGURE 4-6

a Find the total current I_T.

  1 Write the formula.

$$I_T = I_1 + I_2 + I_3 \qquad (4\text{-}2)$$

  2 Substitute numbers.

$$I_T = 2 + 6 + 3$$

  3 Add.

$$I_T = 11 \text{ A} \qquad Ans.$$

b Find the voltage across each device.

  1 Write the formula.

$$E_T = E_1 = E_2 = E_3 \qquad (4\text{-}1)$$

  2 Substitute numbers.

$$E_T = E_1 = E_2 = E_3 = 110 \text{ V} \qquad Ans.$$

c Find the total resistance R_T.

  1 Write the formula.

$$E_T = I_T \times R_T \qquad (3\text{-}7)$$

  2 Substitute numbers.

$$110 = 11 \times R_T$$

  3 Solve for R_T.

$$\frac{110}{11} = R_T$$

  4 Divide.

$$R_T = 10 \text{ } \Omega \qquad Ans.$$

SELF-TEST 4-2 An ammeter carrying 0.06 A is in parallel with a shunt resistor carrying 1.84 A, as shown in Fig. 4-7. If the voltage drop across the combination is 3.8 V find (*a*) the total current and (*b*) the total resistance of the combination.

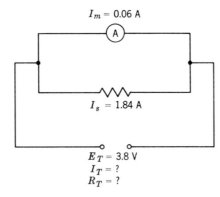

$I_m = 0.06$ A

$I_s = 1.84$ A

$E_T = 3.8$ V
$I_T = ?$
$R_T = ?$

FIGURE 4-7

The shunt prevents large currents from damaging the meter.

SOLUTION

a Find the total current I_T.

   1 Write the formula.

$$I_T = I_m + \underline{\quad} \qquad (4\text{-}2) \qquad\qquad I_s$$

   2 Substitute numbers.

$$I_T = \underline{\quad} + 1.84 \qquad\qquad\qquad 0.06$$

   3 Add.

$$I_T = \underline{\quad} \text{ A} \qquad Ans. \qquad\qquad\qquad 1.9$$

b Find the total resistance R_T.

   1 Write the formula.

$$\underline{\quad} = I_T \times R_T \qquad (3\text{-}7) \qquad\qquad E_T$$

   2 Substitute numbers.

$$3.8 = \underline{\quad} \times R_T \qquad\qquad\qquad 1.9$$

   3 Solve for R_T.

$$\frac{3.8}{?} = R_T \qquad\qquad\qquad\qquad 1.9$$

   4 Divide.

$$R_T = \underline{\quad} \ \Omega \qquad Ans. \qquad\qquad\qquad 2$$

PROBLEMS

1. Two lamps each drawing 2 A and a third lamp drawing 1 A are connected in parallel across a 110-V line. Find (*a*) the total current drawn from the line, (*b*) the voltage across each lamp, and (*c*) the total resistance of the circuit.

2. The ignition coil and the starting motor of an automobile are connected in parallel across a 12-V battery through the ignition switch as shown in Fig. 4-8. Find (*a*) the total current drawn from the

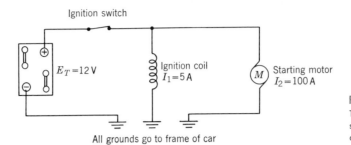

FIGURE 4-8
The ignition coil and the
starting motor of an
automobile are in parallel.

battery, (b) the voltage across the coil and the motor, and (c) the total resistance of the circuit.

3. Find the total current drawn by eight trailer-truck warning lights in parallel if each takes 0.5 A.

4. A motor, a heating coil, and an ultraviolet lamp of a modern clothes drier are connected in parallel across 117 V. The lamp current is 1 A, the coil current is 4 A, and the motor current is 3 A. Find (a) the total current drawn and (b) the total resistance of the circuit.

5. In Table 13-1 the National Electrical Code specifies that No. 14 rubber-covered wire can safely carry only 15 A. How many 0.5-A lamps could be safely operated at a time on a line using this wire? How many lamps could be safely operated at one time if a 5-A electric iron were connected in the circuit?

6. A toaster drawing 2 A, a coffee percolator drawing 3.5 A, and a refrigerator motor drawing 4.5 A are connected in parallel across a 110-V line. Find (a) the total current drawn, (b) the voltage across each device, and (c) the total resistance.

7. A bank of ten 110-V 100-W lamps is connected in parallel in a stage lighting circuit. Each lamp uses 0.91 A. Find the total current drawn. Will a fuse rated at 10 A safely carry this load?

8. A 40-W lamp drawing 0.36 A, a 60-W lamp drawing 0.54 A, and a 100-W lamp drawing 0.9 A are connected in parallel across 110 V. Find (a) the total current, (b) the voltage across each lamp, and (c) the total resistance of the circuit.

9. Two 32-candlepower headlight lamps each drawing 3.9 A and two taillight lamps (4 candlepower, 0.85 A each) are wired in parallel to the 12-V storage battery. Find the total current drawn and the total resistance of the circuit.

10. A washing machine drawing 7.5 A, an electric fan drawing 0.85 A, and an electric clock drawing 0.02 A are in parallel with a 110-V line. Find the total current and the total resistance.

JOB 4-2   USING OHM'S LAW IN PARALLEL CIRCUITS

In some instances, it may be impossible to find the total current by adding the individual currents because the individual currents may be unknown. Therefore, the current in each branch must be found before we can find the total current.

EXAMPLE 4-3   The circuit of an electric clothes drier is shown in Fig. 4-9. The ultraviolet lamp R_1 is 120 Ω and draws 1 A. The heating coil R_2 is 30 Ω, and the motor R_3 draws a current of 4 A. Find (a) the voltage for each part and the total voltage, (b) the current in each part and the total current, and (c) the resistance of each part and the total resistance.

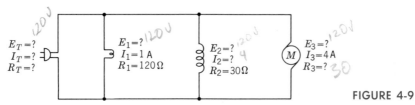

$E_T=?$
$I_T=?$
$R_T=?$

$E_1=?$
$I_1=1$ A
$R_1=120\,\Omega$

$E_2=?$
$I_2=?$
$R_2=30\,\Omega$

$E_3=?$
$I_3=4$ A
$R_3=?$

FIGURE 4-9

SOLUTION

a   Find E_1.

   1   Write the formula.

$$E_1 = I_1 \times R_1 \qquad\qquad (3\text{-}4)$$

   2   Substitute numbers.

$$E_1 = 1 \times 120$$

   3   Multiply.

$$E_1 = 120 \text{ V} \qquad Ans.$$

   Find E_T and the voltage across each part of the circuit.

   1   Write the formula.

$$E_T = E_1 = E_2 = E_3 \qquad\qquad (4\text{-}1)$$

   2   Substitute numbers.

$$E_T = E_1 = E_2 = E_3 = 120 \text{ V}$$

b   Find the current I_2.

   1   Write the formula.

$$E_2 = I_2 \times R_2 \qquad\qquad (3\text{-}5)$$

   2   Substitute numbers.

$$120 = I_2 \times 30$$

   3   Solve for I_2.

$$\frac{120}{30} = I_2$$

   4   Divide.

$$I_2 = 4 \text{ A} \qquad Ans.$$

Find the total current I_T.

1 Write the formula.

$$I_T = I_1 + I_2 + I_3 \qquad\qquad (4\text{-}2)$$

2 Substitute numbers.

$$I_T = 1 + 4 + 4$$

3 Add.

$$I_T = 9 \text{ A} \qquad Ans.$$

c Find the resistance R_3.

1 Write the formula.

$$E_3 = I_3 \times R_3 \qquad\qquad (3\text{-}6)$$

2 Substitute numbers.

$$120 = 4 \times R_3$$

3 Solve for R_3.

$$\frac{120}{4} = R_3$$

4 Divide.

$$R_3 = 30 \ \Omega \qquad Ans.$$

Find the total resistance R_T.

1 Write the formula.

$$E_T = I_T \times R_T \qquad\qquad (3\text{-}7)$$

2 Substitute numbers.

$$120 = 9 \times R_T$$

3 Solve for R_T.

$$\frac{120}{9} = R_T$$

4 Divide.

$$R_T = 13.3 \ \Omega \qquad Ans.$$

In the last example, R_2 and R_3 are both equal to 30 Ω. They both draw 4 A of current. This gives us the following rules.

RULE	If the branches of a parallel circuit have the same resistance, then each will draw the same current.

SELF-TEST 4-4 A 12FQ8 tube whose filament is rated at 12.6 V and 0.15 A is in parallel with a shunt resistor in a filament circuit supplying 1.2 A, as shown in Fig. 4-10. Find (*a*) the voltage in each part and the total voltage, (*b*) the current in the shunt, and (*c*) the resistance of each part and the total resistance.

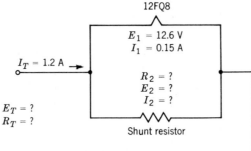

12FQ8

$E_1 = 12.6$ V
$I_1 = 0.15$ A

$I_T = 1.2$ A

$R_2 = ?$
$E_2 = ?$
$I_2 = ?$

$E_T = ?$
$R_T = ?$

Shunt resistor

FIGURE 4-10

SOLUTION

a Find E_T and the voltage across each part of the circuit.

$$E_T = E_1 = E_2 = \underline{\quad} \text{ V} \qquad Ans. \qquad (4\text{-}1)$$

12.6

b Find the current in the shunt I_2.

$$I_T = I_1 + \underline{\quad} \qquad (4\text{-}2)$$

I_2

$$\underline{\quad} = 0.15 + I_2$$

1.2

$$1.2 - \underline{\quad} = I_2$$

0.15

$$I_2 = \underline{\quad} \text{ A} \qquad Ans.$$

1.05

c Find the resistance of each part.

$$E_1 = I_1 \times R_1 \qquad (3\text{-}4)$$

$$\underline{\quad} = 0.15 \times R_1$$

12.6

$$R_1 = \frac{12.6}{?}$$

0.15

$$R_1 = \underline{\quad} \ \Omega \qquad Ans.$$

84

Find R_2. Use E_2 from step $\underline{\quad}$ and I_2 from step $\underline{\quad}$.

a   *b*

$$E_2 = I_2 \times R_2 \qquad (3\text{-}5)$$

$$12.6 = \underline{\quad} \times R_2$$

1.05

$$R_2 = \frac{12.6}{?}$$

1.05

$$R_2 = \underline{\quad} \ \Omega \qquad Ans.$$

Find the total resistance R_T.

$$E_T = \underline{\quad} \times R_T \qquad\qquad (3\text{-}7)$$

$$12.6 = \underline{\quad} \times R_T$$

$$R_T = \frac{12.6}{?}$$

$$R_T = \underline{\quad} \ \Omega \qquad Ans.$$

	12
	I_T
	1.2
	1.2
	10.5

PROBLEMS

1. Two resistors of 3 and 6 Ω are connected in parallel across 18 V. Find (a) the voltage across each resistor, (b) the current in each resistor and the total current, and (c) the total resistance.

2. Find all missing values of voltage, current, and resistance in the circuit shown in Fig. 4-11.

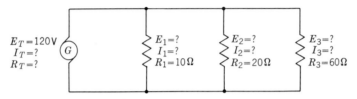

$E_T = 120\text{V}$
$I_T = ?$
$R_T = ?$

$E_1 = ?$
$I_1 = ?$
$R_1 = 10\,\Omega$

$E_2 = ?$
$I_2 = ?$
$R_2 = 20\,\Omega$

$E_3 = ?$
$I_3 = ?$
$R_3 = 60\,\Omega$

FIGURE 4-11

3. A parallel circuit has three branches of 12, 6, and 4 Ω resistance. If the current in the 6-Ω branch is 4 A, what current will flow in each of the other branches? What is the total current?

4. The secondary of a power transformer is connected across the motors of three toy trains in parallel. Motor 1 has a resistance of 50 Ω and draws 0.4 A. Motor 2 has a resistance of 40 Ω. Motor 3 draws a current of 0.3 A. Find (a) the total voltage, (b) the total current, and (c) the total resistance.

5. Three resistors are in parallel. $I_1 = 12$ A, $E_2 = 114$ V, $R_2 = 19\ \Omega$, and $R_3 = 57\ \Omega$. Find (a) the voltage across each resistor and the total voltage, (b) the current in each resistor and the total current, and (c) the resistance of each resistor and the total resistance.

6. Three buzzers are wired in parallel. They draw currents of 0.2, 0.4, and 0.6 A, respectively. If their total resistance is 6 Ω, find (a) the resistance of each buzzer and (b) the voltage across each buzzer.

7. Four 1½-V lamps are wired in parallel. Three of these lamps draw a current of 0.05 A each. The fourth draws a current of 0.1 A. (a) What is the resistance of each filament? (b) What is the total current drawn? (c) What is the total voltage required? (d) What is the total resistance of the four filaments in parallel?

8. Solve the circuit shown in Fig. 4-12 for the values indicated.

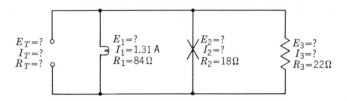

FIGURE 4-12

9. The following GE panel lights are to be wired in parallel from a 6.8-V source: two No. 40 lamps (0.15 A) and three No. 44 lamps (0.25 A). Find the total current, total voltage, and the total resistance of the circuit.

10. What is the total current drawn from the 12-V automobile battery by two 4-Ω headlights and a 12-Ω taillight if they are all connected in parallel?

JOB 4-3   CHECKUP ON ADDITION AND SUBTRACTION OF FRACTIONS (DIAGNOSTIC TEST)

Our next electrical job considers problems which are solved by the addition of fractions. In order to prepare for them, let us try the following problems which are often met by the electrician and electronic technician in his work. If you have any difficulty with any of these, see Job 4-4 which follows.

PROBLEMS

1. What is the total horsepower delivered by a $\frac{1}{3}$-, a $\frac{1}{4}$-, and a $\frac{1}{8}$-hp motor in parallel?

2. Add the following conductances in a circuit to obtain the total conductance: $\frac{1}{60}$, $\frac{1}{20}$, and $\frac{1}{10}$ mho.

3. In rewinding the armature of a motor, the following thicknesses of insulation were used: $\frac{1}{16}$, $\frac{1}{32}$, and $\frac{3}{64}$ in. What was the total thickness of the insulation?

4. What length of a bolt is covered by a lock washer ($\frac{1}{32}$ in), a washer ($\frac{1}{8}$ in), and a nut ($\frac{5}{16}$ in)?

5. What is the total weight of three coils of wire weighing $16\frac{1}{4}$, $4\frac{1}{8}$, and $2\frac{1}{2}$ lb?

6. Add $\frac{1}{5}$, $\frac{1}{3}$, and $\frac{1}{10}$.

7. Add $\frac{3}{4}$, $\frac{7}{8}$, and $\frac{3}{16}$.

8. Add $\frac{3}{4}$, $\frac{5}{6}$, and $\frac{7}{8}$.

9. Add $\frac{5}{6}$, $\frac{1}{9}$, and $\frac{2}{3}$.

10. Add $\frac{1}{2}$, $\frac{5}{7}$, and $\frac{3}{4}$.

11. Subtract $1\frac{1}{2}$ from $3\frac{5}{8}$.

12. What is the difference between $9\frac{3}{8}$ and $4\frac{7}{16}$?

13. Subtract: $8 - 3\sqrt[3]{4}$
14. Subtract: $5\sqrt[1]{4} - 2\sqrt[9]{16}$
15. Subtract: $\sqrt[1]{24} - \sqrt[1]{40}$

JOB 4-4   BRUSHUP ON ADDITION OF FRACTIONS

ADDING FRACTIONS WITH THE SAME DENOMINATOR

EXAMPLE 4-5

1 apple + 3 apples + 2 apples = __ apples.   6

$1\ \Omega + 3\ \Omega + 2\ \Omega = \_\ \Omega.$ 6

$1\ A + 3\ A + 2\ A = 6\_.$ A

$1\ V + 3\ V + 2\ V = 6\_.$ V

Apparently, in order to add the same *kind* of thing, it is only necessary to add the numbers involved. Thus

one-*eighth* + three-*eighths* + two-*eighths* = six-_____   eighths

or

$$\frac{1}{8} + \frac{3}{8} + \frac{2}{8} = ?$$ $\frac{6}{8}$

And $\frac{6}{8}$ may be simplified to $\frac{3}{4}$ *Ans.*

RULE	To add fractions with the same denominator, add the numerators and place the sum over the same denominator.

EXAMPLE 4-6   Add $\sqrt[3]{16}$, $\sqrt[5]{16}$, and $\sqrt[7]{16}$.

SOLUTION

$$\frac{3}{16} + \frac{5}{16} + \frac{7}{16} = \frac{3+5+7}{16} = \frac{15}{?}$$ 16

ADDING FRACTIONS WITH DIFFERENT DENOMINATORS

Procedure

1 Find the *least common denominator.* (See below.)
2 Change the fractions to *equivalent* fractions using this new denominator.
3 Add these fractions with the same denominator.

EXAMPLE 4-7   Add $\sqrt[1]{4} + \sqrt[3]{8}$.

SOLUTION

The least common denominator is a number *into which* all the denominators will evenly divide. Both the 4 and the 8 will divide into 8 evenly. Therefore, 8 is the least common denominator. Since $\frac{1}{4} = \frac{2}{8}$, we have

$$\frac{2}{8} + \frac{3}{8} = \frac{5}{8} \qquad Ans.$$

In this problem, it was very easy to change all the fractions into equivalent fractions with the same denominator. All problems are not so simple. One of the difficulties will be to decide on what the new denominator will be. The least common denominator is abbreviated as the LCD.

HOW TO FIND THE LEAST COMMON DENOMINATOR

EXAMPLE 4-8   Find the LCD for $\frac{1}{2} + \frac{1}{3} + \frac{1}{8}$.

SOLUTION

1   Start with the largest denominator—the 8.
2   Try to divide the other denominators into the 8. They must divide exactly. If not,
3   Multiply the 8 by 2 to get 16.
4   Try to divide the other denominators into the 16. If they all divide evenly, then 16 is the LCD. If not, multiply the 8 by 3 and then 4, etc., until you find a number into which all the denominators will evenly divide. This last number will be the LCD.

Following this method, we multiply the 8 by 2 and get 16. The 2 and the 8 will divide evenly into the 16, but the 3 will not. We multiply the 8 by 3 and get 24. The 2, the 3, and the 8 all divide into 24 evenly. Therefore,

$$24 \text{ is the LCD} \qquad Ans.$$

EXAMPLE 4-9   Add: $\frac{1}{7} + \frac{1}{2} + \frac{1}{4}$.

SOLUTION

1   Find the LCD. Start with the 7. This is not the LCD because the 2 and the 4 do not divide evenly into 7. Multiply the 7 by 2 to get 14. This is not the LCD because the 4 does not divide evenly into 14. Multiply the 7 by 3 to get 21. This is not the LCD because neither the 2 nor the 4 will divde evenly into 21. Multiply the 7 by 4 to get 28. This *is* the LCD because the numbers 2, 4, and 7 *all divide evenly into* 28.
2   Set up the problem like this:

$$\begin{array}{r} 28 \text{ (LCD)} \\ \frac{1}{7} \left| \rule{0pt}{40pt} \right. \\ \frac{1}{2} \\ \frac{1}{4} \end{array}$$

3   Divide each denominator into the LCD, and then multiply the quotient by the numerator of the fraction.

    a   7 into 28 is 4. $4 \times 1 = 4$. Therefore $\frac{1}{7} = \frac{4}{28}$.

    b   2 into 28 is 14. $14 \times 1 = 14$. Therefore $\frac{1}{2} = \frac{14}{28}$.

    c   4 into 28 is 7. $7 \times 1 = 7$. Therefore, $\frac{1}{4} = \frac{7}{28}$.

The problem now looks like this. Add the equivalent fractions and express in lowest terms or divide to a decimal.

$$
\begin{array}{r|l}
 & 28 \\ \hline
\frac{1}{7} & \frac{4}{28} \\
+\frac{1}{2} & \frac{14}{28} \\
\frac{1}{4} & \frac{7}{28} \\ \hline
 & \frac{25}{28} \quad Ans.
\end{array}
$$

EXAMPLE 4-10   Add $\frac{3}{4} + \frac{5}{6} + \frac{7}{8}$.

SOLUTION

1   Find the LCD. The LCD is not 8. The LCD is not $8 \times 2 = 16$. The LCD *is* $8 \times 3 = 24$ because the 4, 6, and 8 will divide evenly into 24.

2   Find the equivalent fractions and put them in the proper form.

    a   4 into 24 is 6. $6 \times 3 = 18$.   Therefore, $\frac{3}{4} = \frac{18}{24}$.

    b   6 into 24 is 4. $4 \times 5 = 20$.   Therefore, $\frac{5}{6} = \frac{20}{24}$.

    c   8 into 24 is 3. $3 \times 7 = 21$.   Therefore, $\frac{7}{8} = \frac{21}{24}$.

3   The problem now looks like this. Add the equivalent fractions, and express in lowest terms or divide to a decimal as shown.

$$
\begin{array}{r|l}
 & 24 \\ \hline
\frac{3}{4} & \frac{18}{24} \\
+\frac{5}{6} & \frac{20}{24} \\
\frac{7}{8} & \frac{21}{24} \\ \hline
 & \frac{59}{24} = 2\frac{11}{24} = 2.46 \quad Ans.
\end{array}
$$

SELF-TEST 4-11   What length of cable is needed to install the lighting outlets shown in Fig. 4-13?

SOLUTION

The total length required is equal to the _____ of all the lengths. The total length $= 9\frac{3}{4} + 8\frac{1}{2} + 14\frac{5}{8} + 6\frac{5}{12}$.

                    sum, or addition

1   Find the LCD. Start with the number ____. This is not the LCD because the denominator __ will not divide evenly into it. Multiply the 12 by __ to get 24. This number *is* the LCD because ____ the denominators divide _____ into 24.

                    12

                    8   2

                    all   evenly

2   Set up the problem like this:

$$
\begin{array}{r|l}
 & 24 \text{ (LCD)} \\ \hline
9\frac{3}{4} & \\
8\frac{1}{2} & \\
14\frac{5}{8} & \\
6\frac{5}{12} & \\ \hline
\end{array}
$$

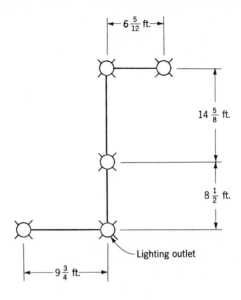

FIGURE 4-13

3   Divide each denominator into the _____, and then multiply the quotient by the _____ of the fraction.

    a 4 into 24 is 6.   6 × 3 = 18.   Therefore, $3/4 = {}^{18}/_{24}$.
    b 2 into 24 is 12.   12 × 1 = 12.   Therefore, $1/2 =$ _____.
    c 8 into 24 is 3.   3 × 5 = 15.   Therefore, $5/8 =$ _____.
    d 12 into 24 is 2.   2 × 5 = 10.   Therefore, $5/12 =$ _____.

4   The problem now looks like this. Add the equivalent fractions and then add the whole numbers.

$$\begin{array}{rl}
 & 24 \\
 9\ \frac{3}{4} & \overline{\ \frac{18}{24}} \\
 8\ \frac{1}{2} & \frac{12}{24} \\
 14\ \frac{5}{8} & \frac{15}{24} \\
 6\ \frac{5}{12} & \frac{10}{24} \\
 \overline{\ 37} & \frac{?}{24}
\end{array}$$

5   Change $^{55}/_{24}$ to a mixed number by _____ 24 into 55. This will give 2 and ____. Add the whole number 2 to the 37 to give the final answer which is ___$^{7}/_{24}$ ft.   *Ans.*

Margin notes:

LCD
numerator

$^{12}/_{24}$
$^{15}/_{24}$
$^{10}/_{24}$

55

dividing
$^{7}/_{24}$
39

PROBLEMS

Add the following fractions and express in lowest terms.

1. $^{1}/_{8} + {}^{3}/_{8} + {}^{7}/_{8}$ 2. $^{3}/_{4} + {}^{5}/_{6} + {}^{9}/_{16}$ 3. $^{1}/_{4} + {}^{5}/_{6} + {}^{3}/_{8}$
4. $^{5}/_{6} + {}^{1}/_{9} + {}^{2}/_{3}$ 5. $^{1}/_{60} + {}^{1}/_{20} + {}^{1}/_{10}$ 6. $^{1}/_{3} + {}^{1}/_{6} + {}^{1}/_{9}$

7. $\frac{1}{4} + \frac{1}{12} + \frac{1}{15}$ 8. $\frac{1}{5} + \frac{1}{7} + \frac{1}{9}$ 9. $\frac{1}{200} + \frac{1}{300}$

10. $\frac{1}{50} + \frac{1}{100}$ 11. $\frac{3}{16} + \frac{5}{64} + \frac{5}{8}$ 12. $\frac{5}{32} + \frac{3}{8} + \frac{9}{16}$

13. $\frac{1}{10} + \frac{1}{30} + \frac{1}{60}$ 14. $\frac{1}{500} + \frac{1}{200} + \frac{1}{400}$ 15. $\frac{3}{4} + \frac{9}{32} + \frac{5}{16}$

16. $1\frac{3}{8} + 3\frac{1}{2} + 2\frac{3}{16}$ 17. $1\frac{3}{4} + 8\frac{5}{16} + 5\frac{3}{8}$ 18. $1\frac{5}{8} + 3\frac{2}{3}$

19. A carbon brush $\frac{29}{32}$ in thick is coated with copper to a thickness of $\frac{1}{64}$ in on each side. Find the total thickness.

20. What is the total thickness of insulation made by $\frac{1}{64}$-in fish paper, $\frac{1}{32}$-in tufflex, $\frac{3}{64}$-in varnished cambric, and $\frac{1}{8}$-in top stick?

21. In Fig. 4-14, the reciprocal of the resistance is known as the conductance, whose symbol is G. If the total conductance of a parallel circuit is the sum of the conductances, find the total conductance G_T.

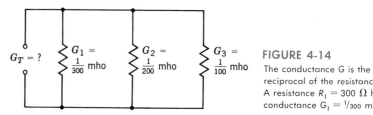

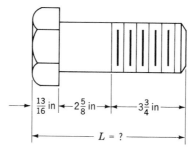

FIGURE 4-14

The conductance G is the reciprocal of the resistance R. A resistance $R_1 = 300\ \Omega$ has a conductance $G_1 = \frac{1}{300}$ mho.

22. Find the total resistance of a series circuit containing a $2\frac{1}{2}$-MΩ (megohm), a $1\frac{3}{10}$-MΩ, and a $\frac{9}{100}$-MΩ resistor.

23. Find the total length of the bolt shown in Fig. 4-15.

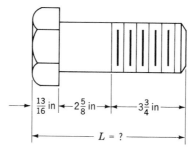

FIGURE 4-15

24. In a layout similar to that shown in Fig. 4-13, find the total length of cable needed if the measurements between outlets are: $6\frac{1}{4}$ ft, $8\frac{7}{12}$ ft, $10\frac{5}{8}$ ft, and $4\frac{5}{10}$ ft.

JOB 4-5   BRUSHUP ON SUBTRACTION OF FRACTIONS

SUBTRACTING FRACTIONS WITH THE SAME DENOMINATOR

RULE	To subtract fractions with the same denominator, subtract the numerators and place the difference over the same denominator.

EXAMPLE 4-12   Subtract $3/8$ from $5/8$.

SOLUTION

$$\frac{5}{8} - \frac{3}{8} = \frac{5-3}{8} = \frac{2}{8} = \frac{1}{4} \quad Ans.$$

SUBTRACTING FRACTIONS WITH DIFFERENT DENOMINATORS

Procedure

1   Find the *least common denominator.*
2   Change the fractions to *equivalent* fractions using this new denominator.
3   Subtract these fractions with the same denominator.

EXAMPLE 4-13   Subtract $3/16$ from $3/4$.

SOLUTION

1   Find the LCD, which is 16.
2   Set up the problem as shown below and change the fractions to equivalent fractions as described in Examples 4-9 to 4-11.

$$
\begin{array}{r|l}
 & 16 \\
\hline
3/4 & 12/16 \\
-\,3/16 & 3/16 \\
\hline
\end{array}
$$

3   Subtract these fractions with the same denominator and reduce to lowest terms.

$$\frac{12}{16} - \frac{3}{16} = \frac{9}{16} \quad Ans.$$

EXAMPLE 4-14   Subtract $3\,1/4$ from 9.

SOLUTION

1   Set up the problem as shown below.

$$
\begin{array}{r}
9 \\
-3\ 1/4 \\
\hline
\end{array}
$$

Since $1/4$ cannot be subtracted from nothing, *borrow* one unit from the 9, leaving 8, and replace this unit as the fraction $4/4$. The unit that is borrowed is always replaced as a fraction with identical numerator and denominator, each being equal to the denominator of the fraction being subtracted.

$$
\begin{array}{r}
9 \\
-3\ 1/4 \\
\hline
\end{array}
=
\begin{array}{r}
8 \\
\cancel{9}\ 4/4 \\
-3\ 1/4 \\
\hline
\end{array}
$$

2   Subtract the fractions ($4/4 - 1/4 = 3/4$).   Subtract the whole numbers ($8 - 3 = 5$).

3   Write the answer.

$$5^3/_4 \quad Ans.$$

EXAMPLE 4-15   Subtract $2^5/_8$ from $8^3/_{16}$.

SOLUTION

1   Set up the problem as shown below.

$$\begin{array}{r} 8\ ^3/_{16} \\ -2\ ^5/_8 \\ \hline \end{array}$$

2   Find the LCD, which is 16.
3   Change the fractions to equivalent fractions using this new denominator.

$$\begin{array}{r} 8\ ^{\cdot 3}/_{16} \\ -\ 2\ ^5/_8 \\ \hline \end{array} = \begin{array}{c|c} & 16 \\ \hline 8 & ^3/_{16} \\ -\ 2 & ^{10}/_{16} \\ \hline \end{array}$$

4   As you can see, $^{10}/_{16}$ cannot be subtracted from only $^3/_{16}$. Therefore, we shall *borrow* one unit from the 8 as in Example 4-14, and replace it as $^{16}/_{16}$ as shown below.

$$\begin{array}{r} 8\ ^3/_{16} \\ -2\ ^5/_8 \\ \hline \end{array} = \begin{array}{c|c} 7 & 16 \\ \hline \cancel{8} & ^3/_{16} + {}^{16}/_{16} \\ -2 & ^{10}/_{16} \\ \hline \end{array}$$

5   Combine the $^3/_{16} + {}^{16}/_{16}$ into $^{19}/_{16}$ and subtract the $^{10}/_{16}$ from the $^{19}/_{16}$ as shown below.

$$\begin{array}{c|c} & 16 \\ \hline 7 & ^3/_{16} + {}^{16}/_{16} = {}^{19}/_{16} \\ -2 & ^{10}/_{16} \\ \hline 5 & ^9/_{16} \quad Ans. \end{array}$$

EXAMPLE 4-16   Subtract $3^2/_3$ from $7^1/_4$.

SOLUTION

$$\begin{array}{r} 7\ ^1/_4 \\ -3\ ^2/_3 \\ \hline \end{array} = \begin{array}{c|c} & 12 \\ \hline 7 & ^3/_{12} \\ -3 & ^8/_{12} \\ \hline \end{array} = \begin{array}{c|c} 6 & 12 \\ \hline \cancel{7} & ^3/_{12} + {}^{12}/_{12} = {}^{15}/_{12} \\ -3 & ^8/_{12} \\ \hline 3 & ^7/_{12} \quad Ans. \end{array}$$

SELF-TEST 4-17   In Fig. 4-16, what resistance must be placed in series with a $12^3/_4$-Ω bell in order to provide a total resistance of $84^3/_5$ Ω?

SOLUTION
The required resistance may be found by _____ the $12^3/_4$ Ω from the total of $84^3/_5$ Ω.   The number after the word "from" is written on the (top/bottom)   of the subtraction problem.   The LCD for the denominators 4 and 5 is ____.

subtracting

top
20

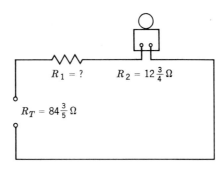

FIGURE 4-16

1   Set up the problem as shown below.

$$\begin{array}{r} 20 \\ \hline 84\ ^3/_5 \\ -\ 12\ ^3/_4 \end{array}$$

2   Change the fractions to equivalent fractions using _____ as the new denominator.

$$\begin{array}{c} 84\ ^3/_5 \\ -\ 12\ ^3/_4 \end{array} = \begin{array}{r} 20 \\ \hline 84\ ^3/_5 \quad = \ ? \\ -\ 12\ ^3/_4 \quad = \ ? \end{array}$$

	20
	$12/_{20}$
	$15/_{20}$

3   As you can see, $^{15}/_{20}$ cannot be subtracted from only $^{12}/_{20}$. Therefore, we must _____ one unit from the 84 and replace it as ____ as shown below.

borrow	$20/_{20}$

$$84\ \frac{3}{5} \quad = \quad \overset{3}{84}\ \frac{3}{5}\ \begin{array}{c} \overset{20}{\overline{\frac{12}{20} + \frac{?}{20}}} \end{array}$$
$$-\ 12\ \frac{3}{4} \qquad\qquad -\ 12\ \frac{3}{4}\ \begin{array}{c} \frac{15}{20} \end{array}$$

20

4   Combine the $^{12}/_{20}$ and the $^{20}/_{20}$ into _____ and subtract the $^{15}/_{20}$ from it. Complete the problem as shown below.

$32/_{20}$

$$\begin{array}{r} 20 \\ \hline 83\ \frac{12}{20} + \frac{20}{20} = \frac{32}{20} \\ -\ 12\ \frac{15}{20} \\ \hline 71\ \frac{?}{20}\ \Omega \quad \textit{Ans.} \end{array}$$

17

PROBLEMS

Subtract the following fractions and express in lowest terms.

1. $^3/_4 - ^1/_4$ 2. $^7/_8 - ^3/_8$ 3. $^{11}/_{16} - ^5/_{16}$ 4. $5^5/_8 - 1^3/_8$
5. $^9/_{16} - ^1/_4$ 6. $^5/_6 - ^1/_3$ 7. $^3/_4 - ^2/_3$ 8. $5^5/_6 - 2^2/_3$
9. $^1/_2 - ^1/_3$ 10. $^1/_{50} - ^1/_{100}$ 11. $^1/_{10} - ^1/_{60}$ 12. $^1/_{90} - ^1/_{100}$
13. $^1/_{40} - ^1/_{80}$ 14. $^1/_{12} - ^1/_{60}$ 15. $^1/_{250} - ^1/_{500}$ 16. $^1/_{480} - ^1/_{2,400}$

17. $7 - 2\frac{1}{4}$ 18. $13 - 5\frac{3}{8}$ 19. $8 - \frac{2}{3}$ 20. $5\frac{1}{4} - 2\frac{5}{8}$
21. $8\frac{3}{16} - 2\frac{3}{4}$ 22. $5\frac{2}{3} - 3\frac{5}{8}$ 23. $\frac{1}{200} - \frac{1}{600}$ 24. $\frac{1}{1,000} - \frac{1}{2,500}$

25. How many feet of push-back wire are left from a 100-ft roll if a radio mechanic used $23\frac{1}{4}$ feet?
26. Find the distance marked A in the eccentric cam shown in Fig. 4-17.

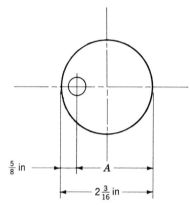

FIGURE 4-17

27. Find the inside diameter of an electrical conduit shown in Fig. 4-18 if its outside diameter is $2\frac{1}{4}$ in and the thickness of the conduit is $\frac{3}{16}$ in.

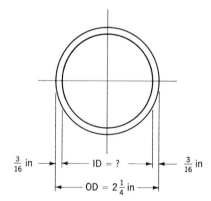

FIGURE 4-18
Cross section of an electrical conduit.

28. Kirchhoff's law states that the current that enters a point in a circuit is equal to the sum of the currents that leave the point. In the circuit shown in Fig. 4-19, find the current I_2.

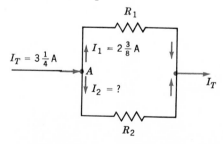

FIGURE 4-19
The current that enters point A is equal to the sum of the currents that leave the point.

JOB 4-6 CHECKUP ON SOLUTION OF FORMULAS INVOLVING FRACTIONS (DIAGNOSTIC TEST)

In addition to adding fractions, our next electrical job will require that we be able to solve formulas which contain fractions. Following are some problems of this type. If you have any difficulty solving any of them, see Job 4-7 which follows.

PROBLEMS

1. Using the formula $f = PS/120$, find the speed S of an alternator if the frequency f is 60 Hz and the number of poles P is 4.
2. $R_1/R_2 = L_1/L_2$ is a formula used to compare the resistances of different lengths of wire. Find R_1 if $R_2 = 100$, $L_1 = 500$, $L_2 = 800$.
3. $E_1/E_2 = I_2/I_1$ is the formula for the relation between the voltages and the currents in the primary and secondary windings of a transformer. Find I_1 if $E_1 = 110$ V, $E_2 = 22$ V, and $I_2 = 10$ A.
4. The fundamental equation for the Wheatstone bridge (a resistance-measuring device) is $R_1/R_2 = R_3/R_x$. Find R_x if $R_1 = 1,000$, $R_2 = 10,000$, and $R_3 = 84.3$.
5. In series circuits, the voltage drops are proportional to the resistances. This is stated mathematically as $E_1/E_2 = R_1/R_2$. Find E_1 if $E_2 = 8$ V, $R_1 = 3$ Ω, and $R_2 = 4$ Ω.

JOB 4-7 BRUSHUP ON SOLUTION OF FRACTIONAL EQUATIONS

Solving simple fractional equations. Many electrical formulas are stated in the form of a fraction. After substituting the given numbers for the letters of the formula, we might get an equation like $E/4 = 5$. To find the value of E, we must get the letter E all by itself on one side of the equality sign. In other words, we must eliminate the number 4. We can do this by applying the general rule which says that we may do anything to one side of an equality sign provided we do the same thing to the other side.

Is the statement "$4 = 4$" a true equation?   (yes/no)   Suppose that we multiply each side of the equation by 2. It would look like this.

$$2 \times 4 = 4 \times 2$$

$$\text{or } 8 = \underline{}$$

Is the equation still true?   (yes/no)   Suppose that we multiply each side of the equation by 5. It would look like this.

$$5 \times 4 = 4 \times 5$$

$$\text{or } \underline{} = 20$$

yes
8
yes
20

Is the equation still true? _____(yes/no)_____   yes

Is the statement "$^1/_2 = {}^2/_4$" a true equation? _____(yes/no)_____   Suppose that   yes
we multiply each side of the equation by 4. It would look like this.

$$\overset{2}{\cancel{4}} \times \underset{1}{\dfrac{1}{\cancel{2}}} = \underset{1}{\dfrac{2}{\cancel{4}}} \times \overset{1}{\cancel{4}}$$

which results in the statement

$$2 = \underline{\quad}$$ 2

Is the equation still true? _____(yes/no)_____   yes

These examples will give us the following rule.

RULE	Both sides of an equality sign may be multiplied by the same number without destroying the equality.

SELF-TEST 4-18   Find the value of E in the equation

$$\frac{E}{4} = 5$$

SOLUTION

Solving an equation means to get the letter all alone on one side of the equality
sign. We can get E alone on the left side of the equality sign if we can get rid of
the denominator 4. We can eliminate the denominator 4 by _____   multiplying
both sides of the equality sign by that same number 4.

1   Write the equation.

$$\frac{E}{4} = 5$$

2   Multiply both sides by 4.

$$\overset{1}{\cancel{4}} \times \underset{1}{\dfrac{E}{\cancel{4}}} = 5 \times \underline{\quad}$$ 4

3   Multiply each side separately.

$$1 \times E = \underline{\quad}$$ 20

$$\text{or } E = \underline{\quad} \quad Ans.$$ 20

SELF-TEST 4-19   Using the formula $I = \dfrac{E}{R}$, find E if $I = 2$ and $R = 6$.

SOLUTION

1   Write the formula.

$$I = \frac{E}{R}$$

2   Substitute numbers.

$$2 = \frac{E}{?}$$

6

Step 2 asks the question, "what number divided by 6 gives 2 as an answer?"
We can find E if we can eliminate the denominator 6. This may easily be done
by _____ both sides of the equality sign by ____.

multiplying   6

3   Multiply both sides by 6.

$$6 \times 2 = \frac{E}{\cancel{6}} \times \cancel{6}^{\,1}$$
$$\phantom{6 \times 2 = \frac{E}{6}}{}_{1}$$

4   Multiply both sides separately.

$$\underline{} = E \times 1$$

12

$$\text{or } E = \underline{} \qquad Ans.$$

12

SELF-TEST 4-20   Find the effective value of an ac voltage wave whose
maximum value $E_{max} = 160$ V. Use the approximate formula

$$\frac{E}{0.7} = E_{max}$$

SOLUTION

1   Write the formula.

$$\frac{E}{0.7} = E_{max}$$

2   Substitute numbers.

$$\frac{E}{0.7} = \underline{}$$

160

3   Multiply both sides by ____.

0.7

$$0.7 \times \frac{E}{0.7} = 160 \times \underline{}$$

0.7

4   Multiply both sides separately.

$$1 \times E = \underline{}$$

112

$$\text{or } E = \underline{} \text{ V} \qquad Ans.$$

112

Notice that in each of the last three examples we eliminated the number in the denominator by *multiplying both sides by that same number.*
If we were to multiply both sides by any other number, we would still
be left with a number in the denominator and the letter would not stand
alone. Therefore, to eliminate a number in the denominator of a fraction, we use the following rule:

RULE	To eliminate a number divided into a letter, multiply both sides of the equality sign by that same number.

PROBLEMS

Find the value of the unknown letter in each problem.

1. $\dfrac{E}{3} = 8$

2. $4 = \dfrac{E}{10}$

3. $\dfrac{P}{6} = 2$

4. $0.5 = \dfrac{E}{3}$

5. $\dfrac{M}{0.2} = 5$

6. $\dfrac{A}{10} = 0.35$

7. $\dfrac{E}{3} = \dfrac{2}{3}$

8. $0.4 = \dfrac{M}{0.8}$

9. $\dfrac{P}{1/2} = 16$

10. $\dfrac{E}{4} = 2\frac{1}{2}$

11. $150 = \dfrac{x}{45}$

12. $117 = \dfrac{P}{4.7}$

13. In the formula $I = E/R$, find E if $I = 3$ and $R = 18$.
14. In the formula $E = P/I$, find P if $E = 110$ and $I = 5$.
15. In the formula $Q = X_L/R$, find X_L if $Q = 100$ and $R = 40$.
16. In the formula Eff $= 0/I$, find 0 if $I = 36$ and Eff $= 0.85$.
17. In the formula $Z = E/I$, find E if $Z = 2,000$ and $I = 0.015$.
18. In the formula $\cos \theta = I_R/I_T$, find I_R if $I_T = 10$ and $\cos \theta = 0.866$.
19. In the formula $\sin \theta = i/I_{max}$, find i if $I_{max} = 100$ and $\sin \theta = 0.9397$.
20. In the formula $R_1 + R_2 = E_T/I_T$, find E_T if $R_1 = 25$, $R_2 = 85$, and $I_T = 2$.

USING THE LEAST COMMON DENOMINATOR TO SOLVE FRACTIONAL EQUATIONS

EXAMPLE 4-21   Find E in the equation

$$\frac{2E}{9} = \frac{4}{3}$$

SOLUTION

When fractions appear on both sides of the equality sign, the solution will be simplified if we eliminate *all* denominators first. We could do this one denominator at a time by the method used in Examples 4-18, 4-19, and 4-20, but it is faster if we eliminate both denominators at the same time. In order to eliminate *both* the 9 and the 3 at the same time, we must multiply both sides of the equality sign by some number so that *both* denominators will be canceled out. This must be a number into which *both* denominators will evenly divide—which is the *least common denominator*. In this problem, the LCD of 9 and 3 is 9.

1   Write the equation.

$$\frac{2E}{9} = \frac{4}{3}$$

2   Multiply both sides by the LCD (9).

$$\overset{1}{\cancel{9}} \times \frac{2E}{\underset{1}{\cancel{9}}} = \frac{4}{\underset{1}{\cancel{3}}} \times \overset{3}{\cancel{9}}$$

3   Multiply each side separately.

$$2E = 12$$

4   Solve for E.

$$E = \frac{12}{2}$$

5   Divide.

$$E = 6 \qquad Ans.$$

EXAMPLE 4-22   Find R in the equation

$$\frac{2R}{3} = \frac{9}{4}$$

SOLUTION
The LCD for 3 and 4 is 12. That is, both 3 and 4 will divide evenly into
12. In general, the LCD is equal to the product of the denominators.

1   Write the equation.

$$\frac{2R}{3} = \frac{9}{4}$$

2   Multiply both sides by the LCD (12).

$$\overset{4}{\cancel{12}} \times \frac{2R}{\underset{1}{\cancel{3}}} = \frac{9}{\underset{1}{\cancel{4}}} \times \overset{3}{\cancel{12}}$$

3   Multiply each side separately.

$$8R = 27$$

4   Solve for R.

$$R = \frac{27}{8}$$

5   Divide.

$$R = 3\frac{3}{8} \qquad Ans.$$

EXAMPLE 4-23   Find L in the equation

$$\frac{6}{L} = \frac{2}{3}$$

SOLUTION

The LCD is $3 \times L$ or $3L$.

1   Write the equation.

$$\frac{6}{L} = \frac{2}{3}$$

2   Multiply both sides by the LCD ($3L$).

$$3\cancel{L} \times \frac{6}{\cancel{L}}_{1} = \frac{2}{\cancel{3}}_{1} \times \cancel{3}L$$

3   Multiply each side separately.

$$18 = 2L$$

4   Solve for L.

$$\frac{18}{2} = L$$

5   Divide.

$$L = 9 \qquad Ans.$$

RULE	When fractions appear on both sides of the equality sign, eliminate the denominators by multiplying both sides by the least common denominator.

SELF-TEST 4-24 $\dfrac{R}{K} = \dfrac{L}{A}$ is a formula that may be used to calculate the length of a wire of particular material and cross section that will provide a definite resistance. Find the length L if $K = 60$ for pure iron wire, $A = 25$ cmil, and $R = 24\ \Omega$.

SOLUTION

1   Write the formula.

$$\frac{R}{K} = \frac{L}{A}$$

2   Substitute numbers.

$$\frac{24}{60} = \frac{L}{25}$$

3   The LCD for the numbers 60 and 25 is ____.

4   Multiply both sides by ____.

300

300

$$\overset{5}{\cancel{300}} \times \frac{24}{\underset{1}{\cancel{60}}} = \frac{L}{25} \times \overset{12}{\cancel{300}}$$
$$\qquad\quad \underset{1}{}$$

5   Multiply each side separately.

$$120 = \underline{\qquad}$$

6   Solve for L.

$$\frac{120}{?} = L$$

7   Divide.

$$L = \underline{\qquad} \text{ ft} \qquad Ans.$$

$12L$

12

10

PROBLEMS

Solve each equation for the value of the unknown letter.

1. $\dfrac{R}{3} = \dfrac{2}{3}$

2. $\dfrac{E}{8} = \dfrac{3}{4}$

3. $\dfrac{2}{3} = \dfrac{P}{6}$

4. $\dfrac{2E}{3} = \dfrac{4}{9}$

5. $\dfrac{M}{5} = \dfrac{2}{3}$

6. $\dfrac{4}{5} = \dfrac{T}{2}$

7. $\dfrac{2E}{5} = \dfrac{3}{0.5}$

8. $\dfrac{2B}{5} = \dfrac{7}{10}$

9. $\dfrac{N}{20} = \dfrac{3}{4}$

10. $\dfrac{4}{7} = \dfrac{S}{2}$

11. $\dfrac{0.3}{E} = \dfrac{1}{4}$

12. $\dfrac{3}{5} = \dfrac{2}{R}$

13. $\dfrac{2}{L} = \dfrac{6}{30}$

14. $\dfrac{10}{C} = \dfrac{150}{200}$

15. $\dfrac{22}{7} = \dfrac{11}{R}$

16. $\dfrac{100}{250} = \dfrac{0.1}{R}$

17. $\dfrac{N}{0.4} = \dfrac{3.9}{0.2}$

18. $\dfrac{9}{L} = \dfrac{0.3}{8.9}$

19. $\dfrac{21}{0.3} = \dfrac{2E}{9}$

20. $\dfrac{37}{250} = \dfrac{74}{R}$

21. $N_1/N_2 = E_1/E_2$ is a formula used in transformer calculations. Find N_2 if $N_1 = 40$ turns, $E_1 = 6$ V, and $E_2 = 18$ V.

22. Using the formula of Prob. 21, find E_1 if $N_1 = 30$ turns, $N_2 = 70$ turns, and $E_2 = 21$ V.

23. $A_2/A_1 = R_1/R_2$ is a formula used to calculate the sizes of wires in electrical installations. Find A_2 if $A_1 = 100$, $R_1 = 1,000$, $R_2 = 3,000$.

24. $I_1/I_2 = R_2/R_1$ is a formula used for calculating the way the current divides in a parallel circuit. Find I_1 if $I_2 = 2$ A, $R_2 = 100$ Ω, and $R_1 = 25$ Ω.

25. Using the same formula as in Prob. 24, find R_2 if $I_1 = 3$ A, $I_2 = 5$ A, and $R_1 = 100$ Ω.

26. $R_1/R_2 = R_3/R_x$ is the formula used for calculations in the Wheatstone-bridge method for measuring resistance. Find R_x if $R_1 = 1,000$, $R_3 = 26.9$, and $R_2 = 10,000$.

27. $E/R = A_1/A_2$ is a formula used to determine the effort required to raise a large weight in a hydraulic lift. Find the effort E required to raise a weight R of 200,000 lb if the area of the small piston A_1 is 4 in² and the area of the large piston A_2 is 1,600 in².

28. $R_1/R_2 = L_2/L_1$ is a formula used to locate the position of a break in an underground cable. Find the length to the break in the cable L_2 if the length of the unbroken cable L_1 is 4,000 ft, R_1 is 10 Ω, and R_2 is 250 Ω.

29. $R_s/R_m = I_m/I_s$ is the formula for finding the shunt resistor needed to extend the range of an ammeter. Find R_s if $I_m = 0.001$, $R_m = 50$, and $I_s = 0.049$.

30. $R_1/R_2 = C_x/C_1$ is a formula used to measure the capacitance of an unknown capacitor. Find C_x if $R_1 = 100$ Ω, $R_2 = 425$ Ω, and $C_1 = 0.5$ μF.

Cross multiplication. When a fractional equation contains *only two fractions* equal to each other, the equation may be solved by a very simple method known as cross multiplication. This method automatically multiplies both sides of the equality sign by the LCD and therefore eliminates one step in the solution. This method is most useful when the unknown letter is in the denominator of one of the fractions.

RULE	To cross-multiply, the product of the numerator of the first fraction and the denominator of the second is set equal to the product of the numerator of the second fraction and the denominator of the first.

It is easier to understand this rule by putting it in picture form. The multiplication of the numbers along one diagonal line is equal to the multiplication of the numbers along the other diagonal line.

$$\frac{2}{3} \times \frac{4}{6}$$

$$2 \times 6 = 4 \times 3$$

or

$$3 \times 4 = 6 \times 2$$

$$\frac{A}{B} \times \frac{C}{D}$$

$$A \times D = C \times B$$

or

$$B \times C = D \times A$$

EXAMPLE 4-25   Find the value of R in the equation

$$\frac{3}{R} = \frac{2}{5}$$

SOLUTION

1   Write the equation.

$$\frac{3}{R} = \frac{2}{5}$$

2   Cross-multiply.

$$2 \times R = 3 \times 5$$

3   Simplify each side.

$$2R = 15$$

4   Solve for R.

$$R = \frac{15}{2}$$

5   Divide.

$$R = 7\frac{1}{2} \quad Ans.$$

PROBLEMS

Find the value of the unknown letter in each equation.

1. $\dfrac{E}{10} = \dfrac{3}{5}$ 2. $\dfrac{8}{3} = \dfrac{R}{6}$ 3. $\dfrac{60}{A} = \dfrac{3}{4}$ 4. $\dfrac{9}{E} = \dfrac{15}{40}$

5. $\dfrac{84}{E} = \dfrac{28}{17}$ 6. $\dfrac{84}{28} = \dfrac{66}{R}$ 7. $\dfrac{E}{18} = \dfrac{3}{2}$ 8. $9 = \dfrac{54}{R}$

9. $\dfrac{50}{T} = 2$ 10. $\dfrac{2R}{3} = \dfrac{10}{5}$ 11. $\dfrac{24}{2} = \dfrac{6M}{5}$ 12. $\dfrac{3P}{0.4} = 6$

13. $\dfrac{3.6}{5} = \dfrac{A}{2}$ 14. $0.88 = \dfrac{R}{3}$ 15. $\dfrac{3}{12} = \dfrac{4}{3T}$ 16. $5 = \dfrac{1}{0.2E}$

17. $\dfrac{1}{R} = 10$ 18. $80 = \dfrac{1}{R}$ 19. $\dfrac{1}{R} = \dfrac{13}{24}$ 20. $\dfrac{10}{R} = 50$

JOB 4-8   TOTAL RESISTANCE IN A PARALLEL CIRCUIT

When resistances are connected in parallel, the total resistance is always *less* than the resistance of any branch. When resistances are added to a circuit in parallel, they merely provide extra paths for the current to follow. Each extra path will draw its own current from the voltage source, *increasing* the total current drawn. But resistance is that quality of a cir-

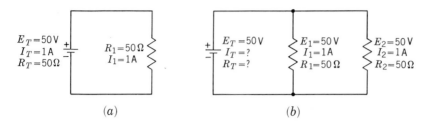

FIGURE 4-20

Adding resistances in parallel reduces the total resistance.

cuit which attempts to stop the flow of current. If the addition of a resistance *increases* the current, then this resistance must have *reduced* the total resistance. For example, in the circuit of Fig. 4-20*a*, the current that flows in the resistor is 1 A and the total resistance R_T is 50 Ω. Now let us add an extra 50-Ω resistor in parallel as shown in Fig. 4-20*b*. Since equal resistors carry equal currents, the total current equals $I_1 + I_2 = 2$ A. The total resistance will be

$$E_T = I_T \times R_T \qquad (3\text{-}7)$$

$$50 = 2 \times R_T$$

$$R_T = \frac{50}{2} = 25 \ \Omega$$

Thus we see that the net effect of adding another resistance in parallel *reduced* the total resistance from 50 to 25 Ω. Also, the current drawn by the new circuit *increased* from 1 to 2 A.

The total resistance in parallel is given by the

FORMULA

$$\frac{1}{R_T} = \frac{1}{R_1} + \frac{1}{R_2} + \frac{1}{R_3} \ \ldots \ \text{etc.} \qquad \boxed{4\text{-}3}$$

where R_T is the total resistance in parallel and R_1, R_2, and R_3 are the branch resistances.

EXAMPLE 4-26   Find the total resistance of a 3-, a 4-, and an 8-Ω resistor in parallel.

SOLUTION
The diagram for the circuit is shown in Fig. 4-21.

1   Write the formula.

$$\frac{1}{R_T} = \frac{1}{R_1} + \frac{1}{R_2} + \frac{1}{R_3} \qquad (4\text{-}3)$$

2   Substitute numbers.

$$\frac{1}{R_T} = \frac{1}{3} + \frac{1}{4} + \frac{1}{8}$$

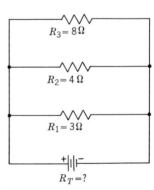

FIGURE 4-21

3   Add fractions.

$$\frac{1}{R_T} = \frac{17}{24}$$

4   Cross-multiply.

$$17 \times R_T = 1 \times 24$$

5   Simplify.

$$17R_T = 24$$

6   Solve for R_T.

$$R_T = \frac{24}{17}$$

7   Divide.

$$R_T = 1.4 \ \Omega \qquad Ans.$$

EXAMPLE 4-27   What resistance must be connected in parallel with a 40-Ω resistance in order to provide a total resistance of 24 Ω?

SOLUTION

Given: $R_T = 24 \ \Omega$ Find: $R_2 = ?$
$R_1 = 40 \ \Omega$

1   Write the formula.

$$\frac{1}{R_T} = \frac{1}{R_1} + \frac{1}{R_2} \qquad\qquad (4\text{-}3)$$

2   Substitute numbers.

$$\frac{1}{24} = \frac{1}{40} + \frac{1}{R_2}$$

3   Transpose the $\frac{1}{40}$ to the left side of the equality sign.

$$\frac{1}{24} - \frac{1}{40} = \frac{1}{R_2}$$

4   Subtract fractions.

$$\frac{1}{60} = \frac{1}{R_2}$$

5   Cross-multiply.

$$R_2 = 60 \ \Omega \qquad Ans.$$

SELF-TEST 4-28   A 40-, a 70-, and a 150-Ω resistor are connected in parallel. Find the total resistance.

SOLUTION

$$\text{Given: } R_1 = 40 \text{ } \Omega \qquad \text{Find: } R_T = ?$$
$$R_2 = 70 \text{ } \Omega$$
$$R_3 = 150 \text{ } \Omega$$

1 Write the formula.

$$\frac{1}{?} = \frac{1}{R_1} + \frac{1}{R_2} + \frac{1}{R_3}$$

R_T

2 Substitute numbers.

$$\frac{1}{R_T} = \frac{1}{40} + \frac{1}{?} + \frac{1}{150}$$

70

The next step would be to add these fractions. However, it is very difficult to find the LCD when the denominators are as large as these. In this situation, it is best to find the decimal equivalent for each fraction and use these decimals instead of the fractions.

$$
\begin{array}{lll}
\,0.025 & \,0.014 & \,0.006\,{}^{2}\!/_{3} = 0.007 \\
1/40 = 40\overline{)1.000} & 1/70 = 70\overline{)1.000} & 1/150 = 150\overline{)1.000} \\
\,\underline{80} & \,\underline{70} & \,\underline{900} \\
\,200 & \,300 & \,100 \\
\,\underline{200} & \,\underline{280} & \\
& \,20 &
\end{array}
$$

3 Substitute the decimals for the fractions.

$$\frac{1}{R_T} = 0.025 + 0.014 + \underline{}$$

0.007

4 Add the decimals.

$$\frac{1}{R_T} = \underline{}$$

0.046

5 Cross-multiply.

$$0.046 R_T = \underline{}$$

1

6 Solve for R_T.

$$R_T = \frac{1}{?}$$

0.046

7 Divide.

$$R_T = \underline{} \text{ } \Omega \qquad Ans.$$

21.7

PROBLEMS

1. Find the total resistance of a 3-, a 4-, and a 12-Ω resistor in parallel.
2. Find the total resistance of the circuit shown in Fig. 4-22.
3. A 12B4A tube is substituted for another tube by placing its 42-Ω

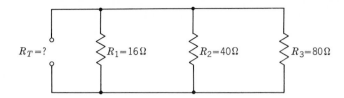

heater in parallel with a shunt of 42 Ω. Find the total resistance of the combination.

4. Three resistances of 3, 6, and 9 Ω are in parallel. What is the combined resistance?

5. Find the total resistance of a 25-Ω coffee percolator and a 30-Ω toaster in parallel.

6. Find the total resistance of 4, 8, 12, and 15 Ω in parallel.

7. Find the total resistance of 6, 8, and 4.8 Ω in parallel.

8. Find the total resistance of 15, 7.5, and 5 Ω in parallel.

9. Find the total resistance of 100, 250, and 500 Ω when connected in parallel.

10. Find the resistance of each group of resistors in the circuit shown in Fig. 4-23.

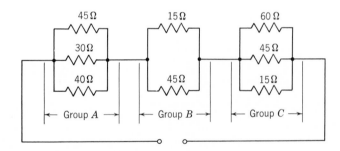

FIGURE 4-23

11. Find the total resistance of 1,000, 1,500, and 2,000 Ω when connected in parallel.

12. What resistance must be connected in parallel with a 20-Ω resistance in order to provide a total resistance of 15 Ω?

13. What resistance must be connected in parallel with a 100-Ω resistance in order to provide a total resistance of 90 Ω?

14. What resistance must be connected in parallel with a 600-Ω resistance in order to provide a total resistance of 400 Ω?

15. A voltage of 120 V is applied across a parallel combination of a 100-Ω resistor and an unknown resistor. If the total current is 1.5 A, find the value of the unknown resistor.

16. A spotlight of unknown resistance is placed in parallel with an automobile cigarette lighter of 80 Ω resistance. If a current of 0.75 A flows when a voltage of 12 V is applied, find the resistance of the spotlight.

TOTAL RESISTANCE OF A NUMBER OF EQUAL BRANCHES

RULE	The total resistance of a number of equal resistors in parallel is equal to the resistance of one resistor divided by the number of resistors.

FORMULA

$$R_T = \frac{R}{N}$$

4-4

where R_T = total resistance of equal resistors in parallel
R = resistance of one of the equal resistors
N = number of equal resistors

EXAMPLE 4-29   Three lamps, each having a resistance of 60 Ω, are connected in parallel. Find the total resistance of the combination.

SOLUTION
Given: $R_1 = R_2 = R_3 = 60 \ \Omega$ Find: $R_T = ?$

$$R_T = \frac{R}{N} \tag{4-4}$$

$$R_T = \frac{60}{3} = 20 \ \Omega \quad Ans.$$

PROBLEMS

1. Find the total resistance of two 100-Ω lamps in parallel.
2. Find the total resistance of three 48-Ω bells in parallel.
3. Find the total resistance of two 1.5-Ω headlight lamps in parallel.
4. If the total resistance of two identical bells in parallel is 20 Ω, what is the resistance of each bell?
5. A toaster, an electric iron, and a coffee percolator, all of 22 Ω resistance, are connected in parallel across a 110-V line. Find (*a*) the total resistance and (*b*) the total current.

Two resistors in parallel. When only two resistors are in parallel, the total resistance may be calculated by a simple rule.

RULE	To find the total resistance of only two resistors in parallel, multiply the resistances and then divide the product by the sum of the resistors.

FORMULA

$$R_T = \frac{R_1 \times R_2}{R_1 + R_2}$$

4-5

where R_T is the total resistance in parallel and R_1 and R_2 are the two resistors in parallel.

EXAMPLE 4-30   Find the total resistance of a 4- and a 12-Ω resistor in parallel.

SOLUTION

$$\text{Given: } R_1 = 4 \ \Omega \qquad \text{Find: } R_T = ?$$
$$R_2 = 12 \ \Omega$$

$$R_T = \frac{R_1 \times R_2}{R_1 + R_2} \qquad\qquad (4\text{-}5)$$

$$R_T = \frac{4 \times 12}{4 + 12}$$

$$R_T = \frac{48}{16} = 3 \ \Omega \qquad Ans.$$

PROBLEMS

1. Find the total resistance of two 40-Ω coils in parallel.
2. Find the total resistance of a 20- and a 60-Ω motor in parallel.
3. An ammeter has a coil whose resistance is 56 Ω and is shunted by a 41-Ω resistor in parallel. Find the equivalent resistance of the combination.
4. Find the total resistance of a 90-Ω galvanometer in parallel with a 10-Ω shunt resistor.
5. A section of the picture-control circuit of a television receiver uses a 10,000- and a 25,000-Ω resistor in parallel. Find the total resistance of the combination.
6. A 24- and a 48-Ω solenoid used in semaphore signals of an H-O electric train set are connected in parallel. Find the total resistance.
7. Find the total resistance of a 5- and a 12-Ω resistor in parallel.
8. Find the total resistance of 9,000 and 2,000 Ω when connected in parallel.
9. A 40-Ω soldering iron and a 100-Ω lamp are connected in parallel. Find the total resistance.
10. Find the total resistance of 20,000 and 27,000 Ω when connected in parallel.

JOB 4-9   TOTAL VOLTAGE IN A PARALLEL CIRCUIT

EXAMPLE 4-31   What voltage is needed to send 3 A through a parallel combination consisting of a 3-, a 4-, and a 12-Ω resistance?

SOLUTION

The diagram for the circuit is shown in Fig. 4-24. In order to find the

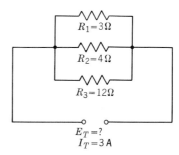

$R_1 = 3\Omega$

$R_2 = 4\Omega$

$R_3 = 12\Omega$

$E_T = ?$
$I_T = 3\,A$

FIGURE 4-24

total voltage E_T, we must know the value of the total current I_T and the total resistance R_T. If either value is unknown, it must be found first.

1 Find the total resistance R_T.

$$\frac{1}{R_T} = \frac{1}{R_1} + \frac{1}{R_2} + \frac{1}{R_3} \qquad (4\text{-}3)$$

$$\frac{1}{R_T} = \frac{1}{3} + \frac{1}{4} + \frac{1}{12}$$

$$\frac{1}{R_T} = \frac{2}{3}$$

$$2R_T = 3$$

$$R_T = \frac{3}{2} = 1.5\ \Omega \qquad Ans.$$

2 Find the total voltage E_T.

$$E_T = I_T \times R_T \qquad (3\text{-}7)$$

$$E_T = 3 \times 1.5 = 4.5\ \text{V} \qquad Ans.$$

PROBLEMS

1. Find the voltage needed to send 2 A through a parallel combination of three 60-Ω resistors.
2. Find the total voltage needed to send 9 A through a parallel circuit of a 25-Ω percolator and a 30-Ω refrigerator motor.
3. Find the voltage needed to send 3 A through a parallel combination of a 2- and an 8-Ω resistor.
4. Find the voltage needed to send 2 A through a parallel combination of a 3- and a 6-Ω resistor.
5. Find the voltage required to send a current of 2.4 A through a 10-Ω coil, a 20-Ω coil, and a 60-Ω motor if they are wired in parallel.
6. In Fig. 4-25, a 25-Ω galvanometer is shunted with a 4-Ω resistor when indicating a current of 0.003 A. What is the voltage across the galvanometer?
7. Two tubes have heaters of 40 and 60 Ω wired in parallel. What voltage is needed to send a current of 0.6 A through the combination?

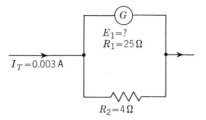

$E_1 = ?$
$R_1 = 25\,\Omega$

$I_T = 0.003\,A$

$R_2 = 4\,\Omega$

FIGURE 4-25
A shunt across the galvanometer carries most of the line current.

8. Find the voltage required to send 2 A through a parallel combination of a 20-, a 30-, and a 40-Ω resistance.

9. Find the total voltage required to send 0.15 A through three coils in parallel if their effective resistances are 200, 400, and 800 Ω, respectively.

10. A faulty resistor R_L in the self-bias circuit shown in Fig. 4-26a was replaced with a 6,000- and a 4,000-Ω resistor in parallel as shown in Fig. 4-26b. If $I_L = 0.002$ A, find the voltage across the parallel combination.

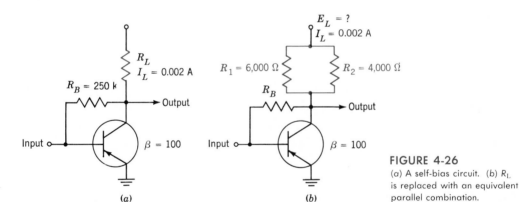

FIGURE 4-26
(a) A self-bias circuit. (b) R_L is replaced with an equivalent parallel combination.

JOB 4-10 DIVISION OF CURRENT IN A PARALLEL CIRCUIT

In our study of Ohm's law we learned that the resistance of a circuit affected the current in the circuit. The greater the resistance, the smaller the current. The smaller the resistance, the greater the current. When the current in a parallel circuit reaches a point at which it may divide and flow in more than one path, the largest current will naturally flow in that portion of the circuit which offers the smallest resistance and the smallest current will flow through the largest resistance. The exact manner in which a current will divide in a parallel circuit is shown in the following example.

EXAMPLE 4-32 Find the current that flows in each branch of the parallel circuit shown in Fig. 4-27.

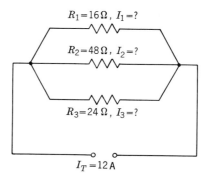

$R_1 = 16\,\Omega,\ I_1 = ?$

$R_2 = 48\,\Omega,\ I_2 = ?$

$R_3 = 24\,\Omega,\ I_3 = ?$

$I_T = 12\,A$

FIGURE 4-27

SOLUTION

1   We can find the current in each branch if we know the voltage and the resistance of each branch by the formulas

$$E_1 = I_1 \times R_1 \tag{3-4}$$

$$E_2 = I_2 \times R_2 \tag{3-5}$$

$$E_3 = I_3 \times R_3 \tag{3-6}$$

2   If the individual voltages are unknown, we can find them if we know E_T, since

$$E_T = E_1 = E_2 = E_3 \tag{4-1}$$

3   If E_T is unknown, it may be found by the formula

$$E_T = I_T \times R_T \tag{3-7}$$

4   If R_T is unknown, it may be found by the formula

$$\frac{1}{R_T} = \frac{1}{R_1} + \frac{1}{R_2} + \frac{1}{R_3} \tag{4-3}$$

$$\text{or } R_T = \frac{R_1 \times R_2}{R_1 + R_2} \tag{4-5}$$

The problem is solved by reversing this plan.

1   Find the total resistance R_T.

$$\frac{1}{R_T} = \frac{1}{R_1} + \frac{1}{R_2} + \frac{1}{R_3} \tag{4-3}$$

$$\frac{1}{R_T} = \frac{1}{16} + \frac{1}{48} + \frac{1}{24}$$

$$\frac{1}{R_T} = \frac{1}{8}$$

$$R_T = 8\ \Omega$$

2   Find the total voltage E_T.

$$E_T = I_T \times R_T \tag{3-7}$$

$$E_T = 12 \times 8 = 96\ V$$

3   Find the branch voltages.

$$E_T = E_1 = E_2 = E_3 = 96 \text{ V} \qquad\qquad (4\text{-}1)$$

4   Find the branch currents.

$$E_1 = I_1 \times R_1 \qquad\qquad\qquad E_2 = I_2 \times R_2$$

$$96 = I_1 \times 16 \qquad\qquad\qquad 96 = I_2 \times 48$$

$$I_1 = \frac{96}{16} = 6 \text{ A} \quad Ans. \qquad I_2 = \frac{96}{48} = 2 \text{ A} \quad Ans.$$

$$E_3 = I_3 \times R_3$$

$$96 = I_3 \times 24$$

$$I_3 = \frac{96}{24} = 4 \text{ A} \qquad Ans.$$

5   Check.

$$I_T = I_1 + I_2 + I_3 \qquad\qquad (4\text{-}2)$$

$$12 = 6 + 2 + 4$$

$$12 = 12 \qquad Check$$

EXAMPLE 4-33   The 16GK6 power pentode in a 0.3-A series heater circuit burned out.   An emergency replacement was made with a tube of 56 Ω resistance in parallel with a shunt of 168 Ω, as shown in Fig. 4-28b.   Find the current flowing in the heater and the shunt.

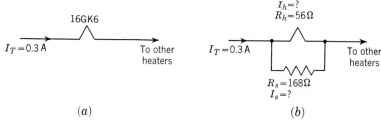

(a)   (b)

FIGURE 4-28

(a) Original heater circuit.
(b) Replacement circuit.

SOLUTION

1   Find the total resistance of the parallel combination.

$$R_T = \frac{R_h \times R_s}{R_h + R_s} \qquad\qquad (4\text{-}5)$$

$$R_T = \frac{56 \times 168}{56 + 168}$$

$$R_T = \frac{9{,}408}{224} = 42 \text{ Ω}$$

2   Find the total voltage.

$$E_T = I_T \times R_T \qquad\qquad (3\text{-}7)$$

$$E_T = 0.3 \times 42 = 12.6 \text{ V}$$

3   Find the branch voltages.

$$E_T = E_h = E_s = 12.6 \text{ V} \qquad (4\text{-}1)$$

4   Find the branch currents.

Heater circuit	Shunt circuit	
$E_h = I_h \times R_h$	$E_s = I_s \times R_s$	(2-1)
$12.6 = I_h \times 56$	$12.6 = I_s \times 168$	
$I_h = \dfrac{12.6}{56}$	$I_s = \dfrac{12.6}{168}$	
$I_h = 0.225 \text{ A} \quad Ans.$	$I_s = 0.075 \text{ A} \quad Ans.$	

DIVISION OF CURRENT IN TWO BRANCHES IN PARALLEL

RULE   When only two branches are involved, the current in one branch will be only some fraction of the total current. This fraction is the quotient of the second resistance divided by the sum of the resistances.

FORMULA

$$I_1 = \frac{R_2}{R_1 + R_2} \times I_T \qquad \boxed{4\text{-}6}$$

$$I_2 = \frac{R_1}{R_1 + R_2} \times I_T \qquad \boxed{4\text{-}7}$$

EXAMPLE 4-34   We can solve Example 4-33 using these formulas.

SOLUTION

Given: $R_h = 56 \ \Omega$ Find: $I_h = ?$
$R_s = 168 \ \Omega$ $I_s = ?$
$I_T = 0.3 \text{ A}$

1   Find the heater current I_h.

$$I_h = \frac{R_s}{R_h + R_s} \times I_T \qquad (4\text{-}6)$$

$$I_h = \frac{168}{56 + 168} \times 0.3 = \frac{168}{224} \times 0.3$$

$$I_h = 0.75 \times 0.3 = 0.225 \text{ A} \qquad Ans.$$

2   Find the shunt current I_s.

$$I_s = \frac{R_h}{R_h + R_s} = I_T \qquad (4\text{-}7)$$

$$I_s = \frac{56}{56 + 168} \times 0.3 = \frac{56}{224} \times 0.3$$

$$I_s = 0.25 \times 0.3 = 0.075 \text{ A} \qquad Ans.$$

SELF-TEST 4-35   A 2N405 in a two-transistor receiver receives 0.036 A from a parallel combination of a 40,000-Ω resistor and a 5,000-Ω headphone, as shown in Fig. 4-29. Find the current flowing in each part.

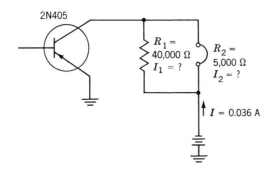

2N405

$R_1 = $ 40,000 Ω
$I_1 = $?

$R_2 = $ 5,000 Ω
$I_2 = $?

$I = 0.036$ A

FIGURE 4-29

Division of current in a parallel circuit.

SOLUTION

1   Find the current I_2 in the headphone.
Write the formula.

$$I_2 = \frac{?}{R_1 + R_2} \times I_T \qquad\qquad R_1$$

Substitute numbers.

$$I_2 = \frac{40,000}{40,000 + ?} \times 0.036 \qquad\qquad 5,000$$

$$I_2 = \frac{40,000}{?} \times 0.036 \qquad\qquad 45,000$$

$$I_2 = \underline{\hspace{1cm}} \text{ A} \qquad Ans. \qquad\qquad 0.032$$

2   Find the current I_1 in the resistor.

Write the formula.

$$I_1 = \frac{?}{R_1 + R_2} \times I_T \qquad\qquad R_2$$

Substitute numbers.

$$I_1 = \frac{5,000}{? + 5,000} \times 0.036 \qquad\qquad 40,000$$

$$I_1 = \frac{5,000}{?} \times 0.036 \qquad\qquad 45,000$$

$$I_1 = \underline{\hspace{1cm}} \text{ A} \qquad Ans. \qquad\qquad 0.004$$

PROBLEMS

1.   Two resistances are connected in parallel. $R_1 = 48 \ \Omega$, $R_2 = 48 \ \Omega$, and $I_T = 8$ A. Find the current flowing in each branch. On the basis of your answers, state a rule about the division of current between equal resistors in parallel.

2. Find the current in each branch of a parallel circuit consisting of a 20-Ω percolator and a 30-Ω toaster if the total current is 9 A.

3. In Fig. 4-30, a 12CX6 tube with a heater resistance of 84 Ω is shunted with an 84-Ω resistor in parallel in order to operate it in series with a 6AL5 detector. The 6AL5 heater draws 0.3 A. Find (*a*) the total resistance of the parallel group, (*b*) the voltage across the 12CX6 heater, (*c*) the current through the 12CX6, and (*d*) the current through the shunt.

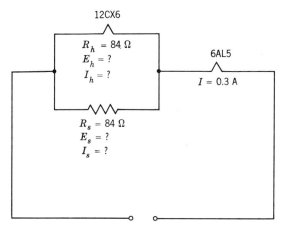

FIGURE 4-30
A resistor must be shunted across the 12CX6 heater in order to operate it in series with a 6AL5 heater.

4. Two 1.5-Ω automobile headlight lamps in parallel draw a total of 8 A. Find the total voltage supplied and the current drawn by each lamp.

5. A galvanometer with a resistance of 48 Ω and a parallel shunt of 2 Ω draw a total current of 0.2 A. Find the current through the galvanometer and through the shunt.

6. A generator supplies a current of 19.5 A to three small electro-plating tanks arranged in parallel. The resistances of the tanks are 8, 12, and 16 Ω. What current does each tank draw?

7. A generator supplies a current of 26 A to three motors arranged in parallel. The resistances of the motors are 24, 36, and 48 Ω. What current does each motor draw?

8. Two resistances are arranged in parallel as shown in Fig. 4-31. Find the current in each resistance.

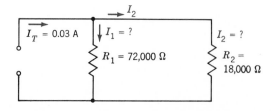

FIGURE 4-31

9. The resistance of an ammeter is 2.8 Ω. A shunt of 0.02 Ω is connected in parallel with it. If the combination is inserted into a line

carrying 10 A, how much current actually flows through the ammeter?

10. In a circuit similar to that shown in Fig. 4-24, $R_1 = 5 \ \Omega$, $R_2 = 7 \ \Omega$, $R_3 = 8 \ \Omega$, and $I_T = 13.1$ A. Find (*a*) the total resistance of the circuit, (*b*) the total voltage of the circuit, (*c*) the voltage across each branch, and (*d*) the current in each branch.

11. A low-power flasher circuit contains a resistor $R_1 = 16,000 \ \Omega$ in parallel with another resistor $R_2 = 4,000 \ \Omega$. If the current entering the combination is 0.003 A, find the current in each resistor.

12. The ballast resistor in a 0.3-A series heater circuit overheated. It was replaced with a 200-Ω and a 300-Ω resistor in parallel. Find (*a*) the total resistance of the parallel group, (*b*) the voltage drop across the group, and (*c*) the current in each resistor of the group.

JOB 4-11 REVIEW OF PARALLEL CIRCUITS

Definition   A parallel circuit is a circuit in which the current may divide so as to flow in _____ than one path.

more

Rules and formulas

1   The total voltage across a parallel circuit is _____ to the voltage across any branch of the circuit.

equal

$$E_T = E_1 = \underline{\ \ \ } = \underline{\ \ \ } \qquad \boxed{4\text{-}1}$$

$E_2 \qquad E_3$

2   The total current in a parallel circuit is equal to the _____ of the currents in all the branches of the circuit.

sum

$$I_T = I_1 + \underline{\ \ \ } + \underline{\ \ \ } \qquad \boxed{4\text{-}2}$$

$I_2 \qquad I_3$

3   The total resistance in a parallel circuit may be found by applying Ohm's law to the _____ values of the circuit.

total

$$E_T = I_T \times \underline{\ \ \ } \qquad \boxed{3\text{-}7}$$

R_T

4   The total resistance may also be found as follows:
For any number of resistors

$$\frac{1}{?} = \frac{1}{R_1} + \frac{1}{R_2} + \frac{1}{R_3} \qquad \boxed{4\text{-}3}$$

R_T

For just two resistors

$$R_T = \frac{R_1 \ ? \ R_2}{R_1 \ ? \ R_2} \qquad \boxed{4\text{-}5}$$

$\times$
$+$

For any number N of equal resistors of $R \ \Omega$ each.

$$R_T = \frac{R}{?} \qquad \boxed{4\text{-}4}$$

N

5   Ohm's law may be used on any branch of a parallel circuit.

$$E_1 = I_1 \times \underline{\ \ \ } \qquad \boxed{3\text{-}4}$$

R_1

$$E_2 = \underline{\quad} \times R_2 \qquad \boxed{3\text{-}5} \qquad \qquad I_2$$

$$\underline{\quad} = I_3 \times R_3 \qquad \boxed{3\text{-}6} \qquad \qquad E_3$$

6   The total resistance in parallel is always __(more/less)__ than the resistance
of any branch.   less

7   Division of current between two branches in parallel

$$I_1 = \frac{?}{R_1 + R_2} \times I_T \qquad \boxed{4\text{-}6} \qquad \qquad R_2$$

$$I_2 = \frac{?}{R_1 + R_2} \times I_T \qquad \boxed{4\text{-}7} \qquad \qquad R_1$$

8   If the branches of a parallel circuit have the same resistance, then each
will draw the _____ current. If the branches of a parallel circuit have different   same
resistances, then each will draw a _____ current. The larger the resist-   different
ance, the _____ the current drawn.   smaller

9   Adding or subtracting fractions.
In order to add or subtract fractions, all the fractions must have the _____   same
denominator.
The LCD is the _____ number into which _____ the denominators   smallest   *all*
will evenly divide.

10   Solving fractional equations:
Simplify fractions whenever possible.
When a fractional equation contains only _____ fractions equal to each other,   two
the equation may be solved by cross_____.   multiplication
To cross-multiply, the product of the numerator of the first fraction and the
denominator of the second is set _____ to the product of the numerator of   equal
the second fraction and the denominator of the first. For example, if

$$\frac{C}{D} = \frac{E}{F}$$

then $C \times \underline{\quad} = E \times D$ F

or $E \times D = \underline{\quad} \times F$ C

PROBLEMS

1.   An electric iron, a radio, and an electric clock are connected to a
     three-way 110-V kitchen outlet which puts the appliances in paral-
     lel. The iron draws 5 A, the radio draws 0.5 A, and the clock draws
     0.25 A. Find (*a*) the total current drawn from the line, (*b*) the volt-
     age across each device, and (*c*) the total resistance of the circuit.
2.   A semaphore signal, a floodlight tower, and a coal loader of a
     model railroad are connected in parallel across the 12-V winding
     of the power transformer. The signal draws 0.1 A and the coal
     loader draws 0.2 A. The floodlight tower has a resistance of 48 Ω.
     Find (*a*) the voltage across each device, (*b*) the resistance of the
     semaphore and the coal loader, (*c*) the total current, and (*d*) the
     total resistance of the circuit.

3. Three motors are wired in parallel across 440 V. Motor 1 draws a current of 10 A, and motor 3 draws 15 A. Motor 2 has a resistance of 20 Ω. Solve the circuit for all missing values of current, voltage, and resistance.

4. Find all missing values of voltage, current, and resistance in the circuit shown in Fig. 4-32.

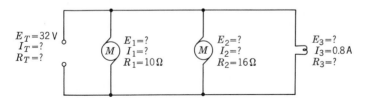

FIGURE 4-32

5. Find the total resistance of a 60-, an 80-, and a 120-Ω resistor in parallel.

6. A 2,000-Ω and a 5,000-Ω resistor are connected in parallel as shown in Fig. 4-33. Find the total resistance of the combination.

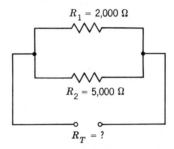

FIGURE 4-33

7. In the circuit shown in Fig. 4-34, find (a) the total resistance R_A of group A and (b) the total resistance R_B of group B. (c) Draw a new circuit using a single resistor (R_A and R_B) in place of the groups they represent. (d) Is the new circuit a series or a parallel circuit? (e) What is the total resistance of the new circuit? (f) Find the total current in the new circuit.

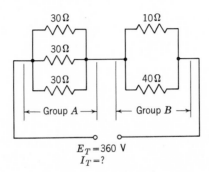

FIGURE 4-34

8. What is the combined resistance of a 480-Ω galvanometer and its parallel 20-Ω shunt?

9. What resistance must be connected in parallel with a 2,400-Ω resistor in order to provide a total resistance of 480 Ω?

10. What resistance must be connected in parallel with a 20- and a 60-Ω resistor in parallel in order to provide a total resistance of 10 Ω?

11. Find the voltage needed to send 2 A through a parallel combination of a 75- and a 100-Ω resistor.

12. A 30-Ω resistor is connected in parallel with an unknown resistor across a 120-V source. If the total current is 5 A, find the value of the unknown resistor.

13. Using a circuit similar to that shown in Fig. 4-31, R_2 equals 3,000 ohms, R_1 equals 17,000 Ω, and I_T equals 0.04 A. Find (a) the total resistance and (b) the total voltage.

14. A generator supplies 26 A to three motors in parallel. The resistances of the motors are 12, 18, and 24 Ω. What current does each motor draw?

15. A 12DQ6B horizontal-deflection amplifier in a color television receiver is substituted for a 6DQ6B tube in a 1.2-A series heater circuit. The 12DQ6B has a heater resistance of 21 Ω and is placed in parallel with a 21-Ω shunt resistor. Find (a) the total resistance of the parallel combination, (b) the voltage drop across the 12DQ6B heater, (c) the current through the heater, and (d) the current through the parallel shunt.

TEST—PARALLEL CIRCUITS

1. Three motors are connected in parallel. $I_1 = 3$ A, $R_1 = 40$ Ω, $R_2 = 30$ Ω, and $I_3 = 1$ A. Find (a) the total voltage, (b) the total current, and (c) the total resistance.

2. What resistance must be connected in parallel with a 2,400-Ω resistor in order to provide a total resistance of 1,600 Ω?

3. Solve for the value of the unknown letter:

$$(a)\ \frac{2M}{5} = \frac{3}{5} \qquad \text{and} \qquad (b)\ \frac{0.8}{R} = \frac{2}{5}$$

4. Find the total voltage needed to send 2 A of current through a parallel combination of a 10-, a 20-, and a 60-Ω motor.

5. A parallel combination of a 5- and a 15-Ω resistor draws 10 A from a line. Find the current in each resistor.

5

COMBINATION CIRCUITS

JOB 5-1 INTRODUCTION TO COMBINATION CIRCUITS

Each simple circuit has its own advantages and disadvantages.

Series circuits. An advantage of a series circuit is that it may be used to connect small voltages to obtain high voltages. Also, high voltages may be reduced by connecting resistances in series. Series circuits provide a means for reducing and controlling the current by connecting resistances in series. However, this series current remains unchanged throughout the circuit. This is a serious disadvantage. Since the current is constant, we are forced to use only those devices which require the same current. Thus it would be impossible to use any two household appliances at the same time because their current requirements range from 0.25 to 10 A. In addition, if any part of a series circuit should burn out, it would cause an open circuit and put the entire circuit out of operation. Lights are never wired in series for this reason, because the circuit demands that we have either *all* the lights on or none at all. Series circuits are used where different voltage drops and a constant current are needed.

Parallel circuits. If a break should occur in any branch of a parallel circuit, it would not affect the other branch circuits. Houses are wired in parallel so that any device may be operated independently of any other device. This is both an advantage and a disadvantage. In a parallel circuit, more branches may be added at any time. Each new load draws current from the line. So much current may be drawn that the original line wires may not be able to carry the new current and the fuse will "blow." In this event, it is necessary to rewire the circuits completely, using wire capable of carrying the larger currents, or to put in extra independent circuits to supply the installation. Parallel circuits are used wherever a constant voltage and a large supply of current are required.

Combination circuits. If we combine series circuits with parallel circuits, we produce a combination circuit which makes use of the best

159

features of each. A combination circuit makes it possible to obtain the different voltages of a series circuit and the different currents of a parallel circuit. This is the condition most generally required, particularly when the different voltages and currents must be supplied from the same source of power. In the electrical system of an automobile, the voltage and current needs of the lights, ignition system, and accessories are all different and yet the power is drawn from a single storage battery. The different voltage and current needs of the different circuits of a radio receiver are all obtained from combination circuits drawing power from a single power supply.

Simple combination circuits are of two types:

1   A *parallel-series* circuit (Fig. 5-1) is a circuit in which one or more *groups* of resistances in series are connected in parallel.

2   A *series-parallel* circuit (Fig. 5-8) is a circuit in which one or more *groups* of resistances in parallel are connected in series.

General method for solving combination circuits

1   A *group* of resistances is a simple combination of two or more resistances which are arranged in either a *simple* series or a *simple* parallel circuit. Locate these groups.

2   Every group must be removed from the circuit as a unit and *replaced* by a single resistor which offers the identical resistance. This equivalent resistance is the total resistance of the group.

3   Redraw the circuit, using the equivalent resistance in place of each group.

4   Solve the resulting simple circuit for all missing values.

5   Go back to the *original* circuit to find the voltage, current, and resistance for each resistance in the circuit.

JOB 5-2   SOLVING PARALLEL-SERIES CIRCUITS

EXAMPLE 5-1   Solve the circuit shown in Fig. 5-1 for all missing values of voltage, current, and resistance.

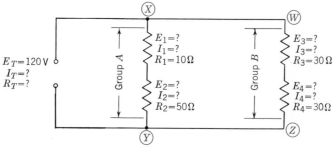

FIGURE 5-1

A parallel-series circuit.

SOLUTION

1   Locate groups A and B as simple series circuits.

2   Find the equivalent resistance of each group. This means that the circuit

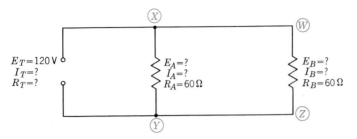

FIGURE 5-2

The resistance R_A replaces the series combination of R_1 and R_2. The resistance R_B replaces the series combination of R_3 and R_4.

is broken at points X and Y; resistors R_1 and R_2 are removed and replaced by a single resistance R_A. This single resistance will do the work of the combination of R_1 and R_2. Similarly, break the circuit at points W and Z; resistors R_3 and R_4 are removed and replaced by a *single* resistance R_B. This single resistance will do the work of the combination of R_3 and R_4.

3   Since the resistors of groups A and B are in *series*,

$$R_A = R_1 + R_2 \tag{3-3}$$

$$R_A = 10 + 50 = 60 \ \Omega \quad \textit{Ans.}$$

$$R_B = R_3 + R_4 \tag{3-3}$$

$$R_B = 30 + 30 = 60 \ \Omega \quad \textit{Ans.}$$

4   Redraw the circuit, using these 60-Ω resistors in place of the series groups as shown in Fig. 5-2.

5   Solve the new *parallel* circuit.

Find the voltage for each group.

$$E_T = E_A = E_B = 120 \text{ V} \quad \textit{Ans.} \tag{4-1}$$

Find the current in each group.

$$E_A = I_A \times R_A \qquad\qquad E_B = I_B \times R_B$$

$$120 = I_A \times 60 \qquad\qquad 120 = I_B \times 60$$

$$I_A = \frac{120}{60} = 2 \text{ A} \quad \textit{Ans.} \qquad I_B = \frac{120}{60} = 2 \text{ A} \quad \textit{Ans.}$$

Find the total current I_T.

$$I_T = I_A + I_B \tag{4-2}$$

$$I_T = 2 + 2 = 4 \text{ A} \quad \textit{Ans.}$$

Find the total resistance R_T.

$$E_T = I_T \times R_T \tag{3-7}$$

$$120 = 4 \times R_T$$

$$R_T = \frac{120}{4} = 30 \ \Omega \quad \textit{Ans.}$$

6   Go back to the original circuit to find the voltage and current for each resistor.

Find the current in each resistor.

$$I_A = I_1 = I_2 = 2 \text{ A} \qquad Ans. \qquad\qquad (4\text{-}2)$$

$$I_B = I_3 = I_4 = 2 \text{ A} \qquad Ans. \qquad\qquad (4\text{-}2)$$

Find the voltage drop across each resistor.

$$E_1 = I_1 \times R_1 \qquad\qquad E_3 = I_3 \times R_3$$

$$E_1 = 2 \times 10 \qquad\qquad E_3 = 2 \times 30$$

$$E_1 = 20 \text{ V} \quad Ans. \qquad E_3 = 60 \text{ V} \quad Ans.$$

$$E_2 = I_2 \times R_2 \qquad\qquad E_4 = I_4 \times R_4$$

$$E_2 = 2 \times 50 \qquad\qquad E_4 = 2 \times 30$$

$$E_2 = 100 \text{ V} \quad Ans. \qquad E_4 = 60 \text{ V} \quad Ans.$$

SELF-TEST 5-2   In Fig. 5-3, find the resistance R_3 that must be connected in parallel with the resistances of group A in order to obtain a
total resistance of 15 Ω.

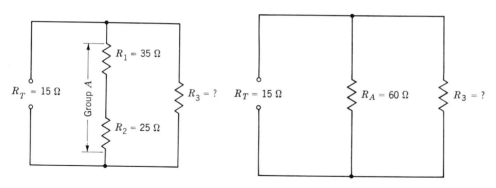

FIGURE 5-3

The series combination of R_1
and R_2 is in parallel with R_3.

FIGURE 5-4

The resistance R_A replaces the
series combination of R_1 and R_2
in Fig. 5-3.

SOLUTION

1   Locate group A as a simple _____ circuit.   series

2   Find the resistance of group A.

$$R_A = R_1 + \underline{\quad} \qquad\qquad (3\text{-}3) \qquad\qquad R_2$$

$$R_A = 35 + \underline{\quad} \qquad\qquad\qquad\qquad 25$$

$$R_A = \underline{\quad} \text{ Ω} \qquad\qquad\qquad\qquad\qquad 60$$

3   Redraw the circuit, using $R_A = 60$ Ω in place of the series group as shown
in Fig. 5-4.

4   Find R_3.

$$\frac{1}{R_T} = \frac{1}{?} + \frac{1}{R_3}$$ (4-3) R_A

$$\frac{1}{15} = \frac{1}{60} + \frac{1}{R_3}$$

$$\frac{1}{15} - ? = \frac{1}{R_3}$$ $\frac{1}{60}$

$$\frac{1}{?} = \frac{1}{R_3}$$ 20

$$R_3 = \underline{\quad} \ \Omega \quad Ans.$$ 20

PROBLEMS

1.   Find all missing values in the circuit shown in Fig. 5-5.

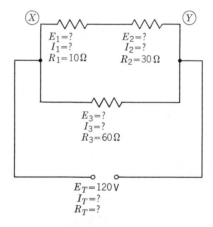

E_1=?   E_2=?
I_1=?   I_2=?
R_1=10Ω   R_2=30Ω

E_3=?
I_3=?
R_3=60Ω

E_T=120 V
I_T=?
R_T=?

FIGURE 5-5

2.   Find the total resistance and the total current for the circuit shown in Fig. 5-6.

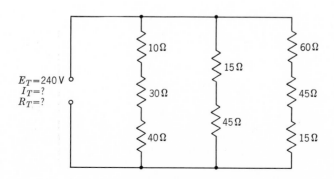

E_T=240 V
I_T=?
R_T=?

10Ω   60Ω
15Ω
30Ω   45Ω
45Ω
40Ω   15Ω

FIGURE 5-6

3. Find the total resistance and the total current for the circuit shown in Fig- 5-7.

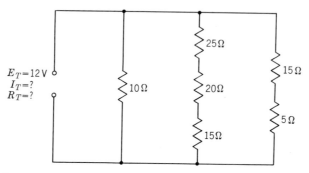

$E_T = 12\,V$
$I_T = ?$
$R_T = ?$

FIGURE 5-7

4. Find all missing values in the circuit shown in Fig. 5-8.

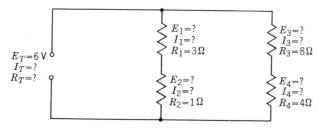

$E_T = 6\,V$
$I_T = ?$
$R_T = ?$

FIGURE 5-8

5. In the circuit shown in Fig. 5-9, find (a) the total resistance, (b) the total current, (c) the voltage E_1, (d) the current I_1, (e) the current I_3, (f) the voltage E_2 and (g) the voltage E_3.

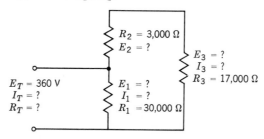

FIGURE 5-9

6. Part of the picture-control circuit of a television receiver is shown in Fig. 5-10. Find the total resistance of the circuit when the variable resistor R_3 has engaged (a) 6,000 Ω, (b) 10,000 Ω, and (c) 5,000 Ω.

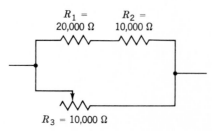

FIGURE 5-10

7. In a circuit similar to that shown in Fig. 5-3, find R_3 if $R_1 = 6\ \Omega$, $R_2 = 18\ \Omega$, and $R_T = 6\ \Omega$.

8. Find R_T in the circuit shown in Fig. 5-11. *Hint:* Find the equivalent resistance of R_3 and R_4 in parallel. Then proceed as in a normal parallel-series circuit. See also Example 5-3.

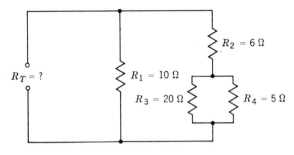

FIGURE 5-11

JOB 5-3 SOLVING SERIES-PARALLEL CIRCUITS

EXAMPLE 5-3 Solve the circuit shown in Fig. 5-12 for all values of voltage, current, and resistance.

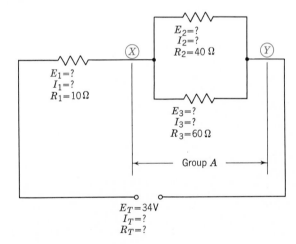

FIGURE 5-12
A series-parallel circuit.

SOLUTION

1 In Fig. 5-12, the resistors R_2 and R_3 form the *parallel* group A. Find the total resistance R_A of group A. This means that the circuit is broken at points X and Y; resistors R_2 and R_3 are removed and replaced by a *single* resistance R_A. This single resistance will do the work of the combination of R_2 and R_3.

2 Since R_2 and R_3 are in parallel,

$$R_A = \frac{R_2 \times R_3}{R_2 + R_3} \qquad (4\text{-}5)$$

$$R_A = \frac{40 \times 60}{40 + 60} = \frac{2,400}{100} = 24\ \Omega \qquad Ans.$$

3   Redraw the circuit using this 24-Ω resistor R_A in place of the combination as shown in Fig. 5-13.

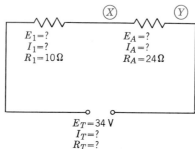

FIGURE 5-13

The resistance R_A replaces the parallel combination of R_2 and R_3 of Fig. 5-12.

4   Solve the new circuit. Notice that we have a simple *series* circuit.

Find the total resistance R_T.

$$R_T = R_1 + R_A \qquad\qquad (3\text{-}3)$$

$$R_T = 10 + 24 = 34\ \Omega \qquad Ans.$$

Find the total current I_T.

$$E_T = I_T \times R_T \qquad\qquad (3\text{-}7)$$

$$34 = I_T \times 34$$

$$I_T = \frac{34}{34} = 1\ A \qquad Ans.$$

Find the current in each part of the series circuit.

$$I_T = I_1 = I_A = 1\ A \qquad Ans. \qquad\qquad (3\text{-}1)$$

Find the voltage in each part of the series circuit.

$$E_1 = I_1 \times R_1 \qquad E_A = I_A \times R_A$$

$$E_1 = 1 \times 10 \qquad E_A = 1 \times 24$$

$$E_1 = 10\ V \qquad E_A = 24\ V \qquad Ans.$$

5   Go back to group A in Fig. 5-12 to find E, I, and R for each resistance in group A as shown in Fig. 5-14.

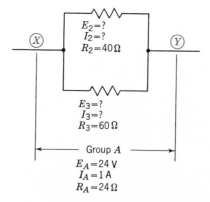

FIGURE 5-14

Since E_A represents the total voltage of the parallel group A,

$$E_A = E_2 = E_3 = 24 \text{ V} \qquad Ans. \qquad\qquad (4\text{-}1)$$

Find the current in each resistor of group A.

$$E_2 = I_2 \times R_2 \qquad\qquad E_3 = I_3 \times R_3$$

$$24 = I_2 \times 40 \qquad\qquad 24 = I_3 \times 60$$

$$I_2 = \frac{24}{40} = 0.6 \text{ A} \qquad I_3 = \frac{24}{60} = 0.4 \text{ A} \qquad Ans.$$

6 Check.

$$I_T = I_2 + I_3 \qquad\qquad\qquad (4\text{-}2)$$

$$I_T = 0.6 + 0.4$$

$$1 = 1 \qquad Check$$

EXAMPLE 5-4   Solve the circuit shown in Fig. 5-15 for all values of voltage, current, and resistance.

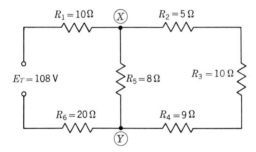

FIGURE 5-15

SOLUTION

1 Find the total resistance. It is usually very helpful if the circuit is redrawn so as to put it in standard form with easily recognizable series or parallel subcircuits. Therefore, redraw Fig. 5-15 to appear as shown in Fig. 5-16.

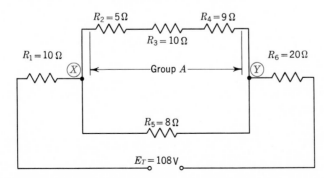

FIGURE 5-16
The circuit of Fig. 5-15 is redrawn in standard form.

a In Fig. 5-16, the resistors R_2, R_3, and R_4 form the *series* group A. Find the total resistance of this group and replace the group with the equivalent resistance R_A as shown in Fig. 5-17.

$$R_A = R_2 + R_3 + R_4 \qquad\qquad (3\text{-}3)$$

$$R_A = 5 + 10 + 9 = 24 \ \Omega \qquad Ans.$$

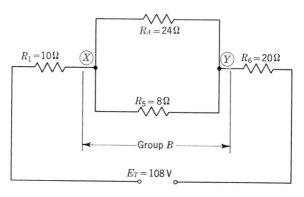

FIGURE 5-17

The resistance R_A replaces the series combination of R_2, R_3, and R_4 of Fig. 5-16.

b In Fig. 5-17, the resistances R_A and R_5 form the *parallel* group B. Find the total resistance of group B and replace the group with the equivalent resistance R_B as shown in Fig. 5-18,

$$R_B = \frac{R_A \times R_5}{R_A + R_5} = \frac{24 \times 8}{24 + 8} = \frac{192}{32} = 6 \ \Omega \qquad Ans.$$

FIGURE 5-18

The resistance R_B replaces the parallel combination of R_A and R_5 of Fig. 5-17.

c In Fig. 5-18, the resistances R_1, R_B, and R_6 form a simple *series* circuit. Find the total resistance of the entire circuit.

$$R_T = R_1 + R_B + R_6 \qquad\qquad (3\text{-}3)$$

$$R_T = 10 + 6 + 20 = 36 \ \Omega \qquad Ans.$$

2   Find the total current I_T.

$$E_T = I_T \times R_T \qquad\qquad (3\text{-}7)$$

$$108 = I_T \times 36$$

$$I_T = \frac{108}{36} = 3 \ A \qquad Ans.$$

3   Find the currents and voltages in each part. Start with the *simplest* circuit obtained in the calculation of the total resistance. This would be Fig. 5-18. In this figure, R_1, R_B, and R_6 are in *series*. Therefore,

$$I_T = I_1 = I_B = I_6 = 3 \ A \qquad\qquad (3\text{-}1)$$

Find the voltage across each part by Ohm's law.

$$E_1 = I_1 \times R_1 \qquad E_B = I_B \times R_B \qquad E_6 = I_6 \times R_6$$

$$E_1 = 3 \times 10 \qquad E_B = 3 \times 6 \qquad E_6 = 3 \times 20$$

$$E_1 = 30 \ V \qquad E_B = 18 \ V \qquad E_6 = 60 \ V$$

These values should be entered on the figure so that it will appear as in Fig. 5-19.

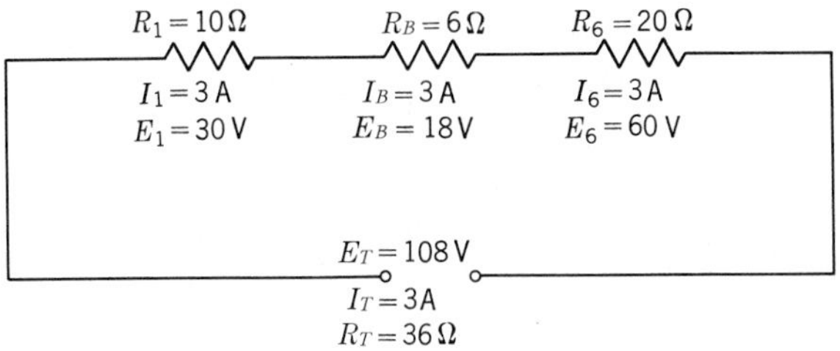

$R_1 = 10\,\Omega$ $R_B = 6\,\Omega$ $R_6 = 20\,\Omega$

$I_1 = 3\,A$ $I_B = 3\,A$ $I_6 = 3\,A$
$E_1 = 30\,V$ $E_B = 18\,V$ $E_6 = 60\,V$

$E_T = 108\,V$
$I_T = 3\,A$
$R_T = 36\,\Omega$

FIGURE 5-19
Values of voltage and current
are entered on the circuit of
Fig. 5-18.

4   We are now ready to find the voltages and currents for group A and resistor R_5. In Fig. 5-17, R_A and R_5 are in parallel. Therefore,

$$E_B = E_A = E_5 = 18\ \text{V} \qquad (4\text{-}1)$$

Find the current in R_A and R_5 by Ohm's law.

$$E_A = I_A \times R_A \qquad\qquad E_5 = I_5 \times R_5$$

$$18 = I_A \times 24 \qquad\qquad 18 = I_5 \times 8$$

$$I_A = \frac{18}{24} = 0.75\ \text{A} \qquad I_5 = \frac{18}{8} = 2.25\ \text{A}$$

Enter these values on Fig. 5-17 so that it will appear as shown in Fig. 5-20.

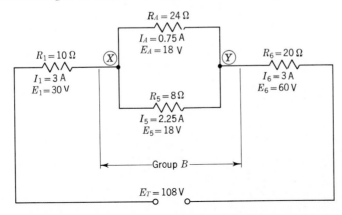

$R_A = 24\,\Omega$
$I_A = 0.75\,A$
$E_A = 18\,V$

$R_1 = 10\,\Omega$ ⓧ   ⓨ $R_6 = 20\,\Omega$
$I_1 = 3\,A$ $I_6 = 3\,A$
$E_1 = 30\,V$ $E_6 = 60\,V$

$R_5 = 8\,\Omega$
$I_5 = 2.25\,A$
$E_5 = 18\,V$

—Group B—

$E_T = 108\,V$

FIGURE 5-20
Values of voltage and current
are entered on the circuit of
Fig. 5-17.

5   We are now ready to find the currents and voltages for the individual resistors of group A. In Fig. 5-16, R_2, R_3, and R_4 are in series. Therefore,

$$I_A = I_2 = I_3 = I_4 = 0.75\ \text{A} \qquad (3\text{-}1)$$

Find the voltage across these resistors by Ohm's law.

$$E_2 = I_2 \times R_2 \qquad E_3 = I_3 \times R_3 \qquad E_4 = I_4 \times R_4$$

$$E_2 = 0.75 \times 5 \qquad E_3 = 0.75 \times 10 \qquad E_4 = 0.75 \times 9$$

$$E_2 = 3.75\ \text{V} \qquad E_3 = 7.5\ \text{V} \qquad E_4 = 6.75\ \text{V}$$

6   Check. The voltage across E_2, E_3, and E_4 should equal E_A.

$$E_A = E_2 + E_3 + E_4 = 18\ \text{V} \qquad (3\text{-}2)$$

$$18 = 3.75 + 7.50 + 6.75$$

$$18 = 18 \quad Check$$

EXAMPLE 5-5 Simplify the circuit shown in Fig. 5-21 and find the total resistance of the circuit.

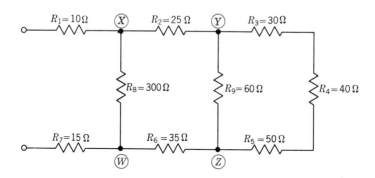

FIGURE 5-21

SOLUTION

1 Redraw the circuit in standard form as shown in Fig. 5-22.

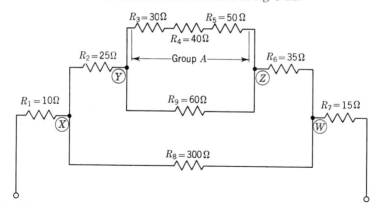

FIGURE 5-22
The circuit of Fig. 5-21 is redrawn in standard form.

2 In Fig. 5-22 the resistors R_3, R_4, and R_5 form the *series* group A. Find the total resistance of the group and replace the group with the equivalent resistance R_A as shown in Fig. 5-23.

$$R_A = R_3 + R_4 + R_5 \tag{3-3}$$

$$R_A = 30 + 40 + 50 = 120 \ \Omega \quad Ans.$$

3 In Fig. 5-23 the resistances R_A and R_9 form the *parallel* group B. Find the total resistance of the group and replace the group with the equivalent resistance R_B as shown in Fig. 5-24.

$$R_B = \frac{R_A \times R_9}{R_A + R_9} \tag{4-5}$$

$$R_B = \frac{120 \times 60}{120 + 60} = \frac{7,200}{180} = 40 \ \Omega \quad Ans.$$

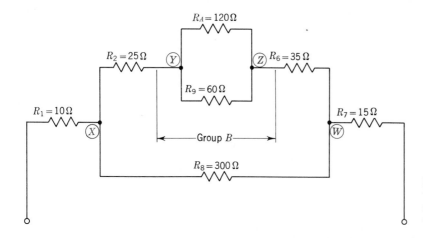

FIGURE 5-23
The resistance R_A replaces the
series combination of R_3, R_4,
and R_5 of Fig. 5-22.

4   In Fig. 5-24 the resistances R_2, R_B, and R_6 form the *series* group C. Find
the total resistance of the group and replace the group with the equivalent resistance R_C as shown in Fig. 5-25.

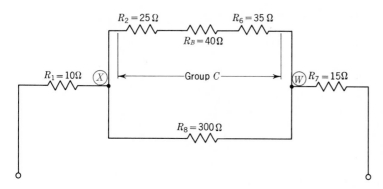

FIGURE 5-24
The resistance R_B replaces the
parallel combination of R_A and
R_9 of Fig. 5-23.

$$R_C = R_2 + R_B + R_6 \qquad (3\text{-}3)$$

$$R_C = 25 + 40 + 35 = 100 \ \Omega \qquad Ans.$$

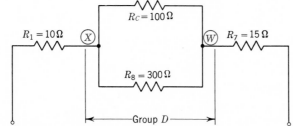

FIGURE 5-25
The resistance R_C replaces the
series combination of R_2, R_B,
and R_6 of Fig. 5-24.

5   In Fig. 5-25 the resistances R_C and R_8 form the *parallel* group D. Find the
total resistance of the group and replace the group with the equivalent resistance R_D as shown in Fig. 5-26.

$$R_D = \frac{R_C \times R_8}{R_C + R_8} \qquad (4\text{-}5)$$

$$R_D = \frac{100 \times 300}{100 + 300} = \frac{30,000}{400} = 75 \ \Omega \qquad Ans.$$

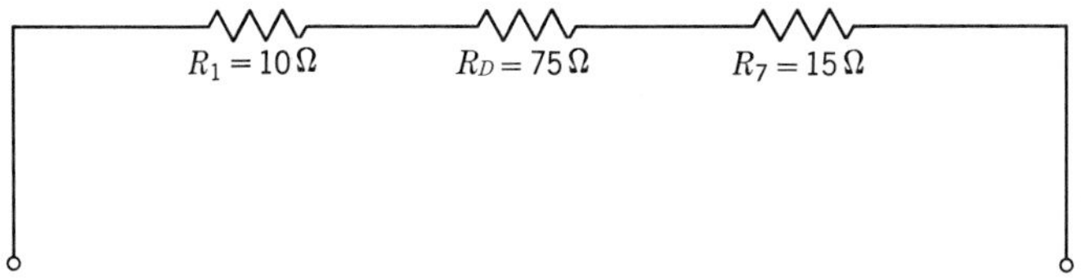

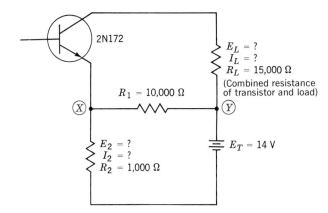

$R_1 = 10\,\Omega$ $R_D = 75\,\Omega$ $R_7 = 15\,\Omega$

FIGURE 5-26
The resistance R_D replaces the parallel combination of R_C and R_8 of Fig. 5-25.

6   In Fig. 5-26 the resistances R_1, R_D, and R_7 form a *series* circuit. Find the resistance of the entire circuit.

$$R_T = R_1 + R_D + R_7 \qquad (3\text{-}3)$$

$$R_T = 10 + 75 + 15 = 100 \ \Omega \qquad Ans.$$

EXAMPLE 5-6   The Emerson color TV chassis 120894 uses a circuit similar to that shown in Fig. 5-27. Find (*a*) the current I_2, (*b*) the voltage E_2, (*c*) the voltage across the load E_L, and (*d*) the load current I_L.

2N172

$E_L = ?$
$I_L = ?$
$R_L = 15,000 \ \Omega$
(Combined resistance of transistor and load)

$R_1 = 10,000 \ \Omega$

(X)

(Y)

$E_2 = ?$
$I_2 = ?$
$R_2 = 1,000 \ \Omega$

$E_T = 14 \ V$

FIGURE 5-27

SOLUTION
Redraw the circuit in the familiar standard form as shown in Fig. 5-28. *Note:* R_L represents the combined resistance of the transistor and the load resistance.

a   Find the current I_2.

1   Find the equivalent resistance of group *A*.

$$R_A = \frac{R_L \times R_1}{R_L + R_1} \qquad (4\text{-}5)$$

$$R_A = \frac{15,000 \times 10,000}{15,000 + 10,000}$$

$$R_A = \frac{150,000,000}{25,000} = 6,000 \ \Omega \qquad Ans.$$

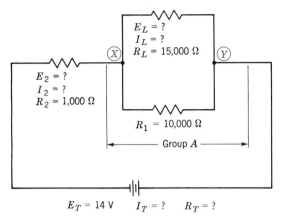

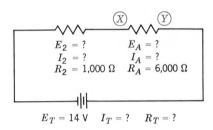

FIGURE 5-28
The circuit of Fig. 5-27 is redrawn in standard form.

2   Redraw the circuit using this 6,000-Ω resistor in place of the combination as shown in Fig. 5-29.

FIGURE 5-29
The resistance R_A replaces the parallel combination R_L and R_1 of Fig. 5-28.

3   Solve the new *series* circuit.
Find the total resistance R_T.

$$R_T = R_2 + R_A \qquad (3\text{-}3)$$

$$R_T = 1,000 + 6,000 = 7,000 \ \Omega \qquad Ans.$$

Find the total current I_T.

$$E_T = I_T \times R_T \qquad (3\text{-}7)$$

$$14 = I_T \times 7,000$$

$$I_T = \frac{14}{7,000} = 0.002 \ \text{A} \qquad Ans.$$

Find the current I_2.

$$I_T = I_2 = I_A = 0.002 \ \text{A} \qquad Ans. \qquad (3\text{-}1)$$

b   Find the voltage E_2.

$$E_2 = I_2 \times R_2 \qquad (3\text{-}4)$$

$$E_2 = 0.002 \times 1,000 = 2 \ \text{V} \qquad Ans.$$

c   Find the voltage across the load E_L.

1   Find the voltage drop across group A. In Fig. 5-29,

$$E_A = I_A \times R_A \qquad\qquad (3\text{-}5)$$

$$E_A = 0.002 \times 6{,}000 = 12 \text{ V}$$

2   In Fig. 5-28, since E_A represents the total voltage of the parallel group A,

$$E_L = E_A = 12 \text{ V} \qquad Ans.$$

d Using group A in Fig. 5-28, find the load current I_L.

$$E_L = I_L \times R_L \qquad\qquad (2\text{-}1)$$

$$12 = I_L \times 15{,}000$$

$$I_L = \frac{12}{15{,}000} = 0.0008 \text{ A} \qquad Ans.$$

SELF-TEST 5-7   Find the total resistance of the circuit shown in Fig. 5-30.

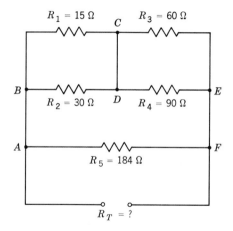

$R_T = ?$

FIGURE 5-30

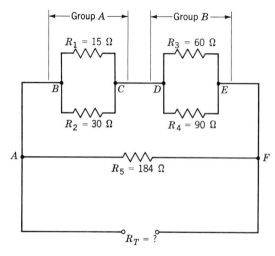

$R_T = ?$

FIGURE 5-31
Figure 5-30 redrawn in
standard form.

SOLUTION

1   Redraw the circuit in standard form as shown in Fig. 5-31.

2   In Fig. 5-31, the resistors R_1 and R_2 are in __(series/parallel)__ , forming
group A. In Fig. 5-31, the resistors R_3 and R_4 are in __(series/parallel)__ , forming
group B.

| parallel |
| parallel |

3   Find the total resistance of each group.

$$R_A = \frac{R_1 \times R_2}{?}$$

$R_1 + R_2$

$$R_A = \frac{15 \times 30}{? + 30}$$

15

$$R_A = \frac{450}{45} = \underline{} \ \Omega \quad Ans.$$

10

$$R_B = \frac{60 \times ?}{60 + 90}$$

90

$$R_B = \frac{5{,}400}{150} = \underline{} \ \Omega \quad Ans.$$

36

4   Redraw the circuit replacing each group with its equivalent resistance
R_A and R_B as shown in Fig. 5-32.

5   In Fig. 5-32, the resistances R_A and R_B form the __(series/parallel)__
group C.

series

Find the total resistance of the group C.

$$R_C = \underline{} \qquad\qquad (3\text{-}3)$$

$R_A + R_B$

$$R_C = 10 + \underline{}$$

36

$$R_C = \underline{} \ \Omega \quad Ans.$$

46

6   Redraw the circuit, replacing R_A and R_B with their equivalent resistance
___ as shown in Fig. 5-33.

R_C

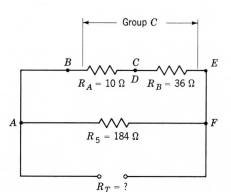

7   In Fig. 5-33, the resistances R_C and R_5 are in __(series/parallel).__   Find R_T.

parallel

$$R_T = \frac{?}{?}$$

$$\frac{R_C \times R_5}{R_C + R_5}$$

FIGURE 5-32

The resistance R_A replaces the
parallel combination of R_1 and
R_2; R_B replaces the parallel
combination of R_3 and R_4 in
Fig. 5-31.

$$R_T = \frac{46 \times ?}{46 + ?}$$

$$R_T = \frac{8{,}464}{230} = \underline{\quad} \ \Omega \qquad Ans.$$

184
184

36.8

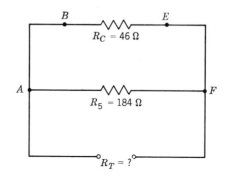

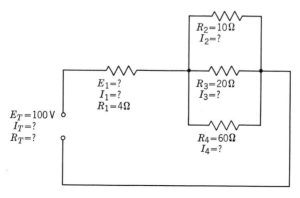

FIGURE 5-33

The resistance R_C replaces the series combination of R_A and R_B in Fig. 5-32.

PROBLEMS

1. In a circuit similar to that shown in Fig. 5-12, $E_T = 130$ V, $R_1 = 10$ Ω, $R_2 = 4$ Ω, and $R_3 = 12$ Ω. Find all missing values of voltage, current, and resistance.

2. Find all missing values in the circuit shown in Fig. 5-34.

FIGURE 5-34

3. In a circuit similar to that shown in Fig. 5-27, $E_T = 17.4$ V, $R_2 = 1{,}000$ Ω, $R_1 = 8{,}000$ Ω, and $R_L = 12{,}000$ Ω. Find (a) I_2, (b) E_2, (c) E_L, and (d) I_L.

4. In a circuit similar to that shown in Fig. 5-27, $R_2 = 1{,}000$ Ω, $R_1 = 10{,}000$ Ω, $R_L = 20{,}000$ Ω, and $I_L = 0.0007$ A. Find (a) E_L, (b) E_1, (c) I_1, (d) I_2, (e) E_2, and (f) E_T.

5. In a circuit similar to that shown in Fig. 5-34, find the total current if $E_T = 8.5$ V, $R_1 = 12$ Ω, $R_2 = 10$ Ω, $R_3 = 15$ Ω, and $R_4 = 30$ Ω.

6. Use a circuit similar to that shown in Fig. 5-15. $E_T = 120$ V, $R_1 = 5$ Ω, $R_2 = 1$ Ω, $R_3 = 3$ Ω, $R_4 = 6$ Ω, $R_5 = 10$ Ω, and $R_6 = 10$ Ω. Find (a) the total resistance, (b) the total current, (c) the current in each resistor, and (d) the voltage drop across each resistor.

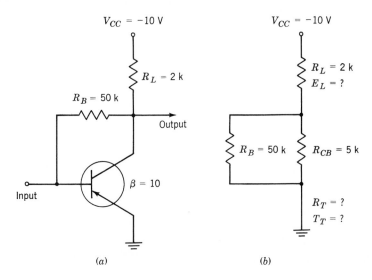

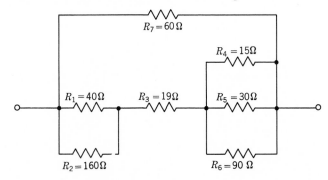

FIGURE 5-35
(a) A self-bias transistor circuit.
(b) The dc equivalent circuit.

7. A self-bias transistor circuit is shown in Fig. 5-35a and its dc equivalent circuit in Fig. 5-35b. Find (a) the total resistance of the circuit, (b) the total current in the circuit, and (c) the voltage across R_L.

8. Use a circuit similar to that shown in Fig. 5-21. $E_T = 400$ V, $R_1 = 50$ Ω, $R_2 = 25$ Ω, $R_3 = 8$ Ω, $R_4 = 2$ Ω, $R_5 = 10$ Ω, $R_6 = 15$ Ω, $R_7 = 105$ Ω, $R_8 = 450$ Ω, and $R_9 = 20$ Ω. Find (a) the total resistance, (b) the total current, (c) the current in each resistor, and (d) the voltage drop across each resistor.

9. Find the total resistance of the circuit shown in Fig. 5-36.

FIGURE 5-36

10. Find the total resistance of the circuit shown in Fig. 5-30 if the 60-Ω resistor were to burn out and open.

11. The Zenith chassis 16J23 television receiver uses a variable-bias type of contrast control similar to that shown in Fig. 5-37. Find (a) the total resistance of the circuit and (b) the resistance in parallel with the entire circuit (connected from point A to ground) which will reduce the total resistance to 4.2 kΩ (kilohms).

12. In Fig. 5-38, (a) draw the equivalent resistance network, (b) find

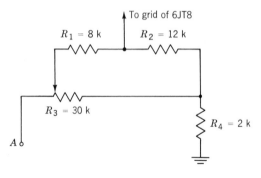

FIGURE 5-37

A variable-bias type of contrast control.

the total resistance between the point P and the ground G, and (c) find the resistance that must be connected between P and G (in parallel with the entire circuit) to reduce the total resistance to 36 k.

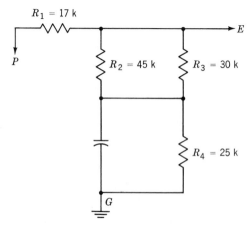

FIGURE 5-38

SUMMARY—COMBINATION CIRCUITS

Finding the total resistance

1 Redraw the circuit in _____ form if necessary.   standard

2 First simplification.

    a Locate the combination of resistors which form a simple _____ or parallel circuit.   series

    b Indicate the beginning and ____ of the group with a dimension line and name it "group ____."   end A

    c Calculate the resistance of this group and label it ____. R_A

3 Redraw the circuit, substituting ____ in place of the group. R_A

4 Second simplification.

    a Repeat steps 2a, 2b, and 2c, using the name group ____ and R_B in the circuit of step 3. B

5 Repeat steps 2 and 3 using the names group C, D, etc., until the circuit is reduced to the total resistance named ____. R_T

Solving combination circuits

1 Find the total resistance R_T by repeated simplification of the original circuit.

2 Find the total current I_T using the formula

$$E_T = \underline{\hspace{1cm}} \times R_T \qquad (3\text{-}7) \qquad I_T$$

3 Find the current and voltage in each resistor.

  a Start with the __(simplest/most complicated)__ circuit obtained in the calculations for R_T. ⎢ simplest

  b The value of current in this circuit will be the _____ current. Enter this value of I_T on this circuit diagram. ⎢ total

  c Calculate the voltage drops across all resistors of this circuit by the formula

$$\underline{\hspace{3cm}} \qquad E = I \times R$$

  d Enter these values on the next simplest circuit obtained in the original calculation for ___. ⎢ R_T

  e Solve this circuit for all missing values of current and _____. ⎢ voltage

  f Repeat steps *d* and *e* on successive circuits found in the _____ simplification until all parts have been found. ⎢ resistance

TEST—COMBINATION CIRCUITS

1. A 50-Ω resistor is connected in series with a parallel combination of a 40- and a 60-Ω resistor. The entire circuit is placed across a total voltage of 37 V. Find (*a*) the total resistance of the parallel group, (*b*) the total resistance of the entire circuit, (*c*) the total current, and (*d*) the current and the voltage drop in each resistor.

2. A 50- and a 30-Ω resistor are connected in series. In parallel with this series group is another series group consisting of a 20- and a 28-Ω resistor. The two groups are supplied from a 120-V source. Find (*a*) the total resistance and total voltage for each series group, (*b*) the total current for each series group, (*c*) the total current for the entire combination, (*d*) the total resistance of the entire combination, and (*e*) the current and the voltage drop in each resistor.

3. A television receiver damper circuit consists of a 30- and a 50-Ω resistor in parallel. In series with this group is another parallel group of a 60- and an 80-Ω resistor. Find the total resistance of the entire circuit.

4. The brightness-control circuit of the Philco-Ford TV chassis 19P22 is essentially a 220,000-Ω resistor in series with a parallel combination of a 100,000- and a 180,000-Ω resistor. Find the total resistance of the circuit.

5. Use a circuit similar to that shown in Fig. 5-15. $E_T = 100$ V, $R_1 = 14$ Ω, $R_2 = 3$ Ω, $R_3 = 6$ Ω, $R_4 = 15$ Ω, $R_5 = 48$ Ω, and $R_6 = 20$ Ω. Find (*a*) the total resistance, (*b*) the total current, (*c*) the current in each resistor, and (*d*) the voltage drop across each resistor.

JOB 5-4   LINE DROP

Meaning of line drop. In our last two jobs, we worked with circuits in which the connecting wires were very short. The resistances of these short lengths were so very small that we did not bother to include them in our calculations. In home and factory installations, however, where long lines of wire (feeders) are used, the resistance of these long lengths must be included in all calculations.

In Fig. 5-39, the voltage that is needed to force the current through the resistance of the line wires is called the *line drop.* For example, if a generator delivers 120 V but the voltage available at a motor some distance away is only 116 V, then there has been a "drop" in voltage of 4 V. The connecting wires apparently had enough resistance to use up 4 V of electrical pressure.

We must be very careful about the kind and size of wires used in any installation. If the wires are poorly chosen, then the *line drop* may be very large and the voltage available to the electrical apparatus will be too low for proper operation. The national and city electrical codes permit definite amounts of line drop for specific installations. This limitation of the line drop is accomplished by specifying definite sizes of wire to be used in specific installations. We shall study this in detail in Chap. 13.

You may have noticed the effect of line drop in your home. The lights may suddenly get dim when the refrigerator motor starts. The large current drain required to start the motor increases the line drop in the house wiring so that the voltage left over for the lights is less than normal. Since the running current is much less than the starting current, as soon as the motor has started the current drain decreases—the line drop decreases—and the lights once again come up to full brilliance.

DEFINITIONS

1   Generator voltage (E_G): The total voltage supplied to the circuit from the source of voltage.

2   Load voltage (E_L): The voltage which is available to operate the devices or loads.

3   Line drop (E_l): The voltage which is lost in sending the current through the line wires.

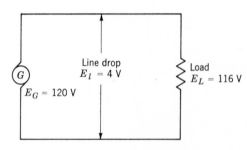

FIGURE 5-39

Voltage is lost in the line wires between a generator and a load.

RULES AND FORMULAS

1   By Ohm's law, the total line drop is equal to the line current multiplied by the total line resistance.

$$E_{\text{line}} = I_{\text{line}} \times R_{\text{line}}$$

or

Formula

$$E_l = I_l \times R_l \qquad \boxed{5\text{-}1}$$

2   The generator voltage is the total voltage of the series circuit made up of the line drop and the load voltage.

$$E_T = E_1 + E_2 \qquad (3\text{-}2)$$

or

$$E_{\text{generator}} = E_{\text{line}} + E_{\text{load}}$$

Formula

$$E_G = E_l + E_L \qquad \boxed{5\text{-}2}$$

3   The load voltage is equal to the generator voltage minus the line drop. From

$$E_l + E_L = E_G \qquad (5\text{-}2)$$

we get, by transposing the E_l,

Formula

$$E_L = E_G - E_l \qquad \boxed{5\text{-}3}$$

and, by transposing the E_L,

Formula

$$E_l = E_G - E_L \qquad \boxed{5\text{-}4}$$

When using these formulas, be sure that

1   The line current I_l is the current flowing in the line wires and *not* the current in the load.
2   The line drop E_l is the voltage lost in the line wires only.
3   The line resistance is the resistance of the connecting wires only. The resistance of *both* lead and return wires must be considered when finding the total resistance of the line.

EXAMPLE 5-8   A lamp bank consisting of three lamps, each drawing 2 A is connected to a 120-V source. Each line wire has a resistance of 0.2 Ω. Find the drop in voltage in the line and the voltage available at the load.

SOLUTION

The diagram for the circuit is shown in Fig. 5-40.

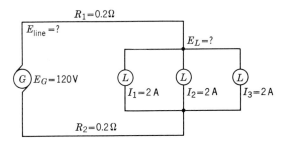

FIGURE 5-40

1 Find the current drawn by the load.

$$I_L = I_1 + I_2 + I_3 \qquad (4\text{-}2)$$

$$I_L = 2 + 2 + 2 = 6 \text{ A} \qquad Ans.$$

2 Find the line current. Since the line wires are in series with the load,

$$I_l = I_L = 6 \text{ A} \qquad Ans. \qquad (3\text{-}1)$$

3 Find the resistance of the line wires. Since the line wires are in series,

$$R_l = R_1 + R_2 \qquad (3\text{-}3)$$

$$R_l = 0.2 + 0.2 = 0.4 \text{ } \Omega \qquad Ans.$$

4 Find the total line drop.

$$E_l = I_l \times R_l \qquad (5\text{-}1)$$

$$E_l = 6 \times 0.4 = 2.4 \text{ V} \qquad Ans.$$

5 Find the voltage available at the load.

$$E_L = E_G - E_l \qquad (5\text{-}3)$$

$$E_L = 120 - 2.4 = 117.6 \text{ V} \qquad Ans.$$

EXAMPLE 5-9 Find the generator voltage required for the circuit shown in Fig. 5-41.

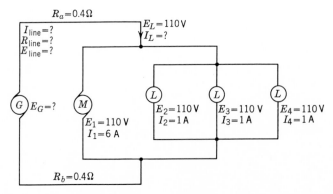

FIGURE 5-41

SOLUTION

1 Find the current drawn by the load.

$$I_L = I_1 + I_2 + I_3 + I_4 \tag{4-2}$$

$$I_L = 6 + 1 + 1 + 1 = 9 \text{ A} \quad \textit{Ans.}$$

2 Find the line current.

$$I_l = I_L = 9 \text{ A} \quad \textit{Ans.} \tag{3-1}$$

3 Find the resistance of the line wires.

$$R_l = R_a + R_b \tag{3-3}$$

$$R_l = 0.4 + 0.4 = 0.8 \ \Omega \quad \textit{Ans.}$$

4 Find the total line drop.

$$E_l = I_l \times R_l \tag{5-1}$$

$$E_l = 9 \times 0.8 = 7.2 \text{ V} \quad \textit{Ans.}$$

5 Find the generator voltage.

$$E_G = E_l + E_L \tag{5-2}$$

$$E_G = 7.2 + 110 = 117.2 \text{ V} \quad \textit{Ans.}$$

SELF-TEST 5-10 Find the resistance of each line wire in the circuit shown in Fig. 5-42.

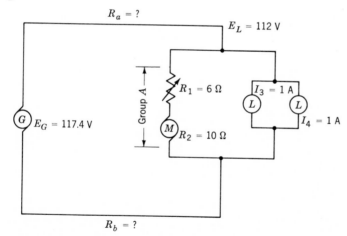

FIGURE 5-42

SOLUTION

In order to find the line resistance we must know the voltage drop in the line and the current in the line. Find the current distribution by investigating group A first.

1 Find the total resistance of group A.

$$R_A = R_1 + R_2 \tag{3-3}$$

$$R_A = 6 + 10 = \underline{\quad} \; \Omega$$

16

2   Since E_A is in parallel with the lamp load and the load voltage E_L,

$$E_A = E_L \tag{4-1}$$

$$E_A = \underline{\quad} \; V$$

112

3   Find the current in group A.

$$E_A = I_A \times R_A \tag{3-7}$$

$$112 = I_A \times \underline{\quad}$$

16

$$I_A = \frac{112}{16} = \underline{\quad} \; A$$

7

4   Find the total load current I_L.

$$I_L = I_A + I_3 + I_4 \tag{4-2}$$

$$I_L = \underline{\quad} + 1 + 1$$

7

$$I_L = \underline{\quad} \; A$$

9

5   Since the line wires are in series with the load,

$$I_l = I_L \tag{3-1}$$

$$I_l = \underline{\quad} \; A$$

9

6   Find the voltage drop in the line wires.

$$E_l = E_G - E_L \tag{5-4}$$

$$E_l = 117.4 - 112$$

$$E_l = \underline{\quad} \; V$$

5.4

7   Find the resistance of the line wires.

$$E_l = I_l \times R_l \tag{5-1}$$

$$5.4 = \underline{\quad} \times R_l$$

9

$$R_l = \frac{5.4}{9} = \underline{\quad} \; \Omega$$

0.6

8   Find the resistance of each line wire.

$$R_a = R_b = \frac{1}{2} \times R_l$$

$$R_a = R_b = \frac{1}{2} \times 0.6 = \underline{\quad} \; \Omega \quad Ans.$$

0.3

PROBLEMS

1. In a circuit similar to that shown in Fig. 5-40, the generator voltage
    is 117 V. Each line wire has a resistance of 0.4 Ω, and each lamp
    draws 1 A. Find the line drop and the voltage available at the lamps.

2. A motor is connected by two wires of 0.15 Ω each to a generator. The motor takes 30 A at 211 V. What must be the generator voltage?

3. If the voltage at a load drawing 6 A is 117 V while the generator voltage is 120 V, what is the resistance of each line wire? *Hint:* Find the line drop, then the line resistance, and finally the resistance of each wire.

4. Home wiring is often done with No. 16 wire, which has a resistance of 0.401 Ω for a 100-ft length. What is the loss in voltage from the house meter to an electric broiler using 12 A and located 100 ft from the meter?

5. What would be the voltage drop if No. 14 wire (0.252 Ω/100 ft) were used in Prob. 4? Which size of wire is better for wiring homes?

6. In a circuit similar to that shown in Fig. 5-40, the generator voltage is 117 V. Each line wire has a resistance of 0.45 Ω, and the lamps draw currents of 0.9, 1.4, and 1.8 A. Find the line drop and the voltage available at the lamps.

7. In a circuit similar to that shown in Fig. 5-41, the motor draws 8.2 A and each of the three lamps draws 0.92 A. Each line wire has a resistance of 0.15 Ω. Find the generator voltage if the load voltage must be 110 V.

8. In a circuit similar to that shown in Fig. 5-40, the generator voltage is 117 V, the resistance of each line wire is 0.2 Ω, and the total resistance of the lamp bank is 16.1 Ω. Find (*a*) the total resistance of the circuit, (*b*) the current delivered to the lamp bank, and (*c*) the voltage across the lamp bank.

JOB 5-5 DISTRIBUTION SYSTEMS

In order to distribute current throughout an installation, the various loads are connected in parallel across the feeder lines. The feeder lines form various combination circuits with the loads. To solve circuits like these, we must first break down the combination into simple series or parallel circuits. It is best to follow a definite system like the following:

1 Find the current distribution. Start with the section *farthest* from the generator. Find the current in this section and work backward toward the generator, finding the current in the different parts of the circuit.

2 Name the sections. Call the section nearest to the generator section *A*, the next section *B*, etc.

3 Find the resistance of each *pair* of line wires for each section using formula (3-3).

4 Find the line drop for each section of the circuit using formula (5-1). The line wires connecting the generator to section *A* are called line 1, the next line wire pair is called line 2, etc.

5   Find the voltage across each section.   Start where the voltage is known, and apply formulas (5-2) and (5-3).

EXAMPLE 5-11   Find the voltage across the motor and across the lamp bank of the circuit shown in Fig. 5-43.

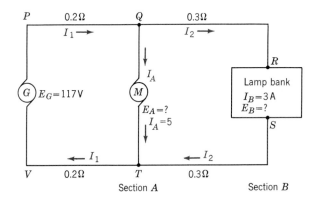

Section A   Section B   **FIGURE 5-43**

SOLUTION

1   Find the current distribution.   Start with the section B farthest from the generator. $I_B = 3$ A.   Line 2, from Q to R and from S to T, must carry these 3 A. Therefore, $I_2 = 3$ A.   Since $I_A = 5$ A, the wire from Q to T must carry these 5 A. At point Q, we have the beginning of a parallel circuit made of the motor (section A) and the lamp bank (section B).

$$I_1 = I_A + I_2 \qquad\qquad (4\text{-}2)$$

$$I_1 = 5 + 3 = 8 \text{ A}$$

Thus, the current in line 1 from P to Q equals 8 A.   Similarly, at T, the current I_A from the motor and the current I_2 from the lamp bank will combine.

$$I_1 = I_A + I_2 \qquad\qquad (4\text{-}2)$$

$$I_1 = 5 + 3 = 8 \text{ A}$$

Thus, the current in line 1 from T to V equals 8 A.
2   Find the resistance of the *pairs* of line wires.

$$R_{l_1} = 0.2 + 0.2 = 0.4 \ \Omega \qquad R_{l_2} = 0.3 + 0.3 = 0.6 \ \Omega \qquad (3\text{-}3)$$

3   Find the line drop for each section.

$$E_{l_1} = I_1 \times R_{l_1} \qquad\qquad E_{l_2} = I_2 \times R_{l_2} \qquad\qquad (5\text{-}1)$$

$$E_{l_1} = 8 \times 0.4 = 3.2 \text{ V} \qquad E_{l_2} = 3 \times 0.6 = 1.8 \text{ V}$$

4   Find the load voltages.

$$E_A = E_G - E_{l_1} \qquad\qquad (5\text{-}3)$$

$$E_A = 117 - 3.2 = 113.8 \text{ V} \qquad Ans.$$

$$E_B = E_A - E_{l_2} \qquad\qquad (5\text{-}3)$$

$$E_B = 113.8 - 1.8 = 112 \text{ V} \qquad Ans.$$

EXAMPLE 5-12 Find the generator voltage and the voltage across the motor in the circuit shown in Fig. 5-44.

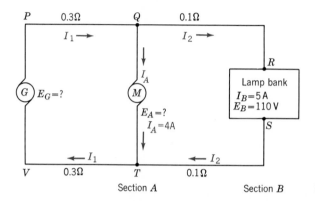

FIGURE 5-44

SOLUTION

1 Find the current distribution. Start with the section B farthest from the generator. $I_B = 5$ A. Line 2, from Q to R and from S to T, must carry these 5 A. Therefore, $I_2 = 5$ A.
Since $I_A = 4$ A, the wire from Q to T must carry these 4 A.

At point Q: At point T:

$I_1 = I_A + I_2$ $I_1 = I_A + I_2$ (4-2)

$I_1 = 4 + 5 = 9$ A $I_1 = 4 + 5 = 9$ A

2 Find the resistance of the *pairs* of line wires.

$R_{l_1} = 0.3 + 0.3 = 0.6$ Ω $R_{l_2} = 0.1 + 0.1 = 0.2$ Ω   (3-3)

3 Find the line drop for each section.

$E_{l_1} = I_1 \times R_{l_1}$ $E_{l_2} = I_2 \times R_{l_2}$ (5-1)

$E_{l_1} = 9 \times 0.6 = 5.4$ V $E_{l_2} = 5 \times 0.2 = 1$ V

4 Find the load and generator voltages.

$E_A = E_{l_2} + E_B$ (5-2)

$E_A = 1 + 110 = 111$ V   *Ans.*

$E_G = E_{l_1} + E_A$

$E_G = 5.4 + 111 = 116.4$ V   *Ans.*

SELF-TEST 5-13 Find the voltage across (*a*) the lamp bank, (*b*) motor 1, and (*c*) motor 2, in the circuit shown in Fig. 5-45.

SOLUTION

1 Find the current distribution. Start with section ____. I_3, from Q to R, and from S to T, = ____ A. At point Q, the incoming current I_2 divides into two branches, ____ and ____.

C
20
I_3 I_B

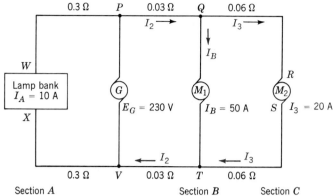

FIGURE 5-45

$$I_2 = I_3 + \underline{\quad} \qquad\qquad I_B$$

$$I_2 = 20 + \underline{\quad} \qquad\qquad 50$$

$$I_2 = \underline{\quad} A \qquad\qquad 70$$

Thus, the current from P to $Q = \underline{\quad}$ A. At point T, I_3 and I_B combine to form | 70
____. Thus, the current from T to $V = \underline{\quad}$ A. The current I_A, from W to P and | I_2 70
from V to X equals ____ A. | 10

2   Find the resistance of the *pairs* of line wires.

$$R_{l_A} = 0.3 + 0.3 = \underline{\quad} \ \Omega \qquad\qquad 0.6$$

$$R_{l_2} = 0.03 + \underline{\quad} = \underline{\quad} \ \Omega \qquad\qquad 0.03 \quad 0.06$$

$$R_{l_3} = \underline{\quad} + \underline{\quad} = 0.12 \ \Omega \qquad\qquad 0.06 \quad 0.06$$

3   Find the line drop for each section.

$$E_{l_A} = I_A \times \underline{\quad} \qquad\qquad R_{l_A}$$

$$E_{l_A} = 10 \times \underline{\quad} = \underline{\quad} \ V \qquad\qquad 0.6 \quad 6$$

$$E_{l_2} = \underline{\quad} \times R_{l_2} \qquad\qquad I_2$$

$$E_{l_2} = 70 \times \underline{\quad} = \underline{\quad} \ V \qquad\qquad 0.06 \quad 4.2$$

$$E_{l_3} = I_3 \times \underline{\quad} \qquad\qquad R_{l_3}$$

$$E_{l_3} = \underline{\quad} \times 0.12 = \underline{\quad} \ V \qquad\qquad 20 \quad 2.4$$

4   Find the load voltages. The voltage across the lamp bank is called E_A.

$$E_A = E_G - \underline{\quad} \qquad\qquad (5\text{-}3) \qquad E_{l_A}$$

$$E_A = \underline{\quad} - 6 = \underline{\quad} \ V \quad Ans. \qquad\qquad 230 \quad 224$$

The voltage across motor 1 is called E_B.

$$E_B = \underline{\quad} - E_{l_2} \qquad\qquad (5\text{-}3) \qquad E_G$$

$$E_B = 230 - \underline{\quad} = 225.8 \ V \quad Ans. \qquad\qquad 4.2$$

The voltage across motor 2 is called ____.

$$E_C = E_B - \underline{\quad} \qquad\qquad (5\text{-}3) \qquad E_C$$

$$E_C = 225.8 - 2.4 = \underline{\quad} \ V \quad Ans. \qquad\qquad E_{l_3}$$

$$\qquad\qquad 223.4$$

PROBLEMS

1. In the circuit shown in Fig. 5-46, the motor takes 30 A and the lamp bank takes 8 A. The generator voltage is 117 V. Find (*a*) the line drop in each section, (*b*) the voltage across the motor, and (*c*) the voltage across the lamp bank.

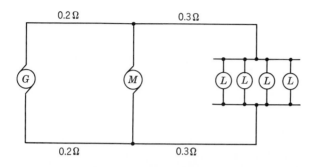

FIGURE 5-46

2. Each lamp in the circuit shown in Fig. 5-46 takes 1.5 A. The motor takes 12 A. The generator voltage is 115 V. Find (*a*) the line drop in each section, (*b*) the voltage across the motor, and (*c*) the voltage across the lamp bank.

3. Each lamp in the diagram shown in Fig. 5-47 takes 0.5 A. Find E_A and E_B.

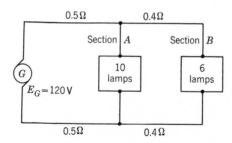

FIGURE 5-47

4. In the circuit shown in Fig. 5-48, the resistance of the wires *AB* is 0.3 Ω, *BC* is 0.5 Ω, *EF* is 0.5 Ω, and *DE* is 0.3 Ω. If each lamp takes 1 A, what is the terminal voltage of the generator? The voltage across *CF* is 105 V.

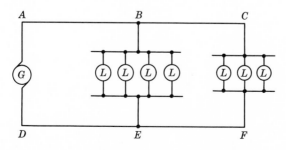

FIGURE 5-48

5. In the circuit shown in Fig. 5-49, each lamp takes 1.2 A. $E_A = 113$ V, and $I_A = 12$ A. Find E_G and E_B.

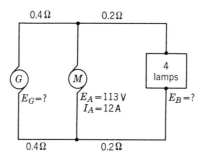

FIGURE 5-49

6. In the circuit shown in Fig. 5-50, each lamp takes 1 A. $E_A = 114$ V, and $E_G = 117$ V. Find E_B and I_A.

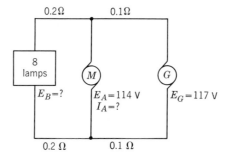

FIGURE 5-50

7. Find the generator voltage in the circuit shown in Fig. 5-51.

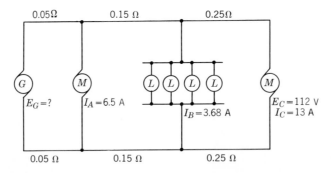

FIGURE 5-51

8. Each line wire of a two-wire distribution system has a resistance of 0.2 Ω. A motor drawing 10 A is connected by two of these wires to a generator delivering 121 V. Two more of these lines wires continue from the motor and carry current to a lamp bank drawing 4.5 A. Find (a) the voltage at the motor and (b) the voltage at the lamp bank.

9. In Fig. 5-52, find (*a*) the voltage across motor 1 and (*b*) the voltage across motor 2. *Hint:* $E_{M_1} = E_G - (E_{l_1} + E_{l_2} + E_{l_4})$, and $E_{M_2} = E_G - (E_{l_1} + E_{l_3} + E_{l_2})$.

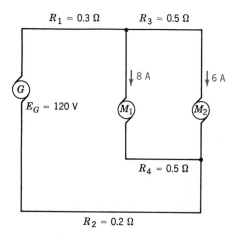

FIGURE 5-52

TEST—DISTRIBUTION SYSTEMS

1. In a circuit similar to that shown in Fig. 5-46, the motor draws 22 A and the lamp bank draws 10 A from the 132-V generator. Find (*a*) the voltage across the motor and (*b*) the voltage across the lamp bank.
2. In a circuit similar to that shown in Fig. 5-47, $E_G = 135$ V and each lamp draws 0.91 A. Find (*a*) E_A and (*b*) E_B.
3. In a circuit similar to that shown in Fig. 5-49, each lamp draws 1.4 A, $E_A = 115$ V, and $I_A = 10$ A. Find (*a*) E_G and (*b*) E_B.
4. In a circuit similar to that shown in Fig. 5-50, each lamp draws 1 A at 110 V and the motor draws 12 A. Find (*a*) the voltage at the motor and (*b*) the generator voltage.

ELECTRICAL POWER

JOB 6-1   ELECTRICAL POWER IN SIMPLE CIRCUITS

Meaning of electrical power. Did you know that it is possible to push a candle through a wooden board? You may not be successful when you try it because you may omit an essential element necessary to do this. This missing quantity is *speed.* Power depends on *how fast* a certain amount of work is done. Thus, if you *shoot* the candle from a shotgun, it will have the necessary speed to penetrate the board.

More than speed, however, is necessary to increase the power. In recognition of this fact, the Roman gladiators of long ago wrapped strips of lead around their fists to increase the power of their blows. Our modern boxers are not permitted to increase the weight of their gloves, but they increase their hitting power by punching with short, *fast* blows rather than with looping, slow swings.

Power, then, depends on two quantities—the work done (or the weight moved) and the speed of doing it.

$$\text{Power} = \text{work done} \times \text{speed}$$

In electrical work,

$$\text{Work done} = Q \times E$$

$$\text{Speed} = \frac{1}{t}$$

Therefore,

$$P = Q \times E \times \frac{1}{t}$$

or

$$P = \frac{Q \times E}{t} = \frac{Q}{t} \times E$$

but since $Q/t = I$

$$P = I \times E$$

RULE	The electrical power in any part of a circuit is equal to the current in that part multiplied by the voltage across that part of the circuit.

FORMULA

$$P = I \times E \qquad \boxed{6\text{-}1}$$

where P = power, W
I = current, A
E = voltage, V

A *watt* of electrical power is the power used when one volt causes one ampere of current to flow in a circuit. A *kilowatt* of power is equal to 1,000 watts.

TABLE 6-1
POWER USED BY ELECTRICAL DEVICES MEASURED IN WATTS

Electric clocks	1–3	Vacuum cleaners	300–700
Door chimes	15	Washers	350–450
Electric fans	50–300	Toasters	600–1,100
Lamp bulbs	15–200	Air conditioners	800–1,500
Sewing machines	40–80	Broilers	800–1,500
Radios	50–100	Electric ironers	1,000–1,500
Televisions	150–250	Clothes driers	4,000–4,700
Refrigerators	200–300	Electric ranges	Up to 23,000

EXAMPLE 6-1   A variable resistor in the volume control of a code practice oscillator passes 0.05 A with a voltage drop of 30 V. Find the power consumed.

SOLUTION
Given: $E = 30$ V   Find: $P = ?$
$\qquad I = 0.05$ A

$$P = I \times E \qquad\qquad (6\text{-}1)$$

$$P = 0.05 \times 30$$

$$P = 1.5 \text{ W} \qquad Ans.$$

EXAMPLE 6-2   A 1,000-Ω resistor in a power-supply filter circuit carries 0.06 A at 60 V. How many watts of power are developed in the resistor? What must be the wattage rating of the resistor in order to dissipate this power safely as heat?

SOLUTION
Given: $I = 0.06$ A   Find: $P = ?$
$\qquad E = 60$ V   Wattage rating $= ?$

$$P = I \times E \tag{6-1}$$

$$P = 0.06 \times 60 = 3.6 \text{ W} \qquad Ans.$$

The wattage rating of a resistor describes its ability to dissipate the heat produced in it by the passage of an electric current without itself overheating. For example, a 2-W resistor could dissipate 2 W of heat energy without overheating. However, if 3 W of power were to be developed in it, it would overheat because of the 1 W of power which it could not dissipate. Owing to the lack of ventilation in the close quarters of most television receivers, the wattage ratings of these resistors is usually at least twice the wattage developed in them.

$$\text{Wattage rating} = 2 \times P$$

$$\text{Wattage rating} = 2 \times 3.6 = 7.2 \text{ W} \qquad Ans.$$

SELF-TEST 6-3   A 56-Ω resistor is shunted with a 168-Ω resistor in a 0.3 A circuit as shown in Fig. 6-1. Find the wattage rating of the 168-Ω resistor.

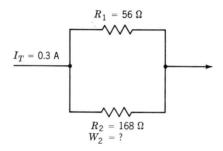

$R_1 = 56 \ \Omega$

$I_T = 0.3$ A

$R_2 = 168 \ \Omega$
$W_2 = ?$

FIGURE 6-1
The wattage rating of a resistor is equal to at least twice the wattage developed in it.

SOLUTION
In order to find the wattage developed in R_2 we must know the value of E_2 and ____.

$$I_2 = \frac{?}{R_1 + R_2} \times I_T \tag{4-6}$$

I_2

$$I_2 = \frac{56}{56 + ?} \times 0.3$$

R_1

168

$$I_2 = \frac{56}{224} \times 0.3 = \text{\_\_\_\_\_} \text{ A}$$

0.075

2 Find E_2.

$$E_2 = I_2 \times \text{\_\_\_\_}\tag{3-4}$$

R_2

$$E_2 = \text{\_\_\_\_} \times 168$$

0.075

$$E_2 = \text{\_\_\_\_} \text{ V}$$

12.6

3 Find the wattage developed in R_2.

$$P = I \times E \tag{6-1}$$

$$P = 0.075 \times \underline{\hspace{1cm}}$$

$$P = \underline{\hspace{1cm}} \text{ W}$$

4   Find the wattage rating.

$$\text{Wattage rating} = \underline{\hspace{1cm}} \times \text{wattage}$$

$$\text{Wattage rating} = 2 \times 0.945$$

$$= \underline{\hspace{1cm}} \text{ W}$$

$$\text{or Wattage rating} = \underline{\hspace{1cm}} \text{ W} \qquad Ans.$$

	12.6
	0.945
	2
	1.89
	2

PROBLEMS

1. An automobile starting motor draws 80 A at 6 V. How much power is drawn from the battery?
2. A 20-hp motor takes 74 A at 230 V when operating at full load. Find the power used.
3. What is the wattage dissipated as heat by a 550-Ω resistor operating at 110 V and 0.2 A?
4. What is the power consumed by an automobile headlight if it takes 2.8 A at 6 V?
5. Find the power used by a 3.4-A soldering iron at 110 V.
6. The heater of a 12B4A vertical-deflection-amplifier tube uses 12.6 V and 0.3 A. Find the power consumed.
7. The high contact resistance of a poorly wired electric toaster plug reduced the current by 1 A on a 110-V line. Find the power wasted in the plug.
8. How much power is consumed by an electric clock using 0.02 A at 110 V?
9. If the voltage drop across a spark-plug air gap is 30 V, find the power consumed in sending 0.002 A across the gap.
10. Find the power dissipated by the collector of a transistor that passes 0.25 A at 9.2 V.
11. A power supply delivers 0.16 A at 250 V to a public-address amplifier. Find the watts of power delivered.
12. A 180-Ω line cord resistor carrying 0.15 A causes a voltage drop of 27 V. How much power must be dissipated as heat? What must be the wattage rating of the line cord?
13. A window air conditioner is rated at 7.5 A and is operated on a 120-V line. Find the wattage used by the conditioner.
14. An electric oven uses 36.3 A at 117 V. Find the wattage generated by the oven.
15. An emitter bias resistor carries 0.045 A at 10 V. What must be its wattage rating?
16. An electric enameling kiln takes 9.2 A from a 117-V line. Find the power used.

17. How much power is used by a ³⁄₄-ton air conditioner drawing 11.4 A from a 220-V line?
18. A cathode bias resistor causes a drop of 26.4 V when 0.45 A flows through it. What power must be dissipated by the resistor?
19. How many watts are dissipated as heat by a 135-Ω line cord resistor if it carries 0.22 A at 30 V?
20. Fifteen lamps in parallel each take 1.67 A when connected to a 120-V line. Find the wattage of each lamp and the total wattage used.

JOB 6-2 TOTAL POWER IN AN ELECTRICAL CIRCUIT

When using Ohm's law, we found that it could be used for total values in a circuit as well as for the individual parts of the circuit. In the same way, the formula for power may be used for total values.

FORMULA

$$P_T = I_T \times E_T \qquad \boxed{\text{6-2}}$$

where P_T = total power, W
   I_T = total current, A
   E_T = total voltage, V

EXAMPLE 6-4   Two 0.62-A lamps, each drawing 120 V, are connected in series. Find the total power used.

SOLUTION
Given: $I_1 = I_2 = 0.62$ A   Find: $P_T = ?$
   $E_1 = E_2 = 120$ V

1 Find the total voltage.

$$E_T = E_1 + E_2 = 120 + 120 = 240 \text{ V} \qquad (3\text{-}2)$$

2 Find the total current.

$$I_T = I_1 = I_2 = 0.62 \text{ A} \qquad (3\text{-}1)$$

3 Find the total power.

$$P_T = I_T \times E_T \qquad (6\text{-}2)$$

$$P_T = 0.62 \times 240 = 148.8 \text{ W} \qquad Ans.$$

EXAMPLE 6-5   If the same lamps were connected in parallel across 120 V, find the total power used and compare it with the power used when the lamps were connected in series as in Example 6-4.

SOLUTION

Given: $I_1 = I_2 = 0.62$A   Find: $P_T = ?$

$E_1 = E_2 = 120$ V

1   Find the total voltage.

$$E_T = 120 \text{ V} \quad \text{(given)}$$

2   Find the total current.

$$I_T = I_1 + I_2 = 0.62 + 0.62 = 1.24 \text{ A} \qquad (4\text{-}2)$$

3   Find the total power.

$$P_T = I_T \times E_T \qquad (6\text{-}2)$$

$$P_T = 1.24 \times 120 = 148.8 \text{ W} \qquad Ans.$$

The total power in parallel is the same as the total power in series.

If the power used by the parts of a circuit is known, the total power may be found by the following

FORMULA

$$P_T = P_1 + P_2 + P_3 \qquad \boxed{6\text{-}3}$$

where P_T = total power, W.

P_1, P_2, P_3 are the power used by the parts of the circuit.

SELF-TEST 6-6   Two resistors in series form the base-bias voltage divider for an audio amplifier. The voltage drops across them are 2.4 V and 6.6 V, respectively, in the 0.0015-A circuit. Find the power used by the circuit.

SOLUTION

Given: $E_1 = 2.4$ V   Find: $P_T = ?$

$E_2 = \underline{\quad}$ V	6.6
$I_T = I_1 = I_2 = \underline{\quad\quad}$ A	0.0015

1   Find P_1.

$P_1 = I_1 \times E_1$	(6-1)	
$P_1 = 0.0015 \times \underline{\quad}$		2.4
$P_1 = \underline{\quad}$ W		0.0036

2   Find P_2.

$P_2 = I_2 \times E_2$	(6-1)	
$P_2 = 0.0015 \times 6.6 = \underline{\quad}$ W		0.0099

3 Find the total power.

$$P_T = P_1 + P_2 \qquad\qquad (6\text{-}3)$$

$$P_T = 0.0036 + 0.0099 = \underline{\qquad} \text{ W} \qquad Ans. \qquad\qquad 0.0135$$

The problem can be solved by another method.

1 Find the total voltage used by both resistors. Since they are in series,

$$E_T = E_1 + ? \qquad\qquad (3\text{-}2) \qquad E_2$$

$$E_T = 2.4 + ? \qquad\qquad\qquad 6.6$$

$$E_T = \underline{\qquad} \text{ V} \qquad\qquad\qquad 9$$

2 Find the total power.

$$P_T = I_T \times \underline{\qquad} \qquad\qquad (6\text{-}2) \qquad E_T$$

$$P_T = \underline{\qquad} \times 9 \qquad\qquad\qquad 0.0015$$

$$P_T = \underline{\qquad} \text{ W} \qquad Ans. \qquad\qquad 0.0135$$

PROBLEMS

1. Seven Christmas-tree lamps are connected in series. Each lamp requires 16 V and 0.1 A. Find the total power used.
2. If the same lamps were connected in parallel across a 16-V source, what would be the power taken?
3. A certain transistor must pass a maximum of 0.3 A. If it is rated at 0.15 W maximum, will it be able to withstand a 0.45-V collector-emitter voltage?
4. What is the total power used by a 4.5-A electric iron, a 0.85-A fan, and a 2.2-A refrigerator motor if they are all connected in parallel across a 115-V line?
5. A 1AD2 high-voltage rectifier in a television receiver is in series with a 3.3-Ω ballast resistor. What is the total power used by the circuit if the 1AD2 uses 1.25 V at 0.2 A?
6. Find the power drawn from a 6-V battery by a parallel circuit of two headlights (4 A each) and two taillights (0.9 A each).
7. In Fig. 5-49, the generator voltage is 120 V. The motor takes 12.4 A, and each lamp takes 0.92 A. Neglecting the line drop, find the total power used by the devices.
8. An electric percolator drawing 9 A and an electric toaster drawing 10.2 A are connected in parallel to the 117-V house line. Find the total power consumed.
9. In a circuit similar to that shown in Fig. 5-1, $E_T = 200$ V, $R_1 = 10\ \Omega$, $R_2 = 15\ \Omega$, $R_3 = 40\ \Omega$, and $R_4 = 60\ \Omega$. Find (a) the total current, (b) the power used by each resistor, and (c) the total power.
10. In a circuit similar to that shown in Fig. 5-15, $E_T = 13$ V, $R_1 = 2\ \Omega$, $R_2 = 1\ \Omega$, $R_3 = 6\ \Omega$, $R_4 = 3\ \Omega$, $R_5 = 40\ \Omega$, and $R_6 = 3\ \Omega$. Find (a) the

total current, (b) the power used by each resistor, and (c) the total power.

JOB 6-3   SOLVING THE POWER FORMULA FOR CURRENT OR VOLTAGE

In Job 2-8 we learned how to solve Ohm's law for the current or the resistance. The power formula is the same general type of equation, and we can use the methods learned in Job 2-8 to solve it for values of current or voltage.

EXAMPLE 6-7   What is the operating voltage of an electric toaster rated at 600 W if it draws 5 A?

SOLUTION
Given: $P = 600$ W   Find: $E = ?$
       $I = 5$ A

$$P = I \times E \qquad\qquad (6\text{-}1)$$

$$600 = 5 \times E$$

$$E = \frac{600}{5} = 120 \text{ V} \qquad Ans.$$

SELF-TEST 6-8   A stabilizing resistor in the emitter circuit of a 2N109 output transistor develops a voltage drop of 1.2 V while consuming 0.06 W of power. Find the current through the resistor.

SOLUTION
Given: $P = 0.06$ W   Find: ___ = ? | I
       $E = $ ___ V | 1.2

$$P = I \times E \qquad\qquad (6\text{-}1)$$ |

$$\text{\underline{\hphantom{xx}}} = I \times 1.2$$ | 0.06

$$I = \frac{0.06}{?}$$ | 1.2

$$I = \text{\underline{\hphantom{xx}}} \text{ A} \qquad Ans.$$ | 0.05

PROBLEMS

1. A 550-W neon sign operates on a 110-V line. Find the current drawn.
2. What current is drawn by a 480-W soldering iron from a 120-V line?

3. Find the current drawn by a 1,200-W aircraft system from a 24-V source.

4. A resistor is capable of dissipating 10 W of power. If the current is 0.3 A, what is the maximum voltage drop permitted across the resistor?

5. The quiescent point of a transistor is at a collector current of 0.06 A and a collector voltage of 20 V. Find the transistor power dissipation with no signal applied.

6. What current is drawn by a 1,500-W electric ironing machine from a 120-V line?

7. What current is drawn by a 55-candlepower 110-V lamp if it uses 1 W per candlepower?

8. Two resistors, each dissipating 2 W, are connected in series with a 40-V source. What is the total current drawn? What is the current in each resistor?

9. Twenty 60-W lamps are connected in parallel to light a stage. Find the current drawn from a 220-V source.

10. A washing-machine motor requires 350 W. If it draws $3\frac{1}{8}$ A, find the operating voltage.

11. An electric broiler rated at 1,550 W operates from a 117-V line. The available fuses are rated at 20, 30, 50, and 60 A. Which fuse should be used in the circuit to protect the broiler?

12. A 6EM5 tube is used in the vertical output stage of a television receiver and delivers 3.4 W. If the current is 0.032 A, what is the voltage across the circuit?

13. How much current is drawn from a 110-V line by a soldering gun rated at 135 W?

14. In the circuit shown in Fig. 6-2, find (*a*) the current in the load I_L and (*b*) the voltage drop across R_A.

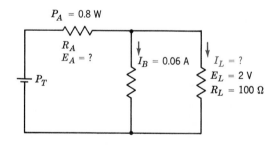

FIGURE 6-2

JOB 6-4 INTERMEDIATE REVIEW OF POWER

In some problems, the power cannot be found because either the voltage or the current is unknown. In these instances, the unknown value is found by Ohm's law.

EXAMPLE 6-9   Find the power taken by a soldering iron of 60 Ω resistance if it draws a current of 2 A.

SOLUTION

Given: $R = 60 \ \Omega$ Find: $P = ?$
       $I = 2 \ A$

1   Find the voltage.

$$E = I \times R \qquad\qquad (2\text{-}1)$$

$$E = 2 \times 60 = 120 \ V$$

2   Find the power.

$$P = I \times E \qquad\qquad (6\text{-}1)$$

$$P = 2 \times 120 = 240 \ W \qquad Ans.$$

SELF-TEST 6-10   Find the power used by the 11-Ω resistance element
of an electric furnace if the voltage is 110 V.

SOLUTION

Given: $R = 11 \ \Omega$ Find: $P = ?$
       $E = \underline{\quad} \ V$ 110

1   Find the current.

$$E = I \times R \qquad\qquad (2\text{-}1)$$

$$110 = I \times \underline{\quad} \qquad\qquad\qquad 11$$

$$I = \frac{110}{11} = \underline{\quad} \ A \qquad\qquad\qquad 10$$

2   Find the power.

$$P = \underline{\quad} \times E \qquad\qquad (6\text{-}1) \qquad\qquad I$$

$$P = 10 \times 110 = \underline{\quad\quad} \ W \qquad Ans. \qquad\qquad 1{,}100$$

PROBLEMS

1.   A 20-Ω neon sign operates on a 120-V line. Find the power used
     by the sign.
2.   Find the power used by a 55-Ω electric light which draws 2 A.
3.   What is the wattage dissipated by a 10,000-Ω voltage divider if
     the voltage across it is 250 V? What is its wattage rating?
4.   What is the maximum power obtainable from a Grenet cell of 2 V
     which has an internal resistance of 0.02 Ω?
5.   A 240-Ω resistor in the emitter circuit of the output stage of a
     transistor radio carries 0.005 A. Find the wattage developed in
     the resistor.
6.   The resistance of an ammeter is 0.025 Ω. Find the power used by
     the meter when it reads 4 A.
7.   What is the power consumed by a 90-Ω subway-car heater if the
     operating voltage is 550 V?

8. A 40-Ω pilot light is to be operated in a 0.15-A circuit. How many watts are developed in the lamp?

9. A 20-Ω toaster operates on a 115-V line. Find the power used.

10. A 12FX5 tube is used as an audio output tube in the RCA model KCS 176 television receiver. If it has a cathode resistor of 180 Ω which develops a bias of 5 V, find the power used by the bias resistor.

11. A voltmeter has an internal resistance of 220,000 Ω. How much power does it use when the meter reads 110 V?

12. In the Magnavox TV chassis T928 series, a 4,000-Ω dropping resistor is used to feed voltage to the screen of the 6BQ6 horizontal output tube. If the screen current is 0.03 A, how many watts are developed in the resistor?

13. In the circuit shown in Fig. 6-3, find (a) the total resistance, (b) the total current, and (c) the total power.

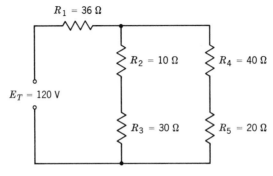

$R_1 = 36\ \Omega$

$R_2 = 10\ \Omega$ $R_4 = 40\ \Omega$

$E_T = 120$ V

$R_3 = 30\ \Omega$ $R_5 = 20\ \Omega$

FIGURE 6-3

14. In a circuit similar to that shown in Fig. 5-15, $E_T = 188$ V, $R_1 = 22\ \Omega$, $R_2 = 18\ \Omega$, $R_3 = 70\ \Omega$, $R_4 = 80\ \Omega$, $R_5 = 56\ \Omega$, and $R_6 = 30\ \Omega$. Find (a) the total current, (b) the power used by each resistor, and (c) the total power.

15. In Fig. 6-4, find (a) the total resistance, (b) the total current, and (c) the total power.

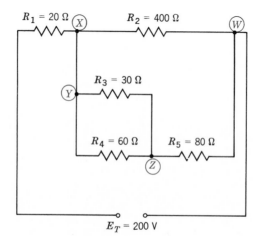

$R_1 = 20\ \Omega$ (X) $R_2 = 400\ \Omega$ (W)

$R_3 = 30\ \Omega$
(Y)

$R_4 = 60\ \Omega$ $R_5 = 80\ \Omega$
(Z)

$E_T = 200$ V

FIGURE 6-4

TEST—POWER

1. Find the power used by a 4.5-A soldering iron when it is operated from a 110-V line.
2. A motor drawing 5 A is connected in parallel with another motor drawing 8 A. The line voltage is 120 V. Find the total power consumed.
3. A 6GK6 power pentode delivers 4.5 W. If the current is 0.038 A, what is the voltage across the circuit?
4. A 22-Ω electric toaster operates from a 110-V line. Find the power used.
5. A 40-Ω neon sign operates on a 120-V line. Find the power used.

JOB 6-5   CHECKUP ON USING FORMULAS WITH EXPONENTS (DIAGNOSTIC TEST)

Many problems in electrical work are solved with formulas which use special mathematical symbols called *exponents*. The following problems involve the use of formulas which contain exponents. If you have any difficulty with these problems, see Job 6-6 which follows.

PROBLEMS

1. Using the formula $P = E^2/R$, find the value of P if $E = 100$ and $R = 50$.
2. Using the formula $P = I^2R$, find the value of P if $I = 3$ and $R = 40$.
3. Using the formula emf $= (L \times n)/10^8$, find the value of emf if $L = 50 \times 10^6$ and $n = 40$.
4. Using the formula $R = (k \times l)/D^2$, find the value of R if $k = 10.4$, $l = 100$, and $D = 4$.
5. Using the formula $F = \mu F/10^6$, find the number of farads equal to 0.5 μF.

JOB 6-6   BRUSHUP ON FORMULAS CONTAINING EXPONENTS

   Meaning of an exponent. Exponents provide a convenient shorthand method for writing and expressing many mathematical operations. For example, $2 \times 2 \times 2$ may be written as 2^3. The number 3 above and to the right of the 2 is called an *exponent*. The exponent says, "Write the number beneath it as many times as the exponent indicates, and then multiply." An exponent may be used with letters as well as numbers. Thus, R^3 means $R \times R \times R$. The exponent 2 is read as the word "square." The exponent 3 is read as the word "cube." When the exponent is any other number, it is read as "to the fourth power," "to the seventh power," etc. For example:

$$3^2 \text{ (3 square)} = 3 \times 3 = 9$$
$$5^3 \text{ (5 cube)} = 5 \times 5 \times 5 = 125$$
$$2^4 \text{ (2 to the fourth power)} = 2 \times 2 \times 2 \times 2 = 16$$
$$10^1 \text{ (10 to the first power)} = 10$$
$$10^2 \text{ (10 square)} = 10 \times 10 = 100$$
$$10^3 \text{ (10 cube)} = 10 \times 10 \times 10 = 1,000$$
$$10^6 \text{ (10 to the sixth power)} = 10 \times 10 \times 10 \times 10 \times 10 \times 10 = 1,000,000$$

EXAMPLE 6-11   The formula for the area of a circle is $A = \pi R^2$. Find the area of a circle if the radius R equals 5 in and $\pi = 3.14$.

SOLUTION
Given: $A = \pi R^2$ Find: $A = ?$
      $R = 5$ in
      $\pi = 3.14$

1   Write the formula.

$$A = \pi R^2$$

2   Substitute numbers.

$$A = 3.14 \times 5^2$$

3   Simplify the exponent.

$$A = 3.14 \times 25$$

4   Multiply.

$$A = 78.5 \text{ in}^2 \quad Ans.$$

SELF-TEST 6-12   The resistance R of a copper wire is found by the formula $R = \dfrac{10.4 \times L}{D^2}$, in which $D =$ the diameter of the wire in mils (1 mil $= 0.001$ in) and $L =$ the length of the wire in feet. Find the resistance of 5,000 ft of wire whose diameter is 50 mils.

SOLUTION
Given: $L = 5,000$ ft   Find: ___ $= ?$ R
        $D =$ ___ mils   50

1   Write the formula.

$$R = \frac{10.4 \times L}{D^2}$$

2   Substitute numbers.

$$R = \frac{10.4 \times ?}{(?)^2}$$ 5,000
                                                                         50

3   Simplify the exponent.

$$R = \frac{10.4 \times 5,000}{?}$$ 2,500

4 Cancel.

$$R = 10.4 \times \_\_\_$$

2

5 Multiply.

$$R = \_\_\_ \ \Omega \quad Ans.$$

20.8

SELF-TEST 6-13   The formula for the power gain of a common-base transistor circuit is

$$PG = \alpha^2 \times \frac{R_L}{R_i}$$

Find the power gain of a transistor if the current gain $\alpha = 0.96$, the load resistance $R_L = 15,000 \ \Omega$, and the input resistance $R_i = 300 \ \Omega$.

SOLUTION

Given: $\alpha = 0.96$ Find: PG = ?
    $R_L = 15,000 \ \Omega$
    $R_i = 300 \ \Omega$

1   Write the formula.

$$PG = \alpha^2 \times \frac{R_L}{R_i}$$

2   Substitute numbers.

$$PG = (0.96)^2 \times \frac{15,000}{?}$$

300

3   Simplify the exponent.

$$PG = \_\_\_ \times \frac{15,000}{300}$$

0.92

4   Simplify the fraction.

$$PG = 0.92 \times \_\_\_$$

50

5   Multiply.

$$PG = \_\_\_ \quad Ans.$$

46

PROBLEMS

1.   Using the formula $A = D^2$, find the area A, in circular mils, of a wire whose diameter $D = 60$ mils.
2.   Using the formula for the volume of a cube, $V = S^3$, find the volume of a cube whose side $S = 10$ in.
3.   The volume of a sphere is given by the formula $V = 4.2R^3$, in which V is the volume in cubic inches and R is the radius of the sphere. Find the volume of a sphere whose radius is 4 in.
4.   Using the formula $S = \frac{1}{2}gt^2$, find the distance S that a body will

fall if the acceleration of gravity $g = 32$ feet per second per second and the time $t = 8$ s.

5. Using the formula $A = \pi R^2$, find the value of A if $\pi = 3.14$ and $R = 9$.

6. Using the formula for the volume of a cylinder, $V = \pi R^2 H$, find the volume V if $\pi = {}^{22}/_7$, $R = 3.5$, and $H = 14$.

7. Using the formula $A = mA/10^3$, change 450 mA into amperes.

8. The force F between two magnetic poles of strength S and s when separated by a distance d cm is given by the formula $F = (S \times s)/d^2$ dyn (dyne). Find F if $S = 70$, $s = 50$, and $d = 10$.

9. Using the formula for the horsepower rating of a gasoline engine, $H = (nD^2)/2.5$, find the horsepower rating H of an engine if the number of cylinders $n = 6$ and the diameter of each cylinder $D = 3$ in.

10. Using the formula $E = (L \times n)/10^8$, find the value of E if $L = 40,000$ and $n = 80$.

11. Using the formula $V^2 = 2gh$, find h if $V = 25$ and $g = 32$.

12. The formula for the volume of a cone is

$$V = \frac{1}{3}\pi R^2 H$$

Find the volume of a cone if $\pi = 3.14$, $R = 7$ in, and $H = 12$ in.

JOB 6-7 THE EXPONENTIAL POWER FORMULA

In Job 6-4, either the voltage or the current was unknown. These values were found by Ohm's law and then used to find the power. The two steps involved in solving problems of this type may be combined into a single formula. The power is given by

$$P = I \times E \tag{6-1}$$

But by Ohm's law,

$$E = I \times R \tag{2-1}$$

Therefore, we may substitute the quantity $I \times R$ for E. This gives

$$P = I \times I \times R$$

FORMULA

$$P = I^2 R \qquad \boxed{6\text{-}4}$$

Also by Ohm's law, $I = E/R$. Therefore, we may substitute the quantity E/R for I. Thus,

$$P = I \times E \tag{6-1}$$

Substituting,

$$P = \frac{E}{R} \times E$$

FORMULA

$$P = \frac{E^2}{R}$$

6-5

EXAMPLE 6-14   A 4,000-Ω base bias resistor in a silicon NPN amplifier transistor carries a base current of 0.005 A. Find the power consumed and the wattage rating required by the resistor.

SOLUTION
The diagram for the circuit is shown in Fig. 6-5.

$$P = I^2R \qquad\qquad (6\text{-}4)$$

$$P = (0.005)^2 \times 4,000$$

$$P = 0.005 \times 0.005 \times 4,000$$

$$P = 0.000025 \times 4,000$$

$$P = 0.1 \text{ W} \qquad Ans.$$

$$\text{Wattage rating} = 2 \times P$$

$$= 2 \times 0.1 = 0.2 \text{ W} \qquad Ans.$$

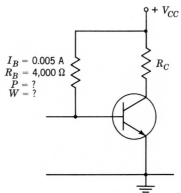

FIGURE 6-5

EXAMPLE 6-15   A motor has a total resistance of 20 Ω and operates on a 120-V line. Find the power used.

SOLUTION
Given: $R = 20 \ \Omega$ Find: $P = ?$
    $E = 120$ V

$$P = \frac{E^2}{R} \qquad\qquad (6\text{-}5)$$

$$P = \frac{(120)^2}{20} = \frac{120 \times 120}{20} = 720 \text{ W} \qquad Ans.$$

SELF-TEST 6-16   Find the wattage rating of R_1 and R_2 in the voltage divider circuit shown in Fig. 6-6.

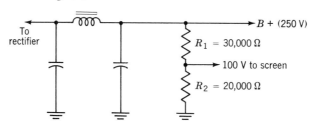

FIGURE 6-6

A simple voltage-divider circuit.

SOLUTION

The voltage drop across R_1 is equal to the difference between the B+ voltage (250) and the screen voltage (100). Therefore, $E_1 = \underline{\hspace{1cm}}$ V.

$$P_1 = \frac{E_1^2}{R_1}$$

$$P_1 = \frac{(150)^2}{?}$$

$$P_1 = \frac{150 \times 150}{30,000}$$

$$P_1 = \underline{\hspace{1cm}} \text{ W}$$

$$\text{Wattage rating} = \underline{\hspace{1cm}} \times P_1$$

$$= 2 \times 0.75 = 1.5 \text{ W}$$

However, since the 1.5-W size is not usually stocked, we must use a 2-W 30,000-Ω resistor.   *Ans.*

For R_2, the voltage drop $E_2 = \underline{\hspace{1cm}}$ V

$$P_2 = \frac{100 \times 100}{?}$$

$$P_2 = \underline{\hspace{1cm}} \text{ W}$$

Therefore,

$$\text{Wattage rating} = \underline{\hspace{1cm}} \text{ W} \qquad Ans.$$

150
30,000
0.75
2
100
20,000
1/2
1

PROBLEMS

1. A 30-Ω electric toaster draws 4 A. Find the power used.
2. If the voltage drop across a 10,000-Ω voltage divider is 90 V, find the power used.
3. Find the power consumed by a 100-Ω electric iron when operating on a 115-V line.
4. A poorly soldered joint has a contact resistance of 100 Ω. What is the power lost in the joint if the current is 0.5 A?

5. Two 2N406 transistors operating in push-pull deliver an average current of 0.05 A through a 2,600-Ω load resistance. Find the power developed.
6. Find the power used by a 15-Ω neon sign on a 110-V line.
7. The motor shown in Fig. 6-7 takes 1,400 W at 220 V. Find the current drawn. How many watts are consumed in the line wires if each has a resistance of 0.2 Ω?

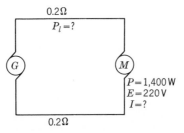

FIGURE 6-7

8. How much power is dissipated in the form of heat in a ballast resistor of 60 Ω if the current is 0.3 A?
9. A 100- and a 260-Ω resistor are connected in series to a 120-V source. Find the power used by each resistor.
10. Find the total voltage across the circuit shown in Fig. 6-8. What is the voltage across each resistor? What is the power taken by each resistor?

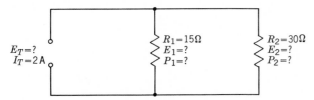

FIGURE 6-8

JOB 6-8   CHECKUP ON SQUARE ROOT (DIAGNOSTIC TEST)

In the last job we learned two new formulas which use the exponent 2. This exponent is read as the word "square." We can use these formulas to find the current, voltage, or resistance if we know the power. To do this, we must be able to do the opposite of "squaring" a number. This is called "finding the square root." We shall also use "square root" when we get to the study of ac circuits. Can you do the following problems? If you have any difficulty with them, turn to Job 6-9 which follows.

PROBLEMS

Find the square root of each of the following numbers:

1. 64	2. 169	3. 17.64	4. 3,481
5. 12,544	6. 57.76	7. 14	8. 567.9
9. 76,432	10. 30	11. 0.652	12. 870,000

JOB 6-9 BRUSHUP ON SQUARE ROOT

The *square root* of a number is that number which must be multiplied by *itself* in order to obtain the original number. The symbol for the square root is $\sqrt{}$. When a number appears under this symbol, it means that we are to find a number which can be multiplied by itself to give the number under the square-root symbol. For example, the square root of 9 ($\sqrt{9}$) must be the number 3 because only $3 \times 3 = 9$. Also,

$$\sqrt{16} = 4 \text{ because only } 4 \times 4 \text{ will equal } 16$$

$$\sqrt{25} = 5 \text{ because only } 5 \times 5 \text{ will equal } 25$$

$$\sqrt{36} = 6 \text{ because only } 6 \times 6 \text{ will equal } 36$$

These numbers under the square-root sign are called "perfect squares" because the square root of each is a whole number.

We can continue to find the square root of numbers in this manner until our knowledge of the multiplication table is insufficient to keep up with the large numbers involved. For example,

$$\sqrt{49} = 7 \qquad \sqrt{121} = 11$$

$$\sqrt{64} = 8 \qquad \sqrt{144} = 12$$

$$\sqrt{81} = 9 \qquad \sqrt{169} = 13$$

$$\sqrt{100} = 10$$

Somewhere along here we begin to forget whether 14×14 is 196 or not or whether 16×16 is 256 or not. You can see that we will not get very far if we rely on just our knowledge of the multiplication table. Besides, what about all those smaller numbers between these perfect squares like

$$\sqrt{7} = ?$$

$$\sqrt{15} = ?$$

$$\sqrt{32} = ?$$

There doesn't seem to be any number that we can multiply by itself to get 7 or 15 or 32. No, there isn't any *whole* number which is the square root of these numbers, but there are decimal numbers which will satisfy.

Obviously, as the numbers get beyond the range of the ordinary multiplication table, we feel the need for some system that will help us to find the square root of *any* number—large or small, whole number or decimal.

In the following system, it will help if we mark off the numbers into groups of two digits to a group. We start marking off the groups *at the decimal point.* If there is no decimal point indicated, it may be assumed to be at the *end* of the number.

EXAMPLE 6-17   Group the digits in the number 3,456.

SOLUTION

The decimal point is at the end of the number. Starting at the decimal point, the numbers are grouped two to a group as we move to the left.

$$\underset{\smile}{34} \; \underset{\smile}{56}.$$

EXAMPLE 6-18   Group the digits in the number 546.78.

SOLUTION

Starting at the decimal point and proceeding to the left, we find that the digit 5 is left over. In situations like this, the single digit at the extreme left is considered to be a group. Now, return to the decimal point and group the digits to the *right* of the point—two to a group. We should get

$$\underset{\smile}{5} \; \underset{\smile}{46}. \; \underset{\smile}{78}$$

EXAMPLE 6-19   Group the digits in the number 54,819.8.

SOLUTION

The 5 at the extreme left is again considered a group by itself, but a zero must be added after the 8 at the right to complete the group. We should get

$$\underset{\smile}{5} \; \underset{\smile}{48} \; \underset{\smile}{19} . \; \underset{\smile}{80}$$

EXAMPLE 6-20   Find the square root of 5,776.

SOLUTION

1   Locate the decimal point. In a whole number the decimal point is at the end of the number. Place the point in the answer directly above its position in the number.

$$\sqrt{5 \; 7 \; 7 \; 6}\,.$$

2   Separate the digits into groups—two digits to a group. Start at the decimal point, and group the digits to the left.

$$\sqrt{\underset{\smile}{57} \; \underset{\smile}{76}}\,.$$

3   Start with the first group (57). Find a number which when multiplied by itself will give an answer close to or equal to but not larger than 57. 8 squared is 64, but that is too large. 7 squared is 49, which is just right. Place the 7 over the first group in the answer and the 49 under the 57. Draw a line and subtract the 49 from the 57, leaving a remainder of 8.

$$\begin{array}{r} 7. \\ \sqrt{57\ 76}\,. \\ -49 \\ \hline 8 \end{array}$$

4   Bring down the next *group.* *Never* bring down a single number. Make a little box to the left of this new number 876. *Double* the answer at this point (the 7), and place it in this box. This will be the number 14.

$$\begin{array}{r} 7. \\ \sqrt{57\ 76}\,. \\ -49\ \ \text{x} \\ \hline 14\ \ \boxed{8\ 76} \end{array}$$

5   Place your finger over the *last digit* in the number 876. The number there will now appear to be 87. Divide the number in the box (14) into this 87. It will go about 6 times. Place this 6 in the answer above the second group, *and also place it next to the 14 in the box.*

$$\begin{array}{r} 7\ 6. \\ \sqrt{57\ 76}\,. \\ -49\ \ \text{x} \\ \hline 14\ 6\ \ \boxed{8\ 76} \end{array}$$

6   Multiply the 6 by the number just formed (the 146). If the product is larger than 876, we shall be forced to change the 6 to a smaller number. However, $6 \times 146 = 876$. Write this 876 under the 876 already there and subtract. Since there is no remainder, 76 is the exact square root of 5,776. *Check:* $76 \times 76 = 5,776$.

$$\begin{array}{r} 7\ \ 6\,. \\ \sqrt{57\ 76}\,. \\ -49\ \ \text{x} \\ \hline 14\ 6\ \ \boxed{8\ 76} \\ 8\ 76 \\ \hline 0 \end{array}$$

EXAMPLE 6-21   Find the square root of 930.25.

SOLUTION

1   Locate the decimal point. Place the point in the answer directly above its position in the number.

$$\sqrt{9\ \ 30.25}$$

2   Separate the digits into groups—two digits to a group. Start at the decimal point, and group the digits to the left. Return to the decimal point, and group the digits to the right.

$$\sqrt{9\ \ 30\ .25}$$

3   Start with the first group (9). Find a number which when multiplied by

itself will give an answer close to or equal to but not larger than 9. 3 squared is 9, which is exactly right. Place the 3 over the first group in the answer and the 9 under the 9 in the number. Draw a line, and subtract, leaving a remainder of 0.

$$\begin{array}{r} 3 . \\ \sqrt{9\ 30\ .\ 25} \\ -9 \end{array}$$

4   Bring down the next *group* (30). *Never* bring down a single digit. Make a little box to the left of this number. *Double* the answer at this point (the 3), and place it in this box. This will be the number 6.

$$\begin{array}{r} 3 . \\ \sqrt{9\ 30\ .\ 25} \\ 9 \ \ \text{x} \\ 6 \ |\ 30 \end{array}$$

5   Place your finger over the *last digit* in the number 30. The number there will now appear to be 3. Divide the number in the box (6) into this 3. It will go 0 times. Place this 0 in the answer above the second group, *and also place it next to the 6 in the box.*

$$\begin{array}{r} 3 \ \ 0 \ . \\ \sqrt{9\ 30\ .\ 25} \\ -9 \ \ \text{x} \\ 6\ 0 \ |\ 30 \end{array}$$

6   Multiply the 0 by the number just formed (the 60). The answer is 00. Write this 00 under the 30 and subtract, leaving a remainder of 30.

$$\begin{array}{r} 3 \ \ 0 \ . \\ \sqrt{9\ 30\ .\ 25} \\ -9 \ \ \text{x} \\ 6\ 0 \ |\ 30 \\ -00 \\ \overline{30} \end{array}$$

7   Bring down the next group (25). Make a little box to the left of this new number (3025). *Double* the answer up to this point (the 30), and place the product (60) in this box.

$$\begin{array}{r} 3 \ \ 0 \ . \\ \sqrt{9\ 30\ .\ 25} \\ -9 \ \ \text{x} \\ 60 \ |\ 30 \\ -00 \\ 60 \ |\ 30\ 25 \end{array}$$

8   Place your finger over the *last digit* in the number 3025. The number there will now appear to be 302. Divide the number in the box (60) into this 302. It will go 5 times. Place this 5 in the answer above the third group, *and also place it next to the 60 in the box.*

$$\begin{array}{r} 3 \quad 0 \,.\, 5 \\ \sqrt{9 \;\; 30 \,.\, 25} \\ -9 \quad \text{x} \,. \\ \end{array}$$

$$\begin{array}{r|l} 60 & 30 \\ & -00 \\ \hline 60\ 5 & 30\ 25 \end{array}$$

9   Multiply the 5 by the number just formed (the 605). The answer is 3025. Write this 3025 under the 3025 already there and subtract. Since there is no remainder, 30.5 is the exact square root of 930.25. *Check:* 30.5 × 30.5 = 930.25.

$$\begin{array}{r} 3 \quad 0 \,.\, 5 \\ \sqrt{9 \;\; 30 \,.\, 25} \\ -9 \quad \text{x} \\ \end{array}$$

$$\begin{array}{r|l} 60 & 30 \\ & -00 \\ \hline 605 & 30\ 25 \\ & -30\ 25 \\ \hline & 0 \end{array}$$

EXAMPLE 6-22   Find the square root of 12.

SOLUTION

1   Locate the decimal point. In a whole number the decimal point is at the end of the number. Place the point in the answer directly above its position in the number.

$$\sqrt{12\,.}\overline{}$$

2   Separate the digits into groups—two digits to a group. Start at the decimal point, and group the digits to the left.

$$\sqrt{1\ 2\,.}\overline{}$$

3   Start with the first group (12). Find a number which when multiplied by itself will give an answer close to or equal to but not larger than 12. 4 squared is 16, but that is too large. 3 squared is 9, which is less than 12 and so is just right. Place the 3 over the first group in the answer and the 9 under the 12 in the number. Draw a line, and subtract, leaving a remainder of 3.

$$\begin{array}{r} 3 \,. \\ \sqrt{1\ 2\,.} \\ -9 \\ \hline 3 \end{array}$$

4   Since there is a remainder, the square root will be a decimal. Add two *pairs* of zeros after the decimal point. Bring down the next group (00). Make a little box to the left of this number (300). *Double* the answer up to this point (the 3), and place the product (6) in this box.

$$
\begin{array}{r}
3\,. \\
\sqrt{1\,2}\,.\,\underset{\smile}{00}\;\underset{\smile}{00} \\
-\;9 \\
\hline
\end{array}
$$

$$6\;\boxed{\;3\;00}$$

5   Place your finger over the *last digit* in the number 300. The number there will now appear to be 30. Divide the number in the box (6) into this 30. It will go 5 times. Place this 5 in the answer above the second group, *and also place it next to the 6 in the box.* Multiply the 5 by the number just formed (the 65), and place the product (325) under the 300 already there. *But 325 is larger than 300, and we have evidently made an error in using the* 5. Since 5 was too large, use 4 instead of 5.

$$
\begin{array}{r}
3\,.\,5 \\
\sqrt{1\,2}\,.\,\underset{\smile}{00}\;\underset{\smile}{00} \\
-\;9\quad x \\
\hline
\end{array}
$$

$$6\;5\;\boxed{\;3\;00}$$
$$3\;25\qquad\text{Too large!}$$

6   Be sure to change *both* the 5 in the answer and the 5 in the 65 in the box to the number 4. Now multiply the 4 in the answer by the 64 in the box. Place the product (256) under the 300 already there, and subtract, leaving a remainder of 44.

$$
\begin{array}{r}
3\,.\,4 \\
\sqrt{1\,2}\,.\,\underset{\smile}{00}\;\underset{\smile}{00} \\
-\;9\quad x \\
\hline
\end{array}
$$

$$6\;4\;\boxed{\;3\;00}$$
$$\underline{-2\;56}$$
$$44$$

7   Bring down the next group (00). Make a little box to the left of this new number (4400). Double the answer up to this point (the 34) and place the product (68) in this box. Always disregard the decimal point in this step.

$$
\begin{array}{r}
3\,.\,4 \\
\sqrt{1\,2}\,.\,\underset{\smile}{00}\;\underset{\smile}{00} \\
-\;9\quad x\quad x \\
\hline
\end{array}
$$

$$6\;4\;\boxed{\;3\;00}$$
$$\underline{-2\;56}$$
$$68\;\boxed{\;44\;00}$$

8   Place your finger over the *last digit* in the number 4400. The number there will now appear to be 440. Divide the number in the box (68) into this 440. It will go 6 times. Place this 6 in the answer over the third group *and also place it next to the 68 in the box.*

$$
\begin{array}{r}
3\,.\,4\;\;6 \\
\sqrt{1\,2}\,.\,\underset{\smile}{00}\;\underset{\smile}{00} \\
-\;9\quad x\quad x \\
\hline
\end{array}
$$

$$64\;\boxed{\;3\;00}$$
$$\underline{-2\;56}$$
$$68\;6\;\boxed{\;44\;00}$$

9 Multiply the 6 by the number just formed (the 686), and place the product (4116) under the 4400 already there. Draw a line, and subtract, leaving a
remainder of 284. This remainder may be disregarded, as we shall rarely need
an answer more accurate than two decimal places. The problem may be worked
out to any number of decimal places and then "rounded off" to suit.

$$
\begin{array}{r}
3\ .\ 4\ \ 6 \\
\sqrt{1\ 2\ .\ 00\ \ 00} \\
-\ \ 9 \qquad \\
\hline
64\quad \fbox{\ 3\ 00} \\
-2\ 56 \\
\hline
68\ 6\quad \fbox{\ 44\ 00} \\
-41\ 16 \\
\hline
2\ 84
\end{array}
$$

Check: $3.46 \times 3.46 = 11.97$, or practically 12

PROBLEMS

Find the square root of the following numbers:

1. 3,481   2. 17.64   3. 15.21   4. 12,544   5. 18,769
6. 151.29   7. 40   8. 267   9. 65   10. 53.87

JOB 6-10   APPLICATIONS OF THE EXPONENTIAL POWER FORMULA

The formula $P = I^2R$ may be used to find the current I or the resistance
R. The formula $P = E^2/R$ may be used to find the voltage E or the resistance R.

EXAMPLE 6-23   What is the maximum current-carrying capacity of
a resistor marked 1,000 Ω and 10 W?

SOLUTION
Given: $R = 1,000\ \Omega$ Find: $I = ?$
$P = 10$ W

$$P = I^2R \tag{6-4}$$

$$10 = I^2 \times 1,000$$

$$I^2 = \frac{10}{1,000} = 0.01 \text{ A}$$

Now $I^2 = 0.01$ means that some number I multiplied by itself will equal
0.01. Another way to say this is "What number multiplied by itself will
equal 0.01?" This can be written as

$$I = \sqrt{0.01}$$

Actually, we have transformed the equation $I^2 = 0.01$ into $I = \sqrt{0.01}$ by taking the square root of both sides of the equality sign as shown in the following step. Since $\sqrt{I^2} = I$,

$$\sqrt{I^2} = \sqrt{0.01}$$

$$I = \sqrt{0.01}$$

$$I = 0.1 \text{ A} \qquad \textit{Ans.}$$

EXAMPLE 6-24   A 2N1479 transistor delivers an output power of 4 W at an average current of 0.2 A. What is the value of the load resistance?

SOLUTION
Given: $P = 4$ W   Find: $R = ?$
$\qquad I = 0.2$ A

$$P = I^2 R \tag{6-4}$$

$$4 = (0.2)^2 \times R$$

$$4 = 0.04 \times R$$

$$R = \frac{4}{0.04} = 100 \ \Omega \qquad \textit{Ans.}$$

EXAMPLE 6-25   The total resistance of the field coils of a 240-W motor is 60 Ω. Find the voltage needed to operate the motor at its rated power.

SOLUTION
Given: $R = 60 \ \Omega$ Find: $E = ?$
$\qquad P = 240$ W

1   Write the formula.

$$P = \frac{E^2}{R} \tag{6-5}$$

2   Substitute numbers.

$$\frac{240}{1} = \frac{E^2}{60}$$

3   Cross-multiply.

$$E^2 = 240 \times 60$$

4   Multiply.

$$E^2 = 14{,}400$$

5   Take the square root of both sides.

$$\sqrt{E^2} = \sqrt{14{,}400}$$

6   Since $\sqrt{E^2} = E$,

$$E = \sqrt{14,400}$$

7   Voltage is

$$E = 120 \text{ V} \qquad Ans.$$

SELF-TEST 6-26   What is the maximum current-carrying capacity of a resistor marked 5,000 Ω and 5 W?

SOLUTION

Given: $P = \underline{\quad}$ W   Find: $I = ?$

$R = \underline{\qquad}$ Ω

$$P = I^2 \times \underline{\quad}$$

$$5 = I^2 \times \underline{\qquad}$$

$$I^2 = \frac{5}{?}$$

$$I^2 = \underline{\qquad}$$

$$\sqrt{I^2} = \underline{\qquad}$$

$$I = \underline{\qquad} \text{ A} \qquad Ans.$$

5
5,000
R
5,000
5,000
0.001
$\sqrt{0.001}$
0.0316

PROBLEMS

1.   What current flows through a line supplying 1,500 W of power to an electric range of 15 Ω resistance?
2.   What voltage is necessary to operate an 18-W automobile headlight bulb of 2 Ω resistance?
3.   A 6DQ6B horizontal-deflection amplifier tube delivers 12 W of power at an average current of 0.06 A. What is the value of the load resistance?
4.   What is the current flowing through a 50-Ω electromagnet drawing 200 W?
5.   What is the maximum current-carrying capacity of a resistor marked 500 Ω and 10 W?
6.   Find the voltage drop across a corroded connection if its contact resistance is 100 Ω and it uses 4 W of power.
7.   Find the internal resistance of a 2-W electric clock which operates on a 110-V line.
8.   A 60- and a 40-W lamp are in parallel across 120 V. Find the combined resistance of the lamps.
9.   What current flows through the heater of a 6KM6 beam power tube which has a resistance of 4 Ω and uses 10.24 W of power?
10.   The 500-Ω cathode resistor for a 6ET7 television IF amplifier uses 0.2 W of power. Find the current in the resistor.

11. What is the voltage necessary to operate a 600-W neon sign whose resistance is 20 Ω?
12. The screen dropping resistor for a 12GN7 videoamplifier uses 0.36 W at 0.0024 A. Find the resistance of the dropping resistor.
13. An ammeter shunt has a resistance of 0.01 Ω and is rated at 15 W. Find the maximum safe current it can carry.
14. In a circuit similar to that shown in Fig. 6-2, $R_A = 1{,}000$ Ω, $P_T = 9$ W, $P_B = 2$ W, and $P_L = 3$ W. Find the current I_A.
15. The secondary of a filament transformer delivers 1.89 W to a tube filament whose resistance is 21 Ω. Find the voltage drop across the filament.

JOB 6-11   REVIEW OF ELECTRICAL POWER

The power used by any part of a circuit is equal to the _____ in that part multiplied by the _____ across that part.

	current
	voltage

The formula for power is

$$P = I \times \underline{\quad}$$

| | E |

where $P = $ _____, measured in _____.

$I = $ _____, measured in _____.

$E = $ _____, measured in _____.

power	watts
current	amperes
voltage	volts

This formula may be used to find

  P if ___ and E are known

  I if ___ and E are known

  E if P and ___ are known

I
P
I

  The wattage rating of a resistor is equal to ___ times the wattage developed in the resistor.

| 2 |

  The total power in a circuit may be found by the formulas

$$P_T = \underline{\quad} \times E_T$$

or

$$P_T = P_1 + \underline{\quad} + \underline{\quad}$$

I_T
P_2 P_3

In the expression 10^3, the exponent is the number ___.

5^3 means $5 \times 5 \times$ ___ or ___.

$10^3 = $ _____. $10^6 = $ _____.

3
5   125
1,000   1,000,000

  Some other formulas for power are:

$$P = \underline{\quad} \times R$$

and

$$P = \frac{E_2}{?}$$

I^2
R

The square root of a number is that number which must be multiplied by _____ to get the original number.

| itself |

The symbol for square root is ____.

$$\sqrt{16} = \underline{\hspace{1cm}}$$

$$\sqrt{E^2} = \underline{\hspace{1cm}}$$

$$\sqrt{I^2} = \underline{\hspace{1cm}}$$

When finding the square root of a number, the digits should be marked off, ____ digits to a group, starting at the _____ point.

The decimal point in a whole number is at the ____ of the number.

Group the digits in the following numbers preparatory to finding the square root.

a   469.4   _____
b   8062   _____
c   12,345 _____
d   0.012   _____
e   0.002   _____
f   6.05   _____
g   0.00006 _____

$\sqrt{}$

4

E

I

2   decimal

end

4 69. 40
80 62.
1 23 45.
0.01 20
0.00 20
6. 05
0.00 00 60

PROBLEMS

1. Find the power used by an electric toaster if it draws 6 A from a 110-V line.
2. Find the power used by a 22-Ω motor if the current is 10 A.
3. Find the total power drawn by the four lamps shown in Fig. 6-9.

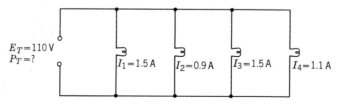

$E_T = 110\,V$
$P_T = ?$

$I_1 = 1.5\,A$ $I_2 = 0.9\,A$ $I_3 = 1.5\,A$ $I_4 = 1.1\,A$

FIGURE 6-9

4. What current is drawn by a 250-W electric vacuum cleaner when operated on 110 V?
5. Three 18-V 0.8-A bells are in series. Find the total power.
6. How many watts of power are dissipated in a 100,000-Ω voltage divider if the voltage across it is 300 V?
7. What voltage is required to operate a 25-W automobile headlight bulb properly if the current drawn is 4 A?
8. Find the resistance of a 1,000-W electric ironing machine if it uses 5 amp.
9. A toy electric train semaphore is made of a 28-Ω lamp in parallel with a solenoid coil with an effective resistance of 42 Ω. If the total current drawn is 0.6 A, find (a) the total resistance and (b) the total power used.
10. The combined resistance of a coffee percolator and toaster in

parallel is 22 Ω. Find the total power used if the line voltage is 110 V.

11. What power is dissipated in the form of heat in a 130-Ω ballast resistor designed to use up 40 V of excess voltage?

12. What is the voltage needed to operate a 10-W electric train accessory whose resistance is 15 Ω?

13. A 100- and a 60-W lamp are connected in parallel across 120 V. Find the combined resistance.

14. What is the maximum current-carrying capacity of a resistor marked 5,000 Ω and 20 W?

15. A number of incandescent lamps in parallel are supplied by a generator delivering 112 V at its brushes. The resistance of each of the two leads carrying current to the lamps is 0.05 Ω and causes a voltage drop of 2 V. If each lamp draws 50 W, how many lamps are lit? *Hint:*

1 Find the line current.

$$E_l = I_l \times R_l \qquad\qquad (5\text{-}1)$$

2 Find the voltage at the load.

$$E_L = E_G - E_l \qquad\qquad (5\text{-}3)$$

3 Find the power supplied to the load.

$$P_L = I_l \times E_L \qquad\qquad (6\text{-}1)$$

4 The number of lamps = $P_L \div$ wattage per lamp.

16. In a circuit similar to that shown in Fig. 5-21, $E_T = 100$ V, $R_1 = 50$ Ω, $R_2 = 25$ Ω, $R_3 = 8$ Ω, $R_4 = 2$ Ω, $R_5 = 10$ Ω, $R_6 = 15$ Ω, $R_7 = 105$ Ω, $R_8 = 450$ Ω, and $R_9 = 20$ Ω. Find (*a*) the total resistance of the circuit, (*b*) the total current in the circuit, and (*c*) the total power used by the circuit.

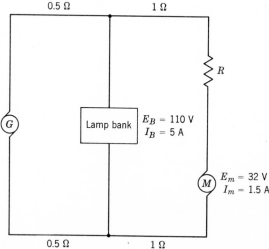

FIGURE 6-10

17. A dc generator supplies a 5-A lamp bank and a 1.5-A motor as shown in Fig. 6-10. The resistor R reduces the voltage to that required by the motor. Find (a) the terminal voltage of the generator, (b) the wattage dissipated by the resistor R, (c) the wattage lost in all the line wires, and (d) the total power supplied to the circuit.

TEST—POWER

1. Find the current drawn by a 1,100-W electric heater when operated on a 110-V line.
2. What should be the wattage rating of a 125-Ω resistor if it must carry 0.2 A?
3. Find the power consumed by a 50-Ω lamp which operates at 110 V.
4. What is the maximum current-carrying capacity of a resistor marked 200 Ω and 10 W?
5. Two 2N407 transistors operating in push-pull deliver 0.36 W to the primary of a transformer. If the current through the primary is 0.012 A, what is its resistance?

ALGEBRA FOR COMPLEX ELECTRICAL CIRCUITS

There are many circuits which cannot be solved by the methods used in Chap. 5. These extremely complicated circuits must be solved by the application of Kirchhoff's laws, which will be discussed in the next chapter. However, the solution of these circuits by Kirchhoff's laws requires an extension of our knowledge of algebra.

JOB 7-1 COMBINING LIKE TERMS

Different quantities of the same item may be added or subtracted. Thus, 2 apples plus 3 apples will equal 5 apples. Similarly, 3 pencils subtracted from 5 pencils will equal 2 pencils. If we use the symbol a for apples and p for pencils, these statements are shortened to read

$$2a + 3a = 5a \qquad \text{and} \qquad 5p - 3p = 2p$$

Quantities involving the *same* letter or letter combinations are called *like terms*. The process of adding or subtracting these like terms is called *combining* terms.

RULE	To combine like terms, combine the numerical quantities and place the result before the common letter.

EXAMPLE 7-1   Combine the following like terms:

$$3x + 4x = 7x$$

$$9y - 2y = 7y$$

$$4I_1 + 5I_1 = 9I_1$$

223

Note: A letter that stands alone such as x, R, or T means $1x$, $1R$, or $1T$. Thus, $4x + x$ means $4x + 1x$ or $5x$.

$$6R + 3R - R = 8R \qquad 1.2x + 3.4x = 4.6x$$
$$4.7R + 2R = 6.7R \qquad 7.8x - 4x = 3.8x$$

SELF-TEST 7-2   Combine the following like terms.

$$2 \text{ mA} + 8 \text{ mA} = \underline{\hspace{1cm}} \text{mA}$$

$$8R + R + 0.2R = 9.2 \underline{\hspace{1cm}}$$

$$5K - 2K + 4K = \underline{\hspace{1cm}}$$

$$8I_2 + 4I_2 - 3I_2 = \underline{\hspace{1cm}}$$

| 10 |
| R |
| $7K$ |
| $9I_2$ |

PROBLEMS

Combine the following like terms.

1. $3x + 5x$
2. $6y - 4y$
3. $8R - 2R$
4. $2I + 5I$
5. $4x + 7x + x$
6. $8y - y + 4y$
7. $4x + 3x - 2x$
8. $2.5R + 1.2R$
9. $5.6R - 1.2R$
10. $2I + 3.7I$
11. $7.5x - 4x$
12. $\frac{1}{2}y + \frac{1}{4}y$
13. $\frac{1}{2}T + \frac{1}{3}T$
14. $x - 0.2x$
15. $1.2R + 5.4R + 2.4R$
16. $3I + 5I + 0.2I$
17. $5.6x + 3.7x - 1.8x$
18. $x + 5x - 0.6x$
19. $7x - 3.5x + x$
20. $y - 0.4y$
21. $5.2R + 1.8R - 0.4R$

Using Fig. 7-1, express the total length D of the block in terms of x.

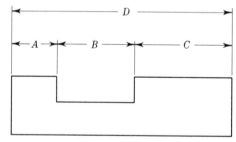

FIGURE 7-1

22. $A = x$, $B = 2x$, and $C = 3x$
23. $A = \frac{3}{4}x$, $B = 1\frac{1}{2}x$, and $C = \frac{5}{8}x$
24. $A = 0.05x$, $B = 1.25x$, and $C = 0.4x$

Using Fig. 7-2, find the measurement B, if

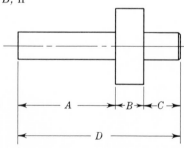

FIGURE 7-2

25. $A = 3x$, $C = x$, and $D = 7x$
26. $A = 2\frac{1}{2}y$, $C = \frac{3}{4}y$, and $D = 5\frac{7}{8}y$
27. $A = 1.6x$, $C = 0.28x$, and $D = 3x$

JOB 7-2 COMBINING UNLIKE TERMS

Unlike terms are those in which the letter portions are *different*. $4R$, $3X$, $3Y$, and $4I$ are all unlike terms. Similarly, $4X$ and the number 6 are unlike terms because the number 6 has no letter.

RULE	To combine several quantities involving unlike terms, combine each group of like terms separately.

EXAMPLE 7-3 Combine terms.

$$2x + 4y + 5x + 7y$$

SOLUTION

1 Combine the similar x terms.

$$2x + 5x = 7x$$

2 Combine the similar y terms.

$$4y + 7y = 11y$$

3 Since unlike terms may *not* be combined, state the answer.

$$7x + 11y \quad Ans.$$

EXAMPLE 7-4 Combine terms.

$$2R + 4I + 7 + 5R - I - 3$$

SOLUTION

1 Combine the similar R terms.

$$2R + 5R = 7R$$

2 Combine the similiar I terms.

$$4I - I = 3I$$

3 Combine the similar "number" terms.

$$7 - 3 = 4$$

4 State the answer.

$$7R + 3I + 4 \quad Ans.$$

EXAMPLE 7-5   Combine terms.

$$8I_1 + 5I_2 + 7I_3 + 2I_1 - I_3 - 3I_2$$

SOLUTION

1   Combine the similar I_1 terms.

$$8I_1 + 2I_1 = 10I_1$$

2   Combine the similar I_2 terms.

$$5I_2 - 3I_2 = 2I_2$$

3   Combine the similar I_3 terms.

$$7I_3 - I_3 = 6I_3$$

4   State the answer.

$$10I_1 + 2I_2 + 6I_3 \qquad Ans.$$

SELF-TEST 7-6   Combine terms.

$3I + 10 + 6I - 2 = 9I + \underline{\hspace{1em}}$	8	
$5R + 3I + 4I - R = \underline{\hspace{1em}}R + \underline{\hspace{1em}}I$	4	7
$12 - 2R - 3 + 7R = \underline{\hspace{1em}} + \underline{\hspace{1em}}$	9	$5R$
$4I_1 + 2I_2 - I_1 + 3I_2 = 3\underline{\hspace{1em}} + \underline{\hspace{1em}}I_2$	I_1	5
$3I_1 + 4I_2 - 3I_1 + 5I_2 + 7 = \underline{\hspace{2em}}$	$9I_2 + 7$	

PROBLEMS

Combine the terms in the following algebraic expressions:

1. $2R + 4I + 3I + 8R$
2. $3R + 2I - R + 5I$
3. $3x + 7 - x + 2$
4. $6x + 2y - y + x$
5. $4R + 3R + 6 - R + 2$
6. $1.5I + 7 + 0.5I - 3$
7. $40 + 30 + 3R - 10$
8. $9I + 16 - 4 + 2I - I$
9. $4.2x + 6y + 1.8x - y$
10. $6R + R - 0.5R + 2I$
11. $1.5I + 0.7R - 0.6I + 1.2R$
12. $2I + 60 - 20 + 3I - 5$
13. $3I_1 + 4I_2 + 5I_1 + 6I_2$
14. $5I_2 + I_2 + 3I_1 - 0.5I_1$
15. $5x + 2y + 7 - x + 3y + 3$
16. $2.5I_1 + 40 - 0.4I_1 + 20$
17. $2.5I_2 + 10 - 1.3I_2 - 8$
18. $8.6R + 7.4 + 2.6 - 1.3R$
19. $3.1 + 4I - 0.7 - 0.6I$
20. $8R - 0.3R + 26 - 9.2$

Find the total voltage E_T of the circuit shown in Fig. 7-3 if

21. $A = 2I, B = 40, C = 4I,$ and $D = 15$
22. $A = 12.6, B = 2.5I, C = I,$ and $D = 35$
23. $A = 0.15R, B = 0.15R, C = 25,$ and $D = 0.15R$

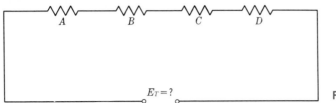

FIGURE 7-3

In Fig. 7-4, find the sum of the voltage drops by tracing around the circuit named in the following problems:

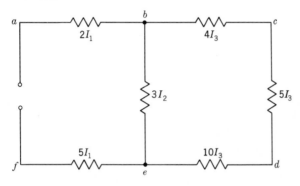

FIGURE 7-4

24. Circuit *abef*
25. Circuit *bcdeb*
26. Circuit *abcdef*

JOB 7-3 SOLVING SIMPLE ALGEBRAIC EQUATIONS

In Job 2-8 we learned to solve the standard equation of the type $3x = 12$. In Job 3-6 we learned to solve equations of the type $R + 2 = 10$ and $x - 3 = 7$. In Job 4-7 we learned to solve equations of the type $E/4 = 5$.

These are the three basic types of equations. The more difficult equations are solved by simplifying them step by step into one or the other of these basic types. The concept of combining like terms should be used whenever possible, as this combination will often simplify the equation into one of the basic types which are readily solved.

EXAMPLE 7-7 Solve the equation

$$2x + 3x = 20$$

SOLUTION

1 Write the equation.

$$2x + 3x = 20$$

2   Combine like terms.

$$5x = 20$$

3   Solve the basic equation.

$$x = 4 \qquad Ans.$$

EXAMPLE 7-8   Solve the equation

$$8x - 2x - 4x = 10$$

SOLUTION

1   Write the equation.

$$8x - 2x - 4x = 10$$

2   Combine like terms.

$$2x = 10$$

3   Solve the basic equation.

$$x = 5 \qquad Ans.$$

EXAMPLE 7-9   Solve the equation

$$21 = 0.7x - 0.4x$$

SOLUTION

1   Write the equation.

$$21 = 0.7x - 0.4x$$

2   Combine like terms.

$$21 = 0.3x$$

3   Solve the basic equation.

$$\frac{21}{0.3} = x$$

4   Write the answer.

$$70 = x \qquad or \qquad x = 70 \qquad Ans.$$

EXAMPLE 7-10   Solve the equation

$$\frac{2x}{5} = 4$$

SOLUTION

1   Complete all fractions by placing whole numbers or decimals over 1.

$$\frac{2x}{5} = \frac{4}{1}$$

2   Cross-multiply.

$$2x = 20$$

3   Solve the basic equation.

$$x = 10 \qquad Ans.$$

EXAMPLE 7-11   Solve the equation

$$3x + 5 = 50$$

SOLUTION

In this equation, as in all equations, our main objective is to get the unknown letter *all alone on one side of the equality sign.* The number that remains on the other side will be the answer. The letter x will remain alone on the left side of the equality sign if we can eliminate the $+5$ and the 3 from that side. We can remove the $+5$ easily by transposing it to the other side as a -5.

1   Write the equation.

$$3x + 5 = 50$$

2   Transpose the $+5$.

$$3x = 50 - 5$$

3   Combine like terms.

$$3x = 45$$

4   Solve the basic equation.

$$x = 15 \qquad Ans.$$

EXAMPLE 7-12   Solve the equation

$$3I - 4 = 20$$

SOLUTION

1   Write the equation.

$$3I - 4 = 20$$

2   Transpose the -4.

$$3I = 20 + 4$$

3   Combine like terms.

$$3I = 24$$

4   Solve the basic equation.

$$I = 8 \qquad Ans.$$

EXAMPLE 7-13   Solve the equation

$$25 = 4x - 3$$

SOLUTION

1   Write the equation.

$$25 = 4x - 3$$

2   Transpose the -3 to the *left* side of the equality sign.

$$25 + 3 = 4x$$

3   Combine like terms.

$$28 = 4x$$

4   Solve the basic equation.

$$7 = x \quad \text{or} \quad x = 7 \quad Ans.$$

EXAMPLE 7-14   Solve the equation

$$3x + 2 + x = 14$$

SOLUTION

1   Write the equation.

$$3x + 2 + x = 14$$

2   Combine like terms.

$$4x + 2 = 14$$

3   Transpose the $+2$.

$$4x = 14 - 2$$

4   Combine like terms.

$$4x = 12$$

5   Solve the basic equation.

$$x = 3 \quad Ans.$$

EXAMPLE 7-15   Solve the equation

$$4x - 6.2 - x = 1.3$$

SOLUTION

1   Write the equation.

$$4x - 6.2 - x = 1.3$$

2   Combine like terms.

$$3x - 6.2 = 1.3$$

3 Transpose the −6.2.

$$3x = 1.3 + 6.2$$

4 Combine like terms.

$$3x = 7.5$$

5 Solve the basic equation.

$$x = \frac{7.5}{3}$$

6 Divide.

$$x = 2.5 \qquad Ans.$$

SELF-TEST 7-16   Solve the equation

$$7x + 9 = 30$$

SOLUTION

1 Write the equation.

$$7x + 9 = 30$$

2 Transpose the number ___.   +9

$$7x = 30 - \underline{\quad}$$ 9

3 Combine like terms.

$$7x = \underline{\quad}$$ 21

4 Solve the basic equation.

$$x = \frac{21}{?}$$ 7

5 Divide.

$$x = \underline{\quad} \qquad Ans.$$ 3

SELF-TEST 7-17   An architect's plan calls for 5 lights laid out as shown in Fig. 7-5. If the total length of electrical conduit used was 58 ft, find the length from B to C.

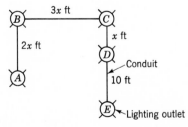

FIGURE 7-5

SOLUTION

1 The total length is equal to the ___ of the individual lengths.   sum
2 Write an equation to describe this.

$$2x + 3x + \underline{\quad} + 10 = 58 \qquad\qquad\qquad x$$

3 Combine like terms.

$$\underline{\quad} + 10 = 58 \qquad\qquad\qquad 6x$$

4 Transpose the $+10$.

$$6x = 58 - \underline{\quad} \qquad\qquad\qquad 10$$

5 Combine like terms.

$$6x = \underline{\quad} \qquad\qquad\qquad 48$$

6 Solve the basic equation.

$$x = \underline{\quad} \qquad\qquad\qquad 8$$

7 The length from B to C is $\underline{\quad}$ ft. $3x$

8 By substituting our answer 8 for x, we get the length from B to $C = 3 \times$
$\underline{\quad} = \underline{\quad}$ ft   *Ans.*   8   24

SELF-TEST 7-18   Solve the circuit shown in Fig. 7-6 for the value of
R_1.

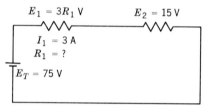

$E_1 = 3R_1$ V $E_2 = 15$ V

$I_1 = 3$ A
$R_1 = ?$

$E_T = 75$ V

FIGURE 7-6

SOLUTION

We obtained the value of E_1 by using the formula

$$E_1 = I_1 \times \underline{\quad} \qquad\qquad (3\text{-}4) \qquad R_1$$

$$E_1 = \underline{\quad} \times R_1 \qquad\qquad\qquad 3$$

$$E_1 = 3R_1$$

1 In this series circuit, the total voltage is equal to the $\underline{\quad}$ of all the voltages.   sum

$$E_T = E_1 + \underline{\quad} \qquad\qquad\qquad E_2$$

2 Substitute numbers.

$$75 = \underline{\quad} + 15 \qquad\qquad\qquad 3R_1$$

3 Transpose the $+15$.

$$75 - 15 = \underline{\quad} \qquad\qquad\qquad 3R_1$$

4 Combine like terms.

$$\underline{\quad} = 3R_1 \qquad\qquad\qquad 60$$

5 Solve the basic equation.

$$20 = R_1 \text{ or } R_1 = 20 \ \Omega \qquad \textit{Ans.}$$

PROBLEMS

Solve the following equations:

1. $3x = 21$
2. $14 = 2R$
3. $2a + 3a = 25$
4. $3I + I = 24$
5. $40 = 3R + 5R$
6. $\dfrac{I}{5} = 6$
7. $\dfrac{2R}{5} = \dfrac{8}{4}$
8. $x - 4 = 6$
9. $\dfrac{2x}{3} = 8$
10. $\dfrac{2x}{3} = 24$
11. $20 = 6x - 2x$
12. $x + 3 = 9$
13. $3x = 16$
14. $10R = 2$
15. $0.2x = 40$
16. $14 = R - 4$
17. $9 = 0.3x$
18. $9R - 5R = 38$
19. $0.3a + 0.2a = 35$
20. $26 = 1.1R + 0.2R$
21. $2.4x - 0.4x = 10$
22. $0.4R + 0.3R = 4.9$
23. $\dfrac{3y}{4} = 0.6$
24. $R - 5.6 = 14$
25. $5x + 2x + x = 40$
26. $3I + 7I - 2I = 56$
27. $26 = 8x + 6x - 2$
28. $0.12x = 0.06$
29. $\dfrac{2R}{7} = 7$
30. $5a - 6 = 4$
31. $25 = 3R + 4$
32. $6 = \dfrac{3x}{5}$
33. $1.9x - 0.4x = 4.5$
34. $3x + 2 = 11$
35. $42 = 6x - x + 2x$
36. $34 = 7R - 8$
37. $29 = 3x + 11$
38. $2R + 3 = 3$
39. $8x + 1 = 3$
40. $2x - 0.3 = 1.1$
41. $4x + 2.6 = 5.4$
42. $4R - R + 2 = 20$
43. $3R - 9 = 11$
44. $59 = 5x - 6$
45. $5y - 17 = 37$
46. $12x - 1 = 8$
47. $5x + 0.2x = 10.4$
48. $x + 1.2x = 4.4$
49. $x + 1.2x + 9 = 97$
50. $2I + 7I + 30 - I = 70$

51. Find the value of each dimension shown in Fig. 7-7.

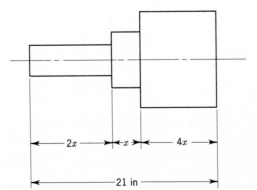

FIGURE 7-7

Using Fig. 7-1, find the value of each dimension if

52. $A = x$, $B = 3x$, $C = 4x$, and $D = 32$
53. $A = 1.3x$, $B = 0.04x$, $C = 2.16x$, and $D = 35$
54. $A = x + 4$, $B = 5$, $C = 2x$, and $D = 21$
55. $A = 1.2y + 8$, $B = 0.8y$, $C = 0.4y$, and $D = 56$

56.   In Fig. 7-8, find the depth of thread h if the outside diameter $D = 1.375$ in and the root diameter $d = 1.171$ in. Use the formula $D = d + 2h$.

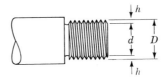

FIGURE 7-8
The depth of the screw thread is represented as the letter h.

57.   The current in a transistor divides according to the formula $I_E = I_B + \beta I_B$. Find the current gain β of the transistor shown in Fig. 7-9.

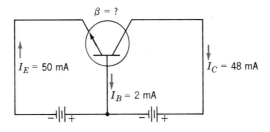

FIGURE 7-9
Division of current in an NPN transistor circuit.

58.   Two equal resistors are connected in series with a 150-Ω resistor to make a total resistance of 200 Ω as shown in Fig. 7-10. (*a*) Form an equation which can be used to solve for R. (*b*) Solve for R.

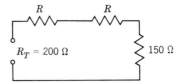

FIGURE 7-10

59.   Two holes, 2.25 in apart on center are to be drilled equidistant from the ends of a steel plate 4.75 in long as shown in Fig. 7-11. How far from the ends should the centers of the holes be marked?

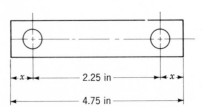

FIGURE 7-11

60. A square bar was milled from a round bar as shown in Fig. 7-12. Find the depth of the cut (h).

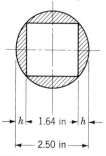

JOB 7-4   SOLVING EQUATIONS BY TRANSPOSITION AND CROSS MULTIPLICATION

EXAMPLE 7-19   Solve the equation

$$\frac{2x}{5} + 3 = 7$$

FIGURE 7-12

SOLUTION

1 Write the equation.

$$\frac{2x}{5} + 3 = 7$$

2 Transpose the $+3$.

$$\frac{2x}{5} = 7 - 3$$

3 Combine like terms.

$$\frac{2x}{5} = 4$$

4 Cross-multiply.

$$2x = 20$$

5 Solve the basic equation.

$$x = 10 \qquad Ans.$$

EXAMPLE 7-20   Solve the equation

$$\frac{x}{4} - 5 = 4$$

SOLUTION

1 Write the equation.

$$\frac{x}{4} - 5 = 4$$

2 Transpose the -5.

$$\frac{x}{4} = 4 + 5$$

3   Combine like terms.

$$\frac{x}{4} = 9$$

4   Cross-multiply.

$$x = 36 \qquad Ans.$$

EXAMPLE 7-21   Solve the equation

$$23 = \frac{2R}{3} + 7$$

SOLUTION

1   Write the equation.

$$23 = \frac{2R}{3} + 7$$

2   Transpose the +7.

$$23 - 7 = \frac{2R}{3}$$

3   Combine like terms.

$$16 = \frac{2R}{3}$$

4   Cross-multiply.

$$2R = 48$$

5   Solve the basic equation.

$$R = 24 \qquad Ans.$$

EXAMPLE 7-22   Solve the equation

$$1\frac{1}{4}x + 1\frac{1}{2}x + 3 = 14$$

SOLUTION

1   Write the equation.

$$1\frac{1}{4}x + 1\frac{1}{2}x + 3 = 14$$

2   Combine like terms.

$$2\frac{3}{4}x + 3 = 14$$

3   Change the mixed number to an improper fraction.

$$\frac{11x}{4} + 3 = 14$$

4 Transpose the +3.

$$\frac{11x}{4} = 14 - 3$$

5 Combine like terms.

$$\frac{11x}{4} = 11$$

6 Cross-multiply.

$$11x = 44$$

7 Solve the basic equation.

$$x = 4 \qquad Ans.$$

SELF-TEST 7-23 Find E_1 in the parallel circuit shown in Fig. 7-13.

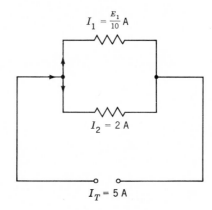

$$I_1 = \frac{E_1}{10} \text{ A}$$

$$I_2 = 2 \text{ A}$$

$$I_T = 5 \text{ A}$$

FIGURE 7-13

SOLUTION

In this parallel circuit, the total current is equal to the ____ of all the currents. | sum

$$I_T = I_1 + \underline{\quad}$$ | I_2

1 Substitute numbers.

$$5 = \frac{E_1}{10} + \underline{\quad}$$ | 2

2 Transpose the +2.

$$5 - \underline{\quad} = \frac{E_1}{10}$$ | 2

3 Combine like terms.

$$\underline{\quad} = \frac{E_1}{10}$$ | 3

4 Cross-multiply.

$$E_1 = \underline{\quad} \text{ V} \qquad Ans.$$ | 30

PROBLEMS

Solve the following equations.

1. $\dfrac{x}{2} + 4 = 9$

2. $\dfrac{x}{3} + 7 = 12$

3. $\dfrac{R}{3} - 2 = 8$

4. $\dfrac{y}{5} - 6 = 3$

5. $9 = \dfrac{x}{2} + 1$

6. $5 = \dfrac{y}{3} - 2$

7. $\dfrac{2R}{3} - 4 = 6$

8. $\dfrac{3R}{5} + 4 = 10$

9. $\dfrac{x}{2} - 1\dfrac{1}{2} = 3\dfrac{1}{2}$

10. $5 = \dfrac{3x}{2} - 7$

11. $\dfrac{x}{3} - 1.2 = 3.2$

12. $\dfrac{x}{5} + 0.2 = 1.8$

13. $\dfrac{5x}{3} + 4 = 9$

14. $\dfrac{4x}{5} - 18 = 22$

15. $32 = \dfrac{3x}{2} - 10$

16. $\dfrac{x}{3} + \dfrac{1}{4} = 1\dfrac{1}{4}$

17. $1\dfrac{1}{4}x - 3 = 12$

18. $2\dfrac{1}{3}x + 4 = 18$

19. In Fig. 7-5, $AB = 1\frac{1}{2}x$, $BC = 3x$, $CD = x$, and $DE = 10$. If the total length of conduit is 87 ft, find the length of CD.

20. In the circuit shown in Fig. 7-14, find the value of E.

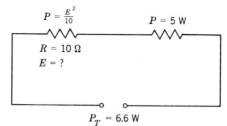

$P = \dfrac{E^2}{10}$ $P = 5\text{ W}$

$R = 10\ \Omega$
$E = ?$

$P_T = 6.6\text{ W}$

FIGURE 7-14

INTERMEDIATE REVIEW

SELF-TEST 7-24   Find the distance x in Fig. 7-15.

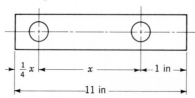

$\dfrac{1}{4}x$ x 1 in

11 in

FIGURE 7-15

SOLUTION

The total length is equal to the ____ of the parts. | sum

$$\frac{1}{4}x + x + 1 = \underline{\hspace{1cm}}$$ | 11

$$\underline{\;\;?\;\;}x + 1 = 11$$ | $1\frac{1}{4}$

$$\frac{5}{4}x = 11 - \underline{\hspace{1cm}}$$ | 1

$$\frac{5}{4}x = \underline{\hspace{1cm}}$$ | 10

$$5x = \underline{\hspace{1cm}}$$ | 40

$$x = \underline{\hspace{1cm}} \text{ in} \quad \textit{Ans.}$$ | 8

SELF-TEST 7-25 Three identical resistors are in series with a 100-Ω and a 300-Ω resistor. If the total resistance of the circuit is 1,600 Ω, find the resistance of each unknown resistor.

SOLUTION

In a series circuit, the total resistance is equal to the ____ of the individual re- | sum
sistances.

$$R_T = R_1 + R_2 + R_3 + \cdots \text{ etc.} \qquad (3\text{-}3)$$

$$1,600 = R + R + \underline{\hspace{1cm}} + 100 + 300$$ | R

$$1,600 = \underline{\hspace{1cm}} + 400$$ | $3R$

$$1,600 - \underline{\hspace{1cm}} = 3R$$ | 400

$$\underline{\hspace{1.5cm}} = 3R$$ | 1,200

$$R = \underline{\hspace{1cm}} \Omega \quad \textit{Ans.}$$ | 400

TEST—SOLVING EQUATIONS

1. $E - 5 = 19$

2. $26 = x + 4$

3. $20R = 4$

4. $\frac{x}{4} = 12$

5. $0.3x = 60$

6. $0.2x + 0.6x = 16$

7. $8R - 28 = 44$

8. $18 = 8a - 2a$

9. $2I + 7I - 3I = 42$

10. $\frac{2R}{5} = 8$

11. $1\frac{1}{2}R = 6$

12. $\frac{3x}{5} + 6 = 24$

13. $3y + 8 + 2y = 30$

14. $3x + 0.7 = 2.8$

15. $31 = 3x + 4$

16. $57 = 8y + 53$

17. $\frac{2y}{3} - 3 = 7$

18. $10 = \frac{3R}{5} + 4$

19. $14 + 4R = 26$

20. $1\frac{1}{4}x - 3 = 7$

JOB 7-5   POSITIVE AND NEGATIVE NUMBERS

Many of the calculations, graphs, and tables used to solve problems in complex dc and ac circuits require an understanding of positive and negative numbers. These numbers, commonly called *signed* numbers, are used to indicate *opposite* amounts, such as a *gain or a loss* in voltage, an *increase or a decrease* in loudness, or currents that flow in *opposite directions*.

Writing positive and negative numbers. In our daily conversations we often indicate opposite quantities by pairs of words such as north or south, up or down, gain or loss, and win or lose. In our electrical work, it is much easier to indicate opposite quantities by the use of the plus sign (+) or the minus sign (−). For example, 5° above zero may be written as +5° and 5° below zero may be written as −5°. A current in one direction is written as +10 A but as −10 A if the flow is in the opposite direction. Numbers preceded by a minus sign are called *negative numbers*. The minus sign must always be written before a negative number. If no sign is written before a number, the quantity is understood to be a positive number. Signed numbers are usually written to agree with the following system. Gains, increases, or directions to the right or upward are written as positive (+). Losses, decreases, or directions to the left or downward are written as negative (−).

PROBLEMS

Write the following quantities as signed numbers:

1. A loss of $3.
2. A temperature of 8° below zero.
3. 23° north latitude.
4. 70° east longitude.
5. An increase in loudness of 2 dB (decibels).
6. A drop of 10° in temperature.
7. Ten miles per hour slower.
8. Eight paces to the right.
9. Five blocks downtown.
10. Twenty feet below sea level.
11. If the voltage of the ground is considered to be 0 V, indicate a voltage of 4 V below ground.
12. Indicate a grid bias of 2 V below ground.

ADDITION OF SIGNED NUMBERS

RULE	To add two positive numbers, add the numbers and place the plus sign before the sum.

EXAMPLE 7-26   A gain of 7 plus a gain of 3 equals a gain of 10 may be indicated as

$$(+7) + (+3) = +10 \qquad Ans.$$

| RULE | To add two negative numbers, add the numbers and place the minus sign before the sum. |

EXAMPLE 7-27   A loss of 5 plus a loss of 2 equals a loss of 7 may be indicated as

$$(-5) + (-2) = -7 \qquad Ans.$$

| RULE | To add two numbers of *different* sign, *subtract* the numbers and place the sign of the larger before the answer. |

EXAMPLE 7-28   A gain of 7 plus a loss of 3 equals a total gain of 4 may be indicated as

$$(+7) + (-3) = +4 \qquad Ans.$$

EXAMPLE 7-29   A loss of 9 plus a gain of 4 equals a total loss of 5 may be indicated as

$$(-9) + (+4) = -5 \qquad Ans.$$

EXAMPLE 7-30   Combine the following signed numbers:

$$7 - 2 - 3 + 5 + 4 - 2$$

SOLUTION
The signs in problems of this type are *never* meant to represent addition or subtraction. These signs are the signs of the numbers. To combine signed numbers *always* means to *add* the signed numbers using the rules for algebraic addition. Therefore, reading from left to right, we shall consider this problem to mean

$+7$ *added to* -2 is $+5$, (7 means $+7$)
$+5$ *added to* -3 is $+2$,
$+2$ *added to* $+5$ is $+7$,
$+7$ *added to* $+4$ is $+11$, and
$+11$ *added to* -2 is $+9$ *Ans.*

SELF-TEST 7-31   Fill in the blank spaces with the correct responses.

1   $(-4) + (-6)$ means to __(add/subtract)__ the numbers and prefix the sum with a _____ sign. The answer is ____.

2   $(+4) + (+8)$ means to ____ the numbers and prefix the sum with a_____ sign. The answer is ____.

add
minus -10
add   plus
$+12$

3 (7) + (+4) means to ____ the numbers and prefix the sum with a _____ sign. The answer is ____.

4 (+6) + (−4) means to _____ the numbers and prefix the difference with a ____ sign because the sign of the larger number is +. The answer is ____.

5 (−12) + (−3) means to ____ the numbers and prefix the answer with a _____ sign. The answer is ____.

6 (−10) + (+4) means to _____ the numbers and prefix the answer with a _____ sign because the sign of the larger is ____. The answer is ____.

7 7 − 4 means (+7) + (___). The answer is ____.

8 (23) + (−5) means to _____ the numbers and prefix the answer with a ____ sign. The answer is ____.

9 −5 − 7 means (−5) + (___). The answer is ____.

10 7 − 3 − 9 − 2 means (+7) + (−3) + (___) + (−2)

+7 added to −3 = ____
+4 added to −9 = ____
−5 added to −2 = ____   *Ans.*

add	plus
+11	
subtract	
plus	+2
add	
minus	−15
subtract	
minus minus	−6
−4 +3	
subtract	
plus +18	
−7 −12	
−9	
+4	
−5	
−7	

PROBLEMS

Add the signed numbers indicated in each problem.

1. (+3) + (+9)   2. (−6) + (−5)   3. (+8) + (−2)
4. (−10) + (+3)   5. (−12) + (−5)   6. (+16) + (+3)
7. (+18) + (−11)   8. (−21) + (+9)   9. (−8) + (−9)

10. +18   11. −26   12. +36
     +14   +12   −14

13. −6   14. −47   15. −75
     +22   −23   +23

16. −8.2   17. −10.5   18. −16.8
     +11.6   +12.4   +7

19. (−¼) + (+½)   20. (+⅝) + (−¼)   21. (−½) + (−⅓)
22. −16⅞   23. +3⁹⁄₁₆   24. −15¾
     +8¾   −9¼   +28½

25. +8 − 2 − 9 + 6   26. −6 − 3 + 11 + 4 − 5
27. 13 − 2 − 3 + 4 − 5   28. −9 + 3 − 2 + 4 − 6
29. −3 − 5 + 2 − 26 + 7   30. 6 − 2 − 9 − 1 + 3
31. 1.4 − 0.2 − 0.7   32. −16 + 4.8 + 3.4
33. 6.4 − 8.5 + 3.2 − 4   34. 3.2 − 8 + 2.5 + 5.7

35. A 6ES5 tube is to operate with a grid bias of −6 V. What is the voltage on the grid when the ac signal input to the grid is (*a*) 6 V, (*b*) 2 V, (*c*) −1 V, (*d*) −2 V?

JOB 7-6 COMBINING UNLIKE TERMS INVOLVING SIGNED NUMBERS

The procedure is exactly the same as that outlined in Job 7-2 except that the *signs* of the quantities must now be taken into account in the addition.

EXAMPLE 7-32   Combine the following terms:

$$40 - 55 + 2x - 10 - 5x$$

SOLUTION

1 Combine the similar "number" terms.

$$+40 - 55 - 10 = -25$$

2 Combine the similar x terms.

$$+2x - 5x = -3x$$

3 State the answer.

$$-25 - 3x \qquad Ans.$$

EXAMPLE 7-33   Combine the following terms:

$$5x - 2y - 5y - 7x + 14 - y - 6$$

SOLUTION

1 Combine the similar x terms.

$$+5x - 7x = -2x$$

2 Combine the similar y terms.

$$-2y - 5y - y = -8y$$

3 Combine the similar "number" terms.

$$+14 - 6 = +8$$

4 State the answer.

$$-2x - 8y + 8 \qquad Ans.$$

EXAMPLE 7-34   Combine the following terms:

$$2I_1 - 6I_2 - 4I_1 - 30 - 4I_1 + 2I_2$$

SOLUTION

1 Combine the similar I_1 terms.

$$+2I_1 - 4I_1 - 4I_1 = -6I_1$$

2 Combine the similar I_2 terms.

$$-6I_2 + 2I_2 = -4I_2$$

3 State the answer.

$$-6I_1 -4I_2 -30 \qquad Ans.$$

SELF-TEST 7-35   An equation that might result from an application of Kirchhoff's laws (which we shall study in the next chapter) is

$$-10 - 2x + 2y - 3x - 5y = 0$$

Combine the terms on the left side of the equation.

SOLUTION

1 Combine the similar x terms.

$$-2x - 3x = \underline{\quad} \qquad\qquad\qquad\qquad\qquad -5x$$

2 Combine the similar y terms.

$$+2y - 5y = \underline{\quad} \qquad\qquad\qquad\qquad\qquad -3y$$

3 State the simplified equation.

$$-5x \underline{\quad} -10 = 0 \qquad Ans. \qquad\qquad\qquad -3y$$

PROBLEMS

Combine the following terms:

1. $3x + 4 - 5x + 3$
2. $16 - 4y - 2y - 7$
3. $2I_1 + 3I_2 - 5I_2 - 6I_1$
4. $3 - 8 + 4x - 2 - x$
5. $2x - 3y - 2y - 4x + y$
6. $8 - 2I_2 - 3 - 4I_2 - 3I_2$
7. $4x - 13 - 5x + 6 - 2x$
8. $2x - y - 3x - 4y + 7 - x$
9. $20 - 35 + 4x - 5 - 6x$
10. $-x - y - 4 + 4x + 2 - 3y$

JOB 7-7   MULTIPLYING AND DIVIDING SIGNED QUANTITIES

The following rules for signs apply to *both* multiplication and division.

RULE	When multiplying or dividing quantities with the same sign, the answer is plus.

RULE	When multiplying or dividing quantities with different signs, the answer is minus.

EXAMPLE 7-36   Perform the indicated operation.

$$(+4) \times (+2) = +8 \qquad (-6) \times (-2) = +12$$

$$(+4) \times (-2) = -8 \qquad (-3) \times (+4) = -12$$

$$(+2) \times (+3R) = +6R \qquad (-4) \times (-2I) = +8I$$

$$(-4) \times (0) = 0 \qquad (+3) \times (0) = 0$$

$$\frac{+20}{+5} = +4 \qquad \frac{-12}{-4} = +3 \qquad \frac{+3}{+6} = +\frac{1}{2} \qquad \frac{-2}{-8} = +\frac{1}{4}$$

$$\frac{+20}{-5} = -4 \qquad \frac{-12}{+4} = -3 \qquad \frac{+3}{-6} = -\frac{1}{2} \qquad \frac{-2}{+8} = -\frac{1}{4}$$

$$\frac{-8R}{-2} = +4R \qquad \frac{-12I}{+6} = -2I \qquad \frac{+6R}{-2} = -3R \qquad \frac{-3R}{-6} = +\frac{1}{2}R$$

PROBLEMS

Multiply:

1. $(+6)$ by $(+3)$
2. (-3) by (-4)
3. $(+4)$ by (-2)
4. (-3) by (6)
5. (-5) by (-6)
6. $(+2)$ by $(3R)$
7. $(6R)$ by $(+3)$
8. (-3) by $(4I)$
9. $(5R)$ by (-2)
10. (-3) by $(-5R)$
11. $(-2R)$ by (-5)
12. (-12) by (-6)
13. (-6) by (0)
14. $(-8T)$ by (0)
15. (8) by (-13)
16. (-25) by (-6)
17. $(-5R)$ by (17)
18. (2) by $(-13I)$
19. $(-4R)$ by (36)
20. (0.2) by (-10)
21. (-0.3) by (20)
22. (-0.2) by $(5R)$
23. (-1.2) by $(2I)$
24. $(-\frac{1}{2})$ by (-20)
25. $(-\frac{1}{4})$ by $(12R)$
26. (-1.2) by (-18)
27. (4.6) by (-3.2)
28. $(-16I)$ by (-0.2)
29. $(3.4R)$ by (-1.5)
30. (-0.6) by $(8.2R)$

Divide:

1. $(+12)$ by $(+3)$
2. (-24) by (-4)
3. $(+8)$ by (-2)
4. (-16) by $(+2)$
5. (-84) by (-7)
6. $(24R)$ by (6)
7. $(24R)$ by (-4)
8. $(-60) \div (15)$
9. $(20) \div (-40)$
10. $(-48) \div (-8)$
11. $(-16) \div (-32)$
12. $(+9) \div (-27)$
13. (0) by (-6)
14. $(0) \div (+7)$
15. $(63) \div (-9)$
16. $(-100) \div (+5)$
17. $(-60) \div (+8)$
18. $(-4) \div (20)$

19. $\dfrac{-3.6}{1.2}$
20. $\dfrac{4}{-7}$
21. $\dfrac{-1.6}{-0.5}$
22. $\dfrac{4.2}{-3}$

23. $\dfrac{-65}{-0.5}$
24. $\dfrac{0.4}{-0.1}$
25. $\dfrac{-2.6}{1.3}$
26. $\dfrac{0.4}{-3.2}$

27. $\dfrac{9.6}{-3}$
28. $\dfrac{-2.4}{-0.6}$
29. $\dfrac{-50}{0.8}$
30. $\dfrac{-10.8}{-0.3}$

JOB 7-8 REMOVING PARENTHESES

In order to solve the equations in the next job, we must first simplify the equation by removing any parentheses in it. A parenthesis is used to indicate that the quantities within it represent a single idea. For example, if a transformer costs $30 and the tax is $1, then the total actual cost is represented as the quantity $(30 + 1)$. Of course, this would be written as $31 because we would naturally combine the similar terms. However, if the cost were unknown, we would represent it as x dollars. If the tax remains constant, then the only way to represent the total cost would be as the quantity $x + 1$ or $(x + 1)$.

Now, if we bought 6 transformers, the total cost would be 6 times the cost of one transformer or $6 \times (x + 1)$. This is usually written as $6(x + 1)$. This means that the 6 is multiplied by the x *and also* by the number 1. Thus,

$$6(x + 1) = 6x + 6$$

We can check the accuracy of this method by using the actual cost.

$$6(30 + 1) = 6(31) = 186$$

or $\qquad 6(30 + 1) = 6 \times 30 + 6 \times 1 = 180 + 6 = 186$

> **RULE**
>
> To multiply a parenthesis by a single quantity:
> 1. Multiply each term of the parenthesis by the multiplier.
> 2. Combine like terms.

EXAMPLE 7-37   Multiply $+3(2R - 7)$.

SOLUTION

1 Multiply each part of the parenthesis by $+3$.

$$(+3) \times (2R) = +6R$$

$$(+3) \times (-7) = -21$$

2 State the answer.

$$6R - 21 \qquad Ans.$$

EXAMPLE 7-38   Remove parentheses and collect terms.

a $8x - 3(2 + x)$	*b* $11 + 2(3x - 9)$	*c* $-3(I + 4) - 5$
$8x - 6 - 3x$	$11 + 6x - 18$	$-3I - 12 - 5$
$5x - 6 \quad Ans.$	$6x - 7 \quad Ans.$	$-3I - 17 \quad Ans.$

EXAMPLE 7-39   Remove parentheses and collect terms.

$$5x + (3 - 8x)$$

SOLUTION

When the parenthesis is preceded by just a plus sign or a minus sign, the number 1 is understood to be present.

1   Write the problem.

$$5x + (3 - 8x)$$

2   Insert the number 1 after the sign.

$$5x + 1(3 - 8x)$$

3   Multiply the parenthesis by +1.

$$5x + 3 - 8x$$

4   Collect terms.

$$-3x + 3 \quad \text{or} \quad 3 - 3x \quad \textit{Ans.}$$

Certain problems are prone to error. Be careful to note the difference between the following examples.

EXAMPLE 7-40   Remove parentheses and collect terms.

$$-9(4x - 3) \qquad\qquad -9 - (4x - 3)$$

$$-36x + 27 \quad \textit{Ans.} \qquad -9 - 1(4x - 3)$$

$$-9 - 4x + 3$$

$$-6 - 4x \quad \textit{Ans.}$$

SELF-TEST 7-41   An equation that results from an application of Kirchhoff's laws to the circuit shown in Fig. 8-22 in the next chapter is

$$-10 - 2(x - y) + 3y = 0$$

Simplify the equation by removing parentheses and collecting like terms.

SOLUTION

$$-10 - 2x \underline{} + 3y = 0 \qquad\qquad\qquad +2y$$

$$-10 - 2x + \underline{} = 0 \quad \textit{Ans.} \qquad\qquad 5y$$

PROBLEMS

Remove parentheses and collect terms.

1. $2(3 - 4x)$
2. $3(5x - 6)$
3. $-3(x - 4)$
4. $4(2x - 3) - 3x$
5. $7 + 3(x - 4)$
6. $2y - (y - 3)$
7. $9I - 3(I + 8)$
8. $6 + (R - 7)$
9. $+(8 - 2R) - 7$
10. $-(2 + 3x) + 5$
11. $14 - 3(x - 5)$
12. $60 - 3(I_1 - 5)$

13. $20 + 2(I_1 + I_2)$ 14. $30 - 4(6 - I_2)$
15. $5R - 2(10 - 4 - R)$ 16. $(x - 2) + 2(x - 4)$
17. $-3(-2 + R) + (R - 1)$ 18. $7x - 3x - 2(x + 4)$
19. $-(I_1 - I_2) + 4(I_1 - 6)$ 20. $3x - 7 - 2(x - 3) + 20$

JOB 7-9 SOLVING EQUATIONS WHICH HAVE UNKNOWNS AND NUMBERS ON BOTH SIDES OF THE EQUALITY SIGN

As noted in Job 7-3, our main objective is to get the unknown letter all alone on one side of the equality sign. If the unknowns appear on *both sides* of the equality sign, we must gather them together as our first step. This will be accomplished by the normal process of transposing. In general then, transpose *all* letters to one side of the equality sign and transpose *all* numbers to the other side. Letters are collected on the left side or on the right side, the side chosen depending on the whim of the solver.

EXAMPLE 7-42   Solve the equation

$$6x = 2x + 12$$

SOLUTION

1   Write the equation.

$$6x = 2x + 12$$

2   Transpose the $2x$.

$$6x - 2x = 12$$

3   Combine like terms.

$$4x = 12$$

4   Solve the basic equation.

$$x = 3 \qquad Ans.$$

EXAMPLE 7-43   Solve the equation

$$7R - 84 = 4R$$

SOLUTION

1   Write the equation.

$$7R - 84 = 4R$$

2   Transpose the $4R$ to the left side and the -84 to the right side.

$$7R - 4R = 84$$

3   Combine like terms.

$$3R = 84$$

4   Solve the basic equation.

$$R = 28 \qquad Ans.$$

EXAMPLE 7-44   Solve the equation

$$8x - 7 = 3x + 8$$

SOLUTION

1   Write the equation.

$$8x - 7 = 3x + 8$$

2   Transpose the $3x$ to the left side and the -7 to the right.

$$8x - 3x = 8 + 7$$

3   Combine like terms.

$$5x = 15$$

4   Solve the basic equation.

$$x = 3 \qquad Ans.$$

EXAMPLE 7-45   Solve the equation

$$3x - 3 = 8x - 18$$

SOLUTION

1   Write the equation.

$$3x - 3 = 8x - 18$$

2   Since the greater number of x's appear on the right side of the equality sign, we shall transpose *all* x's to this right side and *all* numbers to the left side.

$$-3 + 18 = 8x - 3x$$

3   Combine like terms.

$$15 = 5x$$

4   Solve the basic equation.

$$3 = x \qquad \text{or} \qquad x = 3 \qquad Ans.$$

SELF-TEST 7-46   Two identical resistances, each of R_1 Ω resistance are connected as shown in Fig. 7-16. Find the value of R_1.

SOLUTION
In section A, which is a _____ circuit, | series

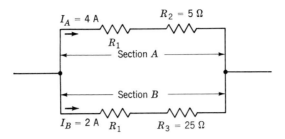

FIGURE 7-16

$$E_1 = I_A \times R_1 = \underline{\quad} \times R_1$$ 4

$$E_1 = \underline{\quad} \text{ V}$$ $4R_1$

$$E_2 = I_A \times R_2 = \underline{\quad} \times 5$$ 4

$$E_2 = \underline{\quad} \text{ V}$$ 20

Therefore, since $E_A = E_1 + E_2$,

$$E_A = 4R_1 + \underline{\quad} \text{ V} \qquad\qquad (1)$$ 20

In section B, which is a $\underline{\hspace{2cm}}$ circuit,   series

$$E_1 = I_B \times R_1 = \underline{\quad} \times R_1$$ 2

$$E_1 = \underline{\quad} \text{ V}$$ $2R_1$

$$E_3 = I_B \times R_3 = \underline{\quad} \times 25$$ 2

$$E_3 = \underline{\quad} \text{ V}$$ 50

Therefore, since $E_B = E_1 + E_3$,

$$E_B = 2R_1 + \underline{\quad} \text{ V} \qquad\qquad (2)$$ 50

The entire circuit is a $\underline{\hspace{2cm}}$ circuit, and   parallel

$$E_A = E_B$$

Substituting $4R_1 + 20$ for E_A from equation (1) and $\underline{\hspace{2cm}}$ for E_B from equa- $2R_1 + 50$
tion (2) we get

$$4R_1 + 20 = 2R_1 + 50$$

$$4R_1 - 2R_1 = 50 - \underline{\quad}$$ 20

$$\underline{\quad} = 30$$ $2R_1$

$$R_1 = \underline{\quad} \ \Omega \qquad Ans.$$ 15

PROBLEMS

Solve the following equations:

1. $7R = 2R + 10$ 2. $8x = 10 + 6x$
3. $4x = 27 + x$ 4. $5R = -2R + 14$
5. $3y + 24 = 9y$ 6. $28 - 2I = 5I$

7. $5x - 20 = 3x$
8. $7R - 48 = 3R$
9. $2x = 35 - 5x$
10. $-x - 19 = -2x$
11. $-2y - 21 = -5y$
12. $6T = 4 - 2T$
13. $3 - R = 8R$
14. $2x = 5x - 39$
15. $y = 9y - 40$
16. $x = 3.9 - 2x$
17. $5R + 1 = 3R + 9$
18. $6x - 4 = 2x + 28$
19. $26 + x = 4x - 1$
20. $7x - 25 = 4x + 23$
21. $R + 10 = 45 - 4R$
22. $2x - 8 = 9x - 50$
23. $7x - x + 8 = 2x + 40$
24. $12R - 5 = 6R - R + 23$
25. $8x - 3 + 9 = 2x + x + 31$
26. $12 + 2x = 8x - 60$
27. $8I - 1 = 3 - 4I$
28. $1 - 3R = 7R - 4$
29. $5T = 3T + 4.2$
30. $1.4x - 12 = -0.6x$

JOB 7-10   SOLVING EQUATIONS WITH POSSIBLE NEGATIVE ANSWERS

Consider the equation

$$2R = -10$$

Solving,
$$R = \frac{-10}{+2}$$

or
$$R = -5 \qquad Ans.$$

The signs in this problem might appear as shown below.

$$-2R = 10 \qquad\qquad -2R = -10$$

Solving,

$$R = \frac{+10}{-2} \qquad\qquad R = \frac{-10}{-2}$$

or $\qquad R = -5 \quad$ *Ans.* $\qquad R = +5 \quad$ *Ans.*

The answers above are not incorrect. It is quite possible for an answer to be a negative number. In the next chapter on complex circuits and in our future study of ac electricity, we shall meet these frequently. The basic equation is solved in a normal manner, but care must be used in dividing the signed numbers. Another method for handling these signs is illustrated in the next example.

EXAMPLE 7-47   Solve the equation

$$-2R = -10.$$

SOLUTION
Since all parts of an equation may be multiplied by the same number without destroying the equality, we can eliminate the cumbersome negative sign of the unknown by multiplying the entire equation by -1.

Therefore,

$$-1(-2R = -10)$$

becomes

$$2R = 10$$

or

$$R = 5 \quad Ans.$$

This operation may be described in the following simple rule.

RULE	All the signs of the individual parts of an equation may be changed without destroying the equality.

EXAMPLE 7-48   Solve the following equations.

$$-R = -6 \qquad -I = 25 \qquad 7 = -R$$
$$R = 6 \qquad I = -25 \qquad -7 = R \qquad Ans.$$

EXAMPLE 7-49   Solve the equation

$$4x - 5 = 5x + 1$$

SOLUTION

1   Write the equation.

$$4x - 5 = 5x + 1$$

2   Transpose.

$$4x - 5x = 1 + 5$$

3   Combine like terms.

$$-x = 6$$

4   Change signs throughout.

$$x = -6 \quad Ans.$$

PROBLEMS

Solve the following equations:

1. $-x = +8$
2. $12 = -R$
3. $3x = -15$
4. $-21 = 3T$
5. $8x = -4$
6. $-5 = 10x$
7. $-2x = 16$
8. $40 = -4x$
9. $-2x = -14$
10. $-24 = -3R$
11. $3x + 17 = 5$
12. $6 - 3x = 18$

13. $9 = 8 - R$
14. $y = 5y + 28$
15. $3R + 10 = R$
16. $5x + 9 = 4x + 1$
17. $5R + 7 = 6R + 18$
18. $3I + 22 = 9I - 20$
19. $-4R - 11 = 6R + 19$
20. $0.4x = -20$
21. $-1.2I = 2.4$
22. $-39 = 0.3T$
23. $1.6R + 10 = 0.6R + 3$
24. $-2I_2 = 10 - 8.58$

TEST—COMBINING TERMS AND SOLVING EQUATIONS

1. Combine terms: $8x - 3y - x + 7 + 5y - 3$
Remove parentheses and collect terms.
2. $5R - 3(6 + 2R) + 7$
3. $4(x - 3) - 3(4 - 2x)$
Solve the following equations:
4. $3x = 8 + 5x$
5. $2R + 3 = 5R - 15$
6. $6.2x - 24 = 3.8x$
7. $x + 1.2x + 9 = 75$
8. $2\frac{1}{3}x + 4 = 18$
9. $-0.04x = 12$
10. $2x - 7 = 6x + 13 - x$

JOB 7-11   SOLVING EQUATIONS CONTAINING PARENTHESES

EXAMPLE 7-50   Solve the equation

$$6x - 2(x - 4) = 32$$

SOLUTION
In order to solve an equation we collect *all* the unknowns on one side of the equality sign and *all* the numbers on the other side. We can't do this in this equation until we release the x and the -4 from the parenthesis. Once this has been done, the solution proceeds normally.

1   Write the equation.

$$6x - 2(x - 4) = 32$$

2   Remove parentheses.

$$6x - 2x + 8 = 32$$

3   Transpose the $+8$.

$$6x - 2x = 32 - 8$$

4   Combine like terms.

$$4x = 24$$

5 Solve the basic equation.

$$x = 6 \qquad Ans.$$

SELF-TEST 7-51   Find R_2 in the circuit shown in Fig. 7-17.

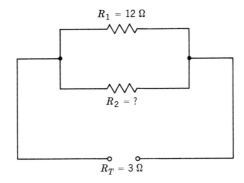

$R_1 = 12\ \Omega$

$R_2 = ?$

$R_T = 3\ \Omega$

FIGURE 7-17

SOLUTION

This is a _____ circuit.   parallel

1 Write the formula for R_T.

$$R_T = \frac{(R_1 \times R_2)}{(R_1 + ?)}$$ R_2

2 Substitute numbers.
                                                                    R_2
$$\frac{3}{1} = \frac{(12 \times ?)}{(? + R_2)}$$ 12

3 Cross-multiply.

$$3(12 + R_2) = \underline{\qquad}$$ $12R_2$

4 Remove parentheses.

$$36 + \underline{\quad} = 12R_2$$ $3R_2$

5 Transpose the $3R_2$.

$$36 = 12R_2 - \underline{\quad}$$ $3R_2$

6 Combine similar terms.

$$36 = \underline{\quad}$$ $9R_2$

7 Solve the basic equation.

$$\underline{\quad} = R_2$$ 4

$$\text{or} \qquad R_2 = 4\ \Omega \qquad Ans.$$

SELF-TEST 7-52   An electric iron uses 90 W more than twice the power used by an electric toaster. Three times the toaster power equals 460 W less than twice the iron wattage. Find the power used by each.

SOLUTION

In order to describe the problem in the language of algebra, we need algebraic names for the power used by each appliance.

Let x = the power used by the toaster.
Then twice this power = ____, and $\qquad$ $2x$
90 W more than this = (_____), or $\qquad$ $2x + 90$
$(2x + 90)$ = the power used by the _____. $\qquad$ iron
Now to make the equation.

$$3 \text{ times the toaster power} = \text{twice the iron power} - 460$$

$$3 \times \underline{\quad} = 2(\underline{\quad\quad}) - 460 \qquad\qquad x \qquad 2x + 90$$

Now solve this equation.

$$3x = 2(2x + 90) - 460$$

1 Remove parentheses.

$$3x = \underline{\quad} + 180 - 460 \qquad\qquad 4x$$

2 Transpose the $4x$.

$$3x - \underline{\quad} = 180 - 460 \qquad\qquad 4x$$

3 Combine similar terms.

$$-x = \underline{\quad\quad} \qquad\qquad -280$$

4 Solve for x.

$$x = \underline{\quad} \qquad\qquad 280$$

5 State the answer. Since x was our algebraic name for the toaster power,

$$\text{The toaster power} = \underline{\quad} \text{ W} \qquad Ans. \qquad\qquad 280$$

Since $(2x + 90)$ was our algebraic name for the iron power, by substituting 280 for x, we get

$$\text{The iron power} = (2 \times 280) + 90$$

$$= \underline{\quad} + 90 \qquad\qquad 560$$

$$= \underline{\quad} \text{ W} \qquad Ans. \qquad\qquad 650$$

PROBLEMS

Solve the following equations:

1. $2(x + 3) = 8$
2. $3(R - 4) = 3$
3. $4(R + 3) = 4$
4. $2(3 - R) = 4$
5. $5(2x + 3) = 35$
6. $7(3y - 2) = 28$
7. $3(2x - 2) = -24$
8. $3(3x - 1) - 4 = 11$
9. $5(3R - 2) + 8 = 43$
10. $3(a - 4) = 2(a + 1)$
11. $7(x + 1) = 5(x + 1)$
12. $2(I - 4) = 5(I + 2)$
13. $3(3x - 2) + 5 = 26$
14. $2(y + 4) + y = 23$

15. $4(x - 3) - 2x = -20$
16. $6x - (x - 3) = 28$
17. $4x - 5(x - 2) = 3$
18. $8R - (R - 4) = 11$
19. $6x - 2(x + 6) = x$
20. $10x = 38 + (4x - 2)$
21. $2R = 15 + 3(R + 2)$
22. $6y = 20 - (y - 8)$
23. $8y = 1 - 2(y - 2)$
24. $5x - 2(x - 3) = 17$
25. $2y + (y - 3) = 18 - 2(y + 3)$
26. $4(R - 2) - 7 = 9 - (R + 4)$
27. $0.4(x - 2) = 1.4$
28. $0.3(5R - 6) = 2.7$
29. $4(x - 0.2) = 2(x + 0.7)$
30. $2(x - 1.2) = 0.2(x - 3)$

31. In a circuit similar to that shown in Fig. 7-9, $I_E = 52$ mA and $I_B = 2$ mA. Find β using the transistor formula $I_E = \dfrac{\beta + 1}{I_B}$.

32. In a circuit similar to that shown in Fig. 7-17, find R_1 if $R_2 = 60\ \Omega$ and $R_T = 15\ \Omega$. Use the formula given in Example 7-51.

33. In a parallel circuit of two resistances, $R_1 = 16\ \Omega$ $I_2 = 2$ A, $I_T = 8$A. Find R_2 using the formula

$$I_2 = \frac{R_1}{(R_1 + R_2)} \times I_T$$

34. Using the formula to change Fahrenheit temperature to Centigrade temperature, $C = \dfrac{5(F - 32)}{9}$, find the number of degrees Fahrenheit F which is equivalent to $20°$ Centigrade C.

35. Each heating element in a cafeteria grill uses 130 W of power less than three times the wattage used by a toaster. When two toasters and three heating elements are in use, they require a total of 2,470 W of power. Find the wattage used by one heating element.

36. Using the formula for the taper per foot $T = \dfrac{12(D - d)}{L}$, find the small diameter d if the taper per foot $T = 0.6$ in, the large diameter $D = 2.75$ in, and the length $L = 4$ in.

37. Using the transistor formula $\beta = \dfrac{\alpha}{1 - \alpha}$, find α if $\beta = 49$.

JOB 7-12　SOLVING EQUATIONS CONTAINING FRACTIONS

In Job 4-7 we learned how to solve some simple fractional equations. These equations were limited to those containing only two fractions which were equal to each other. They were solved by cross multiplication, which is merely a short cut to be used only in the situation where two fractions equal each other. If there are *more* than two fractions, we are forced to use the general method discussed in Examples 4-21 to 4-24 of Job 4-7.

RULE	If an equation contains more than two fractions, eliminate the denominators by multiplying all parts of the equation by the least common denominator.

EXAMPLE 7-53   Solve the equation

$$\frac{x}{2} - \frac{x}{3} = \frac{1}{2}$$

SOLUTION

1   Write the equation.

$$\frac{x}{2} - \frac{x}{3} = \frac{1}{2}$$

2   Multiply all terms by the LCD which is 6.

$$\overset{3}{(\cancel{6})}\frac{x}{\underset{1}{\cancel{2}}} - \overset{2}{(\cancel{6})}\frac{x}{\underset{1}{\cancel{3}}} = \overset{3}{(\cancel{6})}\frac{1}{\underset{1}{\cancel{2}}}$$

3   Multiply.

$$3x - 2x = 3$$

4   Combine like terms.

$$x = 3 \qquad Ans.$$

EXAMPLE 7-54   Solve the equation

$$\frac{x}{4} + \frac{x}{8} = 6$$

SOLUTION

1   Write the equation.

$$\frac{x}{4} + \frac{x}{8} = 6$$

2   Complete all fractions by placing whole numbers or decimals over 1.

$$\frac{x}{4} + \frac{x}{8} = \frac{6}{1}$$

3   Multiply all terms by the LCD which is 8.

$$\overset{2}{(\cancel{8})}\frac{x}{\underset{1}{\cancel{4}}} + \overset{1}{(\cancel{8})}\frac{x}{\underset{1}{\cancel{8}}} = \overset{8}{(\cancel{8})}\frac{6}{\underset{1}{\cancel{1}}}$$

4   Multiply.

$$2x + x = 48$$

5   Combine like terms.

$$3x = 48$$

6   Solve the basic equation.

$$x = 16 \qquad Ans.$$

EXAMPLE 7-55   Solve the equation

$$\frac{2R}{5} + 3 = \frac{R}{4}$$

SOLUTION

1   Write the equation.

$$\frac{2R}{5} + 3 = \frac{R}{4}$$

2   Complete all fractions by placing whole numbers or decimals over 1.

$$\frac{2R}{5} + \frac{3}{1} = \frac{R}{4}$$

3   Multiply all terms by the LCD which is 20.

$$\overset{4}{(\cancel{20})} \frac{2R}{\cancel{5}} + \overset{20}{(\cancel{20})} \frac{3}{\cancel{1}} = \overset{5}{(\cancel{20})} \frac{R}{\cancel{4}}$$
$$\quad 1 \qquad\qquad 1 \qquad\qquad 1$$

4   Multiply.

$$8R + 60 = 5R$$

5   Transpose.

$$8R - 5R = -60$$

6   Combine like terms.

$$3R = -60$$

7   Solve the basic equation.

$$R = -20 \qquad Ans.$$

PROBLEMS

Solve the following equations:

1. $\dfrac{x}{2} - \dfrac{x}{3} = \dfrac{1}{3}$ 2. $\dfrac{x}{2} - \dfrac{x}{4} = \dfrac{1}{2}$

3. $\dfrac{x}{4} - \dfrac{x}{5} = 2$

4. $\dfrac{3R}{4} - \dfrac{2R}{3} = 1$

5. $\dfrac{x}{3} - \dfrac{x}{6} = 5$

6. $\dfrac{x}{2} + \dfrac{x}{3} = 5$

7. $\dfrac{E}{2} + \dfrac{E}{8} = 5$

8. $\dfrac{E}{5} + \dfrac{E}{3} = \dfrac{8}{15}$

9. $\dfrac{10}{3} = \dfrac{x}{3} + \dfrac{x}{7}$

10. $\dfrac{R}{4} + \dfrac{2R}{5} = 13$

11. $\dfrac{5x}{3} - 7 = \dfrac{x}{2}$

12. $\dfrac{E}{30} - 2 = \dfrac{E}{40}$

13. $\dfrac{E}{20} - \dfrac{E}{30} = 5$

14. $\dfrac{E}{20} + \dfrac{E}{10} + \dfrac{E}{60} = 5$

15. $\dfrac{3E}{9} - \dfrac{3E}{10} = \dfrac{1}{3}$

16. $\dfrac{R}{10} + \dfrac{R}{30} + \dfrac{R}{60} = \dfrac{9}{10}$

17. $\dfrac{6x}{50} + \dfrac{3x}{50} = \dfrac{9}{25}$

18. $\dfrac{E}{200} - \dfrac{E}{500} = \dfrac{3}{2}$

19. $\dfrac{R}{8} - \dfrac{R}{15} = 1$

20. $\dfrac{5x}{6} + \dfrac{x}{9} - \dfrac{2x}{3} = \dfrac{5}{9}$

21. $\dfrac{E}{6} + \dfrac{E}{9} + \dfrac{E}{12} = 39$

22. $\dfrac{E}{10} + \dfrac{E}{8} + \dfrac{E}{6} = 18.8$

TEST—EQUATIONS WITH PARENTHESES AND FRACTIONS

Solve the following equations:

1. $3(x - 4) = 24$

2. $5x - (x - 2) = 34$

3. $7R - 2(R - 8) = 5$

4. $3y = 16 - (6 - 5y)$

5. $3I_2 = 2 + 5(I_2 - 4)$

6. $0.3(2x - 5) = 0.2x + 0.5$

7. $\dfrac{x}{3} - \dfrac{x}{6} = \dfrac{1}{6}$

8. $5 = \dfrac{x}{2} + \dfrac{x}{3}$

9. $\dfrac{x}{3} - \dfrac{x}{8} = \dfrac{5}{2}$

10. $\dfrac{3E}{2} + 7 = \dfrac{E}{3}$

JOB 7-13   SOLVING SIMULTANEOUS EQUATIONS BY ADDITION

Simultaneous equations are those that arise at the same time (simultaneously) from the same problem. In simple problems, an equation can usually be found to describe the conditions of the problem. The solution of the equation finds the unknown. In the complex circuits to be discussed in the next chapter, there will be *two* unknowns to find. Suppose that the two unknown currents are represented as x and y and an equation connecting these currents is found to be

$$x + y = 12$$

There is an infinite variety of answers which will fit this equation. If

$x = 2$, then $y = 10$. If $x = 7$, then $y = 5$. If $y = 3$, then $x = 9$, etc. Obviously, then, an equation which contains two unknown quantities *cannot* be solved. However, if a *second* equation connecting the *same* two quantities can be found, we might be able to find a solution by working the two equations simultaneously. In general, *two* unknowns will require *two* equations. *Three* unknowns will require *three* equations, etc.

EXAMPLE 7-56   Solve the pair of simultaneous equations given below for the value of x and y.

SOLUTION

1   The equations are:

$$x + y = 12 \qquad\qquad (1)$$
$$x - y = 4 \qquad\qquad (2)$$

2   Since both equations contain two unknowns and therefore cannot be solved separately, let us *add* the equations. Since only like terms may be added, we must be sure to have the equations arranged so that the like terms are one under the other. If they are not so arranged, we must transpose one equation so as to agree with the other.

Adding, $2x = 16$

Note that the sum of $+y$ and $-y$ equals zero, and that the letter y disappears. The resulting equation contains *only one unknown,* and is easily solved.

Solving, $x = 8$ *Ans.*

3   Substitute this value of x in *either* of the original equations to find the value of y.

Using equation (1), $x + y = 12$ (1)

Substituting, $8 + y = 12$

Transposing, $y = 12 - 8$

Combining like terms. $y = 4$ *Ans.*

We were very lucky in the last problem. The simple act of adding the two equations *eliminated* one letter and provided a *third* equation which contained only *one* unknown which was easily solved. Will this occur all the time, or are certain conditions necessary for the elimination of one unknown by addition?

Consider the following additions: $(+7) + (-7) = 0$; $(+4) + (-4) = 0$; $(-5) + (+5) = 0$; $(+19) + (-19) = 0$. Apparently, the total is zero whenever we add *identical* quantities with *opposite* signs. This is what happened when we added $+y$ and $-y$ in the last problem. The addition totaled zero, which therefore eliminated the unknown y.

The number portion of an algebraic expression is called its numerical coefficient. For example,

2 is the numerical coefficient of the expression $2x$

7 is the numerical coefficient of the expression $7xy$

1 is the numerical coefficient of the expression ab

RULE	To eliminate an unknown by addition, the numerical coefficients of the unknown must be identical, but with opposite signs.

If necessary, one or *both* equations may be multiplied by the proper number and sign to create identical coefficients with opposite signs. Let's see how this works out in the next example.

EXAMPLE 7-57   Solve the pair of simultaneous equations given below for the value of x and y.

SOLUTION

1   The equations are:

$$x + 2y = 10 \tag{1}$$
$$x - y = 1 \tag{2}$$

You can see that neither x nor y will be eliminated by adding these two equations. (x added to $x = 2x$ and *not* zero. $+2y$ added to $-y = +y$ and *not* zero.) However, if the $-y$ in equation (2) were $-2y$, then the total of $+2y$ in equation (1) and $-2y$ in equation (2) *would* total zero. We shall therefore *change* the $-y$ in equation (2) into $-2y$ by multiplying the *entire* equation by the quantity which will change $-y$ into $-2y$. This multiplier must be $+2$.

2   Rewrite the problem as shown.

$$x + 2y = 10$$
$$+2(x - y = 1)$$

3   Multiplication gives

$$x + 2y = 10$$
$$2x - 2y = 2$$

4   Add the equations.

$$3x = 12$$

5   Solve for x.

$$x = 4 \qquad Ans.$$

6   Substitute this value for x in *either* original equation.

$$x + 2y = 10 \tag{1}$$
$$4 + 2y = 10$$

7 Transpose.

$$2y = 10 - 4$$

8 Combine like terms.

$$2y = 6$$

9 Solve the basic equation.

$$y = 3 \qquad Ans.$$

EXAMPLE 7-58   Solve the pair of simultaneous equations given below for the value of a and b.

SOLUTION

1 The equations are:

$$a + b = 5 \qquad\qquad (1)$$
$$\underline{2a + b = 7} \qquad\qquad (2)$$

In order to eliminate the unknown b, we must multiply equation (1) by -1.

$$-1(a + b = 5)$$
$$\underline{2a + b = 7}$$

2 Multiplication gives

$$-a - b = -5$$
$$\underline{2a + b = 7}$$

3 Add the equations.

$$a = 2 \qquad Ans.$$

4 Substitute 2 for a in equation (1).

$$a + b = 5 \qquad\qquad (1)$$

$$2 + b = 5$$

5 Transpose.

$$b = 5 - 2$$

6 Combine like terms.

$$b = 3 \qquad Ans.$$

EXAMPLE 7-59   Solve the pair of simultaneous equations given below for the value of x and y.

SOLUTION

1 The equations are:

$$5x + 2y = 4 \qquad\qquad (1)$$
$$\underline{4x - 3y = 17} \qquad\qquad (2)$$

The elimination of *either* unknown will solve the problem. However, since the signs of the unknown y are exactly what they should be, we shall attempt to eliminate y. It is very difficult to change a 2 into a 3 or a 3 into a 2 by multiplication. However, it is not necessary that the coefficients of y remain what they were in the original problem.

All that is necessary is that the coefficients be the same number, but with opposite signs.

We shall therefore change $+2y$ in equation (1) into $+6y$ by multiplying it by 3 and the $-3y$ in equation (2) into $-6y$ by multiplying it by 2.

$$3(5x + 2y = 4)$$
$$2(4x - 3y = 17)$$

2 Multiplication gives

$$15x + 6y = 12$$
$$8x - 6y = 34$$

3 Add the equations.

$$23x = 46$$

4 Solve for x.

$$x = 2 \qquad Ans.$$

5 Substitute this value for x in equation (1).

$$5x + 2y = 4 \tag{1}$$
$$5(2) + 2y = 4$$

6 Multiply.

$$10 + 2y = 4$$

7 Transpose.

$$2y = 4 - 10$$

8 Combine like terms.

$$2y = -6$$

9 Solve for y.

$$y = -3 \qquad Ans.$$

SELF-TEST 7-60 Solve the pair of simultaneous equations given below for the value of x and y.

SOLUTION

1 The equations are:

$$2x + 3y = -8 \tag{1}$$
$$7x + 4y = 11 \tag{2}$$

2 We plan to eliminate one letter by _____ the equations. | adding

3   The letter will disappear if the addition of the coefficients of that letter is equal to _____.

zero

4   The addition of these coefficients will equal zero if
   a   The coefficients are _____ in value
   b   The signs are _____

equal
opposite

5   The coefficients of x __(do/do not)__ satisfy these conditions. The coefficients of y __(do/do not)__ satisfy these conditions.

do not
do not

6   Yet, if we are going to solve the equations, the coefficients of one of these letters *must* be _____ and with _____ signs.

equal   opposite

7   Let us try to attain this condition for the letter y.

8   The smallest number into which we can change both 3 and 4 by multiplication is ____.

12

9   If we change the $3y$ of equation (1) into $12y$, then we must change the $4y$ of equation (2) into ____.

$-12y$

10   To get $12y$, we must multiply equation (1) by ___ because only $4 \times 3y = 12y$. To get $-12y$, we must multiply equation (2) by ___ because only $-3 \times 4y = -12y$.

4
-3

11   Indicate the plan by placing the entire equation in parentheses with the proper multiplier in front.

$$\underline{\quad} (2x + 3y = -8)$$

4

$$\underline{\quad} (7x + 4y = 11)$$

-3

16   Multiply each equation by its multiplier to give

$$8x + 12y = \underline{\quad}$$

-32

$$\underline{\quad} - 12y = -33$$

$-21x$

13   Add the equations. This will give

$$-13x = \underline{\quad}$$

-65

14   Solve this equation.

$$x = \frac{-65}{?}$$

-13

$$x = \underline{\quad} \quad Ans.$$

$+5$

15   Substitute this value for x in Equation (1).

$$2x + 3y = -8$$

$$2(\underline{\quad}) + 3y = -8$$

5

16   Multiply.

$$\underline{\quad} + 3y = -8$$

10

17   Transpose.

$$3y = -8 \underline{\quad}$$

-10

18   Combine terms.

$$3y = \underline{\quad}$$

-18

19 Solve for y.

$$y = \underline{} \qquad Ans.$$

20 *Check.* If we are correct, then the substitution of these values in the original equations should make true statements. Substitute $x = 5$ and $y = -6$ in equation (1).

$$2x + 3y = -8 \qquad (1)$$

$$2(5) + 3(\underline{}) = -8$$

$$\underline{} - 18 = -8$$

$$\underline{} = -8 \qquad Check$$

Substitute $x = 5$ and $y = -6$ in equation (2).

$$7x + 4y = 11 \qquad (2)$$

$$7(\underline{}) + 4(-6) = 11$$

$$35 - \underline{} = 11$$

$$\underline{} = 11 \qquad Check$$

Right margin values:
-6
-6
10
-8
5
24
11

PROBLEMS

Solve the following sets of equations:

1. $2x + y = 8$
   $x - y = 1$

2. $x + y = 6$
   $x - y = 4$

3. $2x + y = 12$
   $x + y = 7$

4. $x + y = 1$
   $x - y = 5$

5. $I_1 + I_2 = 8$
   $I_1 - 2I_2 = 2$

6. $x + y = 8$
   $x - y = 0$

7. $E - 4R = -1$
   $E - 2R = 3$

8. $x + 2y = 7$
   $x - 2y = 3$

9. $2I + 3E = 8$
   $4I - 3E = 34$

10. $7x + 4y = 26$
    $2x - 4y = -8$

11. $5a + 4b = -7$
    $a - 2b = 7$

12. $3I_1 - I_2 = 5$
    $2I_1 + 3I_2 = 18$

13. $2x - 3y = 7$
    $3x + 4y = 19$

14. $3I_1 + 7I_2 = 5$
    $2I_1 + 3I_2 = 5$

15. $3a + 4b = 58$
    $5a - 2b = 10$

16. $12I_2 + 3I_1 = 75$
    $4I_2 - I_1 = 7$

17. $4I_2 + I_3 = 25$
    $-3I_2 + 8I_3 = -45$

18. $20x - 7y = -36$
    $-4x - 2y = -20$

19. $6I_2 + 5I_3 = 40$ 20. $5I_1 + 2I_2 = 36$
     $-4I_2 + 7I_3 = -6$ $3I_1 - 4I_2 = -20$

JOB 7-14 SOLVING SIMULTANEOUS EQUATIONS BY SUBSTITUTION

There are some pairs of equations which may be solved more efficiently by this method of substitution than by the addition method discussed in Job 7-13.

EXAMPLE 7-61   Solve the pair of simultaneous equations given below for the value of x and y.

SOLUTION

1 The equations are:

$$x = 4 \tag{1}$$
$$2x + y = 11 \tag{2}$$

2 Since x is given equal to 4, we may *substitute* this value for x in equation (2).
    a Write the equation.

$$2x + y = 11 \tag{2}$$

    b Substitute 4 for x.

$$2(4) + y = 11$$

    c Multiply.

$$8 + y = 11$$

    d Transpose.

$$y = 11 - 8$$

    e Combine like terms.

$$y = 3 \quad Ans.$$

EXAMPLE 7-62   Solve the pair of simultaneous equations given below for the value of x and y.

SOLUTION

1 The equations are:

$$y = 2x \tag{1}$$
$$x + 2y = 20 \tag{2}$$

2 Since y is given equal to $2x$, we may *substitute* this value for y in equation (2).

   a Write the equation.

$$x + 2y = 20 \qquad (2)$$

   b Substitute $2x$ for y.

$$x + 2(2x) = 20$$

   c Multiply.

$$x + 4x = 20$$

   d Combine like terms.

$$5x = 20$$

   e Solve the basic equation.

$$x = 4 \qquad Ans.$$

3 Substitute this value for x in equation (1) to find y.
   a Write the equation.

$$y = 2x \qquad (1)$$

   b Substitute 4 for x.

$$y = 2(4)$$

   c Multiply.

$$y = 8 \qquad Ans.$$

EXAMPLE 7-63 Solve the pair of simultaneous equations given below for the value of x and y.

SOLUTION

1 The equations are:

$$3x + y = 6 \qquad (1)$$
$$y = 2x + 1 \qquad (2)$$

2 In equation (2), y is given equal to the *quantity* $2x + 1$, which is best written as $(2x + 1)$. We can substitute *this* value for y in equation (1).
   a Write the equation.

$$3x + y = 6 \qquad (1)$$

   b Substitute $(2x + 1)$ for y.

$$3x + (2x + 1) = 6$$

   c Remove parentheses.

$$3x + 2x + 1 = 6$$

   d Transpose.

$$3x + 2x = 6 - 1$$

e Combine like terms.

$$5x = 5$$

f Solve the basic equation.

$$x = 1 \qquad Ans.$$

3 Substitute this value for x in equation (2) to find y.
 a Write the equation.

$$y = 2x + 1 \tag{2}$$

b Substitute 1 for x.

$$y = 2(1) + 1$$

c Multiply.

$$y = 2 + 1$$

d Combine like terms.

$$y = 3 \qquad Ans.$$

EXAMPLE 7-64   Solve the pair of simultaneous equations given below for the value of x and y.

SOLUTION

1 The equations are:

$$2x + y = 6 \tag{1}$$
$$3x + 0.5y = 5 \tag{2}$$

2 Solve equation (1) so as to obtain a value for y expressed in terms of x.
 a Write the equation.

$$2x + y = 6 \tag{1}$$

b Transpose *all* quantities *except* y to the other side.

$$y = 6 - 2x$$

3 Since y is now expressed as the *quantity* $(6 - 2x)$, we may substitute *this* value for y in equation (2).
 a Write the equation.

$$3x + 0.5y = 5 \tag{2}$$

b Substitute $(6 - 2x)$ for y.

$$3x + 0.5(6 - 2x) = 5$$

c Remove parentheses.

$$3x + 3 - 1x = 5$$

d Transpose.

$$3x - x = 5 - 3$$

e   Combine like terms.

$$2x = 2$$

f   Solve the basic equation.

$$x = 1 \qquad Ans.$$

4   Substitute this value for x in the equation found in step 2.
   a   Write the equation.

$$y = 6 - 2x$$

   b   Substitute 1 for x.

$$y = 6 - 2(1)$$

   c   Multiply.

$$y = 6 - 2$$

   d   Combine like terms.

$$y = 4 \qquad Ans.$$

SUMMARY OF METHOD

1.   Write the equations.
2.   Solve either equation for one of the unknowns in terms of the other.
3.   Substitute this value in the other equation.
4.   Solve the resulting equation.
5.   Substitute the value found in step 4 in the equation found in step 2.
6.   Solve the resulting equation for the value of the second unknown.
7.   Check.

SELF-TEST 7-65   Solve the pair of simultaneous equations given below for the value of x and y.

SOLUTION

The equations are:

$$5x + 3y = 6.5 \qquad\qquad (1)$$
$$2x - \ y = 7 \qquad\qquad (2)$$

1   Solve one of these equations for one letter in terms of the other. The better equation to use for this purpose is equation (___) in which we shall solve the equation for the letter ___ because the coefficient of y is already 1.

                                                                                            2
                                                                                           y

2   *a*   Write the equation.

$$2x - y = 7 \qquad\qquad (2)$$

   b   Transpose to get $+y$ even if it is on the right side.

$$2x - \underline{\quad} = y$$

    or $\qquad\qquad\qquad\qquad y = \underline{\qquad\qquad}$

                                                                                           7
                                                                                           $2x - 7$

3   Since y is now expressed as the quantity _____, we may now _____ this value for y in equation (1).

   a   Write the equation.

$$5x + 3y = 6.5 \qquad (1)$$

   b   Substitute.

$$5x + 3(\underline{\qquad}) = 6.5$$

   c   Remove parentheses.

$$5x + \underline{\quad} - \underline{\quad} = 6.5$$

   d   Transpose.

$$5x + 6x = 6.5 + \underline{\quad}$$

   e   Combine like terms.

$$11x = \underline{\quad}$$

   f   Solve the basic equation.

$$x = \frac{27.5}{?}$$

   g   Divide.

$$x = \underline{\quad} \qquad Ans.$$

4   Substitute this value for x in the equation found in step 2.

   a   Write the equation.

$$y = 2x - 7$$

   b   Substitute.

$$y = 2(\underline{\quad}) - 7$$

   c   Multiply.

$$y = \underline{\quad} - 7$$

   d   Combine like terms.

$$y = \underline{\quad} \qquad Ans.$$

5   Check. Substitute these values for x and y in the original equations (1) and (2).

Substitute $x = \underline{\quad}$ and $y = \underline{\quad}$ in equation (1).

$$5x + 3y = 6.5 \qquad (1)$$

$$5(\underline{\quad}) + 3(\underline{\quad}) = 6.5$$

$$\underline{\quad} - 6 = 6.5$$

$$\underline{\quad} = 6.5 \qquad Check$$

Substitute $x = 2.5$ and $y = -2$ in equation (2).

Right margin annotations:

$(2x - 7)$ substitute

$2x - 7$

$6x$ 21

21

27.5

11

2.5

2.5

5

-2

2.5 -2

2.5 -2

12.5

6.5

$$2x - y = 7 \qquad\qquad (2)$$

$$2(\underline{}) - (\underline{}) = 7$$

$$5\underline{} = 7$$

$$\underline{} = 7 \qquad Check$$

$$\begin{array}{rr} 2.5 & -2 \\ +2 & \\ 7 & \end{array}$$

PROBLEMS

Solve the following sets of equations:

1. $y = 3$
    $4x + y = 23$

2. $4y - x = 9$
    $x = 3$

3. $x = 5$
    $4x - y = 18$

4. $2x + y = 10$
    $y = 3x$

5. $y = 3x + 1$
    $2x + y = 11$

6. $3x + 2y = 17$
    $y = x - 4$

7. $2y - x = 1$
    $x = y + 2$

8. $2x + 5y = 31$
    $x + y = 8$

9. $y - x = 3$
    $2x + y = 6$

10. $2x - y = 7$
    $x - y = 3$

11. $x + 2y = 9$
    $x + 3y = 13$

12. $11x - y = 18$
    $5x + 3y = 22$

JOB 7-15   REVIEW OF ALGEBRA

1 *Like* terms are those which contain the _____ letter portions.   same

2 *Unlike* terms are those in which the letter portions are _____.   different

3 Adding signed numbers.
   a To add two signed numbers of the *same* sign, _____ the numbers and use the common sign.   add
   b To add two signed numbers of *different* sign, _____ the smaller from the larger and use the sign of the _____ number.   subtract   larger

4 To combine a string of signed numbers means to _____ the individual signed numbers using the rules for _____.   add   addition

5 Multiplying and dividing signed numbers.
   a Two signed numbers with the *same* sign yield a (plus/minus) answer.   plus
   b Two signed numbers with *different* signs yield a (plus/minus) answer.   minus

6 A parenthesis is removed by _____ the signed number in front of the parenthesis by each and every quantity within the parenthesis.   multiplying

7 To combine several quantities involving *unlike* terms, combine each group of _____ terms separately.

8 Solving equations.

    a Fractional equations containing one fraction.

        (1) Transpose any other number to the other side of the equality sign.

        (2) Combine like terms.

        (3) Make two fractions by placing any whole numbers or decimals over the number ____.

        (4) Cross-multiply.

        (5) Solve the basic equation.

    b Fractional equations containing two fractions.

        (1) Cross _____.

        (2) Solve the basic equation.

    c Fractional equations with more than two fractions.

        (1) Find the least common _____.

        (2) Multiply each term of the equation by this ____.

        (3) Transpose *all* unknowns to one side of the _____ sign and *all* numbers to the other side.

        (4) Combine the _____ terms on each side separately.

        (5) Solve the basic equation.

    d Equations with parentheses.

        (1) Remove parentheses.

        (2) _____ *all* unknowns to one side of the equality sign and *all* numbers to the other side.

        (3) _____ the like terms on each side separately.

        (4) Solve the basic equation.

    e Simultaneous equations solved by addition.

        (1) In each equation, transpose *all* unknowns to one side of the equality sign and *all* _____ to the other side.

        (2) Combine the _____ terms on each side separately.

        (3) Arrange the _____ letters under each other in both equations.

        (4) Eliminate one letter by _____ one or both equations by the proper number and sign so as to obtain the _____ coefficient with _____ signs.

        (5) ____ the two equations to eliminate the letter.

        (6) Solve the resulting equation which will now contain only ____ letter.

        (7) Substitute this value in *either* of the two _____ equations.

        (8) Solve this equation to obtain the value of the second letter.

    f Simultaneous equations solved by substitution.

        (1) Solve either equation for one of the unknowns in terms of the _____ unknown.

        (2) Substitute this expression for the letter in the other _____.

        (3) Solve the resulting equation.

        (4) Substitute the value found in step 3 in the equation found in step ____.

        (5) Solve the resulting equation for the value of the _____ unknown.

Margin answers:

like

1

multiply

denominator
LCD
equality

like

Transpose

Combine

numbers
like
same
multiplying
same
different or opposite
Add
one

original

other
equation

1
second

TEST—ALGEBRAIC EQUATIONS

Solve the following equations:

1. $10 + \dfrac{3x}{5} = 4$

2. $\dfrac{2E}{5} - 3 = \dfrac{E}{2}$

3. $2(x - 0.2) = 0.8x + 2$

4. $4x - 3y = 22$
   $\underline{3x + 5y = 2}$

5. $2I_1 - 6I_2 = -30$
   $\underline{3I_1 + I_2 = -5}$

8

KIRCHHOFF'S LAWS

JOB 8-1 KIRCHHOFF'S FIRST LAW

RULE	At any point in an electrical circuit, the sum of the currents that enter a junction is equal to the sum of the currents that leave it.

FORMULA

$$\Sigma I_e = \Sigma I_l \qquad \boxed{8\text{-}1}$$

where ΣI_e = summation of all currents *entering* a point
ΣI_l = summation of all currents *leaving* a point

In Fig. 8-1, three resistors meet at point X. The figure shows three ways in which this condition may be drawn. In each, the current I_3 that *enters* point X is equal to the *sum* of the currents I_1 and I_2 that *leave* the junction. This fact may be expressed as the formula $I_3 = I_1 + I_2$. You will probably recognize this as the formula for the total current in a parallel circuit.

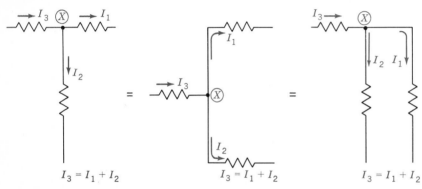

FIGURE 8-1
The current that enters a point is equal to the current that leaves it.

FINDING THE CURRENT IN BRANCH WIRES

EXAMPLE 8-1 Find the current in R_2 of the circuit shown in Fig. 8-2.

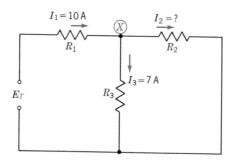

FIGURE 8-2

SOLUTION
At point X,

$$\Sigma I_e = \Sigma I_l \tag{8-1}$$

$$I_1 = I_2 + I_3$$

$$10 = I_2 + 7$$

$$10 - 7 = I_2$$

$$3 = I_2 \quad \text{or} \quad I_2 = 3 \text{ A} \quad Ans.$$

EXAMPLE 8-2 Find the current I_2 in the circuit shown in Fig. 8-3.

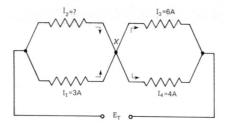

FIGURE 8-3

SOLUTION
The current that enters point X is equal to the current that leaves it. Since I_1 and I_2 enter point X and I_3 and I_4 leave point X, we can apply formula (8-1).

$$\Sigma I_e = \Sigma I_l \tag{8-1}$$

$$I_1 + I_2 = I_3 + I_4$$

$$3 + I_2 = 6 + 4$$

$$I_2 = 10 - 3 = 7 \text{ A} \quad Ans.$$

JOB 8-2   KIRCHHOFF'S SECOND LAW

RULE	The voltage supplied to a circuit is always equal to the sum of the voltage drops across the individual parts of the circuit.

This fact was used when we studied series circuits and was expressed as the formula $E_T = E_1 + E_2 + E_3$. Kirchhoff's second law explains that the sum of the voltage *gains* supplied to a circuit from a generator, battery, etc., is always equal to the sum of the voltage *drops* (E_1, E_2, E_3, etc.) in the circuit. Since the gains are equal to the losses, the total sum of the gains plus the losses must equal zero. The quantities involved must be added *algebraically* in order to include the *direction* of the various voltages. Kirchhoff's second law may now be expressed as follows.

RULE	The *algebraic* sum of all the voltages in any complete electrical circuit is equal to zero.

FORMULA

$$E_1 + E_2 + E_3 + \text{etc.} = 0 \qquad \boxed{8\text{-}2}$$

Direction of voltages. If two equal voltages oppose each other, they may be expressed as $+E_1$ and $-E_2$, where the minus sign in $-E_2$ represents the opposition to $+E_1$. Their algebraic sum would be indicated as

$$+E_1 + (-E_2)$$

or
$$E_1 - E_2$$

Therefore, as we go around a circuit, adding the voltages, we must be very careful to indicate voltage *gains* as *plus* values and voltage *losses* as *minus* values. The following procedure will determine the sign of the voltage.

1 Note the direction of the electron flow around the circuit. Electrons *leave* the negative terminal of the voltage source and *enter* the positive terminal. This is illustrated in Fig. 8-4a.

2 Mark the circuit to indicate the electron flow through *each* resistance. This is shown in Fig. 8-4b. In more complicated circuits, the direction may be unknown. In this event, we shall *assume* a direction. If our assumption is incorrect, the error will be indicated by a minus sign when the resulting equation is solved. A minus current therefore tells us that the true direction is *opposite* to the direction originally assumed. The value of the current will *not* be affected.

3 We intend to move around a circuit to combine all the voltages encountered. We shall start at some convenient point and move around the *complete*

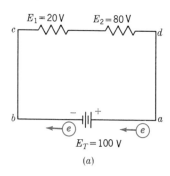

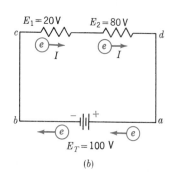

FIGURE 8-4

Electrons *leave* the negative terminal of a voltage source and *enter* the positive terminal.

circuit until we return to the original starting point. The direction of this movement is usually in the direction of the electron flow.

4 *Source voltages* are *positive* (+) if we move through them from the positive (+) to the negative (−) terminal. *Source voltages* are *negative* (−) if we move through them from the negative (−) to the positive (+) terminal. Therefore, in Fig. 8-4b, if we start at point *a* and move around the circuit in the direction *abcd*, we shall go through E_T from (+) to (−) and $E_T = +100$ V. However, if we start at point *a* and move around the circuit in the direction *adcb*, we shall go through E_T from (−) to (+) and $E_T = -100$ V.

5 The voltage across any resistance will be *negative* if we go through it *in the direction of the assumed electron flow*. Thus, in Fig. 8-4b, if we go through the circuit in the direction *abcd*, $E_1 = -20$ V and $E_2 = -80$ V.

6 The voltage in any resistance will be *positive* if we go through it in a direction *opposite* to the assumed electron flow. Thus, in Fig. 8-4b, if we go through the circuit in the direction *adcb*, $E_2 = +80$ V and $E_1 = +20$ V.

EXAMPLE 8-3   Find the signs of the voltages encountered when tracing the circuits shown in Fig. 8-5a.

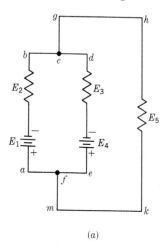

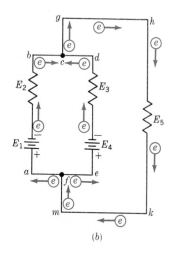

SOLUTION

1 Determine the direction of the electron flow around the circuit. Since electrons leave the negative terminal, the direction of flow will be *up* to point *c*

FIGURE 8-5

Electrons leave the negative terminal of a voltage source.

from both E_1 and E_4. At point c, since the electrons that enter point c must also leave it, the electrons must flow *out* of point c *up* to point g and continue around to point f. At f, the current divides, part going to point a and the rest to point e. This is indicated in Fig. 8-5b.

2   Determine the direction of the voltages around the circuit *abcdef*.
    a E_1 is +, since we go through it from + to −.
    b E_2 is −, since we go through it in the direction of the electron flow.
    c E_3 is +, since we go through it in a direction *opposite* to the electron flow.
    d E_4 is −, since we go through it from − to +.
3   Determine the direction of the voltages around the circuit *abcghkmf*.
    a E_1 is +, since we go through it from + to −.
    b E_2 is −, since we go through it in the direction of the electron flow.
    c E_5 is −, since we go through it in the direction of the electron flow.
4   Determine the direction of the voltages around the circuit *fedcghkm*.
    a E_4 is +, since we go through it from + to −.
    b E_3 is −, since we go through it in the direction of the electron flow.
    c E_5 is −, since we go through it in the direction of the electron flow.

SELF-TEST 8-4   Find the signs of the voltages encountered when tracing the circuit *abcdefa* shown in Fig. 8-6.

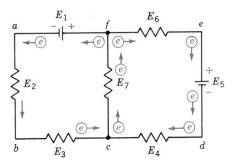

FIGURE 8-6
The direction of the electron flow is assumed.

SOLUTION
1   Assume that the direction of the electron flow is that shown on the diagram.
2   Determine the signs of the voltages. The direction of our trace is in a counterclockwise direction starting from point a.
    a E_2 and E_3 are both ____, since we are going through them both in the (same/opposite) direction as the electron flow.
    b E_4 and E_6 are both ____, since we are going through them both in the (same/opposite) direction as the electron flow.
    c E_5 is ____, since we go through it from ____ to ____.
    d E_1 is ____, since we go through it from ____ to ____.

                                             −
                                           same
                                           +
                                         opposite
                                         −   −   +
                                           +   +   −

JOB 8-3   USING KIRCHHOFF'S LAWS IN SERIES CIRCUITS

EXAMPLE 8-5   Find the current in the series circuit shown in Fig. 8-7a.

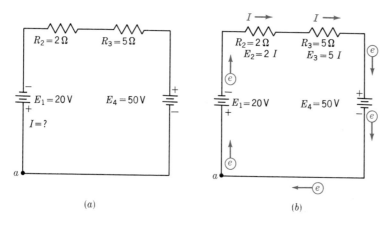

FIGURE 8-7

The sources are connected so as to aid each other.

(a)   (b)

SOLUTION

1   Determine the direction of the electron flow. E_1 and E_4 are connected so that the electron flow comes out of one source and continues through the other in the same direction. This connection of sources aiding each other causes an electron flow moving *clockwise* around the circuit.

2   Mark this direction on the circuit as shown in Fig. 8-7b.

3   By Ohm's law, the voltages in R_2 and R_3 will equal $2I$ and $5I$, respectively.

4   Determine the direction of the voltages. Trace the circuit in a clockwise direction starting at point a.

  a E_1 and E_4 are both +, since we go through them from + to —.

  b E_2 and E_3 are both —, since we go through them in the direction of the electron flow.

5   Apply Kirchhoff's second law. The *algebraic* sum of all the voltages around a circuit will equal zero. Add the voltages starting at point a.

$$E_1 + E_2 + E_3 + E_4 = 0$$

$$+20 - 2I - 5I + 50 = 0$$

$$-2I - 5I = -20 - 50$$

$$-7I = -70$$

$$7I = 70$$

$$I = 10 \text{ A} \qquad Ans.$$

6   *Check:* If we trace the circuit in a counterclockwise direction starting from point a, the voltages through the sources are now negative and the voltages through the resistors are positive, since we are now going through them in a direction *opposite* to the electron flow.

$$E_4 + E_3 + E_2 + E_1 = 0$$

$$-50 + 5I + 2I - 20 = 0$$

$$5I + 2I = 50 + 20$$

$$7I = 70$$

$$I = 10 \text{ A} \qquad Check$$

EXAMPLE 8-6   Find the current in the series circuit shown in Fig. 8-8a.

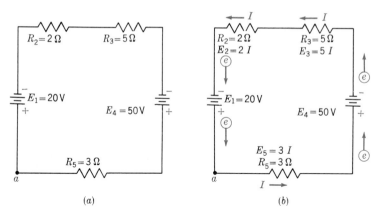

(a)   (b)

FIGURE 8-8
The sources are connected
so as to oppose each other.

SOLUTION

1   Determine the direction of the electron flow. E_1 and E_4 are connected so that they oppose each other. E_4 (50 V) is stronger than E_1 (20 V), and the electron flow is therefore governed by E_4. This will cause the electron flow to be in a *counterclockwise* direction.

2   Mark this direction on the circuit as shown in Fig. 8-8b.

3   By Ohm's law, the voltages in R_2, R_3, and R_5 will equal $2I$, $5I$, and $3I$, respectively.

4   Determine the direction of the voltages. Trace the circuit in a counterclockwise direction starting at point *a*.

   a E_5, E_3, and E_2 are all −, since we go through them in the direction of the electron flow. E_4 is +, since we go through it from + to −. E_1 is −, since we go through it from − to +.

5   Apply Kirchhoff's second law.

$$E_5 + E_4 + E_3 + E_2 + E_1 = 0$$

$$-3I + 50 - 5I - 2I - 20 = 0$$

$$-3I - 5I - 2I = 20 - 50$$

$$-10I = -30$$

$$10I = 30$$

$$I = 3 \text{ A} \qquad Ans.$$

EXAMPLE 8-7   Use the circuit shown in Fig. 8-9a. Find (*a*) the total current and (*b*) the voltage drop across each resistance.

SOLUTION

a   Find the total current.

1   Determine the direction of the electron flow. E_1 and E_3 aid each other, and since their total (70 V) is greater then the opposing E_5 (30 V), the flow will be in a counterclockwise direction.

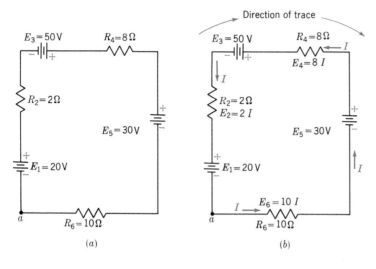

FIGURE 8-9

2   Mark this direction on the circuit as shown in Fig. 8-9*b*.
3   By Ohm's law, the voltages in R_2, R_4, and R_6 will equal $2I$, $8I$, and $10I$, respectively.
4   Determine the direction of the voltages.   Trace the circuit in a *clockwise* direction starting at point *a*.
E_1 and E_3 are $-$, since we go through them from $-$ to $+$.
E_5 is $+$, since we go through it from $+$ to $-$.
E_2, E_4, and E_6 are all $+$, since we go through them in a direction *opposite* to the electron flow.
5   Apply Kirchhoff's second law.

$$E_1 + E_2 + E_3 + E_4 + E_5 + E_6 = 0$$

$$-20 + 2I - 50 + 8I + 30 + 10I = 0$$

$$2I + 8I + 10I = 20 + 50 - 30$$

$$20I = 40$$

$$I = 2 \text{ A} \qquad Ans.$$

b   Find the voltage drop across each resistance.

$$E_2 = IR_2 \qquad E_4 = IR_4 \qquad E_6 = IR_6$$

$$E_2 = 2 \times 2 \qquad E_4 = 2 \times 8 \qquad E_6 = 2 \times 10$$

$$E_2 = 4 \text{ V} \qquad E_4 = 16 \text{ V} \qquad E_6 = 20 \text{ V} \qquad Ans.$$

Check: The sum of the voltages around the complete circuit should equal zero.   Add the voltages in a counterclockwise direction starting from point *a*.

$$E_6 + E_5 + E_4 + E_3 + E_2 + E_1 = 0$$

$$-20 - 30 - 16 + 50 - 4 + 20 = 0$$

$$0 = 0 \qquad Check$$

SELF-TEST 8-8   In Fig. 8-10, R_2 represents the internal resistance of the generator. Find (*a*) the total current in the circuit, (*b*) the voltage drop across each resistance, and (*c*) the emf of the generator.

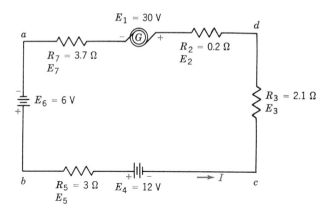

FIGURE 8-10
R_2 represents the internal resistance of the generator.

SOLUTION

a   Find the total current.

1   Determine the direction of the electron flow. E_1 and E_4 __(aid/oppose)__ | aid
each other, and since their total $(30 + 12 = 42)$ is greater than E_6 (6 V), which
__(aids/opposes)__ them, the flow will be in a __(clockwise/counterclockwise)__ | opposes counterclockwise
direction.

2   Mark this direction on the circuit diagram.

3   By Ohm's law, the voltages in the resistances are

$$E_2 = 0.2I \qquad E_3 = \underline{\qquad}$$ | 2.1*I*

$$E_5 = \underline{\qquad} \qquad E_7 = \underline{\qquad}$$ | 3*I*   3.7*I*

4   Determine the direction of the voltages. Trace the circuit in the same
direction as the electron flow, which will be _____. Start at | counterclockwise
point *a*.

E_6 is ____, since we go through it from ____ to ____. | −   −   +
E_4 and E_1 are both __:__, since we go through them both from ____ to ____. | +   +   −
E_5, E_3, E_2, and E_7 are all ____, since we go through them all in the __(same/__ | −   same
__opposite)__ direction as the electron flow.

5   Apply Kirchhoff's second law.

$$E_6 + E_5 + E_4 + E_3 + E_2 + E_1 + E_7 = \underline{\qquad}$$ | 0

$$-6 - 3I + 12 - 2.1I - 0.2I + 30 - \underline{\qquad} = 0$$ | 3.7*I*

$$36 - \underline{\qquad} = 0$$ | 9*I*

$$36 = \underline{\qquad}$$ | 9*I*

$$I = \underline{\qquad} A \qquad Ans.$$ | 4

b   Find the voltage drop across each resistance.

$$E_2 = IR_2 \qquad\qquad E_3 = IR_3$$

$$E_2 = 4 \times 0.2 = 0.8 \text{ V} \qquad E_3 = 4 \times 2.1 = \underline{\qquad} \text{ V}$$ | 8.4

$$E_5 = IR_5 \qquad\qquad E_7 = IR_7$$

$$E_5 = 4 \times 3 = 12 \text{ V} \qquad E_7 = 4 \times \underline{\hspace{1em}} = \underline{\hspace{1em}} \text{ V}$$

| | 3.7 | 14.8 |

Check. The sum of the voltages around the circuit should equal _____. Add the voltages in a clockwise direction starting from point *a*. In this direction, R_7, R_2, R_3, and R_5 will all be ____ because we go through them in a direction _____ to the flow of electrons.

E_1 and E_4 will both be ____ because we go through them from ____ to ____.
E_6 will be ____ because we go through it from ____ to ____.

$$E_7 + E_1 + E_2 + E_3 + E_4 + E_5 + E_6 = 0$$

$$14.8 - 30 \underline{\hspace{2em}} + 8.4 - 12 + 12 + 6 = 0$$

$$0 = 0 \qquad Check$$

| zero |
| + |
| opposite |
| − − + |
| + + − |
| + 0.8 |

Find the emf of the generator.

$$\text{emf} = E_1 + E_2 = 30 + 0.8 = \underline{\hspace{1em}} \text{ V} \qquad Ans.$$

| 30.8 |

PROBLEMS

In each of the circuits shown, find (*a*) the total current, and (*b*) the voltage drop across each resistor.

1. See Fig. 8-11.

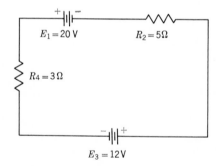

$E_1 = 20$ V $R_2 = 5\Omega$ $R_4 = 3\Omega$ $E_3 = 12$ V

FIGURE 8-11

2. See Fig. 8-12.

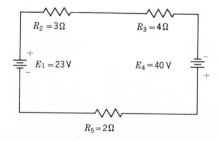

$R_2 = 3\Omega$ $R_3 = 4\Omega$ $E_1 = 23$ V $E_4 = 40$ V $R_5 = 2\Omega$

FIGURE 8-12

3. Use a circuit similar to that shown in Fig. 8-12. $E_1 = 20$ V, $R_2 = 6\ \Omega$, $R_3 = 4\ \Omega$, $E_4 = 16$ V, and $R_5 = 5\ \Omega$.

4. Use a circuit similar to that shown in Fig. 8-12. $E_1 = 45$ V, $R_2 = 2\ \Omega$, $R_3 = 4\ \Omega$, $R_5 = 6\ \Omega$, and $E_4 = 9$ V with the polarity reversed.
5. See Fig. 8-13.

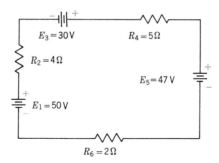

FIGURE 8-13

6. See Fig. 8-14.

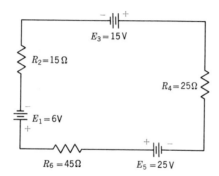

FIGURE 8-14

7. Find the total current flowing in the circuit shown in Fig. 8-15. Be sure to include the internal resistance of the batteries and generator.

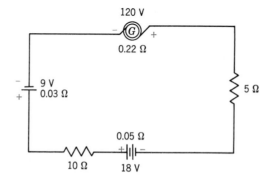

FIGURE 8-15
The circuit includes the internal resistances of the voltage sources.

8. A current of 4 A flows in the circuit shown in Fig. 8-16. Find the value of R.

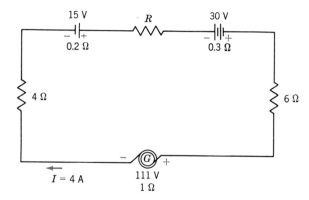

FIGURE 8-16

JOB 8-4   USING KIRCHHOFF'S LAWS IN PARALLEL CIRCUITS

EXAMPLE 8-9   Find all missing values of voltage, current, and resistance in the circuit shown in Fig. 8-17.

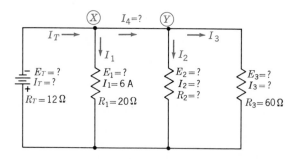

FIGURE 8-17

Using Kirchhoff's first law in parallel circuits.

SOLUTION

1   Start at the point where the greatest amount of information is available. This will be branch R_1. Find E_1.

$$E_1 = I_1 \times R_1$$

$$E_1 = 6 \times 20 = 120 \text{ V} \qquad Ans.$$

2   Find the other voltages. Since this is a parallel circuit,

$$E_T = E_1 = E_2 = E_3 = 120 \text{ V} \qquad Ans.$$

3   Find I_T and I_3 by Ohm's law.

$$E_T = I_T \times R_T \qquad\qquad E_3 = I_3 \times R_3$$

$$120 = I_T \times 12 \qquad\qquad 120 = I_3 \times 60$$

$$I_T = \frac{120}{12} = 10 \text{ A} \qquad I_3 = \frac{120}{60} = 2 \text{ A}$$

4   Find the current I_2 by applying Kirchhoff's first law.
   a   Assume the direction of the currents at point X to be as shown on the

diagram. $I_T = 10$ A *entering* point X, $I_1 = 6$ A *leaving* point X, and $I_4 = ?$ *leaving* point X.

$$\Sigma I_e = \Sigma I_l \qquad\qquad (8\text{-}1)$$

$$I_T = I_4 + I_1$$

$$10 = I_4 + 6$$

$$10 - 6 = I_4$$

$$I_4 = 4 \text{ A } \textit{leaving} \text{ point } X$$

b At point Y, I_4 enters the point, and I_2 and I_3 leave the point.

$$\Sigma I_e = \Sigma I_l \qquad\qquad (8\text{-}1)$$

$$I_4 = I_2 + I_3$$

$$4 = I_2 + 2$$

$$I_2 = 2 \text{ A } \textit{leaving} \text{ point } Y \qquad \textit{Ans.}$$

5 Find R_2 by Ohm's law.

$$E_2 = I_2 \times R_2$$

$$120 = 2 \times R_2$$

$$R_2 = \frac{120}{2} = 60 \ \Omega \qquad \textit{Ans.}$$

EXAMPLE 8-10 Find the total voltage of the circuit shown in Fig. 8-18.

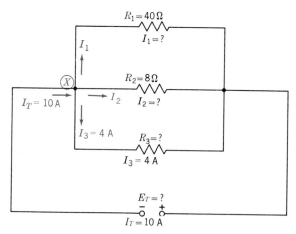

FIGURE 8-18

SOLUTION

The total voltage E_T in this parallel circuit will be equal to any of the branch voltages. E_1 or E_2 may be found if we can determine the value of either I_1 or I_2.

1 Find I_2. Assume the direction of the currents to be as shown on the diagram. At point X, by Kirchhoff's first law,

$$\Sigma I_l = \Sigma I_e \qquad (8\text{-}1)$$

$$4 + I_1 + I_2 = 10$$

$$I_2 = 10 - 4 - I_1$$

$$\text{or} \qquad I_2 = (6 - I_1) \qquad (1)$$

2   Apply Kirchhoff's second law. Trace around the circuit through R_1 in a clockwise direction starting at E_T.

$$+E_T - 40I_1 = 0$$

$$\text{or } E_T = 40I_1 \qquad (2)$$

Trace the circuit again, but this time through R_2.

$$+E_T - 8I_2 = 0$$

$$\text{or } E_T = 8I_2 \qquad (3)$$

3   In equation (1), we found that $I_2 = (6 - I_1)$. Substitute this value for I_2 in equation (3).

$$E_T = 8I_2 \qquad (3)$$

$$E_T = 8(6 - I_1)$$

$$E_T = 48 - 8I_1 \qquad (4)$$

4   Set the values for E_T found in equations (2) and (4) equal to each other.

$$40I_1 = 48 - 8I_1$$

$$40I_1 + 8I_1 = 48$$

$$48I_1 = 48$$

$$I_1 = 1 \text{ A} \qquad Ans.$$

5   Find E_1 by Ohm's law.

$$E_1 = I_1 \times R_1 = 1 \times 40 = 40 \text{ V}$$

6   Find E_T. Since this is a parallel circuit,

$$E_T = E_1 = E_2 = E_3 = 40 \text{ V} \qquad Ans.$$

SELF-TEST 8-11   A voltage source supplies 12 A to a parallel combination of 60 Ω and 20 Ω, as shown in Fig. 8-19. Find I_1, I_2, and E_T.

SOLUTION

1   Apply Kirchhoff's second law. Trace around the circuit in the direction *fabcdef.*

$$E_T - 60I_1 = 0$$

$$E_T = \underline{} \qquad (1)$$

$60I_1$

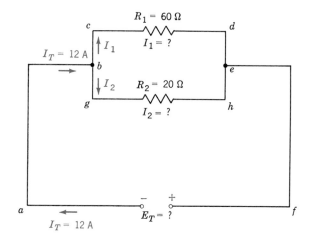

FIGURE 8-19

Trace around the circuit in the direction *fabghef.*

$$\underline{\quad\quad} - 20I_2 = 0 \qquad\qquad\qquad E_T$$

$$E_T = \underline{\quad\quad} \qquad\qquad (2) \qquad\qquad 20I_2$$

These two expressions for E_T may be set _____ to each other, which gives   equal

$$20I_2 = \underline{\quad\quad} \qquad\qquad\qquad 60I_1$$

$$I_2 = \frac{60I_1}{?} \qquad\qquad\qquad\qquad 20$$

$$I_2 = \underline{\quad\quad} I_1 \qquad\qquad (3) \qquad\qquad 3$$

2   Now apply Kirchhoff's first law.

$$\Sigma I_l = \Sigma I_e \qquad\qquad (8\text{-}1)$$

At point b,

$$I_1 + I_2 = \underline{\quad\quad} \qquad\qquad (4) \qquad\qquad 12$$

Now, according to equation (3), we can substitute $3I_1$ for I_2 in equation (4). This will give

$$I_1 + \underline{\quad\quad} = 12 \qquad\qquad\qquad 3I_1$$

$$\underline{\quad\quad} = 12 \qquad\qquad\qquad 4I_1$$

$$I_1 = \underline{\quad\quad} A \quad\quad Ans. \qquad\qquad 3$$

Now we can go back to equation (3) to find I_2.

$$I_2 = 3I_1$$

$$I_2 = 3 \times \underline{\quad\quad} \qquad\qquad\qquad 3$$

$$I_2 = \underline{\quad\quad} A \quad\quad Ans. \qquad\qquad 9$$

3   Find E_2. By Ohm's law,

$$E_2 = I_2 \times R_2$$

$$E_2 = 9 \times \underline{\hspace{1cm}}$$

$$E_2 = \underline{\hspace{1cm}} \text{ V}$$

But in a parallel circuit,

$$E_2 = E_T, \tag{4-1}$$

$$E_T = \underline{\hspace{1cm}} \text{ V} \quad Ans.$$

20	
180	
180	

PROBLEMS

1. In a circuit similar to that shown in Fig. 8-17, $R_T = 6\ \Omega$, $I_1 = 9$ A, $R_1 = 10\ \Omega$, and $R_3 = 60\ \Omega$. Find all missing values of voltage, current, and resistance.

2. In a circuit similar to that shown in Fig. 8-17, $R_T = 8\ \Omega$, $I_1 = 5$ A, $I_2 = 1$ A, and $R_2 = 80\ \Omega$. Find all missing values of voltage, current, and resistance.

3. In a circuit similar to that shown in Fig. 8-17, $R_T = 15\ \Omega$, $I_1 = 10$ A, $R_1 = 30\ \Omega$, and $R_3 = 40\ \Omega$. Find all missing values of voltage, current, and resistance.

4. In a circuit similar to that shown in Fig. 8-18, $I_T = 40$ A, $R_1 = 4\ \Omega$, $R_2 = 12\ \Omega$, and $I_3 = 20$ A. Find the total voltage E_T and R_3.

5. In a circuit similar to that shown in Fig. 8-18, $I_T = 39$ A, $R_1 = 12\ \Omega$, $R_2 = 9\ \Omega$, and $I_3 = 18$ A. Find the total voltage E_T and R_3.

6. In a circuit similar to that shown in Fig. 8-18, $I_T = 15$ A, $I_1 = 9$ A, $R_2 = 10\ \Omega$, and $R_3 = 30\ \Omega$. Find the total voltage E_T and R_1.

7. In a circuit similar to that shown in Fig. 8-19, $R_1 = 4\ \Omega$, $R_2 = 12\ \Omega$, and $I_T = 2.6$ A. Find I_1, I_2, and E_T.

8. In a circuit similar to that shown in Fig. 8-19, $R_1 = 100\ \Omega$, $R_2 = 45\ \Omega$, and $I_T = 7.975$ A. Find I_1, I_2, and E_T.

9. A generator supplies 12 A to three resistors of 16 Ω, 48 Ω, and 24 Ω connected in parallel. Find (*a*) the current in each resistor and (*b*) the generator voltage.

10. In Fig. 8-20, find (*a*) I_1, (*b*) I_2, and (*c*) E_T.

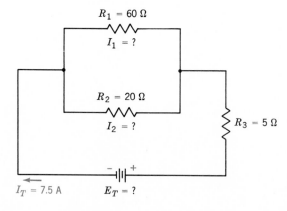

$R_1 = 60\ \Omega$

$I_1 = ?$

$R_2 = 20\ \Omega$

$I_2 = ?$

$R_3 = 5\ \Omega$

$I_T = 7.5$ A $E_T = ?$

FIGURE 8-20

11. Problems 7 and 8 above may be solved by another method. What formula should be used?
12. Check these problems using this formula.

JOB 8-5 USING KIRCHHOFF'S LAWS IN COMPLEX CIRCUITS

As the circuits under consideration become more complicated, it is generally easier to designate the currents in the various branches as x, y, and z, rather than I_1, I_2, or I_3.

EXAMPLE 8-12   Solve the circuit shown in Fig. 8-21 for the values of the currents x, y, and z.

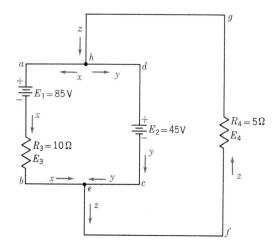

FIGURE 8-21
In complex circuits, the branch currents are designated as x, y, and z A.

SOLUTION

1   Assume the direction of the electron flow to be that indicated on the diagram.
2   Apply Kirchhoff's second law. Trace around the circuit in the direction *abcd*.

$$E_1 + E_3 + E_2 = 0$$
$$85 - 10x - 45 = 0$$
$$-10x = 45 - 85$$
$$-10x = -40$$
$$x = 4 \text{ A} \qquad Ans.$$

Trace around the circuit in the direction *abefgh*.

$$E_1 + E_3 + E_4 = 0$$
$$85 - 10x - 5z = 0$$

Substitute 4 for x.

$$85 - 10(4) - 5z = 0$$

$$85 - 40 - 5z = 0$$

$$-5z = 40 - 85$$

$$-5z = -45$$

$$z = 9 \text{ A} \quad Ans.$$

3 Find the current y by applying Kirchhoff's first law. At point e,

$$\Sigma I_e = \Sigma I_l \qquad (8\text{-}1)$$

$$x + y = z$$

$$4 + y = 9$$

$$y = 9 - 4 = 5 \text{ A} \quad Ans.$$

4 Check by tracing the circuit $dcefgh$, using Kirchhoff's second law.

$$E_2 + E_4 = 0 \qquad (8\text{-}2)$$

$$45 - 5z = 0$$

$$45 - 5(9) = 0$$

$$45 - 45 = 0$$

$$0 = 0 \quad Check$$

EXAMPLE 8-13 Solve the circuit shown in Fig. 8-22 for the values of the currents x, y, and z.

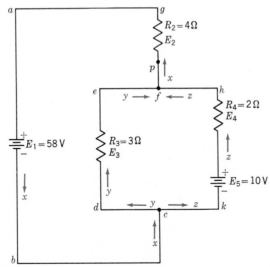

FIGURE 8-22

Since E_1 is stronger than E_5, the electron flow is *in* to point c from the source E_1.

SOLUTION

1 Since E_1 is greater than E_5, the electron flow x is assumed to be *in* to point

c from E_1. At point c, the flow is assumed to be as shown on the diagram. If we are incorrect in these assumptions, a minus sign for a calculated current will advise us to change the direction.

2 Express the current z in terms of currents x and y. At point c,

$$\Sigma I_l = \Sigma I_e \qquad (8\text{-}1)$$

$$y + z = x$$

$$z = x - y \qquad (a)$$

3 Apply Kirchhoff's second law. Trace around the circuit in the direction *abcdefg*.

$$58 - 3y - 4x = 0$$

$$-3y - 4x = -58$$

$$\text{or } 3y + 4x = 58 \qquad (1)$$

Trace around the circuit in the direction *khfedck*.

$$-10 - 2z + 3y = 0$$

Substitute $(x - y)$ for z from equation (a).

$$-10 - 2(x - y) + 3y = 0$$

$$-10 - 2x + 2y + 3y = 0$$

$$5y - 2x - 10 = 0$$

$$\text{or } 5y - 2x = 10 \qquad (2)$$

4 Solve equations (1) and (2) simultaneously.

$$3y + 4x = 58 \qquad (1)$$
$$5y - 2x = 10 \qquad (2)$$

Multiplying equation (2) by 2,

$$3y + 4x = 58$$
$$10y - 4x = 20$$

Add
$$\overline{13y \qquad\ = 78}$$

$$y = 6 \text{ A} \qquad Ans.$$

5 Substitute $y = 6$ in equation (2) to find x.

$$5y - 2x = 10 \qquad (2)$$

$$5(6) - 2x = 10$$

$$30 - 2x = 10$$

$$-2x = 10 - 30$$

$$-2x = -20$$

$$x = 10 \text{ A} \qquad Ans.$$

6 Substitute the values for x and y in equation (a) to find the current z.

$$z = x - y \qquad\qquad (a)$$

$$z = 10 - 6 = 4 \text{ A} \qquad Ans.$$

7   Find the voltage drops in each resistor.

$$E_2 = 4x \qquad E_3 = 3y \qquad E_4 = 2z$$

$$E_2 = 4(10) \qquad E_3 = 3(6) \qquad E_4 = 2(4)$$

$$E_2 = 40 \text{ V} \qquad E_3 = 18 \text{ V} \qquad E_4 = 8 \text{ V}$$

8   Check by tracing the circuit *abckhfg*, using Kirchhoff's second law.

$$E_1 + E_5 + E_4 + E_2 = 0$$

$$58 - 10 - 8 - 40 = 0$$

$$58 - 58 = 0$$

$$0 = 0 \qquad Check$$

In order to illustrate the technique of handling problems in which the assumed direction of electron flow proves to be incorrect, let us investigate the following example.

EXAMPLE 8-14   Solve the circuit shown in Fig. 8-23 for the values of the currents *x*, *y*, and *z*.

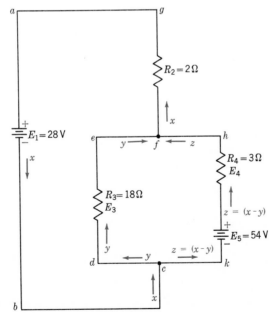

FIGURE 8-23

SOLUTION

1   Assume the direction of the electron flow to be that shown on the diagram.

2   Express the current *z* in terms of currents *x* and *y*. At point *c*,

$$\Sigma I_l = \Sigma I_e \tag{8-1}$$

$$y + z = x$$

$$z = x - y \tag{a}$$

3   Apply Kirchhoff's second law. Trace around the circuit in the direction *abcdefg*.

$$28 - 18y - 2x = 0$$

$$-2x - 18y = -28$$

Divide the equation by -2 in order to simplify. This gives

$$x + 9y = 14 \tag{1}$$

Trace around the circuit in the direction *khfedc*.

$$-54 - 3z + 18y = 0$$

Substitute $(x - y)$ for z from equation (*a*).

$$-54 - 3(x - y) + 18y = 0$$

$$-54 - 3x + 3y + 18y = 0$$

$$-3x + 21y = 54$$

Divide the equation by 3 in order to simplify. This gives

$$-x + 7y = 18 \tag{2}$$

4   Solve equations (1) and (2) simultaneously.

$$x + 9y = 14 \tag{1}$$

$$\underline{-x + 7y = 18} \tag{2}$$

Add.

$$16y = 32$$

$$y = 2 \text{ A} \qquad Ans.$$

5   Substitute $y = 2$ in equation (1) to find x.

$$x + 9y = 14 \tag{1}$$

$$x + 9(2) = 14$$

$$x + 18 = 14$$

$$x = 14 - 18 = -4 \text{ A} \qquad Ans.$$

The fact that the current x is *minus* 4 A means that current x does *not* flow *into* point *c* but *does* flow *out* of this point. Similarly, the current x does *not* flow *out* of point *f* but *does* flow *into* this point.

6   Substitute the values for x and y in equation (*a*) to find the current z.

$$z = x - y \tag{a}$$

$$z = -4 - 2 = -6 \text{ A} \qquad Ans.$$

Since z is *minus* 6 A, the actual direction of flow of current z is *into* point *c* and *out* of point *f*.

7   Find the voltage drops in each resistor.

$$E_2 = 2x \qquad E_3 = 18y \qquad E_4 = 3z$$

$$E_2 = 2(-4) \qquad E_3 = 18(2) \qquad E_4 = 3(-6)$$

$$E_2 = -8 \text{ V} \qquad E_3 = 36 \text{ V} \qquad E_4 = -18 \text{ V}$$

8   Check by tracing the circuit *abckhfg*, using Kirchhoff's second law.

$$E_1 + E_5 + E_4 + E_2 = 0$$

Note:

$E_5 = -54$ V because we go through it from $-$ to $+$.

$E_4 = -(-18)$ V because we go through R_4 in the direction of the assumed current flow.

$E_2 = -(-8)$ V because we go through R_2 in the direction of the assumed current flow.

$$28 - 54 - (-18) - (-8) = 0$$

$$28 - 54 + 18 + 8 = 0$$

$$54 - 54 = 0$$

$$0 = 0 \qquad Check$$

EXAMPLE 8-15   Solve the circuit shown in Fig. 8-24 for the values of the currents *x*, *y*, and *z*.

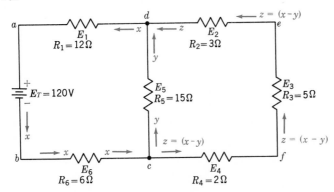

FIGURE 8-24

SOLUTION

1   Assume the direction of the electron flow to be that shown on the diagram. Please remember that these directions could be assumed to point in *other* directions without affecting the validity of the calculations. As we have seen, the truth of our assumptions will be determined by the signs of the calculated currents.

2   Express current *z* in terms of currents *x* and *y*. By Kirchhoff's first law, operating at point *c*,

$$y + z = x$$

$$\text{or } z = x - y \qquad\qquad (a)$$

3   Apply Kirchhoff's second law. Trace around the circuit in the direction *cdef*. Note that in tracing from point *d* around to point *c*, we shall be tracing a *series* circuit made of the resistors R_2, R_3, and R_4. We can therefore simplify our calculations by considering these three resistors to be one resistor of $3+5+2$, or $10\ \Omega$.

$$-15y + 10z = 0$$

Substitute $(x-y)$ for z from equation (*a*).

$$-15y + 10(x-y) = 0$$

$$-15y + 10x - 10y = 0$$

$$-25y + 10x = 0$$

$$-25y = -10x$$

$$y = \frac{-10}{-25}x = \frac{2}{5}x \qquad\qquad (1)$$

4   Trace around the circuit in the direction *abcd*.

$$120 - 6x - 15y - 12x = 0$$

$$-18x - 15y = -120$$

Divide the equation by -3 in order to simplify. This gives

$$6x + 5y = 40 \qquad\qquad (2)$$

5   Substitute the value of y from equation (1) in equation (2).

$$6x + 5y = 40 \qquad\qquad (2)$$

$$6x + 5\left(\frac{2}{5}x\right) = 40$$

$$6x + 2x = 40$$

$$8x = 40$$

$$x = 5\ \text{A} \qquad Ans.$$

6   Substitute $x = 5$ in equation (1).

$$y = \frac{2}{5}x \qquad\qquad (1)$$

$$y = \frac{2}{5}(5) = 2\ \text{A} \qquad Ans.$$

7   Substitute the values for x and y in equation (*a*) to find the current z.

$$z = x - y \qquad\qquad (a)$$

$$z = 5 - 2 = 3\ \text{A} \qquad Ans.$$

8   Find the voltage drops in each resistor.

$$E_1 = 12x \qquad E_2 = 3z \qquad E_3 = 5z$$

$$E_1 = 12(5) \qquad E_2 = 3(3) \qquad E_3 = 5(3)$$

$$E_1 = 60\ \text{V} \qquad E_2 = 9\ \text{V} \qquad E_3 = 15\ \text{V}$$

$$E_4 = 2z \qquad E_5 = 15y \qquad E_6 = 6x$$

$$E_4 = 2(3) \qquad E_5 = 15(2) \qquad E_6 = 6(5)$$

$$E_4 = 6 \text{ V} \qquad E_5 = 30 \text{ V} \qquad E_6 = 30 \text{ V}$$

9   Check by tracing the circuit *abcfeda*, using Kirchhoff's second law.

$$E_T + E_6 + E_4 + E_3 + E_2 + E_1 = 0$$

$$120 - 30 - 6 - 15 - 9 - 60 = 0$$

$$120 - 120 = 0$$

$$0 = 0 \qquad Check$$

EXAMPLE 8-16   Solve the circuit shown in Fig. 8-25 for the values of the currents w, x, y, and z.

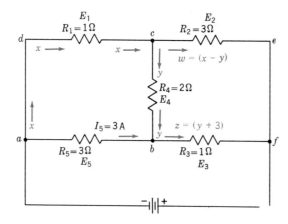

FIGURE 8-25

SOLUTION

1   Assume the direction of the electron flow to be that shown on the diagram.

2   Express current w in terms of currents x and y. By Kirchhoff's first law, operating at point c,

$$w + y = x$$

$$\text{or } w = x - y \qquad (a)$$

At point b, $\qquad\qquad\qquad z = y + 3 \qquad (b)$

3   Apply Kirchhoff's second law.   Trace around the circuit in the direction *abcd*.

$$-3(3) + 2y + 1(x) = 0$$

$$-9 + 2y + x = 0$$

$$\text{or } x + 2y = +9 \qquad (1)$$

4   Trace around the circuit in the direction *bcef*.

$$+2y - 3w + 1z = 0$$

Substitute $(x - y)$ for w from equation (a) and $(y + 3)$ for z from equation (b).

$$+2y - 3(x - y) + 1(y + 3) = 0$$

$$+2y - 3x + 3y + y + 3 = 0$$

$$-3x + 6y = -3$$

Divide the equation by 3 in order to simplify. This gives

$$-x + 2y = -1 \qquad (2)$$

5 Solve equations (1) and (2) simultaneously.

$$x + 2y = 9 \qquad (1)$$
$$\underline{-x + 2y = -1} \qquad (2)$$

Add.

$$4y = 8$$

$$y = 2 \text{ A} \qquad Ans.$$

6 Substitute this value for y in equation (1) to find x.

$$x + 2y = 9 \qquad (1)$$

$$x + 2(2) = 9$$

$$x + 4 = 9$$

$$x = 9 - 4 = 5 \text{ A} \qquad Ans.$$

7 Substitute these values for x and y in equation (a) to find w.

$$w = x - y \qquad (a)$$

$$w = 5 - 2 = 3 \text{ A} \qquad Ans.$$

8 Substitute $y = 2$ in equation (b) to find z.

$$z = y + 3 \qquad (b)$$

$$z = 2 + 3 = 5 \text{ A} \qquad Ans.$$

9 Find the voltage drops in each resistor.

$$E_1 = 1x \qquad E_2 = 3w \qquad E_3 = 1z$$

$$E_1 = 1(5) \qquad E_2 = 3(3) \qquad E_3 = 1(5)$$

$$E_1 = 5 \text{ V} \qquad E_2 = 9 \text{ V} \qquad E_3 = 5 \text{ V}$$

$$E_4 = 2y \qquad\qquad E_5 = 3(3)$$

$$E_4 = 2(2) = 4 \text{ V} \qquad E_5 = 9 \text{ V}$$

10 Check by tracing the circuit *abfecd* using Kirchhoff's second law.

$$E_5 + E_3 + E_2 + E_1 = 0$$

$$-9 - 5 + 9 + 5 = 0$$

$$0 = 0 \qquad Check$$

EXAMPLE 8-17 Solve the unbalanced bridge circuit shown in Fig. 8-26 for the values of the currents x, y, v, and w and the total voltage.

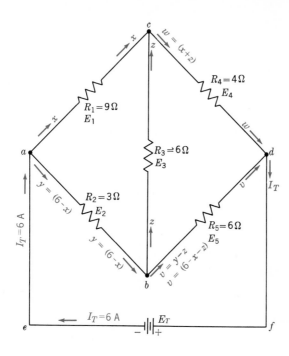

FIGURE 8-26
An unbalanced bridge circuit.

SOLUTION

1 Assume the direction of the electron flow to be that shown on the diagram.

2 Express current y in terms of x and the total current. By Kirchhoff's first law, operating at point a,

$$y + x = 6$$

$$\text{or } y = 6 - x \qquad\qquad (a)$$

At point c: $\qquad\qquad\qquad w = x + z \qquad\qquad\qquad\qquad (b)$

At point b: $\qquad\qquad\qquad v + z = y$

$$\text{or } v = y - z$$

And substituting $6 - x$ for y from equation (a),

$$v = 6 - x - z \qquad\qquad (c)$$

3 Apply Kirchhoff's second law. Trace around the circuit in the direction *abca*.

$$-3y - 6z + 9x = 0$$

Substitute $(6 - x)$ for y from equation (a).

$$-3(6 - x) - 6z + 9x = 0$$

$$-18 + 3x - 6z + 9x = 0$$

$$12x - 6z = 18$$

Divide the equation by 6 in order to simplify. This gives

$$2x - z = 3 \qquad\qquad (1)$$

4　Trace around the circuit in the direction *bcdb*.

$$-6z - 4w + 6v = 0$$

Substitute $(x + z)$ for w from equation (*b*) and $(6 - x - z)$ for v from equation (*c*).

$$-6z - 4(x + z) + 6(6 - x - z) = 0$$

$$-6z - 4x - 4z + 36 - 6x - 6z = 0$$

$$-10x - 16z = -36$$

Divide the equation by -2 in order to simplify.　This gives

$$5x + 8z = 18 \qquad (2)$$

5　Solve equations (1) and (2) simultaneously.

$$2x - z = 3 \qquad (1)$$
$$\underline{5x + 8z = 18} \qquad (2)$$

Multiply equation (1) by 8.

$$16x - 8z = 24$$
$$\underline{5x + 8z = 18}$$
Add.　　　$$21x \quad\;\; = 42$$

$$x = 2 \text{ A} \qquad Ans.$$

6　Substitute this value for x in equation (1) to find z.

$$2x - z = 3 \qquad (1)$$

$$2(2) - z = 3$$

$$4 - z = 3$$

$$-z = 3 - 4$$

$$-z = -1$$

$$z = 1 \text{ A} \qquad Ans.$$

7　Substitute $x = 2$ in equation (*a*) to find y.

$$y = 6 - x$$

$$y = 6 - 2 = 4 \text{ A} \qquad Ans.$$

8　Substitute $x = 2$ and $z = 1$ in equation (*b*) to find w.

$$w = x + z \qquad (b)$$

$$w = 2 + 1 = 3 \text{ A} \qquad Ans.$$

9　Substitute $x = 2$ and $z = 1$ in equation (*c*) to find v.

$$v = 6 - x - z \qquad (c)$$

$$v = 6 - 2 - 1 = 3 \text{ A} \qquad Ans.$$

10　Find the voltage drops in each resistor.

$$E_1 = 9x \qquad E_2 = 3y \qquad E_3 = 6z$$
$$E_1 = 9(2) \qquad E_2 = 3(4) \qquad E_3 = 6(1)$$
$$E_1 = 18 \text{ V} \qquad E_2 = 12 \text{ V} \qquad E_3 = 6 \text{ V}$$

$$E_4 = 4w \qquad\qquad E_5 = 6v$$
$$E_4 = 4(3) = 12 \text{ V} \qquad E_5 = 6(3) = 18 \text{ V}$$

11   Check by tracing the circuit in the direction *abdca*, using Kirchhoff's second law.

$$E_2 + E_5 + E_4 + E_1 = 0$$
$$-12 - 18 + 12 + 18 = 0$$
$$0 = 0 \qquad Check$$

12   Find the total voltage. Trace the circuit in the direction *feabd*.

$$E_T + E_2 + E_5 = 0$$
$$E_T - 12 - 18 = 0$$
$$E_T = 12 + 18 = 30 \text{ V} \qquad Ans.$$

SELF-TEST 8-18   In Fig. 8-27, find (*a*) the currents *x*, *y*, and *z* and (*b*) the voltage drops across all the resistors. (*c*) Check the problem.

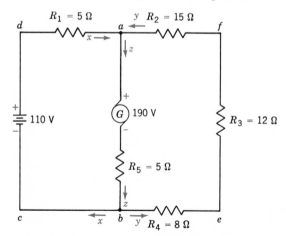

FIGURE 8-27
Opposing voltage sources.

SOLUTION

1   Since the generator voltage (190 V) is greater than the battery voltage (110 V), it is assumed that the current *z* will flow __(up/down)__ from point *a* to point *b*. Assume the remaining currents to be directed as shown. | down

2   Apply Kirchhoff's first law to point *a*.

$$x + \underline{\quad} = \underline{\quad}$$ | *y*   *z*

$$\text{or } y = z - \underline{\quad}$$ *(a)* | *x*

3   Apply Kirchhoff's second law. Trace the circuit *abcda*.

$$190 - 5z - 110 - 5\underline{\quad} = 0$$

$$-5z - 5x = \underline{\quad}$$

Divide the equation by -5 in order to simplify. This gives

$$z + x = \underline{\quad} \tag{1}$$

4   Trace the circuit *abefa*. In this path, R_4, R_3, and R_2 are in _____ and may be considered to be one resistance of ____ Ω.

$$190 - 5z - \underline{\quad} = 0$$

$$-5z - 35y = \underline{\quad}$$

Divide the equation by ____ in order to simplify. This gives

$$z + 7y = \underline{\quad} \tag{2}$$

5   At this point we would solve equations (1) and (2) simultaneously. However, these two equations contain three letters at this point—z, x, and y. One of them must be expressed in terms of the other two letters. We shall express y in terms of z and x by using equation (*a*), and substituting $z - x$ for y in equation (2),

$$z + 7y = 38 \tag{2}$$

$$z + 7(\underline{\qquad}) = 38$$

$$z + 7z - \underline{\quad} = 38$$

$$\underline{\quad} - 7x = 38 \tag{3}$$

6   Now, since they contain the same letters, z and x, we can solve equations (____) and (____) simultaneously.

$$\begin{aligned} z + \ x &= 16 \tag{1} \\ 8z - 7x &= 38 \tag{3} \end{aligned}$$

Multiplying equation (1) by ____,

$$\begin{aligned} 7z + 7x &= \underline{\quad} \\ 8z - 7x &= 38 \\ \hline \end{aligned}$$

Adding, $15z \qquad = \underline{\quad}$

$$z = \underline{\quad} \text{ A} \qquad Ans.$$

7   Substitute this value for z in equation (1) to find x.

$$z + x = 16 \tag{1}$$

$$\underline{\quad} + x = 16$$

$$x = 16 - \underline{\quad}$$

$$x = \underline{\quad} \text{ A} \qquad Ans.$$

8   Substitute these values for x and z in equation *a* to find y.

Margin answers:

x
-80
16
series
35
$35y$
-190
-5
38

$z - x$
$7x$
$8z$

1   3

7
112
150
10

10
10
6

$$y = z - x \qquad\qquad\qquad (a)$$

$$y = 10 - 6 = \underline{} \text{ A} \qquad Ans. \qquad\qquad 4$$

9 Find the voltage drops across the resistors.

$$E_1 = x \times R_1 \qquad\qquad E_5 = z \times R_5$$

$$E_1 = \underline{} \times 5 \qquad\qquad E_5 = \underline{} \times 5 \qquad\qquad 6 \qquad 10$$

$$E_1 = 30 \text{ V} \quad Ans. \qquad E_5 = \underline{} \text{ V} \qquad Ans. \qquad\qquad 50$$

$$E_2 = y \times R_2 \qquad\qquad E_3 = y \times R_3 \qquad\qquad E_4 = y \times R_4$$

$$E_2 = \underline{} \times 15 \qquad E_3 = \underline{} \times 12 \qquad E_4 = \underline{} \times 8 \qquad\qquad 4 \qquad 4 \qquad 4$$

$$E_2 = 60 \text{ V} \quad Ans. \qquad E_3 = 48 \text{ V} \quad Ans. \qquad E_4 = \underline{} \text{ V} \quad Ans. \qquad\qquad 32$$

10 Check. Trace the circuit *abcda*.

$$190 - 50 - 110 - \underline{} = 0 \qquad\qquad 30$$

$$\underline{} = 0 \qquad Check \qquad\qquad 0$$

Trace the circuit *abefa*.

$$190 - 50 - 32 - \underline{} - 60 = 0 \qquad\qquad 48$$

$$\underline{} = 0 \qquad Check \qquad\qquad 0$$

PROBLEMS

SET NO. 1

1. In a circuit similar to that shown in Fig. 8-21, $E_1 = 22$ V, $E_2 = 20$ V, $R_3 = 1$ Ω, and $R_4 = 4$ Ω. Find the currents x, y, and z, and check your answer.

2. In a circuit similar to that shown in Fig. 8-22, $E_1 = 75$ V, $R_2 = 3$ Ω, $R_3 = 12$ Ω, $R_4 = 4$ Ω, and $E_5 = 28$ V. Find the currents x, y, and z, and check your answer.

3. In a circuit similar to that shown in Fig. 8-24, $E_T = 25$ V, $R_1 = 1$ Ω, $R_2 = 3$ Ω, $R_3 = 6$ Ω, $R_4 = 1$ Ω, $R_5 = 5$ Ω, and $R_6 = 4$ Ω. Find the currents x, y, and z, and check your answer.

4. In a circuit similar to that shown in Fig. 8-25, $R_1 = 2$ Ω, $R_2 = 7$ Ω, $R_3 = 9$ Ω, $R_4 = 4$ Ω, $R_5 = 5$ Ω, and $I_5 = 4$ A. Find the currents w, x, y, and z, and check your answer.

5. In a circuit similar to that shown in Fig. 8-26, $R_1 = 10$ Ω, $R_2 = 8$ Ω, $R_3 = 15$ Ω, $R_4 = 18$ Ω, $R_5 = 2$ Ω, and $I_T = 15$ A. Find the currents v, w, x, y, and z and the total voltage.

6. Solve the circuit shown in Fig. 8-28 for the value of the currents x, y, and z.

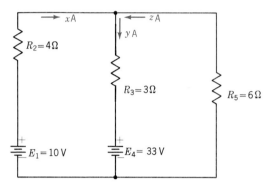

FIGURE 8-28

7. Solve the circuit shown in Fig. 8-29 for the value of the currents x, y, and z.

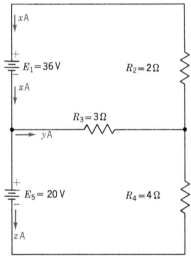

FIGURE 8-29

8. Solve the circuit shown in Fig. 8-30 for the value of the currents x, y, and z.

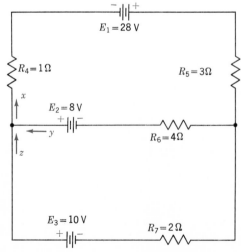

FIGURE 8-30

SET NO. 2

1. In a circuit similar to that shown in Fig. 8-21, $E_1 = 32$ V, $E_2 = 12$ V, $R_3 = 5$ Ω, and $R_4 = 2$ Ω. Find the currents x, y, and z, and check your answer.
2. In a circuit similar to that shown in Fig. 8-22, $E_1 = 28$ V, $R_2 = 1$ Ω, $R_3 = 15$ Ω, $R_4 = 5$ Ω, and $E_5 = 12$ V. Find the currents x, y, and z, and check your answer.
3. In a circuit similar to that shown in Fig. 8-24, $E_T = 11$ V, $R_1 = 2$ Ω, $R_2 = 3$ Ω, $R_3 = 1$ Ω, $R_4 = 6$ Ω, $R_5 = 10$ Ω, and $R_6 = 4$ Ω. Find the currents x, y, and z, and check your answer.
4. In a circuit similar to that shown in Fig. 8-25, $R_1 = 10$ Ω, $R_2 = 18$ Ω, $R_3 = 2$ Ω, $R_4 = 15$ Ω, $R_5 = 8$ Ω, and $I_5 = 10$ A. Find the currents w, x, y, and z, and check your answer.
5. In a circuit similar to that shown in Fig. 8-26, $R_1 = 30$ Ω, $R_2 = 10$ Ω, $R_3 = 5$ Ω, $R_4 = 16$ Ω, $R_5 = 15$ Ω, and $I_T = 11$ A. Find the currents v, w, x, y, and z and the total voltage.
6. In a circuit similar to that shown in Fig. 8-28, $E_1 = 22$ V, $R_2 = 2$ Ω, $R_3 = 4$ Ω, $E_4 = 60$ V, and $R_5 = 16$ Ω. Find the currents x, y, and z.
7. In a circuit similar to that shown in Fig. 8-29, $E_1 = 76$ V, $R_2 = 10$ Ω, $R_3 = 2$ Ω, $R_4 = 15$ Ω, and $E_5 = 54$ V. Find the currents x, y, and z.
8. In a circuit similar to that shown in Fig. 8-30, $E_1 = 23$ V, $E_2 = 11$ V, $E_3 = 8$ V, $R_4 = 5$ Ω, $R_5 = 2$ Ω, $R_6 = 2$ Ω, and $R_7 = 3$ Ω. Find the currents x, y, and z.

SET NO. 3

1. In a circuit similar to that shown in Fig. 8-21, $E_1 = 10$ V, $E_2 = 5$ V, $R_3 = 10$ Ω, and $R_4 = 2.5$ Ω. Find the currents x, y, and z, and check your answer.
2. In a circuit similar to that shown in Fig. 8-22, $E_1 = 12$ V, $R_2 = 2.5$ Ω, $R_3 = 3.4$ Ω, $R_4 = 3$ Ω, and $E_5 = 38$ V. Find the currents x, y, and z, and check your answer.
3. In a circuit similar to that shown in Fig. 8-24, $E_T = 10$ V, $R_1 = 5$ Ω, $R_2 = 6$ Ω, $R_3 = 8$ Ω, $R_4 = 4$ Ω, $R_5 = 6$ Ω, and $R_6 = 3$ Ω. Find the currents x, y, and z, and check your answer.
4. In a circuit similar to that shown in Fig. 8-25, $R_1 = 5$ Ω, $R_2 = 40$ Ω, $R_3 = 10$ Ω, $R_4 = 10$ Ω, $R_5 = 3$ Ω, and $I_5 = 2$ A. Find the currents w, x, y, and z, and check your answer.
5. In a circuit similar to that shown in Fig. 8-26, $R_1 = 32$ Ω, $R_2 = 2$ Ω, $R_3 = 5$ Ω, $R_4 = 4$ Ω, $R_5 = 20$ Ω, and $I_T = 3.5$ A. Find the currents v, w, x, y, and z and the total voltage.
6. In a circuit similar to that shown in Fig. 8-28, $E_1 = 12$ V, $R_2 = 10$ Ω, $R_3 = 30$ Ω, $E_4 = 41$ V, and $R_5 = 20$ Ω. Find the currents x, y, and z.
7. In a circuit similar to that shown in Fig. 8-29, $E_1 = 31$ V, $R_2 = 2$ Ω, $R_3 = 10$ Ω, $R_4 = 4$ Ω, and $E_5 = 6$ V *with polarity opposite to that shown in Fig. 8-29*. Find the currents x, y, and z.

8. In a circuit similar to that shown in Fig. 8-29, $E_1 = 17$ V, $R_2 = 20\ \Omega$, $R_3 = 10\ \Omega$, $R_4 = 40\ \Omega$, and $E_5 = 13$ V. Find the currents x, y, and z.

JOB 8-6 REVIEW OF KIRCHHOFF'S LAWS

1 Kirchhoff's first law.

| RULE | At any point in an electrical circuit, the sum of the currents that _____ a junction is equal to the sum of the currents that _____ it. | enter
leave |

FORMULA

$$\Sigma I_e = \Sigma I_l \qquad \boxed{8\text{-}1}$$

2 Direction of electron flow.
   a If the total known electron flow *in* to a point is *greater* than the total known flow *out* of the point, then the direction of any unknown flow must be __(into/out of)__ the point.

out of

   b If the total known electron flow *into* a point is *less* than the total known flow *out of* the point, then the direction of any unknown flow must be __(into/out of)__ the point.

into

3 Kirchhoff's second law.

| RULE | The _____ sum of all the voltages in any complete electrical circuit is equal to _____. | algebraic
zero |

FORMULA

$$E_1 + E_2 + E_3 + \text{etc.} = 0 \qquad \boxed{8\text{-}2}$$

4 Direction of voltages.
   a *Source* voltages are positive (+) if we move through them from the _____ (__) terminal to the negative (−) terminal.

positive +
negative −

   b *Source* voltages are _____ (__) if we move through them from the negative (−) terminal to the positive (+) terminal.
   c A voltage across a resistance is *negative* (−) if we go through it in the __(same/opposite)__ direction as that of the assumed electron flow.

same

   d A voltage across a resistance is _____ (__) if we go through it in a direction *opposite* to the assumed electron flow.

positive +

5 Using Kirchhoff's laws.
   a Determine the _____ of the electron flow. If insufficient data are given, *assume* directions of flow in each branch of the circuit. A minus sign for the solution indicates that the assumed direction was __(correct/incorrect)__. The value of the current found __(is/is not)__ affected by an incorrect choice of direction.

direction

incorrect
is not

   b Mark the diagram to indicate all _____ of electron flow and all polarities of sources of voltage.

directions

c   If possible, express the current in the various branches in terms of the
_____ in other branches.

d   Trace around a _____ circuit, totaling the _____ sum
of *all* voltages encountered. Set the sum equal to _____. Be careful to
note the correct sign for each voltage.

e   Trace around a *second complete* circuit, obtaining a second equation.

f   Solve the set of _____ obtained in steps d and e simultaneously.

g   Find all voltage drops in all resistances by _____ law.

h   Check the solution by tracing around a *complete third* circuit, setting
the algebraic sum of the voltages equal to _____.

currents

complete algebraic
zero

equations
Ohm's

zero

SELF-TEST 8-19   In Fig. 8-31, find the generator voltage E which will
reduce the current through R_3 to zero.

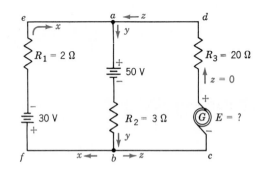

FIGURE 8-31
Find the generator voltage
that will reduce the current
through R_3 to zero.

SOLUTION

1   Since the two batteries   (aid/oppose)   each other, it is assumed that the
current y will flow   (up/down)   from point a to point b. Assume the currents
x and z to be directed as shown.

aid
down

2   Apply Kirchhoff's first law to point b.

$$y = x + \_\_\_$$ z

$$y = x + \_\_\_$$ 0

$$\text{or } y = x \qquad (a)$$

3   Apply Kirchhoff's second law to the circuit *efbae*.

$$+2x - 30 \ \underline{(+/-)} \ 3y - 50 = 0$$ +

$$2x + 3y = \_\_\_$$ 80

Now, since $y = \_\_\_$ from equation (a),   x

$$2x + 3\_\_\_ = 80$$ x

$$\_\_\_ = 80$$ 5x

$$x = \_\_\_ \text{ A}$$ 16

And, since $y = x$, $y = \_\_\_$ A.   16

4   Trace the circuit *abcda*.

$$50 - 3y - \_\_\_ - 20z = 0$$ E

Substitute 0 for z as given.

$$50 - 3y - E - 20(0) = 0$$

$$50 - 3y - E = 0$$

Substitute 16 for y in this equation.

$$50 - 3(16) - E = 0$$

$$50 - 48 = \underline{}$$ E

$$2 = E$$

$$\text{or } E = 2 \text{ V} \qquad Ans.$$

5 *Check.* Trace the circuit *efbcdae.*

$$2x - 30 - E - 20z = 0$$

$$2(16) - 30 - \underline{} - 20(\underline{}) = 0$$ 2   0

$$32 - 30 - 2 - \underline{} = 0$$ 0

$$\underline{} = 0 \qquad Check$$ 0

Now try just one more problem before you take the following test.

9 In Fig. 8-32, find the power consumed in R_5.

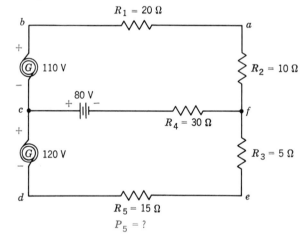

FIGURE 8-32

TEST—KIRCHHOFF'S LAWS

1. In a circuit similar to that shown in Fig. 8-12, $E_1 = 48$ V, $R_2 = 10$ Ω, $R_3 = 30$ Ω, $E_4 = 18$ V, and $R_5 = 20$ Ω. Find (*a*) the total current and (*b*) the voltage drops across each resistor.

2. In a circuit similar to that shown in Fig. 8-18, $I_T = 8$ A, $R_1 = 12$ Ω, $R_2 = 60$ Ω, and $I_3 = 2$ A. Find the total voltage and R_3.

3. In a circuit similar to that shown in Fig. 8-22, $E_1 = 62$ V, $R_2 = 6$ Ω, $R_3 = 5$ Ω, $R_4 = 4$ Ω, and $E_5 = 8$ V. Find the currents x, y, and z.

4. In a circuit similar to that shown in Fig. 8-26, $R_1 = 10$ Ω, $R_2 = 4$ Ω, $R_3 = 8$ Ω, $R_4 = 2$ Ω, $R_5 = 7$ Ω, and $I_T = 5$ A. Find the currents w, x, y, and z.

5. Solve the circuit shown in Fig. 8-33 for the value of the currents *x, y,* and *z.*

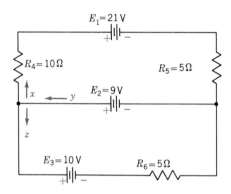

FIGURE 8-33

JOB 8-7 EQUIVALENT DELTA AND STAR CIRCUITS

Example 8-17 of the last job can be greatly simplified by the application of the theory of delta and star circuits. We shall solve this problem again at the conclusion of this job.

The three resistors R_1, R_2, and R_3 of Fig. 8-26 are shown in Fig. 8-34a and are said to be connected in *delta* because the connection resembles the Greek letter delta (Δ). The resistors R_a, R_b, and R_c in Fig. 8-34b are connected in *star,* or Y formation. Most delta circuits will be much easier to solve if we can change them into *equivalent* star circuits. *Note:* Although the same nomenclature is used, these circuits are not to be confused with those of three-phase systems.

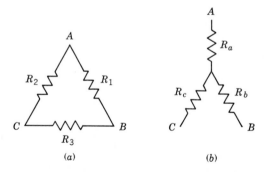

FIGURE 8-34
(a) R_1, R_2, and R_3 are connected in *delta* formation.
(b) R_1, R_b, and R_c are connected in *star* or Y formation.

Now the word "equivalent" means that the circuits must do the same job as they did before. That is, the resistance between A and B, B and C, and C and A must be the same in each circuit.

The resistance from A to B in Fig. 8-34a is found by redrawing the circuit as shown in Fig. 8-35a. This reduces to a circuit in which R_1 is in parallel with the series combination of $(R_2 + R_3)$, as in Fig. 8-35b. Thus,

$$R_{AB} = \frac{R_1(R_2 + R_3)}{R_1 + R_2 + R_3} \tag{1}$$

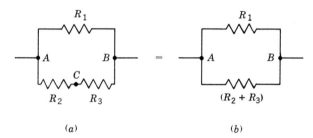

FIGURE 8-35
(a) Figure 8-34a redrawn in standard form. (b) R_2 and R_3 are added since they are in series.

In Fig. 8-34b, the resistance from A to B is simply the series combination of $R_a + R_b$, or

$$R_{AB} = R_a + R_b \qquad (2)$$

Since the two resistances must be equal, we can set equation (2) equal to equation (1) and get

$$R_a + R_b = \frac{R_1R_2 + R_1R_3}{R_1 + R_2 + R_3}$$

If we use the symbol ΣR_Δ (read as "the summation of resistances in delta") to mean $R_1 + R_2 + R_3$, we get

$$R_a + R_b = \frac{R_1R_2 + R_1R_3}{\Sigma R_\Delta} \qquad (3)$$

In a similar manner,

$$R_b + R_c = \frac{R_1R_3 + R_2R_3}{\Sigma R_\Delta} \qquad (4)$$

$$R_a + R_c = \frac{R_1R_2 + R_2R_3}{\Sigma R_\Delta} \qquad (5)$$

When equations (3), (4), and (5) are solved simultaneously, we get the following

FORMULAS

$$R_a = \frac{R_1R_2}{\Sigma R_\Delta} \qquad \boxed{8\text{-}3}$$

$$R_b = \frac{R_1R_3}{\Sigma R_\Delta} \qquad \boxed{8\text{-}4}$$

$$R_c = \frac{R_2R_3}{\Sigma R_\Delta} \qquad \boxed{8\text{-}5}$$

Do not attempt to memorize these formulas. They depend on the positions of the letters A, B, and C and the positions of R_1, R_2, and R_3.

An easy way to develop these formulas is shown in Fig. 8-36a. Each equivalent Y resistance is obtained by multiplying the two adjacent delta resistances and then dividing by the sum of the delta resistances (ΣR_Δ). For example, the resistors R_2 and R_3 are adjacent (next) to R_c. Therefore,

$$R_c = \frac{R_2 \times R_3}{\Sigma R_\Delta}$$

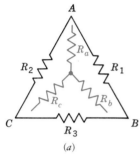

(a)

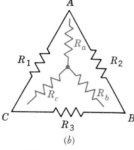

(b)

But, in Fig. 8-36b, in which the positions of R_1 and R_2 have been interchanged, R_1 and R_3 are adjacent to R_c. Therefore,

$$R_c = \frac{R_1 R_3}{\Sigma R_\Delta}$$

EXAMPLE 8-20   In Fig. 8-34a, $R_1 = 10\ \Omega$, $R_2 = 8\ \Omega$, and $R_3 = 2\ \Omega$. Find the resistances of the equivalent Y circuit of Fig. 8-34b.

SOLUTION

1

$$\Sigma R_\Delta = R_1 + R_2 + R_3$$

$$\Sigma R_\Delta = 10 + 8 + 2 = 20\ \Omega$$

2

$$R_a = \frac{R_1 R_2}{\Sigma R_\Delta} \quad (8\text{-}3) \qquad R_b = \frac{R_1 R_3}{\Sigma R_\Delta} \quad (8\text{-}4) \qquad R_c = \frac{R_2 R_3}{\Sigma R_\Delta} \quad (8\text{-}5)$$

$$R_a = \frac{10 \times 8}{20} \qquad\qquad R_b = \frac{10 \times 2}{20} \qquad\qquad R_c = \frac{8 \times 2}{20}$$

$$R_a = 4\ \Omega \qquad\qquad R_b = 1\ \Omega \qquad\qquad R_c = 0.8\ \Omega \quad Ans.$$

SELF-TEST 8-21   Find the total resistance between points A and D in the circuit shown in Fig. 8-37a.

SOLUTION

1   Change the delta circuit ABC into its equivalent Y circuit as shown in Fig. 8-37b. Note that R_1 and R_2 are *not* in the same position as they were in Fig. 8-34a. Develop the correct formula for R_a, R_b, and R_c as shown above.

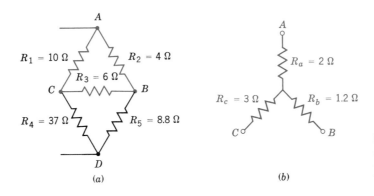

FIGURE 8-37
(a) An unbalanced bridge circuit. (b) The Y equivalent of the delta circuit ABC.

$$\Sigma R_\Delta = R_1 + R_2 + R_3$$

$$\Sigma R_\Delta = 10 + 4 + 6 = \underline{\quad} \ \Omega$$

$$R_a = \frac{R_1 R_2}{\Sigma R_\Delta} \qquad R_b = \frac{R_2 R_3}{\Sigma R_\Delta} \qquad R_c = \frac{R_1 R_3}{\Sigma R_\Delta}$$

$$R_a = \frac{10 \times ?}{20} \qquad R_b = \frac{4 \times ?}{20} \qquad R_c = \frac{10 \times ?}{20}$$

$$R_a = \underline{\quad} \ \Omega \qquad R_b = \underline{\quad} \ \Omega \qquad R_c = \underline{\quad} \ \Omega$$

20		
4	6	6
2	1.2	3

2 Redraw the delta circuit as a Y circuit and connect it to the remainder of the original circuit as shown in Fig. 8-38a.

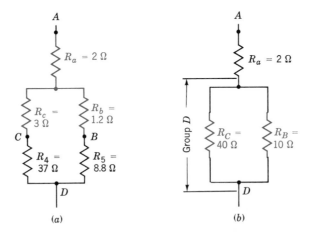

FIGURE 8-38
(a) The Y equivalent of delta ABC is attached to the remainder of the bridge circuit BDC. (b) R_C is the series equivalent of $R_c + R_4$. R_B is the series equivalent of $R_b + R_5$.

3 In Fig. 8-38b, R_C represents the series resistance of R_c plus R_4, which equals $3 + 37 = \underline{\quad} \ \Omega$. Also, R_B represents the series resistance of $\underline{\quad}$ plus R_5, which equals $1.2 + 8.8 = \underline{\quad} \ \Omega$.

4 In Fig. 8-38b, R_C and R_B are connected in $\underline{\quad\quad\quad}$. The total resistance for this group is

40	R_b
10	
parallel	

$$R_D = \frac{R_C \times R_B}{R_C + R_B} \qquad (4\text{-}5)$$

$$R_D = \frac{40 \times 10}{40 + 10} = \underline{\quad} \ \Omega \qquad\qquad\qquad 8$$

5   In Fig. 8-38*b*, the total resistance for the circuit from *A* to *D* is made of
the ___(series/parallel)___ combination of R_a and R_D.   series

$$R_T = R_a + \underline{\quad} \qquad\qquad\qquad\qquad R_D$$

$$R_T = 2 + 8 = \underline{\quad} \ \Omega \qquad \textit{Ans.} \qquad\qquad 10$$

6   If the voltage across points *A* to *D* equals 120 V, then we can find the
total current by _____ law.   Ohm's

$$E_T = I_T \times R_T \qquad (3\text{-}7)$$

$$120 = I_T \times \underline{\quad} \qquad\qquad\qquad\qquad 10$$

$$I_T = \underline{\quad} \ A \qquad \textit{Ans.} \qquad\qquad\qquad 12$$

SELF-TEST 8-22   Solve the unbalanced bridge circuit given in Example 8-17 for the values of the currents *x*, *y*, *v*, *z*, and *w*, and the total
voltage.

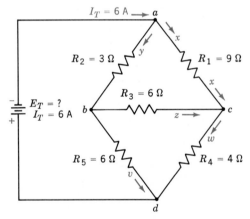

FIGURE 8-39
Figure 8-26 of Example 8-17
is redrawn.

SOLUTION
The circuit is redrawn for your convenience as Fig. 8-39.

1   Find the total resistance between points *a* and *d*.
    a   Change the delta circuit *abc* into its equivalent Y circuit as shown in
    Fig. 8-40*a*.

$$\Sigma R_\Delta = R_1 + R_2 + R_3$$

$$\Sigma R_\Delta = 9 + \underline{\quad} + 6 = \underline{\quad} \ \Omega \qquad\qquad 3 \qquad 18$$

$$R_a = \frac{3 \times ?}{?} \qquad R_b = \frac{? \times 6}{18} \qquad R_c = \frac{6 \times ?}{18} \qquad\qquad \begin{array}{ccc} 9 & 3 & 9 \\ 18 \end{array}$$

$$R_a = \underline{\quad} \ \Omega \qquad R_b = \underline{\quad} \ \Omega \qquad R_c = \underline{\quad} \ \Omega \qquad\qquad 1.5 \quad 1 \quad 3$$

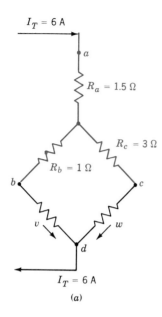

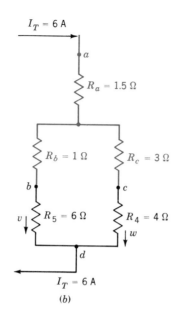

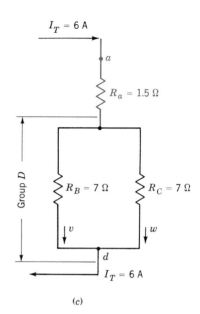

(a)   (b)   (c)

FIGURE 8-40
(a) Delta abc converted to Y formation. (b) Y formation of abc connected to cdb in standard form. (c) R_B is the series equivalent of $R_b + R_5$. R_C is the series equivalent of $R_c + R_4$.

b Connect the equivalent Y circuit to the remainder of the circuit as shown in Fig. 8-40*b*. Label all the parts with their respective values.

c In Fig. 8-40*c*, R_C represents the ___(series/parallel)___ resistance of R_c | series
and R_4, which equals ___ Ω. Also, R_B represents the series resistance of | 7
___ and R_5, which equals ___ Ω. | R_b 7

d In Fig. 8-40*c*, R_C and R_B are connected in _____. | parallel

$$R_D = \_\_ \; \Omega$$ | 3.5

e The total resistance for the circuit from *a* to *d* equals $R_a + R_D =$
$1.5 + 3.5 = ?\ \Omega$. | 5

2 Find the total voltage E_T.

$$E_T = I_T \times R_T = 6 \times 5 = \_\_ \; V \qquad Ans.$$ | 30

3 Find the currents *v* and *w*.
In Fig. 8-40*c*, since $R_C = R_B = 7\ \Omega$, the total current $I_T = 6$ A will divide so that

$$v = w = \_\_ \; A \qquad Ans.$$ | 3

4   Find E_5 and E_4. In Fig. 8-40b,

$$E_5 = v \times R_5 \qquad\qquad E_4 = w \times R_4$$

$$E_5 = 3 \times 6 = \rule{1cm}{0.4pt} \text{ V} \qquad E_4 = 3 \times 4 = \rule{1cm}{0.4pt} \text{ V} \qquad\qquad 18 \qquad 12$$

5   Trace the circuit cbd in Fig. 8-39.

$$6z - E_5 + E_4 = 0$$

$$6z - \rule{1cm}{0.4pt} + 12 = 0 \qquad\qquad 18$$

$$6z = \rule{1cm}{0.4pt} \qquad\qquad 6$$

$$z = \rule{1cm}{0.4pt} \text{ A} \qquad Ans. \qquad\qquad 1$$

6   Find the currents x and y in Fig. 8-39.
Apply Kirchhoff's first law to point c.

$$x + z = \rule{1cm}{0.4pt} \qquad\qquad w$$

$$x + 1 = 3 \text{ (from step 3)}$$

$$x = \rule{1cm}{0.4pt} \text{ A} \qquad Ans. \qquad\qquad 2$$

Apply Kirchhoff's first law to point a.

$$y + x = \rule{1cm}{0.4pt} \qquad\qquad 6$$

$$y + \rule{1cm}{0.4pt} = 6 \qquad\qquad 2$$

$$y = \rule{1cm}{0.4pt} \text{ A} \qquad Ans. \qquad\qquad 4$$

7   $Check.$

$$E_1 = 9x = 9(\rule{0.7cm}{0.4pt}) = 18 \text{ V} \qquad\qquad 2$$

$$E_2 = 3\rule{0.7cm}{0.4pt} = 3(4) = 12 \text{ V} \qquad\qquad y$$

$$E_3 = \rule{0.7cm}{0.4pt} z = 6(1) = 6 \text{ V} \qquad\qquad 6$$

$$E_4 = (\rule{0.7cm}{0.4pt})(\rule{0.7cm}{0.4pt}) = 4(3) = 12 \text{ V} \qquad\qquad 4 \qquad w$$

$$E_5 = 6(\rule{0.7cm}{0.4pt}) = 6(3) = 18 \text{ V} \qquad\qquad v$$

Trace the circuit $abdca$.

$$-E_2 - E_5 + E_4 + E_1 = 0$$

$$-12 - 18 + 12 + 18 = 0$$

$$\rule{1cm}{0.4pt} = 0 \qquad Check \qquad\qquad 0$$

PROBLEMS

1. In the circuit shown in Fig. 8-34a, $R_1 = R_2 = R_3 = 60 \ \Omega$. Find the resistances of the equivalent Y circuit.
2. In the circuit shown in Fig. 8-34a, $R_1 = 50 \ \Omega$, $R_2 = 40 \ \Omega$, and $R_3 = 10 \ \Omega$. Find the resistances of the equivalent Y circuit.

3. In the circuit shown in Fig. 8-34a, $R_1 = 20\ \Omega$, $R_2 = 12\ \Omega$, and $R_3 = 8\ \Omega$. Find the resistances of the equivalent Y circuit.

4. In the circuit shown in Fig. 8-34a, $R_1 = 20\ \Omega$, $R_2 = 10\ \Omega$, and $R_3 = 15\ \Omega$. Find the resistances of the equivalent Y circuit.

5. In a circuit similar to that shown in Fig. 8-37a, $R_1 = 2\ \Omega$, $R_2 = 4\ \Omega$, $R_3 = 6\ \Omega$, $R_4 = 5\ \Omega$, and $R_5 = 4\ \Omega$. Find the total resistance from A to D.

6. In a circuit similar to that shown in Fig. 8-37a, $R_1 = 12\ \Omega$, $R_2 = 18\ \Omega$, $R_3 = 10\ \Omega$, $R_4 = 1\ \Omega$, and $R_5 = 1.5\ \Omega$. Find the total resistance from A to D.

7. In a circuit similar to that shown in Fig. 8-37a, $R_1 = 30\ \Omega$, $R_2 = 12\ \Omega$, $R_3 = 8\ \Omega$, $R_4 = 10.2\ \Omega$, and $R_5 = 3.08\ \Omega$. Find the total resistance from A to D.

8. In a circuit similar to that shown in Fig. 8-37a, $R_1 = 10\ \Omega$, $R_2 = 30\ \Omega$, $R_3 = 5\ \Omega$, $R_4 = 15\ \Omega$, and $R_5 = 16\ \Omega$. Find the total resistance from A to D.

9. In a circuit similar to that shown in Fig. 8-39, $R_1 = 10\ \Omega$, $R_2 = 8\ \Omega$, $R_3 = 2\ \Omega$, $R_4 = 1\ \Omega$, and $R_5 = 1.2\ \Omega$. If $I_T = 10$ A, find (a) the total resistance of the circuit, (b) the currents v, w, x, y, and z, and (c) the total voltage.

10. In a circuit similar to that shown in Fig. 8-39, $R_1 = 10\ \Omega$, $R_2 = 10\ \Omega$, $R_3 = 20\ \Omega$, $R_4 = 19\ \Omega$, and $R_5 = 3\ \Omega$. If $I_T = 16$ A, find (a) the total

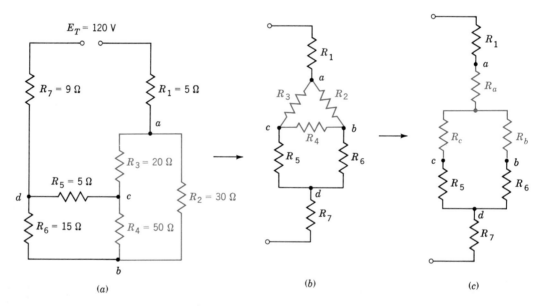

(a)

(b)

(c)

FIGURE 8-41
(a) Original circuit. (b) R_2, R_3, and R_4 in delta formation.
(c) Delta abc in Y formation and connected to the remainder of the circuit.

resistance of the circuit, (*b*) the currents *v*, *w*, *x*, *y*, and *z*, and (*c*) the total voltage.

11. In a circuit similar to that shown in Fig. 8-39, $R_1 = 10\ \Omega$, $R_2 = 50\ \Omega$, $R_3 = 15\ \Omega$, $R_4 = 8\ \Omega$, and $R_5 = 5\ \Omega$. If $I_T = 10$ A, find (*a*) the total resistance of the circuit, (*b*) the currents *v*, *w*, *x*, *y*, and *z*, and (*c*) the total voltage.

12. Fig. 8-41 shows the original circuit and the transformations necessary to find the total resistance. Find (*a*) the total resistance, (*b*) the total current, (*c*) the current in R_5, and (*d*) the current in R_6.

JOB 8-8   THEVENIN'S THEOREM

The main objective in the solution of a circuit is usually the calculation of the values for the load voltage and the load current. As we have seen, this usually involves many intermediate steps. Thevenin's theorem will eliminate many of these intermediate steps and permit us to calculate the load values directly.

Fig. 8-42*a* is the same as Fig. 8-24 of Example 8-15 except that the resistances R_2, R_3 and R_4 have been combined into the load resistance $R_L = 10\ \Omega$. In the solution of Example 8-15, we found

$$z = I_L = 3 \text{ A}$$

$$E_2 + E_3 + E_4 = E_L$$

$$9 + 15 + 6 = E_L = 30 \text{ V}$$

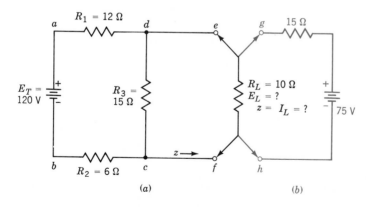

(*a*)   (*b*)

FIGURE 8-42

As far as the load R_L is concerned, circuit (*a*) is equivalent to circuit (*b*).

Now if this same load $R_L = 10\ \Omega$ were connected by a switching arrangement to become the load of circuit Fig. 8-42*b*, then $R_T = 10 + 15 = 25\ \Omega$, and

$$I_L = \frac{E_T}{R_T} = \frac{75}{25} = 3 \text{ A}$$

and

$$E_L = I_L \times R_L$$
$$E_L = 3 \times 10$$
$$E_L = 30 \text{ V}$$

Thus, the *same* values for E_L and I_L were obtained when R_L was connected as part of circuit (*a*) or when R_L was connected as part of circuit (*b*). Therefore, as far as R_L is concerned, circuit (*b*) could be substituted for circuit (*a*) and the same results obtained. Since the two circuits produce the same results, they may be said to be equivalent. Obviously, if we had a choice, we would rather work with circuit (*b*) than with circuit (*a*).

Thevenin's theorem is a method for changing a complex circuit into a simple *equivalent* circuit. Then the simple circuit may be solved with a minimum of effort.

Thevenin's theorem: Any linear network of voltage sources and resistances, if viewed from any two points in the network, can be replaced by an equivalent resistance R_{TH} in series with an equivalent source E_{TH}. Actually, then, the problem consists of three steps.

1 Find the equivalent voltage E_{TH}.
2 Find the equivalent resistance R_{TH}.
3 Place the R_{TH} in series with the load and solve the simple series circuit.

METHOD

1 Disconnect the part of the circuit which is considered as the load.
2 Find the voltage that would appear across the load terminals when the load is disconnected. In Fig. 8-42*a* this would be the voltage across terminals *e* and *f*. This open-circuit voltage is called Thevenin's voltage (E_{TH}). See Fig. 8-43*a*.

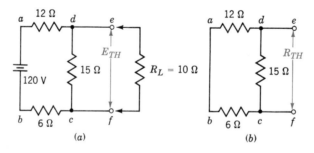

FIGURE 8-43

(*a*) When the load is removed, the equivalent voltage E_{TH} = the voltage across the terminals *ef* or *dc*. (*b*) The equivalent resistance R_{TH} equals the total resistance with all sources of emf shorted and the load removed.

3 Replace each voltage source with a short, reducing the voltage to zero, and remove the load as shown in Fig. 8-43*b*.
4 Find the total resistance that would appear across the load terminals. This will be Thevenin's resistance (R_{TH}), as shown in Fig. 8-43*b*.
5 Draw the equivalent circuit consisting of R_{TH} in series with R_L and connected across the equivalent voltage E_{TH}, as shown in Fig. 8-44.
6 Solve for the load current and the load voltage.

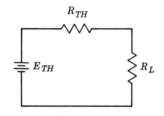

FIGURE 8-44
Thevenin's equivalent circuit
supplying a load R_L.

EXAMPLE 8-23   Solve the circuit shown in Fig. 8-42a for the values
of I_L and E_L.

SOLUTION

1   Disconnect the load R_L as shown in Fig. 8-43a.
2   Find the voltage across the terminals ef. This is equal to the voltage across
terminals dc. In the circuit $abcd$,

$$R_t = 6 + 15 + 12 = 33 \ \Omega \tag{3-3}$$

$$I_t = \frac{120}{33} = 3.63 \ A$$

Therefore,

$$E_{dc} = 3.63 \times 15 = 54.45 \ V$$

$$\text{or } E_{TH} = 54.45 \ V$$

3   Replace each voltage source with a short and remove the load as shown
in Fig. 8-43b.
4   Find the value of R_{TH}. In Fig. 8-43b, the 12 Ω is in series with the 6 Ω for
a total of 18 Ω. This 18 Ω is in parallel with the 15 Ω.

$$R_{TH} = \frac{18 \times 15}{18 + 15} = 8.18 \ \Omega \tag{4-5}$$

5   Draw the equivalent circuit as shown in Fig. 8-45.

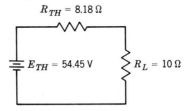

FIGURE 8-45
E_{TH} is in series with R_{TH} and R_L.

6   Solve for I_L.

$$R_t = 8.18 + 10 = 18.18 \ \Omega$$

$$I_L = \frac{E_{TH}}{R_t} = \frac{54.45}{18.18} = 3 \ A \quad Ans.$$

Solve for E_L.

$$E_L = I_L \times R_L$$

$$E_L = 3 \times 10 = 30 \ V \quad Ans.$$

The true value of Thevenin's theorem is apparent when we compare the small effort involved here with the lengthy calculations needed to solve the same problem of Example 8-15.

   EXAMPLE 8-24   Solve the circuit of Example 8-13 by Thevenin's theorem.

   SOLUTION
Fig. 8-22 is repeated here for your convenience.

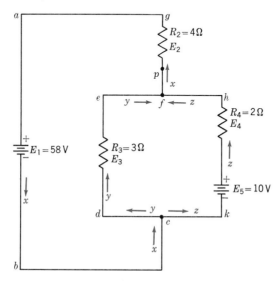

   1   We must redraw the figure so that the load may be separated from the rest of the circuit at only two terminals. See Fig. 8-46. Consider the load to be R_3.

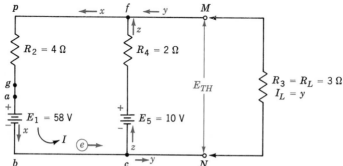

FIGURE 8-46
The circuit of Fig. 8-22 is redrawn to present only two terminals to the load.

   2   Find E_{TH} with the load removed. This will be the voltage across the terminals M and N which is equal to the voltage across the terminals f and c.
   a   In the series circuit $pbcf$, the circulating current I is

$$I = \frac{E}{R} = \frac{58 - 10}{4 + 2} = \frac{48}{6} = 8 \text{ A}$$

b Find the voltage from *f* to *c*.

$$E_{fc} = IR_4 + E_5$$

$$E_{fc} = 8(2) + 10 = 26 \text{ V}$$

Therefore, $E_{TH} = 26 \text{ V}$

3 Replace each voltage source with a short, and remove the load as shown in Fig. 8-47.

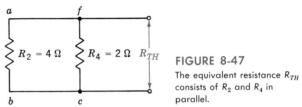

FIGURE 8-47
The equivalent resistance R_{TH} consists of R_2 and R_4 in parallel.

4 Find R_{TH}.

$$R_{TH} = \frac{4 \times 2}{4 + 2} = 1.33 \ \Omega$$

5 Draw the equivalent circuit as shown in Fig. 8-48.

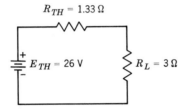

FIGURE 8-48
Thevenin's equivalent circuit. E_{TH} is in series with R_{TH} and R_L.

6 Solve for I_L.

$$R_t = 1.33 + 3 = 4.33 \ \Omega$$

$$I_L = \frac{E_{TH}}{R_t} = \frac{26}{4.33} = 6 \text{ A} \qquad Ans.$$

Solve for E_L.

$$E_L = I_L \times R_L$$

$$E_L = 6 \times 3 = 18 \text{ V} \qquad Ans.$$

7 Find the currents *x* and *z*. In Fig. 8-46, since $E_{pb} = E_{fc} = E_L = 18 \text{ V}$ (all in parallel),

$$-4x + 58 = 18$$

$$-4x = -40$$

$$x = 10 \text{ A} \qquad Ans.$$

Also, since $E_{fc} = 18 \text{ V}$,

$$2z + 10 = 18$$

$$2z = 8$$

$$z = 4 \text{ A} \qquad Ans.$$

EXAMPLE 8-25   Find the load current and the load voltage in the circuit shown in Fig. 8-49*a*.

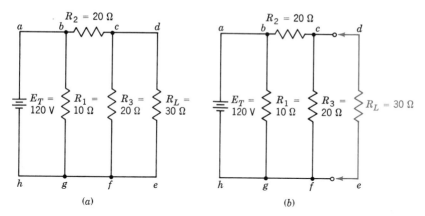

FIGURE 8-49

(*a*) Original circuit. (*b*) The circuit with the load removed.

SOLUTION

1   Remove the load from the circuit as shown in Fig. 8-49*b*.
2   Find E_{TH} with the load removed. This will be the voltage across R_3.
 a   The resistors R_2 and R_3 between points *b* and *f* are in series. Therefore, $R_{bf} = 20 + 20 = 40 \ \Omega$.
 b   The path from *b* to *f* is in parallel with the 120-V source. Therefore,

$$I_{bf} = \frac{120}{40} = 3 \text{ A}$$

$$E_3 = E_{TH} = I_3 \times R_3$$

$$E_{TH} = 3 \times 20 = 60 \text{ V}$$

3   Replace each voltage source with a short and remove the load as shown in Fig. 8-50*a*. Be careful to note that *when the battery is replaced with a short, it also shorts out the resistor* R_1, which results in the circuit shown in Fig. 8-50*b*.

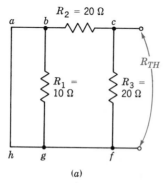

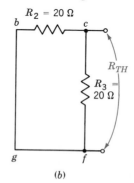

FIGURE 8-50

(*a*) The equivalent R_{TH} = the total resistance with the source shorted and the load removed. (*b*) The short across *ab* of Fig. 8-50*a* also shorts out R_1. R_{TH} is found from this circuit.

4   Find R_{TH}. Since R_2 and R_3 are now in parallel,

$$R_{TH} = \frac{R_2 \times R_3}{R_2 + R_3} \qquad\qquad (4\text{-}5)$$

$$R_{TH} = \frac{20 \times 20}{20 + 20} = 10 \ \Omega$$

5 Draw the equivalent circuit as shown in Fig. 8-51.

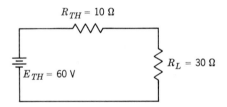

$R_{TH} = 10 \ \Omega$

$E_{TH} = 60 \ V$

$R_L = 30 \ \Omega$

FIGURE 8-51

Thevenin's equivalent circuit. E_{TH} is in series with R_{TH} and R_L.

6 Solve for I_L.

$$R_t = 10 + 30 = 40 \ \Omega$$

$$I_L = \frac{E_{TH}}{R_t} = \frac{60}{40} = 1.5 \ A \qquad Ans.$$

Solve for E_L.

$$E_L = I_L \times R_L$$

$$E_L = 1.5 \times 30 = 45 \ V \qquad Ans.$$

EXAMPLE 8-26   Solve the circuit shown in Fig. 8-29 for the load current y and the load voltage E_3 by Thevenin's theorem.

SOLUTION
Fig. 8-29 is repeated here for your convenience.

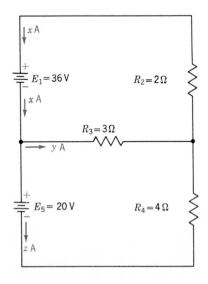

x A

$E_1 = 36$ V

x A

$R_2 = 2\Omega$

$R_3 = 3\Omega$

y A

$E_5 = 20$ V

$R_4 = 4\Omega$

z A

1 Remove the load R_3 from the circuit as shown in Fig. 8-52a.

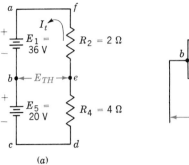

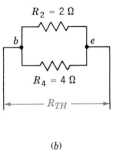

FIGURE 8-52

(a) E_{TH} is the voltage across the terminals from which the load has been removed. (b) The equivalent R_{TH} is the total resistance with all sources of emf shorted and the load removed.

2 Find E_{TH} with the load removed. This will be the voltage between points e and b.

a The circuit $abcdef$ is a simple series circuit in which

$$E_t = 36 + 20 = 56 \text{ V}$$

$$R_t = 4 + 2 = 6 \ \Omega$$

$$I_t = \frac{56}{6} = 9.33 \text{ A}$$

b The voltage from e to b around the path $efab = E_{TH}$.

$$E_{TH} = -I_t R_2 + E_1$$

$$E_{TH} = -(9.33 \times 2) + 36$$

$$E_{TH} = -18.66 + 36 = 17.34 \text{ V}$$

3 Replace each voltage source with a short and remove the load as shown in Fig. 8-52b. In this parallel circuit,

$$R_{TH} = \frac{2 \times 4}{2 + 4} = 1.33 \ \Omega$$

4 Draw the equivalent circuit as shown in Fig. 8-53.

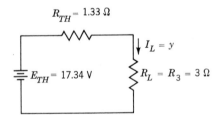

FIGURE 8-53

Thevenin's equivalent circuit. E_{TH} is in series with R_{TH} and R_3.

5 Solve for the load current y.

$$R_t = 1.33 + 3 = 4.33 \ \Omega$$

$$y = I_L = \frac{E_{TH}}{R_t}$$

$$y = \frac{17.34}{4.33} = 4 \text{ A} \qquad Ans.$$

Solve for the load voltage E_3.

$$E_3 = y \times R_3 = 4 \times 3 = 12 \text{ V} \qquad Ans.$$

SELF-TEST 8-27   Find the load current and the load voltage in the circuit shown in Fig. 8-54.

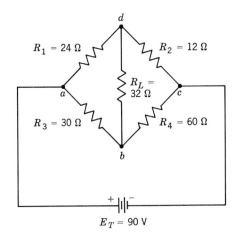

$E_T = 90$ V   **FIGURE 8-54**

SOLUTION

1   Remove the load from the circuit as shown in Fig. 8-55. Move $E_T = 90$ V to the inside of the figure for greater clarity.

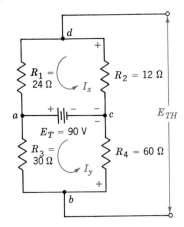

FIGURE 8-55

E_{TH} is the voltage across the terminals from which the load has been removed.

2   Find E_{TH} with the load removed. This will be the voltage across the terminals ____ and ____.

     a   In the circuit *acd*, R_1 and R_2 are in _____.

$$R_x = 24 + \underline{\quad} = \underline{\quad} \ \Omega$$

$$I_x = \frac{E_T}{R_x} = \frac{90}{?} = 2.5 \text{ A}$$

     b   In the circuit *abc*, R_3 and R_4 are in _____.

b	*d*
series	
12	36
36	
series	

$$R_y = \underline{\quad} + 60 = \underline{\quad} \; \Omega$$

$$I_y = \frac{?}{90} = 1 \text{ A}$$

30	90
90	

c Find E_2 and E_4.

$$E_2 = \underline{\quad} \times R_2 \qquad E_4 = \underline{\quad} \times R_4$$

$$E_2 = \underline{\quad} \times 12 \qquad E_4 = \underline{\quad} \times 60$$

$$E_2 = 30 \text{ V} \qquad E_4 = 60 \text{ V}$$

I_x	I_y
2.5	1

d E_{TH} is equal to the *algebraic* sum of the voltages around the path *bcd*. Be careful to note the polarities as indicated on the figure.

$$E_{bcd} = E_{TH} = E_4 \;\underline{\;(+/-)\;}\; E_2$$

$$E_{TH} = 60 - 30 = \underline{\quad} \text{ V}$$

—
30

3   Replace each voltage source with a _____ and remove the _____ as shown in Fig. 8-56a. The circuit should now be redrawn in standard form as shown in Fig. 8-56b.

short	load

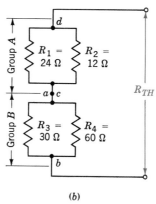

(a)   (b)

FIGURE 8-56
(a) Fig. 8-54 with the load removed and the battery shorted. (b) Fig. 8-56a redrawn in standard form.

4   Find R_{TH}. In Fig. 8-56b,
R_1 and R_2 form a __(series/parallel)__ group *A*.
R_3 and R_4 form a __(series/parallel)__ group *B*.
Group *A* is in __(series/parallel)__ with group *B*.

parallel
parallel
series

$$R_{TH} = \frac{R_1 \times R_2}{R_1 + R_2} + \underline{\quad ? \quad}$$

$$R_{TH} = \frac{24 \times 12}{24 + 12} + \frac{30 \times 60}{30 + 60}$$

$$R_{TH} = \underline{\quad} + \underline{\quad}$$

$$R_{TH} = \underline{\quad} \; \Omega$$

$\dfrac{R_3 \times R_4}{R_3 + R_4}$	
8	20
28	

5   Complete the drawing of the equivalent circuit of Fig. 8-57.
6   Solve for I_L.

$$R_t = \underline{\quad} + \underline{\quad} = 60 \; \Omega$$

28	32

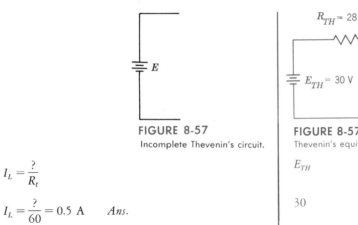

FIGURE 8-57
Incomplete Thevenin's circuit.

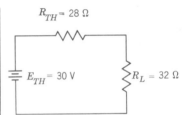

FIGURE 8-57a
Thevenin's equivalent circuit.

$$I_L = \frac{?}{R_t}$$

$$I_L = \frac{?}{60} = 0.5 \text{ A} \qquad Ans.$$

Solve for E_L.

$$E_L = \underline{\quad} \times \underline{\quad}$$

$$E_L = 0.5 \times \underline{\quad}$$

$$E_L = \underline{\quad} \text{ V} \qquad Ans.$$

E_{TH}

30

$I_L \qquad R_L$

32

16

PROBLEMS

Solve the following problems by applying Thevenin's theorem to the circuit.

1. In a circuit similar to that shown in Fig. 8-42a, $E_T = 25$ V, $R_1 = 1$ Ω, $R_2 = 4$ Ω, $R_3 = 5$ Ω, and $R_L = 10$ Ω. Find I_L and E_L.
2. In a circuit similar to that shown in Fig. 8-22, $E_1 = 75$ V, $R_2 = 3$ Ω, $R_4 = 4$ Ω, and $E_5 = 28$ V. If the load $R_3 = 12$ Ω, find the currents x, y, and z, and the load voltage E_3.
3. In a circuit similar to that shown in Fig. 8-49a, $E_T = 120$ V, $R_1 = 2$ Ω, $R_2 = 4$ Ω, $R_3 = 6$ Ω, and $R_L = 3.6$ Ω. Find I_L and E_L.
4. In a circuit similar to that shown in Fig. 8-29, $E_1 = 76$ V, $R_2 = 10$ Ω, $R_3 = 2$ Ω, $R_4 = 15$ Ω, and $E_5 = 54$ V. Find the current y and the voltage across R_3.

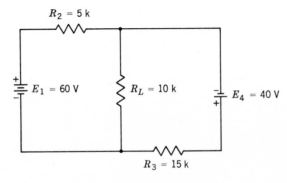

FIGURE 8-58

5. In a circuit similar to that shown in Fig. 8-54, $R_1 = 30\ \Omega$, $R_2 = 70\ \Omega$, $R_3 = 10\ \Omega$, $R_4 = 15\ \Omega$, and $E_T = 100$ V. If $R_L = 23\ \Omega$, find I_L and E_L.
6. Solve Example 8-14 by Thevenin's theorem.
7. Using Fig. 8-28, find I_5 and E_5 by Thevenin's theorem.
8. Using Fig. 8-25, find the current w and E_2 by Thevenin's theorem.
9. Solve the circuit shown in Fig. 8-58 for the values of I_L and E_L.
10. Solve the circuit shown in Fig. 8-59 for the values of I_L and E_L.

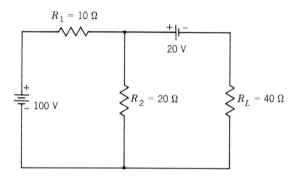

FIGURE 8-59

JOB 8-9   REVIEW AND TEST

In Fig. 8-39, circuit abc is in __(delta/Y)__ formation.

$$\Sigma R_\Delta = \underline{\hspace{2cm}}$$

$$R_a = \frac{?}{\Sigma R_\Delta}$$

$$R_b = \frac{?}{\Sigma R_\Delta}$$

$$R_c = \frac{?}{\Sigma R_\Delta}$$

delta

$R_1 + R_2 + R_3$

$R_1 \times R_2$

$R_2 \times R_3$

$R_1 \times R_3$

THEVENIN'S THEOREM
Any two-terminal network can be replaced by an _____ simple series circuit of one resistance and one voltage.

   1   The equivalent voltage is the terminal voltage of the complex circuit when the _____ is removed. Its symbol is ____.

   2   The equivalent resistance is the resistance between the terminals of the complex circuit when the load is _____, and all sources of emf are _____. Its symbol is ____.

equivalent

load E_{TH}

removed
shorted R_{TH}

PROCEDURE
   1   Determine the load whose current I_L and whose voltage (___) are to be found. In order to simplify the problem, a voltage source __(may/may not)__ be included in the load.

   2   Disconnect the _____ from the circuit at two points and label these points as Thevenin's terminals.

E_L
may

load

3 Find the open-circuit output voltage that would appear across these terminals. The symbol for this voltage is ____.

E_{TH}

4 Replace each voltage source with a _____ and _____ the load.

short   remove

5 Redraw the remaining circuit in standard form.

6 Find the total resistance that would appear across the Thevenin terminals. This is the symbol ____.

R_{TH}

7 Draw the equivalent circuit consisting of E_{TH} in _____ with R_{TH} and the _____.

series
load

8 If the "load" has included any voltage source, it must be (included/ excluded) in the equivalent Thevenin circuit with its original polarity.

included

9 Solve the circuit for the load _____ and the load _____. The total resistance of this circuit is the sum of R_{TH} and the _____ resistance.

current   voltage
load

TEST—DELTA CIRCUITS AND THEVENIN'S THEOREM

1. Use the delta-to-Y transformation method. In a circuit similar to that shown in Fig. 8-39, $I_T = 10$ A, $R_1 = 40$ Ω, $R_2 = 30$ Ω, $R_3 = 30$ Ω, $R_4 = 28$ Ω, $R_5 = 51$ Ω. Find the currents v, w, x, y, and z, and the total voltage E_T.

2. Solve the following problem by Thevenin's Theorem. In Fig. 8-30, find (a) the current z, and (b) the voltage drop across R_7.

APPLICATIONS
OF SERIES AND PARALLEL
CIRCUITS

JOB 9-1   POWERS OF TEN

In many problems in electronics the usual units of amperes, volts, and ohms are either too large or too small. It has been found more convenient to use new units of measurement. These new units are formed by placing a special word or prefix in front of the unit. Each of these prefixes has a definite meaning.

Milli unit (m unit) means one one-thousandth of the unit

Kilo unit (k unit) means one thousand of these units

Micro unit (μ unit) means one one-millionth of the unit

Pico unit (p unit) means one-millionth of one-millionth of the unit

Mega unit (M unit) means one million of these units.

As we learned in Job 6-6, these numbers may be written as powers of ten.

$$10 = 10^1 = 10 \text{ to the } \textit{first} \text{ power}$$
$$100 = 10^2 = 10 \text{ to the } \textit{second} \text{ power}$$
$$1,000 = 10^3 = 10 \text{ to the } \textit{third} \text{ power}$$
$$10,000 = 10^4 = 10 \text{ to the } \textit{fourth} \text{ power}$$
$$100,000 = 10^5 = 10 \text{ to the } \textit{fifth} \text{ power}$$
$$1,000,000 = 10^6 = 10 \text{ to the } \textit{sixth} \text{ power}$$

The use of these units will clearly involve multiplying and dividing by numbers of this size and notation. Our work will be considerably simplified if we learn to apply the following rules.

MULTIPLYING BY POWERS OF 10

RULE	To multiply values by numbers like 100, 1,000, 1,000,000 etc., move the decimal point one place to the right for every zero in the multiplier.

EXAMPLE 9-1

$1.59 \times 10 = 1\odot5.9 = 15.9$ (move point one place to the right)

$4.76 \times 100 = 4\odot76. = 476.$ or 476 (move point two places to the right)

A decimal point is ordinarily not written at the end of a whole number. However, it may be written if desired. In the following example, the point must be written in together with two zeros so that we can move the decimal point past the required number of places.

$$34 \times 100 = 34\odot00. = 3,400. \text{ or } 3,400$$

If the decimal point must be moved past more places than are available, zeros are added at the end of the number to make up the required number of places. This is shown in the following example.

$$0.0259 \times 1,000,000 = \odot025900. = 25,900$$

RULE	To multiply values by numbers expressed as 10 raised to some power, move the decimal point to the right as many places as the exponent indicates.

EXAMPLE 9-2

$0.345 \times 10^2 = \odot34.5$ or 34.5 (move point two places right)

$0.345 \times 10^3 = \odot345.$ or 345 (move point three places right)

$0.345 \times 10^6 = \odot345000.$ or 345,000 (move point six places right)

$0.0065 \times 10^3 = \odot006.5$ or 6.5 (move point three places right)

PROBLEMS

1.	$0.0072 \times 1,000$	2.	45.76×100
3.	$3.09 \times 1,000$	4.	0.0045×100
5.	37×100	6.	0.08×10^2
7.	0.0006×10^3	8.	0.00056×10^6
9.	27×10^2	10.	15×10^3
11.	0.00078×10^2	12.	7.8×10^6
13.	15.4×10^3	14.	$3 \times 15 \times 10^2$
15.	$0.005 \times 2 \times 10^2$	16.	6×10^4

17. 0.008×10^4 18. 0.009×10^5
19. 2.34×10^5 20. 0.0000005×10^8

DIVIDING BY POWERS OF 10

RULE	To divide values by numbers like 10, 100, 1,000, etc., move the decimal point one place to the left for every zero in the divisor.

EXAMPLE 9-3

$17.4 \div 10 = 1.7\odot4 = 1.74$ (move point one place left)

$45 \div 100 = .45\odot = 0.45$ (move point two places left)

$6.5 \div 1,000 = .006\odot5 = 0.0065$ (move point three places left)

RULE	To divide values by numbers expressed as 10 raised to some power, move the decimal point to the left as many places as the exponent indicates.

EXAMPLE 9-4

$467.9 \div 10^2 = 4.67\odot9 = 4.679$ (move point two places left)

$59 \div 10^2 = .59\odot = 0.59$ (move point two places left)

$8.5 \div 10^3 = .008\odot5 = 0.0085$ (move point three places left)

$5,500,000 \div 10^8 = .05500000\odot = 0.055$ (move point eight places left)

PROBLEMS

1. $6,500 \div 100$ 2. $7,500 \div 10^3$
3. $880,000 \div 1,000$ 4. $32 \div 10^2$
5. $6 \div 10^2$ 6. $17.8 \div 10$
7. $835 \div 10^3$ 8. $550 \div 10^6$
9. $653.8 \div 10^3$ 10. $100,000,000 \div 10^6$
11. $0.45 \div 10^2$ 12. $0.08 \div 10$
13. $8.5 \div 10^3$ 14. $7 \div 10^6$

15. $\dfrac{28.6}{10^3}$ 16. $\dfrac{2 \times 1,000}{10^3}$

17. $0.02 \div 10^3$ 18. $\dfrac{180}{2 \times 10^2}$

NEGATIVE POWERS OF TEN

By definition:

$$10^{-n} = \frac{1}{10^n} \quad \text{and} \quad \frac{1}{10^n} = 10^{-n}$$

Thus, $50 \times \frac{1}{10^2}$ is the same as 50×10^{-2}

or, $\frac{50}{10^2}$ is the same as 50×10^{-2}

Therefore, if dividing by 10^2 means to move the decimal point to the left for two places, then the $-$ sign in the exponent (-2) must mean to do the same thing.

MULTIPLYING BY NEGATIVE POWERS OF TEN

RULE   To multiply values by numbers expressed as 10 raised to some negative power, move the decimal point to the *left* as many places as the exponent indicates.

EXAMPLE 9-5

$50 \times 10^{-2} = .50 \odot$ or 0.5 (move point two places left)

$64.9 \times 10^{-2} = .64 \odot 9$ or 0.649 (move point two places left)

$50,000 \times 10^{-6} = .050000 \odot$ or 0.05 (move point six places left)

$0.2 \times 10^{-3} = .000 \odot 2$ or 0.0002 (move point three places left)

PROBLEMS

1. $25,000 \times 10^{-3}$
2. 250×10^{-2}
3. 1.5×10^{-1}
4. 0.5×10^{-2}
5. $6,250 \times 10^{-3}$
6. $100,000 \times 10^{-5}$
7. $250,000 \times 10^{-8}$
8. 6×10^{-3}
9. 75.4×10^{-4}
10. 16.5×10^{-2}

DIVIDING BY NEGATIVE POWERS OF TEN

Since by definition,

$$\frac{1}{10^n} = 1 \times 10^{-n}$$

and

$$1 \times 10^{-n} = \frac{1}{10^n}$$

we can transfer any power of 10 from numerator to denominator, or vice versa, by simply changing the sign of the exponent.

EXAMPLE 9-6

$$\frac{15}{10^{-2}} = 15 \times 10^2 = 1,500$$

$$\frac{0.05}{10^{-3}} = 0.05 \times 10^3 = 50$$

$$\frac{15,000}{10^3} = 15,000 \times 10^{-3} = 15$$

$$\frac{5 \times 0.2}{10^{-4}} = 1.0 \times 10^4 = 10,000$$

PROBLEMS

1. $\dfrac{19.2}{10^{-2}}$

2. $\dfrac{25.6}{10^2}$

3. $\dfrac{0.85}{10^{-3}}$

4. $\dfrac{85}{10^3}$

5. $\dfrac{0.0072}{10^{-6}}$

6. $\dfrac{0.9}{10^{-4}}$

7. $\dfrac{0.0045}{10^2}$

8. $\dfrac{0.96}{10^{-3}}$

9. $\dfrac{880,000}{10^{-2}}$

10. $\dfrac{0.005}{10^{-2} \times 10^{-3}}$

11. $\dfrac{6 \times 5}{10^{-2}}$

12. $\dfrac{0.5 \times 0.04}{10^{-3}}$

13. $\dfrac{30 \times 10^3}{10^{-2}}$

14. $\dfrac{50 \times 10^2}{10^{-3}}$

15. $\dfrac{60 \times 10^{-2}}{10^3}$

16. $\dfrac{64.9 \times 10^3}{10^5}$

EXPRESSING NUMBERS AS POWERS OF 10

As you have seen, multiplying and dividing numbers by powers of 10 is just a set of simple mental problems. It certainly will be to our advantage then if we can express the numbers in any problem as powers of 10 before we multiply or divide.

Expressing numbers larger than 1 as a small number times a power of 10

RULE	To express a large number as a smaller number times a power of 10, move the decimal point to the *left* as many places as desired. Then multiply the number obtained by 10 to a power which is equal to the number of places moved.

EXAMPLE 9-7

a $3{,}000 = 3.000 \odot$ (Moved three places left)

$3{,}000 = 3 \times 10^3$

b $4{,}500 = 45.00 \odot$ (Moved two places left)

$4{,}500 = 45 \times 10^2$

c $4{,}500 = 4.500 \odot$ (Moved three places left)

$4{,}500 = 4.5 \times 10^3$

d $770{,}000 = 77.0000 \odot$ (Moved four places left)

$770{,}000 = 77 \times 10^4$

e $800{,}000 = 8.00000 \odot$ (Moved five places left)

$800{,}000 = 8 \times 10^5$

f $5{,}005.2 = 5.005 \odot 2$ (Moved three places left)

$5{,}005.2 = 5.0052 \times 10^3$

g Express the following number to three significant figures and express it as a number between 1 and 10 times the proper power of 10.

$7{,}831 = 7{,}830$ (Since only three significant figures are wanted)

$7{,}830 = 7.830 \odot$ (Moved three places left)

$7{,}830 = 7.83 \times 10^3$

h Express 62,495 using three significant figures as a number between 1 and 10 times the proper power of 10.

$62{,}495 = 62{,}500$ (Written as three significant figures)

$62{,}500 = 6.2500 \odot$ (Moved four places left)

$62{,}500 = 6.25 \times 10^4$

PROBLEMS

Express the following numbers to three significant figures and write them as numbers between 1 and 10 times the proper power of 10.

1.	6,000	2.	5,700	3.	150,000
4.	500,000	5.	235,000	6.	7,350,000
7.	4,960	8.	62,500	9.	980
10.	175	11.	12.5	12.	7,303
13.	48.2	14.	12,600	15.	880,000,000
16.	54,009	17.	38,270	18.	8,019.7
19.	1,754,300	20,	2,395,000	21.	482,715

Expressing numbers less than 1 as a whole number times a power of 10

RULE

To express a decimal as a whole number times a power of 10, move the decimal point to the right as many places as desired. Then multiply the number obtained by 10 to a *negative* power which is equal to the number of places moved.

EXAMPLE 9-8

a $0.005 = 0 \odot 005.$ (Moved three places right)

$0.005 = 5 \times 10^{-3}$

b $0.00672 = 0 \odot 006.72$ (Moved three places right)

$0.00672 = 6.72 \times 10^{-3}$

c $0.758 = 0 \odot 75.8$ (Moved two places right)

$0.758 = 75.8 \times 10^{-2}$

d $0.0758 = 0 \odot 07.58$ (Moved two places right)

$0.0758 = 7.58 \times 10^{-2}$

e $0.0000089 = 0 \odot 000008.9$ (Moved six places right)

$0.0000089 = 8.9 \times 10^{-6}$

f Express the number 0.0003578 to three significant figures and then write it as a number between 1 and 10 times the proper power of 10.

$0.0003578 = 0.000358$ (Written as three significant figures)

$0.000358 = 0 \odot 0003.58$ (Moved four places right)

$0.000358 = 3.58 \times 10^{-4}$

PROBLEMS

Express the following numbers to three significant figures and write them as numbers between 1 and 10 times the proper power of 10.

1. 0.006   2. 0.0075

3.	0.0035	4.	0.08
5.	0.456	6.	0.0357
7.	785×10^{-2}	8.	0.00000012
9.	0.0965	10.	0.00482
11.	0.5	12.	0.0003743
13.	0.008147	14.	0.000007949
15.	0.000725×10^5	16.	0.01333
17.	0.0006×10^3	18.	$3,200 \times 10^{-5}$
19.	360×10^{-4}	20.	0.000008×10^4

MULTIPLYING WITH POWERS OF TEN

If x^3 means $x \cdot x \cdot x$, and x^2 means $x \cdot x$, then $x^3 \cdot x^2$ means $x \cdot x \cdot x \cdot x \cdot x = x^5$ or, $x^3 \cdot x^2 = x^{(3+2)} = x^5$, which gives us the following rule.

RULE	The multiplication of two or more powers using the *same* base is equal to that base raised to the sum of the powers.

EXAMPLE 9-9

a $a^4 \times a^5 = a^{(4+5)} = a^9$

b $10^2 \times 10^3 = 10^5$

c Multiply $10,000 \times 1,000$:
if $10,000 = 10^4$ and $1,000 = 10^3$, then

$$10,000 \times 1,000 = 10^4 \times 10^3 = 10^{(4+3)} = 10^7 \quad Ans.$$

d Multiply $25,000 \times 4,000$:
if $25,000 = 25 \times 10^3$ and $4,000 = 4 \times 10^3$, then

$$25,000 \times 4,000 = 25 \times 10^3 \times 4 \times 10^3$$
$$= 25 \times 4 \times 10^3 \times 10^3$$
$$= 100 \times 10^6$$
$$= 10^2 \times 10^6 = 10^8 \quad Ans.$$

e Multiply 0.00005×0.003:
if $0.00005 = 5 \times 10^{-5}$ and $0.003 = 3 \times 10^{-3}$, then

$$0.00005 \times 0.003 = 5 \times 10^{-5} \times 3 \times 10^{-3}$$
$$= 5 \times 3 \times 10^{-5} \times 10^{-3}$$
$$= 15 \times 10^{[-5+(-3)]}$$
$$= 15 \times 10^{-8} \quad Ans.$$

f Multiply $7,000 \times 0.00091$:
if $7,000 = 7 \times 10^3$ and $0.00091 = 9.1 \times 10^{-4}$, then

$$7,000 \times 0.00091 = 7 \times 10^3 \times 9.1 \times 10^{-4}$$

$$= 7 \times 9.1 \times 10^3 \times 10^{-4}$$

$$= 63.7 \times 10^{[3+(-4)]}$$

$$= 63.7 \times 10^{-1}$$

$$= 6.37 \quad Ans.$$

g   Multiply $0.00005 \times 20,000 \times 1,500$:

if $0.00005 = 5 \times 10^{-5}$, and $20,000 = 2 \times 10^4$, and $1,500 = 1.5 \times 10^3$, then

$$0.00005 \times 20,000 \times 1,500 = 5 \times 10^{-5} \times 2 \times 10^4 \times 1.5 \times 10^3$$

$$= 5 \times 2 \times 1.5 \times 10^{-5} \times 10^4 \times 10^3$$

$$= 15 \times 10^2$$

$$= 1,500 \quad Ans.$$

PROBLEMS

Multiply the following numbers.

1. $5,000 \times 0.001$
2. $850 \times 2,000$
3. $16 \times 10^2 \times 4 \times 10^3$
4. $0.0004 \times 5 \times 10^2$
5. $250 \times 4,000 \times 3 \times 10^{-2}$
6. $1,000 \times 10^{-4} \times 0.02$
7. $3 \times 10^{-5} \times 4 \times 10^6$
8. $15 \times 10^{-4} \times 20,000 \times 0.04$
9. $200,000 \times 0.000005 \times 3 \times 10^{-2}$
10. $0.004 \times 0.0005 \times 5,000$
11. $0.005 \times 5 \times 10^{-3} \times 0.02$
12. $6,000,000 \times 0.00025 \times 0.3 \times 10^{-2}$
13. $0.3 \times 10^{-2} \times 800,000 \times 400 \times 10^{-3}$
14. $(500)^2 \times 0.0002 \times 4,000$
15. $500,000,000 \times 0.000004 \times 3.14 \times 10^2$
16. As we shall see in Job 16-2, the inductive reactance of a coil is given by the formula

$$X_L = 6.28 \, fL$$

where $f =$ frequency, Hz
$L =$ inductance of the circuit, H
$X_L =$ reactance, Ω

Find the inductive reactance when:
a. $f = 60$ Hz and $L = 0.025$ H
b. $f = 1,000,000$ Hz and $L = 0.25$ H
c. $f = 10,000$ Hz and $L = 0.000025$ H

DIVISION WITH POWERS OF 10

As noted in the section on Dividing by Negative Powers of 10 of this job, we can transfer any power of 10 from numerator to denominator, or vice versa, by simply changing the sign of the exponent. This will permit us to change *all* division problems into multiplications, which are generally easier to do.

EXAMPLE 9-10

a $10^6 \div 10^2 = \dfrac{10^6}{10^2} = 10^6 \times 10^{-2} = 10^4$ *Ans.*

b $\dfrac{4,000}{10^2} = 4 \times 10^3 \times 10^{-2} = 4 \times 10^1 = 40$ *Ans.*

c $\dfrac{35,000}{0.005} = \dfrac{35 \times 10^3}{5 \times 10^{-3}} = 7 \times 10^3 \times 10^3$

$\qquad\qquad\qquad = 7 \times 10^6$ *Ans.*

d $\dfrac{144,000}{12 \times 10^3} = \dfrac{144 \times \overset{1}{\cancel{10^3}}}{12 \times \underset{1}{\cancel{10^3}}} = 12$ *Ans.*

Note that *any* factor divided by itself cancels out to 1, and that it is not necessary to transfer any powers. That is, $10^3/10^3 = 10^{(3-3)} = 10^0 = 1$.

e $\dfrac{0.00075}{500} = \dfrac{75 \times 10^{-5}}{5 \times 10^2} = 15 \times 10^{-5} \times 10^{-2}$

$\qquad\qquad\qquad = 15 \times 10^{-7}$ *Ans.*

f $\dfrac{60}{0.0003 \times 40,000} = \dfrac{60}{3 \times 10^{-4} \times 4 \times 10^4} = \dfrac{5}{10^0}$

Now, since $10^0 = 1$, $\dfrac{5}{10^0} = \dfrac{5}{1} = 5$ *Ans.*

PROBLEMS

Divide the following numbers.

1. $\dfrac{10^8}{10^3}$

2. $\dfrac{10^3}{10^5}$

3. $\dfrac{60,000}{5 \times 10^2}$

4. $\dfrac{50,000}{0.05}$

5. $\dfrac{10}{50,000}$

6. $\dfrac{20}{0.0005}$

7. $\dfrac{0.0001}{500}$

8. $\dfrac{20}{4,000 \times 0.005}$

9. $\dfrac{1,000 \times 0.008}{0.002 \times 500}$

10. $\dfrac{150,000}{3 \times 10^5}$

11. $\dfrac{0.00015}{3 \times 10^{-2}}$

12. $\dfrac{1}{4 \times 100,000 \times 0.00005}$

13. As we shall see in Job 17-4, the capacitive reactance of a capacitor is given by the formula

$$X_c = \frac{1}{2\pi f C}$$

where f = frequency, Hz

$$C = \text{capacitance, F}$$
$$\pi = 3.14$$
$$X_C = \text{reactance, } \Omega$$

Find the capacitive reactance when:

a. $f = 60$ Hz and $C = 0.00005$ F

b. $f = 1,000$ Hz and $C = 0.0000025$ F

c. $f = 1,000,000$ Hz and $C = 0.00000005$ F

TEST—POWERS OF TEN

Express the following as a number between 1 and 10 times the proper power of 10.

1. 140,000	2. 1,750,000
3. 0.0845	4. 350×10^{-4}
5. 0.0000096	6. 0.00007×10^3

Perform the indicated operations.

7. 0.00034×10^3	8. $0.040 \times 10^3 \times 3 \times 10^2$
9. 6.4×10^{-3}	10. 0.078×10^{-2}
11. $\dfrac{10.7}{10^{-3}}$	12. $\dfrac{40 \times 10^2}{10^{-3}}$
13. $2 \times 1,000 \times 6 \times 10^{-2}$	14. $0.006 \times 5 \times 10^4 \times 0.02$
15. $(100)^2 \times 0.02 \times 5,000$	16. $50,000 \div (5 \times 10^2)$
17. $\dfrac{4,000 \times 0.008}{0.02 \times 10^2}$	18. $\dfrac{160,000}{4 \times 10^5}$
19. $\dfrac{1}{4 \times 10 \times 10^3 \times 0.5 \times 10^{-6}}$	20. $200,000,000 \times 4 \times 10^{-6} \times 10^2$

JOB 9-2   UNITS OF MEASUREMENT IN ELECTRONICS

Ohm's law and other electrical formulas use the simple electrical units of volts, amperes, and ohms. However, if the measurements given or obtained in a problem were stated in kilovolts, milliamperes, or megohms, it would be necessary to change these units of measurement into the units required by the formula.

Changing units of measurement. There are two factors to be considered when describing any measurement: (1) how many of the measurements and (2) what *kind* of measurement. For example, $1 may be described as 2 half-dollars, 4 quarters, 10 dimes, 20 nickels, or 100 pennies. When the $1 was changed into each of the new measurements, *both* the unit of measurement as well as the number of them were changed. For example:

Since 3 ft = 1 yd,   2 yd   = 2 × 3   = 6 ft
Since 2,000 lb = 1 ton,   3 tons   = 3 × 2,000 = 6,000 lb
Since 100¢ = 1 dollar   4 dollars = 4 × 100   = 400¢

Notice that a *small number* of *large units* is always changed into a *large number* of *small units* by *multiplying* by the number showing the relationship between the units.

RULE	To change from a large unit into a small unit, multiply by the number showing the relationship between the units.

This rule is illustrated for various units in Table 9-1.

TABLE 9-1
CHANGING LARGE UNITS INTO SMALL UNITS

TO CHANGE	INTO	MULTIPLY BY
Mega units	Units	10^6
Mega units	Kilo units	10^3
Kilo units	Units	10^3
Units	Milli units	10^3
Units	Micro units	10^6
Units	Pico units	10^{12}
Milli units	Micro units	10^3
Milli units	Pico units	10^9
Micro units	Pico units	10^6

EXAMPLE 9-11

1   $2.4 \text{ V} = 2.4 \times 10^3 = 2,400 \text{ mV}$
2   $0.56 \text{ A} = 0.56 \times 10^3 = 560 \text{ mA}$
3   $0.5 \text{ W} = 0.5 \times 10^3 = 500 \text{ mW}$
4   $0.3 \text{ kV} = 0.3 \times 10^3 = 300 \text{ V}$
5   $0.15 \text{ kW} = 0.15 \times 10^3 = 150 \text{ W}$
6   $880 \text{ kHz} = 880 \times 10^3 = 880,000 \text{ Hz}$
7   $0.0004 \text{ A} = 0.0004 \times 10^6 = 400 \text{ } \mu\text{A}$
8   $0.00005 \text{ F} = 0.00005 \times 10^6 = 50 \text{ } \mu\text{F}$
9   $0.25 \text{ M}\Omega = 0.25 \times 10^6 = 250,000 \text{ }\Omega$
10 $3.2 \text{ MHz} = 3.2 \times 10^6 = 3,200,000 \text{ Hz}$
11 $0.00035 \text{ } \mu\text{F} = 0.00035 \times 10^6 = 350 \text{ pF}$
12 $0.000000005 \text{ F} = 0.000000005 \times 10^{12} = 5,000 \text{ pF}$

Now let us reverse the process and change small units into large units. For example:

$$\text{Since 3 ft} = 1 \text{ yd,} \qquad 6 \text{ ft} = 6 \div 3 \qquad\qquad = 2 \text{ yd}$$
$$\text{Since 2,000 lb} = 1 \text{ ton,} \qquad 6,000 \text{ lb} = 6,000 \div 2,000 = 3 \text{ tons}$$
$$\text{Since 100¢} = 1 \text{ dollar} \qquad 400 \text{ ¢} = 400 \div 100 \qquad = 4 \text{ dollars}$$

small unit ⟶ Large unit

Large number ⟶ small number

Notice that a *large number* of *small units* is always changed into a *small number* of *large units* by *dividing* by the number showing the relationship between the units.

RULE	To change from a small unit into a large unit, divide by the number showing the relationship between the units.

This rule is illustrated for various units in Table 9-2.

TABLE 9-2
CHANGING SMALL UNITS INTO LARGE UNITS

TO CHANGE	INTO	DIVIDE BY	OR	MULTIPLY BY
Units	Mega units	10^6		10^{-6}
Kilo units	Mega units	10^3		10^{-3}
Units	Kilo units	10^3		10^{-3}
Milli units	Units	10^3		10^{-3}
Micro units	Units	10^6		10^{-6}
Pico units	Units	10^{12}		10^{-12}
Micro units	Milli units	10^3		10^{-3}
Pico units	Milli units	10^9		10^{-9}
Pico units	Micro units	10^6		10^{-6}

EXAMPLE 9-12

1 $500,000 \ \Omega = 500,000 \div 10^6 = 0.5 \ M\Omega$
   $\qquad \text{or} = 500,000 \times 10^{-6} = 0.5 \ M\Omega$
2 $660 \ kHz = 660 \times 10^{-3} = 0.66 \ MHz$
3 $600 \ V = 600 \times 10^{-3} = 0.6 \ kV$
4 $14.5 \ mA = 14.5 \times 10^{-3} = 0.0145 \ A$
5 $2.5 \ \mu F = 2.5 \times 10^{-6} = 0.0000025 \ F$
6 $30,000,000 \ pF = 30,000,000 \times 10^{-12} = 0.00003 \ F$
7 $400 \ \mu V = 400 \times 10^{-3} = 0.4 \ mV$
8 $350 \ pF = 350 \times 10^{-6} = 0.00035 \ \mu F$
9 $4,000 \ W = 4,000 \times 10^{-3} = 4 \ kW$
10 $1,010,000 \ Hz = 1,010,000 \times 10^{-3} = 1,010 \ kHz$
11 $356 \ mV = 356 \times 10^{-3} = 0.356 \ V$
12 $15,000 \ \mu V = 15,000 \times 10^{-6} = 0.015 \ V$

PROBLEMS

Change the following units of measurement.

1.	225 mA to A	2.	0.076 V to mV
3.	3.5 MΩ to Ω	4.	5 kW to W
5.	550 kHz to Hz	6.	700,000 Hz to kHz
7.	70,000 Ω to MΩ	8.	0.00008 F to μF
9.	0.065 A to mA	10.	6,500 W to kW
11.	75 mV to V	12.	2.3 MHz to Hz
13.	6,000 μA to A	14.	0.007 F to μF
15.	3.9 mA to A	16.	75,000 W to kW
17.	0.005 μF to pF	18.	¼ A to mA
19.	1,000 kHz to Hz	20.	0.5 MΩ to Ω
21.	0.008 V to mV	22.	0.0045 W to mW
23.	0.00006 μF to pF	24.	0.15 A to mA
25.	0.15 μF to F	26.	125 mV to V
27.	8,000 W to kW	28.	4.16 kW to W
29.	0.000004 A to μA	30.	0.6 MHz to Hz

JOB 9-3   USING ELECTRONIC UNITS OF MEASUREMENT IN SIMPLE CIRCUITS

All the formulas for Ohm's law, series circuits, parallel circuits, and power demand that the measurements be given in the units of amperes, volts, and ohms only. If a certain problem gives the measurements in units other than these, we must change all the measurements into amperes, volts, and ohms before we can use any of these formulas.

EXAMPLE 9-13   Find the voltage that will force 28.6 μA of current through a 70 kΩ resistor in the base circuit of a transistor.

SOLUTION
Given: $I = 28.6\ \mu A$ Find: $E = ?$
             $R = 70\ k\Omega$

1   Change μA to A.

$$28.6\ \mu A = 28.6 \times 10^{-6}\ A$$

2   Change 70 kΩ to Ω.

$$70\ k\Omega = 70 \times 10^{3}\ \Omega$$

3   Find the voltage E.

$$E = I \times R \qquad\qquad (2\text{-}1)$$
$$E = 28.6 \times 10^{-6} \times 70 \times 10^{3}$$
$$E = 28.6 \times 7 \times 10^{-2}$$

$$E = 200.2 \times 10^{-2}$$

$$E = 2 \text{ V} \quad Ans.$$

SELF-TEST 9-14   A bias voltage of 300 mV is developed across a 2-MΩ resistor. Find the current flowing.

SOLUTION

Given: $E = 300$ mV   Find: $I = ?$

$R = $ ____

2 MΩ

1   Change 300 mV to V.

$$300 \text{ mV} = 300 \times \underline{\quad} \text{ V}$$

10^{-3}

2   Change 2 MΩ to Ω.

$$2 \text{ MΩ} = 2 \times \underline{\quad} \text{ Ω}$$

10^{6}

3   Find the current I.

$$E = I \times R \qquad\qquad (2\text{-}1)$$

$$300 \times 10^{-3} = I \times 2 \times 10^{6}$$

$$I = \frac{300 \times 10^{-3}}{?}$$

2×10^{6}

$$= 150 \times 10^{-?}$$

9

$$= 0.15 \times 10^{-?} \text{ A}$$

6

$$I = 0.15 \underline{\quad} \text{A} \quad Ans.$$

μ

PROBLEMS

1.   How many milliamperes of current will flow through a 100-Ω resistor if the voltage across its ends is 20 mV?
2.   Two microamperes of current flow in an antenna whose resistance is 50 Ω. Find the voltage drop in the antenna.
3.   An emf of 200 μV sends 10 mA of current through the primary of a transformer. Find the total resisting effect of the coil.
4.   Find the number of microamperes flowing through a 2-MΩ grid leak if the voltage drop across it is 1,000 mV.
5.   Find the voltage drop across the 5-kΩ load of a transistor if the collector current is 2 mA.
6.   Find the total current in a parallel circuit if the currents in the branches are 40 mA, 6,000 μA, and 0.013 A.
7.   A 0.2-MΩ, a 5-kΩ, and a 10,000-Ω resistor are connected in series. Find the total resistance.
8.   Using the formula for capacitances in parallel, $C_T = C_1 + C_2$, find the total capacity of a 0.0025 μF and a 125-pF capacitor in parallel.
9.   Find the total resistance of a 1,000-Ω and a 4-kΩ resistor in parallel.

10. The time constant of an *RC* circuit is equal to the product of the resistance (ohms) and the capacitance (farads). Find the time constant of a circuit if $R = 10$ kΩ and $C = 0.004$ μF.

11. How many ohms of resistance are used in the volume control of a complementary-coupled audio amplifier if it passes 0.0002 A at 1.5 V?

12. The Lafayette LR-1500T radio uses an output stage similar to that shown in Fig. 9-1. If the dc resistance of the primary of the transformer is 0.2 kΩ and it passes 5 mA of current, find the voltage V_C which is available at the collector.

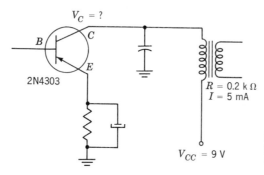

FIGURE 9-1
The output stage of a transistor radio.

13. The radiation resistance of a shortwave antenna is 100 Ω. If the transmitter delivers 900 mA to the antenna, find the number of watts radiated.

14. A 470-kΩ resistor in the base circuit of a 2N2924 phase-shift oscillator circuit carries a current of 30 μA. Find the voltage drop across the resistor.

15. A photoelectric cell circuit contains a resistance of 0.12 MΩ and carries a current of 50 μA. Find the voltage drop in the resistor.

TEST—ELECTRONIC UNITS OF MEASUREMENT

Change the following units of measurement as indicated.

1. 50,000 Ω to MΩ
2. 770 kHz to Hz
3. 100 mV to V
4. 3.7 mA to A
5. 400 pF to μF
6. 0.00005 A to μA
7. 0.0025 μF to F
8. 0.08 V to mV
9. 6,000 μA to A
10. 2.5 MΩ to Ω
11. Find the voltage drop across a 10-kΩ resistor carrying 0.2 mA.
12. Find the number of microamperes passing through a 0.1 MΩ resistor if the voltage drop across the resistor is 0.1 V.
13. Find the total resistance of a 1,000-Ω and a 5-kΩ resistor connected in parallel.
14. Find the cathode resistor needed to create 4 V of bias with a cathode current of 50 mA.

15. What is the voltage drop across a 5-kΩ transistor load resistor carrying 1.2 mA?

16. Find the bias voltage created by 30 mA of current passing through a 1-kΩ resistance.

17. Find the resistance of a screen-dropping resistor if it must use 100 V at 40 mA.

18. A 50-Ω antenna develops 0.2 mV. Find the current flowing.

19. Add 0.00025 μF and 100 pF. State the answer in microfarads.

20. Find the total series resistance of 0.5 MΩ, 10 kΩ, and 15,000 Ω.

JOB 9-4   DC EQUIVALENT CIRCUITS FOR SELF-BIASED TRANSISTOR CIRCUITS

Solid-state diodes. As we learned in Job 1-1, many metals have free electrons in the outer shells of their atoms. The ability of these free electrons to move about make most metals fine conductors of electricity. On the other hand, insulators such as glass and rubber do not have many free electrons. A semiconductor material such as germanium has some free electrons whose number can be considerably increased by the addition of small amounts of arsenic atoms as an impurity. These many loosely held electrons in the outer shells of the germanium atoms cause it to be referred to as N germanium. This does not mean that it is negatively charged, but merely that there are free electrons present.

If gallium is added as an impurity instead of arsenic, the outer shells of the germanium atoms will be filled except for one electron. This missing electron constitutes a "hole" which the atom wants to fill to reach a stable state. This material is known as P germanium. Because N germanium wants to "give" electrons and P germanium wants to "accept" them, both materials act as fairly good electron conductors.

Now suppose that we press these two materials together, as shown

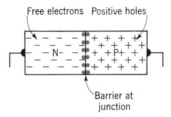

Free electrons Positive holes

Barrier at junction

FIGURE 9-2
A barrier is formed at the junction of N- and P-type materials.

in Fig. 9-2. The free electrons at the junction will meet with the positive holes and cancel each other's charge. After a very short time, the field produced by this zero-charged area repels both the electrons and the holes and acts as a barrier to both. Of course, no current will flow. In Fig. 9-3a, we have connected the − terminal of a battery to the N material, and the +terminal to the P material. The forward push of the many

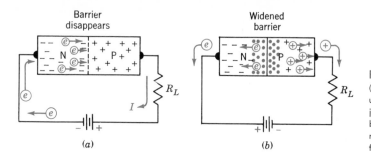

FIGURE 9-3

(a) The barrier disappears under forward-biasing and the junction conducts. (b) The barrier is widened under reverse biasing and no current flows.

electrons from the battery helps the free electrons to overcome the barrier, and the combination acts as a good conductor. Connected in this way, the combination is said to be *forward-biased,* and current flows through the load resistor.

In Fig. 9-3 *b,* we have reversed the polarity, connecting the + of the battery to the N material and the − of the battery to the P material. The + battery pulls the free electrons away from the junction and the − battery pulls the positive holes away from the junction. This has the effect of widening the barrier at the junction, and no current will flow. This is called *reverse bias.*

This combination is called a diode, the symbol for which is shown in Fig. 9-4. When connected as shown, current will flow only from left to right.

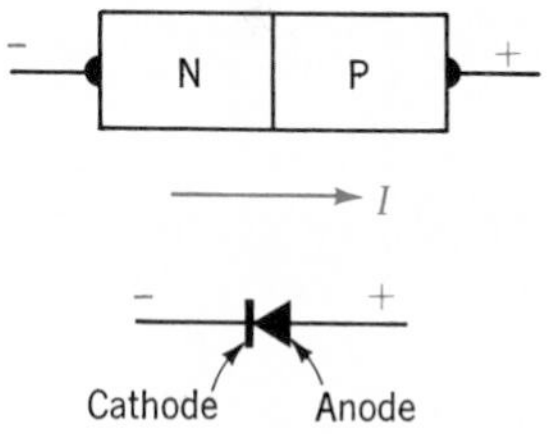

FIGURE 9-4
The diode symbol.

Transistors. A transistor is very similar to a semiconductor diode except that the transistor has two junctions instead of one. In Fig. 9-5, the "emitter" is an N-type material which forms a junction with a P-type material called the "base." This base in turn forms another junction with the "collector," an N-type material. Such a combination is called an NPN-type transistor.

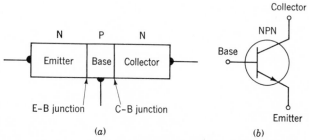

FIGURE 9-5
(a) NPN transistor. (b) Symbol for NPN transistor.

If the emitter and collector are made of P-type material and the base is N-type as shown in Fig. 9-6, the transistor would be called a PNP type. The only difference between the two types is the direction in which the current flows in the emitter. In the symbols, the electron current is *against* the arrowheads.

Transistor operation. In Fig. 9-7, when the voltage $-V_{EE}$ is applied,

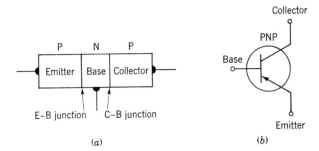

FIGURE 9-6

(a) PNP transistor. (b) Symbol for PNP transistor.

the electrons move out into the emitter lead and enter the emitter material. These electrons, together with the free electrons of the emitter material, are pushed toward the base region. The greater the forward bias, the greater the number of electrons that enter the base region. The number of holes in the base region is very small because it is so very thin and also because it is so slightly doped. A few electrons will find holes and combine to form a small base current. The rest of the electrons (about 98 percent) will not find a hole and will be pushed across the junction by the electrons newly arriving from the emitter. Once they get past the collector-base junction, they are attracted by the large collector voltage (V_{CC}) and become part of the collector current. They return to the battery, join up with I_B, enter V_{EE}, and start around again. As you can see, the emitter current is the sum of the base current and the collector current. An increase in the forward bias will cause an increase in the emitter current and a corresponding increase in the collector current and the base current. Conversely, a decrease in the forward bias results in a decrease of both base and collector current.

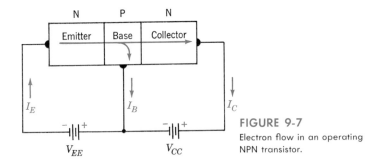

FIGURE 9-7

Electron flow in an operating NPN transistor.

Transistor current gain. As an amplifying device, the transistor is now replacing many of the functions of the vacuum tube. In Fig. 9-8a, a small change in the input signal to the grid controls a large change in the current that flows through the load. Similarly, in Fig. 9-8b, a small change in the input signal to the base of the transistor controls a large change in the current that flows through the collector and the load. This base-to-collector current gain is defined as β(beta).

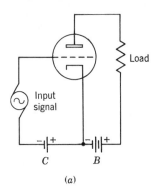
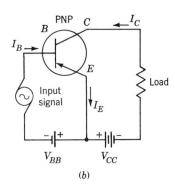

FIGURE 9-8

Comparison of (a) triode circuit, and (b) transistor circuit. Small changes in the input signal control large currents through the load.

$$\beta = \frac{\Delta I_C}{\Delta I_B} \qquad \boxed{9\text{-}1}$$

where β = current gain
   ΔI_C = change in the dc collector current
   ΔI_B = change in the dc base current

In order to solve a transistor circuit by the equivalent resistance-circuit-analysis method, we must first find the collector-to-base resistance R_{CB} for the particular transistor. For the self-bias circuit shown in Fig. 9-9a, the formula for R_{CB} is

$$R_{CB} = \frac{R_B}{\beta} \qquad \boxed{9\text{-}2}$$

where R_{CB} = collector-to-base resistance
   R_B = base-bias resistor
   β = current gain

SELF-BIAS CIRCUITS

EXAMPLE 9-15   Solve the circuit shown in Fig. 9-9a for (a) the load current I_{RL}, (b) the voltage across R_L, and (c) the collector voltage V_C.

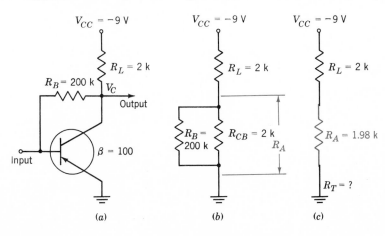

FIGURE 9-9

(a) Self-bias circuit. (b) Dc equivalent circuit. (c) R_A replaces the parallel combination of R_B and R_{CB}.

SOLUTION

The diagram for the circuit is shown in Fig. 9-9a.

1 Find R_{CB}.

$$R_{CB} = \frac{R_B}{\beta} \qquad\qquad (9\text{-}2)$$

$$R_{CB} = \frac{200 \text{ k}\Omega}{100} = 2 \text{ k}\Omega$$

2 Find the load current I_{RL}. This is the current that will flow through the series-parallel circuit shown in Fig. 9-9b. This circuit is further simplified into that shown in Fig. 9-9c, in which R_A replaces the parallel combination of R_B and R_{CB} of Fig. 9-9b.

   a Find R_A in Fig. 9-9b. Since R_B and R_{CB} are in parallel,

$$R_A = \frac{R_B \times R_{CB}}{R_B + R_{CB}} \qquad\qquad (4\text{-}5)$$

$$= \frac{200 \text{ k}\Omega \times 2 \text{ k}\Omega}{200 \text{ k}\Omega + 2 \text{ k}\Omega}$$

$$= \frac{400 \times 10^6}{202 \times 10^3} = 1.98 \times 10^3$$

$$R_A = 1.98 \text{ k}\Omega$$

   b Find R_T in Fig. 9-9c. Since R_L and R_A are in series,

$$R_T = R_L + R_A \qquad\qquad (3\text{-}3)$$

$$= 2 + 1.98$$

$$R_T = 3.98 \text{ k}\Omega$$

   c Find the total current in the circuit of Fig. 9-9c.

$$I_T = \frac{V_{CC}}{R_T} = \frac{9}{3.98 \times 10^3} = 2.26 \times 10^{-3}$$

$$I_T = 2.26 \text{ mA}$$

   d Find I_{RL}.

$$I_{RL} = I_T = 2.26 \text{ mA} \qquad Ans. \qquad\qquad (3\text{-}1)$$

3 Find the voltage across R_L.

$$E_{RL} = I_{RL} \times R_L \qquad\qquad (2\text{-}1)$$

$$= 2.26 \times 10^{-3} \times 2 \times 10^3$$

$$E_{RL} = 4.52 \text{ V} \qquad Ans.$$

4 Find the collector voltage V_C. As indicated in Fig. 9-9a, the collector voltage V_C, referred to ground, is equal to the difference between V_{CC} and E_{RL}.

$$V_C = -V_{CC} + E_{RL} = -9.0 + 4.52 = -4.48 \text{ V} \qquad Ans.$$

SELF-BIAS CIRCUITS WITH EMITTER RESISTANCE

EXAMPLE 9-16

Solve the circuit shown in Fig. 9-10a for (a) the collector current I_C, (b) the emitter current I_E, (c) the voltage across R_L, (d) the collector voltage V_C, (e) the voltage across R_E, and (f) the collector-to-emitter voltage V_{CE}.

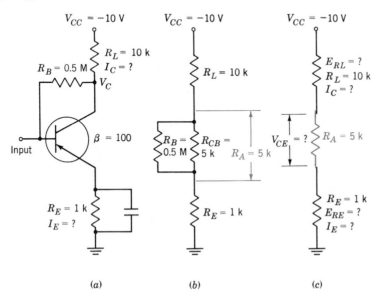

(a)   (b)   (c)

FIGURE 9-10

(a) Self-bias circuit with R_E.
(b) Dc equivalent circuit.
(c) $R_A = R_{CB}$ since R_B is so large in comparison with R_{CB}.

SOLUTION

The diagram for the circuit is shown in Fig. 9-10a.

1 Find R_{CB}.

$$R_{CB} = \frac{R_B}{\beta} \qquad\qquad (9\text{-}2)$$

$$= \frac{0.5 \times 10^6}{10^2}$$

$$= 0.5 \times 10^4$$

$$= 5 \times 10^3$$

$$R_{CB} = 5 \text{ k}\Omega$$

2 Find the collector current I_C. This is the current that will flow through the series-parallel circuit shown in Fig. 9-10b. This circuit is further simplified into that shown in Fig. 9-10c, in which R_A replaces the parallel combination of R_B and R_{CB} of Fig. 9-10b.

   a Find R_A in Fig. 9-10b. Since R_B (0.5 MΩ = 500,000 Ω) is so much larger than R_{CB} (5 k = 5,000 Ω), the effect of R_B on the value of the parallel combination is negligible. We may therefore consider $R_A = R_{CB} = 5$ k.

The student should work out the actual value of R_A to satisfy himself on this point.

b   Find R_T in Fig. 9-10c. Since R_L, R_A, and R_E are in series,

$$R_T = R_L + R_A + R_E \qquad (3\text{-}3)$$

$$= 10 + 5 + 1$$

$$R_T = 16 \text{ k}\Omega$$

Find the total current in the circuit of Fig. 9-10c.

$$I_T = \frac{V_{CC}}{R_T} = \frac{10}{16 \times 10^3}$$

$$= 0.625 \times 10^{-3}$$

$$I_T = 0.625 \text{ mA}$$

d   In the series circuit of Fig. 9-10c,

$$I_T = I_C = I_E = 0.625 \text{ mA} \qquad (3\text{-}1)$$

$$I_C = 0.625 \text{ mA} \qquad Ans.$$

$$I_E = 0.625 \text{ mA} \qquad Ans.$$

3   Find the voltage across R_L.

$$E_{RL} = I_C \times R_L \qquad (2\text{-}1)$$

$$= 0.625 \times 10^{-3} \times 10 \times 10^3$$

$$E_{RL} = 6.25 \text{ V} \qquad Ans.$$

4   Find the collector voltage V_C. As indicated in Fig. 9-10a, the collector voltage V_C, referred to ground, is equal to the difference between V_{CC} and E_{RL}.

$$V_C = -V_{CC} + E_{RL}$$

$$V_C = -10 + 6.25 = -3.75 \text{ V} \qquad Ans.$$

5   Find the voltage across the emitter resistor E_{RE}.

$$E_{RE} = I_E \times R_E \qquad (2\text{-}1)$$

$$= 0.625 \times 10^{-3} \times 1 \times 10^3$$

$$E_{RE} = 0.625 \text{ V} \qquad Ans.$$

6   Find the collector-to-emitter voltage drop V_{CE}. As indicated in Fig. 9-10c, V_{CE} is the drop across R_{CB} and is equal to the difference between V_{CC} and the sum of E_{RL} and E_{RE}.

$$V_{CE} = V_{CC} - (E_{RL} + E_{RE})$$

$$= 10 - (6.25 + 0.625)$$

$$V_{CE} = 10 - 6.88 = 3.12 \text{ V} \qquad Ans.$$

PROBLEMS

1. In a circuit similar to that shown in Fig. 9-9a, $V_{CC} = -10$ V, $R_L = 5$ kΩ, $R_B = 100$ kΩ, and $\beta = 50$. Find (a) the load current I_{RL}, (b) the voltage across R_L, and (c) the collector voltage V_C.
2. Repeat Prob. 1 with the following values: $V_{CC} = -10$ V, $R_B = 80$ kΩ, $R_L = 2$ kΩ, and $\beta = 20$.
3. In a circuit similar to that shown in Fig. 9-10a, $V_{CC} = -13$ V, $R_B = 1$ MΩ, $R_L = 40$ kΩ, $R_E = 2$ kΩ, and $\beta = 100$. Find (a) the collector current I_C, (b) the emitter current I_E, (c) the voltage across R_L, (d) the collector voltage V_C, (e) the voltage across R_E, and (f) the collector-to-emitter voltage V_{CE}.
4. Repeat Prob. 3 with the following values: $V_{CC} = -14$ V, $R_B = 0.5$ MΩ, $R_L = 20$ kΩ, $R_E = 5$ kΩ, and $\beta = 50$.

JOB 9-5 DC EQUIVALENT CIRCUITS FOR FIXED-BIAS TRANSISTOR CIRCUITS

In the fixed-bias circuit shown in Fig. 9-11a, the load resistor R_L is included in the beta-dependent loop, and it must therefore be included in the formula for R_{CB}. For the fixed-bias circuit shown in Fig. 9-11a, the formula for R_{CB} is

$$R_{CB} = \frac{R_B}{\beta} - R_L \qquad \boxed{9\text{-}3}$$

where R_{CB} = collector-to-base resistance
R_B = base-bias resistor
R_L = collector or load resistance
β = current gain

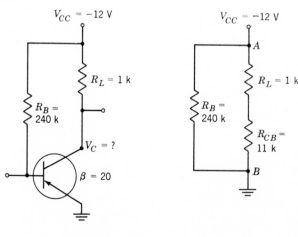

(a)   (b)

FIGURE 9-11

(a) Fixed-bias circuit. (b) Dc equivalent circuit.

FIXED-BIAS CIRCUITS

EXAMPLE 9-17   Solve the circuit shown in Fig. 9-11*a* for (*a*) the collector current I_C, (*b*) the voltage across R_L, and (*c*) the collector voltage V_C.

SOLUTION
The diagram for the circuit is shown in Fig. 9-11*a*.

1   Find R_{CB}.

$$R_{CB} = \frac{R_B}{\beta} - R_L \qquad\qquad (9\text{-}3)$$

$$= \frac{240}{20} - 1$$

$$R_{CB} = 12 - 1 = 11 \text{ k}\Omega$$

2   Find I_C. The collector current is the current through the series group of R_L and R_{CB} as shown in Fig. 9-11*b*. Since R_B is in parallel with this series group, the voltage across this group is equal to the total voltage $V_{CC} = -12$ V.

$$I_C = \frac{E}{R_T}$$

$$I_C = \frac{12}{11 + 1} = \frac{12}{12\text{k}}$$

$$= 1 \times 10^{-3}$$

$$I_C = 1 \text{ mA} \qquad Ans.$$

3   Find E_{RL}.

$$E_{RL} = I_C \times R_L$$

$$E_{RL} = 0.001 \times 1,000 = 1 \text{ V} \qquad Ans.$$

4   Find V_C. As shown in Fig. 9-11*a*, the collector voltage V_C, referred to ground, is equal to the difference between V_{CC} and E_{RL}.

$$V_C = -12 + 1 = -11 \text{ V} \qquad Ans.$$

FIXED-BIAS CIRCUITS WITH EMITTER RESISTANCE

EXAMPLE 9-18   Solve the circuit shown in Fig. 9-12*a* for (*a*) the emitter current I_E, (*b*) the emitter voltage V_E, (*c*) the collector current I_C, (*d*) the voltage across R_L, and (*e*) the collector voltage V_C.

SOLUTION
The diagram for the circuit is shown in Fig. 9-12.

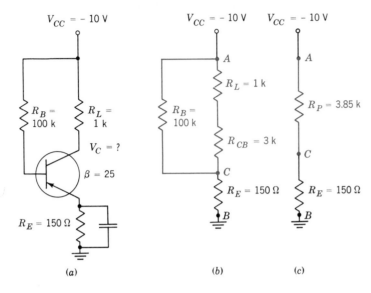

FIGURE 9-12
(a) Fixed-bias circuit with R_E.
(b) Dc equivalent circuit.
(c) R_P replaces the series-parallel combination of Fig. 9-12b.

1 Find R_{CB}.

$$R_{CB} = \frac{R_B}{\beta} - R_L \qquad (9\text{-}3)$$

$$= \frac{100}{25} - 1$$

$$R_{CB} = 4 - 1 = 3 \text{ k}\Omega$$

2 Find I_E, the emitter current. This is the current that flows through the series-parallel circuit shown in Fig. 9-12b and which must be simplified into the circuit shown in Fig. 9-12c. In Fig. 9-12b, the series resistance of R_{CB} and R_L is equal to 3 k + 1 k = 4 k. This 4 k is in parallel with the 100 k of R_B. The total resistance of this parallel combination is

$$R_P = \frac{100 \times 4}{100 + 4} \qquad (4\text{-}5)$$

$$R_P = \frac{400}{104} = 3.85 \text{ k}\Omega$$

Now we can find the total resistance between points A and B.

$$R_T = R_P + R_E$$

$$R_T = 3.85 + 0.15 = 4 \text{ k}\Omega$$

The emitter current I_E is equal to the total current that flows between points A and B.

$$I_E = I_T = \frac{V_{CC}}{R_T}$$

$$I_E = \frac{10}{4 \text{ k}} = 2.5 \text{ mA} \qquad Ans.$$

3   Find the emitter voltage V_E. This is the voltage, referred to ground, which is equal to the drop across R_E.

$$V_E = I_E \times R_E$$

$$V_E = 0.0025 \times 150 = -0.375 \text{ V} \qquad Ans.$$

4   In Fig. 9-12b, the collector current is the current flowing between the points A and C, and is equal to the voltage between A and C divided by the resistance of the series group made of R_L and R_{CB}. The voltage between A and C (V_{AC}) is equal to the difference between V_{CC} and V_E.

$$V_{AC} = V_{CC} - V_E$$

$$V_{AC} = 10 - 0.375 = 9.625 \text{ V}$$

The resistance of the series group between A and C was found to be 4 kΩ. Therefore,

$$I_C = \frac{V_{AC}}{R_{AC}} = \frac{9.625}{4,000} = 2.4 \text{ mA} \qquad Ans.$$

5   Find E_{RL}. In Fig. 9-12a,

$$E_{RL} = I_C \times R_L$$

$$E_{RL} = 0.0024 \times 1,000 = 2.4 \text{ V} \qquad Ans.$$

6   Find V_C.

$$V_C = -V_{CC} + E_{RL}$$

$$V_C = -10 + 2.4 = -7.6 \text{ V} \qquad Ans.$$

PROBLEMS

1. In a circuit similar to that shown in Fig. 9-11a, $V_{CC} = -10$ V, $R_L = 1$ kΩ, $R_B = 200$ kΩ, and $\beta = 20$. Find (a) the collector current I_C, (b) the voltage across R_L, and (c) the collector voltage V_C.
2. Repeat Prob. 1 with the following values: $V_{CC} = -8$ V, $R_L = 2$ kΩ, $R_B = 120$ kΩ, and $\beta = 30$.
3. In a circuit similar to that shown in Fig. 9-12a, $V_{CC} = -8$ V, $R_L = 1$ kΩ, $R_B = 200$ kΩ, $R_E = 200$ Ω, and $\beta = 100$. Find (a) the emitter current I_E, (b) the emitter voltage V_E, (c) the collector current I_C, (d) the voltage across R_L, and (e) the collector voltage V_C.
4. Repeat Prob. 3 with the following values: $V_{CC} = -10$ V, $R_L = 2$ kΩ, $R_B = 100$ kΩ, $R_E = 140$ Ω, and $\beta = 20$.

JOB 9-6   EXTENDING THE RANGE OF AN AMMETER

An ammeter is a device which is used to measure the current in an electrical circuit. To do this, it must always be inserted directly into the line whose current is to be measured. It is essentially a coil of very fine wire which turns in proportion to the current flowing through it. A pointer attached to the coil moves over a dial and indicates the value of the current. The weight of the coil must be very small in order that it be able to react to the current in it. This weight factor necessitates the use of very fine wire which can carry only about 0.05 A at best. Yet we can use this ammeter to measure much larger currents by taking advantage of the fact that current in a parallel circuit will divide—the large current flowing through the small resistance and the small current flowing through the large resistance.

Range of an ammeter. The *range* of an ammeter indicates the value of current required to cause the pointer to swing over the entire scale. This is called "full-scale deflection." Ranges are indicated as "0–1 mA," "0–100 mA," etc. Thus:

0–1 mA requires 1 mA for full-scale deflection

0–100 mA requires 100 mA for full-scale deflection

0–10 A requires 10 A for full-scale deflection

Extending the range of an ammeter. Suppose we had a milliammeter whose range was 0–1 mA. This means that we can use it to measure currents only up to 1 mA but *not larger* than 1 mA. If we had to measure currents larger than 1 mA, we would need another meter. But this would not be necessary if we could extend the ability of our present meter to read and measure larger currents.

This can be accomplished by connecting a low-resistance resistor called a *shunt* in parallel with the meter. If we keep the shunt resistance small enough, most of the current in the line will pass through the shunt and *not* through the delicate coil of the meter. The object is to use a shunt of such a value that the current in the line will divide so as to keep the current flowing in the coil unchanged. Thus, using a 0–1-mA milliammeter, if the range is to be extended to read 0–50 mA, the shunt should carry 49 mA and the coil should carry its original 1 mA. If the range is to be extended to read 100 mA, then the shunt should carry 99 mA and the coil of the meter should carry its original 1 mA. In general, with *any* shunt, the current through the coil for full-scale deflection is the current necessary for full-scale deflection *before* using the shunt.

Problem. Extend the range of a 0–1-mA milliammeter to carry currents up to 50 mA. In order to carry currents larger than 1 mA, a shunt must be placed in *parallel* with the meter as shown in Fig. 9-13. The line current I will divide at point A. If the correct shunt is used, the original 1 mA will flow through the meter and the remaining 49 mA will flow through the shunt. In effect, the pointer will cover the full scale (owing to the 1 mA) but it will be indicating the full 50 mA. We shall need a formula to find the shunt needed to extend the range to any value.

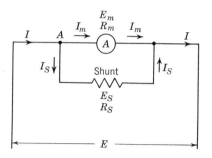

FIGURE 9-13
A shunt is placed in parallel with an ammeter. I = line current to be measured, E_m = voltage drop across meter, I_m = current through meter, R_m = resistance of meter, E_S = voltage across shunt, I_S = current through shunt, R_S = resistance of shunt.

In Fig. 9-13,

$$R_s = \frac{E_s}{I_s} \qquad (2\text{-}1)$$

but since the meter and the shunt are in parallel,

$$E_s = E_m \qquad (4\text{-}1)$$

therefore,

$$R_s = \frac{E_m}{I_s} \qquad (a)$$

but

$$E_m = I_m \times R_m \qquad (2\text{-}1)$$

By substituting $I_m \times R_m$ for E_m in equation (a) above, we obtain the

FORMULA

$$R_s = \frac{I_m \times R_m}{I_s} \qquad \boxed{9\text{-}4}$$

And since

$$I = I_m + I_s \qquad (4\text{-}2)$$

by transposing,

$$I_s = I - I_m \qquad \boxed{9\text{-}5}$$

By substituting this value of I_s in formula (9-4), we obtain the

FORMULA

$$R_s = \frac{I_m \times R_m}{I - I_m} \qquad \boxed{9\text{-}6}$$

In this formula, the resistance of the meter must be known, and it can usually be obtained from the manufacturer.

EXAMPLE 9-19   A Weston model 430 0–1-mA milliammeter has a resistance of 92 Ω. What shunt is necessary to extend its range up to 50 mA?

SOLUTION
Given: $I_m = 1$ mA $= 0.001$ A   Find: $R_s = ?$
          $R_m = 92$ Ω
              $I = 50$ mA $= 0.05$ A

$$R_s = \frac{I_m \times R_m}{1 - I_m} = \frac{0.001 \times 92}{0.05 - 0.001} = \frac{0.092}{0.049} = 1.88 \ \Omega \qquad \textit{Ans.}$$

A simpler formula to extend the range of ammeters may be found by a series of algebraic manipulations on formula (9-6).

$$R_s = \frac{I_m \times R_m}{1 - I_m} \qquad\qquad (9\text{-}6)$$

or
$$R_s = R_m \frac{I_m}{1 - I_m}$$

Inverting and dividing the multiplier of R_m gives

$$R_s = R_m \div \frac{1 - I_m}{I_m}$$

Dividing $1 - I_m$ by I_m,

$$R_s = R_m \div \left(\frac{I}{I_m} - 1\right) \qquad\qquad (b)$$

The fraction I/I_m is the ratio of the maximum *new* range as compared with the maximum *old* range. As such, it represents the amount by which the range of the meter has been multiplied. If N is used to represent this multiplying factor,

$$N = \frac{I}{I_m}$$

FORMULA

$$N = \frac{\text{max new range}}{\text{max old range}} \qquad \boxed{9\text{-}7}$$

By substituting N for I/I_m in equation (b) above, we obtain

$$R_s = R_m \div (N - 1)$$

FORMULA

$$R_s = \frac{R_m}{N - 1} \qquad \boxed{9\text{-}8}$$

where R_s = shunt resistor
$\quad R_m$ = resistance of the meter
$\quad N$ = multiplying factor

SELF-TEST 9-20 A Weston model 433 0–100-mA milliammeter has a resistance of 49 Ω. Find the shunt resistor necessary to extend the range to give maximum deflection at 750 mA.

SOLUTION

Given: Old range = _____ mA   Find: $R_s = ?$

New range = _____ mA

$R_m = $ _____ Ω

Multiplying factor $N = \dfrac{\text{max ? range}}{\text{max ? range}}$

$$N = \frac{750}{?} = 7.5 \qquad\qquad (9\text{-}7)$$

$$R_s = \frac{R_m}{N-1} \qquad\qquad (9\text{-}8)$$

$$R_s = \frac{?}{7.5-1}$$

$$R_s = \_\_\ \Omega \qquad Ans.$$

100
750
49
new
old
100
49
7.5

PROBLEMS

1. Find the shunt necessary to extend the range of a 0–1-mA milli-ammeter whose resistance is 27 Ω to read 0 –10 mA.
2. A 0–1-mA milliammeter has a resistance of 5 Ω. What shunt resistor is necessary to give a full scale reading of 51 mA?
3. Find the shunt needed for the milliammeter of Prob. 2 which will permit full-scale deflection at 0.1 A.
4. A Weston model 45, 0–100-mA milliammeter has a resistance of 0.5 Ω. Find the shunt needed to extend its range to read 0–300 mA.
5. A Weston model 1, 0–15-mA milliammeter has a resistance of 2.24 Ω. Find the shunt needed to extend its range to read 0–60 mA.
6. Full-scale deflection results when 25 mA flows through an ammeter of 25 Ω resistance. Find the shunt resistance needed to extend its range to read (a) 250 mA, (b) 500 mA, and (c) 1 A.
7. A Weston model 45, 0–3-A ammeter has a resistance of 5 Ω. Find the shunt needed to extend its range to read 0–75 A.
8. When the coil current in a meter is 10 mA, the pointer deflects past a full scale of 100 divisions. If the coil resistance is 15 Ω, find the shunts needed to extend its range to read (a) 0–1 A and (b) 0–5 A.

JOB 9-7   READING AMMETERS OF EXTENDED RANGE

EXAMPLE 9-21   The range of a 0–100-mA milliammeter was increased to read 0 to 1 A. Find the true current flowing when the meter reads 60 mA.

SOLUTION

Given: Old range $= 100$ mA   Find: $I = ?$
New range $= 1$ A $= 1,000$ mA
$I_m = 60$ mA

The increase in range was from 100 to 1,000 mA.

$$N = \frac{\text{max new range}}{\text{max old range}} = \frac{1,000}{100} = 10 \qquad (9\text{-}7)$$

Therefore all readings will be increased 10 times, or a reading of 60 mA really means

$$60 \times 10 = 600 \text{ mA, or } 0.6 \text{ A} \qquad Ans.$$

EXAMPLE 9-22   A model 221-T Triplett 0-1-mA milliammeter has a resistance of 55 Ω. When it is shunted with a 2-Ω resistor, the meter reads 0.5 mA. Find the true current.

SOLUTION

Given: $I_m = 0.5$ mA   Find: $I = ?$
$R_m = 55$ Ω
$R_s = 2$ Ω

In this problem we do not know the increase in range and cannot use the method shown in the last example. However, we can find the shunt current by formula (9-4). The line current I may then be found by formula (4-2).

$$R_s = \frac{I_m \times R_m}{I_s} \qquad (9\text{-}4)$$

$$\frac{2}{1} = \frac{0.5 \times 55}{I_s}$$

$$2 \times I_s = 0.5 \times 55$$

$$I_s = \frac{27.5}{2} = 13.8 \text{ mA}$$

The line current may now be found.

$$I = I_m + I_s = 0.5 + 13.8 = 14.3 \text{ mA} \qquad Ans. \qquad (4\text{-}2)$$

Note: Since the shunt usually carries most of the line current, the shunt current is very often used as the line current.

PROBLEMS

1. The range of a 0-1-mA milliammeter was increased to read 0-50 mA. Find the true current when the meter reads 0.3 mA.
2. The range of a 0-0.1-A ammeter was increased to read 0-1 A. Find the true current when the meter reads 0.07 A.

3. A 0–1-mA milliammeter of 25 Ω resistance is used with a 0.25-Ω shunt. What is the true current when the meter reads 0.4 mA?

4. A Weston model 45, 0–3-A ammeter of 5 Ω resistance is used with a 0.1-Ω shunt. What is the true current when the meter reads 0.6 A?

5. A 0–1-A ammeter of 10 Ω resistance is used with a 0.1-Ω shunt. What is the true current when the meter reads 0.7 A?

6. A 0–10-mA milliammeter of 10 Ω resistance is used with a 0.2-Ω shunt. What is the true current when the meter reads 2 mA?

JOB 9-8 EXTENDING THE RANGE OF VOLTMETERS

A voltmeter is a device which is used to measure the difference in electrical pressure across two points in a circuit. To do this, the instrument must be placed in parallel with the portion of the circuit being tested as shown in Fig. 9-14. If the resistance of the voltmeter is low, the current in the line will divide at A and the large current will flow through the moving coil of the meter and burn it out. To avoid this, the resistance of the moving coil is increased by adding a *high* resistance in *series* with the coil. These resistors are called *multipliers*. Essentially, a voltmeter is really an ammeter with a series resistor. This extra resistance holds down the current to the value required for full-scale deflection when the full-scale voltage is applied to it. It is possible to use one meter to read many different voltage ranges if the correct resistances can be placed in the instrument with an arrangement for disconnecting one resistance and connecting another in series. Commercial meters are available which do this by a variety of switching arrangements.

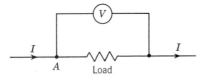

FIGURE 9-14
A voltmeter is always connected in parallel across the terminals of the part being tested.

Ohms per volt. A perfect meter should only measure the current but should not use any of the current in the circuit for itself. This is actually impossible, since some current, however small, is needed to operate the meter. The best, or most sensitive, meters are those which use as little current as possible. The more resistance that can be placed in a meter and still have it read 1 V, the less the current that is drawn. This means that the meter will use very little current for itself and will have a high sensitivity. Sensitivity is usually expressed as the number of ohms needed to read 1 V, or the ohms per volt.

FORMULA

$$\frac{R}{v} = \frac{R_T}{E_T}$$

9-9

where $R/v = \Omega/V$

R_T = total meter resistance, Ω

E_T = maximum scale voltage, V

EXAMPLE 9-23   A 50,000-Ω voltmeter reads 50 V at full scale. What is its sensitivity in ohms per volt?

SOLUTION

Given: $R_T = 50,000\ \Omega$ Find: $\dfrac{R}{v} = ?$

$E_T = 50$ V

$$\frac{R}{v} = \frac{R_T}{E_T} = \frac{50,000}{50} = 1,000\ \Omega/V \qquad Ans. \qquad (9\text{-}9)$$

EXAMPLE 9-24   A 1,000 Ω/V voltmeter has a range of 0–10 V. What is the total resistance of the meter?

SOLUTION

Given: $\dfrac{R}{v} = 1,000\ \Omega$ Find: $R_T = ?$

$E_T = 10$ V

$$\frac{R}{v} = \frac{R_T}{E_T} \qquad\qquad (9\text{-}9)$$

$$1,000 = \frac{R_T}{10}$$

$$R_T = 1,000 \times 10$$

$$R_T = 10,000\ \Omega \qquad Ans.$$

Extending the range of a voltmeter. A 0–150-V voltmeter has a 150,000-Ω resistor in series with its moving coil. How can it be altered so as to read up to 750 V?

SOLUTION

Since 750 V is five times as much as 150 V, we shall therefore require five times as much resistance as is in the meter for the 150-V range. The resistance already in the meter may then be subtracted from the total required resistance to find the needed *additional* resistance to increase the range to 750 V. The increase in voltage (the five times) represents the multiplying power we desire.   Therefore, the series resistor R_s which must be added to extend the range of an existing voltmeter is given by

$$R_s = (\text{multiplying power} \times R_{\text{meter}}) - R_{\text{meter}}$$

Another way to write this is the

FORMULA

$$R_s = (MP - 1) \times R_{\text{meter}}$$ $\boxed{9\text{-}10}$

where R_s = series resistor to be added, Ω

$$MP = \frac{\text{max new voltage}}{\text{max old voltage}}$$ $\boxed{9\text{-}11}$

R_{meter} = resistance of the meter, Ω

Let us use this formula to solve the problem above.

$$MP = \frac{\text{max new voltage}}{\text{max old voltage}} = \frac{750}{150} = 5 \qquad (9\text{-}11)$$

$$R_s = (MP - 1) \times R_m \qquad (9\text{-}10)$$

$$= (5 - 1) \times 150{,}000 = 4 \times 150{,}000 = 600{,}000 \ \Omega \qquad \textit{Ans.}$$

Note: The resistance of the meter must be known in order to use formula (9-10). If it is not given, it may be found by connecting the meter in series with a milliammeter across some voltage within its range as

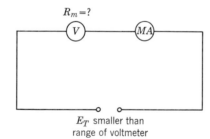

$R_m = ?$

E_T smaller than
range of voltmeter

FIGURE 9-15
Circuit to find the
resistance of a voltmeter.

shown in Fig. 9-15. The resistance of the meter may then be found by the

FORMULA

$$R_m = \frac{\text{voltmeter reading (V)}}{\text{ammeter reading (A)}}$$ $\boxed{9\text{-}12}$

EXAMPLE 9-25   A 0–10-V 10,000-Ω voltmeter is to be extended to read 100 V. What additional series resistance is needed?

SOLUTION

Given: Max new voltage = 100 V   Find: $R_s = ?$
        Max old voltage = 10 V
              $R_{\text{meter}} = 10{,}000 \ \Omega$

$$MP = \frac{\text{max new voltage}}{\text{max old voltage}} = \frac{100}{10} = 10 \qquad (9\text{-}11)$$

$$R_s = (MP - 1) \times R_m \hspace{4cm} (9\text{-}10)$$

$$= (10 - 1) \times 10,000 = 9 \times 10,000 = 90,000 \ \Omega \hspace{1cm} Ans.$$

EXAMPLE 9-26   A 1,000 Ω/V 0-10-V voltmeter is to be extended to read 0-100 V. What is the needed series resistance?

SOLUTION

Given: $\hspace{3cm} \dfrac{R}{v} = 1,000 \ \Omega \hspace{1cm}$ Find: $R_s = ?$

Max new voltage = 100 V
Max old voltage = 10 V

Before we can find the series resistance, we must know the resistance of the meter and the multiplying power.

$$\frac{R}{v} = \frac{R_T}{E_T} \hspace{4cm} (9\text{-}9)$$

$$1,000 = \frac{R_T}{10}$$

$$R_T = 10 \times 1,000 = 10,000 \ \Omega$$

$$R_m = 10,000 \ \Omega \hspace{1cm} Ans.$$

$$MP = \frac{\text{max new voltage}}{\text{max old voltage}} = \frac{100}{10} = 10 \hspace{1cm} Ans. \hspace{1cm} (9\text{-}11)$$

$$R_s = (MP - 1) \times R_m \hspace{4cm} (9\text{-}10)$$

$$= (10 - 1) \times 10,000 = 9 \times 10,000 = 90,000 \ \Omega \hspace{1cm} Ans.$$

SELF-TEST 9-27   A 0-10-V voltmeter of 1,000 Ω resistance is extended to read 100 V. Find the true voltage when the meter reads 5.5 V.

SOLUTION

Given: $\hspace{2cm} R_m =$ _____ $\Omega \hspace{1cm}$ Find: True voltage = ? $\hspace{3cm}$ 1,000
$\hspace{2cm}$ Max new voltage = ____ V $\hspace{6.5cm}$ 100
$\hspace{2cm}$ Max old voltage = ____ V $\hspace{6.5cm}$ 10
$\hspace{2cm}$ Meter reading = 5.5 V

$$MP = \frac{\text{max new voltage}}{\text{max old voltage}} = \frac{?}{10} = 10 \hspace{4cm} 100$$

therefore all readings will be increased 10 times, or a reading of 5.5 V means

$$5.5 \times \text{\_\_\_} = 55 \text{ V} \hspace{1cm} Ans. \hspace{4cm} 10$$

PROBLEMS

1. A 1,000 Ω/V 0-10-V voltmeter is to be extended to read 300 V. Find (a) the series resistor needed and (b) the true voltage when the meter reads 5.6 V.

2. A 0−7.5-mV millivoltmeter whose resistance is 1 Ω is to be extended to read 15 V. Find (*a*) the series resistor needed and (*b*) the true voltage when the meter reads 6 mV.

3. A 0−50-mV millivoltmeter of 5 Ω resistance is to be extended to read up to 30 V. Find (*a*) the series resistor needed and (*b*) the true voltage when the meter reads 36 mV.

4. A 0−100-V voltmeter of 12,000 Ω resistance is to read up to 300 V. Find the multiplying resistor needed.

5. A voltmeter with a full-scale deflection of 150 V has a resistance of 17,000 Ω. Find the external series resistance necessary to extend it to read (*a*) 300 V and (*b*) 600 V.

6. A 1,000 Ω/V 0−1-V voltmeter is to be extended to read up to 100 V. Find (*a*) the series resistor needed and (*b*) the true voltage when the meter reads 0.7 V.

7. If the current taken by a 5,000-Ω meter is 1 mA, find the series resistor needed to extend its range to read up to (*a*) 50 V, (*b*) 100 V, and (*c*) 150 V. *Hint:* Find *E* of the meter by $E = I \times R$.

8. Find the series resistor to be used with a 15,000-Ω voltmeter in order to have its readings multiplied by 5.

JOB 9-9 REVIEW OF METERS

Extending the range of an ammeter. Ammeters may be used to measure currents larger than their full-scale deflections by connecting appropriate shunts in parallel with the meter. The value of this shunt resistor may be found by the following formulas:

$$R_s = \frac{I_m \times R_m}{I_s} \qquad \boxed{9\text{-}4}$$

$$R_s = \frac{I_m \times R_m}{I - I_m} \qquad \boxed{9\text{-}6}$$

$$R_s = \frac{R_m}{N - 1} \qquad \boxed{9\text{-}8}$$

where R_s = resistance of the _____, Ω   shunt
  I_s = current in the _____, A   shunt
  R_m = resistance of the _____, Ω   meter
  I_m = current in the _____, A   meter
  I = line current to be measured, A
  N = multiplying factor which indicates the number of times that the range of the meter is increased

$$N = \frac{\text{max} \underline{\quad} \text{range}}{\text{max} \underline{\quad} \text{range}} \qquad \boxed{9\text{-}7}$$ new
                                                                                         old

READING AMMETERS OF EXTENDED RANGE

1 If the multiplying factor N is known, the true current is equal to the actual reading multiplied by ___. N

$$\text{True reading} = \text{actual reading} \times N \qquad \boxed{9\text{-}13}$$

2 If N is unknown,

a Find the shunt current by

$$R_s = \frac{I_m \times R_m}{?} \qquad \boxed{9\text{-}4}$$

I_s

b Find the true current by

$$I = I_m + ? \qquad \boxed{4\text{-}2}$$

I_s

Extending the range of voltmeters. The range of a voltmeter may be extended by placing it in series with the appropriate series multiplier resistor.

$$R_s = (MP - 1) \times \underline{\quad} \qquad \boxed{9\text{-}10}$$

R_{meter}

where R_s = series resistor to be added, Ω
R_{meter} = resistance of meter, Ω

$$MP = \frac{\text{max ___ voltage}}{\text{max ___ voltage}} \qquad \boxed{9\text{-}11}$$

new
old

Meter sensitivity. The sensitivity of a meter is expressed as its resistance in ohms for every volt measured on its scale. For the same reading of 1 V, the meter with the larger resistance will draw (more/less) current for itself and therefore give more accurate measurements. less

$$\frac{R}{v} = \frac{R_T}{E_T} \qquad \boxed{9\text{-}9}$$

where R/v = ___________, Ω/V sensitivity
R_T = total meter resistance, Ω
E_T = maximum scale voltage, V

FINDING THE TOTAL RESISTANCE OF THE METER

1 Use formula (9-9) to find R_T of the meter. Or,

2 Connect the voltmeter in series with an ammeter across some voltage within its range. The meter resistance is given by

$$R_m = \frac{\text{voltmeter reading (V)}}{\text{ammeter reading (A)}} \qquad \boxed{9\text{-}12}$$

PROBLEMS

1. A 0–2-mA milliammeter has a resistance of 18 Ω. Find the parallel shunt resistor which will permit measurements of currents up to 200 mA.
2. The range of a 12-Ω 0–5-mA milliammeter was increased to read 0–50 mA. Find the true current when the meter reads 4.5 mA.
3. A 0–1-mA milliammeter of 20 Ω resistance is used with a 0.2-Ω

shunt in parallel. Find the true current when the meter reads 0.6 mA.

4. A 10,000-Ω voltmeter reads 100 V at full-scale deflection. Find its sensitivity in ohms per volt.

5. A Weston model 5 dc voltmeter has a sensitivity of 100 Ω/V and a range of $0-15$ V. Find the total resistance of the meter.

6. A $0-30$-V voltmeter is to be extended to read 150 V. If the resistance of the meter is 3,000 Ω, find (a) the sensitivity, (b) the series resistor needed, and (c) the true voltage when the meter reads 12 V.

7. A 100 Ω/V $0-7.5$-V voltmeter is to be extended to read $0-30$ V. Find (a) the series multiplier needed and (b) the true voltage when the meter reads 3.2 V.

8. If the current taken by a 1,000-Ω meter is 15 mA, find (a) the voltage indicated by the full-scale deflection, (b) the sensitivity in ohms per volt, and (c) the series multiplier resistor needed to extend the range to read (1) 120 V and (2) 180 V.

9. The resistance of a $0-15$-mA milliammeter is 3.2 Ω. Find the parallel shunt required to extend the range to $0-100$ mA.

10. The range of an 18-Ω $0-3$-mA milliammeter was increased to read up to 50 mA. Find the true current when the meter reads 1.7 mA.

TEST—METERS

1. A $0-5$-mA milliammeter has a resistance of 12 Ω. Find the shunt resistor which must be connected in parallel in order to increase the range up to 75 mA.

2. The range of a $0-1$-mA milliammeter was increased to $0-50$ mA. Find the true current when the meter reads 0.65 mA.

3. If the current taken by a 5,000-Ω meter is 3 mA, find (a) the voltage indicated by the full-scale deflection, (b) the sensitivity in ohms per volt, and (c) the series multiplier needed to extend the range to read 90 V.

4. .A $0-10$-V voltmeter of 1,000 resistance is to be extended to read up to 100 V. Find (a) the needed series multiplier resistor and (b) the true voltage when the meter reads 5.8 V.

5. A 1,000 Ω/V $0-25$-V voltmeter is to be extended to read up to 200 V. Find (a) the needed series multiplier resistor and (b) the true voltage when the meter reads 13.5 V.

JOB 9-10 VOLTAGE DIVIDERS

The filter circuit of a radio receiver is designed to smooth out the dc voltage delivered from the rectifier. This voltage may be 300 V. However, although some circuits in the receiver may require these 300 V, other tubes and circuits may need only 180 or only 90 V. These dif-

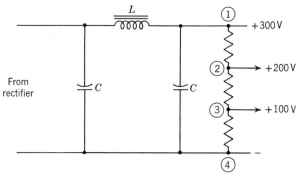

FIGURE 9-16
A power-supply voltage divider.

ferent voltages may be obtained by placing a large resistor across the filter output as shown in Fig. 9-16 and tapping the resistor at various points. This resistor is called a *voltage divider*.

The total voltage of 300 V appears across points 1 and 4. If the resistor is divided into three equal parts by taps at points 2 and 3, at point 2, which is one-third of the resistor, one-third of the total voltage ($\frac{1}{3} \times 300 = 100$) has been used up. Therefore only

$$300 - 100 = 200 \text{ V}$$

will be available at point 2. At point 3, which is two-thirds of the resistor, two-thirds of the 300 V ($\frac{2}{3} \times 300 = 200$) has been used up and at point 3 only $300 - 200 = 100$ V will be available. This will all be true only if the current in all parts of the voltage divider is the same current. However, the different voltages must be available at different currents, and so the calculations for a working voltage divider are a bit more complicated.

EXAMPLE 9-28   Calculate the resistances for the sections of a voltage divider which is to deliver 40 mA at 300 V, 30 mA at 180 V, and 20 mA at 90 V.

SOLUTION
The diagram for the circuit is shown in Fig. 9-17.

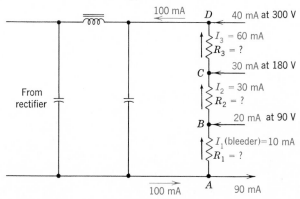

FIGURE 9-17

1 Determine the current distribution. Some current will always flow through the voltage divider even when there is no load on it. This current is called the *bleeder current*. The bleeder current may be assumed to be the difference between 90 percent of the current rating of the power transformer and the total current drawn by the receiver. In this problem, the receiver needs $40 + 30 + 20$, or 90 mA, and the transformer is rated at 110 mA.

90 percent of 110 mA $= 0.90 \times 110 = 99$ mA $= 100$ mA approximately

At A:

$$I_1 = I \text{ from rectifier} - \text{current to loads}$$

$$I_1 = 100 - 90 = 10 \text{ mA}$$

At B:

$$I_2 = I_1 + \text{current from load}$$

$$I_2 = 10 + 20 = 30 \text{ mA}$$

At C:

$$I_3 = I_2 + \text{current from load}$$

$$I_3 = 30 + 30 = 60 \text{ mA}$$

At D:

$$I_T = I_3 + \text{current from load}$$

$$I_T = 60 + 40 = 100 \text{ mA}$$

2 Find the sectional resistances.
For R_3: The voltage drop from D to $C = 300 - 180 = 120$ V.

$$E_3 = I_3 \times R_3 \tag{3-6}$$

$$120 = 0.06 \times R_3$$

$$R_3 = \frac{120}{0.06} = 2,000 \ \Omega \qquad Ans.$$

For R_2: The voltage drop from C to $B = 180 - 90 = 90$ V.

$$E_2 = I_2 \times R_2 \tag{3-5}$$

$$90 = 0.03 \times R_2$$

$$R_2 = \frac{90}{0.03} = 3,000 \ \Omega \qquad Ans.$$

For R_1: The voltage drop from B to $A = 90 - 0 = 90$ V.

$$E_1 = I_1 \times R_1 \tag{3-4}$$

$$90 = 0.01 \times R_1$$

$$R_1 = \frac{90}{0.01} = 9,000 \ \Omega \qquad Ans.$$

SELF-TEST 9-29 Find the resistance of the sections R_1, R_2, R_3, and R_4 of the voltage divider shown in Fig. 9-18. The -50-V bias terminal draws no current, and the bleeder current is 10 percent of the total load current.

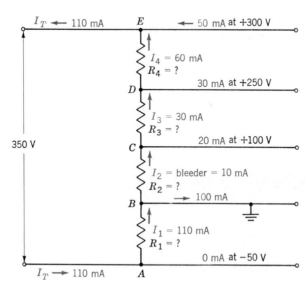

FIGURE 9-18
Voltage divider circuit for
Example 9-29.

SOLUTION

1 Determine the current distribution.

The total load current $= 50 + 30 +$ ____ mA | 20

$I_L =$ ____ mA | 100

The bleeder current $= 10$ percent $\times 100$

$=$ ____ $\times 100$ | 0.1

$I_b =$ ____ mA | 10

The total current $=$ bleeder current $+$ load current

At B: $I_T = I_1 = I_b +$ load currents

$I_T = 10 +$ ____ | 100

$I_T = 110$ mA $=$ ____ A | 0.11

At C: $I_3 = I_2 +$ current from load

$= 10 +$ ____ | 20

$I_3 =$ ____ mA | 30

At D: $I_4 =$ _____ + current from load I_3

                                 $= 30 +$ _____   30

                                 $I_4 =$ _____ mA   60

At E: $I_T =$ _____ + current from load I_4

                                 $= 60 +$ _____   50

                                 $I_T =$ _____ mA $=$ _____ A   110   0.11

2   Find the sectional resistances.
For R_1: The voltage drop between A and $B = 50 - 0$

                  $E_1 = 50$ V

                  $R_1 = \dfrac{50}{?}$ 0.11

                  $R_1 =$ _____ Ω *Ans.*   455

For R_2: The voltage drop between B and $C =$ _____ V   100

                  $R_2 = \dfrac{100}{?}$ 0.01

                  $R_2 =$ _____ Ω *Ans.*   10,000

For R_3: The voltage drop between _____ and _____ C D

                  $= 250 -$ _____   100

                  $=$ _____ V   150

                  $R_3 = \dfrac{?}{0.03}$ 150

                  $R_3 =$ _____ Ω *Ans.*   5,000

For R_4: The voltage drop between D and $E =$ _____ V   50

                  $R_4 = \dfrac{?}{0.06}$ 50

                  $R_4 =$ _____ Ω *Ans.*   833

PROBLEMS

1. Find the resistance of the sections R_1, R_2, and R_3 of the voltage divider shown in Fig. 9-19a.
2. Find the resistance of the sections R_1, R_2, R_3, and R_4 of the voltage divider shown in Fig. 9-19b. *Hint:* Find the current distribution starting from point A and working up to point E.
3. A power supply is to deliver 45 mA at 150 V, 30 mA at 100 V, and 10 mA at 50 V. Assuming a bleeder current of 5 mA, calculate the resistance of the sections of the voltage divider needed.

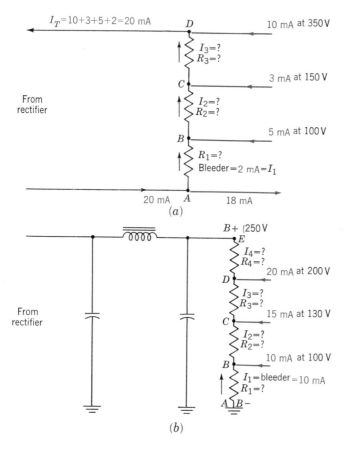

$I_T=10+3+5+2=20$ mA

D   10 mA at 350 V

$I_3=?$
$R_3=?$

C   3 mA at 150 V

From rectifier

$I_2=?$
$R_2=?$

B   5 mA at 100 V

$R_1=?$
Bleeder$=2$ mA$=I_1$

20 mA   A   18 mA

(a)

B+ (250 V
E

$I_4=?$
$R_4=?$

D   20 mA at 200 V

$I_3=?$
$R_3=?$

C   15 mA at 130 V

From rectifier

$I_2=?$
$R_2=?$

B   10 mA at 100 V

$I_1=$bleeder$=10$ mA
$R_1=?$

A   B−

(b)

FIGURE 9-19

4. Design a voltage divider to deliver 70 mA at 350 V, 40 mA at 250 V, and 20 mA at 100 V if the power supply transformer is rated at 155 mA and operates at 90 percent of its rated value.

5. A power supply is to deliver 60 mA at 250 V, 5 mA at 100 V, and 2 mA at 50 V. The transformer is rated at 80 mA and operates at 90 percent of its rated value. Design a voltage divider to deliver the required currents and voltages.

6. In the voltage divider shown in Fig. 9-20, the bias bleeder current is 60 mA. Find the value of R_1, R_2, R_3, and R_4.

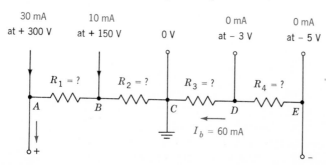

30 mA
at + 300 V

10 mA
at + 150 V

0 V

0 mA
at − 3 V

0 mA
at − 5 V

$R_1 = ?$ $R_2 = ?$ $R_3 = ?$ $R_4 = ?$

A   B   C   D   E

$I_b = 60$ mA

FIGURE 9-20

JOB 9-11 RESISTANCE MEASUREMENT BY THE VOLTAGE-COMPARISON METHOD. THE POTENTIOMETER RULE

In Fig. 9-21, the value of the unknown resistor R_x may be found by connecting it in series with a known standard resistance R_k and measuring the voltage drops across each.

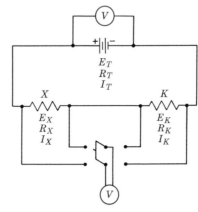

FIGURE 9-21
Voltage-comparison method of measuring resistance. $X =$ unknown resistance, $K =$ known standard resistance, $R_T =$ total resistance.

$$E_x = I_x \times R_x \qquad (3\text{-}4)$$

$$E_k = I_k \times R_k \qquad (3\text{-}5)$$

$$E_T = I_T \times R_T \qquad (3\text{-}7)$$

$$I_T = I_x = I_k \qquad (3\text{-}1)$$

Dividing Eq. (3-4) by Eq. (3-5), and canceling out the equal currents—$I_x = I_k$,

$$\frac{E_x = \overset{1}{\cancel{I_x}} \times R_x}{E_k = \cancel{I_k} \times R_k}_{1}$$

we obtain the

FORMULA

$$\frac{E_x}{E_k} = \frac{R_x}{R_k} \qquad \boxed{9\text{-}14}$$

Similarly, by dividing Eq. (3-4) by Eq. (3-7), we obtain the

FORMULA

$$\frac{E_x}{E_T} = \frac{R_x}{R_T} \qquad \boxed{9\text{-}15}$$

These formulas mean that in a series circuit, the voltage across any

resistance depends on the value of the resistance—a large voltage appearing across a large resistance and a small voltage appearing across a small
resistance. This is discussed in greater detail in Job 12-2.

EXAMPLE 9-30   Using Fig. 9-21, find the value of the unknown resistance K if the known resistance $R_k = 1{,}000$ Ω, $E_x = 100$ V, and $E_k = 25$ V.

SOLUTION
Given: $R_k = 1{,}000$ Ω   Find: $R_x = ?$
    $E_x = 100$ V
    $E_k = 25$ V

$$\frac{E_x}{E_k} = \frac{R_x}{R_k} \tag{9-14}$$

$$\frac{100}{25} = \frac{R_x}{1{,}000}$$

$$25 \times R_x = 100 \times 1{,}000$$

$$R_x = \frac{100{,}000}{25} = 4{,}000 \text{ Ω} \qquad Ans.$$

EXAMPLE 9-31   A horizontal hold-control circuit of a television receiver is essentially that shown in Fig. 9-22. Find (a) the voltage drop
across the 27,000-Ω resistor, (b) the voltage drop across the 75,000-Ω
resistor, and (c) the voltage drop across the 68,000-Ω resistor.

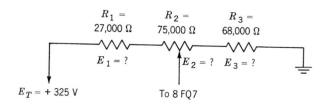

FIGURE 9-22
A horizontal hold-control circuit
in a television receiver.

SOLUTION
a   Find the total resistance of the circuit.

$$R_T = R_1 + R_2 + R_3 \tag{3-3}$$

$$R_T = 27{,}000 + 75{,}000 + 68{,}000 = 170{,}000 \text{ Ω} \qquad Ans.$$

Find E_1.

$$\frac{E_1}{E_T} = \frac{R_1}{R_T} \tag{9-15}$$

$$\frac{E_1}{325} = \frac{27{,}000}{170{,}000}$$

$$\frac{E_1}{325} = \frac{27}{170}$$

$$170 \times E_1 = 325 \times 27$$

$$E_1 = \frac{8,775}{170} = 51.6 \text{ V} \qquad Ans.$$

b   Find E_2.

$$\frac{E_1}{E_2} = \frac{R_1}{R_2} \qquad\qquad (9\text{-}14)$$

$$\frac{51.6}{E_2} = \frac{27,000}{75,000}$$

$$27 \times E_2 = 51.6 \times 75$$

$$E_2 = \frac{3,870}{27} = 143.3 \text{ V} \qquad Ans.$$

c   Find E_3.

$$\frac{E_1}{E_3} = \frac{R_1}{R_3} \qquad\qquad (9\text{-}14)$$

$$\frac{51.6}{E_3} = \frac{27,000}{68,000}$$

$$27 \times E_3 = 51.6 \times 68$$

$$E_3 = \frac{3,508.8}{27} = 129.9 \text{ V} \qquad Ans.$$

THE POTENTIOMETER RULE

When a number of resistances are connected in series, the voltage drop across any one of them may be found by using another form of formula (9-15).

$$\frac{E_x}{E_T} = \frac{R_x}{R_T} \qquad\qquad (9\text{-}15)$$

By cross-multiplying, we get

$$E_x \times R_T = R_x \times E_T$$

Dividing both sides by R_T will give the

FORMULA

$$E_x = \frac{R_x}{R_T} \times E_T \qquad\qquad \boxed{9\text{-}16}$$

In effect, this formula says that the voltage across any part of a series circuit is some fractional part of the total voltage. The numerator of the fraction is the resistance of the part of the circuit and the denominator is the total resistance of the circuit.

SELF-TEST 9-32   A voltage divider in the base circuit of a transistor is shown in Fig. 9-23. Find the voltage drop across $R_{B'}$.

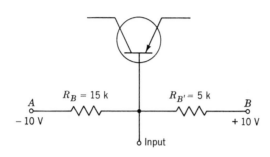

FIGURE 9-23
A voltage divider in the base circuit of a transistor.

SOLUTION

Since R_B and $R_{B'}$ are in _____, the potentiometer rule may be used. The total voltage between the points B and A is the difference in potential between these points. Thus,

$$V_T = +10 - (-10) = \underline{} \text{ V}$$

Formula (9-16) may now be rewritten using the symbols given in our circuit. Thus,

$$E_x = \frac{R_x}{R_T} \times E_T \tag{9-16}$$

will become

$$E_{RB'} = \frac{R_{B'}}{R_T} \times \underline{}$$

Substituting values will give

$$E_{RB'} = \frac{5}{5 + ?} \times 20$$

$$E_{RB'} = \frac{5 \text{ k}\Omega}{20 \text{ k}\Omega} \times 20$$

$$E_{RB'} = \underline{} \text{ V} \quad Ans.$$

series

+20

V_T

15

5

PROBLEMS

In Probs. 1 to 6, R_k and R_x are connected in series. Find the missing values in each problem.

PROBLEM	R_k	E_k	E_x	R_x	E_T
1	500	10	25	?	
2	50	15.5	70.2	?	
3	10	36.4	40.3	?	
4	100	15	?	250	
5	1,000	?	?	2,000	100 V
6	15,000	?	?	20,000	120 V

7. In a circuit similar to that shown in Fig. 9-22, $R_1 = 22,000\ \Omega$, $R_2 = 50,000\ \Omega$, and $R_3 = 100,000\ \Omega$. Find (*a*) E_1, (*b*) E_2, and (*c*) E_3 if $E_T = 200$ V.

8. In the picture-control circuit shown in Fig. 9-24, find the voltage drop across R_1 and R_2.

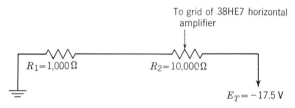

To grid of 38HE7 horizontal amplifier

$R_1 = 1,000\ \Omega$ $R_2 = 10,000\ \Omega$

$E_T = -17.5$ V   FIGURE 9-24

9. A brightness-control circuit in the Admiral TV chassis model NA1-1A is essentially that shown in Fig. 9-25. Find the voltage between ground and point *A*.

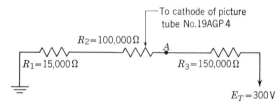

To cathode of picture tube No.19AGP 4

$R_2 = 100,000\ \Omega$ *A*

$R_1 = 15,000\ \Omega$ $R_3 = 150,000\ \Omega$

$E_T = 300$ V

FIGURE 9-25
A brightness-control circuit in a television receiver.

10. In a circuit similar to that shown in Fig. 9-23, $R_B = 35$ kΩ, $R_{B'} = 5$ kΩ, and the total voltage from *A* to *B* is 30 V. Find the voltage drop across $R_{B'}$.

11. The volume control of a transistorized phono amplifier is essentially a 470-kΩ and a 5-kΩ resistor in series across 9.5 V. Find the voltage drop across the 5-kΩ resistor.

12. In a brightness-control circuit, the total resistance of the potentiometer equals 5 MΩ and E_T equals 145 V. Find the cathode voltage when the potentiometer arm has covered (*a*) 1 MΩ and (*b*) 3.5 MΩ.

JOB 9-12   RESISTANCE MEASUREMENT USING THE WHEATSTONE BRIDGE

The Wheatstone bridge is a device for obtaining accurate measurements of resistance. A diagrammatic sketch of the circuit is shown in Fig. 9-26. The resistors R_1, R_2, R_3, and R_x are arranged in two parallel branches.

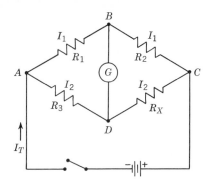

FIGURE 9-26
The Wheatstone-bridge circuit.

R_1, R_2, and R_3 are variable *known* resistors, and R_x is the *unknown* resistance. A galvanometer G is connected across the two branches between points B and D. A battery supplies the total current I_T.

OPERATION OF THE BRIDGE

1   When the circuit is closed, a current I_T will flow through the circuit which divides at point A, current I_1 flowing through the branch ABC (R_1 and R_2) and current I_2 flowing through the branch ADC (R_3 and R_x).

2   The variable resistors are adjusted until the galvanometer indicates no deflection. R_1 and R_2 are usually fixed at some convenient ratio, and then R_3 is varied until the galvanometer reads zero.

3   When there is no deflection of the galvanometer, it indicates that there is no current flowing between points B and D and therefore B and D are at the same voltage level. Under these conditions, we find that

Voltage across AB = voltage across AD or $I_1 \times R_1 = I_2 \times R_3$

Voltage across BC = voltage across DC or $I_1 \times R_2 = I_2 \times R_x$

Dividing one equation by the other gives us the fundamental equation for the Wheatstone bridge.

$$\frac{I_1 \times R_1}{I_1 \times R_2} = \frac{I_2 \times R_3}{I_2 \times R_x}$$

Canceling out the currents I_1 and I_2, we obtain

FORMULA

$$\frac{R_1}{R_2} = \frac{R_3}{R_x} \qquad \boxed{9\text{-}17}$$

EXAMPLE 9-33   When a Wheatstone bridge was used, the following readings were obtained: $R_1 = 1,000\ \Omega$, $R_2 = 10,000\ \Omega$, and $R_3 = 67.4\ \Omega$. Find the unknown resistance.

SOLUTION
Given: $R_1 = 1,000\ \Omega$ Find: $R_x = ?$
      $R_2 = 10,000\ \Omega$
      $R_3 = 67.4\ \Omega$

$$\frac{R_1}{R_2} = \frac{R_3}{R_x} \qquad\qquad (9\text{-}17)$$

$$\frac{1,000}{10,000} = \frac{67.4}{R_x}$$

$$\frac{1}{10} = \frac{67.4}{R_x}$$

$$R_x = 67.4 \times 10 = 674 \ \Omega \qquad Ans.$$

PROBLEMS

Find the value of R_x for each problem.

PROBLEM	R_1	R_2	R_3	R_x
1	1,000	10,000	84.3	?
2	10,000	1,000	952.7	?
3	100	10	60.4	?
4	10	1	175.3	?
5	1	10	128.9	?
6	5,000	10,000	823.7	?
7	100	1,000	46.5	?
8	1,000	100	9.16	?
9	10	1	1.6	?
10	1	10	35.79	?

TEST—VOLTAGE DIVIDERS AND RESISTANCE MEASUREMENT

1. In a voltage divider similar to that shown in Fig. 9-19a, the loads are 15 mA at 300 V at D, 10 mA at 175 V at C, 5 mA at 100 V at B, and the bleeder current is 2 mA. Find R_3, R_2, and R_1.
2. A 500- and a 700-Ω resistor are connected in series across 120 V. Find the voltage drop across the 700-Ω resistor.
3. Two resistors are connected in series. If $R_1 = 100 \ \Omega$, $E_1 = 125$ V, and $E_2 = 500$ V, find R_2.
4. In a diagram similar to that shown in Fig. 9-25, $R_1 = 30,000 \ \Omega$, $R_2 = 50,000 \ \Omega$, and $R_3 = 160,000 \ \Omega$. If the total voltage is $E_T = 270$ V, find the voltage between ground and point A.
5. When a Wheatstone bridge was used, the following readings were obtained: $R_1 = 100 \ \Omega$, $R_2 = 1,000 \ \Omega$, and $R_3 = 148 \ \Omega$. Find R_x.

JOB 9-13 ATTENUATORS

An attenuator pad is a combination of resistors whose purpose is (1) to reduce the source voltage to the lower voltage required by the load but (2) to keep the original source current unchanged.

The first of these requirements may be met very easily by inserting a resistance in series with the source as explained in Example 3-31 in

Job 3-7. In this example, a lamp rated at 12 V and 40 Ω is to operate from a 24-V source. Therefore, the original 24-V source voltage must be reduced to the 12 V required by the lamp. This reduction is accomplished by the insertion of a 40-Ω resistor in series with the lamp. If the lamp had been connected directly to the 24-V source, the current would have been

$$I_L = \frac{E_L}{R_L} = \frac{24}{40} = 0.6 \text{ A}$$

But, with the 40-Ω series resistor added,

$$R_T = R_1 + R_L \tag{3-3}$$

$$R_T = 40 + 40 = 80 \ \Omega$$

and

$$I_L = \frac{E_L}{R_T} = \frac{24}{80} = 0.3 \text{ A}$$

Notice that although the voltage was reduced from 24 to 12 V, the current drawn from the source was *also reduced* from 0.6 to 0.3 A. An attenuator circuit would also reduce the voltage from 24 to 12 V but *not* change the original current. Actually, this means that the resistance that the load presents to the source would remain unchanged. Thus, if the lamp resistance was 40 Ω, an attenuator circuit would reduce the voltage but would *not* change the total resistance of the circuit, and would therefore *not* change the original current. Now how can this be done?

Consider the circuit shown in Fig. 9-27. $E_T = 24$ V, and $I_T = E_T \div R_T$ or $24/40 = 0.6$ A. We wish to have $E_L = 12$ V, but *keep* $I_T = 0.6$ A. In order to do this, we shall insert resistors R_1 and R_2 as shown in Fig. 9-28 on p. 382. The current drawn by the lamp when $E_L = 12$ V is

$$I_L = \frac{E_L}{R_L} = \frac{12}{40} = 0.3 \text{ A}$$

By Kirchhoff's first law,

$$I_2 = I_T - I_L$$

$$I_2 = 0.6 - 0.3 = 0.3 \text{ A}$$

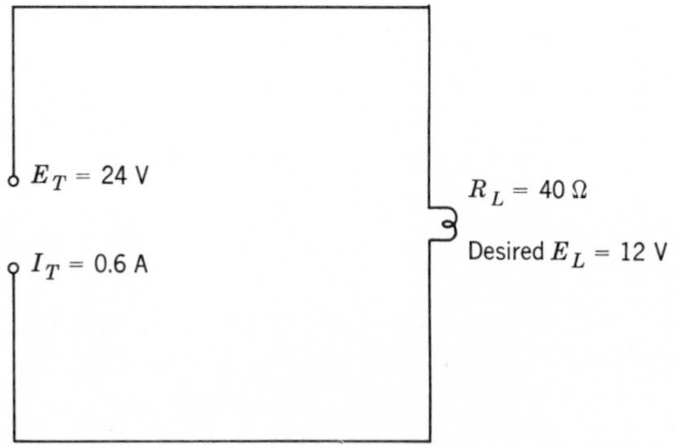

FIGURE 9-27
A 24-V source is to produce a load voltage of 12 V.

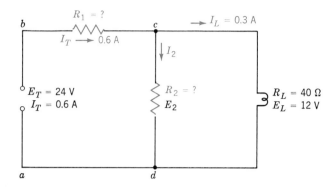

FIGURE 9-28

An L pad is inserted in the circuit of Fig. 9-27.

Since E_2 and E_L are in parallel, $E_2 = E_L = 12$ V. Therefore,

$$R_2 = \frac{E_2}{I_2} = \frac{12}{0.3} = 40 \ \Omega \qquad Ans.$$

In order to find R_1, apply Kirchhoff's second law, and trace around the circuit in the direction *abcd*.

$$E_T - E_1 - E_2 = 0$$
$$24 - E_1 - 12 = 0$$
$$24 - 12 = E_1$$
$$E_1 = 12 \text{ V}$$

R_1 may now be found.

$$R_1 = \frac{E_1}{I_1} = \frac{12}{0.6} = 20 \ \Omega \qquad Ans.$$

Check: If we are correct, the total resistance of the series-parallel combination of R_1, R_2, and R_L will exactly equal the original R_L. Since R_2 and R_L are in parallel, the effective resistance of the group equals

$$\frac{R_2 \times R_L}{R_2 + R_L} = \frac{40 \times 40}{40 + 40} = \frac{1{,}600}{80} = 20 \ \Omega$$

This 20-Ω effective resistance is in series with $R_1 = 20 \ \Omega$. R_T therefore equals $20 + 20 = 40 \ \Omega$, which is exactly what the total resistance was *before* the insertion of the attenuator resistors. If the total resistance of the entire combination is 40 Ω, then $I_T = E_T \div R_T$, or $I_T = 24/40 = 0.6$ A. Notice that I_T is *still* 0.6 A but that E_L is now reduced to 12 V. This combination of R_1 and R_2 when inserted as shown in Fig. 9-28 is called an L pad due to its resemblance to an inverted letter L.

EXAMPLE 9-34   Insert an L pad in the circuit shown in Fig. 9-29 which will reduce the load voltage to 4 V while maintaining a constant resistance to the source.

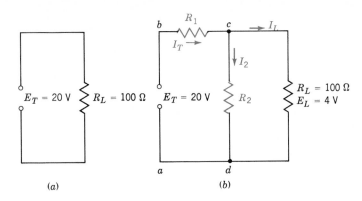

(a)   (b)

FIGURE 9-29
(a) Original circuit. (b) With
L pad inserted.

SOLUTION

Insert R_1 and R_2 as shown in Fig. 9-29b. The total current I_T *before* the insertion of the pad was

$$I_T = \frac{E_T}{R_T} = \frac{20}{100} = 0.2 \text{ A}$$

If the voltage at the load is to be 4 V,

$$I_L = \frac{E_L}{R_L} = \frac{4}{100} = 0.04 \text{ A}$$

Find I_2 by Kirchhoff's first law.

$$I_2 = I_T - I_L = 0.2 - 0.04 = 0.16 \text{ A}$$

Find R_2. Since R_2 and R_L are in parallel, $E_2 = E_L = 4$ V.

$$R_2 = \frac{E_2}{I_2} = \frac{4}{0.16} = 25 \text{ } \Omega \qquad Ans.$$

Find R_1. Apply Kirchhoff's second law to find E_1 by tracing around the circuit in the direction *abcd*.

$$E_T - E_1 - E_2 = 0$$

$$20 - E_1 - 4 = 0$$

$$E_1 = 16 \text{ V}$$

Therefore,

$$R_1 = \frac{E_1}{I_1} = \frac{16}{0.2} = 80 \text{ } \Omega \qquad Ans.$$

Check: The total resistance of R_1, R_2, and R_L connected as shown must equal R_L or 100 Ω.

$$R_T = R_1 + \frac{R_2 \times R_L}{R_2 + R_L}$$

$$= 80 + \frac{25 \times 100}{25 + 100}$$

$$= 80 + \frac{2,500}{125}$$

$$R_T = 80 + 20 = 100 \ \Omega \qquad Check$$

SELF-TEST 9-35 The resistance of a 40-V source is 50 Ω. In order to reduce the volume to a 50-Ω speaker, an L pad is inserted to reduce the voltage to 4 V. Find R_1 and R_2.

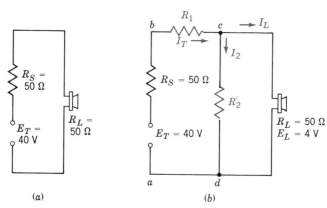

FIGURE 9-30
(a) Original circuit. (b) With L pad inserted.

(a)

(b)

SOLUTION
The diagram for the circuit is shown in Fig. 9-30. In Fig. 9-30a, the total current *before* the pad is inserted is

$$I_T = \frac{E_T}{R_T} = \frac{E_T}{R_S + ?}$$	R_L
$$I_T = \frac{40}{?}$$	100
$$I_T = \underline{\quad} \ A$$	0.4

In Fig. 9-30b, after R_1 and R_2 are in the circuit,

$$I_L = \frac{E_L}{R_L} = \frac{4}{50} = \underline{\quad} \ A$$	0.08

Find I_2 by Kirchhoff's first law. At point c,

$$I_2 = I_T - I_L = 0.4 - ? = 0.32 \ A$$	0.08

Find R_2. Since $E_2 = E_L = \underline{\quad}$ V,

4

$$R_2 = \frac{E_2}{I_2} = \frac{4}{0.32} = \underline{\quad} \ \Omega$$	12.5

Find R_1. Apply Kirchhoff's second law to find E_1 by tracing around the circuit in the direction *abcd*.

$$E_T - E_S - E_1 - ? = 0$$

$$E_T - I_T R_S - E_1 - E_2 = 0$$

$$40 - (?)(50) - E_1 - 4 = 0$$

$$40 - \underline{\quad} - E_1 - 4 = 0$$

$$\underline{\quad} - E_1 = 0$$

$$E_1 = \underline{\quad} \text{ V}$$

Therefore,

$$R_1 = \frac{E_1}{I_1} = \frac{E_1}{I_T} = \frac{16}{?}$$

$$R_1 = \underline{\quad} \Omega \quad Ans.$$

Check: The total resistance of R_1, R_2, and R_L connected as shown must equal R_L or 50 Ω.

$$R_T = R_1 + \frac{R_2 \times ?}{R_2 + ?}$$

$$= ? + \frac{12.5 \times 50}{12.5 + 50}$$

$$= 40 + ?$$

$$R_T = 50 \ \Omega \quad Check$$

Side column values:

E_2

0.4

20

16

16

0.4

40

R_L
R_L

40

10

PROBLEMS

Insert an L pad into the following circuits. Find the value of R_1 and R_2 which will provide the required reduction in voltage.

PROBLEM	CIRCUIT FIG. NO.	E_T, V	R_S, Ω	R_L, Ω	E_L, V
1	9-29a	60	. . . .	15	12
2	9-30a	60	60	60	15
3	9-29a	120	. . . .	10	60
4	9-30a	120	100	100	30
5	9-30a	120	60	60	24
6	9-30a	100	20	20	5
7	9-30a	250	100	100	100
8	9-29a	6	. . . .	10	1.5
9	9-30a	40	100	100	5
10	9-30a	6.3	20	20	2.1

T-TYPE ATTENUATORS

As we have seen, the L-type attenuator maintains a constant resistance to the source even though the voltage across the load is changed.

However, the position of the source and the load may not be inter-changed, because the resistance presented on one side of the pad is different from the resistance on the other side. If it is desired that the pad present a constant resistance on *each* side of it, a T-type of pad is needed. This is a symmetrical pad and offers the *same* resistance on both sides. When this type of pad is used, the source and the load *may* be interchanged, because the resistance presented by each side of the pad is constant.

In the T-type, $R_1 = R_3$ and $R_S = R_L$.

EXAMPLE 9-36   In Fig. 9-31*a*, it is desired to reduce the voltage across R_L to 20 V. Design a T-type attenuator pad to achieve this result.

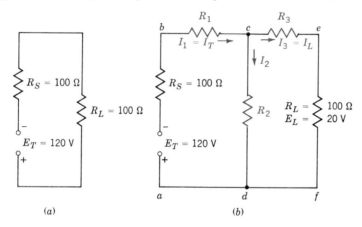

(a)   (b)

FIGURE 9-31

(a) Original circuit. (b) With T pad inserted. $R_1 = R_3$.

SOLUTION

In Fig. 9-31*a*, the total current *before* the pad is inserted is

$$I_T = \frac{E_T}{R_T} = \frac{E_T}{R_S + R_L} = \frac{120}{100 + 100} = \frac{120}{200} = 0.6 \text{ A}$$

In Fig. 9-31*b*, after R_1, R_2, and R_3 have been inserted,

$$I_L = \frac{E_L}{R_L} = \frac{20}{100} = 0.2 \text{ A}$$

Find I_2 by Kirchhoff's first law operating at point *c*.

$$I_2 = I_1 - I_L = 0.6 - 0.2 = 0.4 \text{ A}$$

R_1, R_2, and R_3 may be found by applying Kirchhoff's second law to different loops of the circuit of Fig. 9-31*b*. Trace the circuit *abcd*, assuming the currents to be in the directions indicated on the diagram.

$$120 - 0.6(100) - 0.6R_1 - 0.4R_2 = 0$$

$$120 - 60 - 0.6R_1 - 0.4R_2 = 0$$

$$- 0.6R_1 - 0.4R_2 = -60 \tag{1}$$

Now trace the circuit *cefdc*.

$$-0.2R_3 - 20 + 0.4R_2 = 0$$

$$-0.2R_3 + 0.4R_2 = 20$$

but since $R_1 = R_3$, we can substitute R_1 for R_3 in this equation.

$$-0.2R_1 + 0.4R_2 = 20 \tag{2}$$

Solve equations (1) and (2) simultaneously.

$$-0.6R_1 - 0.4R_2 = -60 \tag{1}$$
$$-0.2R_1 + 0.4R_2 = 20 \tag{2}$$

Adding, $-0.8R_1 = -40$

$$R_1 = \frac{-40}{-0.8} = 50 \ \Omega \qquad Ans.$$

and $R_3 = 50 \ \Omega \qquad Ans.$

Substitute this value for R_1 in equation (2).

$$-0.2R_1 + 0.4R_2 = 20$$

$$-0.2(50) + 0.4R_2 = 20$$

$$-10 + 0.4R_2 = 20$$

$$0.4R_2 = 20 + 10$$

$$0.4R_2 = 30$$

$$R_2 = \frac{30}{0.4} = 75 \ \Omega \qquad Ans.$$

Check: The total resistance of R_1, R_2, and R_L connected as shown must equal R_L, or 100 Ω.

The resistance from c to $f = R_3 + R_L$

$$= 50 + 100 = 150 \ \Omega$$

This 150 Ω is in parallel with R_2. The resistance of this group is equal to

$$\frac{75 \times 150}{75 + 150} = \frac{11,250}{225} = 50 \ \Omega$$

This 50 Ω is in series with R_1. The total resistance is

$$R_T = 50 + R_1$$

$$R_T = 50 + 50 = 100 \ \Omega$$

which is equal to R_L.   *Check*

PROBLEMS

Insert a T pad into the following circuits similar to that shown in Fig. 9-31a. Find the value of R_1, R_2, and R_3 which will provide the required reduction in voltage.

PROBLEM	E_T, V	R_S, Ω	R_L, Ω	E_L, V
1	120	60	60	30
2	12	200	200	4
3	60	60	60	15
4	100	400	400	30
5	60	10	10	5
6	200	400	400	20
7	24	100	100	1.5

TEST—ATTENUATOR CIRCUITS

1. In a circuit similar to that shown in Fig. 9-29a, $E_T = 120$ V and $R_L = 48$ Ω. Insert an L pad which will reduce the voltage of E_L to 6 V.

2. In a circuit similar to that shown in Fig. 9-31a, $E_T = 60$ V, $R_S = 15$ Ω, $R_L = 15$ Ω, and E_L is to be reduced to 15 V. Insert a T pad to provide this reduction.

3. In a circuit similar to that shown in Fig. 9-30a, $E_T \doteq 32$ V, $R_S = 800$ Ω, and $R_L = 800$ Ω. Insert an L pad whch will reduce the voltage of E_L to 4 V.

4. In a circuit similar to that shown in Fig. 9-31a, $E_T = 80$ V, $R_S = 200$ Ω, $R_L = 200$ Ω, and E_L is to be reduced to 20 V. Insert a T pad to provide this reduction.

EFFICIENCY

JOB 10-1 CHECKUP ON PERCENT (DIAGNOSTIC TEST)

The efficiency of electrical machinery is expressed as a percent. The concept of percent is used throughout the fields of electricity and electronics to describe and compare electrical effects. Can you solve the following problems which use percent? If you have difficulty with any of these problems, turn to Job 10-2, which follows.

PROBLEMS

1. What is the possible error in a resistor marked 1,000 Ω if the indicated error (tolerance) is 10 percent?
2. A solenoid exerts a pull of 0.9 lb at its rated voltage. What pull is exerted at 85 percent of its rated voltage?
3. A 15-A fuse carried a 15 percent overload for 3 s. What current flowed through the fuse during this time?
4. The plate voltage on a tube might normally vary up to 10 percent of the rated value. Is a voltage of 200 V within the normal variation if the rated voltage is 230 V?
5. The peak voltage of an ac wave is 141 percent of the ac meter reading. Find the peak voltage if the meter reads 50 V.
6. What is the efficiency of a motor if it uses 20 units of energy and delivers 18 units of energy?
7. What is the efficiency of a transmission line if the power supplied is 4,500 W and the power delivered is 4,200 W?
8. A transformer has an efficiency of 96 percent. If the transformer uses 60 W, what power will it deliver?
9. The National Electrical Code specifies a maximum of 2 percent voltage drop in a house line. What is the minimum voltage at a load if the supply voltage is 120 V?
10. A television mechanic bought $125 worth of tubes at a 35 percent discount. What did he pay for the tubes?

11. If he was also allowed 2 percent discount for payment within 10 days, what was his actual cost?
12. A television mechanic charged the list price of $2.25 for a tube. If the tube cost him $1.80, what was his percent of profit?
13. A television mechanic estimated that his overhead expenses equaled 20 percent of his cost. If he charges the list price of $4 for an item, what is the most that he should pay for it?
14. Some storage batteries are shipped dry and filled with electrolyte by the seller. In making up a batch of electrolyte to contain 40 percent acid, how much acid should be used to make 32 oz of electrolyte?
15. What percent of the 250 V rated voltage is a tube receiving if it receives only 225 V?

JOB 10-2 BRUSHUP ON PERCENT

The word *percent* is used to indicate some portion of 100. A mark of 92 percent on an examination indicates that the student got 92 points out of a possible 100 points. This may also be written as a decimal fraction (0.92) or as a common fraction ($^{92}/_{100}$), both of which are read as 92 *hundredths*. A percent indicated by a percent sign (%) cannot be used in a calculation until it has been changed into an equivalent decimal fraction.

Changing percents to decimals. Since 92 percent means $^{92}/_{100}$, the change to a decimal is made by dividing 92 by 100. This is easily accomplished by moving the decimal point two places to the left as shown in Job 9-1.

RULE	To change a percent into a decimal, move the decimal point two places to the left and drop the percent sign.

EXAMPLE 10-1 Change the following percents into decimals.

SOLUTION

$$32\% = 32.\% = 0.32 \quad Ans.$$
$$8\% = 8.\% = 0.08 \quad Ans.$$
$$16\frac{1}{2}\% = 16.5\% = 0.165 \quad Ans.$$

PROBLEMS

Change the following percents into decimals:

1. 38%   2. 60%   3. 6%   4. 19%   5. 4%
6. 26.4%   7. 3.6%   8. 100%   9. 125%   10. 0.5%

11. $16^2/3\%$ 12. $^3/4\%$ 13. 62.5% 14. 1% 15. 12.5%
16. 0.9% 17. 2.25% 18. $5^1/2\%$ 19. $4^1/4\%$ 20. $^1/2\%$

Changing decimals into percents. To change a decimal into a percent is to reverse the process of changing a percent into a decimal.

RULE	To change a decimal into a percent, move the decimal point two places to the right and add a percent sign.

EXAMPLE 10-2   Change the following decimals into percents:

SOLUTION

$$0.20 = 20.\% = 20\% \quad Ans.$$

$$0.06 = 6.\% = 6\% \quad Ans.$$

$$0.125 = 12.5\% \quad Ans.$$

$$1.1 = 110.\% = 110\% \quad Ans.$$

$$2 = 2.00 = 200.\% = 200\% \quad Ans.$$

PROBLEMS

Express the following decimals as percents:

1. 0.50   2. 0.04   3. 0.2   4. 0.075   5. 1.45
6. 0.008   7. 1.00   8. 0.87   9. 0.625   10. 0.092
11. 0.222   12. 0.15   13. 0.7   14. 3   15. 0.055

Changing common fractions to percents

RULE	To change a common fraction to a percent, express the fraction as a decimal; then move the decimal point two places to the right and add a percent sign.

The decimal equivalents for many of the common fractions may be found in Table 2-4.

EXAMPLE 10-3   Express the following fractions as percents.

SOLUTION

$$^3/4 = 0.75 = 75\% \quad Ans.$$

$$^1/2 = 0.50 = 50\% \quad Ans.$$

$$^5/8 = 0.625 = 62.5\% \quad Ans.$$

If the fraction is not on the decimal equivalent chart, change the fraction into a decimal by dividing the numerator by the denominator as shown in Job 2-5.

EXAMPLE 10-4   Express $8/25$ as a percent.

SOLUTION

$$8/25 = 25 \overline{)\begin{array}{r} 0.32 = 32\% \quad Ans. \\ 8.00 \\ -7\,5 \\ \hline 50 \\ -50 \\ \hline 0 \end{array}}$$

PROBLEMS

Express the following common fractions as percents:

1. $1/4$	2. $3/8$	3. $2/5$	4. $4/5$	5. $5/8$
6. $3/16$	7. $3/10$	8. $3/5$	9. $3/6$	10. $9/10$
11. $13/20$	12. $3/32$	13. $2/3$	14. $5/6$	15. $5/11$
16. $3/7$	17. $16/48$	18. $12/30$	19. $2/9$	20. $13/15$

Using percent in problems. There are three parts to every problem involving percent.

1   The *base B* is the entire amount.
2   The *rate R* is the percent of the base.
3   The *part P* is the portion of the base.

These three parts are combined in the following

FORMULA

$$B \times R = P \qquad\qquad \boxed{10\text{-}1}$$

Finding the part

EXAMPLE 10-5   How much is 20 percent of $80?

SOLUTION
Given: $B = \$80$ Find: $P = ?$
       $R = 20\% = 0.20$

$$B \times R = P \qquad\qquad (10\text{-}1)$$
$$80 \times 0.20 = P$$
$$P = \$16 \quad Ans.$$

EXAMPLE 10-6   What is the profit on an article costing $30 if it is sold at a profit of 15 percent?

SOLUTION
Given: $B = \$30$ Find: $P = ?$
     $R = 15\% = 0.15$

$$B \times R = P \qquad\qquad (10\text{-}1)$$

$$30 \times 0.15 = P$$

$$P = \$4.50 \qquad Ans.$$

SELF-TEST 10-7   The voltage lost in a line supplying a motor is 5 percent of the generator voltage of 220 V. Find (*a*) the voltage lost and (*b*) the voltage supplied to the motor load.

SOLUTION
Given: $E_G = $ base $B = $ _____   Find: $E_l = $ part $P = ?$ 220
     $R = 5\% = $ _(decimal)_ $E_L = ?$ 0.05

a $B \times R = P$ (10-1)

            $220 \times$ ____ $= P$ 0.05

                   $P = $ ____ V   11

                 $E_l = $ ____ V   *Ans.*   11

b $E_L = E_G - $ ____   (5-3) E_l

               $E_L = $ ____ $- 11$ 220

               $E_L = $ ____ V   *Ans.*   209

PROBLEMS

1.   How much is 22 percent of 150? *33%*
2.   How much is 6 percent of $500?
3.   How much is 2.5 percent of $300?
4.   What is the amount of sales tax on an order of $7.50 if the tax rate is 3 percent?
5.   A television benchman earned $250 per week. He received an increase of 15 percent. Find the amount of the increase.
6.   A TV mechanic used 30 percent of a 1,000-ft roll of push-back wire. How many feet of wire did he use?
7.   A 15-A fuse carried a 15 percent overload for 2 s. What current flowed through the fuse during this time?
8.   What is the possible error in a 500-Ω resistor if it is marked with a silver band indicating only 10 percent accuracy?
9.   The effective value of an ac wave is 70.7 percent of the peak value.

What is the effective voltage of a wave which reaches a peak of 165 V?

10. In a brightness-control circuit, 6 percent of the 525 horizontal lines were blanked out. How many lines were blanked out?

11. Out of a lot of 200 transistors, 2½ percent were rejected as being defective. How many were rejected?

12. The voltage drop in a line supplied by a 220-V generator is 2 percent of the generator voltage. Find the voltage drop and the voltage supplied to the load.

13. How many watts of power are lost in a transformer rated at 250 W if 3 percent of the energy is lost as heat?

14. What is the interest for 1 year at 2½ percent on $125?

15. If you are allowed a discount of 15 percent on a bill amounting to $127.85, how much is the discount?

16. A zener diode rated at 10 W is used as a regulator in a power supply as shown in Fig. 10-1. The power supply delivers 20 V to the load. Find the largest current which the zener should be allowed to pass if only 70 percent of the rated current is permitted.

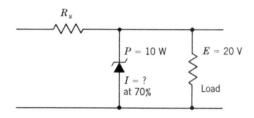

FIGURE 10-1
A zener diode used as a regulator in a power supply.

Finding the rate

EXAMPLE 10-8   20 is what percent of 80?

SOLUTION
Given: $B = 80$ Find: $R = ?$
$\quad\quad\ P = 20$

$$B \times R = P \tag{10-1}$$

$$80 \times R = 20$$

$$R = \frac{20}{80} = \frac{1}{4} = 0.25 = 25\% \quad Ans.$$

EXAMPLE 10-9   A man earns $120 per week. If he saves $10 per week, what percent of his wages does he save?

SOLUTION
Given: $B = \$120$ Find: $R = $ percent saved $= ?$
$\quad\quad\ P = $ part saved $= \$10$

$$B \times R = P \tag{10-1}$$

$$120 \times R = 10$$

$$R = \frac{10}{120} = \frac{1}{12} = 0.083 = 8.3\% \qquad Ans.$$

PROBLEMS

1. 30 is what percent of 120?
2. 30 is what percent of 80?
3. What percent of 60 is 24?
4. What percent of 85 is 12?
5. What percent of 25 is 0.5?
6. What percent of 30 is 40?
7. 150 is what percent of 100?
8. 24.5 is what percent of 70?
9. What percent of 25½ is 8½?
10. What percent of 18.5 is 3.5?
11. A discount of $2 was given on a bill of $16. Find the rate of discount.
12. If three tubes out of a lot of 90 tubes are defective, what percent are defective?
13. If 100 ft of a 250-ft roll of wire has been used, what percent has been used?
14. A signal generator costing $65 was sold at a loss of $25. Find the rate of loss.
15. In transmitting 50 hp by a belt system, 1.2 hp was lost due to slippage. What percent of the power was lost?
16. A team played 18 games and won 15 of them. What percent of the games played did they win?
17. An electrician used 40 ft of BX cable from a 200-ft-long coil. What percent did he use?
18. A man earning $80 per week received an increase of $2.50 per week. Find the percent of increase.
19. The voltage loss in a supply line is 5.5 V. If the generator voltage is 110 V, find the rate of loss.
20. A 15-A fuse carried 18 A for 2 s. What was the percent of overload?

Finding the base

EXAMPLE 10-10   5 is 25 percent of what number?

SOLUTION

Given: $P = 5$ Find: $B = ?$

$R = 25\% = 0.25$

$$B \times R = P \qquad\qquad\qquad (10\text{-}1)$$

$$B \times 0.25 = 5$$

$$B = \frac{5}{0.25} = 20 \qquad Ans.$$

EXAMPLE 10-11   A mechanic is able to save $18.50 each week. This amount is equal to 12½ percent of his weekly wages. How much does he earn each week?

SOLUTION

Given: P = amount saved = \$18.50   Find: B = total wages = ?
         R = percent saved = 12½% = 0.125

$$B \times R = P \qquad\qquad (10\text{-}1)$$

$$B \times 0.125 = 18.50$$

$$B = \frac{18.50}{0.125} = \$148 \quad \textit{Ans.}$$

PROBLEMS

1. 10 is 50 percent of what number?
2. 20 is 4 percent of what number?
3. 16 is 40 percent of what number?
4. 25 is 2.5 percent of what number?
5. 70 is 3½ percent of what number?
6. The voltage loss in a line is 3 V. If this is 2 percent of the generator voltage, what is the generator voltage?
7. A mechanic received a 15 percent increase in his wages amounting to \$12.30. What were his wages before the increase?
8. A motor has an output of 5 hp. This amount is 85 percent of the power put into the motor. Calculate the power input.
9. A fuse carried 16.5 A. This was 110 percent of the fuse rating. What is the fuse rating?
10. What must be the generator voltage if only 98 percent of the generator voltage is delivered to a 117-V line?

REVIEW OF PERCENT PROBLEMS

RULE	To change a percent into a decimal, move the decimal point _____ places to the _____ and drop the percent sign.	two	left
RULE	To change a decimal into a percent, move the decimal point _____ places to the _____ and add a percent sign.	two	right
RULE	To change a common fraction into a percent, express the fraction as a decimal; then move the decimal point _____ places to the right and add a _____ sign.	two	percent

All percent problems contain three parts:

1	The base B is the _____ amount.	total
2	The rate R is a percent of the _____.	base
3	The part P is the portion of the _____.	base

The relationship among these parts is given by the formula

$$\_\_\_ \times \_\_\_ = \_\_\_$$

| 10-1 | | B | R | P |

PROBLEMS

1. Change the following percents to decimals: (*a*) 62%, (*b*) 3%, (*c*) 5.6%, (*d*) 0.8%, (*e*) 116%, (*f*) 4½%, and (*g*) 6¼%.
2. Change the following decimals to percents: (*a*) 0.4, (*b*) 0.08, (*c*) 0.6, (*d*) 2.00, (*e*) 0.625, (*f*) 0.045, and (*g*) 5.
3. Change the following fractions to percents: (*a*) ¾, (*b*) ⅗, (*c*) 3/7, (*d*) 3/10, (*e*) 3/13, (*f*) ⅙, and (*g*) 24/52.
4. What is 18 percent of 96?
5. How much is 4.5 percent of $2,000?
6. 20 is what percent of 120?
7. What percent of 30 is 12?
8. 8 is 40 percent of what number?
9. How much is 3¼ percent of $1,500?
10. 10 is 2½ percent of what number?
11. What percent of 38.4 is 8?
12. How much is 0.6 percent of 75?
13. In the transmission of 6 hp by a belt system, 0.09 hp was lost owing to slippage. What percent was lost?
14. The plate voltage on an amplifier tube may vary up to 10 percent of its rated value and still be satisfactory. A tube rated at 200 V has a plate voltage of 185 V. Is this within the normal variation?
15. Of the 60 men in a shop, 80 percent got production bonuses. How many men got a bonus?
16. If only a 2 percent voltage drop is permitted in a line, what is the maximum loss in voltage at the end of a line supplied by a 120-V source? What is the voltage at the end of the line?
17. A man received 150 percent of his hourly wage for every hour that he worked above 40 h. If he worked 50 h in a certain week, at a base rate of $2/h, what was his overtime pay? What was his total salary? How much was withheld from his salary for social security at a 5.2 percent tax rate?
18. A man earning $85/wk received an increase of 8 percent. Find the amount of the increase and his new salary.
19. Emitter bias resistors usually have a wattage rating about 80 percent higher than the calculated wattage. What should be the wattage rating of an emitter bias resistor developing 0.5 W?
20. The cost of rewinding an armature is $34. If the electrician wishes

to make a profit of 20 percent, at what price must he bill the customer?

TEST—PERCENT

1. Change each of the following to a percent: (*a*) 3.75, (*b*) 0.68, (*c*) 0.007, and (*d*) 1½.
2. Change each of the following percents to decimals: (*a*) 1.5%, (*b*) 8%, (*c*) 35%, and (*d*) 37½%.
3. A television mechanic bought $85 worth of tubes at a 25 percent discount. What was the amount of the discount? How much did he pay?
4. What percent of the power taken by a transformer is delivered if it takes 200 W and delivers 190 W?
5. The effective value of an ac wave is 70.7 percent of its peak value. What is the peak value of an ac wave if the effective value is 110 V?

JOB 10-3   CONVERSION FACTORS FOR ELECTRICAL AND MECHANICAL POWER

A *motor* is a device which uses electrical power and converts this power into the mechanical power of a rotating shaft. The electrical power supplied to a motor is measured in watts or kilowatts; the mechanical power delivered by a motor is measured in horsepower. One horsepower is equivalent to 746 watts of electrical power. For most calculations, it is sufficiently accurate to consider 1 hp equal to 750 W.

A *generator* is a device which uses mechanical power and converts this power into electrical power. The mechanical power supplied to a generator is measured in horsepower; the electrical power delivered by a generator is measured in watts or kilowatts.

Tables of conversion factors. Tables 10-1 and 10-2 are based on the following relationships.

$$1 \text{ kW} = 1,000 \text{ W}$$

$$1 \text{ hp} = 750 \text{ W}$$

TABLE 10-1

	TO CHANGE	INTO	MULTIPLY BY
1	Kilowatts (kW)	Watts (W)	1,000
2	Horsepower (hp)	Watts (W)	750
3	Kilowatts (kW)	Horsepower (hp)	4/3
4	Horsepower (hp)	Kilowatts (kW)	3/4

TABLE 10-2

	TO CHANGE	INTO	DIVIDE BY
5	Watts (W)	Kilowatts (kW)	1,000
6	Watts (W)	Horsepower (hp)	750

Items 3 and 4 are derived as follows:

Since hp = W/750 (item 6) and W = kW × 1,000 (item 1), we can substitute (kW × 1,000) for watts in item 6. This gives

$$hp = \frac{kW \times 1,000}{750}$$

or

$$hp = kW \times \frac{4}{3}$$

Similarly, since kW = W/1,000 (item 5) and W = hp × 750 (item 2), we can substitute (hp × 750) for watts in item 5. This gives

$$kW = \frac{hp \times 750}{1,000}$$

or

$$kW = hp \times \frac{3}{4}$$

EXAMPLE 10-12

1   1.5 kW = 1.5 × 1,000 = 1,500 W   *Ans.*
2   ½ hp = ½ × 750 = 375 W   *Ans.*
3   1½ kW = 1½ × 4/3 = 3/2 × 4/3 = 2 hp   *Ans.*
4   1½ hp = 1½ × ¾ = 3/2 × ¾ = 9/8 = 1.125 kW   *Ans.*
5   1,800 W = 1,800 ÷ 1,000 = 1.8 kW   *Ans.*
6   1,125 W = 1,125 ÷ 750 = 1.5 hp   *Ans.*

PROBLEMS

Change the following units of measurement.

1.   6.5 kW to watts
2.   2 hp to watts
3.   2,300 W to kilowatts
4.   2,625 W to horsepower
5.   0.05 kW to watts
6.   1 kW to horsepower
7.   1 hp to kilowatts
8.   1¾ kW to horsepower
9.   2¼ hp to kilowatts
10.   7.5 kW to horsepower
11.   ⅛ hp to kilowatts
12.   ¾ hp to watts
13.   4,000 W to horsepower
14.   4½ hp to kilowatts
15.   10 kW to horsepower
16.   8.75 kW to horsepower

JOB 10-4   EFFICIENCY OF ELECTRICAL APPARATUS

Most machines are designed to do a specific job. A motor takes in electrical energy and delivers mechanical energy in the form of a rotating shaft. If it could change *all* the electrical energy into mechanical energy, it would be said to be 100 percent efficient. Unfortunately, not all the electrical energy put into the motor appears as mechanical energy at the shaft. Some of the energy is used in overcoming friction, and some appears as heat energy. *No energy is lost*—it merely does not appear at the shaft as *useful* energy. The amount of useful energy (the power output) is therefore always *less* than the energy received by the machine (the power input). This means that the power output is always some fractional part of the power input. This fraction, obtained by dividing the output by the input, is called the *efficiency* of the machine. It is always expressed as a percent by multiplying the fraction by 100. The efficiency of electrical devices is generally large, ranging from 75 to 98 percent.

FORMULA

$$\text{Efficiency} = \frac{\text{output}}{\text{input}} \qquad \boxed{10\text{-}2}$$

In this formula, the output and the input must *both* be expressed in the *same units of measurement*. This will ordinarily necessitate a change in the units of measurement, since for a motor,

Output is measured in horsepower
Input is measured in watts or kilowatts

For a generator,

Output is measured in watts or kilowatts
Input is measured in horsepower

EXAMPLE 10-13   Find the efficiency of a motor which receives 4 kW and delivers 4 hp.

SOLUTION
Given: Output = 4 hp   Find: Percent eff = ?
         Input = 4 kW

1   Express all measurements in the same kind of units.

$$\text{Output} = 4 \text{ hp} = 4 \times 750 = 3,000 \text{ W}$$

$$\text{Input} = 4 \text{ kW} = 4 \times 1,000 = 4,000 \text{ W}$$

2   Find the efficiency.

$$\text{Eff} = \frac{\text{output}}{\text{input}} = \frac{3,000}{4,000} = 0.75 = 75\% \qquad Ans.$$

SELF-TEST 10-14   A generator receives 7 hp and delivers 20 A at 230 V. Find its efficiency.

SOLUTION

Given: Output $\begin{cases} E = \underline{\quad} \text{ V} \\ I = \underline{\quad} \text{ A} \end{cases}$ Find: Percent eff = ?

Input = $\underline{\quad}$ hp

230
20
7

1   Express all measurements in the same kind of unit.

Output: $P = I \times E = 20 \times 230 = 4,600 \underline{\quad}$ W

Input: $7 \text{ hp} = 7 \times 750 = 5,250 \underline{\quad}$ W

2   Find the efficiency.

$$\text{Eff} = \frac{?}{?}$$ output
input

$$\text{Eff} = \frac{4,600}{5,250}$$

$$\text{Eff} = 0.876 = \underline{\quad} \% \qquad Ans.$$ 87.6

SELF-TEST 10-15   A 6HB5 power tube requires a plate current of 44 mA at 125 V. If its power output is 2.2 W, find the plate efficiency of the tube.

SOLUTION

Given: Output = $\underline{\quad}$ W   Find: Plate eff = ?

Input = $\begin{cases} E = \underline{\quad} \text{ V} \\ I = \underline{\quad} \text{ mA} \end{cases}$

2.2
125
44

1   Express all measurements in the same kind of unit.

Input: $P = I \times E = \underline{\quad\quad} \times 125$ 0.044

Input $P = 5.5 \underline{\quad}$ W

Output: $P = 2.2 \underline{\quad}$ W

$$\text{Plate eff} = \frac{\text{output}}{?}$$ input

$$\text{Plate eff} = \frac{2.2}{5.5} = 0.40 = \underline{\quad} \% \qquad Ans.$$ 40

PROBLEMS

1.   A motor rated at 2 hp (delivers 2 hp) receives 1.8 kW of energy. Find its efficiency.
2.   A motor delivers 3 hp and receives 2.4 kW. Find its efficiency.
3.   A 6CW5 power tube requires a plate current of 70 mA at 275 V. If its power output is 11.55 W, find the plate efficiency.
4.   A 6HB5 power tube requires a plate current of 50 mA at 130 V. If its power output is 3.9 W, find the plate efficiency.
5.   A "power" transformer draws 0.5 kW from a line and delivers 480 W. Find its efficiency.

6. A filament transformer draws 60 W and supplies 50 W to the tube filaments. Find its efficiency.

7. A generator rated at 10 kW (delivers 10 kW) receives 15 hp. Find its efficiency.

8. A generator delivers 1¼ kW and receives 2 hp. What is its efficiency?

9. A transmission line receives 230 kW and delivers 210 kW. What is the efficiency of transmission?

10. A shunt motor takes 24 A at 220 V and delivers 5 hp. Find the watt output of the motor and its efficiency.

11. A 2-hp motor requires 17 A at 110 V. What percent of the input is delivered at the shaft? What percent is wasted?

12. A "power" transformer draws 1.4 A from a 117-V line. What is the efficiency of the transformer if it delivers 235 V at 0.65 A?

JOB 10-5 FINDING THE OUTPUT AND INPUT OF ELECTRICAL DEVICES

The formula for the percent efficiency may be used to find the values of both the output and the input of electrical devices. The percent efficiency must be expressed as a decimal by moving the decimal point two places to the left.

Finding the output

EXAMPLE 10-16   Find the kilowatt output of a generator if it receives 6 hp and operates at an efficiency of 90 percent.

SOLUTION

Given: Input $= 6$ hp   Find: Output $= ?$

Eff $= 90\% = 0.90$

1   Write the formula.

$$Eff = \frac{output}{input} \qquad (10\text{-}2)$$

2   Substitute.

$$\frac{0.90}{1} = \frac{output}{6}$$

3   Cross-multiply.

$$Output = 6 \times 0.90 = 5.4 \text{ hp}$$

But the output of a generator must be measured in kilowatts. Therefore,

$$5.4 \text{ hp} = 5.4 \times \frac{3}{4} = \frac{16.2}{4} = 4.05 \text{ kW} \qquad Ans.$$

EXAMPLE 10-17   A motor has an efficiency of 87 percent. If it draws 20 A from a 220-V line, what is it hp output?

SOLUTION

Given: Input $\begin{cases} I = 20 \text{ A} \\ E = 220 \text{ V} \end{cases}$ Find: Output = ?

$$\text{Eff} = 87\% = 0.87$$

1   Find the watt input.

$$P = I \times E = 20 \times 220 = 4{,}400 \text{ W input}$$

2   Find the watt output.

$$\text{Eff} = \frac{\text{output}}{\text{input}} \qquad (10\text{-}2)$$

$$\frac{0.87}{1} = \frac{\text{output}}{4{,}400}$$

$$\text{Output} = 4{,}400 \times 0.87 = 3{,}828 \text{ W output}$$

But the output of a motor must be measured in horsepower. Therefore,

$$3{,}828 \text{ W} = 3{,}828 \div 750 = 5.1 \text{ hp} \qquad Ans.$$

Finding the input

EXAMPLE 10-18   How much power is needed to operate a 5-kW generator if its efficiency is 92 percent?

SOLUTION

Given: Output = 5 kW   Find: Input = ?
       Eff = 92% = 0.92

$$\text{Eff} = \frac{\text{output}}{\text{input}} \qquad (10\text{-}2)$$

$$\frac{0.92}{1} = \frac{5}{\text{input}}$$

$$0.92 \times \text{input} = 5$$

$$\text{Input} = \frac{5}{0.92} = 5.43 \text{ kW}$$

But the input to a generator is measured in horsepower. Therefore,

$$5.43 \text{ kW} = 5.43 \times \frac{4}{3} = \frac{21.72}{3} = 7.24 \text{ hp} \qquad Ans.$$

SELF-TEST 10-19   How much current is drawn by a 2½-hp motor if it has an efficiency of 90 percent and operates on 110 V?

SOLUTION

Given: Output = 2½ ____   Find: Input $I = ?$ hp

Eff = 90% = ___(decimal)___   0.90

Input $E = 110$ V

1   Find the power input.

$$\text{Eff} = \frac{\text{output}}{\text{input}} \qquad (10\text{-}2)$$

$$\frac{0.90}{1} = \frac{2.5}{?} \qquad \text{input}$$

$$0.90 \times ? = 2.5 \qquad \text{input}$$

$$\text{Input} = \frac{2.5}{?} \qquad 0.90$$

$$\text{Input} = 2.78 \,\_\_\_\_ \qquad \text{hp}$$

But the input to a motor is measured in watts or _____. Therefore,   kilowatts

$$2.78 \text{ hp} = 2.78 \times \_\_\_\_ \text{ W} \qquad 750$$

or $2.78 \text{ hp} = \_\_\_\_ \text{ W} \quad Ans.$ 2,085

2   Find the current input.

$$P = I \times E \qquad (6\text{-}1)$$

$$\_\_\_\_ = I \times 110 \qquad 2{,}085$$

$$I = \_\_ \text{ A} \quad Ans. \qquad 19$$

PROBLEMS

1. Find the horsepower output of a motor drawing 3 kW and operating at an efficiency of 90 percent.
2. An 80 percent efficient "power" transformer delivers 50 W. Find its power input.
3. Find the horsepower output of a motor drawing 5 A at 110 V and operating at an efficiency of 80 percent.
4. A motor operates at an efficiency of 92 percent and draws 5.5 A from a 110-V line. Find the horsepower output.
5. A transmission line operating at an efficiency of 98 percent receives 20 A at 230 V. Find the power delivered.
6. How much power is delivered by a transformer operating at an efficiency of 88 percent if it draws 0.08 kW?
7. Find the input to a 3-hp motor if its efficiency is 85 percent.
8. Find the horsepower input to a generator delivering 5 kW at an efficiency of 90 percent.
9. A generator delivers 20 A at a voltage of 110 V. Find its output in watts. If it has an efficiency of 90 percent, find the horsepower input.

10. How much current is drawn by a 2-hp motor if it has an efficiency of 87 percent and operates at 110 V?
11. What voltage is necessary to operate a 3-hp motor if it draws 11.37 A and its efficiency is 90 percent?
12. Find the kilowatt output of a generator which uses 9 hp and has an operating efficiency of 92 percent.

JOB 10-6 REVIEW OF CONVERSION FACTORS AND EFFICIENCY

$1 \text{ kW} = \underline{\hspace{1cm}} \text{ W}$	1,000
$1 \text{ hp} = 750 \underline{\hspace{1cm}}$	W
$\text{W} = \text{kW} \times \underline{\hspace{1cm}}$	1,000
$\text{W} = \text{hp} \times \underline{\hspace{1cm}}$	750
$\text{hp} = \text{kW} \times ?$	$\dfrac{4}{3}$
$\text{kW} = \text{hp} \times ?$	$\dfrac{3}{4}$
$\text{kW} = \text{W} \div \underline{\hspace{1cm}}$	1,000
$\text{hp} = \text{W} \div \underline{\hspace{1cm}}$	750

The *efficiency* of a machine is the ratio of the power _____ to the power _____ and is usually expressed as a percent.

output
input

$$\text{Eff} = \frac{\text{output}}{\text{input}} \qquad \boxed{10\text{-}2}$$

Units of measurement

For a generator:

Output is in kilowatts or _____ or voltamperes

Input is in _____

watts
horsepower

For a motor:

Output is in _____

Input is in kilowatts or watts or _____

horsepower
voltamperes

PROBLEMS

1. Change (*a*) 500 W to kilowatts, (*b*) 500 W to horsepower, (*c*) 1.5 kW to watts, (*d*) 1.5 hp to watts, (*e*) 10 kW to horsepower, and (*f*) 10 hp to kilowatts.
2. Find the efficiency of a 1½-hp induction motor using 1.3 kW of power.
3. Find the efficiency of a generator if it delivers 20 A at 120 V and uses 3.5 hp.

4. What is the efficiency of a ¾-hp motor if it draws 5.5 A from a 110-V line?

5. Find the horsepower output of a motor drawing 5 A at 110 V if it operates at an efficiency of 85 percent.

6. Find the kilowatt output of a generator which uses 12 hp and operates at an efficiency of 92 percent.

7. Find the power needed to operate a ¾-hp motor if its efficiency is 90 percent.

8. How much current is drawn from a 120-V line by a 3-hp motor if it operates at an efficiency of 87 percent?

TEST—CONVERSION FACTORS AND EFFICIENCY

1. Change (*a*) 700 W to kilowatts, (*b*) 1¾ hp to watts, (*c*) 3.6 kW to horsepower, and (*d*) 8 hp to kilowatts.

2. What is the efficiency of a 2-hp motor which takes 1.8 kW from a 220-V line?

3. Calculate the horsepower output of a 90 percent efficient motor if it draws 10 A from a 220-V line.

4. How many kilowatts of power are needed to operate a 2½-hp motor if its efficiency at full load is 85%?

5. Find the current drawn from a 110-V line by a 1-hp motor if its efficiency is 89 percent.

11

ELECTRICAL ENERGY

JOB 11-1 FINDING MECHANICAL AND ELECTRICAL ENERGY

One horsepower or one kilowatt represents a certain amount of power. An electric iron which uses 600 W of power is more expensive to operate than a 60-W lamp. However, it would cost more to burn the lamp for 20 h than to use the iron for 1 h. The *cost* of energy depends not only on how much power is used but also on *how long it is used*. Thus, the light used 60 W for 20 h, or $60 \times 20 = 1{,}200$ units of energy. The iron used 600 W for 1 h, or $600 \times 1 = 600$ units of energy. The units of energy are the horsepower-hour (hp · h) and the kilowatthour (kWh).

Mechanical energy. One horsepower-hour is the work done in one hour by a machine delivering one horsepower.

FORMULA

$$\text{hp} \cdot \text{h} = \text{hp} \times \text{h} \qquad \boxed{11\text{-}1}$$

Electrical energy. One kilowatthour is the work done in one hour by a machine using one kilowatt.

FORMULA

$$\text{kWh} = \text{kW} \times \text{h} \qquad \boxed{11\text{-}2}$$

EXAMPLE 11-1 How much work is done by a 5-hp motor which is in operation for 3 h?

SOLUTION

$$\text{hp} \cdot \text{h} = \text{hp} \times \text{h} \qquad (11\text{-}1)$$

$$\text{hp} \cdot \text{h} = 5 \times 3$$

$$\text{Work done} = 15 \text{ hp} \cdot \text{h} \qquad \textit{Ans.}$$

EXAMPLE 11-2   How much energy is delivered in 3 h by a generator rated at 10 kW?

SOLUTION

$$kWh = kW \times h \qquad (11\text{-}2)$$

$$kWh = 10 \times 3$$

$$\text{Energy delivered} = 30 \text{ kWh} \qquad Ans.$$

EXAMPLE 11-3   How much energy is drawn from a 110-V line by two motors in parallel if they draw 4 and 5 A, respectively? The motors are in operation for 2 h.

SOLUTION
The diagram for the circuit is shown in Fig. 11-1.

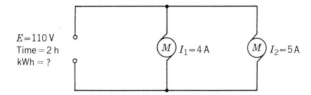

$E = 110$ V
Time $= 2$ h
kWh $= ?$

M) $I_1 = 4$ A M) $I_2 = 5$ A

FIGURE 11-1

1   Find the total current drawn.

$$I_T = I_1 + I_2 \qquad (4\text{-}2)$$

$$I_T = 4 + 5 = 9 \text{ A}$$

2   Find the total power used.

$$P_T = I_T \times E_T \qquad (6\text{-}2)$$

$$P_T = 9 \times 110 = 990 \text{ W}$$

3   Change watts to kilowatts.

$$990 \text{ W} = 990 \div 1{,}000 = 0.99 \text{ kW}$$

4   Find the energy used.

$$\text{Energy} = kW \times h \qquad (11\text{-}2)$$

$$\text{Energy} = 0.99 \times 2 = 1.98 \text{ kWh} \qquad Ans.$$

PROBLEMS

1.   Find the work done by a 3-hp motor operating for 6 h.
2.   Find the energy delivered by a 10-kW generator in 8 h.
3.   Find the work done by three 1½-hp motors in 4 h.
4.   How much energy is delivered in 7½ h by a 40-kW generator?
5.   How much electrical energy is used in 2 h by a bank of six 200-W lamps?

6. The motor in a washing machine uses about 1,200 W. How much energy is used by a Laundromat with six washers if they are all in use 10 h/day for a 6-day week?

7. A radio receiver draws 0.85 A at 110 V. If the set is used 4 h/day, how much energy does it use in 7 days?

8. Seven Christmas-tree lights rated at 15 V and 0.15 A are connected in series. If the lights are used for 7 h/day, how much energy is used per day?

9. A 20-Ω motor drawing 4 A is in operation for 2 h. Find the energy used.

10. How much energy is drawn from a 110-V line by a 22-Ω electric iron in 3 h?

JOB 11-2 COST OF ELECTRICAL ENERGY

A watthour meter is a meter designed to measure the total electrical *energy* used. These meters are installed by the utility companies near the service entrance of a building to record the energy used. The utility company bills the consumer by multiplying the number of units of energy (kWh) by the cost of 1 kWh.

FORMULA

$$\text{Total cost} = \text{kWh} \times \text{unit cost} \qquad \boxed{11\text{-}3}$$

EXAMPLE 11-4   A 5-hp motor has an efficiency of 90 percent. Find the kilowatt input to the motor. What is the cost to run this motor for 2 h at a cost of 5 cents/kWh?

SOLUTION

Given: Output = 5 hp   Find: Input = ?
         Eff = 90% = 0.90   Total cost = ?
       Time = 2 h
   Unit cost = 5¢/kWh

1   Find the input.

$$\text{Eff} = \frac{\text{output}}{\text{input}} \qquad (10\text{-}2)$$

$$\frac{0.90}{1} = \frac{5}{\text{input}}$$

$$0.90 \times \text{input} = 5$$

$$\text{Input} = \frac{5}{0.90} = 5.56 \text{ hp}$$

2   Change horsepower to kilowatts.

$$5.56 \text{ hp} = 5.56 \times \frac{3}{4} = \frac{16.68}{4} = 4.17 \text{ kW}$$

3   Find the energy input.

$$\text{Energy} = \text{kW} \times \text{h} = 4.17 \times 2 = 8.34 \text{ kWh} \qquad (11\text{-}2)$$

4   Find the total cost.

$$\text{Total cost} = \text{kWh} \times \text{unit cost} \qquad (11\text{-}3)$$

$$\text{Total cost} = 8.34 \times 0.05 = \$0.42 \qquad Ans.$$

PROBLEMS

1.   A motor uses 10 kW. At 5 cents/kWh, what is the cost to operate this motor for 3 h?
2.   A 3-hp lathe motor runs 8 h/day. At 4 cents/kWh, find the cost to operate it for 1 day.
3.   At 4 cents/kWh, find the cost to operate a 1½-hp motor on a drill press for 4 h.
4.   At 3 cents/kWh, what is the cost of operating a bank of four 25-hp motors for 2 h?
5.   What is the cost of operating a 3-kW electric heater for 6 h at 6 cents/kWh?
6.   What does it cost to operate a 5.5-kW electric range for 3 h at 5 cents/kWh?
7.   An electric clock uses 2 W of power. What does it cost to operate it for 30 days at 5 cents/kWh?
8.   A bank of five 200-W lamps is connected in parallel. How much will it cost to burn these lamps for 5 h at 4 cents/kWh?
9.   A 3-hp motor has an efficiency of 80 percent. Find the kilowatt input to the motor. What is the cost to operate this motor for 3 h at 4 cents/kWh?
10. A ¾-hp motor has an efficiency of 85 percent. Find the kilowatt input to the motor. What is the cost to operate this motor for 2 h at 5 cents/kWh?

EXAMPLE 11-5   At 5 cents/kWh, how much will it cost to operate a 220-V 25-A motor for 4 h?

SOLUTION

Given: $E = 220$ V   Find: Total cost $= ?$

$I = 25$ A

Time $= 4$ h

Unit cost $= 5¢/\text{kWh}$

1   Find the power used.

$$P = I \times E \qquad (6\text{-}1)$$

$$P = 25 \times 220 = 5{,}500 \text{ W}$$

2   Change watts to kilowatts.

$$5,500 \text{ W} = 5,500 \div 1,000 = 5.5 \text{ kW}$$

3   Find the energy used.

$$\text{Energy} = \text{kW} \times \text{h} \tag{11-2}$$

$$\text{Energy} = 5.5 \times 4 = 22 \text{ kWh}$$

4   Find the total cost.

$$\text{Total cost} = \text{kWh} \times \text{unit cost} \tag{11-3}$$

$$\text{Total cost} = 22 \times 0.05 = \$1.10 \qquad Ans.$$

PROBLEMS

1.   What is the cost of operating an electric fan for 9 h at 5 cents/kWh if it draws 0.75 A from a 110-V line?

2.   What is the cost to operate an electroplating tank for 5 h at 4 cents/kWh if it draws 90 A at 24 V?

3.   A Tungar battery charger uses 15 A at 110 V. What is the cost to charge a bank of storage batteries at 5 cents/kWh if it requires 1 h to charge the batteries?

4.   At 7 cents/kWh, what is the cost of running a washing machine for 2 h if it takes 2.1 A at 110 V?

5.   What is the cost of operating a radio receiver for 5 h/day for 1 week at the rate of 4 cents/kWh? The set draws 0.9 A from a 110-V line.

6.   An electric refrigerator is in operation about 2 h/day. If it draws 3.5 A at 110 V, find the cost to operate this refrigerator for 30 days at 5 cents/kWh.

7.   An automobile headlight lamp draws 3 A at 6 V. If it is used for 3 h a day for a year of 300 days, find the cost at 5 cents/kWh. How does this cost compare with the \$16 cost of an ordinary automobile storage battery which can be expected to last for 2 years?

EXAMPLE 11-6   A 22-Ω toaster in a cafeteria draws 5 A. What is the cost to operate this toaster for 3 h/day for 25 days a month at 5 cents/kWh?

SOLUTION

Given: $R = 22 \ \Omega$ Find: Total cost = ?

$I = 5$ A

Unit cost = 5¢/kWh

Time = 3 h/day for 25 days

1   Find the power used.

$$P = I^2 R \tag{6-4}$$

$$P = 5^2 \times 22 = 25 \times 22 = 550 \text{ W}$$

2   Change watts to kilowatts.

$$550 \text{ W} = 550 \div 1,000 = 0.55 \text{ kW}$$

3   Find the hours of use.

$$25 \text{ days} \times 3 \text{ h/day} = 75 \text{ h}$$

4   Find the energy used.

$$\text{Energy} = \text{kW} \times \text{h} \qquad\qquad (11\text{-}2)$$

$$\text{Energy} = 0.55 \times 75 = 41.25 \text{ kWh}$$

5   Find the total cost.

$$\text{Total cost} = \text{kWh} \times \text{unit cost} \qquad\qquad (11\text{-}3)$$

$$\text{Total cost} = 41.25 \times 0.05 = \$2.06 \qquad Ans.$$

PROBLEMS

1. A current of 5 A is passed through an arc lamp for 2 h. If the re-sistance of the lamp is 4 Ω, how much energy has been used? What is the cost at 4 cents/kWh?
2. The resistance of the copper cables connecting a generator to a switchboard is 0.1 Ω, and 2 V is required to send the full-load cur-rent through them. How much energy is expended in the cables in 10 h? What is the cost at 5 cents/kWh?
3. An electric heater has a resistance of 22 Ω. What does it cost to operate it for 9 h on a 110-V line at 5 cents/kWh?
4. A 20-Ω 5-A motor operates for 5 h/day. What does it cost per day at 4 cents/kWh?
5. A bank of five 100-W lamps is in parallel with a motor drawing 4 A from a 110-V line. Find the cost to operate the circuit for 4 h at 5 cents/kWh.

JOB 11-3   REVIEW OF ELECTRICAL ENERGY

RULE	The total energy used by a device is equal to the power consumed multiplied by the _____ it is in operation.	hours
	Mechanical energy (hp $\cdot$ h) = hp $\times$? $\boxed{11\text{-}1}$	h
	Electrical energy (kWh) = ? $\times$ h $\boxed{11\text{-}2}$	kW
RULE	The total cost of electrical energy is equal to the number of kilowatthours of energy multiplied by the cost per _____.	kilowatthour

$$\text{Total} \underline{\hspace{1cm}} = \text{kWh} \times \text{unit cost} \qquad \boxed{11\text{-}3} \qquad | \quad \text{cost}$$

The total power in an electrical circuit is given by the following formulas:

$$P_T = I_T \times E_T \qquad\qquad\qquad (6\text{-}2)$$

$$P_T = P_1 + P_2 + P_3 \qquad\qquad (6\text{-}3)$$

$$P_T = I^2 R \qquad\qquad\qquad\qquad (6\text{-}4)$$

$$P_T = \frac{E^2}{R} \qquad\qquad\qquad\qquad (6\text{-}5)$$

PROBLEMS

1. Find the total work accomplished in 3 h by a ½-hp motor in parallel with a ¾-hp motor.
2. Find the energy delivered in 2½ h by a generator rated at 8 kW.
3. How much electrical energy is used in 2 h by two 100-W lamps and three 75-W lamps in parallel?
4. How many kilowatthours are used in 2¼ h by a motor drawing 2.6 A at 24 V from the secondary of a toy-train transformer?
5. A washing-machine motor draws 4.8 A at 117 V. Find the cost to operate the machine for 2 h/day for 20 days at 5 cents/kWh.
6. How much electrical energy is drawn in 2 h from a 110-V line by a 22-Ω iron in parallel with an electric heater drawing 6 A? '
7. At 5 cents/kWh, find the cost to run a 3-hp motor for 3 h if it operates at an efficiency of 80 percent.
8. Find the cost to operate a 16-Ω electric heater on a 120-V line for 5 h at a rate of 5 cents/kWh.
9. An electric broiler has a resistance of 12 Ω. If it draws 10 A of current, what does it cost to operate it for 2½ h at 5 cents/kWh?
10. Two 100-W lamps are in parallel with a motor drawing 5 A from a 117-V line. Find the cost of operation for 3½ h at 6 cents/kWh.

TEST—COST OF ENERGY

1. How much energy is needed to operate a 2-hp motor for 2 h if its efficiency is 90 percent?
2. A motor drawing 6.5 A at 110 V is in operation for 3 h. At 5 cents/kWh, what is the cost?
3. At 5 cents/kWh, what is the cost to operate a 9-Ω electric range drawing 12 A for 4 h?
4. An electric drier has a resistance of 11 Ω. At 5 cents/kWh, what is the cost to operate it for 2 h from a 110-V line?

12

RESISTANCE OF WIRE

JOB 12-1   CHECKUP ON RATIO AND PROPORTION
(DIAGNOSTIC TEST)

Many complicated ideas may be expressed quite simply when written in formula form. For example, the rule "In a series circuit, the voltage is directly proportional to the resistance" may be written as $E_1/E_2 = R_1/R_2$. Or "The resistance of a wire is inversely proportional to its area" may be written as $R_1/R_2 = A_2/A_1$. The mathematical concepts of *ratio and proportion* enable us to compare voltages, currents, etc., and to show how they depend on each other. We shall be using these ideas in the next and succeeding jobs. Let us check up on what we know about ratio and proportion. If you have any difficulty with any of the following problems, turn to Job 12-2 which follows.

PROBLEMS

1.   What is the ratio of 12 to 30 in?
2.   Two pulleys have diameters of 20 and 5 in, respectively. What is the ratio of their diameters?
3.   If the number of turns of wire on the primary of a bell-ringing transformer is 360 turns and the secondary has 40 turns, what is the turns ratio of primary to secondary?
4.   The power factor (PF) of an ac circuit is described as the ratio of its resistance R to its impedance Z. Find the PF if $R = 500 \ \Omega$ and $Z = 550 \ \Omega$.
5.   What is the ratio of 1 hp to 1 kW?
6.   A wire 30 ft long has a resistance of 0.02 Ω. If the resistance is directly proportional to the length, find the resistance of 10 ft of this wire.
7.   If 60 ft of conduit costs $3.50, how much does 150 ft cost?
8.   The ratio of acid to water in the electrolyte of a storage battery is 2:3. If 30 oz of acid is used to prepare a batch of electrolyte, how much water should be mixed with it?

9. In a simple transformer, the voltage is directly proportional to the number of turns. In a simple step-down transformer, the primary has 240 turns and the secondary has 30 turns. Find the voltage of the secondary if the primary voltage is 120 V.

10. The resistance of a wire is inversely proportional to its cross-sectional area. If a wire whose area is 5,200 units has a resistance of 2 Ω, find the resistance of a wire of the same material whose area is 100 units.

11. In a parallel circuit, the current is inversely proportional to the resistance. Write a formula to state this fact.

12. In a series circuit, the voltage drops are directly proportional to the resistances. What is the voltage across a 100-Ω resistance if the voltage across a 500-Ω resistance is 10 V?

JOB 12-2   BRUSHUP ON RATIO AND PROPORTION

Comparing quantities. In our daily lives there are many situations in which we compare quantities. For example, (1) Mr. Jones is richer than Mr. Smith, (2) Joe is heavier than Jack, (3) a foot is shorter than a yard. These statements are adequate in most instances, but in scientific work we need more information. It is not sufficient to say that one resistor is larger than another. We must know *how much larger* it is. For example, if resistor $A = 40$ Ω and resistor $B = 20$ Ω, by subtraction we could say that A is 20 Ω larger than B. Using division, we could say that A is twice as large as B. The method of comparing by subtraction is not so useful as the method using division. For example, in a school election, one class voted 25 for A and 15 for B. The vote for all classes was 500 for A and 300 for B. How did the class vote in comparison with the voting for the entire school? Using the subtraction method, all we can say is that the class voted in *about* the same way as the school, that is, more for A than for B. However, if we use the method of division,

Class vote: $$\frac{A}{B} = \frac{25}{15} = \frac{5}{3}$$

School vote: $$\frac{A}{B} = \frac{500}{300} = \frac{5}{3}$$

After reducing to lowest terms, we can see that the class voted in *exactly* the same manner as the school. In the class, voting 25 to 15, for every 5 votes for A, there were 3 votes for B. In the school, voting 500 to 300, for every 5 votes for A, there were 3 votes for B.

Ratio. When two quantities are compared by division, the quotient is called the *ratio* of the quantities. In the example above, the ratio of the vote for *A* compared with the vote for *B* is 5 compared with 3. The ratio of the vote for *B* compared with the vote for *A* is 3 compared with 5. The ratio of *A* compared with *B* may be written as a fraction (⁵/₃), using two dots as a ratio sign (5:3), or with words (5 to 3). In every instance, it means that for every 5 for *A* there are 3 for *B*. It also means that *A* has ⁵/₃, or 1²/₃, times as many votes as *B* or that *B* has ³/₅ as many votes as *A*.

Units of a ratio. The comparison, or ratio, of 2 yd to 1 ft is *not* 2 to 1. This would mean that 2 yd is only twice as large as 1 ft, when actually it is six times as large. Therefore, in order to compare two quantities, they must be measured in the *same units* of measurement. Also, the quantities themselves must be of the same *kind*, like two resistances, two voltages, two lengths, or two areas. Since 2 yd and 1 ft are both lengths, we may compare them by division.

$$\frac{2 \text{ yd}}{1 \text{ ft}} = \frac{6 \text{ ft}}{1 \text{ ft}} = \frac{6}{1} = 6:1 = 6 \text{ to } 1$$

Since the units of measurement are identical, they cancel out. Thus, a ratio itself has no units of measurement.

RULE	To find the ratio of two similar quantities:
	  1 Express them in the same units of measurement.
	  2 Form a fraction using the first quantity as the numerator and the second quantity as the denominator.
	  3 Express in lowest terms.

EXAMPLE 12-1   Find the ratio of 1 mV to 1 V.

SOLUTION
Given: The quantities 1 mV and 1 V   Find: Ratio = ?

$$\text{Ratio} = \frac{1 \text{ mV}}{1 \text{ V}} = \frac{1 \text{ mV}}{1{,}000 \text{ mV}} = \frac{1}{1{,}000} \text{ or } 1{:}1{,}000 \text{ (read as 1 to 1,000)}$$

EXAMPLE 12-2   Find the ratio of 1 hp to 1 kW.

SOLUTION
Given: The quantities 1 hp and 1 kW   Find: Ratio = ?

If it is difficult to change one unit into the other or vice versa, then change both units into a third unit. Since 1 hp = 750 W and 1 kW = 1,000 W,

$$\text{Ratio} = \frac{1 \text{ hp}}{1 \text{ kW}} = \frac{750 \text{ W}}{1{,}000 \text{ W}} = \frac{3}{4} \text{ or } 3{:}4 \text{ (read as 3 to 4)} \qquad Ans.$$

Not all ratios are expressed as fractions. It is sometimes more convenient to express the ratio as a decimal or as a percent. Also, the *order* in which the quantities are compared is very important. In trigonometry, the ratio of the side *o* to the side *a* is called the tangent ratio, while the ratio of the side *a* to the side *o* is called the cotangent ratio.

EXAMPLE 12-3   Find the tangent ratio and the cotangent ratio for angle *A* in the triangle shown in Fig. 12-1.

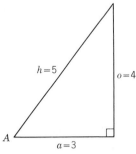

FIGURE 12-1

SOLUTION

$$\text{Tangent ratio} = \frac{o}{a} = \frac{4}{3} \quad Ans.$$

$$\text{Cotangent ratio} = \frac{a}{o} = \frac{3}{4} \quad Ans.$$

EXAMPLE 12-4   The power factor (PF) of an ac circuit is the ratio of its resistance *R* to its impedance *Z*. Find the PF of a circuit if $R = 2.46 \ \Omega$ and $Z = 30 \ \Omega$.

SOLUTION
Given: $R = 2.46 \ \Omega$ Find: PF = ?
        $Z = 30 \ \Omega$

$$\text{PF} = \frac{R}{Z} = \frac{2.46}{30} = 0.082$$

Since PF is often expressed as a percent,

$$\text{PF} = 0.082 \text{ or } 8.2\% \quad Ans.$$

EXAMPLE 12-5   The efficiency of a motor is the ratio of the output to the input and is described as a percent. Find the efficiency of a motor whose output is 5 hp and whose input is 4 kW.

SOLUTION
Given: Output = 5 hp   Find: Eff = ?
        Input = 4 kW

$$\text{Eff} = \frac{\text{output}}{\text{input}} = \frac{5 \text{ hp}}{4 \text{ kW}}$$

$$= \frac{5 \times 750}{4 \times 1,000} = \frac{3,750 \text{ W}}{4,000 \text{ W}} = 0.9375$$

$$\text{Eff} = 0.9375 = 93.75\% \qquad Ans.$$

PROBLEMS

Find the ratio of the quantities in each problem.

1. 3 in to 12 in   2. 6 ft to 2 ft
3. 18 V to 27 V   4. 105 turns to 20 turns
5. 3 ft to 18 in   6. 2 kHz to 500 Hz
7. 0.4 MΩ to 100,000 Ω   8. 2 hp to 3 kW
9. In Fig. 12-2, find (*a*) the ratio of D_2 to D_1 and (*b*) the ratio of D_1 to D_2.

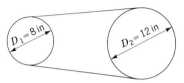

FIGURE 12-2

10. Find the teeth ratio of two gears if the first has 35 teeth and the second has 30 teeth.
11. In Fig. 12-3, the turns ratio of the transformer is the ratio of the number of turns on the primary coil N_p to the number of turns on the secondary coil N_s. Find the turns ratio.

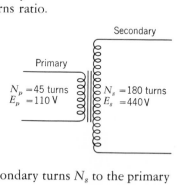

FIGURE 12-3

A step-up transformer.

12. In Fig. 12-3, find the ratio of the secondary turns N_s to the primary turns N_p.
13. In Fig. 12-3, find the ratio of the primary voltage E_p to the secondary voltage E_s.
14. If the primary voltage E_p of a transformer is 125 V and the secondary voltage E_s is 20 V, find the ratio of E_p to E_s.
15. Find the efficiency of a motor if the output is 2 hp and the input is 1.8 kW.

16. The quality Q of a coil is the ratio of its reactance X to its resistance R. Find the Q of an RF coil if its reactance is 2,500 Ω and its resistance is 25 Ω.

17. Find the Q of a tuned circuit if $X = 12,000$ Ω and $R = 70$ Ω.

18. In a triangle similar to that shown in Fig. 12-1, the sine is the ratio of o to h, the cosine is the ratio of a to h, and the tangent is the ratio of o to a. Find the value of all three functions if $o = 7$, $a = 24$, and $h = 25$.

19. β, the current gain of a transistor, is defined as the ratio of the collector current I_C to the base current I_B. Find the β of a transistor if $I_B = 5$ μA and $I_C = 200$ μA.

20. Find the PF of an ac circuit if $R = 56.8$ Ω and $Z = 65$ Ω.

21. The multiplying power of a meter is the ratio of the new voltage to the old voltage. Find the multiplying power of a voltmeter reading 10 V if it is extended to read 100 V.

22. Find the multiplying power of a 150-V 150,000-Ω voltmeter which has been extended to read 750 V.

23. What is the ratio of the distance on a drawing to the actual distance if the scale of the drawing is $\frac{1}{4}$ in equals 1 ft?

24. If 34 oz of acid is mixed with 51 oz of water to make the electrolyte for a storage battery, find (a) the ratio of acid to water and (b) the ratio of water to acid.

25. A generator rated at 117 V supplies 115 V to a motor some distance away. Find (a) the line loss in volts, (b) the ratio of the line loss to the rated voltage in percent, and (c) the ratio of the load voltage to the rated voltage in percent.

Proportion. Consider the following statement. If 3 pencils cost 8 cents, then 6 pencils will cost 16 cents. At the given rate, the cost depends only on the number of pencils bought. The more pencils bought, the larger the cost. The fewer pencils bought, the smaller the cost. When two quantities depend on each other, the relationship between them may be stated as a *proportion*.

A proportion is a mathematical statement that two ratios are equal. In our problem, the two quantities are the number of pencils N and the cost C.

First purchase	Second purchase
$N_1 = 3$ pencils	$N_2 = 6$ pencils
$C_1 = 8$ cents	$C_2 = 16$ cents

The ratio of the number of pencils is

$$\frac{N_1}{N_2} = \frac{3}{6} = \frac{1}{2}$$

The ratio of the costs is

$$\frac{C_1}{C_2} = \frac{8}{16} = \frac{1}{2}$$

Since the two ratios are equal, the proportion may be written mathematically as

$$\frac{N_1}{N_2} = \frac{C_1}{C_2}$$

and is an example of a *direct proportion*.

Direct proportion. When two quantities depend on each other so that one increases as the other increases or one decreases as the other decreases, they are said to be *directly proportional* to each other. Notice that the two ratios are compared in the *same order* so that the items in the first situation (N_1 and C_1) are in the numerator and the items in the second situation (N_2 and C_2) are in the denominator. The proportion may be written as

$$\frac{C_1}{C_2} = \frac{N_1}{N_2} \quad \text{or} \quad \frac{C_2}{C_1} = \frac{N_2}{N_1} \quad \text{or} \quad \frac{N_2}{N_1} = \frac{C_2}{C_1} \quad \text{or} \quad \frac{N_1}{N_2} = \frac{C_1}{C_2}$$

It is not important which ratio is written first. However, once the first ratio is written, the second ratio must be written *in the same order.*

> **RULE**
>
> To set up a direct proportion between two variables:
>
> 1 Make a ratio of one of the variables.
> 2 Make a ratio of the second variable in the same order.
> 3 Set the two ratios equal to each other.

EXAMPLE 12-6 Write as a proportion: The weight of a pipe is directly proportional to its length.

SOLUTION

First pipe | Second pipe
Length $= L_1$ | Length $= L_2$
Weight $= W_1$ | Weight $= W_2$

Since the ratio of the lengths (L_1/L_2) and the ratio of the weights (W_1/W_2) are equal, the proportion may be written as

$$\frac{L_1}{L_2} = \frac{W_1}{W_2} \quad \text{or} \quad \frac{W_1}{W_2} = \frac{L_1}{L_2}$$

or since the ratio of the lengths (L_2/L_1) and the ratio of the weights

(W_2/W_1) are equal, the proportion may also be written as

$$\frac{L_2}{L_1} = \frac{W_2}{W_1} \qquad \text{or} \qquad \frac{W_2}{W_1} = \frac{L_2}{L_1}$$

RULE

To solve problems involving direct proportion:

1 Set up the proportion.
2 Substitute the values.
3 Solve by cross multiplication.

EXAMPLE 12-7   In the series circuit shown in Fig. 12-4, the voltage across any resistor is directly proportional to the resistance of the resistor. Find the value of E_2.

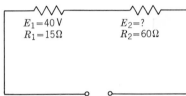

$E_1 = 40$ V
$R_1 = 15\Omega$

$E_2 = ?$
$R_2 = 60\Omega$

FIGURE 12-4

SOLUTION

1 Set up the direct proportion.

$$\frac{E_1}{E_2} = \frac{R_1}{R_2}$$

2 Substitute numbers.

$$\frac{40}{E_2} = \frac{15}{60}$$

3 Cross-multiply.

$$15 \times E_2 = 40 \times 60$$

4 Solve for E_2.

$$E_2 = \frac{2{,}400}{15} = 160 \text{ V} \qquad Ans.$$

SELF-TEST 12-8   An automobile can travel 280 miles in 7 h. At the same rate of speed, how long will it take to travel 200 miles?

SOLUTION

This is an example of a direct proportion, since the distance increases as the time _____ and the distance traveled depends on the _____ spent traveling.

Given: $D_1 =$ ____ mi   Find: $T_2 = ?$
 $T_1 =$ ____ h
 ____ = 200 mi

| |
| increases   time |
| 280 |
| 7 |
| D_2 |

1   Set up the direct proportion.

$$\frac{D_1}{D_2} = \frac{?}{?}$$

T_1
T_2

2   Substitute numbers.

$$\frac{280}{200} = \frac{7}{?}$$

T_2

3   Cross-multiply.

$$280 \times T_2 = 200 \times \underline{\quad}$$

7

4   Solve for T_2.

$$T_2 = \frac{1,400}{?}$$

280

$$T_2 = \underline{\quad} \text{ h} \qquad Ans.$$

5

PROBLEMS

1.   An 8-ft-long steel beam weighs 2,200 lb. What would be the weight of a similar beam 10 ft long?

2.   If 1 gross (144) of resistors costs $2.60, how much do 36 resistors cost?

3.   An airplane can travel 2,040 mi in 6 h. At the same rate, how long would it take the plane to travel 1,530 mi?

4.   The shadows cast by vertical poles are directly proportional to the heights of the poles. If a pole 9 ft high casts a shadow 12 ft long, how high is a tree that casts a shadow 36 ft long?

5.   The volume of a gas is directly proportional to the temperature. If a gas occupies 100 ft³ at 70°F, what volume will it occupy at 50°F, assuming the pressure to be constant?

6.   If 14 lb of cement is used to make 70 lb of concrete, how many pounds of concrete can be made with 30 lb of cement?

7.   Using a diagram similar to Fig. 12-4, find R_1 if $E_1 = 20$ V, $E_2 = 36$ V, and $R_2 = 1,800$ Ω.

8.   If a 500-ft length of wire has a resistance of 30 Ω, find the resistance of an 850-ft length of the same wire. Use the fact that the resistance of identical wires is directly proportional to the length.

9.   In a transformer, the voltage is directly proportional to the number of turns. In a diagram similar to that shown in Fig. 12-3, find the secondary voltage E_s if $N_p = 160$ turns, $E_p = 18$ V, and $N_s = 400$ turns.

10.   The Elco stereo amplifier model 3080 uses a series-circuit base-bias voltage divider similar to that shown in Fig. 12-5. Find the value of the bias voltage E_2.

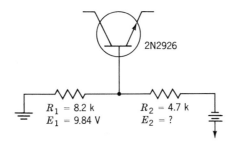

FIGURE 12-5

A series-circuit base-bias
voltage divider.

$R_1 = 8.2$ k $R_2 = 4.7$ k
$E_1 = 9.84$ V $E_2 = ?$

Inverse proportion. When two gears are meshed as shown in Fig. 12-6, the smaller the gear, the faster it turns. When gear 1 turns once, its

Gear No. 1   Gear No. 2

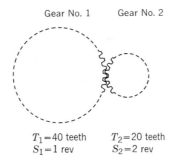

$T_1 = 40$ teeth $T_2 = 20$ teeth
$S_1 = 1$ rev $S_2 = 2$ rev

FIGURE 12-6

The speed is inversely
proportional to the number
of teeth.

40 teeth must engage 40 teeth on gear 2. Therefore, gear 2 must turn *twice* in order for 40 teeth (2×20) to mesh with the 40 teeth on gear 1. When two quantities depend on each other so that one *increases* as the other *decreases* or one *decreases* as the other *increases,* they are said to be *inversely proportional* to each other. This may be written mathematically as

$$\frac{T_1}{T_2} = \frac{S_2}{S_1}$$

Notice that the two ratios are compared in the *opposite,* or *inverse,* order. The proportion will be correct regardless of which ratio is written first *provided* the second ratio is written in the *opposite order.* Thus, the proportion may be written as

$$\frac{T_1}{T_2} = \frac{S_2}{S_1} \quad \text{or} \quad \frac{T_2}{T_1} = \frac{S_1}{S_2} \quad \text{or} \quad \frac{S_1}{S_2} = \frac{T_2}{T_1} \quad \text{or} \quad \frac{S_2}{S_1} = \frac{T_1}{T_2}$$

RULE

To set up an inverse proportion between two variables:

1 Make a ratio of one variable.
2 Make a ratio of the second variable in the opposite order.
3 Set the two ratios equal to each other.

EXAMPLE 12-9   Write as a proportion: "The speeds of pulleys are inversely proportional to the diameters."

SOLUTION
The diagram for the problem is shown in Fig. 12-7.

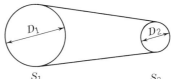

S_1 S_2 **FIGURE 12-7**

$$\frac{D_1}{D_2} = \frac{S_2}{S_1} \quad \text{or} \quad \frac{S_1}{S_2} = \frac{D_2}{D_1} \quad \text{or} \quad \frac{D_2}{D_1} = \frac{S_1}{S_2} \quad \text{or} \quad \frac{S_2}{S_1} = \frac{D_1}{D_2}$$

RULE	To solve problems involving inverse proportion: 1 Set up the proportion. 2 Substitute the values. 3 Solve by cross multiplication.

EXAMPLE 12-10   The resistance of a length of wire is inversely proportional to its cross-sectional area. A certain copper wire has a resistance of 32 Ω and a cross-sectional area of 20 units. Find the resistance of another wire of the same length whose area is 100 units.

SOLUTION
Given: $R_1 = 32\ \Omega$ Find: $R_2 = ?$
$\quad\quad\quad A_1 = 20$
$\quad\quad\quad A_2 = 100$

$$\frac{R_1}{R_2} = \frac{A_2}{A_1}$$

$$\frac{32}{R_2} = \frac{100}{20}$$

$$100R_2 = 32 \times 20$$

$$R_2 = \frac{640}{100} = 6.4\ \Omega \quad \textit{Ans.}$$

SELF-TEST 12-11   In a parallel circuit, the currents are inversely proportional to the resistances. In the circuit shown in Fig. 12-8, find I_2.

SOLUTION
1   The variables in this problem are the current and the _____.   resistance

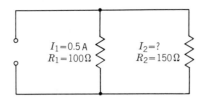

FIGURE 12-8

2   Set up a ratio comparing the currents I_1 to I_2.

$$\frac{?}{?}$$

I_1
I_2

3   Since the currents are *inversely* proportional to the resistances, set up an *inverse* ratio of resistances.

$$\frac{?}{?}$$

R_2
R_1

4   Since the two variables are proportional, the ratios may be set _____ to each other.

equal

$$\frac{I_1}{I_2} = \frac{?}{?}$$

R_2
R_1

5   Substitute numbers.

$$\frac{0.5}{I_2} = \frac{150}{?}$$

100

6   Solve for I_2.

$$150 I_2 = 0.5 \times 100$$

$$I_2 = \frac{50}{?}$$

150

$$I_2 = \underline{\quad} \text{ A} \qquad Ans.$$

0.33

PROBLEMS

The speeds of pulleys are inversely proportional to their diameters. Using Fig. 12-7,

1.   Find D_1 if $S_1 = 40$ rpm, $S_2 = 100$ rpm, and $D_2 = 2$ in.
2.   Find S_1 if $D_1 = 5$ in, $D_2 = 6$ in, and $S_2 = 120$ rpm.

The resistance of a wire is inversely proportional to its cross-sectional area.

3.   Find R_2 if $A_1 = 200$, $R_1 = 50$ Ω, and $A_2 = 150$.
4.   Find A_2 if $A_1 = 200$, $R_1 = 50$ Ω, and $R_2 = 10$ Ω.
5.   Find A_1 if $R_1 = 20$ Ω, $A_2 = 10,000$, and $R_2 = 1$ Ω.
6.   Find R_1 if $A_1 = 30$, $A_2 = 600$, and $R_2 = 16$ Ω.

In a parallel circuit, the currents are inversely proportional to the resistances. Using a diagram similar to Fig. 12-8,

7. Find I_1 if $I_2 = 0.06$ A, $R_1 = 30\ \Omega$, and $R_2 = 40\ \Omega$.
8. Find R_2 if $I_1 = 2$ A, $I_2 = 4.5$ A, and $R_1 = 90\ \Omega$.
9. Find R_1 if $I_1 = 2.25$ A, $I_2 = 3.5$ A, and $R_2 = 0.6\ \Omega$.

In a transformer, the currents in the primary and secondary coils are inversely proportional to the voltages. Using a diagram similar to that shown in Fig. 12-3,

10. Find E_s if $E_p = 120$ V, $I_p = 5$ A, and $I_s = 2$ A.
11. Find I_p if $E_p = 120$ V, $E_s = 15$ V, and $I_s = 2$ A.
12. Find I_s if $E_p = 120$ V, $I_p = 4$ A, and $E_s = 6$ V.

JOB 12-3   REVIEW OF RATIO AND PROPORTION

A *ratio* is the _____ of two quantities of the same kind.	comparison
A ratio is indicated by the _____ of the quantities.	division
A ratio may be written as (1) 8 to 2, (2) 8:2, or (3) $^8/_2$ and is always read as _____.	"8 to 2"
The two quantities of a ratio must always be measured in the _____ units of measurement.	same
A *proportion* is a mathematical statement that two ratios are _____.	equal

In a *direct proportion*, the two quantities increase or decrease together. This is indicated by comparing the two ratios in the <u>(same/opposite)</u> order. Thus, if A is directly proportional to B,

$$\frac{A_1}{A_2} = \frac{B_1}{B_2} \quad \text{or} \quad \frac{B_1}{B_2} = \frac{?}{?}$$

or

$$\frac{A_2}{A_1} = \frac{?}{?}$$

or

$$\frac{B_2}{B_1} = \frac{?}{?}$$

same

A_1
A_2

B_2
B_1

A_2
A_1

In an *inverse proportion*, as one quantity increases, the other _____, and vice versa. This is indicated by comparing the two ratios in the <u>(same/opposite)</u> order. Thus, if C is inversely proportional to D,

$$\frac{C_1}{C_2} = \frac{D_2}{D_1} \quad \text{or} \quad \frac{D_2}{D_1} = \frac{?}{?}$$

or

$$\frac{C_2}{C_1} = \frac{?}{?}$$

or

$$\frac{D_1}{D_2} = \frac{?}{?}$$

decreases

opposite

C_1
C_2

D_1
D_2

C_2
C_1

PROBLEMS

1. Find the ratio of (*a*) 6 to 18 in, (*b*) 1 ft to 2 yd, (*c*) 100 mA to 1 A, (*d*) 500 Hz to 0.8 kHz, and (*e*) 4 hp to 4 kW.
2. In a series circuit, the voltage across a resistance is directly pro-

portional to the resistance. Using a circuit similar to that shown in Fig. 12-4, find R_1 if $E_1 = 90$ V, $E_2 = 48$ V, and $R_2 = 80$ Ω.

In Probs. 3 to 6, A is directly proportional to B.

3. Find B_2 if $A_1 = 15$, $A_2 = 6$, and $B_1 = 90$.
4. Find B_1 if $A_1 = 35$, $A_2 = 45$, and $B_2 = 63$.
5. Find A_2 if $A_1 = 27$, $B_1 = 3$, and $B_2 = 8$.
6. Find A_1 if $A_2 = 56$, $B_1 = 4$, and $B_2 = 7$.

In a parallel circuit similar to that shown in Fig. 12-8, the current in each branch is inversely proportional to the resistance.

7. Find I_1 if $I_2 = 0.4$ A, $R_1 = 100$ Ω, and $R_2 = 150$ Ω.
8. Find I_2 if $I_1 = 1.8$ A, $R_1 = 225$ Ω, and $R_2 = 75$ Ω.

In a transformer, the currents in the primary and secondary coils are inversely proportional to the voltages. Using a diagram similar to that shown in Fig. 12-3,

9. Find E_p if $E_s = 2,200$ V, $I_p = 50$ A, and $I_s = 2.5$ A.
10. Find I_p if $E_p = 24$ V, $E_s = 120$ V, and $I_s = 0.2$ A.

TEST—RATIO AND PROPORTION

1. Find the ratio of (*a*) 5 dimes to 3 nickels, (*b*) 18 in to 2 yd, (*c*) 3 kW to 8 hp, (*d*) 400 mV to 2 V, and (*e*) 2 h to 15 min.
2. *a.* A baseball team won 30 games and lost 20 games. What is the ratio of the games won to the games played?
   b. In an electronics class, 20 boys passed and 5 boys failed. What is the ratio of the boys passing to the total number of boys? Express this ratio as a percent.
   c. A "power" transformer draws 1.2 A from a 120-V line and delivers 175 V at 0.8 A. Find the ratio of the power output to the power input.
   d. If 1 mA flows through a milliammeter and 99 mA flows through its shunt, find the ratio of the meter current to the line current.
3. In a transformer, the voltage is directly proportional to the number of turns. In a diagram similar to that shown in Fig. 12-3, find the number of turns on the secondary N_s if $N_p = 200$ turns, $E_p = 20$ V, and $E_s = 50$ V.
4. In a parallel circuit similar to that shown in Fig. 12-8, the current in each branch is inversely proportional to the resistance. Find R_2 if $I_1 = 0.3$ A, $I_2 = 1.05$ A, and $R_1 = 490$ Ω.

JOB 12-4   THE AMERICAN WIRE GAGE TABLE

Wires are manufactured in standard sizes which are listed in Table 12-1 and are known as the American Wire Gage (AWG). It has been found

TABLE 12-1

AMERICAN WIRE GAGE TABLE

Resistance of bare annealed copper wire at 20°C (68°F)

AWG NO.	DIAMETER, MILS, d	AREA, CIRMILS, d^2	$\Omega/1,000$ FT
0000	460.0	211,600	0.0490
000	409.6	167,800	0.0618
00	364.8	133,100	0.0779
0	324.9	105,500	0.0983
1	289.3	83,690	0.1239
2	257.6	66,360	0.1563
3	229.4	52,630	0.1970
4	204.3	41,740	0.2485
5	181.9	33,100	0.3133
6	162.0	26,250	0.3951
7	144.3	20,820	0.4982
8	128.5	16,510	0.6282
9	114.4	13,090	0.7921
10	101.9	10,380	0.9989
11	90.74	8,234	1.260
12	80.81	6,530	1.588
13	71.96	5,178	2.003
14	64.08	4,107	2.525
15	57.07	3,257	3.184
16	50.82	2,583	4.016
17	45.26	2,048	5.064
18	40.30	1,624	6.385
19	35.89	1,288	8.051
20	31.96	1,022	10.15
21	28.46	810.1	12.80
22	25.35	642.4	16.14
23	22.57	509.5	20.36
24	20.10	404.0	25.67
25	17.90	320.4	32.37
26	15.94	254.1	40.81
27	14.20	201.5	51.47
28	12.64	159.8	64.90
29	11.26	126.7	81.83
30	10.03	100.5	103.2
31	8.928	79.70	130.1
32	7.950	63.21	164.1
33	7.080	50.13	206.9
34	6.305	39.75	260.9
35	5.615	31.52	329.0
36	5.000	25.00	414.8
37	4.453	19.83	523.1
38	3.965	15.72	659.6
39	3.531	12.47	831.8
40	3.145	9.888	1,049

that calculations involving these wires may be simplified by expressing their diameters and cross-sectional areas in new units of measurement.

Mils. The diameter of wires is expressed in terms of *mils* instead of inches.

$$1,000 \text{ mils} = 1 \text{ in} \quad \text{or} \quad 1 \text{ mil} = \frac{1}{1,000} \text{ in}$$

CHANGING UNITS

To change inches to mils: Multiply the number of inches by 1,000.

To change mils to inches: Divide the number of mils by 1,000.

EXAMPLE 12-12   A wire has a diameter of 0.162 in.   Change the diameter to mils and find the AWG number.

SOLUTION

$$0.162 \text{ in} = 0.162 \times 1,000 = 162 \text{ mils} \quad \text{Ans.}$$

In the second column of the AWG table marked "Diameter, mils," read down until you find 162 mils. Read to the left to the column marked "AWG No." to find No. 6 wire.   *Ans.*

EXAMPLE 12-13   A wire has a diameter of ⅛ in. Change the diameter to mils and find the AWG number.

SOLUTION

$$⅛ = 0.125 \text{ in}$$

$$0.125 \text{ in} = 0.125 \times 1,000 = 125 \text{ mils} \quad \text{Ans.}$$

In the second column, read down until you find the number closest to 125. This number is 128.5. Read to the left to the first column to find No. 8 wire.   *Ans.*

EXAMPLE 12-14   Express the diameter of No. 18 wire in mils and inches.

SOLUTION

Read down in the first column until you find No. 18. Read to the right to the second column to find 40.30 mils.

$$40.30 \text{ mils} = 40.30 \div 1,000 = 0.0403 \text{ in} \quad \text{Ans.}$$

PROBLEMS

Using Table 12-1, find the missing values in the following problems.

PROBLEM	GAGE NO.	DIAMETER, MILS	DIAMETER, IN
1	?	28.46	?
2	10	?	?
3	?	?	$1/4$
4	?	?	0.05082
5	?	?	$162/1{,}000$
6	?	204.3	?
7	14	?	?
8	12	?	?
9	?	40.30	?
10	?	?	$1/16$

Circular mils. The circular mil (cirmil) is the unit of area which is used to measure the cross-sectional area of wires. The circular-mil area is used rather than the ordinary units of area because of the ease of obtaining the circular-mil area when the diameter is given in mils.

RULE	To obtain the circular-mil area of a wire, express the diameter in mils and then square the resulting number.

FORMULA

$$A = D_m{}^2$$

12-1

where A = area, cirmils
   D_m = diameter, mils

EXAMPLE 12-15   Find the circular-mil area A of No. 12 wire.

SOLUTION
Read across to the right from No. 12 in the first column to find the circular-mil area in column 3.

   Area of No. 12 wire = 6,530 cirmils   *Ans.*

EXAMPLE 12-16   Find the circular-mil area A of a wire whose diameter is 0.005 in.

SOLUTION

$$0.005 \text{ in} = 0.005 \times 1{,}000 = 5 \text{ mils} = D_m$$

$$A = D_m{}^2 \tag{12-1}$$

$$A = 5^2 = 25 \text{ cirmils} \quad \textit{Ans.}$$

| RULE | To obtain the diameter of a wire in mils, find the square root of the circular-mil area. |

FORMULA

$$D_m = \sqrt{\text{cirmil}}$$

$$\boxed{12\text{-}2}$$

EXAMPLE 12-17   Find the diameter of a wire whose cross-sectional area is 25,000 cirmils.

SOLUTION

$$D_m = \sqrt{\text{cirmil}} \qquad\qquad (12\text{-}2)$$

$$D_m = \sqrt{25,000} = 158 \text{ mils} \qquad Ans.$$

(Review Job 6-9 on square root.)

If the diameter is wanted in inches,

$$158 \text{ mils} = \frac{158}{1,000} = 0.158 \text{ in} \qquad Ans.$$

PROBLEMS

Find the missing values in the following problems:

PROBLEM	DIAMETER, IN	DIAMETER, MILS	AREA, CIRMILS
1	?	10	?
2	0.05	?	?
3	?	?	4,096
4	?	60	?
5	0.032	?	?
6	?	?	9,500
7	?	87.2	?
8	1/4	?	?
9	?	?	30,000
10	0.102	?	?

JOB 12-5   RESISTANCE OF WIRES OF DIFFERENT MATERIALS

All materials differ in their atomic structure and therefore in their ability to resist the flow of an electric current. The measure of the ability of a specific material to resist the flow of electricity is called its *specific resistance.*

The *specific resistance K* of a material is the resistance offered by a wire of this material which is 1 ft long with a diameter of 1 mil. The specific resistances of different materials are given in Table 12-2.

TABLE 12-2
SPECIFIC RESISTANCE OF MATERIALS IN OHMS PER MIL-FOOT AT 20°C

MATERIAL	K	MATERIAL	K
Silver	9.7	Tantalum	93.3
Copper	10.4	German silver (18%)	200
Gold	14.7	Monel metal	253
Aluminum	17.0	Manganin	265
Tungsten	34.0	Magnesium	276
Brass	43.0	Constantan	295
Iron (pure)	60.0	Nichrome	600
Tin	69.0	Nickel	947

RULE   The resistance of a wire is directly proportional to the specific resistance of the material.

FORMULA

$$\frac{R_1}{R_2} = \frac{K_1}{K_2}$$

$\boxed{12\text{-}3}$

where R_1 and K_1 = resistance and specific resistance of a wire of one material, respectively

R_2 and K_2 = resistance and specific resistance of a wire of another material, respectively

EXAMPLE 12-18   A copper wire has a resistance of 5 Ω. What is the resistance of a nichrome wire of the same length and cross-sectional area?

SOLUTION
Given: Copper wire, $R_1 = 5\ \Omega$ Find: R_2 of nichrome = ?
$K_1 = 10.4$
Nichrome wire, $K_2 = 600$

$$\frac{R_1}{R_2} = \frac{K_1}{K_2} \qquad (12\text{-}3)$$

$$\frac{5}{R_2} = \frac{10.4}{600}$$

$$10.4R_2 = 5 \times 600$$

$$10.4R_2 = 3,000$$

$$R_2 = \frac{3,000}{10.4} = 288 \ \Omega \qquad Ans.$$

PROBLEMS

1. A copper wire has a resistance of 12 Ω. What is the resistance of an aluminum wire of the same length and diameter?
2. A tungsten wire has a resistance of 40 Ω. What is the resistance of a nichrome wire of the same length and diameter?
3. A nichrome wire has a resistance of 125 Ω. What is the resistance of an iron wire of the same length and diameter?
4. A copper wire has a resistance of 2.5 Ω. What is the resistance of a manganin wire of the same length and diameter?

JOB 12-6   RESISTANCE OF WIRES OF DIFFERENT LENGTHS

Consider two wires of the same material and diameter but of different lengths. A length of wire may be considered to be made of a large number of small lengths all connected in series. The total resistance of the length of wire is then equal to the sum of the resistances of all the small lengths. Therefore, the longer the wire, the greater its resistance.

RULE	The resistance of a wire is directly proportional to its length.

FORMULA

$$\frac{R_1}{R_2} = \frac{L_1}{L_2} \qquad \boxed{12\text{-}4}$$

where R_1 and L_1 = resistance and length of the first wire, respectively
R_2 and L_2 = resistance and length of the second wire, respectively

EXAMPLE 12-19   If 1,000 ft of No. 16 copper wire has a resistance of 4 Ω, find the resistance of 1,800 ft of the same wire.

SOLUTION
Given: $R_1 = 4 \ \Omega$ Find: $R_2 = ?$
$\qquad L_1 = 1,000$ ft
$\qquad L_2 = 1,800$ ft

$$\frac{R_1}{R_2} = \frac{L_1}{L_2} \qquad\qquad (12\text{-}4)$$

$$\frac{4}{R_2} = \frac{1,000}{1,800}$$

$$1,\overline{0}00R_2 = 1,800 \times 4$$

$$1,000R_2 = 7,200$$

$$R_2 = \frac{7,200}{1,000} = 7.2\ \Omega \qquad Ans.$$

SELF-TEST 12-20   Find the resistance of 700 ft of No. 20 copper wire. What current flows through the wire when there is a voltage drop of 14.2 V across the ends of the wire?

SOLUTION

Given: $L =$ _____ ft of No. 20 copper wire   Find: $R = ?$ | 700
    $E =$ _____ V $I = ?$ | 14.2

1   Find the resistance of No. 20 copper wire. From the Table 12-1, No. 20 wire has a resistance of _____ $\Omega/1,000$ ft. | 10.15

2   Find the resistance of 1 ft of this wire.

$$\frac{R}{\text{ft}} = \frac{10.15}{1,000} = \underline{\hspace{2cm}}\ \Omega/\text{ft}$$ | 0.01015

3   Find the resistance of _____ ft of this wire. | 700

$$R = \frac{R}{\text{ft}} \times \text{ft} = 0.01015 \times 700 = \underline{\hspace{1cm}}\ \Omega \qquad Ans.$$ | 7.1

4   Find the current.

$$E = IR \qquad\qquad (2\text{-}1)$$

$$14.2 = I \times \underline{\hspace{1cm}}$$ | 7.1

$$I = \frac{14.2}{?}$$ | 7.1

$$I = \underline{\hspace{1cm}}\ A \qquad Ans.$$ | 2

PROBLEMS

1.   If 1,000 ft of No. 12 copper wire has a resistance of 1.6 Ω, find the resistance of 2,300 ft of this wire.
2.   Find the resistance of 800 ft of No. 16 copper wire.
3.   Find the resistance of 400 ft of No. 20 copper wire.
4.   What is the resistance of the primary coil of a transformer if it is wound with 600 ft of No. 20 copper wire?
5.   The coil of an electromagnet is wound with 300 ft of No. 16 copper

wire. What is the resistance of the coil? What current will be drawn from a 6-V battery?

6. The coil of an outboard motor is wound with 100 ft of No. 18 copper wire. What current will it draw from a 6-V battery?

7. The four field windings of a motor are connected in series. If each winding uses 50 ft of No. 32 copper wire, find the total resistance of the field windings. What current is drawn when the motor is used on a 110-V line?

8. Find the resistance of a two-wire service line 100 ft long if No. 8 copper wire is used.

9. What is the resistance of a telephone line 1 mi long if No. 18 copper wire is used? What is the voltage drop across this line if the current is 200 mA?

10. Find the resistance of 10 ft of No. 22 copper wire. What is the resistance of the same length of No. 22 nichrome wire? If this nichrome wire is used as the resistance element in an electric furnace, what current is drawn from a 110-V line?

JOB 12-7 RESISTANCE OF WIRES OF DIFFERENT AREAS

The flow of electricity in a wire is very similar to the flow of water in a pipe. A large-diameter pipe can carry more water than a small-diameter pipe. Similarly, a large-diameter wire can carry more current than a small-diameter wire. But the ability of a wire to carry a large current means that its resistance is small. Thus, a large-diameter wire has a small resistance while a small-diameter wire has a large resistance. As we have learned, when two quantities depend on each other so that one increases as the other decreases, and vice versa, the relationship is called an *inverse ratio*.

RULE	The resistance of a wire is inversely proportional to its cross-sectional area.

FORMULA

$$\frac{R_1}{R_2} = \frac{A_2}{A_1} \qquad \boxed{12\text{-}5}$$

where R_1 and A_1 = resistance and area of the first wire, respectively
R_2 and A_2 = resistance and area of the second wire, respectively

EXAMPLE 12-21 A wire has a resistance of 20 Ω and a cross-sectional area of 320 cirmils. Find the resistance of a wire of the same length but with an area of 800 cirmils.

SOLUTION

Given: $R_1 = 20 \ \Omega$ Find: $R_2 = ?$
   $A_1 = 320$ cirmils
   $A_2 = 800$ cirmils

$$\frac{R_1}{R_2} = \frac{A_2}{A_1} \qquad\qquad (12\text{-}5)$$

$$\frac{20}{R_2} = \frac{800}{320}$$

$$800R_2 = 320 \times 20$$

$$R_2 = \frac{6{,}400}{800} = 8 \ \Omega \qquad Ans.$$

EXAMPLE 12-22   A certain length of No. 36 copper wire has a resistance of 200 Ω. Find the resistance of the same length of No. 30 wire.

SOLUTION

Given: First wire: No. 36 $= 200 \ \Omega = R_1$ Find: $R_2 = ?$
   Second wire: No. 30

1 From Table 12-1, find the circular-mil area of each wire.

   A_1 of No. 36 $= 25$ cirmils

   A_2 of No. 30 $= 100$ cirmils (approx)

2 Set up the inverse ratio.

$$\frac{R_1}{R_2} = \frac{A_2}{A_1} \qquad\qquad (12\text{-}5)$$

$$\frac{200}{R_2} = \frac{100}{25}$$

$$100R_2 = 200 \times 25$$

$$R_2 = \frac{5{,}000}{100} = 50 \ \Omega \qquad Ans.$$

PROBLEMS

1. If $R_1 = 21 \ \Omega$, $A_1 = 10{,}000$ cirmils, and $A_2 = 4{,}000$ cirmils, find R_2.
2. A wire has a resistance of 30 Ω and a cross-sectional area of 100 cirmils. Find the resistance of the same length of a wire whose area is 320 cirmils.
3. A certain length of No. 30 wire has a resistance of 50 Ω. Find the resistance of the same length of No. 40 wire.
4. A certain length of No. 36 wire has a resistance of 1.5 Ω. Find the resistance of the same length of No. 34 wire.
5. A certain length of No. 12 wire has a resistance of 3.2 Ω. Find the resistance of the same length of No. 18 wire.

JOB 12-8   RESISTANCE OF WIRES OF ANY DIAMETER, ANY LENGTH, OR ANY MATERIAL

In the last three jobs we learned that

1   The resistance is directly proportional to the specific resistance K of the material
2   The resistance is directly proportional to the length L
3   The resistance is inversely proportional to the area A

These three concepts may be combined into one rule.

RULE	The resistance R of a wire is equal to the specific resistance K multiplied by the length in feet L, and divided by the circular-mil area of the wire A.

FORMULA

$$R = \frac{K \times L}{A} \qquad \boxed{12\text{-}6}$$

where R = resistance of wire, Ω
K = specific resistance for a particular material
L = length of the wire, ft
A = area of the wire, cirmils

EXAMPLE 12-23   Find the resistance of a tungsten wire 10 ft long whose diameter is 0.005 in.

SOLUTION
Given: Tungsten $K = 34$ $\qquad$ Find: $R = ?$
$\qquad\qquad\qquad L = 10$ ft
$\qquad\qquad\qquad D = 0.005$ in

1   Change the diameter to mils.

$$0.005 \text{ in} = 0.005 \times 1{,}000 = 5 \text{ mils}$$

2   Find the circular-mil area.

$$A = D_m{}^2 = 5^2 = 25 \text{ cirmils} \qquad (12\text{-}1)$$

3   Find the resistance of the wire.

$$R = \frac{K \times L}{A} \qquad (12\text{-}6)$$

$$R = \frac{34 \times 10}{25} = \frac{340}{25} = 13.6 \ \Omega \qquad Ans.$$

EXAMPLE 12-24   An electric heater is made with a heating element of 4 ft of No. 30 nichrome wire. (*a*) What is the resistance of the heating coil? (*b*) What current will it draw from a 120-V line? (*c*) How much power will it use?

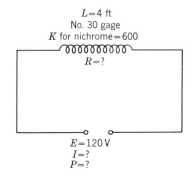

$L=4$ ft
No. 30 gage
K for nichrome $=600$
$R=?$

$E=120$ V
$I=?$
$P=?$

FIGURE 12-9

SOLUTION

The diagram for the problem is shown in Fig. 12-9.

a For the resistance of the heating coil,

1 Find the circular-mil area. From Table 12-1,

No. 30 = 100.5 cirmils = 100 cirmils   (approx)

2 Find the resistance of the coil.

$$R = \frac{K \times L}{A} \qquad (12\text{-}6)$$

$$R = \frac{600 \times 4}{100} = \frac{2{,}400}{100} = 24 \ \Omega \qquad Ans.$$

b Find the current drawn.

$$E = IR \qquad (2\text{-}1)$$

$$120 = I \times 24$$

$$I = \frac{120}{24} = 5 \text{ A} \qquad Ans.$$

c Find the power used.

$$P = I \times E \qquad (6\text{-}1)$$

$$P = 5 \times 120 = 600 \text{ W} \qquad Ans.$$

PROBLEMS

1. Find the resistance of a 0.1-in-diameter copper wire which is 100 ft long.
2. Find the resistance of 150 ft of No. 32 copper wire.
3. Find the resistance of 10 ft of ⅛-in-diameter silver wire.
4. What is the resistance of 20 ft of No. 20 gage manganin wire? What current will flow through the wire if the voltage is 6 V?
5. Find the resistance of 30 ft of No. 24 iron wire. What current will flow through the wire if it is used as a resistance element across 110 V? What is the power used?

6. What is the resistance of ½ ft of No. 40 nichrome wire?
7. A winding made of 400 ft of No. 30 copper wire is placed across 6 V. Find (a) the current drawn and (b) the power used.
8. Find the resistance of 200 ft of copper annunciator wire whose diameter is 0.04 in.
9. The ½-in-diameter copper leads from a welding control are each 1 ft long. What is the voltage drop along these leads when the welding current is 2,500 A?

JOB 12-9 FINDING THE LENGTH OF WIRE NEEDED TO MAKE A CERTAIN RESISTANCE

EXAMPLE 12-25   How many feet of No. 20 gage nichrome wire are required to make a heater coil of 10 Ω resistance?

SOLUTION
Given: K for nichrome $= 600$ Find: $L = ?$
 Gage $=$ No. 20
 $R = 10 \ \Omega$

1 Find the circular-mil area. From Table 12-1, for No. 20 gage,

$$A = 1{,}022 \ \text{cirmils}$$

2 Find the length of the wire.

$$R = \frac{K \times L}{A} \qquad\qquad (12\text{-}6)$$

$$\frac{10}{1} = \frac{600 \times L}{1{,}022}$$

$$600L = 1{,}022 \times 10$$

$$L = \frac{10{,}220}{600} = 17.03 \ \text{ft} \qquad Ans.$$

EXAMPLE 12-26   How much resistance must be placed in series with a 50-V 50-Ω lamp in order to operate it from a 110-V line? How many feet of No. 18 German silver wire are required to make this limiting resistor?

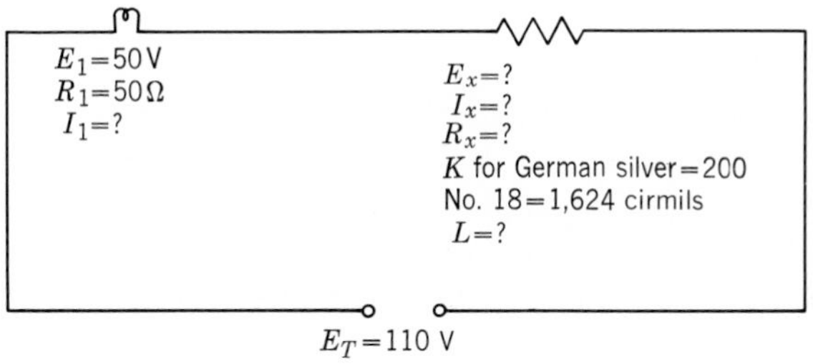

$E_1 = 50 \text{V}$
$R_1 = 50 \Omega$
$I_1 = ?$

$E_x = ?$
$I_x = ?$
$R_x = ?$
K for German silver $= 200$
No. $18 = 1{,}624$ cirmils
$L = ?$

$E_T = 110 \text{ V}$

FIGURE 12-10

SOLUTION

The diagram for the circuit is shown in Fig. 12-10.

1   Find the series current.

$$E_1 = I_1 \times R_1 \qquad\qquad (3\text{-}4)$$

$$50 = I_1 \times 50$$

$$I_1 = \frac{50}{50} = 1 \text{ A}$$

Therefore, $$I_x = I_1 = 1 \text{ A} \qquad\qquad (3\text{-}1)$$

2   Find E_x.

$$E_T = E_1 + E_x \qquad\qquad (3\text{-}2)$$

$$110 = 50 + E_x$$

$$E_x = 110 - 50 = 60 \text{ V}$$

3   Find R_x.

$$E_x = I_x \times R_x \qquad\qquad (3\text{-}5)$$

$$60 = 1 \times R_x$$

$$R_x = 60 \text{ } \Omega \qquad Ans.$$

4   Find the length of wire needed to make a 60-Ω resistor.

$$R = \frac{K \times L}{A} \qquad\qquad (12\text{-}6)$$

$$\frac{60}{1} = \frac{200 \times L}{1{,}624}$$

$$200L = 1{,}624 \times 60$$

$$L = \frac{97{,}440}{200} = 487.2 \text{ ft} \qquad Ans.$$

PROBLEMS

1.   What is the resistance of an aluminum wire 200 ft long if its circular-mil area is 2,000?
2.   What is the resistance of a 100-ft-long constantan wire if its diameter is 80 mils?
3.   How many feet of 0.01-in-diameter copper wire are required to make a resistance of 10 Ω?
4.   A 0.02-in-diameter nichrome wire is used for the coils of an electric heater. If the resistance of the coils is to be 18 Ω, how many feet of wire are needed? What are the current and power drawn when the heater is used on a 110-V line?

5. How many feet of No. 28 copper wire are needed to make an ammeter shunt of 0.2 Ω?

6. What would be the length of the wire in Prob. 5 if manganin wire were used instead of copper?

7. A subway-car heater is made of No. 24 iron wire. It is to operate on 550 V and 10 A. How many feet of wire are needed to make the heater?

8. What resistance must be inserted in series with the heater of a 2BJ2 tube in order to operate it from two dry cells connected in series? The tube takes 2.3 V at 0.3 A. What length of No. 20 iron wire is needed to make the resistance?

9. Which of the following has the greater resistance: (a) 50 ft of No. 20 iron wire or (b) 10 ft of No. 18 nichrome wire?

JOB 12-10   FINDING THE DIAMETER OF WIRE NEEDED TO MAKE A CERTAIN RESISTANCE

EXAMPLE 12-27   What must be the diameter and gage number of a nichrome heating element 40 ft long if the resistance is to be 20 Ω?

SOLUTION
Given: K for nichrome $= 600$ Find: $D = ?$
$\qquad\qquad R = 20\ \Omega$ Gage No. $= ?$
$\qquad\qquad L = 40\ \text{ft}$

1 Find the required circular-mil area.

$$R = \frac{K \times L}{A} \qquad\qquad (12\text{-}6)$$

$$\frac{20}{1} = \frac{600 \times 40}{A}$$

$$20A = 24{,}000$$

$$A = \frac{24{,}000}{20} = 1{,}200 \text{ cirmils}$$

2 Find the diameter in mils.

$$D_m = \sqrt{\text{cirmil}} \qquad\qquad (12\text{-}2)$$

$$D_m = \sqrt{1{,}200} = 34.6 \text{ mils} \qquad Ans.$$

3 Find the gage number. This may be found by looking up the table for either the diameter of 34.6 mils or the area of 1,200 cirmils.

$$\text{No. } 18 = 40.3 \text{ mils} \qquad \text{No. } 18 = 1{,}624 \text{ cirmils}$$

$$? \quad = 34.6 \text{ mils} \qquad ? \quad = 1{,}200 \text{ cirmils}$$

$$\text{No. } 19 = 35.89 \text{ mils} \qquad \text{No. } 19 = 1{,}288 \text{ cirmils}$$

Using either method, the closest gage number is No. 19. However, common practice is always to use the smaller gage number so as to select a wire of smaller resistance and larger current-carrying ability. Therefore, use No. 18 wire.   *Ans.*

EXAMPLE 12-28 Find the size of copper wire to be used in a two-wire system 100 ft long if the total resistance of the system is to be 1.3 Ω.

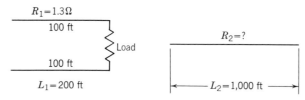

$R_1 = 1.3 \Omega$
100 ft

Load

100 ft

$L_1 = 200$ ft

$R_2 = ?$

$L_2 = 1,000$ ft

FIGURE 12-11

SOLUTION

The diagram for the problem is shown in Fig. 12-11. When the wire is made of copper, we can use the Table 12-1 to simplify our calculations. If we can find the resistance per 1,000 ft, we can look up the table to find the wire which has this resistance. The total length L_1 of the two-wire system equals $2 \times 100 = 200$ ft.

Find the resistance per 1,000 ft.

$$\frac{R_1}{R_2} = \frac{L_1}{L_2} \tag{12-4}$$

$$\frac{1.3}{R_2} = \frac{200}{1,000}$$

$$200 R_2 = 1.3 \times 1,000$$

$$R_2 = \frac{1,300}{200} = 6.5 \ \Omega/1,000 \text{ ft}$$

In column 4 of Table 12-1, the next *smaller* resistance per 1,000 ft is 6.385 Ω. Reading to the left to column 1, we find the gage number to be No. 18.   *Ans.*

PROBLEMS

1. What diameter of constantan wire should be used to make a coil of 10 Ω resistance if only 3 ft of wire is used?
2. What must be the diameter of an aluminum wire 2,000 ft long if its resistance is to be 3 Ω?
3. What must be the diameter of an iron wire 40 ft long if the resistance is to be 50 Ω?
4. What size of copper wire should be used for a single line 200 ft long if the allowable resistance is 1 Ω?
5. What diameter of copper wire should be used for a two-wire system 500 ft long if the total resistance is not to exceed 10 Ω?

6. The heating coil of an electric heater using 4 ft of nichrome wire is to have a resistance of 24 Ω. What gage wire should be used?

7. A rheostat is to be wound with 500 ft of German silver wire to produce a resistance of 60 Ω. What gage wire should be used?

JOB 12-11 REVIEW OF RESISTANCE OF WIRES

A *mil* is the unit used to measure the _____ of round wires. A *mil* is equal to one-_____ of an inch. A *circular mil* (cirmil) is the unit used to measure the cross-sectional _____ of wires.

	diameter
	thousandth
	area

FORMULAS

	1,000
	1,000

$$\boxed{12\text{-}1}$$

$$\boxed{12\text{-}2}$$

where A = area of the wire, _____   cirmils
      D_m = diameter of the wire, _____   mils

The specific resistance K of a wire is the resistance of a wire 1 ft long with a diameter of 1 ____. The specific resistance of different materials is given in Table 12-2.   mil

The resistance of a wire is directly proportional to its specific resistance.

$$\frac{R_1}{R_2} = \frac{K_?}{K_?} \qquad \boxed{12\text{-}3} \qquad \frac{1}{2}$$

The resistance of a wire is directly proportional to its length.

$$\frac{R_1}{R_2} = \frac{L_?}{L_?} \qquad \boxed{12\text{-}4} \qquad \frac{1}{2}$$

The resistance of a wire is inversely proportional to its area.

$$\frac{R_1}{R_2} = \frac{A_?}{A_?} \qquad \boxed{12\text{-}5} \qquad \frac{2}{1}$$

The general formula for the resistance of any wire is

$$R = \frac{K \times L}{?} \qquad \boxed{12\text{-}6} \qquad A$$

where R = resistance of the wire, Ω
      K = specific resistance of the material
      L = length of the wire, ____   ft
      A = area of the wire, _____   cirmils

PROBLEMS

1. Find the diameter in mils and gage number of the wires whose diameters are (*a*) 0.025 in, (*b*) 0.102 in, (*c*) ⅛ in, and (*d*) 128/1,000 in.

2. Find the area in circular mils of wires whose diameters are (a) 15 mils, (b) 40 mils, (c) 0.01 in, and (d) 0.204 in.

3. A constantan wire has a resistance of 50 Ω. What is the resistance of a manganin wire of the same length and area?

4. Find the resistance of a two-wire line 500 ft long using No. 20 copper wire. Find the voltage drop across this line if the current is 150 mA.

5. A length of No. 12 copper wire has a resistance of 3.6 Ω. What is the resistance of the same length of No. 8 wire?

6. Find the resistance of 6 in of No. 20 nichrome wire.

7. A resistance element designed to operate at 110 V and 6 A is to be made of No. 30 nichrome wire. Find the length of wire needed.

8. What diameter of iron wire 12 ft long is needed to make a resistance of 80 Ω?

TEST—RESISTANCE OF WIRES

1. A copper wire has a resistance of 0.4 Ω. What is the resistance of a nichrome wire of the same length and cross-sectional area?

2. A winding made of 100 ft of No. 26 iron wire is placed across 10 V. Find (a) the resistance of the circuit, (b) the current, and (c) the power dissipated.

3. A resistance element for an electric enameling kiln is designed to operate at 120 V and 12 A. How many feet of nichrome wire 0.01 in in diameter are needed to make the required resistance?

4. What diameter of copper wire should be used for a two-wire system 400 ft long if the total resistance of the line is not to exceed 1 Ω? Give the answer in mils and inches.

13

SIZE OF WIRING

JOB 13-1 MAXIMUM CURRENT-CARRYING CAPACITY OF WIRES

Heat is produced whenever a current flows in a wire. The larger the current, the greater the amount of heat that is produced. This heat must be given up to the surrounding atmosphere, or the wire may get hot enough to burst into flame.

The heat produced in a wire depends not only on the current but also on the resistance to that flow of current. Thick wires, because of their low resistance, can carry more current than thin wires before they dangerously overheat. But exactly how many amperes can be safely carried by a particular wire? Can a No. 20 wire carry 30 A, or is a No. 12 or larger wire required? Many tests have been made by the National Board of Fire Underwriters to determine the largest current which may be safely carried by wires of different sizes and different insulation. The National Electrical Code has set forth these values as shown in Table 13-1. This table gives the *maximum* current permitted in any size wire insulated as indicated.

Using the table of allowable current capacities

EXAMPLE 13-1   What is the largest current that may be safely carried by No. 12 rubber-covered wire?

SOLUTION

1   Locate No. 12 wire in column 1 of Table 13-1.
2   Read across to the right to column 5 for rubber-covered wire.
3   The answer (20 A) means that No. 12 rubber-covered wire should never be permitted to carry more than 20 A.   *Ans.*

EXAMPLE 13-2   What is the allowable current-carrying capacity of No. 14 varnished-cambric-insulated wire?

TABLE 13-1

TABLE OF ALLOWABLE CURRENT-CARRYING CAPACITIES OF COPPER CONDUCTORS (AMPACITIES)

National Electrical Code 1968

(1) AWG NO.	(2) DIAMETER, MILS	(3) CROSS SECTION, CIRMILS	(4) RESISTANCE, Ω/1,000 FT	ALLOWABLE CARRYING CAPACITY, A		
				(5) RUBBER-COVERED, TYPE RH	(6) VARNISHED CAMBRIC, TYPE V	(7) ASBESTOS, TYPE A
14	64.1	4,107	2.53	15	25	30
12	80.8	6,530	1.59	20	30	40
10	101.9	10,380	0.999	30	40	55
8	128.5	16,510	0.628	45	50	70
6	162.0	26,250	0.395	65	70	95
4	204.3	41,740	0.249	85	90	120
3	229.4	52,630	0.197	100	105	145
2	257.6	66,370	0.156	115	120	165
1	289.3	83,690	0.124	130	140	190
0	325	105,500	0.0983	150	155	225
00	364.8	133,100	0.0779	175	185	250
000	409.6	167,800	0.0618	200	210	285
0000	460	211,600	0.0490	230	235	340

SOLUTION

1 Locate No. 14 wire in column 1.
2 Read across to the right to column 6 for varnished-cambric-insulated wire.
3 The answer is 25 A.

EXAMPLE 13-3   What is the smallest rubber-covered wire that should be used to carry 16 A?

SOLUTION

1 Read down column 5 for rubber-covered wire until you find a number *larger* than 16 A. This will be 20 A.
2 Read to the left until you get to column 1. No. 12 gage is the smallest wire that can be used.   *Ans.*

EXAMPLE 13-4   What gage wire should be used if the circular-mil area required is 3,000 cirmils?

SOLUTION

1 Read down column 3 until you get to the number which is *just larger* than 3,000 cirmils. This number is 4,107 cirmils.
2 Read to the left until you get to column 1. No. 14 gage is the smallest wire that may be used.   *Ans.*

EXAMPLE 13-5   What gage wire should be used if the resistance required is 0.5 Ω/1,000 ft?

SOLUTION

1   Read down column 4 until you get to a number which is *just smaller* than 0.5 Ω. This number is 0.395 Ω.
2   Read to the left until you get to column 1. No. 6 gage is the smallest wire that may be used.   *Ans.*

SELF-TEST 13-6   Find the voltage drop along 1,000 ft of No. 10 rubber-covered wire if it is carrying its maximum current.

SOLUTION

1   Find the maximum current for No. 10 rubber-covered wire. This is found in column 5 to be ____ A.   30

2   Find the resistance per 1,000 ft of No. 10 rubber-covered wire. Read across to the right from No. 10 in column 1 to find _____ Ω in column ____.   0.999   4

3   Find the voltage drop.

$$E = IR \qquad\qquad (2\text{-}1)$$

$$E = \text{\_\_\_} \times 0.999$$ 30

$$E = \text{\_\_\_\_\_} \text{ V} \qquad Ans.$$ 29.97

SUMMARY

Always choose the wire

1   Which can carry (more/less) current than is required   more
2   Which has the (smaller/larger) circular-mil area   larger
3   Which has the (smaller/larger) resistance   smaller

PROBLEMS

1.   What is the maximum current that may be safely carried by No. 8 varnished-cambric-insulated wire?
2.   What is the smallest rubber-covered wire that should be used to carry 50 A?
3.   What gage wire should be used if the circular-mil area required is 18,000 cirmils?
4.   What gage wire should be used if the required resistance is not to exceed 0.91 Ω/1,000 ft?
5.   Find the voltage drop along 1,000 ft of No. 8 varnished-cambric-insulated wire when it is carrying its maximum current.
6.   What is the smallest varnished-cambric-insulated wire that should be used to carry 62 A safely?
7.   What is the resistance per foot of the smallest rubber-covered wire that should be used to carry 66 A safely?
8.   What size of asbestos-covered wire should be used to carry 42 A safely?
9.   What size of wire should be used if the circular-mil area required is 42,000 cirmils?

10. What is the diameter in mils and inches of the smallest rubber-covered wire that can be used to carry 80 A safely?

JOB 13-2 FINDING THE MINIMUM SIZE OF WIRE TO SUPPLY A GIVEN LOAD

The minimum size of wire that may be used in any installation depends on two factors: (1) the total current load and (2) the voltage drop in the wire. In this job we shall determine the size of wire needed to carry the given current. In the next job, we shall take the voltage drop into consideration.

Procedure

1 Determine the total current load.
2 Consult Table 13-1 to find the smallest wire to carry this load.

EXAMPLE 13-7 What is the smallest size of rubber-covered wire that may be used to supply two 10-Ω heating elements operated in parallel from a 220-V line?

SOLUTION
Given: $R_1 = 10\ \Omega$ Find: Smallest size of rubber-covered wire = ?
$\quad\quad\quad R_2 = 10\ \Omega$
$\quad\quad\quad E_T = 220\ V$

1 Find the total resistance.

$$R_T = \frac{R}{N} = \frac{10}{2} = 5\ \Omega \qquad\qquad (4\text{-}4)$$

2 Find the total current.

$$I_T = \frac{E_T}{R_T} = \frac{220}{5} = 44\ A \qquad\qquad (3\text{-}7)$$

3 Find the gage number to handle 44 A.
  a Read down column 5 until you get to the first number *larger* than 44 A. This number is 45 A.
  b Read to the left from 45 A until you get to column 1, where we read the gage number as No. 8.   *Ans.*

EXAMPLE 13-8 What is the smallest size of slow-burning weather-proof cable that may be used to carry current to a 10-hp motor from a 100-V source?

SOLUTION
Given: $P = 10\ hp$ Find: Smallest size of slow-burning cable = ?
$\quad\quad\quad E = 100\ V$

1   Find the watts of power to be delivered by the cable. Assume an input to the motor equal to 110 percent of the rated hp.

$$\text{Input hp} = 1.1 \times 10 = 11 \text{ hp}$$

$$\text{Watts} = \text{hp} \times 750 = 11 \times 750 = 8{,}250 \text{ W}$$

2   Find the current drawn.

$$P = I \times E \qquad\qquad (6\text{-}1)$$

$$8{,}250 = I \times 100$$

$$I = \frac{8{,}250}{100} = 82.5 \text{ A}$$

3   Find the gage number to handle 82.5 A. *Note:* For any wire other than rubber-covered or varnished-cambric-insulated wire, use the data for asbestos-covered wire in column 7.

   a   Read down column 7 until you get to the first number *larger* than 82.5 A. This number is 95 A.

   b   Read to the left from 95 A until you get to column 1, where we read the gage number as No. 6.   *Ans.*

PROBLEMS

1.   What is the minimum size of rubber-covered wire that may be used to supply a load of 60 lamps each drawing 0.91 A?
2.   What is the minimum size of asbestos-covered wire that may be used to supply a load of three 5-Ω electric ovens operated in parallel from a 110-V line?
3.   What is the minimum size of varnished-cambric-covered wire that may be used to supply a load of thirty 200-W lamps and twenty 100-W lamps if they are all operated in parallel from the same 110-V line?
4.   A 30-hp motor is to be used on a 220-V line. If the efficiency of the motor is 90 percent, what is the smallest size of varnished-cambric-covered wire that may be used?
5.   A 220-V generator supplies motors drawing 5, 10, and 12 kW of power. What is the minimum size of rubber-covered wire that may be used?

JOB 13-3   FINDING THE SIZE OF WIRE NEEDED TO PREVENT EXCESSIVE VOLTAGE DROPS

A wire not only must be able to carry a current without overheating but must also be able to carry this current without too many volts being used up in the wire itself. If the voltage drop in the line is too large, the voltage available at the load will be too small for proper operation of the load. For example, a 117-V generator is used to supply current to a bank of lamps some distance away. If the supply line should use up 17 V in supplying this current, then only 100 V would be available at the lamps and they would be dim. Not only that, but the loss in the line represents wasted power and a very inefficient system. To cover this, the National Electrical Code stipulates that the voltage drop in a line must not be more than 2 percent of the rated voltage for lighting purposes and not more than 5 percent of the rated voltage for power installations.

EXAMPLE 13-9   A bank of lamps draws 32 A from a 117-V source 300 ft away. Find the smallest gage of rubber-covered wire that may be safely used.

SOLUTION
The diagram for the circuit is shown in Fig. 13-1.

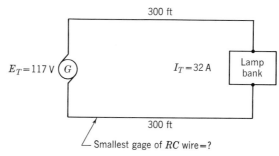

FIGURE 13-1

1   Find the allowable voltage drop. For lighting purposes, the Code permits only a 2 percent drop. Therefore,

$$\text{Allowable drop} = 2\% \text{ of } 117 = 0.02 \times 117 = 2.34 \text{ V}$$

2   Find the line resistance for this drop.

$$E_l = I_l \times R_l \qquad\qquad (5\text{-}1)$$

$$2.34 = 32 \times R_l$$

$$R_l = \frac{2.34}{32} = 0.0731 \ \Omega$$

3   Find the circular-mil area of the wire that has this resistance. Since there are two wires, $L = 2 \times 300 = 600$ ft. Also, the K for copper is 10.4.

$$R = \frac{K \times L}{A} \qquad\qquad (12\text{-}6)$$

$$\frac{0.0731}{1} = \frac{10.4 \times 600}{A}$$

$$0.0731 \times A = 10.4 \times 600$$

$$0.0731A = 6{,}240$$

$$A = \frac{6{,}240}{0.0731} = 85{,}360 \text{ cirmils}$$

4 Find the gage number of the wire whose circular-mil area is *larger* than 85,360 cirmils.

    a Read down column 3 until you get to a number *just larger* than 85,360. This number is 105,500.

    b Read across to the left to find gage No. 0 in column 1.   *Ans.*

EXAMPLE 13-10   A bank of lathes is operated by individual motors in a machine shop. The motors draw a total of 60 A at 110 V from the distributing panel box. What size of rubber-covered wire is required for the two-wire line between the panel box and the switchboard located 100 ft away if the switchboard voltage is 115 V?

SOLUTION

The diagram for the circuit is shown in Fig. 13-2.

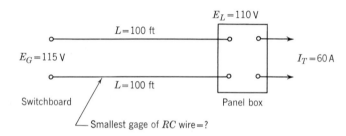

FIGURE 13-2

1 Find the line drop between the switchboard and the panel box.

$$E_G = E_l + E_L \qquad\qquad (5\text{-}2)$$

$$115 = E_l + 110$$

$$E_l = 115 - 110 = 5 \text{ V}$$

2 Find the line resistance for this drop.

$$E_l = I_l \times R_l \qquad\qquad (5\text{-}1)$$

$$5 = 60 \times R_l$$

$$R_l = \frac{5}{60} = 0.0833 \ \Omega$$

3 Find the circular-mil area of the wire that has this resistance. Since there are two wires, $L = 2 \times 100 = 200$ ft.

$$R = \frac{K \times L}{A} \qquad\qquad (12\text{-}6)$$

$$\frac{0.0833}{1} = \frac{10.4 \times 200}{A}$$

$$0.0833A = 10.4 \times 200$$

$$A = \frac{2,080}{0.0833} = 25,000 \text{ cirmils}$$

4 Find the gage number of the wire whose circular-mil area is *larger* than 25,000 cirmils.

    a Read down column 3 until you get to a number *just larger* than 25,000 cirmils. This number is 26,250.

    b Read across to the left to find gage No. 6 in column 1. This No. 6 wire can safely carry the 60 A without overheating, since its maximum current-carrying capacity is 65 A as found in column 5 for rubber-covered wire. *Ans.*

SELF-TEST 13-11 A 10-hp motor is operated at an efficiency of 90 percent from a 232-V source 100 ft away. What is the minimum size of slow-burning insulated wire that may be used for the line supplying the motor?

SOLUTION

The diagram for the circuit is shown in Fig. 13-3.

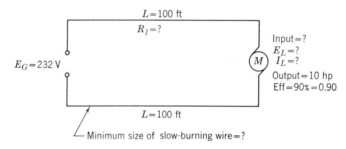

FIGURE 13-3

1 Find the allowable voltage drop. For power installations, the Code permits a 5 percent drop. Therefore,

$$E_l = \text{allowable drop} = 5 \text{ percent of } \underline{\quad}$$ 232

$$= \underline{\quad} \times 232$$ 0.05

$$E_l = \underline{\quad} \text{ V}$$ 11.6

2 Find the voltage at the motor load.

$$E_L = E_G - \underline{\quad} \tag{5-3}$$ E_l

$$E_L = 232 - \underline{\quad} = 220.4 \text{ V}$$ 11.6

3 Find the input to the motor.

$$\text{Eff} = \frac{\text{output}}{\text{input}} \tag{10-2}$$

$$\underline{\quad} = \frac{10 \times 750}{\text{input}}$$ 0.90

$$0.90 \text{ input} = \underline{\quad}$$ 7,500

$$\text{input} = \frac{7,500}{0.90} = \underline{\quad} \text{ W}$$ 8,333

4   Find the current drawn.

$$P_L = I_L \times E_L \tag{6-1}$$

$$8{,}333 = I_L \times \underline{\hspace{1cm}} \qquad\qquad\qquad 220.4$$

$$I_L = \frac{8{,}333}{220.4} = \underline{\hspace{0.5cm}} \text{ A} \qquad\qquad 37.8$$

5   Find the resistance of the line wires. Since $I_l = I_L$,

$$E_l = I_l \times R_l \tag{5-1}$$

$$\underline{\hspace{1cm}} = 37.8 \times R_l \qquad\qquad\qquad 11.6$$

$$R_l = \frac{11.6}{37.8} = \underline{\hspace{1cm}} \ \Omega \qquad\qquad 0.3069$$

6   Find the circular-mil area of the wire that has this resistance. Since there are two wires, $L = 2 \times 100 = 200$ ft.

$$R = \frac{K \times L}{A} \tag{12-6}$$

$$\frac{0.3069}{1} = \frac{? \times 200}{A} \qquad\qquad\qquad 10.4$$

$$0.3069A = 10.4 \times 200$$

$$A = \frac{2{,}080}{0.3069} = \underline{\hspace{1cm}} \text{ cirmils} \qquad 6{,}777$$

7   Find the gage number of the wire whose circular-mil area is __(smaller/larger)__ than 6,777 cirmils.   larger
   a   Read down column 3 until you get to a number just __(smaller/larger)__   larger
   than 6,777 cirmils. This number is _____.   10,380
   b   Read across to the left to find gage No. ___ in column ____. This No.   10   1
   10 wire can safely carry the required 37.8 A without overheating, since
   its maximum current-carrying capacity is ____ A as found in column ___   55   7
   for slow-burning wire.   *Ans.*

PROBLEMS

1.   What is the minimum size of rubber-covered wire that may be used
     to carry 40 A if the allowable voltage drop is 10 V per 1,000 ft
     of wire?
2.   A 50-ft two-wire extension line is to carry 30 A with a voltage drop
     of only 5 V. What is the smallest size of weatherproof cable that
     may be used?
3.   A bank of lamps draws 90 A from a 110-V line. What size of
     rubber-covered wire should be used if the voltage drop along 150
     ft of the two-wire system must not exceed 3 V?
4.   A bank of lamps draws 50 A from a 117-V source 40 ft away. Find
     the smallest gage rubber-covered wire that may be used for this

two-wire system if the voltage drop must not exceed 2 percent of the voltage at the source.

5. A 20-kW motor load is 100 ft from a 230-V source. If the allowable voltage drop is 5 percent, what is the smallest size of varnished-cambric-covered wire that may be used?

6. A load 400 ft from a generator requires 80 A. The generator voltage is 115.6 V, and the load requires 110 V. What is the smallest size of rubber-covered wire that may be used?

7. A 10-hp motor is located 20 ft from a 225-V generator. What is the smallest size of slow-burning wire that may be used?

8. A 10-hp motor operates at an efficiency of 85 percent at a distance of 100 ft from a 122-V generator. What is the smallest size of varnished-cambric-covered wire that may be used?

9. A generator supplies 5.5 kW at 125 V to a motor 500 ft away. The motor delivers 6.3 hp at an efficiency of 90 percent. Find (a) the watt input to the motor, (b) the watts lost in the line, (c) the current delivered to the line, (d) the voltage drop in the line, and (e) the smallest size of rubber-covered wire that may be used.

10. Calculate the smallest size of weatherproof wire required to conduct current to one hundred 220-Ω lamps in parallel which are located 125 ft from a generator delivering 112 V. The lamps must receive 110 V.

11. A portable tree-cutting saw requires 4 A at 120 V. If the line drop in the No. 10 cable used must not exceed 3 percent of the motor voltage, what is the maximum length of cable that may be used? *Hint:* Use Table 13-1 to get the resistance per foot.

12. A two-wire No. 10 AWG branch circuit carries 10 A from the main distribution panel to a load 100 ft away. Find (a) the total resistance of the line wires, (b) the voltage at the load when the voltage at the panel is 120 V, and (c) the maximum distance that this branch could carry a peak load of 15 A if the line drop must not exceed 3 percent.

JOB 13-4   REVIEW OF SIZE OF WIRING

The size of a wire depends on (1) the total current load and (2) the voltage drop in the wires.

To find the smallest wire that may be used in a given job

1 Find the total current drawn by the load.
2 Find the voltage drop in the supply wires.
3 Find the maximum resistance of the line wires.
4 Find the circular-mil area of the required wire.
5 Look up Table 13-1 to find the wire which has the next larger circular-mil area.

6   Look up the table to find the wire which can carry *more* current than that required by the load.

7   Choose the larger of the two wires found in steps 5 and 6.

PROBLEMS

1. What is the maximum current that may be safely carried by No. 10 varnished-cambric-covered wire?

2. What is the smallest asbestos-covered (type A) wire that should be used to carry 56 A?

3. What gage number wire should be used if the circular mil area required is 52,000 cirmils?

4. What is the diameter in mils of the smallest rubber-covered wire that should be used to carry 22 A?

5. What size of varnished-cambric-insulated wire is needed to supply a 5-hp motor operating at an efficiency of 90 percent from a 220-V line?

6. What size of rubber-covered wire is needed to supply a bank of ten 200-W lamps and two ½-hp motors connected in parallel across a 110-V line?

7. Find the size of rubber-covered wire needed to supply two 8-Ω heaters in parallel across 122 V.

8. What is the smallest gage of rubber-covered wire that may be used to carry a current of 32 A if the allowable voltage drop is 6 V per 1,000 ft of wire?

9. A 50-A 112-V load is located 200 ft from a switchboard delivering 115 V. Find the smallest varnished-cambric-covered wire that may be safely used in this two-wire system.

10. A lamp bank draws 60 A from a 230-V source 500 ft away. Assuming a maximum voltage drop of 2 percent, what is the smallest rubber-covered wire that may be used?

11. A 5-hp motor operates at an efficiency of 87 percent at a distance of 50 ft from a 232-V source. Find the smallest size of rubber-covered wire that may be safely used.

12. The 1¼-hp motor of an industrial floor-scraping machine operates at an efficiency of 87 percent from a 220-V line. If the line drop in the No. 14 gage wire used must not exceed 5 percent of the line voltage, find the maximum radius of operation of the scraper.

TEST—SIZE OF WIRING

1. *a.* What is the maximum current that may be safely carried by No. 12 weatherproof cable?

   b. What is the smallest rubber-covered wire that should be used to carry 31 A?

    c. What gage number wire should be used if the circular-mil area required is 17,000 cirmils?

    d. What is the diameter in mils of the smallest varnished-cambric-insulated wire that should be used to carry 27 A?

2. What size of rubber-covered wire should be used to supply a bank of six 150-W lamps and a ¾-hp motor connected in parallel across a 120-V line?

3. A 15-kW motor load is located 75 ft from a 230-V source. If the allowable voltage drop is 5 percent, what is the smallest rubber-covered wire that may be used?

4. A welding transformer located 250 ft from the power cabinet draws a maximum of 145 A from the 220-V line. What is the minimum size of RH cable required if the permissible voltage drop may not exceed 3 percent of the line voltage?

14

TRIGONOMETRY FOR ALTERNATING-CURRENT ELECTRICITY

JOB 14-1 TRIGONOMETRIC FUNCTIONS OF A RIGHT TRIANGLE

Trigonometry is the study of the relationships that exist among the sides and angles of a triangle. These relationships will form a basic mathematical tool used in the solution of ac electrical problems.

Angles. An angle is a figure formed when two lines meet at a point. In Fig. 14-1, the lines OA and OC are the sides of the angle. They meet at the point O, which is the vertex of the angle.

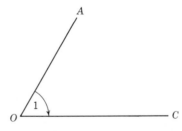

FIGURE 14-1
Naming an angle. Angle AOC or angle O or angle 1.

Naming angles. The angle shown in Fig. 14-1 may be named in three ways. (1) Use three capital letters, setting them down in order from one end of the angle to the other. Thus the angle may be named $\angle AOC$ or $\angle COA$. (2) Use only the capital letter at the vertex of the angle, as $\angle O$. (3) Use a small letter or number inside the angle, as $\angle 1$.

Measuring angles. When a straight line *turns* about a point from one position to another, an angle is formed. When the minute hand of a clock turns from the 1 to the 3, the hand has turned through an angle approximately equal to $\angle AOC$. An angle is measured *by the amount of rotation of a line about a fixed point*. The end of the minute hand of a clock describes a circle as it revolves around the dial. The circumference

457

of this circle is divided into 60 parts. In Fig. 14-2*a*, the angle formed by a rotation through $\frac{1}{60}$ part of the circle is called one minute of time. In ordinary angular measurement, a circle is divided into 360 parts, as shown in Fig. 14-2*b*. The angle formed by a rotation through $\frac{1}{360}$ part of the circle is called one degree (1°).

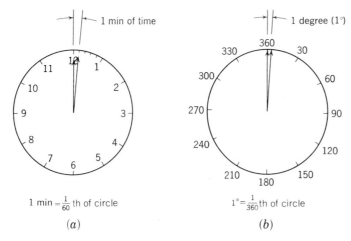

1 min $= \frac{1}{60}$ th of circle

(*a*)

1° $= \frac{1}{360}$ th of circle

(*b*)

FIGURE 14-2

An angle is measured by the amount of rotation of a line about a fixed point.

A *right angle* is an angle formed by a rotation through one-fourth of a circle, as $\angle ABC$ in Fig. 14-3. Since a complete circle contains 360°, a right angle contains $\frac{1}{4} \times 360$, or 90°.

An *acute angle* is an angle containing *less* than 90°, as $\angle AOC$ in Fig. 14-1.

Triangles. A triangle is a closed plane figure of three sides. Triangles are named by naming the three vertices of the triangle using capital letters. The letters are then given in order around the triangle. Thus in Fig. 14-3, the triangle is named $\triangle ACB$ or $\triangle CBA$ or $\triangle BAC$ or $\triangle ABC$ or $\triangle BCA$ or $\triangle CAB$.

A *right triangle* is a triangle which contains a right angle, as $\triangle ABC$ in Fig. 14-3. The little square at $\angle B$ is used to indicate a right angle.

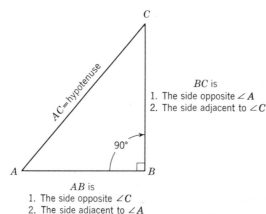

AC = hypotenuse

BC is
1. The side opposite $\angle A$
2. The side adjacent to $\angle C$

90°

AB is
1. The side opposite $\angle C$
2. The side adjacent to $\angle A$

FIGURE 14-3

Naming the sides of a right triangle.

Naming the sides of a right triangle. In trigonometry, the sides of a right triangle are named depending on which of the *acute* angles are used. In Fig. 14-3,

For angle *A:*

1   The side opposite the right angle is called the *hypotenuse* (*AC*).
2   The side opposite angle *A* is called the *opposite side* (*BC*).
3   The side of angle *A* which is *not* the hypotenuse is called the *adjacent side* (*AB*).

For angle *C:*

1   The side opposite the right angle is called the hypotenuse (*AC*).
2   The side opposite angle *C* is called the opposite side (*AB*).
3   The side of angle *C* which is *not* the hypotenuse is called the *adjacent side* (*BC*).

THE TRIGONOMETRIC FORMULAS

The tangent of an angle. In addition to degrees, the size of an angle may also be described in terms of the lengths of the sides of a right triangle formed from the angle. Refer to Fig. 14-4, in which each space represents one unit of length. From various points on one side of angle

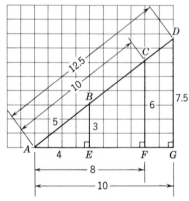

FIGURE 14-4
Diagram used to obtain the trigonometric formulas.

A, lines have been drawn making right angles with the other side. These lines have formed the right triangles *ABE, ACF,* and *ADG.* Notice that all these triangles contain the same angle *A.*

	In △*ABE*	In △*ACF*	In △*ADG*
Hypotenuse =	*AB* = 5	*AC* = 10	*AD* = 12.5
Side opposite ∠*A* =	*BE* = 3	*CF* = 6	*DG* = 7.5
Side adjacent ∠*A* =	*AE* = 4	*AF* = 8	*AG* = 10

In each triangle, let us divide the side *opposite* ∠*A* by the side *adjacent* to ∠*A*.

In △*ABE:* $\dfrac{\text{Side opposite} \angle A}{\text{Side adjacent} \angle A} = \dfrac{BE}{AE} = \dfrac{3}{4} = 0.75$

In $\triangle ACF$: $\dfrac{\text{Side opposite } \angle A}{\text{Side adjacent } \angle A} = \dfrac{CF}{AF} = \dfrac{6}{8} = 0.75$

In $\triangle ADG$: $\dfrac{\text{Side opposite } \angle A}{\text{Side adjacent } \angle A} = \dfrac{DG}{AG} = \dfrac{7.5}{10} = 0.75$

Notice that this particular division of the opposite side by the adjacent side always results in the *same* answer *regardless* of the size of the triangle. This is true because *all* the triangles contain the same angle A. The ratio of these sides remains constant because they all describe the same angle A. This constant number describes the size of angle A and is called the *tangent of angle A*. Therefore, if the tangent of an *unknown* angle were calculated to be 0.75, then the angle would be equal to angle A, or about 37°. If the angle changes, then the number for the tangent of the angle will also change. However, the tangent of every angle is a specific number which never changes. These numbers are found in Table 14-1.

RULE	The tangent of an angle $= \dfrac{\text{side opposite the angle}}{\text{side adjacent to the angle}}$

FORMULA

$$\tan \angle = \frac{o}{a}$$

$$\boxed{14\text{-}1}$$

The sine of an angle. In each triangle shown in Fig. 14-4, let us divide the side *opposite* angle A by the side called the *hypotenuse*.

In $\triangle ABE$: $\dfrac{\text{Side opposite } \angle A}{\text{Hypotenuse}} = \dfrac{BE}{AB} = \dfrac{3}{5} = 0.6$

In $\triangle ACF$: $\dfrac{\text{Side opposite } \angle A}{\text{Hypotenuse}} = \dfrac{CF}{AC} = \dfrac{6}{10} = 0.6$

In $\triangle ADG$: $\dfrac{\text{Side opposite } \angle A}{\text{Hypotenuse}} = \dfrac{DG}{AD} = \dfrac{7.5}{12.5} = 0.6$

Once again, the resulting quotients are fixed regardless of the size of the triangles. This number is called the *sine of angle A* and is *another* way to describe the size of the angle. If the angle changes, then the number for the sine of the angle will also change. However, the sine of every angle is a specific number which never changes. These numbers are also found in Table 14-1.

RULE	The sine of an angle $= \dfrac{\text{side opposite the angle}}{\text{hypotenuse}}$

FORMULA

$$\sin \angle = \frac{o}{h}$$

14-2

The cosine of an angle. In each triangle shown in Fig. 14-4, let us divide the side *adjacent* to the angle A by the *hypotenuse*.

In $\triangle ABE$: $\dfrac{\text{Side adjacent } \angle A}{\text{Hypotenuse}} = \dfrac{AE}{AB} = \dfrac{4}{5} = 0.8$

In $\triangle ACF$: $\dfrac{\text{Side adjacent } \angle A}{\text{Hypotenuse}} = \dfrac{AF}{AC} = \dfrac{8}{10} = 0.8$

In $\triangle ADG$: $\dfrac{\text{Side adjacent } \angle A}{\text{Hypotenuse}} = \dfrac{AG}{AD} = \dfrac{10}{12.5} = 0.8$

Here, too, the resulting quotients are fixed regardless of the size of the triangles. This number is called the *cosine of angle A* and is a third way to describe the size of the angle. If the angle changes, then the number for the cosine of the angle will also change. However, the cosine of every angle is a specific number which never changes. These numbers are found in Table 14-1.

RULE	The cosine of an angle $= \dfrac{\text{side adjacent to the angle}}{\text{hypotenuse}}$

FORMULA

$$\cos \angle = \frac{a}{h}$$

14-3

EXAMPLE 14-1   Find the sine, cosine, and tangent of $\angle A$ in the triangle shown in Fig. 14-5.

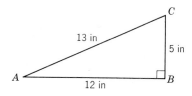

FIGURE 14-5

SOLUTION

1 Name the sides using $\angle A$ as the reference angle.

$$\text{Hypotenuse} = AC = 13 \text{ in}$$

$$\text{Opposite side} = BC = 5 \text{ in}$$

$$\text{Adjacent side} = AB = 12 \text{ in}$$

2   Find the values of the three functions.

$$\sin \angle A = \frac{o}{h} \qquad \cos \angle A = \frac{a}{h} \qquad \tan \angle A = \frac{o}{a}$$

$$\sin \angle A = \frac{5}{13} \qquad \cos \angle A = \frac{12}{13} \qquad \tan \angle A = \frac{5}{12}$$

$$\sin \angle A = 0.384 \qquad \cos \angle A = 0.923 \qquad \tan \angle A = 0.417 \qquad Ans.$$

EXAMPLE 14-2   Find the sine, cosine, and tangent of $\angle B$ in the triangle shown in Fig. 14-6.

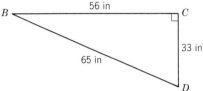

FIGURE 14-6

SOLUTION

1   Name the sides, using $\angle B$ as the reference angle.

$$\text{Hypotenuse} = BD = 65 \text{ in}$$
$$\text{Opposite side} = CD = 33 \text{ in}$$
$$\text{Adjacent side} = BC = 56 \text{ in}$$

2   Find the values of the three functions.

$$\sin \angle B = \frac{o}{h} \qquad \cos \angle B = \frac{a}{h} \qquad \tan \angle B = \frac{o}{a}$$

$$\sin \angle B = \frac{33}{65} \qquad \cos \angle B = \frac{56}{65} \qquad \tan \angle B = \frac{33}{56}$$

$$\sin \angle B = 0.5077 \qquad \cos \angle B = 0.8615 \qquad \tan \angle B = 0.5893 \qquad Ans.$$

PROBLEMS

Calculate the sine, cosine, and tangent of the angles named in each triangle in Fig. 14-7.

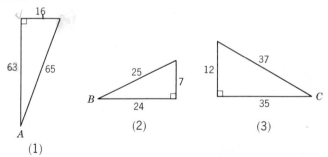

(1)   (2)   (3)

FIGURE 14-7

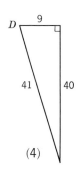

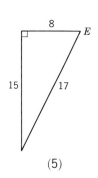

(4)   (5)   **FIGURE 14-7** (Cont.)

JOB 14-2 USING THE TABLE OF TRIGONOMETRIC FUNCTIONS

Since the values of the trigonometric functions of an angle never change, it is possible to set these values down in a table such as Table 14-1.

EXAMPLE 14-3   Find the value of sin 50°.

SOLUTION
Follow down the column marked "Angle" in Table 14-1 until you reach 50°. Read across to the right to find the number 0.7660 in the sine column. Therefore,

$$\sin 50° = 0.7660 \qquad Ans.$$

EXAMPLE 14-4   Find the value of tan 30°.

SOLUTION
Follow down the column marked "Angle" until you get to 30°. Read across to the right to find the number 0.5774 in the tangent column. Therefore,

$$\tan 30° = 0.5774 \qquad Ans.$$

FINDING THE ANGLE WHEN THE FUNCTION IS GIVEN

EXAMPLE 14-5   Find $\angle A$ if $\cos A = 0.7314$.

SOLUTION
Follow down the column marked "cos" until you find the number 0.7314. Read across to the left to find 43° in the column marked "Angle." Therefore,

$$\angle A = 43° \qquad Ans.$$

EXAMPLE 14-6   Find $\angle B$ if $\tan B = 1.8807$.

SOLUTION
Follow down the column marked "tan" until you find the number 1.8807.

TABLE 14-1
VALUES OF THE TRIGONOMETRIC FUNCTIONS

ANGLE	SIN	COS	TAN	ANGLE	SIN	COS	TAN
0°	0.0000	1.0000	0.0000	46°	0.7193	0.6947	1.0355
1°	0.0175	0.9998	0.0175	47°	0.7314	0.6820	1.0724
2°	0.0349	0.9994	0.0349	48°	0.7431	0.6691	1.1106
3°	0.0523	0.9986	0.0524	49°	0.7547	0.6561	1.1504
4°	0.0698	0.9976	0.0699	50°	0.7660	0.6428	1.1918
5°	0.0872	0.9962	0.0875	51°	0.7771	0.6293	1.2349
6°	0.1045	0.9945	0.1051	52°	0.7880	0.6157	1.2799
7°	0.1219	0.9925	0.1228	53°	0.7986	0.6018	1.3270
8°	0.1392	0.9903	0.1405	54°	0.8090	0.5878	1.3764
9°	0.1564	0.9877	0.1584	55°	0.8192	0.5736	1.4281
10°	0.1736	0.9848	0.1763	56°	0.8290	0.5592	1.4826
11°	0.1908	0.9816	0.1944	57°	0.8387	0.5446	1.5399
12°	0.2079	0.9781	0.2126	58°	0.8480	0.5299	1.6003
13°	0.2250	0.9744	0.2309	59°	0.8572	0.5150	1.6643
14°	0.2419	0.9703	0.2493	60°	0.8660	0.5000	1.7321
15°	0.2588	0.9659	0.2679	61°	0.8746	0.4848	1.8040
16°	0.2756	0.9613	0.2867	62°	0.8829	0.4695	1.8807
17°	0.2924	0.9563	0.3057	63°	0.8910	0.4540	1.9626
18°	0.3090	0.9511	0.3249	64°	0.8988	0.4384	2.0503
19°	0.3256	0.9455	0.3443	65°	0.9063	0.4226	2.1445
20°	0.3420	0.9397	0.3640	66°	0.9135	0.4067	2.2460
21°	0.3584	0.9336	0.3839	67°	0.9205	0.3907	2.3559
22°	0.3746	0.9272	0.4040	68°	0.9272	0.3746	2.4751
23°	0.3907	0.9205	0.4245	69°	0.9336	0.3584	2.6051
24°	0.4067	0.9135	0.4452	70°	0.9397	0.3420	2.7475
25°	0.4226	0.9063	0.4663	71°	0.9455	0.3256	2.9042
26°	0.4384	0.8988	0.4877	72°	0.9511	0.3090	3.0777
27°	0.4540	0.8910	0.5095	73°	0.9563	0.2924	3.2709
28°	0.4695	0.8829	0.5317	74°	0.9613	0.2756	3.4874
29°	0.4848	0.8746	0.5543	75°	0.9659	0.2588	3.7321
30°	0.5000	0.8660	0.5774	76°	0.9703	0.2419	4.0108
31°	0.5150	0.8572	0.6009	77°	0.9744	0.2250	4.3315
32°	0.5299	0.8480	0.6249	78°	0.9781	0.2079	4.7046
33°	0.5446	0.8387	0.6494	79°	0.9816	0.1908	5.1446
34°	0.5592	0.8290	0.6745	80°	0.9848	0.1736	5.6713
35°	0.5736	0.8192	0.7002	81°	0.9877	0.1564	6.3138
36°	0.5878	0.8090	0.7265	82°	0.9903	0.1392	7.1154
37°	0.6018	0.7986	0.7536	83°	0.9925	0.1219	8.1443
38°	0.6157	0.7880	0.7813	84°	0.9945	0.1045	9.5144
39°	0.6293	0.7771	0.8098	85°	0.9962	0.0872	11.4300
40°	0.6428	0.7660	0.8391	86°	0.9976	0.0698	14.3010
41°	0.6561	0.7547	0.8693	87°	0.9986	0.0523	19.0810
42°	0.6691	0.7431	0.9004	88°	0.9994	0.0349	28.6360
43°	0.6820	0.7314	0.9325	89°	0.9998	0.0175	57.2900
44°	0.6947	0.7193	0.9657	90°	1.0000	0.0000	
45°	0.7071	0.7071	1.0000				

Read across to the left to find 62° in the column marked "Angle." Therefore,

$$\angle B = 62° \quad Ans.$$

PROBLEMS

Find the number of degrees in each angle.

1. $\tan A = 0.3249$ 2. $\sin B = 0.6428$ 3. $\cos C = 0.1736$
4. $\cos D = 0.9877$ 5. $\sin E = 0.5000$ 6. $\tan F = 1.0724$
7. $\tan G = 0.5774$ 8. $\cos H = 0.7071$ 9. $\sin J = 0.8660$

FINDING THE ANGLE WHEN THE FUNCTION IS NOT IN THE TABLE

EXAMPLE 14-7   Find $\angle A$ if $\tan A = 0.5120$.

SOLUTION
The number 0.5120 is not in the table under the column "tan" but lies between 0.5095 (27°) and 0.5317 (28°). Choose the number closest to 0.5120.

$$\left.\begin{array}{l} \tan 27 = 0.5095 \\ \tan A = 0.5120 \\ \tan 28 = 0.5317 \end{array}\right\} \begin{array}{l} \text{difference} = 0.0025 \\ \text{difference} = 0.0197 \end{array}$$

The smaller difference indicates the closer number. Therefore,

$$\angle A = 27° \quad Ans.$$

PROBLEMS

Find the number of degrees in each angle correct to the nearest degree.

1. $\tan A = 0.2700$ 2. $\cos B = 0.7500$ 3. $\sin C = 0.8500$
4. $\sin D = 0.2350$ 5. $\cos E = 0.4172$ 6. $\tan F = 1.9120$
7. $\tan G = 0.2783$ 8. $\cos H = 0.1645$ 9. $\sin J = 0.7250$

JOB 14-3   FINDING THE ACUTE ANGLES OF A RIGHT TRIANGLE

In order to find the value of an angle in any problem, it is only necessary to find the number for the sine *or* the cosine *or* the tangent of the angle. If we know *any one* of these values, we can determine the angle by finding the number in the appropriate column of the table.

EXAMPLE 14-8   Find $\angle A$ and $\angle B$ in the triangle of Fig. 14-8.

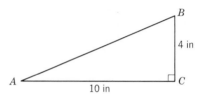

FIGURE 14-8

SOLUTION

1   Name the sides which have values, using $\angle A$ as the reference angle.

$$4 \text{ in} = \text{the side } \textit{opposite } \angle A$$

$$10 \text{ in} = \text{the side } \textit{adjacent } \angle A$$

2   We can find $\angle A$ if we can find *any* of the three functions of the angle. However, the only function that can *actually* be found is the one for which we have *known* values. In this problem, the only known values are those for the opposite and adjacent sides. The only formula that uses these particular sides is the *tangent* formula.

$$\tan A = \frac{o}{a} = \frac{4}{10} = 0.4000 \qquad (14\text{-}1)$$

3   Find the number in the tangent table closest to 0.4000.

$$\angle A = 22° \text{ (nearest angle)} \qquad \textit{Ans.}$$

4   Since the two acute angles of any right triangle always total 90°,

$$\angle B = 90° - \angle A \qquad \boxed{14\text{-}4}$$

$$\angle B = 90° - 22° = 68° \qquad \textit{Ans.}$$

EXAMPLE 14-9   The phase angle in an ac circuit may be represented by $\angle \theta$ (angle theta), as shown in Fig. 14-9.   Find $\angle \theta$ and $\angle B$.

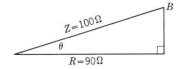

FIGURE 14-9
The angle theta (θ) is the phase angle in an inductive ac circuit.

SOLUTION

1   Name the sides which have values, using $\angle \theta$ as the reference angle.

$$100 \ \Omega = \text{hypotenuse}$$

$$90 \ \Omega = \text{side adjacent } \angle \theta$$

2   Choose the trigonometric formula which uses the adjacent side and the hypotenuse.

$$\cos \theta = \frac{a}{h} = \frac{90}{100} = 0.9000 \qquad (14\text{-}3)$$

3   Find the number in the cosine table closest to 0.9000.

$$\angle \theta = 25° \text{ (nearest angle)} \qquad \textit{Ans.}$$

4   Since the two acute angles of a right triangle always total 90°,

$$\angle B = 90° - \angle\theta \qquad (14\text{-}4)$$

$$\angle B = 90° - 25° = 65° \quad Ans.$$

SELF-TEST 14-10   An electrician must bend a pipe to make a 3½-ft rise in a 5-ft horizontal distance. What is the angle at each bend?

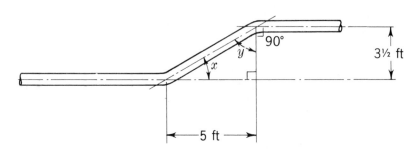

FIGURE 14-10

SOLUTION
The diagram describing the conditions is shown in Fig. 14-10.

1   Name the sides which have values, using $\angle x$ as the reference angle.

The side opposite $\angle x =$ ___ ft	3½
The side adjacent $\angle x =$ ___ ft	5

2   Choose the trigonometric formula which uses the opposite side and the adjacent side. The only formula that uses these two sides is the _____.   tangent

$$\tan x = \frac{?}{?} \qquad (14\text{-}1)$$ $\dfrac{o}{a}$

$$\tan x = \frac{3.5}{5} = \underline{\qquad}$$ 0.7000

3   Find the number in the _____ table that is closest to 0.7000.   tangent

$$\angle x = \underline{\quad}° \quad Ans.$$ 35

4   Since the two acute angles of a right triangle always total ___°,   90

$$\angle y = 90° - \underline{\quad} \qquad (14\text{-}4)$$ $\angle x$

$$\angle y = 90° - 35° = \underline{\quad}$$ 55°

5   The angle at the top bend $= \angle y +$ ___, or   90°

$$\text{The angle at the top bend} = 55° + 90°$$

$$= \underline{\quad}° \quad Ans.$$ 145

PROBLEMS

1.   Find $\angle A$ and $\angle B$ in the right triangle shown in Fig. 14-11.

Using Fig. 14-11, find ∠A and ∠B if

2. $AC = 100$ ft and $BC = 70$ ft
3. $BC = 4$ in and $AB = 8$ in
4. $BC = 40 \ \Omega$ and $AC = 25 \ \Omega$
5. $AC = 200 \ \Omega$ and $AB = 350 \ \Omega$
6. $BC = 300$ W and $AB = 1,000$ W
7. $AC = 600 \ \Omega$ and $AB = 960 \ \Omega$
8. $BC = 7.5$ V and $AC = 12.5$ V
9. $BC = 12.4$ A and $AB = 67.8$ A
10. $AC = 62.5 \ \Omega$ and $BC = 100 \ \Omega$

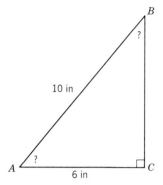

FIGURE 14-11

11. At what angles must a pipe be bent in order to make a 7-ft rise in a 3-ft horizontal distance?
12. At what angles must a pipe be bent in order to make a rise of 4 ft 6 in. in a 2-ft 3-in. horizontal distance?
13. A car rises 50 ft while traveling along a road 1,000 ft long. At what angle is the road inclined to the horizontal?
14. Find angle x in the taper shown in Fig. 14-12.

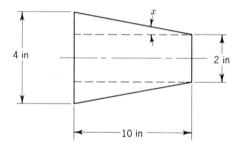

FIGURE 14-12
Angle x is equal to one-half of the taper angle.

15. A guy wire 120 ft long reaches from the top of a pole to a point 64 ft from the foot of the pole. What angle does the wire make with the ground?

JOB 14-4 FINDING THE SIDES OF A RIGHT TRIANGLE

EXAMPLE 14-11   Find (a) side BC and (b) ∠B of the right triangle shown in Fig. 14-13.

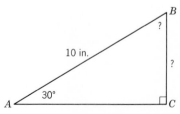

FIGURE 14-13

SOLUTION

a   Find the side *BC*.

1   Select the angle to be used ($\angle A = 30°$).
2   Select the side to be found (*BC*).
3   Select one other side whose value is known ($AB = 10$ in).
4   Name these two sides.

$$BC = \text{side } \textit{opposite} \angle A$$

$$10 \text{ in} = AB = \textit{hypotenuse}$$

5   Select the correct trigonometric formula. It will be the formula that uses these two sides—the *opposite* and the *hypotenuse*. Only the *sine* formula uses the *opposite* side and the *hypotenuse*.

$$\sin A = \frac{o}{h} \qquad\qquad (14\text{-}2)$$

$$\sin 30° = \frac{BC}{10}$$

From Table 14-1, the sin $30° = 0.5000$. Therefore,

$$\frac{0.5000}{1} = \frac{BC}{10}$$

$$BC = 0.5000 \times 10 = 5 \text{ in} \qquad \textit{Ans.}$$

b   Find $\angle B$.

$$\angle B = 90° - \angle A \qquad\qquad (14\text{-}4)$$

$$\angle B = 90° - 30° = 60° \qquad \textit{Ans.}$$

EXAMPLE 14-12   Find side *BC* in the right triangle shown in Fig. 14-14.

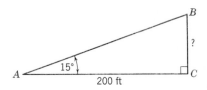

A   15°   C
                  200 ft   **FIGURE 14-14**

SOLUTION

Find the side *BC*.

1   Select the angle to be used ($\angle A = 15°$).
2   Select the side to be found (*BC*).
3   Select one other side whose value is known ($AC = 200$ ft).
4   Name these two sides.

$$BC = \text{the side } \textit{opposite} \angle A$$

$$200 \text{ ft} = AC = \text{the side } \textit{adjacent} \angle A$$

5   Select the correct trigonometric formula. It will be the formula that uses

these two sides—the *opposite* and the *adjacent*. Only the tangent formula uses the *opposite* side and the *adjacent* side.

$$\tan A = \frac{o}{a} \qquad (14\text{-}1)$$

$$\tan 15° = \frac{BC}{200}$$

From Table 14-1, the tan 15° = 0.2679. Therefore,

$$\frac{0.2679}{1} = \frac{BC}{200}$$

$$BC = 0.2679 \times 200 = 53.58 \text{ ft} \qquad Ans.$$

EXAMPLE 14-13   The relationship among the impedance Z, the resistance R, and the capacitive reactance X_C of an ac circuit is shown in Fig. 14-15. Find the impedance.

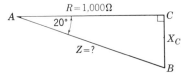

FIGURE 14-15

SOLUTION

Find the impedance Z represented by side AB.

1   Select the angle to be used ($\angle A = 20°$).
2   Select the side to be found (AB).
3   Select one other side whose value is known ($AC = 1,000 \ \Omega$).
4   Name these two sides.

$$AB = hypotenuse$$

$$1,000 \ \Omega = AC = \text{side } adjacent \ \angle A$$

5   Select the correct trigonometric formula. It will be the formula that uses these two sides—the *adjacent* and the *hypotenuse*. Only the cosine formula uses the *adjacent* side and the *hypotenuse*.

$$\cos A = \frac{a}{h} \qquad (14\text{-}3)$$

$$\cos 20° = \frac{1,000}{AB}$$

From Table 14-1, the cos 20° = 0.9397. Therefore,

$$\frac{0.9397}{1} = \frac{1,000}{AB}$$

$$AB \times 0.9397 = 1,000$$

$$AB = \frac{1,000}{0.9397} = 1,064 \ \Omega$$

$$\text{Impedance } Z = 1,064 \ \Omega \qquad Ans.$$

SELF-TEST 14-14   As shall be discussed in Job 18-1, the current and voltage of an ac circuit do not always appear at the same time. They are said to be "out of phase." In Fig. 14-16a, the current "leads" the voltage by a phase angle of 37°. In order to cope with this situation, the current "phasor" $I = 20$ A is resolved into its "in-phase" component I_x and its "reactive" component I_y, as shown in Fig. 14-16b. Find I_x and I_y. A further discussion of the resolution of phasors may be found in Job 19-5.

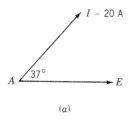
(a)

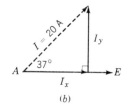
(b)

FIGURE 14-16
(a) The current I "leads" the voltage E by 37°. (b) I is resolved into its "in-phase" component I_x and its "reactive" component I_y.

SOLUTION
Find I_x. In Fig. 14-16b,

1   The angle to be used = ____.   37°
2   The side to be found = ____. I_x
3   Another side whose value is known is $I =$ ____.   20
4   Name these two sides using $\angle A = 37°$ as the reference angle.

$$I_x = \text{the side} \underline{\hspace{2cm}} \angle A$$ adjacent

$$I = 20 = \text{the} \underline{\hspace{2cm}}$$ hypotenuse

5   Select the correct trigonometric formula that uses these two particular sides. The adjacent side and the hypotenuse are connected by the _____   cosine
formula.

$$\cos \angle A = \frac{a}{h} \tag{14-2}$$

$$\cos 37° = \frac{?}{20}$$ I_x

From Table 14-1, the $\cos 37° =$ _____. Therefore,   0.7986

$$\frac{0.7986}{1} = \frac{I_x}{20}$$

and $$I_x = 0.7986 \times 20 = \underline{\hspace{1cm}} \text{A} \quad Ans.$$ 16

Find I_y.

1   Using $\angle A = 37°$, the sides to be used are I_y and ____.   20
2   Using $\angle A$ as the reference angle, these sides are named as follows:

$$I_y = \text{the side} \underline{\hspace{2cm}} \angle A$$ opposite

$$I = 20 = \text{the} \underline{\hspace{2cm}}$$ hypotenuse

3   The only formula that uses these two sides is the _____ formula.   sine

$$\sin A = \frac{?}{h}$$ 0

$$\sin 37° = \frac{I_y}{?}$$ 20

From Table 14-1, the sin 37° = _____. Therefore,   0.6018

$$\frac{0.6018}{1} = \frac{I_y}{20}$$

and $I_y = 0.6018 \times 20 = $ ____ A   *Ans.*   12

PROBLEMS

Use the triangle shown in Fig. 14-13 for the following problems.

1.   Find AC and $\angle B$ if $AB = 20$ in and $\angle A = 60°$.
2.   Find BC and $\angle B$ if $AB = 26$ ft and $\angle A = 40°$.
3.   Find AC and $\angle A$ if $BC = 75$ ft and $\angle B = 50°$.
4.   Find AC and $\angle B$ if $AB = 400$ W and $\angle A = 28°$.
5.   Find AB and $\angle B$ if $BC = 75.5$ Ω and $\angle A = 30°$.
6.   Find AB and $\angle B$ if $AC = 30$ Ω and $\angle A = 25°$.
7.   Find BC and $\angle A$ if $AC = 500$ ft and $\angle B = 28°$.
8.   Find AC and $\angle A$ if $AB = 36.8$ in and $\angle B = 35°$.
9.   Find BC and $\angle B$ if $AB = 475$ Ω and $\angle A = 15°$.
10. Find AC and $\angle A$ if $AB = 92.8$ V and $\angle B = 15°$.
11. A guy wire reaches from the top of an antenna pole to a point 30 ft from the foot of the pole and makes an angle of 70° with the ground. How long is the wire? How tall is the pole?
12. Use Fig. 14-12. If the small diameter equals 3 in, the length equals 12 in, and angle x equals 4°, find the large diameter.
13. Four holes are drilled evenly spaced around a 5-in-diameter circle. Find the distance between the centers of the holes.
14. How long is each side of the largest square bar that can be made from a piece of 6-in-diameter round stock?
15. A ladder 30 ft long leans against the side of a building and makes an angle of 65° with the ground. How high up the building does it reach?
16. In an ac circuit, the current $I = 10$ A leads the voltage by 53°. Resolve the current into its in-phase current I_x and its reactive current I_y.
17. In an ac circuit, the current $I = 14$ A leads the voltage by 25°. Resolve the current into its in-phase current I_x and its reactive current I_y.
18. At a point 40 ft from the foot of a tree, the line of sight to the top

of the tree makes an angle of 60° with the ground. Find the height of the tree to the nearest foot.

19. In an impedance triangle similar to that shown in Fig. 14-15, find the reactance X_C if $R = 2,000 \ \Omega$ and angle $A = 20°$.

20. Find the impedance Z in the triangle used for Prob. 19.

JOB 14-5 REVIEW OF TRIGONOMETRY

FORMULAS

1 Tangent of an angle $= \dfrac{\underline{\hspace{1.5cm}} \text{ side}}{\underline{\hspace{1.5cm}} \text{ side}}$.

opposite
adjacent

$$\tan \angle = \frac{o}{a} \qquad \boxed{14\text{-}1}$$

2 Sine of an angle $= \dfrac{\underline{\hspace{1.5cm}} \text{ side}}{\underline{\hspace{1.5cm}}}$.

opposite
hypotenuse

$$\sin \angle = \frac{o}{h} \qquad \boxed{14\text{-}2}$$

3 Cosine of an angle $= \dfrac{\underline{\hspace{1.5cm}} \text{ side}}{\underline{\hspace{1.5cm}}}$.

adjacent
hypotenuse

$$\cos \angle = \frac{a}{h} \qquad \boxed{14\text{-}3}$$

4 The sum of the two acute angles of a right triangle equals ___.

90°

$$\angle A + \angle B = 90° \qquad \boxed{14\text{-}4}$$

PROCEDURE FOR FINDING ANGLES IN A RIGHT TRIANGLE

1 Name the sides which have values, using the angle to be found as the reference angle.

2 Choose the trigonometric formula which uses these sides.

3 Substitute values, and divide.

4 Find the number in the table closest to this quotient. Be certain to look in the column indicated by step 2.

5 Find the angle in the angle column corresponding to this number.

6 Use formula (14-4) to find the other acute angle.

PROCEDURE FOR FINDING SIDES IN A RIGHT TRIANGLE

1 Select the angle to used.

2 Select the side to be found.

3 Select one other side whose value is known.

4 Name these two sides.

5 Select the correct trigonometric formula which uses these sides.

6   Substitute values, using Table 14-1.
7   Solve the equation.

PROBLEMS

Find the value of the following functions.

1. $\sin 36°$ 2. $\cos 78°$ 3. $\tan 69°$ 4. $\sin 52°$ 5. $\cos 25°$

Find angle A, correct to the nearest degree.

6. $\sin A = 0.5878$ 7. $\cos A = 0.4226$ 8. $\tan A = 5.7500$
9. $\cos A = 0.9800$ 10. $\sin A = 0.7200$ 11. $\tan A = 0.3113$
12. $\tan A = 0.1340$ 13. $\cos A = 0.2868$ 14. $\sin A = 0.7240$

Use the triangle shown in Fig. 14-13 for the following problems:

15.   Find $\angle A$ if $BC = 30$ and $AC = 40$.
16.   Find $\angle B$ if $AC = 50$ and $AB = 100$.
17.   Find $\angle B$ if $BC = 25$ and $AB = 75$.
18.   Find $\angle A$ if $BC = 16$ and $AB = 65$.
19.   Find $\angle B$ if $AC = 22.5$ and $BC = 14$.
20.   Find $\angle A$ if $AC = 4.5$ and $AB = 20.5$.
21.   Find BC if $AB = 2{,}200$ W and $\angle A = 25°$.
22.   Find AC if $AB = 600$ W and $\angle A = 8°$.
23.   Find AB if $BC = 28.6$ and $\angle B = 42°$.
24.   Find AB if $AC = 9.3$ Ω and $\angle A = 34°$.
25.   Find BC if $AC = 750$ Ω and $\angle A = 48°$.
26.   Find AC if $BC = 17.6$ ft and $\angle B = 60°$.
27.   Find AC if $AB = 4{,}000$ W and $\angle B = 45$ °.
28.   Find BC if $AB = 2{,}500$ W and $\angle A = 45°$.
29.   Find AB if $BC = 142$ V and $\angle A = 37°$.
30.   Find AC if $AB = 85.8$ Ω and $\angle A = 83°$.
31.   A pipe must be bent to provide a 6-ft rise in a 1-ft horizontal distance. Find the angle at each bend.
32.   The foot of a ladder 30 ft long rests on the ground 12 ft from the side of a building. What angle does the ladder make with the ground?
33.   In a taper similar to that shown in Fig. 14-12, the large diameter equals 0.75 in and the small diameter equals 0.47 in. Find angle x if the length equals 2.8 in.
34.   How long is a ladder that reaches 20 ft up the side of a building if the angle between the ladder and the ground is 65°?
35.   Use Fig. 14-12. If the small diameter equals 1.25 in, the length equals 2.25 in, and angle x equals 6°, find the large diameter.
36.   How many inches of wire are needed to wind a single layer coil of 20 turns around a core whose cross section is a square with a diagonal equal to 1.414 in?

37. A rectangle measures 3 by 7 in. Find the angle that the diagonal makes with the longer side.
38. Find the length of the diagonal in Prob. 37.
39. In an impedance triangle similar to that shown in Fig. 14-15, find the impedance Z if $R = 150 \ \Omega$ and angle $A = 50°$.
40. In an inductive ac circuit, the current $I = 15$ A leads the voltage by $30°$. Resolve the current into its in-phase current I_x and its reactive current I_y.

TEST—TRIGONOMETRY

1. Find angle A, correct to the nearest degree, if (a) $\sin A = 0.7416$, (b) $\tan A = 0.9150$, and (c) $\cos A = 0.3333$.

Use a diagram similar to Fig. 14-13 for the Probs. 2 to 5.

2. Find $\angle B$ and $\angle A$ if $BC = 20$ and $AB = 45$.
3. Find BC if $AB = 100$ and $\angle A = 40°$.
4. Find AC if $BC = 60$ and $\angle A = 75°$.
5. Find AB if $BC = 30$ and $\angle A = 30°$.
6. A boy flying a kite lets out 240 ft of string which makes an angle of $28°$ with the ground. How high is the kite above the ground?
7. How long is a ladder that reaches 25 ft up the side of a building if the angle between the ladder and the ground is $70°$?
8. A rectangle measures 5 by 9 in. Find the angle that the diagonal makes with the shorter side.
9. In an impedance triangle similar to that shown in Fig. 14-15, find the impedance Z if $R = 2,000 \ \Omega$ and angle $A = 30°$.
10. Find the capacitive reactance X_C in the triangle used for Prob. 9.

15

INTRODUCTION TO AC ELECTRICITY

JOB 15-1 GRAPHS

In Fig. 15-1, the current that flows through the resistor depends on the voltage that is applied across the ends of the resistor. If the voltage changes, then the current will also change. Let us prepare a table of

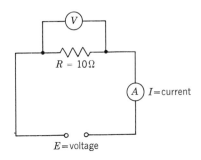

FIGURE 15-1
Changes in the independent variable (voltage) cause corresponding changes in the dependent variable (current).

values of different voltages and the resulting currents using Ohm's law and show them in Table 15-1.

TABLE 15-1

VOLTAGE E	RESISTANCE R	CURRENT I
0	10	0
20	10	2
40	10	4
60	10	6
80	10	8
100	10	10

Quantities like voltages and currents whose values may change are called *variables*. An *independent variable,* like voltage, is one whose value is changed in order to observe the effect on another *dependent variable,* like the current. Tables of information like Table 15-1 are fairly easy to understand and interpret. A glance at the data tells us that the current will double if the voltage is doubled. However, as the information given in a table becomes more complicated, it becomes more difficult to understand and interpret. The relationships between the two variables may be made more evident by presenting the data in the form of a picture, or *graph.*

A graph is a picture that shows the effect of one variable on another. Graphs are used throughout the electronics industry to present information in simple form, to describe the operation of circuits, and to illustrate relationships that cannot be shown by data presented in tabular form.

The scale of a graph. Graphs are drawn on paper ruled with uniformly spaced horizontal and vertical lines. Every fifth line or every tenth line may be heavier than the rest in order to make it easier to read the graph. Figure 15-2, which shows the graph of the data in Table 15-1, is drawn on paper ruled 10 boxes to the inch. The two heavy lines at right angles to each other are the *base lines,* or *reference lines.* The hori-

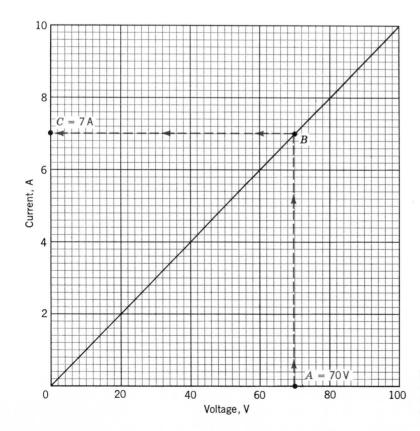

FIGURE 15-2
The current through a 10-Ω resistor depends on the voltage across it.

zontal line, or *abscissa,* is generally used to describe the independent variable, while the vertical base line, or *ordinate,* is used for the dependent variable. The value of each box along each base line must be indicated on the graph. This is called the *scale* for that variable. The highest value of the variable will determine the scale to be used.

For the voltage or abscissa: If we had 100 boxes, we could make each box equal to 1 V and indicate the scale up to 100 V. However, only 50 boxes are available. Therefore, in order to show 100 V, each box must have a value of 100 ÷ 50, or 2 V, for every box. Only every tenth box is numbered in order to keep the graph neat and uncluttered.

For the current or ordinate: The vertical current scale need not be the same as the horizontal scale. Actually, since the highest value of current that must be indicated is only 10 A, we would have a graph only 5 boxes high if we used the same scale. This would cramp the graph and make it difficult to read. Since 50 boxes are available, in order to show 10 A, each box must have a value of 10 ÷ 50, or 0.2 A, for each box. Only every tenth box is numbered.

Reading graphs. As one variable changes, the corresponding value of the other variable may be read from the graph.

EXAMPLE 15-1   Using Fig. 15-2, what is the value of the current when the voltage is 70 V?

SOLUTION
Notice that this information is not included in the table. Without a graph, the information could be obtained only by substitution in the formula for Ohm's law. To get the information from the graph,

1   Locate 70 V on the horizontal voltage scale at *A.*
2   Read straight up along this vertical line until the graph is reached at *B.*
3   Read horizontally to the left along this line to reach the vertical current scale at *C.*
4   Read the value of the current at point *C* as 7 A.   *Ans.*

EXAMPLE 15-2   If a constant voltage is applied across the ends of different resistors, the resulting current may be calculated by Ohm's law. This information may then be shown as a graph such as Fig. 15-3, in which a constant voltage of 10 V was applied across different resistances. Using this graph, find the current when the resistance is (*a*) 5 Ω and (*b*) 7 Ω.

SOLUTION

a
1   Locate 5 Ω at *A* on the horizontal resistance scale.
2   Read straight up to the graph at *B.*
3   Read horizontally to the left to reach the vertical current scale at *C.*

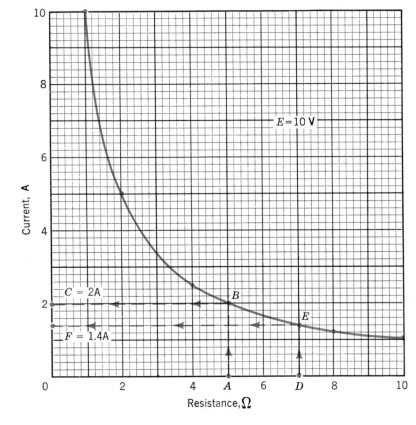

FIGURE 15-3

The relationship between current and resistance at a constant voltage.

4   Read the value of the current at point *C* as 2 A.   *Ans.*

b

1   Locate 7 Ω at *D* on the horizontal resistance scale.
2   Read straight up to the graph at *E*.
3   Read horizontally to the left to reach the vertical current scale at *F*.
4   Read the value of the current at point *F* as slightly more than 1.4 A.
Ans.

PLOTTING GRAPHS

EXAMPLE 15-3   In determining the characteristic curve of a 6J5 tube at 0 V grid bias, the voltage on the plate E_p was varied and the corresponding plate current I_p was measured. The data obtained is shown in the following table. Plot the graph.

Point No.	1	2	3	4	5	6
Plate voltage E_p, V	20	30	40	60	80	100
Plate current I_p, mA	1.0	1.5	2.7	5.5	8.2	11.1

SOLUTION

The finished curve is shown in Fig. 15-4.

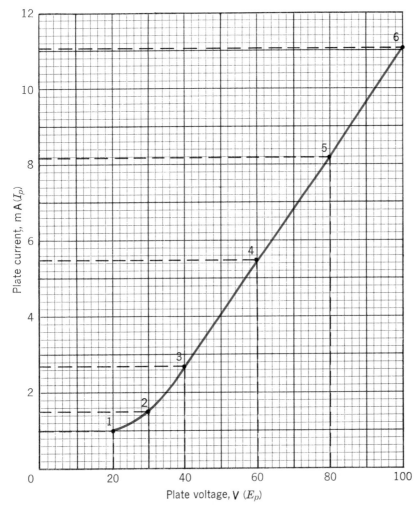

FIGURE 15-4

$E_p - I_p$ curve for a 6J5 tube at 0 V grid bias.

1   Draw two base lines at right angles to each other.

2   Label the horizontal line as the plate voltage in volts and the vertical line as the plate current in milliamperes.

3   Select appropriate scales for each. Since the maximum voltage is 100 V, we can use 1 box to represent 2 V. This will require $100 \div 2$, or 50 boxes. Number every tenth box. On the current scale, to show at least 12 mA, we can use 5 boxes to represent 1 mA, which will require $5 \times 12 = 60$ boxes. Each box will then represent 0.2 mA. Number every tenth box.

4   Plot the individual points. To locate point 1, find 20 V on the horizontal scale. Draw a light line straight up. Now find the corresponding current (1.0 mA) on the vertical scale. Draw a light line straight across. These two lines will intersect at point 1. In the same manner, plot points 2 to 6. Notice that our choice of values for the current scale makes it easy to locate tenths of a milli-ampere. Each box represents 0.2 mA, and half a box represents 0.1 mA.

5   Draw a smooth curve through the points. If all the points do not fall on this smooth curve, draw the curve so that there are as many points over the line as under it.

Graphs with positive and negative values. Many graphs have negative as well as positive values to be considered, and these values must be located on the graph. To do this, the two base lines are extended as shown in Fig. 15-5 to form the horizontal axis XX' and the vertical axis YY'. The two axes meet at the *origin O*. Values along the X axis measured to the *right* of YY' are *positive;* values measured to the *left* of YY' are *negative*. Values along the Y axis measured *upward* from XX' are *positive;* values *downward* from XX' are *negative*. For example, in Fig. 15-5, the points are located depending on the values of X and Y. These

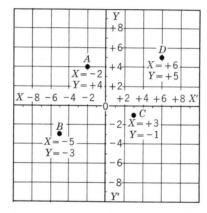

FIGURE15-5

Locating points with positive and negative coordinates.

values are called the coordinates of the point. All points are located starting from the origin O. To locate point A ($X = -2$, $Y = +4$), move two units to the *left* along the X axis, since $X = -2$. Then move four units *up* along this line, since $Y = +4$. To locate point B ($X = -5$, $Y = -3$), move five units to the *left* along the X axis, since $X = -5$. Then move three units *down* along this line, since $Y = -3$. To locate point C ($X = +3$, $Y = -1$), move three units to the *right* along the X axis, since $X = +3$. Then move one unit *down* along this line, since $Y = -1$. To locate point D ($X = +6$, $Y = +5$), move six units to the *right* along the X axis, since $X = +6$. Then move five units *up* along this line, since $Y = +5$.

EXAMPLE 15-4   For a constant plate voltage, the plate current will change when the grid voltage changes. Plot the $E_g I_p$ curve of a tube from the following data.

Grid voltage, V	-3.0	-2.5	-2	-1.5	-1.0	-0.5	0	0.5	1.0
Plate current, mA	0.1	0.3	0.6	1.5	2.4	3.3	4.3	5.1	6.0
Point number	1	2	3	4	5	6	7	8	9

SOLUTION

The curve is shown in Fig. 15-6. Each box along the grid voltage or X axis is worth 0.2 V. Each box along the plate current or Y axis is worth 0.2 mA.

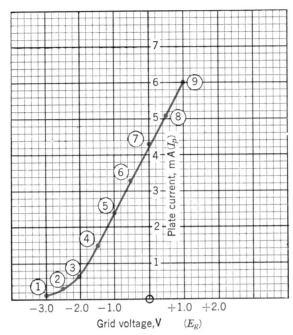

FIGURE 15-6

An $E_g - I_p$ curve. At a constant plate voltage, the plate current depends on the grid voltage.

PROBLEMS

1. Figure 15-7 is a graph showing the current taken by an incandescent lamp at various voltages. Find the current taken at the following

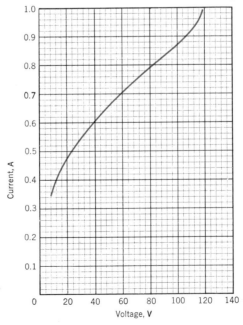

FIGURE 15-7

Current taken by an incandescent lamp at various voltages.

voltages: (*a*) 30 V, (*b*) 45 V, (*c*) 50 V, (*d*) 65 V, (*e*) 80 V, (*f*) 100 V, and (*g*) 120 V.

2. Figure 15-8 is a graph showing the resistance in ohms per 1,000 ft of copper wires of various diameters. Referring to Table 12-1 for the diameter in mils of the gage numbers, find the resistance per 1,000 ft of (*a*) No. 0, (*b*) No. 4, (*c*) No. 6, (*d*) No. 8, (*e*) No. 10, and (*f*) No. 12. Find the resistance per 1,000 ft of wires whose diameters are (*g*) 150 mils, (*h*) 220 mils, (*i*) 250 mils, and (*j*) 0.3 in.

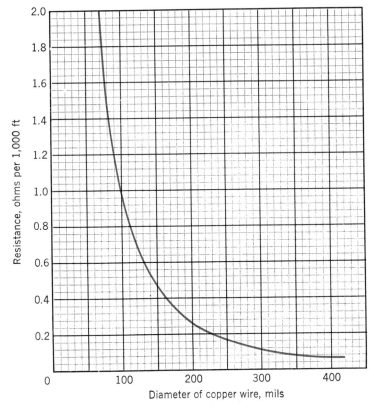

FIGURE 15-8

Graph of a portion of the AWG table, Table 12-1.

Plot a graph for each of the following problems:

3. The volume of a cube when the side is changed.

Side, in	0	1	2	3	4	5
Volume, in³	0	1	8	27	64	125

4. The distance covered by a falling body for increasing units of time.

Time, s	1	2	3	4	5	6	7	8	9	10
Distance, ft	16	64	144	256	400	576	784	1,024	1,296	1,600

5. The efficiency of an engine against its horsepower output. What is the maximum efficiency of the engine? At what horsepower output is this efficiency obtained?

Horsepower output, hp	0	10	20	30	40	50	60	70
Efficiency, percent	0	30	50	64	78	80	78	64

6. The power used by a 100-Ω resistor carrying different currents.

Current, A	0.1	0.2	0.3	0.4	0.5	0.6	0.7	0.8	0.9	1.0
Power, W	1	4	9	16	25	36	49	64	81	100

7. In an inductive circuit, the current does not rise to its Ohm's law value instantaneously. The growth of the current in a certain coil is shown by the following data. Plot the curve.

Time, s	0	0.1	0.2	0.3	0.4	0.5	0.6	0.7	0.8	0.9	1.0
Current, A	0	4.2	6.6	8.0	8.9	9.3	9.6	9.8	9.9	10	10

8. The plate voltage E_p against the plate current I_p for a 6C5 tube at a grid bias of -2 V.

E_p, V	30	50	75	100	125	150	175	200
I_p, mA	0	1.1	2.9	4.9	7.3	10	13.0	16.2

9. The inductive reactance of a 0.01-H coil at different frequencies.

Frequency, Hz	60	100	250	500	1,000
Inductive reactance, Ω	3.7	6.3	15.7	31.4	62.8

10. The capacitive reactance for a 4-μF capacitor at different frequencies.

Frequency, Hz	25	50	60	120	240
Capacitive reactance, Ω	1,590	795	663	331	166

11. The collector voltage V_C against the collector current I_C for a
     2N265 transistor.

V_C, V	5	10	15	20	25	30
I_C, mA	14.1	7.2	4.9	4.1	3.7	3.2

12. The sine of an angle against the number of degrees in the angle.

Angle, deg	0	30	45	60	90	120	135	150	180
Sine of the angle	0	0.5	0.7	0.86	1.0	0.86	0.7	0.5	0

Angle, deg	210	225	240	270	300	315	330	360
Sine of the angle	−0.5	−0.7	−0.86	−1.0	−0.86	−0.7	−0.5	0

JOB 15-2   THE GENERATION OF AN AC VOLTAGE

Magnetism. The phenomenon of magnetism was discovered about
100 B.C. when it was observed that a peculiar stone had the property of
attracting bits of iron to it. This natural magnet was called a *lodestone.*
The lodestone was used to create other magnets artificially by stroking
pieces of iron with it.

Magnetic poles. Every magnet has two points opposite each other
which attract pieces of iron best. These points are called the *poles* of the
magnet: the north pole and the south pole. Just as similar electrical
charges repel each other and opposite charges attract each other, similar
magnetic poles repel each other and unlike poles attract each other.
   A magnet evidently attracts a bit of iron because of some force that
exists around the magnet. This force is called the magnetic field. Although it is invisible to the naked eye, it can be shown to exist by its
effect on bits of iron. Place a sheet of glass or some other nonmagnetic
material over a bar magnet as shown in Fig. 15-9. Sprinkle some iron

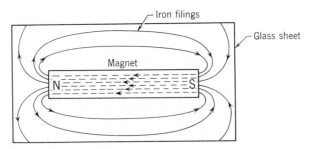

FIGURE 15-9
The iron filings indicate the
pattern of the lines of force
around a bar magnet.

filings over the glass, and tap it gently. The filings will fall back into a definite pattern which describes the field of force around the magnet. The field evidently seems to be made up of *lines* of force which appear to leave the magnet at the north pole, travel through the air around the magnet, and continue through the magnet to the north pole to form a *closed loop* of force. The stronger the magnet, the greater the number of lines of force and the larger the area covered by the field.

Electromagnetism. In 1819, Hans Christian Oersted, a Danish physicist, discovered that a field of magnetic force exists around a wire carrying an electric current. In Fig. 15-10, a wire is passed through a

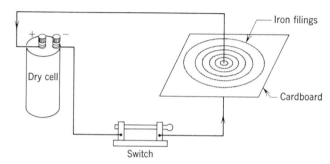

FIGURE 15-10
A circular pattern of magnetic force exists around a wire carrying an electric current.

piece of cardboard and connected through a switch to a dry cell. With the switch open (no current flowing), sprinkle iron filings on the cardboard and tap it gently. The filings will fall back haphazardly. Now close the switch, which will permit a current to flow in the wire. Tap the cardboard again. This time, the magnetic effect of the current in the wire will cause the filings to fall back into a definite pattern of concentric circles with the wire as the center of the circles. Every section of the wire has this field of force around it in a plane perpendicular to the wire as shown in Fig. 15-11.

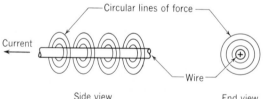

FIGURE 15-11
The circular fields of force around a wire carrying a current are in planes which are perpendicular to the wire.

The strength of the magnetic field. The ability of the magnetic field to attract bits of iron depends on the number of lines of force present. The strength of the magnetic field around a wire carrying a current depends on the current, since it is the current that produces the field. The greater the current, the greater the strength of the field. A large current will produce many lines of force extending far from the wire, while a small current will produce only a few lines close to the wire as shown in Fig. 15-12.

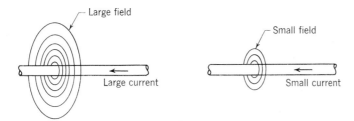

FIGURE 15-12
The strength of the magnetic field around a wire carrying a current depends on the amount of current.

Electromagnetic induction. Michael Faraday is credited with the discovery, in 1831, of the basic principle underlying the operation of ac machinery. Simply stated, he discovered that if a conductor "cut across" lines of magnetic force, or if lines of force "cut across" a conductor, an electromotive force or voltage would be induced across the ends of the conductor. Figure 15-13 represents a magnet with its lines of force

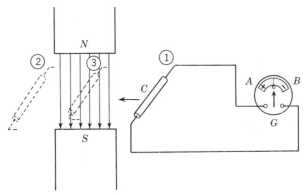

FIGURE 15-13
When a conductor cuts lines of force, an emf is induced in the conductor. The direction in which the conductor cuts the lines determines the direction of the induced emf.

streaming from the north to the south pole. A conductor *C*, which can be moved between the poles, is connected to a galvanometer, which is a very sensitive meter used to indicate the presence of an electromotive force. When the conductor is stationary, the galvanometer indicates zero emf. If the wire is *moved about outside* the magnetic field at position 1, the galvanometer will still indicate zero. However, if the conductor is moved to the *left* to position 2, so that it *cuts across the lines of magnetic force,* the galvanometer pointer will deflect to *A*. This indicates that an emf was induced in the conductor because lines of force were "cut." Upon reaching position 2, the galvanometer pointer swung back to zero because no lines of force were being cut. Now move the conductor to the *right* through the lines of force back to position 1. During this *movement,* the pointer will deflect to *B,* indicating that an emf has again been induced in the wire, but in the *opposite direction.* If the wire is held *stationary* in the middle of the field of force at position 3, the galvanometer reads zero. If the conductor is moved up or down *parallel* to the lines of force so that *none are cut,* no emf will be induced. From experiments similar to these, Faraday deduced the following:

1 When lines of force are cut by a conductor or lines of force cut a conductor, an emf is induced in the conductor.

2   There must be a relative *motion* between the conductor and the lines of force in order to induce an emf.

3   Changing the direction of the cutting will change the direction of the induced emf.

Generating an alternating emf.   Since a voltage is induced in a conductor when lines of force are cut, the amount of the induced emf depends on the number of lines cut in a unit time.   In order to induce an emf of 1 V, a conductor must cut 100,000,000 lines of force per second. To obtain this great number of "cuttings," the conductor is formed into a loop and rotated on an axis at great speed as shown in Fig. 15-14.   The two sides of the loop become individual conductors in series, each side of the loop cutting lines of force and inducing twice the voltage that a single conductor would induce.   In commercial generators, the number of "cuttings" and the resulting emf are increased by (1) increasing the number of lines of force by using more magnets or stronger electromagnets, (2) using more conductors or loops, (3) rotating the loops faster.

Let us follow a single conductor as it rotates at a uniform speed through a uniformly distributed field of force.   In Fig. 15-15, the lines *AD*, *BE*, and *CF* are all equal to *OC* and represent the direction in which the conductor is moving at points *A*, *B*, and *C*, respectively.   At *A*, the conductor is moving parallel to the lines of force.   No lines of force are cut, and zero volts are induced.   At *C*, the conductor has rotated through 90° and is moving in the direction *CF*.   This motion is directly across the lines of force and produces the maximum number of cuttings and the maximum voltage E_{max}.   This maximum voltage may be represented by the distance *CF*.   Since *OC* is equal to *CF*, the maximum voltage may be represented by the radius of the circle *OC*.   At *B*, the conductor has

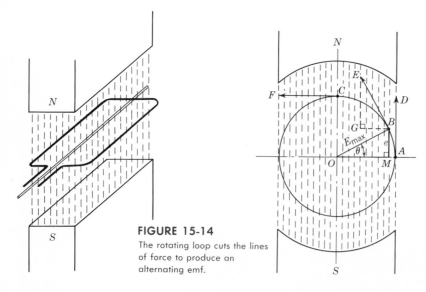

FIGURE 15-14

The rotating loop cuts the lines of force to produce an alternating emf.

FIGURE 15-15

A conductor rotating at a constant speed through a uniform magnetic field.

rotated through some angle θ (theta) and is moving in the direction shown by *BE*. This motion from *B* to *E* may be considered to be made of a motion from *B* to *G* and then from *G* to *E*. However, only one of these motions is useful in cutting lines of force. The motion *GE* is parallel to the lines of force and produces no cuttings. Therefore, the distance *BG* represents the total cuttings produced by the motion *BE*. *BG* therefore represents the voltage produced at the instant that the conductor is passing through point *B*. It can be shown by geometry that $BG = BM$. Thus, the vertical line drawn from the conductor at any instant perpendicular to the base represents the voltage induced in the conductor at that instant. The voltage at any instant of time evidently depends on the position of the conductor at that instant and is known as the instantaneous voltage *e*.

SUMMARY

1   Only that part of the motion of a conductor directly across the field cuts lines and produces voltage.

2   The number of lines cut and the voltage produced are zero at 0° and increase to a maximum at 90°.

3   The vertical distance drawn from the conductor at any point to the horizontal base line represents the voltage produced at the instant that the conductor is passing through that point.

The complete picture of the voltage produced by a rotating conductor may now be drawn. Draw a circle, and divide the circumference into 12 parts, each 30° apart, as shown in Fig. 15-16. A horizontal base line is drawn as shown and labeled in degrees to correspond to the positions of the conductor. The vertical distances represent the voltages produced. As the conductor rotates, the vertical distance at each point is drawn at the corresponding point on the graph. Notice that the motion from 0 to 180° was to the *left*. The motion from 180 to 360° was to the *right* and produced a voltage in the *opposite* direction. This is indicated by *negative* voltages drawn *below* the base line. This graph gives a complete picture of all the changes in voltage during one complete rotation.

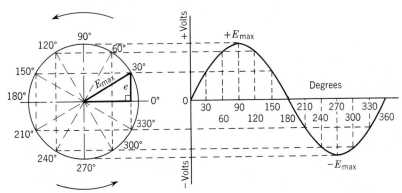

FIGURE 15-16

The voltage wave produced by a conductor rotating at a constant speed through a uniform magnetic field.

1   At 0°, the emf is 0 V.

2   At 90°, the emf is the greatest and is known as $+E_{max}$.

3   At 180°, the emf is again 0 V. The direction of the rotation and voltage changes at this point.

4   At 270°, the emf is again a maximum, but in the *opposite* direction, and is known as $-E_{max}$.

5   At 360°, the emf is 0 V.

6   The voltage passes twice through both the zero value and the maximum value during the cycle.

7   The maximum voltages are equal in value but are of opposite sign.

8   The instantaneous voltage means the voltage at any instant during an ac cycle. The symbol is *e*.

The sine wave. Consider the triangle *OBM* in Fig. 15-15. *OB* is a radius of the circle and is equal to the maximum voltage E_{max}. *BM* is the instantaneous voltage at any angle θ (theta), given as *e*. By trigonometry,

$$\sin \theta = \frac{e}{E_{max}} \qquad \boxed{15\text{-}1}$$

or
$$e = E_{max} \times \sin \theta \qquad \boxed{15\text{-}2}$$

This formula says that the value of the voltage at any instant depends on the maximum voltage and the *sine of the angle at that instant*. If the maximum voltage is 1 V,

$$e = 1 \times \sin \theta$$

or
$$e = \sin \theta \qquad \boxed{15\text{-}3}$$

We can now plot a graph of the changes in the voltage as a conductor rotates in a circle through a uniform field at a constant speed. Figure 15-17 shows the graph obtained by plotting the angles against the values of the sine of the angles. Compare this curve with the curve of Fig. 15-16. They are identical. Most commercial generators are designed to produce alternating waves of this type. They are called sine waves because the voltage at any instant is proportional to the sine of the angle at that instant.

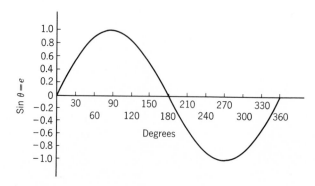

FIGURE 15-17

The voltage is proportional to the sine of the angle in a sine wave.

Cycle, frequency. An alternating wave may be an ac voltage or an alternating current. During one *cycle,* the wave will pass through a complete series of positive and negative values. In one cycle, as shown in Fig. 15-18, an ac voltage starts at 0°, rises to a positive maximum at 90°, and falls to zero at 180°; then *reverses its polarity,* rises to a negative maximum at 270°, and falls to zero at 360°. An alternating current starts at 0°, rises to a positive maximum at 90°, and falls to zero at 180°; then *reverses its direction,* rises to a negative maximum at 270°, and falls to zero at 360°.

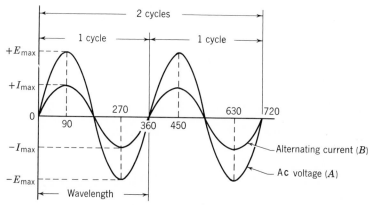

FIGURE 15-18
A cycle describes all the changes of voltage or current during a rotation of 360°.

Each cycle of an ac wave may be repeated over and over. The frequency f of an ac wave means the number of complete cycles that occur *in one second.* In the United States the standard frequency for light and power is 60 cycles/s (60 Hz). Audio frequencies range between 30 and 15,000 Hz. Radio and television frequencies range between 15,000 and 890,000,000 Hz.

Wavelength. The distance traveled by an ac wave during one complete cycle is called its *wavelength.* Its symbol is the Greek letter lambda, λ. This distance may be expressed in any convenient unit of length. However, since most scientific work uses the metric system, the wavelength is usually measured in terms of *meters.* One meter is equal to 39.37 inch.

The speed of radio waves is the same as the speed of light, or 186,000 mi/s. This speed may be expressed in the metric system in terms of meters per second. Since 1 mi = 5,280 ft,

$$186,000 \text{ mi} = 186,000 \times 5,280 \text{ feet}$$

$$= 186,000 \times 5,280 \times 12 \text{ inches}$$

$$= \frac{186,000 \times 5,280 \times 12}{39.37} \text{ meters}$$

$$= 300,000,000 \text{ meters}$$

Therefore, the speed of a radio wave may be expressed as 300,000,000 m/s.

If we divide the speed in meters per second by the frequency in cycles per second, the units of time will cancel out as shown below.

$$\frac{\text{Meters}}{\text{Second}} \div \frac{\text{cycles}}{\text{second}}$$

Inverting and multiplying,

$$\frac{\text{Meters}}{\underset{1}{\cancel{\text{Second}}}} \times \frac{\overset{1}{\cancel{\text{second}}}}{\text{cycles}} = \frac{\text{meters}}{\text{cycle}}$$

The number of meters per cycle is the wavelength.

FORMULA

$$\lambda = \frac{300,000,000}{f} \qquad \boxed{15\text{-}4}$$

where λ = wavelength, m
  f = frequency, Hz

If the frequency is expressed in kilohertz,

$$\lambda = \frac{300,000}{f} \qquad \boxed{15\text{-}5}$$

where λ = wavelength, m
  f = frequency, kHz

EXAMPLE 15-5 What is the wavelength of radio station WCBS, which broadcasts at a frequency of 880 kHz?

SOLUTION
GIVEN: STATION WCBS   FIND: λ = ?
    f = 880 kHz

$$\lambda = \frac{300,000}{f} \qquad (15\text{-}5)$$

$$\lambda = \frac{300,000}{880} = 340.9 \text{ m} \qquad Ans.$$

EXAMPLE 15-6 What is the frequency of a radio wave if its wavelength is equal to 297 m? What New York City station broadcasts at this frequency?

SOLUTION
Given: λ = 297 m   Find: f = ?
                    Name of New York station = ?

$$\lambda = \frac{300,000}{f} \qquad (15\text{-}5)$$

$$297 = \frac{300,000}{f}$$

$$297 \times f = 300,000$$

$$f = \frac{300,000}{297} = 1,010 \text{ kHz} \qquad Ans.$$

The station is WINS.

SUMMARY

A magnet attracts bits of iron or steel. A magnet has a north and a south pole. Like poles repel; unlike poles attract. A magnetic field composed of closed loops of lines of force exists around a magnet.

A field of magnetic force exists around a wire that carries an electric current. The strength of the field is directly proportional to the strength of the current.

Electromagnetic induction. When there is a mutual cutting of lines of force by a conductor, or vice versa, an emf is induced in the conductor. The direction of the induced voltage depends on the direction of the motion of the conductor.

Generating a sine wave emf. An emf will be induced in a conductor if it is rotated at a constant speed through a uniform field of force. The amount of voltage induced depends on the number of lines of force which are cut per second. The number of "cuttings" and the voltage at any instant depend on the position of the conductor at that instant and are proportional to the sine of the angle at that instant. The voltage will rise and fall and change polarity at regular intervals of time. Such a wave is called an alternating wave or an ac wave. An alternating-current wave is one which changes in amount and *direction* at regular intervals of time.

A *cycle* of an ac wave is a record of all the changes that occur during a *single* rotation from 0 to 360°.

The *frequency* of an ac wave is the number of complete cycles that occur in one second. The symbol is f.

The *wavelength* of an ac wave is the distance traveled by the wave during one complete cycle. The symbol is λ.

JOB 15-3 INSTANTANEOUS VALUES, MAXIMUM VALUES, AND PHASE ANGLES OF AN AC WAVE

Since alternating voltage and current waves change in amount and direction at regular intervals, the voltage or current at any instant of time must be calculated. These values are called the *instantaneous values.* For example, in Fig. 15-15, when the conductor has rotated through some angle θ to reach point B, the instantaneous value is indicated by the vertical line BM. The radius of the circle OB indicates the maximum value of the wave. By trigonometry, we obtain

FORMULAS

$$\sin \theta = \frac{e}{E_{max}} \qquad\qquad (15\text{-}1)$$

or
$$e = E_{max} \times \sin \theta \qquad\qquad (15\text{-}2)$$

If this changing voltage wave is impressed across a resistance, each instantaneous voltage e will produce its own value of instantaneous current i. Thus, as shown in Fig. 15-18, the ac voltage wave A produced the ac wave B. This current wave will have the same frequency as the voltage wave which produced it. Using this current wave, we obtain

FORMULAS

$$\sin \theta = \frac{i}{I_{max}} \qquad\qquad \boxed{15\text{-}6}$$

or
$$i = I_{max} \times \sin \theta \qquad\qquad \boxed{15\text{-}7}$$

EXAMPLE 15-7 An ac wave has a maximum value of 100 mA. Find the instantaneous current at $70°$.

SOLUTION
Given: $I_{max} = 100$ mA   Find: $i = ?$
$\qquad\quad \theta = 70°$

$$i = I_{max} \times \sin \theta \qquad\qquad (15\text{-}7)$$
$$i = 100 \times \sin 70° = 100 \times 0.9397 = 93.97 \text{ mA} \qquad Ans.$$

Maximum values. The maximum value of an ac voltage (E_{max}) or an alternating current (I_{max}) is reached twice during each cycle. The positive maximums occur at $90°$, and the negative maximums occur at $270°$. By solving Eqs. (15-2) and (15-7) for the E_{max} and I_{max} we obtain the following formulas:

FORMULAS

$$E_{max} = \frac{e}{\sin \theta} \qquad\qquad \boxed{15\text{-}8}$$

$$I_{max} = \frac{i}{\sin \theta} \qquad\qquad \boxed{15\text{-}9}$$

EXAMPLE 15-8   An ac voltage wave has an instantaneous value of 70 V at 30°. (*a*) Find the maximum value of the wave. (*b*) Can this wave be impressed across a capacitor whose breakdown voltage is 125 V?

SOLUTION

Given: $e = 70$ V   Find: $E_{max} = ?$

$\quad\quad\theta = 30°$

a $E_{max} = \dfrac{e}{\sin \theta} = \dfrac{70}{\sin 30°} = \dfrac{70}{0.5000} = 140$ V   *Ans.*

b   No, since 140 V is larger than the breakdown voltage of 125 V.

Phase angles. The phase angle θ or phase of an ac cycle refers to the value of the electrical angle at any point during the cycle. These angles may be found by solving formula (15-1) or (15-6).

EXAMPLE 15-9   An ac voltage wave has a maximum value of 155.5 V. Find the phase angle at which the instantaneous voltage is 110 V.

SOLUTION

Given: $E_{max} = 155.5$ V   Find: $\theta = ?$

$\quad\quad\quad e = 110$ V

$$\sin \theta = \frac{e}{E_{max}} = \frac{110}{155.5} = 0.7074 \quad\quad\quad (15\text{-}1)$$

$$\theta = 45° \quad\quad \textit{Ans.}$$

PROBLEMS

1. What is the wavelength of an ac wave whose frequency is 30,000 Hz?
2. Find the frequency of a carrier wave whose wavelength is 600 m.
3. Find the instantaneous voltage at 50° in a wave whose maximum value is 165 V.
4. Find the maximum value of an ac wave if the instantaneous voltage is 50 V at 35°.
5. Find the phase angle at which an instantaneous voltage of 72 V appears in a wave whose maximum value is 250 V.
6. Find the instantaneous current at 85° in a wave whose maximum value is 26 A.
7. Find the maximum value of an ac wave if the instantaneous current is 9 A at 12°.
8. Find the phase angle at which an instantaneous current of 3.5 A appears in a wave whose maximum value is 20 A.
9. The maximum current of the current wave of a transmitter is 10 A.

At what instant (angle) will the instantaneous current be (*a*) 5 A, (*b*) 6 A, and (*c*) 8.66 A?

10. The maximum voltage of an ac wave is 100 V. Find the instantaneous voltage at (*a*) 0°, (*b*) 15°, (*c*) 30°, (*d*) 45°, (*e*) 60°, (*f*) 75°, and (*g*) 90°. (*h*) What is the average of these voltages?

JOB 15-4 EFFECTIVE VALUE OF AN AC WAVE

An alternating current is a current that is continually changing in amount and direction. In Fig. 15-19, the current starts at 0 A at 0 time. After 1 s, it reaches 10 A but drops down to 0 after 2 s. At this point, the current reverses its direction and increases negatively to 10 A at 3 s, after which it drops down to 0 after 4 s. The *average* current during these 4 s equals $0 + 10 + 0 - 10 + 0$ divided by 5, or 0 A. Obviously, even though the average of all the currents is zero, this ac wave can be effective in running a motor or lighting a lamp. But how many amperes are actually flowing? If an ac ammeter is used to measure this current, it will read 7.07 A. This meter reading is called the *effective value* of all the changes that occur during one cycle of the wave.

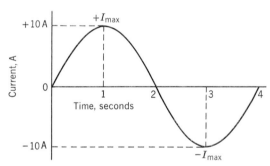

FIGURE 15-19
An ac wave.

One of the effects of the passage of any electrical current through a resistance, whether it be alternating or direct, is the production of heat. To determine the *worth,* or *effectiveness,* of an ac wave, we must compare its effect with the effect of a direct current.

RULE	If an ac wave produces as much heat as 1 A of direct current, we say that the ac wave is as effective as 1 A of direct current.

Thus, as in Fig. 15-20, an ac wave may start at zero and pass through many values of current up to a maximum of 10 A, continuing to fall to zero, change direction, rise to a negative maximum of 10 A, and fall to zero again. If the *effect* of all these changes is to produce only as much heat as 7.07 A of direct current would produce, then the wave is said

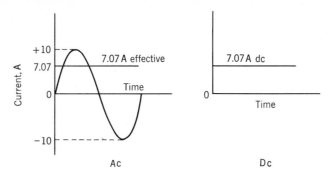

FIGURE 15-20
Effective values of alternating
and direct currents.

to have an *effective* value of only 7.07 A. The effective value of any current wave may be calculated by averaging the *heating* effects of the many individual instantaneous currents. Since $P = I^2R$, the heating effect on any resistance depends on the *square* of the current. Thus,

$$I_{dc}^2 = \text{average of } i^2$$

by taking the square root of both sides,

$$I_{dc} = \sqrt{i_{av}^2}$$

Since the effective alternating current is to have the same heating effect as the direct current,

$$I_{ac} = I_{dc} = \sqrt{i_{av}^2}$$

This equation says that the effective value of an ac wave is equal to the square root of the average (mean) of the squares of the instantaneous currents. For this reason it is sometimes called the rms (root mean square) value. This gives us a method for calculating the effective value of any ac wave. One quarter of a cycle is divided into a number of equal parts, and the instantaneous currents are calculated at each point. These currents are squared, and the average found. The square root of this average is equal to the effective value of the wave. The results of many calculations for waves of different maximums indicate that the effective value of a sine-wave current is always 0.707 times the maximum value of the wave.

FORMULA

$$I = 0.707 \times I_{max} \qquad \boxed{15\text{-}10}$$

where I = effective value of an ac wave
  I_{max} = maximum value of an ac wave

Since alternating currents are the result of ac voltages, the effective values of a voltage wave have an identical relation to the maximum voltages.

FORMULA

$$E = 0.707 \times E_{max}$$

15-11

where E = effective value of an ac voltage wave

E_{max} = maximum value of an ac voltage wave

Notice that the effective values are written as I and E, with no subscripts. Alternating-current meters are designed and calibrated to indicate these effective values. Unless otherwise specified, a value of an alternating current or ac voltage always means the effective value.

Formulas (15-10) and (15-11) may be transformed to obtain formulas for the I_{max} and the E_{max}.

$$I = 0.707 \times I_{max}$$

or $$I_{max} = \frac{I}{0.707}$$

FORMULA

$$I_{max} = 1.414 \times I$$

15-12

Similarly, $$E = 0.707 \times E_{max}$$

or $$E_{max} = \frac{E}{0.707}$$

FORMULA

$$E_{max} = 1.414 \times E$$

15-13

Thus, an effective voltage of 120 V is the effective voltage of a wave whose maximum equals $1.414 \times 120 = 170$ V. This means that if an electric heater were used on a 120-V ac line, it would produce only as much heat as would be produced on a 120-V dc line, even though the ac line reaches the maximum of 170 V twice in each cycle.

EXAMPLE 15-10   An alternating current has a maximum value of 50 A. Find (a) the effective current and (b) the instantaneous current at 10°.

SOLUTION

Given: $I_{max} = 50$ A   Find: $I = ?$

$\qquad\quad \theta = 10°$ $\qquad i = ?$

a $\qquad\qquad\qquad I = 0.707 \times I_{max}$ (15-10)

$\qquad\qquad\qquad I = 0.707 \times 50 = 35.35$ A   *Ans.*

b $\qquad\qquad\qquad i = I_{max} \times \sin \theta$ (15-7)

$\qquad\qquad\qquad i = 50 \times \sin 10°$

$\qquad\qquad\qquad i = 50 \times 0.1736 = 8.68$ A   *Ans.*

EXAMPLE 15-11   An ac voltage wave has an effective value of 110 V. Find (a) the maximum value and (b) the instantaneous value at 40°.

SOLUTION

Given: $E = 110$ V   Find: $E_{max} = ?$
$\qquad \theta = 40°$ $\qquad\qquad\qquad e = ?$

a $\qquad\qquad E_{max} = 1.414 \times E = 1.414 \times 110 = 155$ V   *Ans.*

b $\qquad\qquad\qquad e = E_{max} \times \sin \theta$ $\qquad\qquad\qquad\qquad$ (15-2)

$\qquad\qquad\qquad\quad e = 155 \times \sin 40°$

$\qquad\qquad\qquad\quad e = 155 \times 0.6428 = 99.6$ V   *Ans.*

SELF-TEST 15-12   An ac wave has an instantaneous value of 12.95 A at 15°. Find (a) the maximum value and (b) the effective value.

SOLUTION

Given: $i = 12.95$ A   Find: $I_{max} = ?$ $\qquad\qquad\qquad\qquad\qquad\qquad$ 15°
$\qquad \theta = \underline{\quad}$ $\qquad\qquad\qquad\qquad I = ?$

$a.$ $\qquad\qquad\qquad I_{max} = \dfrac{i}{?}$ $\qquad\qquad\qquad\qquad$ (15-9) $\qquad\qquad$ $\sin \theta$

$\qquad\qquad\qquad\qquad = \dfrac{12.95}{\sin 15°} = \dfrac{12.95}{?}$ $\qquad\qquad\qquad\qquad\qquad\qquad$ 0.2588

$\qquad\qquad\qquad I_{max} = \underline{\quad}$ A $\quad$ *Ans.* $\qquad\qquad\qquad\qquad\qquad\qquad$ 50

$b.$ $\qquad\qquad\quad I = 0.707 \times \underline{\quad}$ $\qquad\qquad\qquad\qquad$ (15-10) $\qquad\qquad$ I_{max}

$\qquad\qquad\quad I = 0.707 \times \underline{\quad} = 35.35$ A $\quad$ *Ans.* $\qquad\qquad\qquad\qquad$ 50

PROBLEMS

Find the values indicated in each problem.

PROBLEM	MAXIMUM VALUE	EFFECTIVE VALUE	PHASE ANGLE	INSTANTANEOUS VALUE
1	35 A	?	30°	?
2	456 V	?	40°	?
3	?	440 V	50°	?
4	?	25 A	60°	?
5	155 V	?	30°	?
6	10 A	?	45°	?
7	?	110 V	65°	?
8	?	20 A	75°	?
9	?	?	50°	26.81 A
10	?	?	15°	120.3 V
11	100 V	?	?	43.84 V
12	20 A	?	?	5.5 A

13. A sine wave has an instantaneous value of 10 V at 30°. What is its value at 60°?

14. What must be the minimum breakdown voltage rating of a capacitor in order to use it on a 110-V ac line?

15. An electric stove draws 7.5 A from a 120-V dc source. (*a*) What is the maximum value of an alternating current which will produce heat at the same rate? (*b*) Find the power drawn from the ac line.

16. An underground cable is designed to operate safely at an effective voltage of 2,200 V. What dc voltage will the line carry safely?

TEST—AC WAVES

1. Using the following data, plot a graph showing the current taken by an incandescent lamp at different voltages.

Voltage, V	10	20	30	40	50	60	70	80	90	100	110
Current, A	0.17	0.24	0.30	0.37	0.44	0.50	0.57	0.64	0.71	0.76	0.84

2. An ac wave has a maximum value of 300 V. Find the effective value and the instantaneous value at 30°.

3. An ac wave has an effective value of 50 mA. Find the maximum value and the instantaneous value at 60°.

4. An ac wave reaches an instantaneous value of 40 V at 18°. Find the maximum and the effective value of the wave.

5. An ac wave has a maximum value of 200 V. Find the angle at which the voltage is 165.8 V. What is the effective value?

16

INDUCTANCE AND TRANSFORMERS

JOB 16-1   INDUCTANCE OF A COIL

Basic ideas. In Chap. 15 we learned the following:

1   A field of force exists around a wire carrying a current.

2   This field has the form of concentric circles around the wire, in planes perpendicular to the wire, and with the wire at the center of the circles.

3   The strength of the field depends on the current. Large currents produce large fields; small currents produce small fields.

4   When lines of force cut across a conductor, a voltage is induced in the conductor.

EFFECT OF INDUCTANCE

Experiment 1. Connect a 20-V source of direct current across a *straight* wire whose resistance is 10 Ω as shown in Fig. 16-1*a*. When the switch is closed, the direct current

$$I = \frac{E}{R} = \frac{20}{10} = 2 \text{ A}$$

will flow. This current will produce *stationary* lines of force perpendicu-

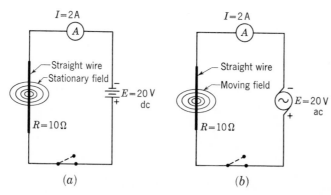

(*a*)   (*b*)

FIGURE 16-1

(*a*) Direct current through a straight wire produces 2 A. (*b*) Alternating current through a straight wire produces the same 2 A.

501

lar to the wire. No cuttings can occur, and therefore no voltage is induced in the wire.

Experiment 2. Remove the 20-V dc source from the circuit of Fig. 16-1*a,* and replace it with a 20-V ac source as in Fig. 16-1*b.* When the switch is closed, the alternating current

$$I = \frac{E}{R} = \frac{20}{10} = 2 \text{ A}$$

will flow. This current will produce lines of force that move *out* from the wire as the alternating current increases and collapse *back* toward the wire as the current decreases. The field expands and contracts with the variations in the current. However, since the lines of force are perpendicular to the wire, no lines of force can cut the wire and no voltage is induced in the wire.

Experiment 3. Remove the 10-Ω wire, and *twist it into a coil.* The resistance of the wire will still be 10 Ω. Replace the 20-V ac source with a 20-V dc source as shown in Fig. 16-2*a.* When the switch is closed, the direct current

$$I = \frac{E}{R} = \frac{20}{10} = 2 \text{ A}$$

will flow. This current will produce *stationary* lines of force perpendicular to the wire. Since the field is stationary, there can be no relative *motion* between the lines and the wire; therefore no cuttings can occur and no voltage is induced in the wire.

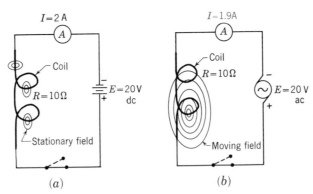

(*a*)   (*b*)

FIGURE 16-2

(*a*) Direct current through a coil produces 2 A. (*b*) Alternating current through a coil *reduces* the current to 1.9 A.

Experiment 4. Remove the 20-V dc source from the circuit of Fig. 16-2*a,* and replace it with the 20-V ac source as shown in Fig. 16-2*b.* When the switch is closed, the alternating current

$$I = \frac{E}{R} = \frac{20}{10} = 2 \text{ A}$$

will not flow! Actually it might be only 1.9 A. This is what happened.

The alternating current produced an expanding and collapsing field of force as in Experiment 2, but *because the wire was twisted into a coil, the moving lines of force could cut the turns of the coil.* These cuttings induced a voltage in the coil *and in a direction so as to oppose the original voltage.* For this reason it is called a *back emf.* If the back emf is 1 V, then the voltage available to force the current through the 10-Ω resistance is only $20 - 1 = 19$ V. The current will therefore be

$$I = \frac{E}{R} = \frac{19}{10} = 1.9 \text{ A}$$

Notice that this back emf can occur *only* when a *coil* is carrying a *changing* current.

Inductance. The inductance of a coil is a measure of its ability to produce a back emf when an ac voltage is impressed across it. If the voltage and resulting current are *increasing,* the induced emf will be in a direction so as to *reduce* the increase. If the voltage and resulting current are *decreasing,* the induced emf will be in a direction so as to *increase* the current. The net effect of inductance is to slow down the speed at which any change occurs. The symbol for inductance is L.

The unit of inductance. The back emf induced in a coil depends on the number of "cuttings" of lines of force by conductors. A rapidly changing current will induce a larger back emf than a slowly changing current because the former will produce more cuttings in the same time. In order to compare two coils, we must pass the same kind of current through both and observe the back emf generated in each. If this same current induces 1 V of back emf in coil A and 2 V of back emf in coil B, then coil B would have twice the inductance of coil A. This enables us to define the unit of inductance.

Definition. If a current changing at the uniform rate of 1 A/s induces a back emf of 1 V, then the inductance is 1 H.

JOB 16-2   REACTANCE OF A COIL

When an ac voltage is impressed across a coil,

   1   The ac voltage will produce an alternating current.
   2   When a current flows in a wire, lines of force are produced around the wire.
   3   Large currents produce many lines of force; small currents produce only a few lines of force.
   4   As the current changes, the number of lines of force will change. The field of force will seem to expand and contract as the current increases and decreases as shown in Fig. 16-3.

Expanding
field of force

Contracting
field of force

FIGURE 16-3
An alternating current produces
a *moving* field of force which
cuts the wires forming the turns
of the coil.

   5   As the field expands and contracts, the lines of force must cut across the
wires which form the turns of the coil.
   6   These "cuttings" induce an emf in the coil.
   7   This emf acts in a direction so as to oppose the original voltage and is
called a "back emf."
   8   The effect of this back emf is to reduce the original voltage impressed
on the coil. The net effect will be to reduce the current below that which would
flow if there were no cuttings or back emf.
   9   In this sense, the back emf is acting as a resistance in reducing the current.
   10   Actually, it is extremely convenient to consider the current-reducing
effect of a back emf as a number of ohms of effective resistance. However, since
a back emf is not actually a resistance but merely *acts* as a resistance, we use the
term *reactance* to describe this effect. The *reactance* of a coil is the number of
ohms of resistance which the coil *seems* to offer as a result of a back emf induced
in it. Its symbol is X to differentiate it from the dc resistance R.

   What factors affect the reactance? (1) If the frequency of the ac
voltage changes, then the number of cuttings and the resulting reactance
will change. (2) If the natural ability of the coil to produce a back emf—
its inductance—changes, then the reactance will also change. The value
of the reactance of a coil is therefore proportional to its inductance and
the frequency of the ac circuit in which it is used. Its actual value may
be found by the formula $X_L = 2\pi fL$. Since $2\pi = 2 \times 3.14 = 6.28$, the
formula for the reactance of a coil becomes

FORMULA

$$X_L = 6.28fL$$

16-1

where X_L = inductive reactance, Ω
       f = frequency, Hz
       L = inductance, H
    6.28 = constant of proportionality

   EXAMPLE 16-1   The primary of a power transformer has an inductance of 150 mH. (*a*) Find its inductive reactance at a frequency of 60
Hz. (*b*) What current will it draw from a 117-V line?

SOLUTION

Given: $L = 150$ mH   Find: $X_L = ?$

$f = 60$ Hz $I_L = ?$

$E = 117$ volts

a.   150 mh $= 150 \times 10^{-3}$ H

$$X_L = 6.28fL \tag{16-1}$$

$$X_L = 6.28 \times 60 \times 150 \times 10^{-3}$$

$$X_L = 56.6 \ \Omega \quad Ans.$$

b.   Since the only resistance in the circuit is the inductive reactance, the formula for Ohm's law, $E = IR$, may be rewritten as the

FORMULA

$$E_L = I_L \times X_L \qquad \boxed{16\text{-}2}$$

$$117 = I_L \times 56.5$$

$$I_L = \frac{117}{56.5} = 2.07 \ \text{A} \quad Ans.$$

EXAMPLE 16-2   A 20-mH coil is in a tank circuit operating at a frequency of 1,500 kHz. Find its inductive reactance.

SOLUTION

Given: $L = 20$ mH   Find: $X_L = ?$

$f = 1,500$ kHz

1   Change units of measurement.

$$20 \ \text{mH} = 20 \times 10^{-3} \ \text{H}$$

$$1,500 \ \text{kHz} = 1,500 \times 10^3 \ \text{Hz}$$

2   Find the inductive reactance.

$$X_L = 6.28fL \tag{16-1}$$

$$X_L = 6.28 \times 1,500 \times 10^3 \times 20 \times 10^{-3}$$

$$X_L = 6.28 \times 1,500 \times 20$$

$$X_L = 188,400 \ \Omega \quad Ans.$$

EXAMPLE 16-3   What must be the inductance of a coil in order that it have a reactance of 942 Ω at a frequency of 60 kHz?

SOLUTION

Given: $X_L = 942 \ \Omega$ Find: $L = ?$

$f = 60$ kHz $= 60 \times 10^3$ Hz

$$X_L = 6.28fL \qquad\qquad (16\text{-}1)$$

$$942 = 6.28 \times 60 \times 10^3 \times L$$

$$942 = 376.8 \times 10^3 \times L$$

$$L = \frac{942}{376.8 \times 10^3}$$

$$L = 2.5 \times 10^{-3} \text{ H}$$

$$L = 2.5 \text{ mH} \qquad Ans.$$

SELF-TEST 16-4   A tuning coil in a radio transmitter has an inductance of 300 μH. At what frequency will it offer a reactance of 3,768 Ω?

SOLUTION

Given: $L = 300\ \mu$H   Find: $f = ?$
         $X_L = \underline{\hspace{1cm}} \Omega$ 3,768

1   Change units of measurement.

$$300\ \mu\text{H} = 300 \times \underline{\hspace{1cm}} \text{ H} \qquad\qquad 10^{-6}$$

2   Find the frequency.

$$X_L = 6.28fL \qquad\qquad (16\text{-}1)$$

$$3{,}768 = 6.28 \times f \times \underline{\hspace{2cm}} \qquad\qquad 300 \times 10^{-6}$$

$$3{,}768 = \underline{\hspace{1cm}} \times 10^{-6} \times f \qquad\qquad 1{,}884$$

$$f = \frac{3{,}768}{1{,}884 \times 10^{-6}}$$

$$f = 2 \times \underline{\hspace{1cm}} \text{ Hz} \qquad\qquad 10^6$$

$$f = \underline{\hspace{1cm}} \text{ MHz} \qquad Ans. \qquad\qquad 2$$

PROBLEMS

1. A 0.7-H coil is in series with a 5-kΩ resistor in a transistorized bass boost circuit. Find the inductive reactance of the coil at (a) 100 Hz and (b) 2 kHz.

2. A loudspeaker coil of 2-H inductance is operating at a frequency of 1 kHz. Find (a) its inductive reactance and (b) the current flowing if the voltage across the coil is 40 V.

3. A 20-H Stancor C1515 choke in the filter circuit of a power supply operates at a frequency of 60 Hz. Find (a) its inductive reactance and (b) the current flowing if the voltage across the coil is 150 V.

4. An RF choke coil whose inductance is 5.5 mH operates at a frequency of 1,200 kHz. Find (a) its inductive reactance and (b) the current flowing if the voltage across the coil is 41.5 V.

5. A Miller 7825 line filter choke used in a noise-control circuit of a flasher sign has an inductance of 0.6 mH. Find its inductive reactance at a frequency of 10 kHz.
6. The primary coil of an antenna transformer has an inductance of 50 μH. At what frequency will the reactance equal 314 Ω?
7. What must be the inductance of a coil in order that it have a reactance of 1,884 ohms at 60 Hz?
8. An antenna circuit has an inductance of 150 μH. What is its reactance to a 1,000-kHz signal?
9. An RF coil in an FM receiver has an inductance of 100 μH. What is its reactance at 100 MHz?
10. What is the reactance of the 10-mH coil in the high-pass filter shown in Fig. 16-4 to (a) a 3,000-Hz AF current and (b) a 600-kHz RF current?

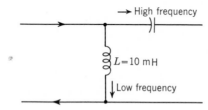

FIGURE 16-4
A simple high-pass filter.

11. A 1-mH coil in the primary of an IF transformer is resonant to 456 kHz. Find its inductive reactance at this frequency.
12. A 0.5-mH coil in the oscillator circuit of a continuous-wave transmitter operates at 30 MHz. Find its reactance at this frequency.
13. What must be the inductance of a coil in order that it have a reactance of 10,000 Ω at 600 kHz?
14. A transmitter tuning coil must have a reactance of 95.6 Ω at 3.8 MHz. What must be the inductance of the coil?
15. A choke coil of negligible resistance is to limit the current through it to 25 mA when 40 V are impressed across it at 1,000 kHz. Find its inductance.

JOB 16-3 THE SQUARE AND SQUARE ROOT OF POWERS OF TEN

Our next job will require that we be able to find the square of a power of ten as well as its square root.

SQUARING POWERS OF TEN

EXAMPLE 16-5 Find the value of $(10^3)^2$.

SOLUTION
An exponent means to multiply its base by itself as many times as the

exponent indicates. If the base happens to be (10^3), then

$$(10^3)^2 \text{ means } (10^3) \times (10^3),$$

and, since exponents are added when multiplying (see page 337),

$$(10^3)^2 = (10^3) \times (10^3) = 10^6 \qquad Ans.$$

The answer may be obtained more directly by applying the following rule.

RULE	To find the power of a power, express the base to a power obtained by multiplying the exponents.

For example:

1 $(10^3)^2 = (10)^{(3 \times 2)} = 10^6$
2 $(10^4)^2 = (10)^{(4 \times 2)} = 10^8$
3 $(10^{-3})^2 = (10)^{(-3 \times 2)} = 10^{-6}$
4 $(10^{-6})^2 = 10^{-12}$

EXAMPLE 16-6 Express the number $(12,000)^2$ as a power of ten.

1 Express 12,000 as a power of ten.

$$12,000 = 12 \times 10^3$$

2 Square this number.

$$(12,000)^2 = (12 \times 10^3)^2$$

$$= (12)^2 \times (10^3)^2$$

Notice that both the 12 and the 10^3 are squared because each is a part of the base (12×10^3) that is being squared.

$$(12,000)^2 = 144 \times 10^6 \qquad Ans.$$

EXAMPLE 16-7 Express $(0.00008)^2$ as a power of ten.

SOLUTION

$$0.00008 = 8 \times 10^{-5}$$

therefore, $$(0.00008)^2 = (8 \times 10^{-5})^2$$

$$= 8^2 \times (10^{-5})^2$$

$$= 64 \times 10^{-10} \qquad Ans.$$

PROBLEMS

Perform the indicated operation.

1. $(10^5)^2$ 2. $(10^{-4})^2$ 3. $(3 \times 10^3)^2$

4. $(5 \times 10^{-3})^2$ 5. $(10^2 \times 10^3)^2$ 6. $(10^6 \times 10^{-2})^2$
7. $(8,000)^2$ 8. $(15,000)^2$ 9. $(1,100)^2$
10. $(0.007)^2$ 11. $(0.00025)^2$ 12. $(0.015)^2$

THE SQUARE ROOT OF A POWER OF TEN

RULE	To find the square root of a power, express the base to a power obtained by dividing the exponent by 2.

For example:

1 $\sqrt{10^6} = 10^{(6 \div 2)} = 10^3$

2 $\sqrt{10^{10}} = 10^{(10 \div 2)} = 10^5$

3 $\sqrt{10^{-12}} = 10^{(-12 \div 2)} = 10^{-6}$

4 $\sqrt{10^{-8}} = 10^{(-8 \div 2)} = 10^{-4}$

EXAMPLE 16-8   Express $\sqrt{250,000}$ as a power of ten.

SOLUTION
Express 250,000 as a power of ten.

$$250,000 = 25 \times 10^4$$

Find the square root of this number. Be careful to find the square root of *both* the 25 and the 10^4.

$$\sqrt{250,000} = \sqrt{25 \times 10^4} = \sqrt{25} \times \sqrt{10^4}$$
$$= 5 \times 10^{(4 \div 2)}$$
$$= 5 \times 10^2 \quad Ans.$$

EXAMPLE 16-9   Express $\sqrt{0.0004}$ as a power of ten.

SOLUTION
$$\sqrt{0.0004} = \sqrt{4 \times 10^{-4}} = \sqrt{4} \times \sqrt{10^{-4}}$$
$$= 2 \times 10^{(-4 \div 2)}$$
$$= 2 \times 10^{-2} \quad Ans.$$

Now let's see what happens if we get an exponent which is *not* exactly divisible by 2. For example, $\sqrt{10^3} = 10^{1.5}$. This decimal exponent, although it has wide use in all the sciences, is very inconvenient, and should be avoided if at all possible. Let's see how this may be done.

EXAMPLE 16-10   Express $\sqrt{500,000}$ as a power of ten.

SOLUTION

When 500,000 is expressed as a power of ten it *must* be written so that the power of ten is an *even* number that can be divided by 2. Thus, 500,000 written as 5×10^5 is not good because the exponent 5 is not evenly divisible by 2. And 500,000 written as 500×10^3 is wrong for the same reason. Therefore, we must write 500,000 as a number $\times 10$ to an *even* exponent.

$$\sqrt{500,000} = \sqrt{50 \times 10^4} = \sqrt{50} \times \sqrt{10^4}$$
$$= 7.07 \times 10^2 \quad Ans.$$

EXAMPLE 16-11   Express $\sqrt{0.00064}$ as a power of ten.

SOLUTION

$$\sqrt{0.00064} = \sqrt{6.4 \times 10^{-4}}$$
$$= \sqrt{6.4} \times \sqrt{10^{-4}}$$
$$= 2.53 \times 10^{-2} \quad Ans.$$

EXAMPLE 16-12

$$\sqrt{0.9 \times 10^3} = \sqrt{9 \times 10^2}$$
$$= 3 \times 10 = 30 \quad Ans.$$

EXAMPLE 16-13

$$\sqrt{0.0016 \times 0.0004} = \sqrt{16 \times 10^{-4} \times 4 \times 10^{-4}}$$
$$= 4 \times 10^{-2} \times 2 \times 10^{-2}$$
$$= 8 \times 10^{-4} \quad Ans.$$

EXAMPLE 16-14

$$\sqrt{8,000 \times 400} = \sqrt{8 \times 10^3 \times 4 \times 10^2}$$
$$= \sqrt{32 \times 10^5}$$
$$= \sqrt{320 \times 10^4}$$
$$= 17.9 \times 10^2 \quad Ans.$$

PROBLEMS

Perform the indicated operation.

1. $\sqrt{10^8}$
2. $\sqrt{10^{-6}}$
3. $\sqrt{16 \times 10^4}$
4. $\sqrt{9 \times 10^{-6}}$
5. $\sqrt{160,000}$
6. $\sqrt{0.0064}$
7. $\sqrt{0.000025}$
8. $\sqrt{20 \times 80}$
9. $\sqrt{120 \times 30}$

10. $\sqrt{200,000}$ 11. $\sqrt{800 \times 500}$ 12. $\sqrt{0.0006}$

13. $\sqrt{0.016 \times 10^3}$ 14. $\sqrt{0.25 \times 10^8}$ 15. $\sqrt{0.4 \times 10^5}$

16. $\sqrt{0.0049 \times 0.0009}$ 17. $\sqrt{6 \times 10^3 \times 500}$ 18. $\sqrt{8 \times 10^{-3} \times 0.08}$

JOB 16-4   THE IMPEDANCE OF A COIL

In a "pure" coil, the opposition to the flow of an alternating current is its reactance. Actually, of course, every coil is made of wire which has some resistance. If this resistance is small in comparison with the reactance, it may be neglected, and the total opposition to the flow of current through the coil is equal to its inductive reactance. If the ohmic resistance of the coil is large, it must be added on to the reactance of the coil to obtain the total opposing effect. This total opposition is called the *impedance Z* of the coil. The addition of the ohms of resistance and the ohms of inductive reactance is *not* accomplished by simple addition but by *phasor (vector) addition,* for reasons which will be explained in Job 18-3.

RULE	The impedance of a coil is the phasor sum of the resistance and the reactance.

FORMULA

$$Z^2 = R^2 + X_L{}^2 \qquad \boxed{16\text{-}3}$$

or

$$Z = \sqrt{R^2 + X_L{}^2} \qquad \boxed{16\text{-}4}$$

where Z = impedance, Ω
R = dc resistance, Ω
X_L = inductive reactance, Ω

The comparative values of the inductive reactance and the resistance are described by a value called the Q, or "quality," of the coil.

RULE	The Q of a coil is the ratio of its inductive reactance to its effective resistance.

FORMULA

$$Q = \frac{X_L}{R} \qquad \boxed{16\text{-}5}$$

If the Q of a coil is greater than 5, then the resistance may be neglected in the calculation of the impedance. If the Q is smaller than 5, then the resistance must be added to the reactance by formula (16-4) to obtain the impedance. Also, if the ratio of R/X_L is larger than 5, the reactance may be neglected and the impedance is equal to the resistance.

EXAMPLE 16-15   A coil has a resistance of 5 Ω and an inductive reactance of 12 Ω at a certain frequency. Find (*a*) the Q of the coil and (*b*) the impedance of the coil.

SOLUTION
Given: $R = 5\ \Omega$ Find: $Q = ?$
$\qquad\quad X_L = 12\ \Omega$ $Z = ?$

a.
$$Q = \frac{X_L}{R} = \frac{12}{5} = 2.4 \qquad Ans. \qquad\qquad (16\text{-}5)$$

b.   Since Q is less than 5, the resistance *must* be included in the calculation of the impedance.
$$Z = \sqrt{R^2 + X_L{}^2} \qquad\qquad\qquad\qquad (16\text{-}4)$$
$$= \sqrt{5^2 + 12^2}$$
$$Z = \sqrt{25 + 144} = \sqrt{169} = 13\ \Omega \qquad Ans.$$

EXAMPLE 16-16   A coil has a resistance of 10 Ω and an inductive reactance of 70 Ω at a certain frequency. Find (*a*) the Q of the coil and (*b*) the impedance of the coil. (*c*) If the resistance is neglected, what is the percent of error?

SOLUTION
Given: $R = 10\ \Omega$ Find: $Q = ?$
$\qquad\quad X_L = 70\ \Omega$ $Z = ?$
$\qquad\qquad\qquad\qquad$ Percent of error $= ?$

a.
$$Q = \frac{X_L}{R} = \frac{70}{10} = 7 \qquad Ans. \qquad\qquad (16\text{-}5)$$

b.   Since Q is larger than 5, the resistance may be neglected and the impedance is equal to the inductive reactance.
$$Z = 70\ \Omega \qquad Ans.$$

c.   If we had included the resistance in the calculation of the impedance,
$$Z = \sqrt{R^2 + X_L{}^2} \qquad\qquad\qquad\qquad (16\text{-}4)$$
$$Z = \sqrt{10^2 + 70^2} = \sqrt{100 + 4{,}900} = \sqrt{5{,}000}$$
$$Z = 70.7\ \Omega$$

The error introduced by *not* including R is equal to $70.7 - 70 = 0.7\ \Omega$. The percent of error is

$$\frac{0.7}{70.7} \times 100 \text{ equals } 0.99 \text{ or } 1 \text{ percent}$$

This error is well within the normal human error incurred in merely taking measurements and is therefore unimportant.

EXAMPLE 16-17 The field coils of a loudspeaker have a resistance of 6,000 Ω and an inductance of 1.592 H. Find (a) the inductive reactance at 800 Hz, (b) the Q of the coils, (c) the impedance of the coils, and (d) the current flowing if the voltage across the coils is 40 V.

SOLUTION

Given: $R = 6,000$ Ω   Find: $X_L = ?$
   $L = 1.592$ H $Q = ?$
   $f = 800$ Hz $Z = ?$
   $E = 40$ V $I = ?$

a. $X_L = 6.28fL = 6.28 \times 800 \times 1.592 = 8,000$ Ω   Ans.

b. $Q = \dfrac{X_L}{R} = \dfrac{8,000}{6,000} = 1.33$ Ans.   (16-5)

c. Since Q is less than 5, the resistance *must* be included in the calculation of the impedance.

$$Z = \sqrt{R^2 + X_L{}^2} \qquad\qquad (16\text{-}4)$$
$$Z = \sqrt{6,000^2 + 8,000^2}$$
$$Z = \sqrt{(6 \times 10^3)^2 + (8 \times 10^3)^2}$$
$$Z = \sqrt{36 \times 10^6 + 64 \times 10^6}$$
$$Z = \sqrt{(36 + 64) \times 10^6}$$
$$Z = \sqrt{100 \times 10^6}$$
$$Z = 10 \times 10^3 = 10^4 = 10,000 \text{ Ω} \qquad Ans.$$

d. Since the total opposition is the impedance, the formula for Ohm's law may be rewritten as the

FORMULA

$$E = IZ \qquad\qquad \boxed{16\text{-}6}$$
$$40 = I \times 10,000$$
$$I = \dfrac{40}{10,000} = 0.004 \text{ A} \qquad Ans.$$

PROBLEMS

1. Find the Q of a coil if $R = 30$ Ω and $X_L = 120$ Ω.
2. Find the Q of a coil if $X_L = 6,000$ Ω and $R = 1,000$ Ω.
3. Find the Q of a coil at 100 Hz if $R = 200$ Ω and $L = 10$ H.

4. Find the impedance of a coil if its resistance is 12 Ω and its reactance is 35 Ω.

5. Find (a) the Q and (b) the impedance of a coil if its resistance is 100 Ω and its reactance is 1,000 Ω.

6. An antenna circuit has an inductance of 30 μH and a resistance of 20 Ω. Find the impedance to a 500-kHz signal.

7. A 40-V emf at a frequency of 1 kHz is impressed across a loudspeaker of 5,000 Ω resistance and 1.5 H inductance. Find (a) the inductive reactance, (b) the impedance, and (c) the current.

8. A 120-V 60-Hz line is connected across a 10-H choke coil whose resistance is 400 Ω. Find (a) the inductive reactance, (b) the Q of the coil, (c) the impedance, and (d) the current.

9. The primary of an AF transformer has a resistance of 100 Ω and an inductance of 50 mH. Find (a) the inductive reactance at 1 kHz and (b) the impedance.

10. A 3,000-Ω resistor has an inductance of 10 mH. Find its impedance at (a) 500 Hz, (b) 5 kHz, (c) 500 kHz, and (d) 1,500 kHz.

11. The primary of an IF coupling transformer has an inductance of 5 mH and a resistance of 100 Ω. If the voltage across the primary is 10 V at 456 kHz, what is the current flowing in the primary?

12. An AF amplifier circuit uses an audio choke of 100-mH inductance and 3,000-Ω resistance. Find the impedance to (a) 500 Hz, (b) 1,000 Hz, and (c) 5,000 Hz.

JOB 16-5   MEASURING THE INDUCTANCE OF A COIL

The inductance of a coil may be calculated by the use of several formulas involving specific dimensions of the coil. However, these dimensions are not always easily obtained, and other methods are substituted. One method uses a standard inductance and a circuit similar to the Wheatstone bridge. Another method obtains the resonant frequency of the combination of the coil with a known capacity, and the inductance is calculated from the formula for the resonant frequency given in Job 18-6. In a third method, called the impedance method, an ac voltage is impressed across the coil and voltage, frequency, and current are measured. The resistance of the coil is obtained by use of an ohmmeter.

EXAMPLE 16-18   What is the inductance of a coil that draws 30 mA from a 120-V 60-Hz ac source? The resistance of the coil is 400 Ω.

SOLUTION
Given: $I = 30$ mA $= 0.03$ A   Find: $L = ?$
$E = 120$ V
$f = 60$ Hz
$R = 400$ Ω

1 Find the impedance.

$$E = IZ \qquad\qquad (16\text{-}6)$$

$$120 = 0.03 \times Z$$

$$Z = \frac{120}{0.03} = 4{,}000\ \Omega \qquad Ans.$$

2 Compare the R and the Z. When the resistance is small in comparison with the impedance, it may be neglected completely, making $X_L = Z$. The resistance is small when Z/R is more than 5.

$$\frac{Z}{R} = \frac{4{,}000}{400} = 10$$

Therefore, since Z/R is larger than 5, the resistance is small when compared with the impedance and $X_L = Z$. If Z/R had been less than 5, the reactance X_L would have been found by applying the formula $Z^2 = R^2 + X_L{}^2$ of Eq. (16-3).

3 Find the inductance.

$$X_L = 6.28 \times 60 \times L \qquad\qquad (16\text{-}1)$$

$$4{,}000 = 376.8 \times L$$

$$L = \frac{4{,}000}{376.8} = 10.6\ \text{H} \qquad Ans.$$

PROBLEMS

1. What is the inductance of a coil whose resistance is 200 Ω if it draws 0.1 A from a 120-V 60-Hz line?
2. What is the inductance of a coil whose resistance is 500 Ω if it draws 20 mA from a 110-V 60-Hz line?
3. What is the inductance of a coil whose resistance is 300 Ω if it draws 10 mA from a 50-V 1,000-Hz ac source?
4. What is the inductance of a coil whose resistance is 200 Ω if it draws 100 mA from a 50-V 1-kHz source?
5. What is the inductance of a coil whose resistance is 50 Ω if it draws 0.55 A from a 110-V 60-Hz line?
6. What is the inductance of a coil whose resistance is 100 Ω if it draws 0.4 A from a 120-V 100-Hz source?

JOB 16-6 REVIEW OF COILS AND INDUCTANCE

1 When an ac voltage is impressed across a coil,
   a The resulting current is an _____ current.   alternating
   b This changing current produces changing fields of force which _____   cut
   the wires of the coil.
   c These cuttings induce a _____ emf in the coil.   back

2 The *inductance* of a coil is a measure of its ability to produce a _____ emf when the current through it is changing. The symbol for inductance is L.

back

3 Unit of inductance. A coil has an inductance of 1 _____ if a current changing at the rate of 1 A/s can induce a back emf of 1 V in the coil.

H

4 The reactance of a coil is the opposition of the coil to the passage of a _____ current.

changing

$$X_L = 6.28fL \qquad \boxed{16\text{-}1}$$

5 The Q of a coil is the comparison of its inductive reactance with its effective resistance.

$$Q = \frac{X_L}{R} \qquad \boxed{16\text{-}5}$$

6 The impedance Z of a coil is the _____ sum of its resistance and its reactance. If Q is _____ than 5, the resistance may be neglected and $Z = X_L$. If Q is _____ than 5, the resistance must be added to the reactance to find Z.

phasor
larger
smaller

$$Z^2 = R^2 + X_L{}^2 \qquad \boxed{16\text{-}3}$$

or $$Z = \sqrt{R^2 + X_L{}^2} \qquad \boxed{16\text{-}4}$$

7 To measure the inductance of a coil, an ac voltage is impressed across the coil and the voltage, frequency, and current are measured. The resistance of the coil is measured with an _____. The inductance is calculated by the following steps.

ohmmeter

    a Find the impedance.

$$E = IZ \qquad \boxed{16\text{-}6}$$

    b Find the reactance.

$$R^2 + X_L{}^2 = Z^2 \qquad \boxed{16\text{-}3}$$

    c Find the inductance.

$$X_L = 6.28fL \qquad \boxed{16\text{-}1}$$

    d If the ratio of Z to R is _____ than 5, the resistance may be neglected and $X_L = Z$.

larger

PROBLEMS

1. Find the inductive reactance of a 0.2-H choke coil at (*a*) 100 Hz, (*b*) 1,000 Hz, (*c*) 10 kHz, and (*d*) 100 kHz.
2. A 5-V 100-kHz ac voltage is impressed across an RF choke whose inductance is 10 mH. Find (*a*) the reactance and (*b*) the current that flows.
3. Find the inductive reactance of a 50-μH coil at a frequency of 10 MHz.
4. What must be the inductance of a coil in order that it have a reactance of 8,000 Ω at 800 Hz?
5. Find the Q of a coil if $R = 80\ \Omega$ and $X_L = 4,800\ \Omega$.

6. Find the impedance of a coil if its resistance is 39 Ω and its reactance is 80 Ω.

7. Find the impedance of a coil to a frequency of 60 Hz if its resistance is 30 Ω and its inductance is 0.2 mH.

8. A coil has an inductance of 50 μH and a resistance of 5 Ω. Find (a) the reactance to a 500-kHz frequency, (b) the impedance, and (c) the current flowing if the voltage is 3 V.

9. A coil of 100 Ω resistance draws 100 mA from a 25-V 60-Hz source. Find its inductance.

10. A coil having a Q of 50 draws 10 mA when connected to a 15-V 1-kHz power supply. Find its inductance.

TEST—COILS

1. A 12-V 200-kHz ac voltage is impressed across a coil whose inductance is 30 mH. Find the reactance and the current in the circuit.

2. Find the impedance of a coil to a frequency of 1 kHz if its resistance is 40 Ω and its inductance is 30 mH.

3. Find the impedance of a Stancor C-2303 coil to a frequency of 10 kHz if its resistance is 100 Ω and its inductance is 2.5 H.

4. A coil of 400 Ω resistance draws 50 mA from a 120-V 60-Hz line. Find its inductance.

5. A coil of 800 Ω resistance draws 120 mA from a 120-V 60-Hz line. Find its inductance.

JOB 16-7 INTRODUCTION TO TRANSFORMERS

It is cheaper to transmit electrical energy at high voltages than at low voltages because of the smaller loss of power in the line at high voltages. For this reason, the 220 V that is delivered by an ac generator may be stepped up to 2,200 or even 220,000 V for transmission over long distances. At its destination, the voltage is stepped down to 240 V for industrial users and to 120 V for ordinary home and power users. The changes in the voltage continue. In our radio and television receiver, the voltage is changed again to 6.3 V to operate the tube heaters or to 350 V for the plate supply of the tubes. Elsewhere, the 120-V supply is reduced to 20 V to operate a toy train or to 12 V to operate a door bell. All these changes in voltage are made by an extremely efficient electrical device called a *transformer*.

Basic construction. As shown in Fig. 16-5, a transformer consists of (1) the *primary coil* which *receives* energy from an ac source, (2) the *secondary coil* which *delivers* energy to an ac load, and (3) a *core* on which the two coils are wound. The core is generally of some highly mag-

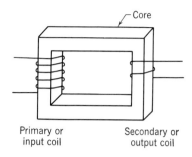

Primary or
input coil

Secondary or
output coil

FIGURE 16-5
Basic transformer construction.

netic material, although cardboard, ceramics, and other nonmagnetic
materials are used for the cores of some radio and television transformers.

Principle of operation. An alternating current will flow when an ac
voltage is applied to the primary coil of a transformer. This current produces a field of force which changes as the current changes. The changing magnetic field is carried by the magnetic core to the secondary coil,
where it cuts across the turns of that coil. These "cuttings" induce a
voltage in the secondary coil. In this way, an ac voltage in one coil is
transferred to another coil, even though there is no electrical connection
between them. The number of lines of force available in the primary is
determined by the primary voltage and the number of turns on the primary—each turn producing a given number of lines. Now, if there are
many turns on the secondary, each line of force will cut *many turns* of wire
and *induce a high voltage.* If the *secondary contains only a few turns,* there
will be few cuttings and a *low induced voltage.* The secondary voltage,
then, depends on the number of secondary turns as compared with the
number of primary turns. If the secondary has twice as many turns as
the primary, the secondary voltage will be twice as large as the primary
voltage. If the secondary has half as many turns as the primary, the secondary voltage will be one-half as large as the primary voltage. This is
stated as the following rule:

RULE	The voltage on the coils of a transformer is directly proportional to the number of turns on the coils.

FORMULA

$$\frac{E_p}{E_s} = \frac{N_p}{N_s}$$

16-7

where E_p = voltage on primary coil
E_s = voltage on secondary coil
N_p = number of turns on primary coil
N_s = number of turns on secondary coil

The ratio E_p/E_s is called the voltage ratio (VR). The ratio N_p/N_s is called the turns ratio (TR). By substituting these terms in formula (16-7), we obtain an equivalent statement.

$$VR = TR \qquad \boxed{16\text{-}8}$$

Nomenclature. A voltage ratio of 1:3 (read as 1 to 3) means that for each volt on the primary, there are 3 V on the secondary. This is called a *"step-up"* transformer. A step-up transformer *receives a low voltage* on the primary and *delivers a high voltage* from the secondary. A voltage ratio of 3:1 (read as 3 to 1) means that for 3 V on the primary, there is only 1 V on the secondary. This is called a *"step-down"* transformer. A step-down transformer *receives a high voltage* on the primary and *delivers a low voltage* from the secondary.

EXAMPLE 16-19 A bell transformer reduces the primary voltage of 120 V to the 18 V delivered by the secondary. If there are 180 turns on the primary and 27 turns on the secondary, find (*a*) the voltage ratio and (*b*) the turns ratio.

SOLUTION
The diagram for the problem is shown in Fig. 16-6.

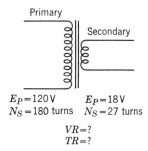

$E_P = 120\,\text{V}$ $E_P = 18\,\text{V}$
$N_S = 180$ turns $N_S = 27$ turns
$VR = ?$
$TR = ?$ FIGURE 16-6

a. $VR = \dfrac{E_p}{E_s}$

    $VR = \dfrac{120}{18} = \dfrac{20}{3}$ (read as 20 to 3)   *Ans.*

b. $TR = \dfrac{N_p}{N_s}$

    $TR = \dfrac{180}{27} = \dfrac{20}{3}$ (read as 20 to 3)   *Ans.*

Note: The ratios are always expressed in fractional form, even if the fraction can be reduced to a whole number.

EXAMPLE 16-20 A "power" transformer has 99 turns on the primary and 315 turns on the secondary. What voltage will it deliver if the primary voltage is 110 V?

SOLUTION

Given: $N_p = 99$ turns   Find: $E_s = ?$
$N_s = 315$ turns
$E_p = 110$ V

$$\frac{E_p}{E_s} = \frac{N_p}{N_s} \qquad (16\text{-}7)$$

$$\frac{110}{E_s} = \frac{99}{315}$$

$$99E_s = 315 \times 110$$

$$E_s = \frac{315 \times 110}{99} = 350 \text{ V} \qquad Ans.$$

EXAMPLE 16-21   The Stancor P-6011 television plate transformer has a voltage ratio of 11:35. If the primary has 242 turns, how many turns must be wound on the secondary?

SOLUTION

Given: VR $= 11:35$ Find: $N_s = ?$
$N_p = 242$

$$\frac{E_p}{E_s} = \frac{N_p}{N_s} \qquad (16\text{-}7)$$

but $$\frac{E_p}{E_s} = \text{VR}$$

therefore, $$\text{VR} = \frac{N_p}{N_s}$$

$$\frac{11}{35} = \frac{242}{N_s}$$

$$N_s = \frac{242 \times 35}{11} = 770 \text{ turns} \qquad Ans.$$

PROBLEMS

1. A "power" transformer has 85 turns on the primary and 255 turns on the secondary. What voltage will it deliver if the primary is connected to a 120-V source?
2. A filament transformer reduces the 110 V on the primary to 10 V on the secondary. Find (a) the voltage ratio and (b) the turns ratio.
3. The Stancor P-6293 universal-type power transformer steps down the voltage from 120 to 2.5 V. Find (a) the voltage ratio and (b) the turns ratio.
4. A Stancor A-4773 transformer whose turns ratio is 1:3 is used as

a plate-to-grid coupling transformer in an amplifier circuit. What is the secondary voltage if the primary voltage is 15 V?

5. A 24:1 welding transformer has 25 turns on the secondary. How many turns are there on the primary?

6. A UTC LS-185 plate transformer steps up the voltage from 100 to 2,500 V. If there are 50 turns on the primary, how many turns are on the secondary?

7. Find the voltage at the spark plugs if a 6-V alternator is connected to a coil with a primary winding of 50 turns and a secondary winding of 50,000 turns.

8. A coil with a primary winding of 100 turns must deliver 4,800 V. If the primary is connected to a 6-V source, find the number of turns on the secondary.

9. The output from a 2N1097 transistor is to be matched to a 13.9-Ω voice coil by a 12:1 matching transformer. If the primary voltage is 18 V, find the voltage across the voice coil.

10. A transformer whose primary is connected to a 120-V source delivers 10 V. If the number of turns on the secondary is 20 turns, find the number of turns on the primary. How many extra turns must be added to the secondary if it must deliver 35 V?

11. A toy-train transformer is connected to a 120-V 60-Hz source. The secondary has 60 turns and delivers 24 V. How many turns are on the primary?

12. The secondary coil of a transformer has 100 turns, and the secondary voltage is 5 V. If the turns ratio is 22:1, find (a) the voltage ratio, (b) the primary voltage, and (c) the primary turns.

13. A step-down transformer is wound with 3,750 turns on the primary and 60 turns on the secondary. What is the delivered voltage if the high-voltage side is 15,000 V?

14. The 117-V primary of a transformer has 250 turns. Two secondaries are to be provided to deliver (a) 12.6 V and (b) 35 V. How many turns are needed on each secondary?

15. A power transformer with 100 turns on the primary is to be connected to a 120-V source of supply. Separate secondary windings are to deliver (a) 2.5 V, (b) 6.3 V, and (c) 600 V. Find the number of turns on each secondary.

16. A transformer bank is used to transform 2,000 kVA (kilovoltampere) from 14,000 to 4,000 V. Find (a) the turns ratio of the transformer, and (b) the primary current.

JOB 16-8 CURRENT IN A TRANSFORMER

In the modern transformer, the power delivered to the primary is transferred to the secondary with practically no loss. For all practical purposes, the power input to the primary is equal to the power output of the secondary, and the transformer is assumed to operate at an efficiency of 100 percent. Thus,

$$\text{Power input} = \text{power output} \qquad \boxed{16\text{-}9}$$

Since

$$\text{Power input} = E_p \times I_p \qquad \boxed{16\text{-}10}$$

and

$$\text{Power output} = E_s \times I_s \qquad \boxed{16\text{-}11}$$

$$E_p \times I_p = E_s \times I_s \qquad \boxed{16\text{-}12}$$

By dividing both sides of the equation by $E_s \times I_p$ and canceling out identical terms,

$$\frac{E_p \times \overset{1}{\cancel{I_p}}}{E_s \times \underset{1}{\cancel{I_p}}} = \frac{\overset{1}{\cancel{E_s}} \times I_s}{\underset{1}{\cancel{E_s}} \times I_p}$$

we obtain

FORMULA

$$\frac{E_p}{E_s} = \frac{I_s}{I_p} \qquad \boxed{16\text{-}13}$$

This formula indicates that the current ratio in a transformer is *inversely proportional* to the voltage ratio. If the *voltage* ratio *increases,* the *current* ratio will *decrease.* If the *voltage ratio decreases,* the *current* ratio will *increase.*

In addition, since

$$\frac{E_p}{E_s} = \frac{N_p}{N_s}$$

we may substitute $\dfrac{N_p}{N_s}$ for $\dfrac{E_p}{E_s}$ in Eq. (16-13). This gives

FORMULA

$$\frac{N_p}{N_s} = \frac{I_s}{I_p} \qquad \boxed{16\text{-}14}$$

EXAMPLE 16-22 The Stancor model P-6293 universal-type power transformer delivers 36 W of power to a rectifier circuit. If the primary voltage is 120 V, how much current is drawn by the transformer?

SOLUTION
Given: Power output $= 36$ W   Find: $I_p = ?$
$\qquad\qquad E_p = 120$ V

$$\text{Power input} = \text{power output} \qquad (16\text{-}9)$$

$$E_p \times I_p = \text{power output}$$

$$120 \times I_p = 36$$

$$I_p = \frac{36}{120} = 0.6 \text{ A} \qquad Ans.$$

EXAMPLE 16-23   The primary of a transformer is connected to a 110-V 60-Hz line. The secondary delivers 250 V at 0.1 A. Find (*a*) the current in the primary and (*b*) the power input to the primary.

SOLUTION
The diagram for the problem is shown in Fig. 16-7.

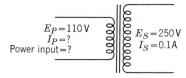

$E_P = 110\,\text{V}$
$I_P = ?$
Power input $= ?$

$E_S = 250\,\text{V}$
$I_S = 0.1\,\text{A}$

FIGURE 16-7

a. $$\frac{E_p}{E_s} = \frac{I_s}{I_p} \qquad (16\text{-}13)$$

$$\frac{110}{250} = \frac{0.1}{I_p}$$

$$110 \times I_p = 250 \times 0.1$$

$$I_p = \frac{25}{110} = 0.227 \text{ A} \qquad Ans.$$

b.   Power input $= E_p \times I_p = 110 \times 0.227 = 24.97$ watts   *Ans.*

EXAMPLE 16-24   A bell transformer with 300 turns on the primary and 45 turns on the secondary draws 0.3 A from the 110 V line. Find (*a*) the current delivered by the secondary, (*b*) the voltage delivered by the secondary, and (*c*) the power delivered by the secondary.

SOLUTION
Given: $N_p = 300$ turns   Find: $I_s = ?$
$\quad\quad\quad N_s = 45$ turns $E_s = ?$
$\quad\quad\quad I_p = 0.3$ A   Power output $= ?$
$\quad\quad\quad E_p = 110$ V

a. $$\frac{N_p}{N_s} = \frac{I_s}{I_p} \qquad (16\text{-}14)$$

$$\frac{300}{45} = \frac{I_s}{0.3}$$

$$45 \times I_s = 300 \times 0.3$$

$$I_s = \frac{90}{45} = 2 \text{ A} \qquad Ans.$$

b.
$$\frac{E_p}{E_s} = \frac{N_p}{N_s} \qquad (16\text{-}7)$$

$$\frac{110}{E_s} = \frac{300}{45}$$

$$300 \times E_s = 110 \times 45$$

$$E_s = \frac{4{,}950}{300} = 16.5 \text{ V} \qquad Ans.$$

c. $\quad$ Power output $= E_s \times I_s = 16.5 \times 2 = 33 \text{ W} \qquad Ans.$

SELF-TEST 16-25 A 120:24 V transformer draws 1.5 A. Find the secondary current.

SOLUTION
Given: VR = 120:24 $\qquad$ Find: $I_s = ?$
$\qquad I_p = 1.5$ A

$$\frac{E_p}{E_s} = \frac{I_?}{I_?} \qquad (16\text{-}13)$$

but
$$\frac{E_p}{E_s} = \text{VR} = \frac{?}{?}$$

therefore, we can substitute this ratio in formula (16-13).

$$\frac{120}{24} = \frac{I_s}{?}$$

$$24 \times I_s = 120 \times \underline{\quad}$$

$$I_s = \frac{180}{24} = \underline{\quad} \text{ A} \qquad Ans.$$

s		
p		
120		
24		
		1.5
		1.5
		7.5

PROBLEMS

1. A bell transformer draws 20 W from a line. What is the secondary current if the secondary voltage is 10 V?
2. A Thermador model 5A6086 power transformer delivers 22.5 W of power. If the primary voltage is 112.5 V, how much current is drawn by the primary?
3. A 120-V 60-Hz line supplies power to a Stancor model P-6297 universal-type transformer. If the secondary delivers 480 V at 0.04 A, find (a) the primary current and (b) the power input.
4. A bell transformer with 240 turns on the primary and 30 turns on

the secondary draws 0.25 A from a 120-V line. Find (a) the secondary current, (b) the secondary voltage, and (c) the secondary power.

5. A transformer is wound with 2,200 turns on the primary and 150 turns on the secondary. (a) If it delivers 2 A, what is the primary current? (b) If the primary voltage is 110 V, what is the secondary voltage?

6. A 230:110-V step-down transformer in a stage-lighting circuit draws 10 A from the line. Find the current delivered.

7. A filament transformer delivers 1.5 A at 6.3 V. If E_p is 110 V, find (a) I_p and (b) the power input.

8. A transformer with 2,400 turns on the primary and 480 turns on the secondary draws 8.5 A from a 230-V line. Find (a) I_s, (b) E_s, and (c) the power output.

9. A transformer has 120 turns on the primary and 1,500 turns on the secondary. (a) If it delivers 0.4 A, what is the primary current? (b) If the primary voltage is 120 V, what is the secondary voltage?

10. A 9:2 step-down transformer draws 1.8 A. Find the I_s.

11. A substation transformer reduces the voltage from the transmission line voltage of 150,000 to 4,400 V. If the transmission line carries 15 A, what current will the transformer deliver?

12. A step-down transformer with a turns ratio of 50,000:250 has its primary connected to a 27,000-V transmission line. If the secondary is connected to a 7.5-Ω load, find (a) the secondary voltage, (b) the secondary current, (c) the primary current, and (d) the power output.

JOB 16-9   EFFICIENCY OF A TRANSFORMER

In Job 10-4 we learned that the efficiency of an electrical machine is equal to the ratio of the power output to the power input. This ratio is expressed as a percent by multiplying it by 100. In general, the efficiency of any device is the ratio of its output to its input and describes the effectiveness of the device in utilizing the energy supplied to it. Thus, a transformer which delivers *all* the power put into it would have an efficiency of 100 percent. In the last job, we assumed that the transformers had an efficiency of 100 percent and delivered all the energy that they received. Actually, because of copper and core losses, the efficiency of even the best transformer is less than 100 percent.

FORMULA

$$\text{Eff} = \frac{\text{power output}}{\text{power input}} \qquad (10\text{-}2)$$

EXAMPLE 16-26   A plate transformer draws 30 W from a 117-V line and delivers 300 V at 90 mA. Find its percent efficiency.

SOLUTION
Given: Power input $= 30$ W   Find: Percent eff $= ?$

$\qquad E_s = 300$ V

$\qquad I_s = 90$ mA $= 0.09$ A

$$\text{Eff} = \frac{\text{power output}}{\text{power input}} \qquad (10\text{-}2)$$

$$\text{Eff} = \frac{300 \times 0.09}{30} = 0.9 = 90\% \qquad Ans.$$

EXAMPLE 16-27   A transformer whose efficiency is 80 percent draws its power from a 120-V line. If it delivers 192 W, find (*a*) the power input and (*b*) the primary current.

SOLUTION
Given: Eff $= 80\% = 0.80$ Find: Power input $= ?$

$\qquad\qquad\qquad E_p = 120$ V $I_p = ?$

$\qquad$ Power output $= 192$ W

a. $$\text{Eff} = \frac{\text{power output}}{\text{power input}} \qquad (10\text{-}2)$$

$$0.80 = \frac{192}{\text{power input}}$$

$$\text{Power input} = \frac{192}{0.80} = 240 \text{ W} \qquad Ans.$$

b. $$\text{Power input} = E_p \times I_p \qquad (16\text{-}10)$$

$$240 = 120 \times I_p$$

$$I_p = \frac{240}{120} = 2 \text{ A} \qquad Ans.$$

PROBLEMS

1. What is the efficiency of a transformer if it draws 800 W and delivers 700 W?
2. A toy transformer draws 150 W from a 110-V line and delivers 24 V at 5 A. Find its efficiency.
3. A transformer draws 1.5 A at 120 V and delivers 7 A at 24 V. Find (*a*) the power input, (*b*) the power output, and (*c*) the efficiency.
4. A power transformer draws 96 W and delivers 420 V at 200 mA. Find (*a*) the efficiency and (*b*) the primary current if the primary voltage is 120 V.

5. In Fig. 16-8, an impedance-matching transformer couples an output transistor delivering 2.1 W to a voice coil which receives 1.68 W. Find its efficiency.

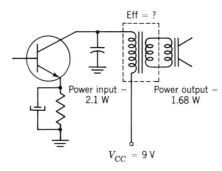

Eff = ?

Power input = 2.1 W

Power output = 1.68 W

V_{CC} = 9 V

FIGURE 16-8
Finding the efficiency of an impedance-matching transformer.

6. A transformer that draws 1,000 W from a 230-V line operates at an efficiency of 92 percent and delivers 50 V. Find (*a*) the watts delivered and (*b*) the secondary current.

7. A transformer that delivers 10,000 W at an efficiency of 96 percent draws its power from a 2,000-V line. Find (*a*) the power input and (*b*) the primary current.

8. A transformer delivers 750 V at 120 mA at an efficiency of 90 percent. If the primary current is 0.8 A, find (*a*) the power input and (*b*) the primary voltage.

9. A transformer delivers 660 V at 98 mA at an efficiency of 84 percent. If the primary current is 875 mA, find (*a*) the power input and (*b*) the primary voltage.

10. The three secondary coils of a power supply transformer deliver 100 mA at 350 V, 2 A at 2.5 V, and 1.2 A at 12.6 V. What is the efficiency of the transformer if it draws 60 W from the 117-V line?

JOB 16-10 IMPEDANCE-MATCHING TRANSFORMERS

The maximum transfer of energy from one circuit to another will occur when the impedances of the two circuits are equal or *matched*. If the two circuits have unequal impedances, a coupling transformer may be used as an intermediate impedance-changing device between the two circuits. In Fig. 16-9, the output of a transistor is used to operate the voice coil of a loudspeaker. The output of the transistor cannot be connected directly to the voice coil because the impedance of the transistor circuit is 4,000 Ω and the impedance of the voice coil is only 10 Ω. The circuits may be *matched* by a transformer with an appropriate turns ratio whose value depends on the values of the impedances involved. In Fig. 16-9,

$$\frac{N_p}{N_s} = \frac{E_p}{E_s} \quad \text{and} \quad \frac{N_p}{N_s} = \frac{I_s}{I_p}$$

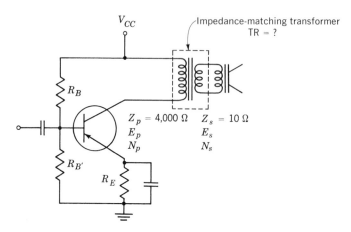

FIGURE 16-9
An impedance-matching transformer is used to couple the output transistor to the voice coil of the speaker.

By multiplying the two equations,

$$\frac{N_p}{N_s} \times \frac{N_p}{N_s} = \frac{E_p}{E_s} \times \frac{I_s}{I_p}$$

or

$$\left(\frac{N_p}{N_s}\right)^2 = \frac{E_p}{I_p} \times \frac{I_s}{E_s}$$

but $E_p/I_p = Z_p$ and $I_s/E_s = 1/Z_s$; therefore

$$\left(\frac{N_p}{N_s}\right)^2 = \frac{Z_p}{Z_s} \qquad \boxed{16\text{-}15}$$

By taking the square root of both sides we obtain the

FORMULA

$$\frac{N_p}{N_s} = \sqrt{\frac{Z_p}{Z_s}} \qquad \boxed{16\text{-}16}$$

where N_p = number of turns on primary
N_s = number of turns on secondary
Z_p = impedance of primary, Ω
Z_s = impedance of secondary, Ω

EXAMPLE 16-28 Find the turns ratio of the transformer shown in Fig. 16-9.

SOLUTION

$$\frac{N_p}{N_s} = \sqrt{\frac{Z_p}{Z_s}} = \sqrt{\frac{4,000}{10}} = \sqrt{400} \qquad (16\text{-}16)$$

$$\frac{N_p}{N_s} = \frac{20}{1} \qquad Ans.$$

EXAMPLE 16-29   A 2N255A transistor in a telephone amplifier supplies a 490-Ω load. If the load is to be matched to a 10-Ω speaker, find the required turns ratio.

SOLUTION

Given: $Z_p = 490 \ \Omega$ Find: $\dfrac{N_p}{N_s} = ?$
$\quad\quad\quad Z_s = 10 \ \Omega$

$$\frac{N_p}{N_s} = \sqrt{\frac{Z_p}{Z_s}} = \sqrt{\frac{490}{10}} = \sqrt{49} \qquad\qquad (16\text{-}16)$$

$$\frac{N_p}{N_s} = \frac{7}{1} \qquad Ans.$$

EXAMPLE 16-30   A carbon microphone whose impedance is 20 Ω is to be coupled to a grid circuit whose impedance is 72,000 Ω. Find the turns ratio of the coupling transformer.

SOLUTION

Given: $Z_p = 20 \ \Omega$ Find: $\dfrac{N_p}{N_s} = ?$
$\quad\quad\quad Z_s = 72{,}000 \ \Omega$

When coupling from a low impedance to a high impedance, it is best to find the turns ratio by comparing N_s with N_p. This can be done by inverting both sides of formula (16-16). This gives the

FORMULA

$$\frac{N_s}{N_p} = \sqrt{\frac{Z_s}{Z_p}} \qquad \boxed{16\text{-}17}$$

$$\frac{N_s}{N_p} = \sqrt{\frac{72{,}000}{20}} = \sqrt{3{,}600} = 60$$

$$\frac{N_s}{N_p} = \frac{60}{1} \qquad \text{or} \qquad \frac{N_p}{N_s} = \frac{1}{60} \qquad Ans.$$

Thus, the microphone is connected to the primary ($N_p = 1$) and the grid is connected to the secondary ($N_s = 60$).

EXAMPLE 16-31   A 1:20 step-up transformer is used to match a microphone with a grid circuit impedance of 40,000 Ω. Find the impedance of the microphone.

SOLUTION

Given: $\dfrac{N_p}{N_s} = \dfrac{1}{20}$ Find: $Z_p = ?$
$\quad\quad\quad Z_s = 40{,}000 \ \Omega$

$$\left(\frac{N_p}{N_s}\right)^2 = \frac{Z_p}{Z_s} \qquad\qquad (16\text{-}15)$$

$$\left(\frac{1}{20}\right)^2 = \frac{Z_p}{40,000}$$

$$\frac{1}{400} = \frac{Z_p}{40,000}$$

$$Z_p = \frac{40,000}{400} = 100 \ \Omega \qquad Ans.$$

PROBLEMS

1. Find the turns ratio of a transformer used to match a 1,600-Ω load to a 4-Ω load.

2. Find the turns ratio of a transformer used to match a 60-Ω load to a 540-Ω line.

3. The impedance of the output circuit of a power stage is 8,000 Ω. What is the turns ratio of a transformer used to transfer the power to a 500-Ω line supplying a public-address system?

4. A 2N265 transistor works into a load impedance of 9,000 Ω. Find the turns ratio of the transformer needed to feed into a 10-Ω voice coil.

5. Find the turns ratio of a microphone transformer required to couple a 20-Ω microphone to a 500-Ω line.

6. Find the turns ratio of a microphone transformer required to couple a 20-Ω microphone to a grid circuit of 50,000 Ω impedance.

7. A 55:1 output transformer is used to match an output tube to a 4-Ω voice coil. Find the impedance of the output circuit.

8. A beam-power amplifier tube is working into a plate-load impedance of 9,800 Ω. Find the turns ratio of the transformer needed to feed into an 8-Ω voice coil.

9. Two 2N406 output transistors work in push-pull into a load impedance of 14,000 Ω. Find the required turns ratio of a transformer to match the output to an 8-Ω voice coil.

10. Find the turns ratio of a Stancor model A-8101 transformer which is used to match a 500-Ω line to an 8-Ω voice coil.

11. Find the turns ratio of the transformer needed to match a load of 4,500 Ω to two 9-Ω speakers in parallel.

12. What would be the turns ratio in Prob. 11 if there were three 9-Ω speakers in parallel?

13. Find the turns ratio of the transformer used to match a 4,200-Ω impedance to a 500-Ω line supplying a distant auditorium loudspeaker.

14. Find the turns ratio of the transformer needed to match a 50-Ω Amperite model PGL dynamic microphone to a 500-Ω line.

15. The secondary load of a step-down transformer with a turns ratio of 6 to 1 is 800 Ω. Find the impedance of the primary.

JOB 16-11 REVIEW OF TRANSFORMERS

1   A transformer transmits energy from one circuit to another by means of electromagnetic induction between two coils.

2   The _____ coil is connected to the source of supply. The *secondary* coil is connected to the _____ .

    primary
    load

3   A step-up transformer _____ the voltage and decreases the current.   A step-down transformer decreases the voltage and _____ the current.

    increases
    increases

4   The turns ratio of a transformer is the comparison (by division) of the number of turns on the _____ with the number of turns on the _____ .

    primary   secondary

$$TR = \frac{N_p}{N_s}$$

The voltage ratio of a transformer is the comparison (by division) of the voltage on the primary with the voltage on the secondary.

$$VR = \frac{E_p}{E_s}$$

5   In a 100 percent efficient transformer

    a   Power input = power output   16-9

    b   Power input $= E_p \times I_p$ 16-10

    c   Power output $= E_s \times I_s$ 16-11

    d   The voltage is directly proportional to the number of turns.

$$\frac{E_p}{E_s} = \frac{?}{?}$$ 16-7

                             N_p
                             N_s

    e   The voltage is inversely proportional to the current.

$$\frac{E_p}{E_s} = \frac{?}{?}$$ 16-13

                             I_s
                             I_p

    f   The number of turns is inversely proportional to the current.

$$\frac{N_p}{N_s} = \frac{?}{?}$$ 16-14

                             I_s
                             I_p

6   The efficiency of a transformer is the ratio of the power output to the power input and is expressed as a percent.

$$Eff = \frac{power\ output}{power\ input}$$ 10-2

7   Impedance-matching transformers permit transfer of power between

loads of different impedance. The turns ratio of such transformers is given by the formulas below:

$$\left(\frac{N_p}{N_s}\right)^2 = \frac{?}{?}$$
$$\boxed{16\text{-}15}$$
$$Z_p$$
$$Z_s$$

or

$$\frac{N_p}{N_s} = \sqrt{\frac{Z_p}{Z_s}}$$
$$\boxed{16\text{-}16}$$

PROBLEMS

1. A bell transformer reduces the voltage from 120 to 15 V. If there are 22 turns on the secondary, find (a) the number of turns on the primary and (b) the turns ratio.

2. Find the voltage at the spark plugs if a 12-V alternator is connected to a coil with 80 turns on the primary and 40,000 turns on the secondary.

3. A UTC LS-185 plate transformer has a turns ratio of 1:25. If there are 70 turns on the primary, how many turns are on the secondary?

4. If the turns ratio of a transformer is 20:3, find the primary voltage if the secondary voltage is 24 V.

5. The 110-V primary of a transformer has 500 turns. Two secondaries are to be provided to deliver (a) 22 V and (b) 5 V. How many turns are needed for each secondary?

6. A power transformer delivers 50 W of power. If the primary voltage is 110 V, find the primary current.

7. A transformer connected to a 120-V 60-Hz line delivers 750 V at 200 mA. Find (a) the primary current and (b) the power drawn by the primary.

8. A 5:1 transformer draws 0.5 A from a 120-V line. Find (a) the secondary current, (b) the secondary voltage, and (c) the power output.

9. A filament transformer delivers 1.2 A at 6.3 V. If the primary voltage is 120 V, find (a) I_p and (b) the power input.

10. A transformer with 1,500 turns on the primary and 375 turns on the secondary draws 3.5 A from a 115-V line. Find (a) the secondary current, (b) the secondary voltage, and (c) the power output.

11. A plate transformer draws 250 mA from a 120-V line and delivers 80 mA at 350 V. Find its efficiency.

12. A transformer drawing 150 W from the line operates at an efficiency of 90 percent and delivers 50 V. Find (a) the power delivered and (b) the secondary current.

13. A 2N321 amplifier feeds into the 500-Ω primary of an audible automobile signal minder. Find the turns ratio of the transformer needed to match it with a 3.2-Ω speaker.

14. A 1:30 step-up transformer is used to match a 50-Ω microphone to a grid circuit. Find the impedance of the grid circuit.

15. A step-down transformer with a turns ratio of 45,000:150 has its primary connected to a 72,000-V transmission line. If the secondary is connected to a 20-Ω load, find (*a*) the secondary voltage, (*b*) the secondary current, (*c*) the primary current, and (*d*) the power output.

TEST—TRANSFORMERS

1. The Stancor model P-6165 rectifier filament transformer has a voltage ratio of 24:1. If the primary has 312 turns, how many turns must be wound on the secondary?
2. A bell transformer with 180 turns on the primary and 27 turns on the secondary draws 0.2 A from a 120-V line. Find (*a*) the secondary current and (*b*) the secondary voltage.
3. A transformer whose efficiency is 90 percent draws its power from a 120-V line. If it delivers 180 W, find (*a*) the power input and (*b*) the primary current.
4. The output of a 2N265 transistor in a common-base amplifier is to be matched to a 1,000-Ω headphone. If the primary impedance is 10 kΩ, find the required turns ratio.
5. A UTC model 0-1 step-up transformer has a turns ratio of 1:10. It is used to couple a 500-Ω line to a grid circuit. Find the impedance of the grid circuit.

CAPACITANCE

JOB 17-1   INTRODUCTION TO CAPACITANCE

What is a capacitor? A capacitor, or "condenser," is formed whenever two pieces of metal are separated by a thin layer of insulating material. To form a capacitor of any appreciable value, however, the area of the metal pieces must be quite large and the thickness of the insulating material, or *dielectric,* must be quite small.

What does a capacitor do? A capacitor is an electrical storehouse. When we wish to store up electricity for a little while, we "charge" the capacitor. When we "discharge" a capacitor, we draw the electrons from it to operate some device. The two plates of the capacitor shown in Fig. 17-1 are electrically neutral, since there are as many protons as electrons on each plate. The capacitor has no "charge." Now let us connect a battery across the plates as shown in Fig. 17-2a. When the switch is closed (Fig. 17-2b), the positive side of the battery pulls electrons from plate A of the capacitor and deposits them on plate B. Electrons will continue to flow from A to B until the number of electrons on plate B exert a force equal to the electromotive force of the battery. The capacitor is now charged. It will remain in this condition even if the battery is removed as shown in Fig. 17-3a. This is a condition of extreme un-

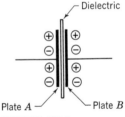

FIGURE 17-1
An electrically neutral capacitor.

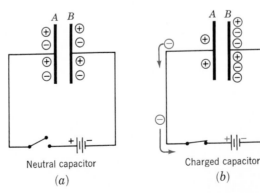

Neutral capacitor

(a)

Charged capacitor

(b)

FIGURE 17-2
A charged capacitor has an excess of electrons on one plate.

534

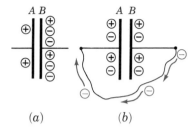

FIGURE 17-3

(a) A charged capacitor has more electrons on one plate than on the other. (b) Discharging a capacitor.

balance, and the electrons on plate B will attempt to return to plate A if they can. The resistance of the dielectric and the surrounding air prevents this from happening, although some electrons do manage to "leak" off plate B and return to plate A. However, if a conductor is placed across the plates as in Fig. 17-3b, then the electrons find an easy path back to plate A and they will return in a rush, thus "discharging" the capacitor. There are many uses for capacitors such as in tuning circuits, filter circuits, coupling circuits, bypasses for alternating currents of high frequency, and blocking devices in audio circuits. In each application, the capacitor operates by storing up electrons and discharging them at the proper time. Capacitors may not be used in dc circuits, since the dielectric of the capacitor acts to present an open circuit. Current will flow in an ac circuit containing a capacitor as shown in Fig. 17-4. During the positive half of the ac cycle, the electrons travel through the lamp and pile up on plate A of the capacitor. During this time, electrons are drawn off plate B of the capacitor by the ac source. During the negative half of the cycle, the direction of the electron flow is reversed. The capacitor discharges through the lamp; the source pulls the electrons from plate A and piles them up on plate B. This action continues with each reversal of the alternating current. There seems to be a continuous flow of electrons through the capacitor which lights the lamp, but it is actually a flow of electrons *around* the capacitor which operates the lamp.

Meaning of capacitance. The measure of the ability of a capacitor to hold electrons is called its capacitance. Since an electron is so small, and since there are so many of them, the *coulomb* is used as the measure of electrical quantity. In Job 1-1 we learned that a coulomb is equal to

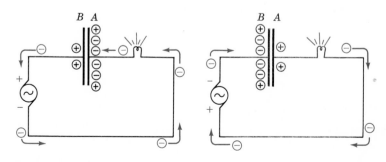

FIGURE 17-4

Electron flow around a capacitor in an ac circuit.

approximately 6 billion billion electrons. The capacitance of a capacitor has been defined as the number of coulombs of electricity that may be held on its plates by a pressure of 1 V. If 1 coulomb is held on the plates by a pressure of 1 V, then the capacitance is called 1 farad (F). If 4 coulombs may be held by 4 V, then 1 coulomb may be held by 1 V and the capacitance will still be 1 F. But if 4 coulombs may be held by only 2 V, then 2 coulombs will be held by 1 V and the capacitance will be 2 F. From this, we can get a formula to find the capacitance of a capacitor.

FORMULA

$$C = \frac{Q}{E}$$

$$\boxed{17\text{-}1}$$

where C = capacitance, F
   Q = number of electrons on plates, coulomb
   E = voltage across the plates, V

It is very inconvenient to discuss capacitances in terms of farads, since a farad is such a tremendous unit of measurement. Always change units of capacitance into microfarads (μF) or picofarads (pF). See Job 9-2 for methods of changing units of measurement.

JOB 17-2   CAPACITORS IN PARALLEL

In the last job we learned that the capacitance depends on the number of coulombs that can be held on the plates by a pressure of 1 V. A capacitor that can hold 3 coulombs will have three times the capacitance of another that can hold only 1 coulomb if the same voltage is applied to both. What is it about a capacitor that enables one to hold more electrons than another? Obviously, the electrons must be held somewhere, and they are usually distributed on the surface of the capacitor plates. If the area of the plates is large, then many electrons can be placed on the large area, but if the plates are small in area, then only a few electrons can be held there and the capacitance will be small. The capacitance of a capacitor depends on this plate area and also on the thickness of the dielectric. The larger the plate area, the larger the capacitance. The *thinner* the dielectric, the *larger* the capacitance.

What is the effect of placing capacitors in parallel? In Fig. 17-5, C_1 and C_2 are connected in parallel. Since plate A and plate B are both connected together, the effect is the same as if we had one big plate whose area is equal to the sum of plates A and B. Similarly, plates C and D on the other side are connected together to form one large plate equal to the sum of C and D. Since the capacitance increases as we increase the plate area, we get the capacitance of the combination by adding the capacitances of the individual capacitors.

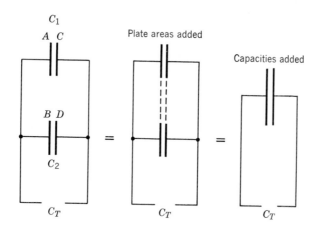

FIGURE 17-5

When capacitors are in parallel, the plate areas are added and the total capacitance C_T equals the *sum* of the individual capacitances.

FORMULA

$$C_T = C_1 + C_2 + C_3 + \cdots + \text{etc.} \qquad \boxed{17\text{-}2}$$

where
C_T = total capacitance
C_1, C_2, C_3, etc. = capacitances of the individual capacitors

All capacitances must be measured in the same units.

Working voltage. There is a limit to the voltage that may be applied across any capacitor. If too large a voltage is applied, it will overcome the resistance of the dielectric and a current will be forced through it from one plate to the other, sometimes burning a hole in the dielectric. In this event, a short circuit exists and the capacitor must be discarded. This applies only to mica or waxed-paper capacitors. If the dielectric is air, the "short" disappears as soon as the voltage is removed. The maximum voltage that may be applied to a capacitor is known as the *working voltage* and must never be exceeded.

EXAMPLE 17-1   A 0.00035-μF tuning capacitor is in parallel with a trimmer capacitor of 0.000075 μF. What is the total capacity?

SOLUTION
The diagram for the circuit is shown in Fig. 17-6.

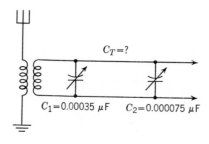

FIGURE 17-6

$$C_T = C_1 + C_2 \qquad\qquad (17\text{-}2)$$

$$C_T = 0.00035 + 0.000075$$

$$C_T = 0.000425 \ \mu F \qquad Ans.$$

Note: Remember to keep the decimal points in line when adding.

EXAMPLE 17-2   What are the total capacitance and working voltage of a 0.0005-μF 50-V capacitor, a 0.015-μF 100-V capacitor, and a 0.00025-μF 100-V capacitor when they are connected in parallel?

SOLUTION
The total capacitance is the sum of the capacities:

$$
\begin{array}{r}
0.0005 \\
0.015 \\
\underline{0.00025} \\
C_T = 0.01575 \ \mu F \qquad Ans.
\end{array}
$$

Just as a chain is only as strong as its weakest link, the working voltage of a group of parallel capacitors is only as great as the *smallest* working voltage. Therefore, the working voltage of the combination is only 50 V.

PROBLEMS

1. A capacitor in a tuning circuit has a capacitance of 0.00032 μF. When the stage is aligned, the trimmer capacitor in parallel with it is adjusted to a capacitance of 0.000053 μF. What is the total capacitance of the combination?

2. A mechanic has the following capacitors available: 0.0003-μF 75-V, 0.00025-μF 50-V, 0.0002-μF 50-V, 0.00015-μF 75-V, and 0.00005-μF 75-V. Which of these should he arrange in parallel to form a combination with a capacitance of 0.0005 μF and 75 V working voltage?

3. What is the total capacitance in parallel of the following capacitors: 35 pF, 0.005 μF, and 0.00003 μF?

4. A capacitor of 0.0003-μF capacitance is connected in parallel with a 0.000005-F capacitor. What is the total capacitance?

5. What is the total capacitance of a 25-pF, a 0.00006-μF, and a 0.00000003-F capacitor?

6. A capacitor of 0.003 μF is in parallel with another which holds a charge of 0.000004 coulomb at 200 V. What is the total capacitance?

7. What amount of capacitance must be added in parallel with a 0.00055-μF capacitor in order to get a total capacitance of 0.0007 μF?

8. What is the total capacitance in parallel of two capacitors if they are charged at 120 V with 0.00006 and 0.0001728 coulomb, respectively?

JOB 17-3   CAPACITORS IN SERIES

It has been found that the thicker the dielectric, or the greater the distance between the plates, the smaller the capacitance. If we were to combine capacitances so that the effective distance between the plates was increased, then the resulting capacitance would necessarily be less than before.

What is the effect of placing capacitors in series? In Fig. 17-7, capacitors C_1 and C_2 are connected in series. When a voltage is impressed on this combination, electrons are drawn from plate A and deposited on plate D. The charges on plates B and C are equal and oppo-

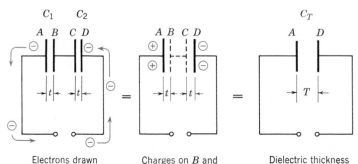

Electrons drawn from A to D

Charges on B and C cancel each other

Dielectric thickness T is equal to $t+t$

FIGURE 17-7
Capacitors in series increase the total dielectric thickness and *decrease* the total capacitance.

site and therefore neutralize each other. In this event, they may be considered to be eliminated and the combination replaced by a single capacitor whose dielectric thickness is equal to the sum of the dielectric thicknesses of the original capacitors. Thus the effect of a series combination is to increase the dielectric thickness and therefore to decrease the capacitance.

FORMULA

$$\frac{1}{C_T} = \frac{1}{C_1} + \frac{1}{C_2} + \frac{1}{C_3} + \cdots \text{etc.} \qquad \boxed{17\text{-}3}$$

All capacitances must be measured in the same units.

Notice the similarity between this formula and the formula for resistances in parallel given in Job 4-8 as formula (4-3). The similarity is continued through the formula for the total resistance in parallel of a number of equal resistors given in the same job as formula (4-4). For equal capacitors in *series,* we have

FORMULA

$$C_T = \frac{C}{N}$$

17-4

where C_T = total capacitance
   C = capacitance of one of the equal capacitors
   N = number of equal capacitors

   Working voltage. Within limits, the total voltage that may be applied across a group of capacitors in series is equal to the sum of the working voltages of the individual capacitors.

   EXAMPLE 17-3   A 4-, a 5-, and a 10-μF capacitor are connected in series. Find the total capacitance.

   SOLUTION
Review Job 4-4 on Addition of Fractions.

$$\frac{1}{C_T} = \frac{1}{C_1} + \frac{1}{C_2} + \frac{1}{C_3} \tag{17-3}$$

$$\frac{1}{C_T} = \frac{1}{4} + \frac{1}{5} + \frac{1}{10}$$

$$\frac{1}{C_T} = \frac{11}{20}$$

$$11 \times C_T = 20$$

$$C_T = \frac{20}{11} = 1.818 \ \mu F \qquad Ans.$$

   EXAMPLE 17-4   A voltage doubler circuit is shown in Fig. 17-8. Only C_1 is charged during the first half of the cycle. When the polarity reverses during the second part of the cycle, C_2 is charged to *twice* the peak

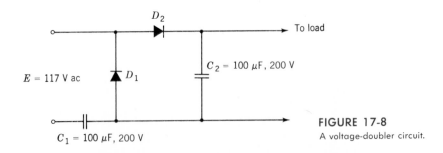

FIGURE 17-8

A voltage-doubler circuit.

voltage of the line because it is in series aiding with the line and C_1. What is the total capacitance and working voltage of the capacitor combination if C_1 and C_2 are both 100-μF 200-V capacitors?

SOLUTION

$$C_T = \frac{C}{N} = \frac{100}{2} = 50 \ \mu F \qquad Ans.$$

$$\text{Working voltage} = 200 + 200 = 400 \text{ V} \qquad Ans.$$

EXAMPLE 17-5   The frequency which beats against the incoming frequency in the superheterodyne receiver is produced by an oscillator circuit. The Colpitts oscillator shown in Fig. 17-9 controls the frequency of oscillation by means of the variable inductance. What is the total capacity of the series combination of C_1 and C_2 if $C_1 = 0.0005 \ \mu F$ and $C_2 = 0.00025 \ \mu F$?

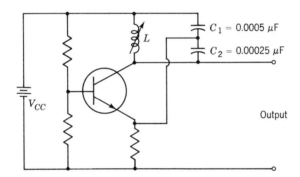

FIGURE 17-9
The Colpitts oscillator.

SOLUTION
When only two capacitors are in series, we can use a formula very similar to the formula for finding the total resistance of two resistors in parallel.

FORMULA

$$C_T = \frac{C_1 \times C_2}{C_1 + C_2} \qquad \boxed{17\text{-}5}$$

In this formula, all the measurements must be in the same units. Since it is easier to use whole numbers than decimals in the formula, all measurements are changed into picofarads.

$$C_1 = 0.0005 \ \mu F = 0.0005 \times 10^6 = 500 \text{ pF}$$

$$C_2 = 0.00025 \ \mu F = 0.00025 \times 10^6 = 250 \text{ pF}$$

$$C_T = \frac{500 \times 250}{500 + 250} = \frac{125,000}{750} = 167 \text{ pF} \qquad Ans.$$

PROBLEMS

1. Capacitors of 3, 4, and 6 μF are connected in series. What is their total capacitance?
2. What is the total capacitance and working voltage of a voltage doubler similar to that shown in Fig. 17-8 if the circuit uses two 40-μF 175-V capacitors?
3. Find the total capacitance of the series capacitors in a Colpitts oscillator similar to that shown in Fig. 17-9 if $C_1 = 0.0004$ μF and $C_2 = 0.00002$ μF.
4. Find the total capacitance of the series capacitors in a Colpitts oscillator if (a) $C_1 = 0.01$ μF and $C_2 = 0.001$ μF, (b) $C_1 = 0.0015$ μF and $C_2 = 800$ pF.
5. What is the range of total capacitances available in an oscillator circuit which uses a tuning capacitor of a 35- to 350-pF range in series with a padder capacitor set at 300 pF?
6. In some vibrator power supplies operating from a storage battery, a pair of "buffer" capacitors are placed across the secondary of the transformer to reduce the voltage peaks. What is the total capacitance and working voltage of a pair of 0.0075-μF 800-V buffer capacitors in series?
7. Find the total capacitance of a 6-, a 10-, and a 15-μF capacitor in series.
8. What is the total capacitance of a 0.00000002-F, a 0.04-μF and a 60,000-pF capacitor in series?

JOB 17-4 REACTANCE OF A CAPACITOR

We learned in Job 17-1 that as a capacitor is charged, electrons are drawn from one plate and deposited on the other. As more and more electrons accumulate on the second plate, they begin to act as an opposing voltage which attempts to stop the flow of electrons just as a resistor would do. This opposing effect is called the *reactance* of the capacitor and is measured in ohms.

WHAT FACTORS DETERMINE THE REACTANCE?

1   The size of the capacitor is one factor. The larger the capacitor, the greater the number of electrons that may be accumulated on its plates. However, because the plate area is large, the electrons do not accumulate in one spot but spread out over the entire area of the plate and do not impede the flow of new electrons on to the plate. Therefore, a large capacitor offers a small reactance. If the capacitance was small, as in a capacitor with a small plate area, the electrons could not spread out and would attempt to stop the flow of electrons coming to the plate. Therefore, a small capacitor offers a large reactance. The reactance is therefore *inversely* proportional to the capacitance.

2   If an ac voltage is impressed across the capacitor, electrons are accumulated first on one plate and then on the other. If the frequency of the changes

in polarity is low, the time available to accumulate electrons will be large. This means that a large number of electrons will be able to accumulate, which will result in a large opposing effect, or a large reactance. If the frequency is high, the time available to accumulate electrons will be small. This means that there will be only a few electrons on the plates, which will result in only a small opposing effect, or a small reactance. The reactance is therefore *inversely* proportional to the frequency.

3 A special constant of proportionality is necessary to change the current-reducing effect of the electron accumulation into ohms of reactance. This number is 2π. The formula for the capacitive reactance is

$$X_C = \frac{1}{2\pi f C}$$

with C measured in farads. If the capacitance is measured in microfarads,

$$X_C = \frac{1}{2 \times 3.14 \times f \times (C/1,000,000)} = \frac{1,000,000}{6.28 \times f \times C}$$

and since

$$\frac{1,000,000}{6.28} = \text{approx } 159,000$$

FORMULA

$$X_C = \frac{159,000}{f \times C}$$

$\boxed{17\text{-}6}$

where X_C = capacitive reactance, Ω
f = frequency, Hz
C = capacitance, μF

Note: The larger the capacitance, the smaller the reactance. The larger the frequency, the smaller the reactance.

EXAMPLE 17-6 . The antenna circuit of a two-transistor AM receiver is shown in Fig. 17-10. Find the capacitive reactance of the tuning capacitor to a frequency of 500 kHz when it is set at 300 pF.

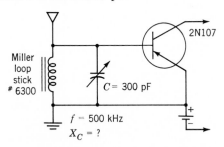

FIGURE 17-10
Find the capacitive reactance of the tuning capacitor.

SOLUTION
1 Change the measurements to the required units.

$$500 \text{ kHz} = 500 \times 10^3 \text{ Hz}$$

$$300 \text{ pF} = 300 \times 10^{-6} \ \mu\text{F}$$

2   Find the capacitive reactance.

$$X_C = \frac{159,000}{f \times C} \qquad\qquad (17\text{-}6)$$

$$X_C = \frac{159 \times 10^3}{500 \times 10^3 \times 300 \times 10^{-6}}$$

$$X_C = \frac{159}{15 \times 10^4 \times 10^{-6}}$$

$$X_C = 10.6 \times 10^2 = 1,060 \ \Omega \qquad Ans.$$

EXAMPLE 17-7   A capacitor is formed whenever two metal pieces are separated by a dielectric. A capacitor formed by two wires of a circuit or two turns of a coil produces a *distributed capacitance.* This is extremely undesirable, because even a very small distributed capacitance can transfer energy from one circuit to another at radio frequencies, since the reactance at radio frequencies is very small. This unwanted transfer of energy represents wasted power. What is the current lost through a distributed capacitance of 10 pF formed by two parallel wires, one of which carries a 1,000-kHz current? The difference in potential between the wires is 1 V.

SOLUTION
The diagram of the circuit is shown in Fig. 17-11.

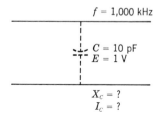

f = 1,000 kHz

C = 10 pF
E = 1 V

X_C = ?
I_C = ?

FIGURE 17-11

1   Change the measurements to the required units.

$$1,000 \text{ kHz} = 10^3 \times 10^3 = 10^6 \text{ Hz}$$

$$10 \text{ pF} = 10 \times 10^{-6} = 10^{-5} \ \mu\text{F}$$

2   Find the capacitive reactance.

$$X_C = \frac{159,000}{f \times C} = \frac{159,000}{10^6 \times 10^{-5}} = \frac{159,000}{10} = 15,900 \ \Omega$$

3   Find the current. Since the only opposition to the flow of current around a capacitor is its reactance, the formula for Ohm's law, $E = IR$, may be rewritten as

$$E_C = I_C \times X_C \qquad \boxed{17\text{-}7}$$

$$1 = I_C \times 15,900$$

$$I_C = \frac{1}{15,900} = 0.000062 \text{ A}$$

$$I_C = 0.062 \text{ mA} \quad Ans.$$

EXAMPLE 17-8 Find the size of filter capacitor necessary to provide a capacitive reactance of 159 Ω at a frequency of 60 Hz.

SOLUTION
The diagram for the circuit is shown in Fig. 17-12.

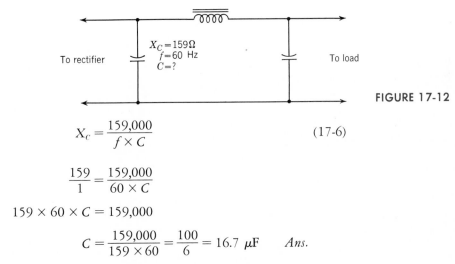

FIGURE 17-12

$$X_C = \frac{159,000}{f \times C} \qquad (17\text{-}6)$$

$$\frac{159}{1} = \frac{159,000}{60 \times C}$$

$$159 \times 60 \times C = 159,000$$

$$C = \frac{159,000}{159 \times 60} = \frac{100}{6} = 16.7 \ \mu F \qquad Ans.$$

Use the commercially available 16-μF 500-V capacitor.

SELF-TEST 17-9 A capacitance of 30 pF draws 20 mA when connected across a 106-V source. Find the frequency of the ac voltage.

SOLUTION
Given: $C = 30$ pF   Find: $f = ?$
$\quad\quad I = \underline{\hspace{1cm}}$ 20 mA
$\quad\quad E = 106$ V

1   Change the measurements into the required units.

$$30 \text{ pF} = 30 \times \underline{\hspace{1cm}} \ \mu F \qquad\qquad 10^{-6}$$

$$20 \text{ mA} = 20 \times 10^{-3} = \underline{\hspace{1cm}} \text{ A} \qquad\qquad 0.02$$

2   Find the capacitive reactance.

$$E_C = I_C \times X_C \qquad (17\text{-}7)$$

$$106 = 0.02 \times X_C$$

$$X_C = \frac{106}{0.02} = \underline{\hspace{1cm}} \ \Omega \qquad\qquad 5{,}300$$

3   Find the frequency.

$$X_C = \frac{159,000}{f \times C} \qquad (17\text{-}6)$$

$$5,300 = \frac{159 \times 10^3}{f \times 30 \times 10^{-6}}$$

$$f = \frac{159 \times 10^3}{30 \times 10^{-6} \times 53 \times 10^2}$$

$$f = \frac{159 \times 10^3}{159 \times \text{?}} \qquad\qquad 10^{-3}$$

$$f = 1 \times 10^3 \times \underline{} \qquad\qquad 10^3$$

$$f = 1 \underline{} \qquad Ans. \qquad\qquad \text{MHz}$$

PROBLEMS

1. What is the reactance of a 0.0003-μF capacitor at (*a*) 30 kHz, (*b*) 100 kHz, and (*c*) 800 kHz?
2. What is the reactance of an oscillator capacitor of 0.0004 μF to a frequency of 456 kHz?
3. A 10-μF capacitor in the emitter circuit of a 2N322 transistor used in a 12-V audio amplifier produces a voltage drop of 3 V at 1 kHz. Find the current passed by the capacitor.
4. What is the reactance of a 20-μF coupling capacitor to an audio frequency of 1 kHz? What current will flow if the voltage across the capacitor is 2.38 V as shown in Fig. 17-13?

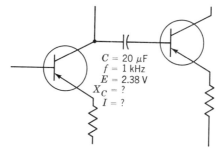

$$C = 20\ \mu F$$
$$f = 1\ kHz$$
$$E = 2.38\ V$$
$$X_C = \text{?}$$
$$I = \text{?}$$

FIGURE 17-13

5. A 0.00035-μF tuning capacitor is in parallel with a 0.00005-μF trimmer capacitor. Find the total capacitance of the combination and its reactance to a frequency of 100 kHz.
6. A capacitor draws 4 A when connected across a 120-V 60-Hz line. What will be the current drawn if both the capacitance and frequency are doubled?
7. What should be the capacitance of a thyratron control circuit if the reactance must be 1,590 Ω at 60 Hz?
8. A capacitor in a telephone circuit has a capacitance of 2 μF. What

current flows through it when an emf of 15 V at 795 Hz is impressed across it?

9. A pocket radio uses a 10-μF coupling capacitor in the base circuit of a 2N35 NPN transistor. Find its reactance to a frequency of (*a*) 1 kHz, (*b*) 5 kHz, and (*c*) 20 kHz.

10. The emitter resistor for a 2N1265 transistor is bypassed with a 5-μF capacitor. What is the reactance of this capacitor to a 1.5-kHz frequency? If the voltage across the capacitor is 10.6 V, what current will flow?

11. Find the capacitive reactance between two wires if the stray capacitance between them is 8 pF and one wire carries a radio frequency of 1,500 kHz.

12. A 2N218 transistor acting as an FM sound detector has its emitter resistor bypassed with a 4-μF capacitor. What is the reactance of the capacitor to the 500-Hz AF current?

13. Find the capacitance required for a power triode bypass capacitor if the reactance should be 200 Ω at 600 kHz.

14. A capacitance of 1.1 μF draws 0.05 A when connected across a 120-V line. Find the frequency of the ac voltage.

15. An antenna tuning capacitor has a capacitance of 250 pF. What current flows through it when 41.8 V are impressed across it at 7.6 MHz?

16. A 2N190 PNP transistor used as an audio amplifier has its emitter stabilizing resistor bypassed with a 50-μF capacitor. Find the reactance of the capacitor to a frequency of (*a*) 100 Hz, and (*b*) 5 kHz.

17. In the Admiral transistorized television receiver, model NA1-2B, the first sound IF transistor 2SC460 has its emitter resistor bypassed with a 0.01 μF capacitor. What is its reactance to a frequency of 21.25 MHz?

18. Find the bypass capacitor required for a 2N109 audio output transistor if it is to have a reactance of 795 Ω at 10 kHz.

19. A "leading" current of 5 A is to be obtained from a 220-V, 60-Hz line by means of a capacitor. Find the required capacitance.

20. A static capacitor capable of passing 40 A at 240 V and 60 Hz is added to a line to correct the power factor. What must be its capacitance?

JOB 17-5 IMPEDANCE OF A CAPACITOR

In the last job, the opposition to the flow of current offered by a capacitor was considered to be its reactance. Actually, however, it is impossible to obtain a circuit which contains only reactance. The plates of the capacitor and its connecting leads all have some resistance. The *impedance* is the total opposition to the flow of current and is equal to the *phasor* (*vector*) *sum* of the resistance and the reactance. The symbol for the impedance is Z. The complete explanation of impedance and the derivation of the formula are given in Job 18-4.

FORMULA

$$Z = \sqrt{R^2 + X_C^{\,2}}$$

17-8

where Z = impedance, Ω
    R = resistance, Ω
    X_C = capacitive reactance, Ω

EXAMPLE 17-10   Find the impedance offered by a 10-μF filter capacitor to a 60-Hz frequency if its resistance is 200 Ω.

SOLUTION
Given: $C = 10\ \mu$F   Find: $Z = ?$
    $f = 60$ Hz
    $R = 200\ \Omega$

1   Find the capacitive reactance.

$$X_C = \frac{159,000}{f \times C} = \frac{159,000}{60 \times 10} = \frac{1,590}{6} = 265\ \Omega \qquad Ans. \qquad (17\text{-}6)$$

2   Find the impedance.

$$Z = \sqrt{R^2 + X_C^{\,2}} = \sqrt{200^2 + 265^2} = \sqrt{40,000 + 70,225}$$
$$= \sqrt{110,225} = 332\ \Omega \qquad Ans.$$

PROBLEMS

1. Find the impedance of a capacitor if its reactance is 40 Ω and its resistance is 9 Ω.
2. Find the impedance of a capacitor if its reactance is 24 Ω and its resistance is 7 Ω.
3. Using Fig. 17-14, find the impedance of a coupling capacitor circuit to an audio frequency of 1 kHz if the capacitance is 0.01 μF and the resistance of the circuit is 3 kΩ.

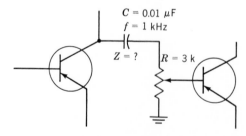

$C = 0.01\ \mu$F
$f = 1$ kHz
$Z = ?$ $R = 3$ k

FIGURE 17-14

4. Find the impedance of the tone control circuit shown in Fig. 17-15.
5. What is the total impedance of the circuit in Fig. 17-15 if $f = 5$ kHz, $C = 0.01\ \mu$F, and $R = 10,000\ \Omega$?

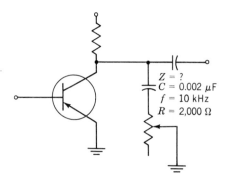

FIGURE 17-15

$Z = ?$
$C = 0.002 \ \mu F$
$f = 10 \ kHz$
$R = 2,000 \ \Omega$

6. A 3,000-Ω resistor is in series with a 0.02-μF capacitance. Find the impedance at (*a*) 500 kHz, (*b*) 5 kHz, and (*c*) 500 Hz.

JOB 17-6 MEASUREMENT OF CAPACITY

Voltmeter-ammeter method. The circuit used to measure the capacitance of a capacitor is shown in Fig. 17-16. The voltmeter measures the voltage across the capacitor, and the ammeter measures the current in the circuit. Since the resistance of the capacitor is so very small when compared with its reactance, we can neglect it in this situation.

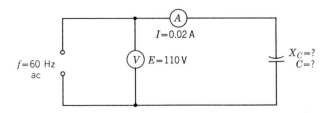

$f=60$ Hz ac

$I=0.02$ A

$E=110$ V

$X_C=?$
$C=?$

FIGURE 17-16

Circuit for measuring capacitance by the voltmeter-ammeter method.

EXAMPLE 17-11 Find the capacitance of the capacitor shown in Fig. 17-16.

SOLUTION

1 Find the capacitive reactance.

$$E_C = I_C \times X_C \qquad (17\text{-}7)$$

$$110 = 0.02 \times X_C$$

$$X_C = \frac{110}{0.02} = 5,500 \ \Omega \qquad Ans.$$

2 Find the capacitance.

$$X_C = \frac{159,000}{f \times C} \qquad (17\text{-}6)$$

$$\frac{5,500}{1} = \frac{159,000}{60 \times C}$$

$$5,500 \times 60 \times C = 159,000$$

$$C = \frac{159,000}{33,000} = 0.482 \ \mu F \qquad Ans.$$

PROBLEMS

Find the capacitance of each capacitor if the measurements obtained by the voltmeter-ammeter method are given below.

PROBLEM	E	I	f
1	110 V	0.11 A	60 Hz
2	110 V	0.5 A	60 Hz
3	18 V	20 mA	60 Hz
4	50 V	10 mA	25 Hz
5	318 mV	20 mA	1 kHz

JOB 17-7   REVIEW OF CAPACITANCE

A capacitor is made of two metallic plates separated by an _____ material, or dielectric.

 A capacitor is used to store up an electrical _____.

 The capacitance of a capacitor is a measure of its ability to store up _____.

 The capacitance _(increases/decreases)_ if the *plate area increases* or the *dielectric thickness* _____.

 The working voltage is the _____ voltage that may be placed across a capacitor before it breaks down. The working voltage in parallel is the working voltage of the _(strongest/weakest)_ capacitor. The working voltage in series is the _____ of the working voltages of the series capacitors.

 A *farad* is the capacitance of a capacitor which can hold 1 coulomb of electricity on its plates under a pressure of 1 _____.

 The *reactance* of a capacitor is the opposition offered by the capacitor to the passage of an _____ current. The reactance decreases as the frequency or capacitance _(increases/decreases)_ .

 Distributed, or "stray," capacitance is the capacity formed when two wires run close together or when any two metal parts are separated by a thin _____ material.

insulating

charge

electrons
increases
decreases
largest

weakest
sum

V

alternating
increases

insulating

FORMULAS
Capacitance:

$$C = \frac{Q}{E} \qquad \boxed{17\text{-}1}$$

where C = capacitance, F
  Q = charge, coulomb
  E = voltage, V

Capacitors in parallel:

$$C_T = C_1 + C_2 + C_3 \qquad \boxed{17\text{-}2}$$

where C_T = total capacitance
   C_1, C_2, C_3 are the individual capacitances, all measured in the
      same units.

Capacitors in series:

$$\frac{1}{C_T} = \frac{1}{C_1} + \frac{1}{C_2} + \frac{1}{C_3} \qquad \boxed{17\text{-}3}$$

where C_T = total capacitance
   C_1, C_2, C_3 are the individual capacitances, all measured in the
      same units.

Equal capacitors in series:

$$C_T = \frac{C}{N} \qquad \boxed{17\text{-}4}$$

where C_T = total capacitance
   C = capacitance of one of the equal capacitors
   N = number of equal capacitors

Two capacitors in series:

$$C_T = \frac{C_1 \times C_2}{C_1 + C_2} \qquad \boxed{17\text{-}5}$$

where C_T = total capacitance
   C_1 and C_2 are the individual capacitances, all measured in the
      same units.

Reactance of a capacitor:

$$X_C = \frac{159{,}000}{f \times C} \qquad \boxed{17\text{-}6}$$

where X_C = reactance, Ω
   f = frequency, Hz
   C = capacitance, μF

Impedance of a capacitor:

$$Z = \sqrt{R^2 + X_C^2} \qquad \boxed{17\text{-}8}$$

where Z = impedance, Ω
   R = resistance, Ω
   X_C = reactance, Ω

PROBLEMS

1. Find the total capacitance in parallel of a 0.0035-μF, a 0.00000004-F, and a 6,200-pF capacitor.

2. What amount of capacitance must be added in parallel to a 0.00035-μF capacitor to obtain a total capacitance of 0.00115 μF?

3. Find the total capacitance in series of a 3-, a 6-, and an 8-μF capacitor.

4. What is the total capacitance and working voltage of two 25-μF 180-V capacitors used in a voltage multiplier?

5. What is the total capacitance of the capacitors in a Colpitts oscillator similar to Fig. 17-9 if $C_1 = 0.0004$ μF and $C_2 = 0.00035$ μF?

6. An oscillator circuit contains a 0.00035- and a 0.00025-μF capacitor in series. Find the total capacitance.

7. Part of the first stage of a hi-fi preamplifier is shown in Fig. 17-17. Find the capacitive reactance of C_E at (a) 30 Hz, and (b) 15,000 Hz.

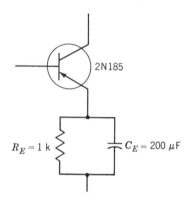

FIGURE 17-17

8. Find the reactance of a 0.0003-μF tuning capacitor to a frequency of 1,350 kHz.

9. Find the impedance of a capacitor if its reactance is 40 Ω and its resistance is 20 Ω.

10. Find the impedance of a capacitive circuit to a 2-kHz audio frequency if the resistance is 2,000 Ω and the capacitance is 0.02 μF.

11. What cathode bypass capacitor is needed to provide a reactance of 1,000 Ω at an audio frequency of 500 Hz?

12. In finding the capacitance of a capacitor by the voltmeter-ammeter method, the current was 0.004 A and the voltage was 110 V at 60 Hz. Find the capacitance.

TEST—CAPACITANCE

1. Find the total capacitance in parallel of a 0.00025-μF and a 750-pF capacitor.

2. Find the total capacitance in series of a 4-, an 8-, and a 12-μF capacitor.

3. Find the impedance of a capacitive circuit to a 10-kHz frequency if its resistance is 400 Ω and its capacitance is 0.0318 μF.

4. In finding the capacitance of a capacitor by the voltmeter-ammeter method, the current was 0.03 A and the voltage was 120 V at 25 Hz. Find the capacitance.

5. What capacitance is necessary to provide a reactance of 318 Ω at a frequency of 600 kHz?

18

SERIES AC CIRCUITS

JOB 18-1 SIMPLE SERIES AC CIRCUITS

Within certain limits (to be explained in Job 18-3), the general rules for solving dc series circuits are also applicable to the solution of ac series circuits.

1 The current in each part is equal to the current in every other part and equal to the total current.

2 The total voltage is equal to the sum of the voltages across all parts of the circuit.

Series circuits containing only resistance. As we have learned, an ac voltage consists of a number of different instantaneous voltages, each instant of time giving rise to a different value of voltage. If this voltage is impressed across a resistor, each instantaneous voltage will cause an instantaneous current to flow at that time. The increasing and decreasing voltages and currents are shown in Fig. 18-1. The current that flows

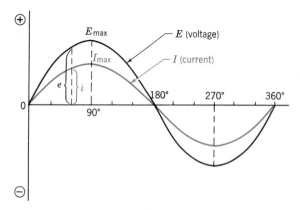

FIGURE 18-1
The voltage and current are in phase in a purely resistive circuit.

as a result of an ac voltage will be an alternating current with the same frequency as the ac voltage. The voltage and the current both start at zero and rise to their maximum values, reaching them at the same instant.

The voltage and current continue to rise and fall in step with each other throughout the entire cycle. We say that the voltage and current are "in phase" or "in step" with each other. It is difficult to draw these curves whenever we wish to indicate this or any other condition, and so we shall use a method in which the voltage and current are indicated by straight lines which are drawn to a definite length and in a definite direction.

Vectors. A vector is a straight line having a definite length and *direction*. Vectors are commonly used to show the amount and *direction* of a quantity. For example, *both* the amount and direction must be indicated to describe adequately a 10-lb force which acts straight up. If 1 in represents 10 lb, then Fig. 18-2*a* describes this force. However, if the force were acting straight *down,* it would be described as shown in Fig. 18-2*b.* We shall use vectors to show the amount and *time* at which a volt-

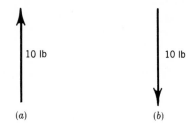

10 lb   10 lb

(a)   (b)

FIGURE 18-2
A vector indicates both amount
and *direction.*

age or current is acting. Vectors which are drawn in the *same direction* will indicate that they are happening at the *same time,* or are "in phase." Vectors which are drawn in *different directions* will indicate that they are happening at *different times* or are "out of phase." In electricity, since different directions really represent *time* expressed as a phase relationship, an electrical vector is called a *phasor.*

In a circuit containing only resistance, we have seen that the voltage and current occur at the *same time,* or are in phase. To indicate this condition by means of phasors, all that is necessary is to draw the phasors for the voltage and the current in the *same direction.* The values of each are indicated by the *length* of the phasor.

Since the current is constant in a series circuit, the current is chosen as the reference line upon which to draw the phasors. Draw a line *AC* from left to right as in Fig. 18-3 to represent the current phasor. Place

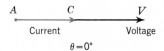

A   *C*   *V*

Current   Voltage

$\theta = 0°$

FIGURE 18-3
The voltage and current
phasors are "in phase" in a
circuit containing only
resistance.

an arrowhead on the phasor at *C* pointing to the right. Point *A* is the "tail" of the phasor, and point *C* is the "head" of the phasor. Since the voltage occurs at the *same time* as the current, the voltage phasor must be drawn in the *same direction* as the current phasor. Draw a line starting from the original point A to the right to point V with an arrow pointing to the right. This voltage phasor is drawn larger than the current phasor because the voltage is larger than the current. When phasors are drawn in the same direction, the angle between the phasors is 0°. This angle is called the phase angle and is denoted by the Greek letter theta (θ).

EXAMPLE 18-1   A 22-Ω electric iron is operated from a 110-V 60-Hz line. Draw a phasor diagram, and find the current and power used by the iron.

SOLUTION
Given: $E = 110$ V   Find: $I = ?$
       $R = 22\ \Omega$ $P = ?$

1   Draw the phasor diagram. Since the iron may be assumed to be made of a purely resistive element, the phasor diagram will be the same as that shown in Fig. 18-3. It is not drawn to scale.

2   In a purely resistive circuit, Ohm's law may be used.

$$E = IR \tag{2-1}$$

$$110 = I \times 22$$

$$I = \frac{110}{22} = 5 \text{ A} \qquad Ans.$$

3   Find the power.

$$P = I \times E \tag{6-1}$$

$$P = 5 \times 110 = 550 \text{ W} \qquad Ans.$$

PROBLEMS

Draw a phasor diagram for each problem (not to scale).

1.   What is the hot resistance of a tungsten lamp if it draws 2 A from a 120-V ac line?
2.   Find the current drawn by a 50-Ω toaster from a 120-V ac line.
3.   What current is carried by a 135-Ω line cord resistor if the voltage drop across it is 30 V?
4.   What is the voltage needed to operate a 600-W neon sign whose resistance is 20 Ω?
5.   An electric soldering iron draws 0.8 A from a 120-V 60-Hz line. What is its resistance? How much power will it consume?
6.   What ac voltage is required to force 0.02 A through an 8,000-Ω radio resistor? What is the power used?
7.   Find the current and power drawn from a 110-V 60-Hz line by a tungsten lamp whose hot resistance is 275 Ω.
8.   What is the current drawn by a 200-W incandescent lamp from a 110-V 60-Hz line? What is the hot resistance of the lamp?

9. Find the power used by a 24-Ω soldering iron which draws 5 A.
10. Find the voltage needed to operate a 500-W electric percolator if it draws 4.5 A. What is its resistance?

Series circuits containing only inductance. When an ac voltage is impressed across a coil, it will produce an alternating current. The changing current will produce changing lines of force around the turns of the coil. The changing lines of force will cut across the wires forming the coil and induce an emf in the coil. This emf is a "back emf" which acts to oppose the original voltage. This opposition, called the inductive reactance, will reduce the current below that which would flow if there were no "cuttings" or back emf. This reactance does more than just reduce the current. It also prevents the current from appearing at the same time as the voltage. The current will be pushed back in *time* as well as in amount. We say that the current "lags" behind the voltage which produces it. In a perfect coil—one which has only inductance and zero resistance—the current will lag behind the voltage by an amount of time equal to the time required for 1/4 cycle. It is easier to discuss this "time lag" in terms of the number of electrical degrees for 1/4 cycle than in units of time. We say that the current lags the voltage by 90°, since 1/4 cycle equals 1/4 $\times$ 360° = 90°.

The current that flows as a result of an ac voltage across a coil will be an alternating current with the same frequency as the ac voltage. The difference between this and the resistive circuit is that in the inductive circuit the current does *not* rise and fall in step with the voltage. The current remains forever 90 electrical degrees *behind* the voltage as shown in Fig. 18-4. The current lags behind the voltage by 90°, or the voltage "leads" the current by 90°. In an inductive circuit, the voltage and current are out of phase by 90°. The phase angle θ in an inductive circuit is 90°.

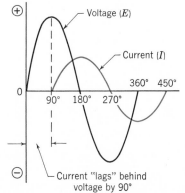

FIGURE 18-4
The voltage and current are out of phase in an ac circuit containing only inductance.

Phasor diagram. Since the voltage and current are out of phase by 90°, the phasors must be drawn in two different directions 90° apart. In addition to this, we must show which phasor is the "leading" phasor and which is the "lagging" phasor. To show quantities occurring "before" or "after" another, we shall use the numbers on a clock. Let us consider the hour hand of a clock as a phasor. A phasor pointing to 3 o'clock occurs after a phasor pointing to 12 o'clock, or noon. Similarly, a phasor pointing to 3 o'clock occurs before a phasor pointing to 6 o'clock.

We can now proceed to draw a phasor diagram for an inductive circuit. Since the current in a series circuit is constant, the current is used as the reference line. Draw a line with an arrow pointing to the right as shown in Fig. 18-5. This will represent the current I in the circuit. Since the voltage leads the current by 90°, we shall be forced to draw the voltage phasor in such a way so as to be 90° before the current phasor. If the current phasor already points to 3 o'clock, the voltage phasor must point to 12 o'clock in order to lead the current phasor by 90°.

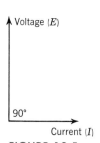

FIGURE 18-5
The voltage phasor leads the current phasor by 90° in a purely inductive circuit.

The amount of current that will flow in a "pure" inductance is found by Ohm's law. However, since a pure inductance contains zero resistance, the R is replaced by X_L. Ohm's law for a pure inductance will then be

$$E_L = I_L \times X_L \qquad (16\text{-}2)$$

Power. In a purely resistive circuit, the voltage and current occur at the same time, or are in phase. The power is equal to the multiplication of the current by the voltage—just as in a dc circuit. However, as we have just seen, the voltage and the current do not always occur at the same time. In this event, only a portion of the current will occur at the same time as the voltage. In these ac circuits in which the voltage and current are *not* in phase, the effective power consumed will be equal to the voltage multiplied by only that portion of the current *in phase with it*. The amount of this *in-phase* current is equal to the current multiplied by the cosine of the phase angle. (See Job 19-5, Examples 19-13 and 19-14.)

$$\text{In-phase current} = I \times \cos \theta \qquad \boxed{18\text{-}1}$$

The general formula for power in an ac circuit is

$$W = E \times \text{in-phase current} \qquad \boxed{18\text{-}2}$$

By substitution, we obtain

FORMULA

$$W = E \times I \times \cos \theta \qquad \boxed{18\text{-}3}$$

where W = effective power, W
E = voltage, V
I = current, A
θ = phase angle of the circuit, deg

In a pure inductance, the power will be

$$W = E \times I \times \cos 90°$$

$$W = E \times I \times 0$$

$$W = 0 \text{ W}$$

Thus, the average power used by a pure inductance is zero. Actually, the inductance uses power to build up its magnetic field during one quarter of a cycle, but it delivers an equal amount of power back to the source while the field is collapsing during the second quarter of its cycle. The net result is that zero power is used by the inductance. A perfect inductance may be considered to be just like a perfect flywheel, which accumulates power during one revolution and delivers an equal amount of power back to the engine during its second revolution.

EXAMPLE 18-2   A 10-H filter choke coil is connected across a 120-V 60-Hz ac line. Assuming that the coil has zero resistance, find the current and the effective power drawn. Draw the phasor diagram.

SOLUTION

Given: $L = 10$ H   Find: $I = ?$
       $E = 120$ V $W = ?$
       $f = 60$ Hz

1   Find the inductive reactance.

$$X_L = 6.28 f L = 6.28 \times 60 \times 10 = 3{,}768 \ \Omega \qquad (16\text{-}1)$$

2   Find the current.

$$E_L = I_L \times X_L \qquad (16\text{-}2)$$

$$120 = I_L \times 3{,}768$$

$$I_L = \frac{120}{3{,}768} = 0.0318 \text{ A} \qquad Ans.$$

3   Draw the phasor diagram. See Fig. 18-5.
4   Find the effective power.

$$W = E \times I \times \cos \theta \qquad (18\text{-}3)$$

$$W = 120 \times 0.0318 \times \cos 90°$$

$$W = 120 \times 0.0318 \times 0 = 0 \text{ W} \qquad Ans.$$

PROBLEMS

Draw a phasor diagram for each problem (not to scale).

1.   Find the current sent through a 0.03-H coil by a voltage of 188.4 V at a frequency of 1 kHz.

2. Find the current and effective power drawn by a 200-mH coil which is connected to a 31.4-V source at a frequency of 1,000 Hz.
3. What voltage is needed to force 0.08 A through an inductance of 0.5 H at a frequency of 100 Hz?
4. What voltage at 10 kHz is necessary to send a current of 20 mA through an inductance of 50 mH? What is the effective power consumed?
5. What must be the reactance of a filter choke in order for it to pass 80 mA of current when the voltage is 240 V? What must be the inductance of the choke if the frequency is 60Hz?

Series circuits containing only capacitance. When an alternating voltage is impressed across a capacitor, the capacitor will be alternately charged and discharged. While it is charging, the flow of electrons to the plate of the capacitor is largest at the instant the charge is begun. This is so because there are no electrons already on the plate to exert an opposing force. As more and more electrons accumulate on the plate of the capacitor, they exert a greater and greater force which tends to stop the flow of electrons to the plate. When the capacitor is fully charged to the voltage of the source, the flow of current falls to zero, since the back pressure is equal to the pressure of the charging source. Notice that the maximum current occurs when the voltage is zero and a zero current flows when the voltage is a maximum. If the capacitor is continually charged and discharged by a source of alternating voltage, the relation between current and voltage will be that which is shown in Fig. 18-6. This indicates that in a capacitive circuit the current *leads* the voltage or the voltage *lags* behind the current. This condition does not exist until the circuit is in operation for a few seconds, as it is obviously impossible for the current to start at any value other than zero. However, once the circuit is in operation, the phase relations are adjusted so that the current will *lead* the voltage by ¼ cycle or 90 electrical degrees. As with an inductance, this applies only to a "perfect" capacitor—one in which there is no resistance due to the resistance of the capacitor plates or leads.

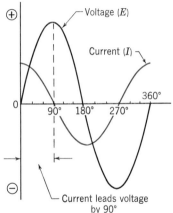

FIGURE 18-6

The voltage and current are out of phase in an ac circuit containing only capacitance.

The current that flows as a result of an ac voltage across a capacitor will be an alternating current with the same frequency as the ac voltage. The current remains forever 90 electrical degrees *ahead* of the voltage. The current *leads* the voltage or the voltage *lags* behind the current by 90°. The phase angle θ in a capacitive circuit is 90°.

Phasor diagram. To express this leading current by phasors, the phasors must be drawn 90° apart. Since the current in a series circuit is constant, the current is used as the reference line. Draw a line with an arrow pointing to the right as shown in Fig. 18-7. This will represent the current I in the circuit. Since the voltage *lags* the current by 90°, we shall be forced to draw the voltage phasor in such a way so as to be 90° *after* the current. Since the current phasor already points to 3 o'clock, the voltage phasor must point to 6 o'clock in order to *lag* the current vector by 90°.

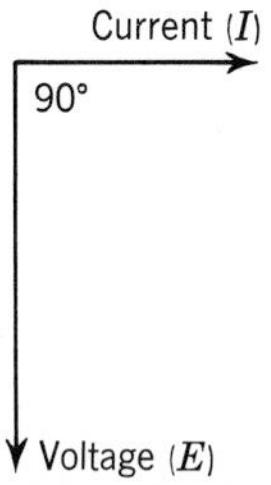

The amount of current in a "pure" capacitance is found by Ohm's law. However, since a pure capacitance contains zero resistance, R is replaced by X_C. Ohm's law for a pure capacitance will then be

$$E_C = I_C \times X_C \qquad (17\text{-}7)$$

Current (I)

90°

Voltage (E)

FIGURE 18-7

The voltage phasor lags the current phasor by 90° in a purely capacitive circuit.

Power. Since the voltage and current in a pure capacitive circuit are 90° out of phase, the power used is equal to zero. This fact is obtained by substituting in formula (18-3) for ac power.

$$W = E \times I \times \cos \theta \qquad (18\text{-}3)$$

$$W = E \times I \times \cos 90°$$

$$W = E \times I \times 0 = 0 \text{ W}$$

EXAMPLE 18-3   A 10-μF coupling capacitor in a transistor record player passes 300 mA at a frequency of 0.4 kHz. Find (*a*) the voltage drop across the capacitor and (*b*) the effective power consumed.

SOLUTION

Given: $C = 10 \ \mu$F   Find: $E = ?$
$\quad\quad\quad I = 300 \text{ mA} = 0.3 \text{ A}$
$\quad\quad\quad f = 0.4 \text{ kHz} = 400 \text{ Hz}$

a. Find the reactance of the capacitor.

$$X_C = \frac{159,000}{f \times C} = \frac{159,000}{400 \times 10} = \frac{159}{4} = 40 \ \Omega \text{ (approx)} \quad (17\text{-}6)$$

Find the voltage drop.

$$E_C = I_C \times X_C \qquad (17\text{-}7)$$

$$E_C = 0.3 \times 40 = 12 \text{ V} \quad\quad \textit{Ans.}$$

b. Find the effective power.

$$W = E \times I \times \cos \theta \qquad\qquad (18\text{-}3)$$

$$W = 12 \times 0.3 \times \cos 90°$$

$$W = 12 \times 0.3 \times 0 = 0 \text{ W} \qquad Ans.$$

PROBLEMS

1. A voltage of 9 V at a frequency of 10 kHz is impressed across a
    4-μF capacitor. Find (*a*) the current and (*b*) the effective power
    used.
2. What current will flow through a 0.000015-F capacitor if the volt-
    age across it is 10.6 V at a frequency of 100 Hz?
3. An absorption-type wave trap in a television receiver is tuned to
    27.25 MHz. What is the reactance of the 47 pF capacitor in the
    trap?
4. What is the reactance of a 0.06-μF coupling capacitor to an audio
    frequency of 2 kHz? What current will flow if the voltage across
    the capacitor is 6 V?
5. What is the reactance of a 0.02-μF coupling capacitor to a frequency
    of 200 kHz? What current will flow if the voltage across the ca-
    pacitor is 4 V?
6. A 4-μF bypass capacitor passes 200 mA at a frequency of 1 kHz.
    Find (*a*) the voltage drop across the capacitor and (*b*) the effective
    power consumed.
7. The potential difference between two wires having a distributed
    capacity of 20 pF is 2 V. Find the flow of current between the wires
    if one of them carries a 1,000-kHz current.
8. Find the voltage across a 10-μF filter capacitor if it passes 1 A at
    a frequency of 60 Hz.
9. What must be the reactance of a capacitor in order for it to pass
    1 A of current when the voltage is 100 V? What is the capacitance
    of the capacitor if the frequency is 1,000 kHz?
10. The plates of a tuning capacitor are set to provide a capacitance of
    200 pF. If the capacitor passes 350 mA at 3 MHz, what is the
    voltage drop across it?

JOB 18-2 THE PYTHAGOREAN THEOREM

In our next job we shall find the total voltage across a series ac circuit
by adding the voltages *even though the voltages do not appear at the same
time!* The formulas for this total voltage and for all our work in ac
power are applications of the *pythagorean theorem.*

This basic mathematical law about a *right triangle* was discovered by
a Greek scholar named Pythagoras about 2,500 years ago. In Fig. 18-8,

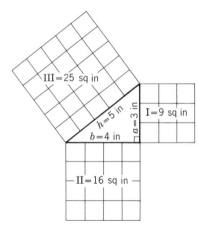

FIGURE 18-8
Pictorial representation of the Pythagorean theorem:
$$a^2 + b^2 = h^2$$

squares are drawn on each of the three sides of the right triangle. The length of the sides of each square is equal to the length of the side of the triangle on which it is drawn. Pythagoras discovered that the *sum of the areas of the squares on the two legs of a right triangle is exactly equal to the area of the square erected on the hypotenuse.* This is true for *any right triangle.* Thus,

$$\text{area I} + \text{area II} = \text{area III}$$

$$9 \quad + \quad 16 \quad = \quad 25$$

Since the area of a square is equal to a side times itself,

$$\text{Area I} = a \times a = a^2$$

$$\text{Area II} = b \times b = b^2$$

$$\text{Area III} = h \times h = h^2$$

The theorem may be stated as the following rule.

RULE	The sum of the squares of the legs of a right triangle is equal to the square of the hypotenuse.

FORMULA

$$a^2 + b^2 = h^2 \qquad \boxed{18\text{-}4}$$

where a and b = legs of a right triangle
   h = hypotenuse of a right triangle

The formula may be solved for h by taking the square root of both sides.

$$\sqrt{a^2 + b^2} = \sqrt{h^2}$$

$$\sqrt{a^2 + b^2} = h \qquad \boxed{18\text{-}4a}$$

EXAMPLE 18-4   Find the hypotenuse of a right triangle whose altitude is 5 in and whose base is 12 in.

SOLUTION
The diagram is shown in Fig. 18-9.

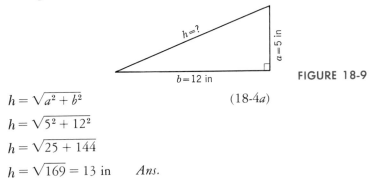

FIGURE 18-9

$$h = \sqrt{a^2 + b^2} \qquad\qquad (18\text{-}4a)$$
$$h = \sqrt{5^2 + 12^2}$$
$$h = \sqrt{25 + 144}$$
$$h = \sqrt{169} = 13 \text{ in} \qquad Ans.$$

EXAMPLE 18-5   Find the altitude a in a right triangle whose hypotenuse h is 17 in and whose base b is 15 in.

SOLUTION
Given: $h = 17$ in   Find: $a = ?$
$\quad\quad\;\; b = 15$ in

$$a^2 + b^2 = h^2$$
$$a^2 + 15^2 = 17^2$$
$$a^2 + 225 = 289$$
$$a^2 = 289 - 225$$
$$a^2 = 64$$
$$a = \sqrt{64} = 8 \text{ in} \qquad Ans.$$

SELF-TEST 18-6   An electrician's tool box measures 16 in × 12 in × 10 in. What is the length of the largest extension bit holder that may be placed in the tool box?

SOLUTION
The tool box is shown in Fig. 18-10.

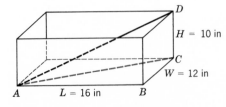

FIGURE 18-10
AD is the longest dimension in the tool box.

1   Find the length of the diagonal AC. Triangle ABC is a right triangle with the right angle at point ___.

$$h = \sqrt{a^2 + b^2} \qquad\qquad (18\text{-}4a)$$

$$AC = \sqrt{16^2 + (?)^2}$$

$$AC = \sqrt{256 + ?}$$

$$AC = \sqrt{400} = \underline{\quad} \text{ in}$$

2   Find the length of the bit holder AD using triangle ___, in which the right angle is at point ___.

$$h = \sqrt{a^2 + b^2} \qquad\qquad (18\text{-}4a)$$

$$AD = \sqrt{10^2 + (?)^2}$$

$$AD = \sqrt{100 + 400} = \sqrt{?}$$

$$AD = \underline{\quad} \text{ in} \qquad Ans.$$

B
12
144
20
ACD
C
20
500
22.3

PROBLEMS

Find the unknown side in each of the following right triangles:

PROBLEM	a	b	h
1	6	8	?
2	7	24	?
3	?	63	65
4	33	?	65
5	14	22.5	?
6	17.5	6	?
7	?	20	20.5
8	6.5	?	42.5

9. A guy wire stretches from the top of an 80-ft-high pole to a stake in the ground 120 ft from the foot of the pole. Find the length of the wire.

10. A 10-ft ladder is placed against a wall with the foot of the ladder 6 ft from the base of the wall. How high above the ground will the ladder reach?

11. A doorway measures 3×7 ft. What is the diameter of the largest circular table that will pass through the doorway?

12. A conduit must be bent to provide a rise of 6 ft in a horizontal distance of 4 ft 6 in. What is the length of conduit between the bends?

13. Find the length of electrical conduit needed to include the 5-ft offset as shown in Fig. 18-11.

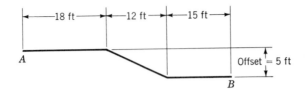

FIGURE 18-11

Find the length of conduit from A to B.

14. Find the distance across the corners of a square nut measuring $3\frac{1}{4}$ in on a side.
15. Find the distance X in Fig. 18-12.

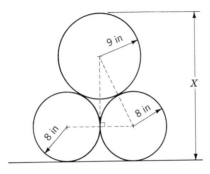

FIGURE 18-12

JOB 18-3   RESISTANCE AND INDUCTANCE IN SERIES

Figure 18-13 shows a 100-Ω resistor connected in series with an inductance whose reactance is 100 Ω at a frequency of 60 Hz. A series current of 0.85 A produces a voltage drop of 85 V across both the resistor and the inductance. In a series circuit, the total voltage is ordinarily

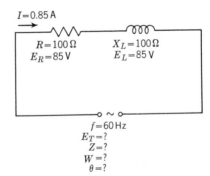

FIGURE 18-13

An ac series circuit containing resistance and inductance.

found by adding the voltages across all the parts of the circuit. This rule was used in dc circuits, but can we use it for ac circuits? Since the current in a series circuit remains unchanged throughout the circuit, we may draw the waveforms for the currents and voltages across each part of the circuit on the same drawing. Figure 18-14 shows the relationship of each voltage to the unchanging current. The voltage across the resistor E_R is *in phase* with the current I; that is, E_R and I reach their maximum and minimum values *at the same time.* The voltage across the inductance E_L *leads* the current I by 90°; that is, E_L reaches its maximum 90° *before I* reaches its maximum. Also, E_L *leads* E_R by 90°; that is, E_L reaches its maximum 90° *before* E_R reaches its maximum.

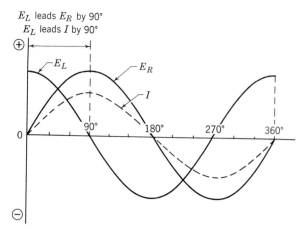

FIGURE 18-14
Voltages and currents in a series ac circuit containing resistance and inductance.

To obtain the total voltage we must add the voltages across all parts of the circuit. But how are we going to add voltages that do not happen at the same time? The only way to do this is to add the *instantaneous* voltages that *do* occur at the same time. Thus, in Fig. 18-15, the instantaneous values of e_R and e_L are added for different instants of time.

At 0°, $e_R = 0$ and e_L is a maximum. Therefore

$$E_T = e_R + e_L$$
$$E_T = 0 + e_L$$
$$E_T = e_L \qquad \text{(point } a)$$

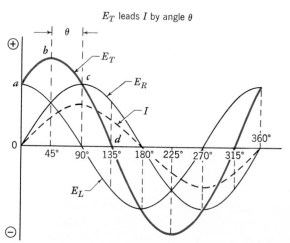

FIGURE 18-15
The total voltage in a series ac circuit is obtained by adding the instantaneous voltages instant by instant.

At $45°$, $e_R = e_L$ and

$$E_T = e_R + e_L$$

or $\qquad E_T =$ twice the value of either $\qquad$ (point b)

At $90°$, $e_L = 0$ and e_R is a maximum. Therefore

$$E_T = e_R + e_L$$
$$E_T = e_R + 0$$
$$E_T = e_R \qquad \text{(point } c)$$

At $135°$, $e_R = e_L$, but they are of opposite polarity. Therefore

$$E_T = e_R + (-e_L)$$
$$E_T = 0 \qquad \text{(point } d)$$

By continuing in this manner, adding the voltages instant by instant the waveform for the total voltage is obtained as shown in Fig. 18-15. Notice that the maximum value of E_T (at $45°$) is *still leading* the current maximum. In this particular problem, since R and X_L are equal, the angle of lead is equal to $45°$. For other values of R and X_L, angle θ will change.

Apparently, then, although we *do* add the voltages to get the total voltage, the addition is not just a simple arithmetic addition. We can see this more clearly if we draw the voltages and currents as phasors on the same unchanging current base as shown in Fig. 18-16a. This phasor diagram shows exactly the same relationships that were shown in Fig. 18-14 in waveform. The constant series current is used as the reference line. The voltage across the resistor E_R is still in phase with the current I, and the voltage across the inductance E_L still leads the current I by $90°$.

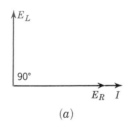

(a)

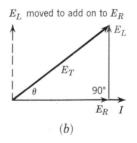

(b)

FIGURE 18-16

(a) Phasor diagram for a series ac circuit containing resistance and inductance. (b) E_T represents the phasor sum of E_R and E_L.

ADDITION OF PHASORS

RULE

Phasors are added by placing the tail of each phasor on the head of the preceding phasor and drawing it in its original direction and length.

In Fig. 18-16b, the total voltage E_T is obtained by adding the phasor E_L to the phasor E_R. Place the tail of E_L on the head of E_R and draw it in its original direction and length. The distance from the origin of the phasors to the head of the final phasor is the *sum* of the phasors. In this instance, the phasor E_T represents the sum of the phasors E_R and E_L. The phase angle θ is the angle by which the total voltage leads the current. In this problem, the angle is $45°$ and is the same angle shown on the waveform diagram of Fig. 18-15.

By applying the pythagorean theorem to Fig. 18-16b, we obtain

FORMULA

$$E_T{}^2 = E_R{}^2 + E_L{}^2$$

$$\boxed{18\text{-}5}$$

Total impedance. To find the impedance of the series ac circuit, we must add R and X_L vectorially as was done with the voltages. This is shown in Fig. 18-17. The voltages in Fig. 18-17a are replaced by their Ohm's law values in Fig. 18-17b. Now, by dropping out the common factor of the current I, we obtain the *impedance triangle* of Fig. 18-17c.

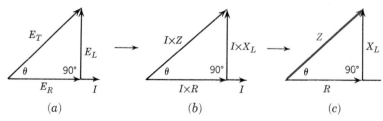

FIGURE 18-17
Z represents the phasor sum of R and X_L.

Applying the pythagorean theorem to Fig. 18-17c, we obtain

FORMULAS

$$Z^2 = R^2 + X_L{}^2$$

$$\boxed{18\text{-}6}$$

and

$$Z = \sqrt{R^2 + X_L{}^2}$$

$$\boxed{18\text{-}7}$$

And by trigonometry,

$$\cos\theta = \frac{a}{h}$$

or

$$\cos\theta = \frac{R}{Z}$$

$$\boxed{18\text{-}8}$$

The power is still given by $W = E \times I \times \cos\theta$ (18-3)

EXAMPLE 18-7   In Fig. 18-13, find (*a*) the total voltage, (*b*) the impedance, (*c*) the phase angle, and (*d*) the power.

SOLUTION

a
$$E_T{}^2 = E_R{}^2 + E_L{}^2 = 85^2 + 85^2 \tag{18-5}$$

$$= 7{,}225 + 7{,}225$$

$$= 14{,}450$$

$$E_T = \sqrt{14{,}450} = 120 \text{ V} \qquad Ans.$$

b
$$Z = \sqrt{R^2 + X_L{}^2} \tag{18-7}$$

$$Z = \sqrt{100^2 + 100^2} = \sqrt{10^4 + 10^4} = \sqrt{2 \times 10^4}$$

$$Z = 1.41 \times 10^2 = 141 \ \Omega \qquad Ans.$$

c
$$\cos\theta = \frac{R}{Z} = \frac{100}{141} = 0.709 \tag{18-8}$$

$$\theta = 45° \qquad Ans.$$

d
$$W = E \times I \times \cos\theta \tag{18-3}$$

$$W = 120 \times 0.85 \times \cos 45° = 120 \times 0.85 \times 0.709$$

$$W = 72.3 \text{ W} \qquad Ans.$$

EXAMPLE 18-8   An inductance of 0.17 H and a resistance of 50 Ω are connected in series across a 110-V 60-Hz line. Find (*a*) the inductive reactance, (*b*) the impedance, (*c*) the total current, (*d*) the voltage drop across the resistor and the coil, (*e*) the phase angle, and (*f*) the power used.

SOLUTION

Given: $L = 0.17$ H   Find: $X_L = ?$
        $R = 50 \ \Omega$ $Z = ?$
        $E_T = 110$ V $I_T = ?$
        $f = 60$ Hz $E_R = ?$
                                $E_L = ?$
                                  $\theta = ?$
                                  $W = ?$

a
$$X_L = 6.28fL = 6.28 \times 60 \times 0.17 = 64 \ \Omega \qquad Ans.$$

b
$$Z = \sqrt{R^2 + X_L{}^2} = \sqrt{50^2 + 64^2} \tag{18-7}$$

$$= \sqrt{2{,}500 + 4{,}096}$$

$$Z = \sqrt{6{,}596} = 81 \ \Omega \qquad Ans.$$

c   Since the total opposition is the impedance Z, formula (3-7) becomes

$$E_T = I_T \times Z \qquad \boxed{18\text{-}9}$$

$$110 = I_T \times 81$$

$$I_T = \frac{110}{81} = 1.36 \text{ A} \qquad Ans.$$

d Since

$$I_T = I_R = I_L = 1.36 \text{ A} \qquad (3\text{-}1)$$

$$E_R = I_R \times R_R \qquad\qquad E_L = I_L \times X_L$$

$$E_R = 1.36 \times 50 = 68 \text{ V} \qquad E_L = 1.36 \times 64 = 87 \text{ V}$$

e

$$\cos\theta = \frac{R}{Z} = \frac{50}{81} = 0.6173 \qquad (18\text{-}8)$$

$$\theta = 52° \qquad Ans.$$

f

$$W = E \times I \times \cos\theta \qquad (18\text{-}3)$$

$$W = 110 \times 1.36 \times \cos 52°$$

$$W = 110 \times 1.36 \times 0.617$$

$$W = 92.5 \text{ W} \qquad Ans.$$

In the series circuit, the total voltage of 110 V leads the total current of 1.36 A by 52°.

SELF-TEST 18-9 Figure 18-18 may be used to represent the plate circuit of an amplifier with transformer coupling. Find the value of E_p when the frequency of the applied voltage is (*a*) 100 Hz and (*b*) 10 Hz.

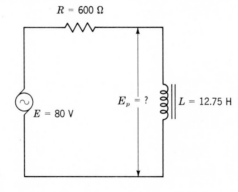

R = 600 Ω

E_p = ?   L = 12.75 H

E = 80 V

FIGURE 18-18
Representation of the plate circuit of a transformer-coupled amplifier.

SOLUTION

a At 100 Hz,

$$X_L = 6.28fL \qquad (16\text{-}1)$$

$$X_L = 6.28 \times 100 \times 12.75 = \underline{\qquad} \ \Omega$$

8,000

The factor that determines whether we should include the 600-Ω resistance in the calculation for *Z* is called the ___ of the circuit. (See page 511.)

Q

$$Q = \frac{X_L}{R} = \frac{8,000}{600} = \underline{\qquad} \qquad (16\text{-}5)$$

13.3

Since Q is greater than 5, we __(should/should not)__ include the resistance in the calculation for Z. Therefore, $Z =$ ____ Ω.

Find the current.

$$E = IZ \qquad (16\text{-}6)$$

$$80 = I \times 8,000$$

$$I = \underline{\quad} \text{ A}$$

Find E_p.

$$E_p = I \times X_L$$

$$= 0.01 \times 8,000$$

$$E_p = \underline{\quad} \text{ V} \qquad Ans.$$

b At 10 Hz,

$$X_L = 6.28 \times \underline{\quad} \times 12.75$$

$$X_L = \underline{\quad} \Omega$$

The Q of the circuit is now $800/\underline{?}$, or

$$Q = \underline{\quad}$$

Since $Q = 1.33$, the resistance __(should/should not)__ be included in the calculation for Z.

$$Z = \sqrt{R^2 + X_L^2} = \sqrt{(600)^2 + (800)^2}$$

$$= \sqrt{36 \times 10^4 + \underline{?} \times 10^4}$$

$$= \sqrt{(36 + 64) \times 10^4}$$

$$Z = \sqrt{100 \times 10^4} = \underline{\quad} \Omega$$

Find the current.

$$E = IZ \qquad (16\text{-}6)$$

$$80 = I \times 1,000$$

$$I = \underline{\quad} \text{ A}$$

Find E_p.

$$E_p = I \times X_L$$

$$= 0.08 \times \underline{\quad}$$

$$E_p = \underline{\quad} \text{ V} \qquad Ans.$$

Answer column (right margin):

should not
8,000

0.01

80

10
800
600
1.33

should

64

1,000

0.08

800
64

PROBLEMS

1.   A resistance of 5 Ω is in series with a coil whose inductive reactance is 12 Ω. If the total voltage is 104 V, find (a) the impedance, (b) the total current, (c) the voltage drop across each part, (d) the phase angle, and (e) the power.

2.   A 112-V 60-Hz ac voltage is applied across a series circuit of a 50-Ω

resistor and a 100-Ω inductive reactance. Find (*a*) the impedance, (*b*) the total current, (*c*) the voltage drop across each part, (*d*) the phase angle, and (*e*) the power.

3. A 66-V 220-Hz ac voltage is applied across a series circuit of a 20-Ω resistor and a 0.05-H coil. Find the total current and the phase angle.

4. A tuning coil has an inductance of 48 μH and a resistance of 20 Ω. Find its impedance to a frequency of 100 kHz.

5. A fluorescent lamp ballast has an inductance of 0.4 H and a resistance of 80 Ω. If the supply frequency is 60 Hz, find (*a*) the reactance of the ballast, (*b*) the impedance of the ballast, and (*c*) the voltage across the ballast when 0.5 A flows through it.

6. The plate circuit of a transformer-coupled amplifier contains a 25,000-Ω resistance and a 20-H coil. At what frequency will the voltage across the coil equal that across the resistance? What current will flow if the impressed voltage is 35 V?

7. Part of the oscillator circuit for a continuous-wave transmitter is shown in Fig. 18-19. Find the current from point *A* to point *B* if the voltage drop is 70 V.

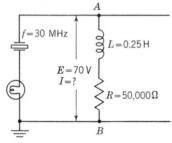

FIGURE 18-19
A portion of the oscillator circuit for a continuous-wave transmitter.

8. A 20-Ω resistor is in series with a 0.03-H dimmer coil. If the 230-V 60-Hz ac voltage is applied to the circuit, find (*a*) the current and (*b*) the power used.

9. A lightning protector circuit contains a 63.7-mH coil in series with a 7-Ω resistor. What current will flow when it is tested with a 110-V 60-Hz ac voltage?

10. The coil of a telephone relay has a resistance of 500 Ω and an inductance of 0.32 H. When operated at a frequency of 500 Hz, find (*a*) the reactance of the coil, (*b*) the impedance of the coil, and (*c*) the voltage that must be impressed across the coil in order to operate the relay at its rated current of 5 mA.

11. The output voltage of an audio oscillator is 37.7 V at 3,000 Hz. It is applied to a series circuit of 200 Ω resistance and 200 mH inductance. Find the impedance of the circuit and the current that flows.

12. A filter choke coil is connected in series with a 400-Ω resistor. When the voltage across the circuit is 120 V, the current is 0.12 A.

Find the inductance of the coil if the frequency is 60 Hz. *Hint:* See Job 16-5.

13. To measure the inductance of an audio choke, a 2,000-Ω resistor is connected in series with the choke. A 110-V 60-Hz voltage is impressed across the circuit, and the current is measured at 10 mA. Find the inductance of the coil.

14. A 40-V emf at 1,000 Hz is impressed across a loudspeaker of 5,000 Ω resistance and 1.5 H inductance. Find the current and power drawn.

15. Find the inductive reactance of a single-phase motor if the line voltage is 220 V, the line current is 20 A, and the resistance of the motor coils is 8 Ω. What is the angle of lag?

JOB 18-4   RESISTANCE AND CAPACITANCE IN SERIES

Figure 18-20 shows a 5-Ω resistor connected in series with a capacitance whose reactance is 12 Ω at a frequency of 60 Hz. A series current of 1 A produces a voltage drop of 5 V across the resistor and 12 V across the capacitor.

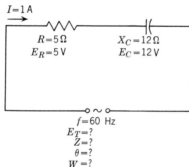

FIGURE 18-20

An ac series circuit containing resistance and capacitance.

The total voltage across the circuit can be found by adding the voltage drops across each part. But, just as in the last job, since the voltages are *not* in phase, they must be added vectorially. The phase relations in a capacitive circuit are shown in Fig. 18-21*a*. The constant series current is used as the reference line. The voltage across the resistor E_R is in

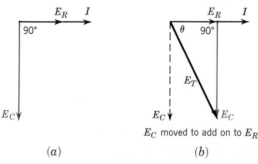

FIGURE 18-21

(a) Phasor diagram for a series ac circuit containing resistance and capacitance. (b) E_T represents the phasor sum of E_R and E_C.

phase with the current I; the voltage across the capacitor E_C *lags* the current I by 90°; E_C *lags* E_R by 90°.

Addition of the phasors. In Fig. 18-21b, the total voltage E_T is obtained by adding the phasor E_C to the phasor E_R. Place the tail of E_C on the head of E_R, and draw it in its original direction and length. The distance from the origin of phasors to the head of the final phasor is the sum of the phasors. In this instance, the phasor E_T represents the sum of the phasors E_R and E_C. The phase angle θ is the angle by which the total voltage *lags* behind the current. By applying the pythagorean theorem to Fig. 18-21b, we obtain

FORMULA

$$E_T{}^2 = E_R{}^2 + E_C{}^2 \qquad \boxed{18\text{-}10}$$

Total impedance. To find the impedance of the series ac circuit, we must add R and X_C vectorially as was done with the voltages. This is shown in Fig. 18-22. The voltages in Fig. 18-22a are replaced by their Ohm's law values in Fig. 18-22b. Now, by dropping out the common factor of the current I, we obtain the *impedance triangle* of Fig. 18-22c.

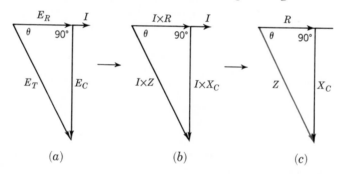

(a)   (b)   (c)

FIGURE 18-22
Z represents the phasor sum of R and X_C.

Applying the pythagorean theorem to Fig. 18-22c, we obtain

FORMULAS

$$Z^2 = R^2 + X_C{}^2 \qquad \boxed{18\text{-}11}$$

and

$$Z = \sqrt{R^2 + X_C{}^2} \qquad \boxed{18\text{-}12}$$

And by trigonometry,

$$\cos \theta = \frac{a}{h}$$

or

$$\cos \theta = \frac{R}{Z} \qquad (18\text{-}8)$$

The power is still given by

$$W = E \times I \times \cos \theta \qquad (18\text{-}3)$$

EXAMPLE 18-10   In Fig. 18-20, find (a) the total voltage, (b) the impedance, (c) the phase angle, and (d) the power.

SOLUTION

a
$$E_T^2 = E_R^2 + E_C^2 = 5^2 + 12^2 \qquad (18\text{-}10)$$
$$= 25 + 144$$
$$= 169$$
$$E_T = \sqrt{169} = 13 \text{ V} \qquad Ans.$$

b
$$Z = \sqrt{R^2 + X_C^2} \qquad (18\text{-}12)$$
$$= \sqrt{5^2 + 12^2}$$
$$= \sqrt{25 + 144}$$
$$Z = \sqrt{169} = 13 \ \Omega \qquad Ans.$$

c
$$\cos \theta = \frac{R}{Z} = \frac{5}{13} = 0.3846 \qquad (18\text{-}8)$$
$$\theta = 67° \quad (\text{approx}) \qquad Ans.$$

d
$$W = E \times I \times \cos \theta \qquad (18\text{-}3)$$
$$W = 13 \times 1 \times \cos 67° = 13 \times 0.385 = 5 \text{ W} \qquad Ans.$$

EXAMPLE 18-11   A capacitance of 4 μF and a resistance of 30 Ω are connected in series across a 100-V 1-kHz ac source. Find (a) the capacitive reactance, (b) the impedance, (c) the total current, (d) the voltage drop across the resistor and the capacitor, (e) the phase angle, and (f) the power.

SOLUTION

Given: $C = 4 \ \mu F$ Find: $X_C = ?$
        $R = 30 \ \Omega$ $Z = ?$
        $E_T = 100 \text{ V}$ $I_T = ?$
        $f = 1 \text{ kHz} = 1,000 \text{ Hz}$ $E_R = ?$
                                       $E_C = ?$
                                       $\theta = ?$
                                       $W = ?$

a
$$X_C = \frac{159,000}{f \times C} = \frac{159,000}{1,000 \times 4} = \frac{159}{4} = 40 \ \Omega \qquad (\text{approx})$$

b
$$Z = \sqrt{R^2 + X_C^2} \qquad (18\text{-}12)$$
$$= \sqrt{30^2 + 40^2}$$
$$= \sqrt{900 + 1,600}$$
$$Z = \sqrt{2,500} = 50 \ \Omega \qquad Ans.$$

c $$E_T = I_T \times Z \qquad (18\text{-}9)$$

$$100 = I_T \times 50$$

$$I_T = \frac{100}{50} = 2 \text{ A} \qquad Ans.$$

d Since $$I_T = I_R = I_C = 2 \text{ A} \qquad (3\text{-}1)$$

$$E_R = I_R \times R_R \qquad\qquad E_C = I_C \times X_C$$

$$E_R = 2 \times 30 = 60 \text{ V} \quad Ans. \qquad E_C = 2 \times 40 = 80 \text{ V} \qquad Ans.$$

e $$\cos \theta = \frac{R}{Z} = \frac{30}{50} = 0.6000 \qquad (18\text{-}8)$$

$$\theta = 53° \quad \text{(approx)} \quad Ans.$$

f $$W = E \times I \times \cos \theta = 100 \times 2 \times 0.6 = 120 \text{ W} \qquad Ans.$$

In the series circuit, the total voltage of 100 V lags the total current of 2 A by 53°.

PROBLEMS

1. A 119-V 60-Hz ac voltage is applied across a series circuit of an 8-Ω resistor and a capacitor whose reactance is 15 Ω. Find (*a*) the impedance, (*b*) the total current, (*c*) the voltage drop across each part, (*d*) the phase angle, and (*e*) the power.
2. A 134-V 60-Hz ac voltage is applied across a series circuit of a 30-Ω resistor and a 60-Ω capacitive reactance. Find (*a*) the impedance, (*b*) the total current, (*c*) the voltage drop across each part, (*d*) the phase angle, and (*e*) the power.
3. A 113-V 100-Hz ac voltage is applied across a series circuit of a 100-Ω resistor and a 15.9-μF capacitor. Find (*a*) the impedance, (*b*) the total current, (*c*) the voltage drop across each part, (*d*) the phase angle, and (*e*) the power.
4. Find the current and angle of lag for a series circuit of a 10-Ω resistor and an 8-μF capacitor if the applied voltage is 110 V at 60 Hz.
5. In the volume-control circuit shown in Fig. 18-23, find the impedance of the control unit to frequencies of (*a*) 1,000 Hz and (*b*) 10 kHz.

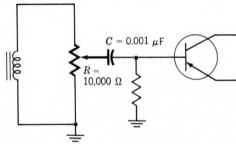

FIGURE 18-23

6. In the resistance-coupled stage shown in Fig. 18-24, the voltage
    drop between points A and B is 1.414 V. If the frequency of the
    current between these points is 10 kHz, find the voltage drop
    across the 1,000-Ω resistor.

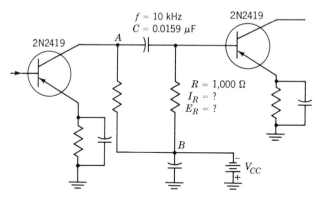

FIGURE 18-24
A resistance-coupled
amplifier stage.

7. When the value of an unknown capacitor was calculated by the
    impedance method, a 300-Ω resistor was placed in series with the
    capacitor. A 110-V, 60-Hz ac voltage caused a current of 0.22 A
    to flow. Find (*a*) the impedance of the circuit, (*b*) the reactance of
    the capacitor, and (*c*) the capacitance of the capacitor.
8. A 10,000-Ω resistor and a capacitor are placed in series across a
    60-Hz line. If the voltage across the resistor is 50 V and across the
    capacitor 100 V, find (*a*) the current in the resistor, (*b*) the current
    in the capacitor, (*c*) the reactance of the capacitor by Ohm's law,
    and (*d*) the capacitance of the capacitor.
9. A 120-V source is connected to a resistance of 50 Ω in series with
    a capacitance of 10 μF. What frequency will permit a current of
    0.8 A to flow?
10. A circuit consisting of a 40-μF capacitance in series with a rheostat
    is connected across a 138-V 60-Hz line. What must be the value
    of the resistance in order to permit a current of 2 A to flow?

JOB 18-5   RESISTANCE, INDUCTANCE, AND CAPACITANCE IN SERIES

Figure 18-25 shows a 16-Ω resistor, an inductive reactance of 80 Ω, and
a capacitive reactance of 50 Ω connected in series across a frequency of
60 Hz. A series current of 0.5 A produces a voltage drop of 8 V across
the resistor, 40 V across the inductance, and 25 V across the capacitance.

The total voltage across the entire circuit may be found by adding the
voltage drops across each part. However, since the voltages are *not* in
phase, they must be added vectorially. The phase relations in the circuit
are shown in Fig. 18-26*a*. The constant series current is used as the refer-

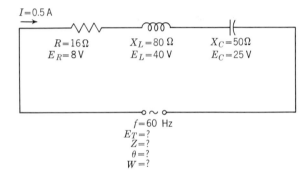

FIGURE 18-25

An ac series circuit containing resistance, inductance, and capacitance.

ence line. The voltage across the resistor E_R is in phase with the current I. The voltage across the inductance E_L *leads* the current I by 90°. The voltage across the capacitance E_C *lags* the current I by 90°. Since E_L and E_C are exactly 180° out of phase and acting in exactly *opposite* directions, the voltage E_C is denoted by a minus sign.

Addition of phasors. When there are three phasors, it is best to add only two at a time. To add the phasor E_C to E_L, place the tail of E_C on the head of E_L and draw it in its original direction and length which will be straight *down* as shown in Fig. 18-26b. Since these phasors are acting in opposite directions, their *sum* is actually the *difference* between the

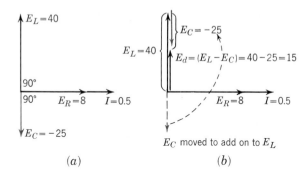

(a)   (b)

FIGURE 18-26

(a) Phasor diagram for a series ac circuit containing resistance, inductance, and capacitance. (b) E_d represents the phasor sum of E_L and E_C.

phasors as indicated by E_d. After this addition, the phasor diagram looks like Fig. 18-27a. Notice that the effect of the capacitor has disappeared. The 40 V of coil voltage have exactly balanced the 25 V of capacitive voltage and have left an excess of 15 V of coil voltage. These 15 V of coil voltage must now be added vectorially to the 8 V of resistance voltage. In Fig. 18-27b, the total voltage E_T is obtained by adding the phasor E_d to the phasor E_R. Place the tail of E_d on the head of E_R, and draw it in the proper direction. If E_C is larger than E_L, the phasor E_d will have a *downward* direction. The distance from the origin of the phasors to the head of the final phasor is the sum of the phasors. In this instance, the phasor E_T represents the sum of the phasors $E_R + E_L + E_C$. The phase

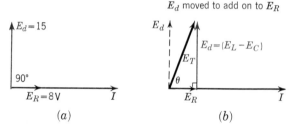

FIGURE 18-27

(a) E_d represents the result of adding E_C to E_L. (b) E_T represents the phasor sum of $E_R + E_L + E_C$.

angle θ is the angle by which the total voltage will lead the current. If E_C were larger than E_L, the total voltage would *lag* behind the current by this angle. By applying the pythagorean theorem to Fig. 18-27*b*, we obtain

FORMULA

$$E_T{}^2 = E_R{}^2 + (E_L - E_C)^2 \qquad \boxed{18\text{-}13}$$

Total impedance. To find the impedance of the series ac circuit, we must add R, X_L, and X_C vectorially as was done with the voltages. This is shown in Fig. 18-28, resulting in the impedance triangle of Fig. 18-28*c*.

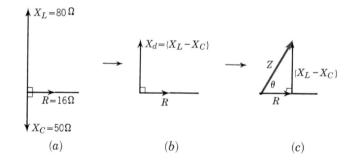

FIGURE 18-28

Z represents the phasor sum of $R + X_L + X_C$.

Applying the pythagorean theorem to Fig. 18-28*c*, we obtain

FORMULAS

$$Z^2 = R^2 + (X_L - X_C)^2 \qquad \boxed{18\text{-}14}$$

and

$$Z = \sqrt{R^2 + (X_L - X_C)^2} \qquad \boxed{18\text{-}15}$$

And by trigonometry,

$$\cos \theta = \frac{a}{h}$$

or

$$\cos \theta = \frac{R}{Z} \qquad (18\text{-}8)$$

The power is still given by

$$W = E \times I \times \cos \theta \qquad (18\text{-}3)$$

EXAMPLE 18-12   In Fig. 18-25, find (a) the total voltage, (b) the impedance, (c) the phase angle, and (d) the power.

SOLUTION

a
$$E_T{}^2 = E_R{}^2 + (E_L - E_C)^2 \tag{18-13}$$
$$E_T{}^2 = 8^2 + (40 - 25)^2$$
$$E_T{}^2 = 8^2 + 15^2 = 64 + 225 = 289$$
$$E_T = \sqrt{289} = 17 \text{ V} \qquad Ans.$$

b
$$Z = \sqrt{R^2 + (X_L - X_C)^2} \tag{18-15}$$
$$Z = \sqrt{16^2 + (80 - 50)^2}$$
$$Z = \sqrt{16^2 + 30^2} = \sqrt{256 + 900} = \sqrt{1,156}$$
$$Z = 34 \text{ } \Omega \qquad Ans.$$

c
$$\cos \theta = \frac{R}{Z} = \frac{16}{34} = 0.4706 \tag{18-8}$$
$$\theta = 62° \qquad (\text{approx}) \qquad Ans.$$

d
$$W = E \times I \times \cos \theta \tag{18-3}$$
$$W = 17 \times 0.5 \times \cos 62° = 17 \times 0.5 \times 0.471 = 4 \text{ W} \qquad Ans.$$

EXAMPLE 18-13   An 18-Ω resistor, a 4-μF capacitor, and a 2.5-mH inductance are connected in series across a 60-V 1-kHz ac source. Find (a) the capacitive reactance, (b) the inductive reactance, (c) the impedance, (d) the total current, (e) the voltage drop across each part, (f) the phase angle, and (g) the power.

SOLUTION
Given: $R = 18 \text{ } \Omega$ 　　　　　　Find: $X_C = ?$
　　　　$C = 4 \text{ } \mu\text{F}$ 　　　　　　　　　$X_L = ?$
　　　　$L = 2.5 \text{ mH} = 0.0025 \text{ H}$ 　　$Z = ?$
　　　　$E_T = 60 \text{ V}$ 　　　　　　　　　$I_T = ?$
　　　　$f = 1 \text{ kHz} = 1,000 \text{ Hz}$ 　　$E_R = ?$
　　　　　　　　　　　　　　　　　　$E_L = ?$
　　　　　　　　　　　　　　　　　　$E_C = ?$
　　　　　　　　　　　　　　　　　　$\theta = ?$
　　　　　　　　　　　　　　　　　　$W = ?$

a
$$X_C = \frac{159,000}{f \times C} = \frac{159,000}{1,000 \times 4} = \frac{159}{4} = 40 \text{ } \Omega \qquad Ans.$$

b
$$X_L = 6.28fL = 6.28 \times 1,000 \times 0.0025 \tag{16-1}$$
$$= 6.28 \times 2.5 = 16 \text{ } \Omega \qquad Ans.$$

c
$$Z = \sqrt{R^2 + (X_C - X_L)^2} \qquad (18\text{-}15)$$

(Notice that X_C is written first because X_C is larger than X_L.)

$$Z = \sqrt{18^2 + (40 - 16)^2} = \sqrt{18^2 + 24^2}$$
$$= \sqrt{324 + 576}$$
$$= \sqrt{900}$$
$$Z = 30 \ \Omega \qquad Ans.$$

d
$$E_T = I_T \times Z \qquad (18\text{-}9)$$
$$60 = I_T \times 30$$
$$I_T = \frac{60}{30} = 2 \ \text{A} \qquad Ans.$$

e Since
$$I_T = I_R = I_L = I_C = 2 \ \text{A} \qquad (3\text{-}1)$$

$$E_R = I_R \times R_R \qquad\qquad E_C = I_C \times X_C$$
$$E_R = 2 \times 18 = 36 \ \text{V} \qquad Ans. \qquad E_C = 2 \times 40 = 80 \ \text{V} \qquad Ans.$$
$$E_L = I_L \times X_L$$
$$E_L = 2 \times 6 = 32 \ \text{V} \qquad Ans.$$

f
$$\cos \theta = \frac{R}{Z} = \frac{18}{30} = 0.6000 \qquad (18\text{-}8)$$

$$\theta = 53° \quad (\text{approx}) \qquad Ans.$$

g
$$W = E \times I \times \cos \theta = 60 \times 2 \times 0.6 = 72 \ \text{W} \qquad Ans.$$

In the series circuit, since the capacitive reactance is larger than the inductive reactance, the total voltage of 60 V *lags* behind the total current of 2 A by 53°.

EXAMPLE 18-14   A rectifier delivers 200 V at 120 Hz to a filter circuit consisting of a 30-H filter choke coil and a 20-μF capacitor connected as shown in Fig. 18-29.   How much 120-Hz voltage appears across the capacitor which feeds into the plate supply?   Has this filter succeeded in removing the ac component from the plate supply?

SOLUTION
The circuit diagram is shown in Fig. 18-29.

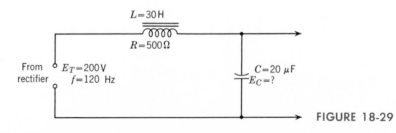

FIGURE 18-29

1   Find the reactance of the coil.

$$X_L = 6.28fL \qquad (16\text{-}1)$$

$$X_L = 6.28 \times 120 \times 30$$

$$X_L = 22{,}600 \ \Omega \qquad Ans.$$

2   Find the reactance of the capacitor.

$$X_C = \frac{159{,}000}{f \times C} = \frac{159{,}000}{120 \times 20} = \frac{1{,}590}{24} = 66 \ \Omega \qquad Ans. \qquad (17\text{-}6)$$

3   Find the total reactance effect X_d so that we may compare it with R. If X_d/R is greater than 5, we shall be able to neglect R and greatly simplify our calculations.

$$X_d = X_L - X_C$$

$$X_d = 22{,}600 - 66 = 22{,}542 \ \Omega \qquad Ans.$$

4   Find the Q of the circuit.

$$Q = \frac{X_d}{R} = \frac{22{,}542}{500} = 45+ \qquad Ans.$$

Therefore, since Q is greater than 5, we shall neglect the resistance of 500 Ω, and

$$Z = X_d = 22{,}542 \ \Omega \qquad Ans.$$

5   Find the series current.

$$E_T = I_T \times Z \qquad (18\text{-}9)$$

$$200 = I_T \times 22{,}542$$

$$I_T = \frac{200}{22{,}542} = 0.0089 \ A \qquad Ans.$$

6   Find the voltage across the capacitor.

$$E_C = I_C \times X_C \qquad (17\text{-}7)$$

$$E_C = 0.0089 \times 66 = 0.59 \ V \qquad Ans.$$

Therefore this is a satisfactory filter, since only 0.59 V out of the total of 200 V of 120-Hz alternating current can get through to the plate supply.

SELF-TEST 18-15   The output voltage of an audio oscillator is 50 V at 3 kHz. It is applied to a series circuit of a 300-Ω resistor, a coil of 531-mH inductance and 75-Ω resistance, a 125-Ω resistor, and a 2,650-pF capacitor. Find (a) the impedance, (b) the total current, and (c) the phase angle.

SOLUTION

Given: $R_1 = 300 \ \Omega$ $C = 2{,}650 \ \text{pF}$ Find: $Z = ?$

Coil $\begin{cases} L = 531 \ \text{mH} \\ R_2 = 75 \ \Omega \end{cases}$ $E_T = 50 \ \text{V}$ $I_T = ?$

       $f = 3 \ \text{kHz}$ $\theta = ?$

$R_3 = 125 \ \Omega$

a In order to find the impedance, we must know the value of R_T, X_L, and ____.

$$R_T = R_1 + R_2 + R_3 = 300 + 75 + \text{\_\_\_\_} \qquad (3\text{-}3)$$

$$R_T = \text{\_\_\_\_} \ \Omega$$

$$X_L = 6.28fL = 6.28 \times 3 \times 10^3 \times 531 \times \text{\_\_\_\_} \qquad (16\text{-}1)$$

$$X_L = \text{_____} \ \Omega \quad Ans.$$

$$X_C = \frac{159,000}{f \times C} = \frac{159 \times 10^3}{3 \times 10^3 \times 2,650 \times ?} \qquad (17\text{-}6)$$

$$= \frac{53 \times 10^6}{2,650}$$

$$X_C = 0.02 \times 10^6 = \text{_____} \ \Omega$$

$$X_d = X_C - X_L = 20,000 - 10,000 = \text{_____} \ \Omega$$

The Q of the circuit $= X_d/R = 10,000/500 = $ ____.   Therefore, $R_T = 500 \ \Omega$ <u>(may/may not)</u> be neglected.

$$Z = X_d = \text{_____} \ \Omega \quad Ans.$$

b $$E_T = I_T \times Z$$

$$I_T = \frac{?}{10,000} = 0.005 \ A \quad Ans.$$

c $$\cos \theta = \frac{R}{Z} = \frac{?}{10,000} \qquad (18\text{-}8)$$

$$\cos \theta = \text{_____}$$

$$\theta = \text{\_\_\_\_} \quad Ans.$$

	X_C
	125
	500
	10^{-3}
	10,000
	10^{-6}
	20,000
	10,000
	20
	may
	10,000
	50
	500
	0.0500
	87°

In this series circuit, since the capacitive reactance is larger than the inductive reactance, the total voltage of 50 V *lags* behind the total current of 0.005 A by 87°.

PROBLEMS

1. A 16-Ω resistor, an 83-Ω inductive reactance, and a 20-Ω capacitive reactance are in series. A 130-V 60-Hz emf is impressed on the circuit. Find (*a*) the impedance, (*b*) the series current, (*c*) the voltage drops across all the parts, (*d*) the phase angle, and (*e*) the power.

2. A coil of 2.07-mH inductance, a 0.3-μF capacitor, and a 36-Ω resistor are connected in series across a 127.5-V 10-kHz ac source. Find (*a*) the impedance, (*b*) the total current, (*c*) the phase angle, and (*d*) the power.

3. A 125-V 100-Hz power supply is connected across a 4,000-Ω resistor, a 0.5-μF capacitor, and a 10-H coil connected in series. Find (*a*) the individual reactances, (*b*) the impedance, (*c*) the total current, (*d*) the phase angle, and (*e*) the power.

4. The antenna circuit of a radio receiver consists of a 0.2-mH inductance and a 0.0001-μF capacitance. If the resistance of the antenna is small enough to be considered to be zero, what is the impedance of the antenna to a 1,200-kHz signal? If this frequency induces a voltage of 100 μV in the antenna, what current will flow?

5. In a circuit similar to Fig. 18-29, $E_T = 250$ V, $f = 120$ Hz, $L = 25$ H, $R = 400$ Ω, and $C = 25$ μF. What amount of the 120-Hz voltage will appear across the capacitor?

6. A wave trap to eliminate a 13-kHz frequency is made of a 30-mH inductance of 40 Ω resistance and a 0.005-μF capacitor in series. What is the impedance of the circuit?

7. A 10.8-V 100-kHz emf is applied across a series circuit of a 6-Ω resistance, a 0.5-mH coil, and a 5,000-pF capacitance. What is the total current?

8. A 300-Ω 100-μH resistor is in series with a capacitance of 2 μF. Find the impedance of the circuit at (a) 500 Hz, (b) 5 kHz, and (c) 500 kHz.

9. A 5-H coil and a 1.67-μF capacitor are in series with an adjustable resistor. What must be the value of the resistance in order to draw 0.3 A from a 120-V 60-Hz line?

10. A 2.8-mH inductance and a 9-μF capacitance are in series with a 50-Ω resistor. At what frequency will the inductive reactance equal the capacitive reactance? What is the impedance of the circuit? What current will be drawn at this frequency from a 10-V source?

JOB 18-6   SERIES RESONANCE

EXAMPLE 18-16   A 30-H coil, a 250-Ω resistor, and a variable capacitor are connected in series across a 110-V 60-Hz line. When the capacitor is adjusted to 0.2344 μF, find the impedance of the circuit.

SOLUTION

Given: $L = 30$ H   Find: $Z = ?$
$\quad\quad\quad R = 250$ Ω
$\quad\quad\quad C = 0.2344$ μF
$\quad\quad\quad E = 110$ V
$\quad\quad\quad f = 60$ Hz

1   Find the inductive reactance.

$$X_L = 6.28fL = 6.28 \times 60 \times 30 = 11{,}304 \ \Omega \quad \textit{Ans.}$$

2   Find the capacitive reactance.

$$X_C = \frac{159{,}000}{f \times C} = \frac{159{,}000}{60 \times 0.2344} = \frac{15{,}900}{1.4064} = 11{,}304 \ \Omega \quad \textit{Ans.}$$

3   Find the impedance.

$$Z = \sqrt{R^2 + (X_C - X_L)^2} = \sqrt{250^2 + (11{,}304 - 11{,}304)^2}$$
$$= \sqrt{250^2 + 0^2}$$
$$= \sqrt{250^2}$$
$$Z = 250 \ \Omega \quad Ans.$$

Notice that for these particular values of L and C, the inductive reactance and the capacitive reactance are exactly equal. Since their actions are directly opposed to each other, the total effect of both is equal to zero and the impedance of the circuit is equal to just the resistance of the circuit. This condition is called *resonance*. Series resonance is the condition of *smallest* circuit resistance. At resonance, since the reactance effect is zero, the *largest* amount of current will flow.

Any change in the values of either L or C would give *different* values of X_L and X_C, whose sum would no longer be zero. Under these conditions, since the reactance effect is *larger* than zero, the current that flows will be *smaller* than the flow at resonance. In addition, since the values of the reactances depend on the frequency, any change in the frequency results in *different* values of reactances whose sum again would *not* be zero. Apparently, for any combination of L and C in series, there is only *one* frequency for which X_L can equal X_C. This frequency is called the *resonant frequency*.

At this frequency, a large current will flow in the series circuit, since the reactance is zero at the resonant frequency. At any other frequency, since the sum of X_L and X_C is *not* equal to zero, the impedance will be *larger* and the current will be *smaller*.

Why is the resonant frequency important? The antenna of a radio receiver is receiving signals from many stations at the same time. Each station broadcasts at a different frequency. Each different frequency induces a signal voltage in the antenna so that at any one time there may be many different signal voltages in the same antenna. How shall we separate one of these signals from all the rest?

We can separate one frequency from the rest if we can find an L and C combination which is *resonant* to that same frequency which we are trying to separate. Only this frequency will encounter a *zero impedance* and therefore will produce a *large* current. All other frequencies will encounter large impedances, and the currents at these frequencies will be practically zero. The tuner of a receiver is a series circuit of an inductance and a capacitance which can be made resonant to different frequencies by changing the values of the capacitance. Thus it will select and pass on to the amplifying system only one frequency at a time.

There are many other uses for the series-resonant circuit. In the superheterodyne receiver, the oscillator must deliver a definite frequency to the mixer tube. Values of L and C are chosen to make the combination resonant to that particular frequency. Bandpass filters and acceptance circuits are other common applications of the series-resonant circuit.

Calculating the resonant frequency. At resonance, the inductive reactance is equal to the capacitive reactance. Write the equation.

$$X_L = X_C \qquad \boxed{\text{18-16}}$$

Substitute reactances.

$$\frac{6.28fL}{1} = \frac{159,000}{f \times C}$$

Cross-multiply.

$$f^2 \times 6.28 \times L \times C = 159,000$$

Solve for f.

$$f^2 = \frac{159,000}{6.28 \times L \times C}$$

Divide.

$$f^2 = \frac{25,318}{L \times C}$$

Take the square root of both sides.

$$f = \sqrt{\frac{25,318}{L \times C}}$$

FORMULA

$$f = \frac{159}{\sqrt{L \times C}} \qquad \boxed{\text{18-17}}$$

where f = frequency, Hz
L = inductance, H
C = capacitance, μF

If we use the units of measurement commonly used in radio and television work, the formula retains the same form *but* both the frequency and the inductance are expressed in different units.

FORMULA

$$f = \frac{159}{\sqrt{L \times C}} \qquad \boxed{\text{18-18}}$$

where f = frequency, kHz
L = inductance, μH
C = capacitance, μF

EXAMPLE 18-17   Calculate the resonant frequency of a tuning circuit if the inductance is 300 μH and the capacitor is set at a capacity of 300 pF.

SOLUTION
The diagram of the circuit is shown in Fig. 18-30. If formula (18-18) is used, 300 pF must be changed into microfarads.

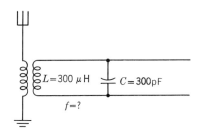

$L = 300\ \mu H$ $C = 300$pF

$f = ?$

FIGURE 18-30
A simple tuning circuit.

$$300\text{ pF} = 300 \times 10^{-6}\ \mu F$$

$$f = \frac{159}{\sqrt{L \times C}} \qquad (18\text{-}18)$$

$$= \frac{159}{\sqrt{300 \times 300 \times 10^{-6}}} = \frac{159}{\sqrt{9 \times 10^{-2}}}$$

$$= \frac{159}{0.3}$$

$$f = 530\text{ kHz} \qquad Ans.$$

PROBLEMS

1. A transmitting antenna has a capacitance of 200 pF, a resistance of 50 Ω, and an inductance of 200 μH. Find (a) the resonant frequency and (b) the impedance of the antenna.
2. Find the resonant frequency of a tuning circuit similar to that shown in Fig. 18-30 if $L = 250\ \mu$H and $C = 40$pF.
3. A series circuit consists of a 12-Ω resistance, an inductance of 0.04 H, and a capacitance of 0.16 μF. Find (a) the resonant frequency, (b) the reactance of the inductance, (c) the reactance of the capacitance, (d) the impedance, (e) the current at resonance if the impressed voltage is 6 V, and (f) the voltage drop across the capacitance.
4. What is the resonant frequency of a series circuit if the inductance is 270 μH and the capacitance is 0.003 μF?
5. What is the resonant frequency of the Hartley-type oscillator shown in Fig. 18-31 if the coil has an inductance of 40 μH and the capacitance is set at 160 pF?

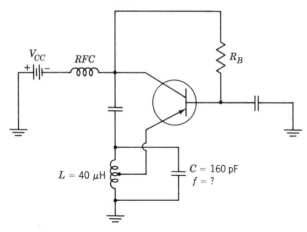

FIGURE 18-31
The Hartley oscillator.

6. Find the resonant frequency of the series-resonant section of the bandpass filter shown in Fig. 18-32.

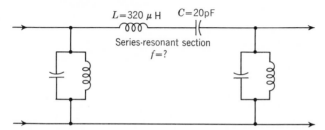

FIGURE 18-32
A bandpass filter.

7. Find the resonant frequency of the series-resonant section of the wave trap or band-elimination filter shown in Fig. 18-33.

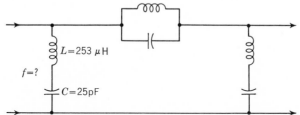

FIGURE 18-33
A band-elimination filter.

8. A 3-mH coil and a 40-pF capacitor are connected as shown in Fig. 18-34 to form the secondary side of an IF transformer. What is its resonant frequency? Explain why the secondary is a series-tuned circuit while the primary is a parallel circuit.

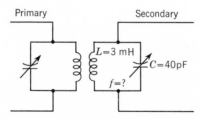

FIGURE 18-34
The secondary of the IF transformer is a series-resonant circuit.

9. Find the resonant frequency of an antenna circuit if the inductance is 50 μH and the capacitance is 0.0002 μF.

10. Find the resonant frequency of a series circuit containing a 300-μH coil and a 365-pF capacitor.

JOB 18-7   FINDING THE INDUCTANCE OR CAPACITANCE NEEDED TO MAKE A SERIES-RESONANT CIRCUIT

Formula (18-18) may be transformed to find formulas which may be used to find the inductance or capacitance needed to form a series-resonant circuit at a given frequency.

FORMULAS

$$L = \frac{25,300}{f^2 \times C} \qquad \boxed{18\text{-}19}$$

$$C = \frac{25,300}{f^2 \times L} \qquad \boxed{18\text{-}20}$$

where L = inductance, μH
C = capacitance, μF
f = frequency, kHz

EXAMPLE 18-18   What value of inductance must be placed in series with a 253-pF tuning capacitor in order to provide resonance for a 500-kHz signal?

SOLUTION
Given: $C = 253$ pF $= 253 \times 10^{-6}$ μF   Find: $L = ?$
$f = 500$ kHz

$$L = \frac{25,300}{f^2 \times C} = \frac{25,300}{(500)^2 \times 253 \times 10^{-6}} \qquad (18\text{-}19)$$

$$= \frac{25,300}{25 \times 10^4 \times 253 \times 10^{-6}}$$

$$= \frac{100 \times 10^2}{25}$$

$$L = 400 \ \mu\text{H} \qquad Ans.$$

EXAMPLE 18-19   An inductance of 40 μH is in series with a capacitor in a Hartley-type oscillator circuit. Find the value of the capacitance needed to produce resonance to a frequency of 5,000 kHz.

SOLUTION
Given: $L = 40$ μH   Find: $C = ?$
$f = 5,000$ kHz

$$C = \frac{25,300}{f^2 \times L} = \frac{25,300}{(5,000)^2 \times 40} \qquad (18\text{-}20)$$

$$= \frac{25,300}{25 \times 10^6 \times 40}$$

$$= \frac{25,300}{10^9}$$

$$= 25,330 \times 10^{-9} \; \mu F$$

$$= 25,300 \times 10^{-9} \times 10^6 \; pF$$

$$C = 25.3 \; pF \qquad Ans.$$

SELF-TEST 18-20   A series circuit has a resistance of 30 Ω, an inductance of 0.382 H, and a capacitance of 0.2 μF. Find (a) the impedance of the circuit to a frequency of 500 Hz, (b) the capacitance that must be added in parallel with the 0.2-μF capacitor to produce resonance at this frequency, and (c) the impedance of the circuit at resonance.

SOLUTION
Given: $R = 30 \; \Omega$ Find: Z at 500 Hz
       $L = 0.382$ H C to be added
       $C = 0.2 \; \mu F$ Z at resonance
       $f = 500$ Hz

a   In order to find Z, we must know X_L and ____. X_C

$$X_L = 6.28 f L = 6.28 \times 500 \times 0.382$$

$$X_L = \underline{\hspace{1cm}} \; \Omega \qquad\qquad\qquad\qquad\qquad\qquad 1,200$$

$$X_C = \frac{159,000}{f \times C} = \frac{159,000}{500 \times 0.2} = \underline{\hspace{1cm}} \; \Omega \qquad\qquad 1,590$$

$$X_d = X_C - X_L = 1,590 - 1,200$$

$$X_d = \underline{\hspace{1cm}} \; \Omega \qquad\qquad\qquad\qquad\qquad\qquad 390$$

$$Q = \frac{X_d}{R} = \frac{390}{30} = 13$$

and we __(should/should not)__ include R in our calculations for Z.   should not

$$Z = X_d = \underline{\hspace{1cm}} \; \Omega \qquad Ans. \qquad\qquad\qquad 390$$

b   Find the C that will produce resonance at 500 Hz.

$$C = \frac{25,300}{f^2 \times L}$$

Changing units to agree with the formula,

$$C = \frac{25,300}{(0.5)^2 \times 0.382 \times 10^6} \qquad\qquad (18\text{-}20)$$

$$= \frac{25{,}300}{? \times 10^6}$$ $\quad\quad$ 0.0955

$$= \frac{25.3 \times 10^3}{95.5 \times ?}$$ $\quad\quad$ 10^3

$$C = \text{\_\_\_\_\_} \ \mu F \quad Ans.$$ $\quad\quad$ 0.265

Since 0.265 μF are needed for resonance, and we have only 0.2 μF, we must add $0.265 - 0.2 = \text{\_\_\_} \ \mu F$.   *Ans.* $\quad\quad$ 0.065

c   At resonance, X_d will equal ___ Ω, and the only resistance in the circuit will $\quad\quad$ zero

be the original resistance of ___ Ω. Therefore, $Z = \text{\_\_\_} \ \Omega$.   *Ans.* $\quad\quad$ 30   30

PROBLEMS

1. What value of inductance must be connected in series with a 0.0003-μF capacitor in order that the circuit be resonant to a frequency of 1,000 kHz?
2. What value of capacitance must be connected in series with a 50-μH coil in order that the circuit be resonant to a frequency of 2,000 kHz?
3. What value of inductance will produce resonance to 50 Hz if it is placed in series with a 20-μF capacitor?
4. What value of capacitance must be used in series with a 30-μH inductance in order to produce an oscillator frequency of 6,000 kHz?
5. What value of capacitance must be added in series with a solenoid of 0.2-H inductance in order to be resonant to 60 Hz?
6. What capacity is necessary in series with a 100-μH coil to produce a wave trap for a 1,200-kHz signal?
7. What is the inductance of the secondary winding of an RF transformer if it is in series with a 0.00035-μF capacitor and is resonant to a frequency of 1,000 kHz?
8. What is the capacity of an antenna circuit whose inductance is 50 μH if it is resonant to 1,500 kHz?
9. A 0.00004-μF capacitance is in series with the secondary of an RF transformer. What must be the inductance of the coil if the secondary is to be resonant to 500 kHz?
10. What must be the minimum and maximum values of the capacitor needed to produce resonance with a 240-μH coil to frequencies between 500 and 1,500 kHz?

JOB 18-8   REVIEW OF SERIES AC CIRCUITS

The voltages and current in a series ac circuit are not usually in phase with each other. Alternating-current voltages may not be added arithmetically but only by means of _____ addition. $\quad\quad$ phasor

A phasor is a straight line drawn with a definite length and in a definite direction. In ac electricity, the direction of the phasor indicates the _____ at which the voltage or current occurs in relation to another voltage or current.

| | time |

Phasors drawn in the _____ direction are in phase.

| | same |

Phasors drawn in _____ directions are out of phase.

| | different |

Phasors are added by placing the tail of one phasor on to the _____ of another and drawing the phasor with its original length and direction.

| | head |

The sum of the phasors is the phasor drawn from the _____ of the phasors to the _____ of the last phasor.

| | origin |
| | head |

In a purely resistive circuit:

The voltage is __(in/out of)__ phase with the current.

| | in |

$$E_T = E_1 + E_2 + E_3 \qquad \boxed{3\text{-}2}$$

$$E_T = I_T \times R_T \qquad \boxed{3\text{-}7}$$

$$R_T = R_1 + R_2 + R_3 \qquad \boxed{3\text{-}3}$$

$$P = E \times I \qquad \boxed{6\text{-}1}$$

In a purely inductive circuit:

The voltage __(leads/lags)__ the current by 90°.

| | leads |

$$E_T = E_1 + E_2 + E_3 \qquad \boxed{3\text{-}2}$$

$$E_L = I_L \times \text{_____} \qquad \boxed{16\text{-}2}$$

| | X_L |

$$X_T = X_1 + X_2 + X_3 \qquad \boxed{18\text{-}21}$$

$$W = E \times I \times \text{_____} \qquad \boxed{18\text{-}3}$$

| | $\cos \theta$ |

In a purely capacitive circuit:

The voltage __(leads/lags)__ the current by 90°.

| | lags |

$$E_T = E_1 + E_2 + E_3 \qquad \boxed{3\text{-}2}$$

$$E_C = I_C \times \text{_____} \qquad \boxed{17\text{-}7}$$

| | X_C |

$$X_T = X_1 + X_2 + X_3 \qquad \boxed{18\text{-}21}$$

$$W = E \times I \times \cos \theta \qquad \boxed{18\text{-}3}$$

In an ac series circuit of resistance and inductance:

The total voltage __(leads/lags)__ the current by some angle θ.

| | leads |

$$E_T^2 = E_R^2 + \text{_____} \qquad \boxed{18\text{-}5}$$

| | E_L^2 |

$$Z = \text{_____} \qquad \boxed{18\text{-}7}$$

| | $\sqrt{R^2 + X_L^2}$ |

$$E_T = I_T \times \text{_____} \qquad \boxed{18\text{-}9}$$

| | Z |

$$\cos \theta = \frac{R}{?} \qquad \boxed{18\text{-}8}$$

| | Z |

$$W = E \times I \times \text{_____} \qquad \boxed{18\text{-}3}$$

| | $\cos \theta$ |

In an ac series circuit of resistance and capacitance:
The total voltage __(leads/lags)__ the current by some angle θ.

lags

$$E_T^2 = E_R^2 + E_C^2 \qquad \boxed{18\text{-}10}$$

$$Z = \underline{\hspace{2cm}} \qquad \boxed{18\text{-}12} \qquad \sqrt{R^2 + X_C^2}$$

$$E_T = I_T \times \underline{\hspace{2cm}} \qquad \boxed{18\text{-}9} \qquad Z$$

$$\cos\theta = \frac{?}{Z} \qquad \boxed{18\text{-}8} \qquad R$$

$$W = E \times I \times \cos\theta \qquad \boxed{18\text{-}3}$$

In an ac series circuit of resistance, inductance, and capacitance:
The total voltage will lead or lag the current, depending on the values of X_L and X_C. If X_L is larger than X_C, the voltage will __(lead/lag)__ the current. If X_L is smaller than X_C, the voltage will __(lead/lag)__ behind the current. The angle of lead or lag is given by the angle θ.

lead
lag

$$E_T^2 = E_R^2 + (E_L - E_C)^2 \qquad \boxed{18\text{-}13}$$

$$Z = \sqrt{R^2 + \underline{\hspace{2cm}}} \qquad \boxed{18\text{-}15} \qquad (X_L - X_C)^2$$

$$E_T = I_T \times \underline{\hspace{2cm}} \qquad \boxed{18\text{-}9} \qquad Z$$

$$\cos\theta = \frac{R}{Z} \qquad \boxed{18\text{-}8}$$

$$W = E \times I \times \cos\theta \qquad \boxed{18\text{-}3}$$

Series resonance is the condition at which the inductive reactance is exactly equal to the capacitive reactance. For any given combination of coil and capacitor, there is only one frequency at which this situation can occur. This frequency is called the resonant frequency.

$$f = \frac{159}{\sqrt{L \times C}} \qquad \boxed{18\text{-}18}$$

where f = frequency, measured in ____
L = inductance, measured in ____
C = capacitance, measured in ____

kHz
μH
μF

The inductance or capacitance needed to make a circuit resonant to a given frequency is given by the formulas

$$L = \frac{25{,}300}{f^2 \times ?} \qquad \boxed{18\text{-}19} \qquad C$$

$$C = \frac{25{,}300}{? \times L} \qquad \boxed{18\text{-}20} \qquad f^2$$

where all units are measured in the units given for formula (18-18).

PROBLEMS

1. What is the voltage drop across a 3,000-Ω resistor carrying 60 mA of current at a frequency of 60 Hz?

2. Find the current and power drawn by a 20-mH coil from a 125.6-V 10-kHz source.

3. A filter choke passes 60 mA of current when it is connected across a 120-V 60-Hz line. What is its inductance?

4. Find the voltage drop across a 0.05-μF capacitor if it passes 50 mA at a frequency of 1 kHz.

5. A 50-V emf at 1-kHz frequency is impressed across a 1,000-Ω resistor in series with a 1-H coil. Find (a) the impedance, (b) the total current, (c) the voltage drop across each part, (d) the phase angle, and (e) the power drawn.

6. A 120-V 1-kHz ac voltage is applied across a series circuit of a 200-Ω resistor and a 1.6-μF capacitor. Find (a) the impedance, (b) the total current, (c) the voltage drop across each part, (d) the phase angle, and (e) the power drawn.

7. An antenna circuit consists of a 10-Ω resistance, a 0.5-mH inductance, and a 50-pF capacitance. Find its impedance to a frequency of (a) 1,000 kHz and (b) 500 kHz.

8. A 1,000-Ω 100-μH coil is in series with a capacitance of 5 μF. Find the impedance at (a) 500 Hz, (b) 5 kHz, and (c) 500 kHz.

9. Find the frequency of operation of the Colpitts oscillator shown in Fig. 18-35. Note that C_1 and C_2 are in series.

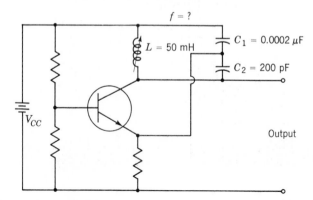

FIGURE 18-35
The Colpitts oscillator.

10. What capacitance is needed in series with a 0.5-mH coil in order to produce resonance to 10 kHz?

TEST—SERIES AC CIRCUITS

1. A phase-shift control circuit is made of a 15,000-Ω rheostat and a 0.04-μF capacitor. If it is connected to a 120-V 500-Hz line, find (a) the impedance, (b) the current, and (c) the phase angle.

2. A 100-V emf at 5 kHz is impressed across a 2,000-Ω resistor in series with a 0.1-H coil. Find (a) the impedance of the circuit, (b) the total current, (c) the voltage drop across each part, (d) the phase angle, and (e) the power drawn by the circuit.

3. A 500-Ω resistor, a 0.5-mH coil, and a 0.02-μF capacitor are connected in series across a 13.8-V 100-kHz ac source. Find (a) the impedance of the circuit, (b) the total current, and (c) the phase angle.

4. What is the resonant frequency of a series ac circuit consisting of a 0.02-mH coil and a 0.0005-μF capacitor?

5. What inductance is needed in series with a 0.00025-μF capacitor in order to produce resonance to a 100-kHz wave?

19

PARALLEL AC CIRCUITS

JOB 19-1   SIMPLE PARALLEL AC CIRCUITS

The general rules for solving dc parallel circuits are also applicable to the solution of ac parallel circuits.

1 The voltages across all branches are equal to each other and to the total voltage.

$$E_T = E_1 = E_2 = E_3 \qquad (4\text{-}1)$$

2 The total current is equal to the sum of all the branch currents.

$$I_T = I_1 + I_2 + I_3 \qquad (4\text{-}2)$$

Parallel circuits containing only resistance. We can add the branch currents as indicated by formula (4-2) only if the branch currents are in phase. If they are out of phase, they may be added *only* by phasor addition. Let us draw the phasor diagrams for each branch of the circuit shown in Fig. 19-3 for Example 19-1 to discover the phase relationships in this type of circuit.

Phasor diagrams. Since the voltage in a parallel circuit is constant, the *voltage* is used as the reference line upon which to draw the phasors. In Fig. 19-1a, the current I_1 is drawn in the same direction as the voltage

(a)   (b)

FIGURE 19-1
Currents in purely resistive parallel branches are in phase with the voltage.

because the current in the purely resistive iron is in phase with the voltage. In Fig. 19-1b, the smaller current through the lamp I_2 is also drawn in the same direction as the voltage because the current through a purely resistive lamp is in phase with the voltage. Now let us draw both sets of phasors on the same voltage base as shown in Fig. 19-2a. This diagram indicates that the current in one resistance is in phase with the current in the other resistance, since they are both drawn in the same direction.

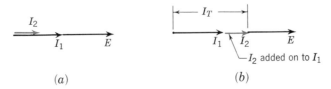

FIGURE 19-2
(a) Resistive branch currents
are in phase with each other.
(b) I_T represents the phasor
sum of I_1 and I_2.

To find the total current, it is necessary only to add the two current phasors. This is done, as with any phasor quantities, by adding the tail of phasor I_2 on to the head of phasor I_1 as shown in Fig. 19-2b. The total current is then the distance from the origin of the phasors to the head of the last phasor. Since the two currents are in phase, the total current may be found by the direct arithmetical addition of the currents, using formula (4-2).

EXAMPLE 19-1   A 20-Ω electric iron and a 100-Ω lamp are connected in parallel across a 120-V 60-Hz ac line. Find (a) the total current, (b) the total resistance, and (c) the total power drawn by the circuit.

SOLUTION
The diagram for the circuit is shown in Fig. 19-3.

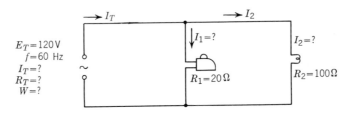

FIGURE 19-3

a   Find the branch currents. Since

$$E_T = E_1 = E_2 = E_3 = 120 \text{ V} \tag{4-1}$$

$$E_1 = I_1 \times R_1 \qquad\qquad E_2 = I_2 \times R_2$$

$$120 = I_1 \times 20 \qquad\qquad 120 = I_2 \times 100$$

$$I_1 = \frac{120}{20} = 6 \text{ A} \qquad I_2 = \frac{120}{100} = 1.2 \text{ A}$$

Find the total current.

$$I_T = I_1 + I_2 = 6 + 1.2 = 7.2 \text{ A} \qquad Ans. \tag{4-2}$$

b

$$E_T = I_T \times R_T \tag{3-7}$$

$$120 = 7.2 \times R_T$$

$$R_T = \frac{120}{7.2} = 16.7 \ \Omega \qquad Ans.$$

c   In a purely resistive set of branch circuits, the total current is in phase with the total voltage. The phase angle is therefore equal to 0°.

$$W = E \times I \times \cos \theta = 120 \times 7.2 \times \cos 0° \qquad (18\text{-}3)$$

$$W = 120 \times 7.2 \times 1 = 864 \text{ W} \qquad Ans.$$

Parallel circuits containing only inductance. This type of circuit is illustrated in Fig. 19-6 for Example 19-2 below.

Phasor diagrams. Since the voltage in a parallel circuit is constant, the *voltage* is used as the reference line upon which to draw the phasors. In Fig. 19-4a, the current I_{L_1} is drawn lagging the voltage by 90°. In

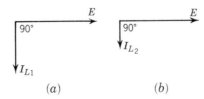

(a)   (b)

FIGURE 19-4
Currents in purely inductive parallel branches lag the voltage by 90°.

Fig. 19-4b, the current I_{L_2} is also drawn lagging the voltage by 90°, since the current in *any* inductance lags the voltage by 90°. Now let us draw both sets of phasors on the same voltage base as shown in Fig. 19-5a. This diagram indicates that the current in one coil is in phase with the current in the second coil, since they are both drawn in the same direction. To find the total current, it is necessary only to add the two current phasors. This is done, as with any phasor quantities, by adding the tail of phasor I_{L_2} on to the head of phasor I_{L_1} as shown in Fig. 19-5b. The

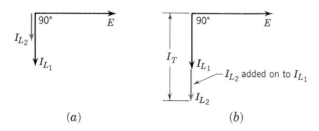

(a)   (b)

FIGURE 19-5
(a) Inductive branch currents are in phase with each other. (b) I_T represents the phasor sum of I_{L_1} and I_{L_2}.

total current is then the distance from the origin of the phasors to the head of the last phasor. Since the two currents are in phase, the total current may be found by the direct arithmetical addition of the currents, using formula (4-2). The difference between this circuit and the purely resistive circuit lies in the fact that the total current *lags* behind the total voltage by 90°. The phase angle $\theta = 90°$.

EXAMPLE 19-2 Two coils of 20 and 30 Ω reactance, respectively, are connected in parallel across a 120-V 60-Hz ac line. Find (*a*) the total current, (*b*) the impedance, and (*c*) the power drawn by the circuit.

SOLUTION
The diagram for the circuit is shown in Fig. 19-6.

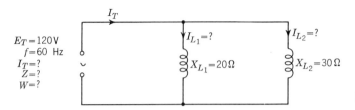

$E_T = 120\text{V}$
$f = 60$ Hz
$I_T = ?$
$Z = ?$
$W = ?$

$I_{L_1} = ?$

$X_{L_1} = 20\,\Omega$

$I_{L_2} = ?$

$X_{L_2} = 30\,\Omega$

FIGURE 19-6

a   Find the branch currents. Since

$$E_T = E_1 = E_2 = 120 \text{ V} \qquad (4\text{-}1)$$

$$E_1 = I_1 \times X_1 \qquad\qquad E_2 = I_2 \times X_2$$

$$120 = I_1 \times 20 \qquad\qquad 120 = I_2 \times 30$$

$$I_1 = \frac{120}{20} = 6 \text{ A} \qquad I_2 = \frac{120}{30} = 4 \text{ A}$$

Find the total current.

$$I_T = I_1 + I_2 = 6 + 4 = 10 \text{ A} \qquad Ans. \qquad (4\text{-}2)$$

b
$$E_T = I_T \times Z \qquad\qquad (18\text{-}9)$$

$$120 = 10 \times Z$$

$$Z = \frac{120}{10} = 12 \;\Omega \qquad Ans.$$

c   In a purely inductive set of branch circuits, the total current lags behind the voltage by 90°. The phase angle is therefore equal to 90°.

$$W = E \times I \times \cos \theta = 120 \times 10 \times \cos 90° \qquad (18\text{-}3)$$

$$W = 120 \times 10 \times 0 = 0 \text{ W} \qquad Ans.$$

Parallel circuits containing only capacitance. This type of circuit
is illustrated in Fig. 19-9 for Example 19-3 below.

Phasor diagrams. Since the voltage in a parallel circuit is constant,
the *voltage* is used as the reference line upon which to draw the phasors.
In Fig. 19-7*a*, the current I_{C_1} is drawn *leading* the voltage by 90°. In Fig.
19-7*b*, the current I_{C_2} is also drawn *leading* the voltage by 90°, since the

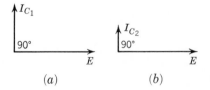

(*a*)   (*b*)

FIGURE 19-7
Currents in purely capacitive
parallel branches lead the
voltage by 90°.

current in *any* capacitance leads the voltage by 90°. Now let us draw
both sets of phasors on the same voltage base, as shown in Fig. 19-8*a*.

This diagram indicates that the current in one capacitor is in phase with the current in the second capacitor, since they are both drawn in the same direction. To find the total current, it is necessary only to add the two current phasors. This is done, as with any phasor quantities, by add-

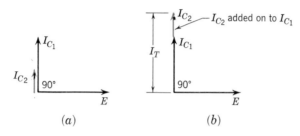

FIGURE 19-8

(a) Capacitive branch currents are in phase with each other. (b) I_T represents the phasor sum of I_{C_1} and I_{C_2}.

ing the tail of phasor I_{C_2} on to the head of phasor I_{C_1} as shown in Fig. 19-8b. The total current is then the distance from the origin of the phasors to the head of the last phasor. Since the two currents are in phase, the total current may be found by the direct arithmetical addition of the currents, using formula (4-2). The difference between this and the other two circuits lies in the fact that the total current *leads* the total voltage by 90°. The phase angle $\theta = 90°$.

EXAMPLE 19-3   Two capacitors of 30 and 40 Ω reactance, respectively, are connected across a 120-V 60-Hz ac line. Find (a) the total current, (b) the impedance, and (c) the power drawn by the circuit.

SOLUTION
The diagram for the circuit is shown in Fig. 19-9.

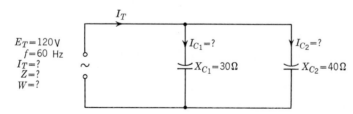

FIGURE 19-9

a   Find the branch currents. Since

$$E_T = E_1 = E_2 = 120 \text{ V} \qquad (4\text{-}1)$$

$$E_1 = I_1 \times X_{C_1} \qquad\qquad E_2 = I_2 \times X_{C_2}$$

$$120 = I_1 \times 30 \qquad\qquad 120 = I_2 \times 40$$

$$I_1 = \frac{120}{30} = 4 \text{ A} \qquad I_2 = \frac{120}{40} = 3 \text{ A}$$

Find the total current.

$$I_T = I_1 + I_2 = 4 + 3 = 7 \text{ A} \qquad Ans. \qquad (4\text{-}2)$$

b
$$E_T = I_T \times Z \qquad (18\text{-}9)$$

$$120 = 7 \times Z$$

$$Z = \frac{120}{7} = 17.1 \ \Omega \qquad Ans.$$

c   In a purely capacitive set of branch circuits, the total current leads the voltage by 90°. The phase angle is therefore equal to 90°.

$$W = E \times I \times \cos \theta = 120 \times 7 \times \cos 90° \qquad (18\text{-}3)$$

$$W = 120 \times 7 \times 0 = 0 \ W \qquad Ans.$$

SUMMARY

In a parallel ac circuit

1   The voltage across any branch is equal to the total voltage.
2   The current in a resistor is   (in/out of)   phase with the voltage.   in
3   The current in an inductance   (leads/lags)   the voltage by ____°.   lags   90
4   The current in a capacitance   (leads/lags)   the voltage by ____°.   leads   90
5   Currents that are in phase with each other are added   (vectorially/
arithmetically)   using formula (4-2).   arithmetically
6   Ohm's law, $E_T = I_T \times Z$ [formula (18-9)], may be used for total values.
7   The power depends on the angle of lead or lag as shown by formula (18-3)
$W = E \times I \times$ _____. $\cos \theta$

PROBLEMS

1.   A 10-Ω electric heater and a 50-Ω incandescent lamp are placed in parallel across a 120-V 60-Hz ac line. Find (*a*) the total current, (*b*) the total resistance, and (*c*) the power drawn.
2.   Two toy-train solenoids used in semaphore signals have inductive reactances of 24 and 48 Ω, respectively. They are connected in parallel across the 12-V winding of the power transformer. Find (*a*) the total current, (*b*) the impedance, and (*c*) the power drawn.
3.   Two capacitors of 100 and 200 Ω capacitive reactance, respectively, are connected in parallel across a 100-V 60-Hz ac line. Find (*a*) the total current, (*b*) the impedance, and (*c*) the power drawn.
4.   A 40-Ω soldering iron and a 100-Ω incandescent lamp are connected in parallel across a 110-V 60-Hz ac line. Find (*a*) the total current, (*b*) the total resistance, and (*c*) the power drawn.
5.   Find the total current, impedance, and power used by the circuit shown in Fig. 19-10.
6.   A mechanic replaced a leaky coupling capacitor with a parallel combination of two capacitors as shown in Fig. 19-11. If the voltage drop across the capacitors is 0.5 V at a frequency of 1 kHz,

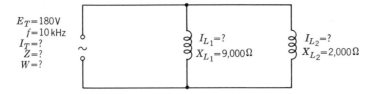

FIGURE 19-10

find the current in each capacitor, the total current, and the impedance of the combination.

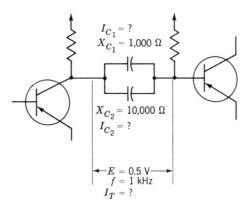

FIGURE 19-11

7. Two pure inductances of 2- and 5-H inductance are connected in parallel across a 120-V 60-Hz line. Find (a) the current in each inductance, (b) the total current, (c) the impedance, and (d) the power drawn.

8. Two pure capacitances of 0.159 and 0.04 μF are connected in parallel across a 50-V 1-kHz line. Find (a) the current in each capacitance, (b) the total current, (c) the impedance, and (d) the power drawn.

JOB 19-2 RESISTANCE AND INDUCTANCE IN PARALLEL

Figure 19-13 shows a 24-Ω resistance and a 30-Ω inductive reactance in parallel across a 12-V 60-Hz ac source. The total current drawn by the circuit can be found by adding the currents in each branch. However, if they are not in phase, they must be added vectorially. The phase relations in the circuit are shown in Fig. 19-12a. The constant voltage is

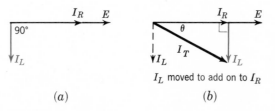

(a)   (b)

FIGURE 19-12

(a) Phasor diagram for a parallel ac circuit containing resistance and inductance. (b) I_T represents the phasor sum of I_R and I_L.

used as the reference line. The current in the resistance is in phase with the voltage, and the current in the inductance lags the voltage by 90°.

Addition of the phasors. In Fig. 19-12b, the total current I_T is obtained by adding the phasor I_L to the phasor I_R. Place the tail of I_L on the head of I_R, and draw it in its original direction and length. The distance from the origin of phasors to the head of the final phasor is the sum of the phasors. In this instance, the phasor I_T represents the sum of the phasors I_R and I_L. The phase angle θ is the angle by which the total current *lags* behind the total voltage. By applying the pythagorean theorem to Fig. 19-12b, we obtain

FORMULA

$$I_T{}^2 = I_R{}^2 + I_L{}^2 \qquad \boxed{19\text{-}1}$$

By Ohm's law,

$$E_T = I_T \times Z \qquad (18\text{-}9)$$

Note that the impedance Z is *not* found by the phasor addition of R and X. The formula $Z^2 = R^2 + X^2$ applies *only* to series ac circuits. In parallel circuits, the *currents* are added vectorially as shown by formula (19-1) above. The impedance Z is found by applying formula (18-9).
  By trigonometry,

$$\cos\theta = \frac{a}{h}$$

FORMULA

$$\cos\theta = \frac{I_R}{I_T} \qquad \boxed{19\text{-}2}$$

The power is still given by

$$W = E \times I \times \cos\theta \qquad (18\text{-}3)$$

EXAMPLE 19-4   A toy electric-train semaphore is made of a 24-Ω lamp in parallel with a solenoid coil of 30 Ω inductive reactance. If it operates from the 12-V winding of the 60-Hz power transformer, find (a) the total current, (b) the impedance, (c) the phase angle, and (d) the power drawn.

SOLUTION
The diagram of the circuit is shown in Fig. 19-13.

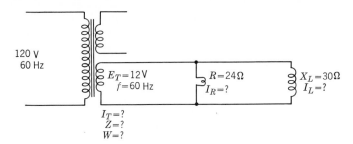

FIGURE 19-13

An ac parallel circuit containing resistance and inductance.

a Find the branch currents. Since

$$E_T = E_R = E_L = 12 \text{ V} \qquad (4\text{-}1)$$

$$E_R = I_R \times R \qquad\qquad E_L = I_L \times X_L$$

$$12 = I_R \times 24 \qquad\qquad 12 = I_L \times 30$$

$$I_R = \frac{12}{24} = 0.5 \text{ A} \qquad I_L = \frac{12}{30} = 0.4 \text{ A}$$

Find the total current.

$$I_T{}^2 = I_R{}^2 + I_L{}^2 = 0.5^2 + 0.4^2 \qquad (19\text{-}1)$$

$$= 0.25 + 0.16$$

$$I_T{}^2 = 0.41$$

$$I_T = \sqrt{0.41} = 0.64 \text{ A} \qquad \textit{Ans.}$$

b $$\qquad E_T = I_T \times Z \qquad (18\text{-}9)$$

$$12 = 0.64 \times Z$$

$$Z = \frac{12}{0.64} = 18.75 \ \Omega \qquad \textit{Ans.}$$

c $$\qquad \cos \theta = \frac{I_R}{I_T} = \frac{0.5}{0.64} = 0.7812 \qquad (19\text{-}2)$$

$$\theta = 39° \qquad \textit{Ans.}$$

d $$W = E \times I \times \cos \theta = 12 \times 0.64 \times \cos 39° \qquad (18\text{-}3)$$

$$= 12 \times 0.64 \times 0.781$$

$$W = 6 \text{ W} \qquad \textit{Ans.}$$

In the parallel circuit, the total current of 0.64 A lags the total voltage of 12 V by 39°.

EXAMPLE 19-5   The purpose of the "high-pass" circuit shown in Fig. 19-14 is to permit high frequencies to pass on to the load but to prevent the passage of low frequencies. Find the effectiveness of the circuit by calculating (*a*) the branch currents, (*b*) the total current, and (*c*) the percent of the total current in the resistor for (1) a 1-kHz audio frequency and (2) a 1,000-kHz radio frequency.

SOLUTION

The diagram for the circuit is shown in Fig. 19-14.

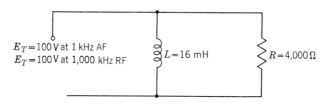

$E_T = 100$ V at 1 kHz AF
$E_T = 100$ V at 1,000 kHz RF

$L = 16$ mH

$R = 4,000\,\Omega$

FIGURE 19-14
A "high-pass" filter.

1   For the 1-kHz audio frequency,

a $X_L = 6.28\,fL = 6.28 \times 10^3 \times 16 \times 10^{-3}$ (16-1)

$$X_L = 6.28 \times 16 = 100 \ \Omega \qquad Ans.$$

Find the branch currents. Since

$$E_T = E_R = E_L = 100 \text{ V} \qquad (4\text{-}1)$$

$E_R = I_R \times R$ $E_L = I_L \times X_L$

$100 = I_R \times 4,000$ $100 = I_L \times 100$

$I_R = \dfrac{100}{4,000} = 0.025$ A $I_L = \dfrac{100}{100} = 1$ A

b   Find the total current.

$$I_T{}^2 = I_R{}^2 + I_L{}^2 = 0.025^2 + 1^2 \qquad (19\text{-}1)$$

$$= 0.000625 + 1$$

$$I_T{}^2 = 1.000625$$

$$I_T = \sqrt{1.000625} = 1 \text{ A} \qquad Ans.$$

c   Find the percent of the total current passing through the resistor.

$$\text{Percent} = \frac{I_R}{I_T} \times 100 = \frac{0.025}{1} \times 100 = 2.5\% \qquad Ans.$$

That is, 2.5 percent of the 1-kHz audio frequency passes through the resistor.

2   For the 1,000-kHz radio frequency: Since 1,000 kHz is 1,000 times as large as the audio frequency of 1 kHz, the X_L at 1,000 kHz will be equal to 1,000 times the X_L at 1 kHz. Therefore,

$$X_L = 1,000 \times 100 = 100,000 \ \Omega$$

Find the branch currents. Since

a $$E_T = E_R = E_L = 100 \text{ V} \qquad (4\text{-}1)$$

$$E_R = I_R \times R \qquad\qquad E_L = I_L \times X_L$$

$$100 = I_R \times 4{,}000 \qquad\qquad 100 = I_L \times 100{,}000$$

$$I_R = \frac{100}{4{,}000} = 0.025 \text{ A} \qquad I_L = \frac{100}{100{,}000} = 0.001 \text{ A}$$

b Find the total current.

$$I_T{}^2 = I_R{}^2 + I_L{}^2 = 0.025^2 + 0.001^2 \qquad (19\text{-}1)$$

$$= (25 \times 10^{-3})^2 + (1 \times 10^{-3})^2$$

$$= 625 \times 10^{-6} + 1 \times 10^{-6}$$

$$I_T{}^2 = 626 \times 10^{-6}$$

$$I_T = \sqrt{626 \times 10^{-6}} = 25 \times 10^{-3}$$

$$I_T = 0.025 \text{ A} \qquad Ans.$$

c Find the percent of the total current passing through the resistor.

$$\text{Percent} = \frac{I_R}{I_T} \times 100 = \frac{0.025}{0.025} \times 100 = 100\% \qquad Ans.$$

That is, practically 100 percent of the 1,000-kHz radio frequency passes through the resistor.

The circuit is evidently a good high-pass circuit, since it passes practically 100 percent of the high radio frequency and only 2.5 percent of the low audio frequency. The majority of the low audio frequency finds an easy path through the coil (I_L for the 1-kHz audio frequency equals the total current of 1 A).

PROBLEMS

1. A 24-Ω resistor and a 10-Ω inductive reactance are in parallel across a 120-V, 60-Hz ac line. Find (a) the total current, (b) the impedance, (c) the phase angle, and (d) the power drawn.
2. Repeat Prob. 1 for a 1,000-Ω resistor and a 100-Ω inductive reactance.
3. A 50-Ω resistor and a 0.2-H coil are in parallel across a 100-V, 100-Hz ac line. Find (a) the total current, (b) the impedance, (c) the phase angle, and (d) the power drawn.
4. In Fig. 19-15a, find the percent of the total AF current that passes through the resistor. Find the percent of the total RF current that passes through the resistor. On the basis of these answers, may the circuit be classified as a high-pass circuit?
5. Repeat Prob. 4 for the circuit shown in Fig. 19-15b.

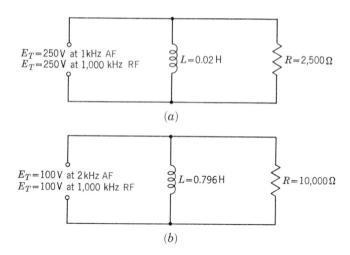

$E_T = 250\,V$ at 1kHz AF
$E_T = 250\,V$ at 1,000 kHz RF

$L = 0.02\,H$

$R = 2,500\,\Omega$

(a)

$E_T = 100\,V$ at 2kHz AF
$E_T = 100\,V$ at 1,000 kHz RF

$L = 0.796\,H$

$R = 10,000\,\Omega$

(b)

FIGURE 19-15

JOB 19-3 RESISTANCE AND CAPACITANCE IN PARALLEL

Figure 19-17 shows a 20-Ω resistance and a 15-Ω capacitive reactance in parallel across a 60-V 60-Hz ac source. The total current drawn by the circuit can be found by adding the currents in each branch. However, if they are not in phase, they must be added vectorially. The phase relations in the circuit are shown in Fig. 19-16a. The constant voltage is used as the reference line. The current in the resistance I_R is in phase with the voltage, and the current in the capacitor I_C leads the voltage by 90°.

Addition of the phasors. In Fig. 19-16b, the total current I_T is obtained by adding the phasor I_C to the phasor I_R. Place the tail of I_C on the head of I_R, and draw it in its original direction and length. The dis-

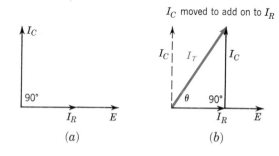

I_C moved to add on to I_R

FIGURE 19-16
(a) Phasor diagram for a parallel ac circuit containing resistance and capacitance. (b) I_T represents the phasor sum of I_R and I_C.

tance from the origin of the phasors to the head of the final phasor is the sum of the phasors. In this instance, the phasor I_T represents the sum of the phasors I_R and I_C. The angle θ is the angle by which the total current *leads* the total voltage. By applying the pythagorean theorem to Fig. 19-16b, we obtain

FORMULA

$$I_T^2 = I_R^2 + I_C^2 \qquad \boxed{19\text{-}3}$$

By Ohm's law,

$$E_T = I_T \times Z \qquad (18\text{-}9)$$

By trigonometry,

$$\cos \theta = \frac{a}{h}$$

$$\cos \theta = \frac{I_R}{I_T} \qquad (19\text{-}2)$$

The power is still given by

$$W = E \times I \times \cos \theta \qquad (18\text{-}3)$$

EXAMPLE 19-6   A 20-Ω resistor and a capacitor of 15 Ω capacitive reactance at 60 Hz are connected in parallel across a 60-V 60-Hz ac source. Find (a) the total current, (b) the impedance, (c) the phase angle, and (d) the power drawn by the circuit.

SOLUTION
The diagram for the circuit is shown in Fig. 19-17.

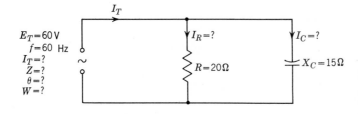

FIGURE 19-17
An ac parallel circuit containing resistance and capacitance.

a Find the branch currents. Since

$$E_T = E_R = E_C = 60 \text{ V} \qquad (4\text{-}1)$$

$$E_R = I_R \times R \qquad\qquad E_C = I_C \times X_C$$

$$60 = I_R \times 20 \qquad\qquad 60 = I_C \times 15$$

$$I_R = \frac{60}{20} = 3 \text{ A} \qquad I_C = \frac{60}{15} = 4 \text{ A}$$

Find the total current.

$$I_T^2 = I_R^2 + I_C^2 = 3^2 + 4^2 \qquad (19\text{-}3)$$

$$= 9 + 16$$

$$I_T^2 = 25$$

$$I_T = \sqrt{25} = 5 \text{ A} \qquad Ans.$$

b

$$E_T = I_T \times Z \qquad (18\text{-}9)$$

$$60 = 5 \times Z$$

$$Z = \frac{60}{5} = 12 \ \Omega \qquad Ans.$$

c

$$\cos \theta = \frac{I_R}{I_T} = \frac{3}{5} = 0.6000 \qquad (19\text{-}2)$$

$$\theta = 53° \qquad Ans.$$

d

$$W = E \times I \times \cos \theta = 60 \times 5 \times \cos 53° \qquad (18\text{-}3)$$

$$= 60 \times 5 \times 0.6$$

$$W = 180 \ \text{W} \qquad Ans.$$

In the parallel circuit, the total current of 5 A leads the total voltage of 60 V by 53°.

EXAMPLE 19-7   The purpose of the "low-pass" circuit shown in Fig. 19-18 is to permit low frequencies to pass on to the load but to prevent the passage of high frequencies. Find the effectiveness of the circuit by calculating the percent of the total current in the resistor for (1) a 1-kHz audio frequency and (2) a 1,000-kHz radio frequency.

SOLUTION
The diagram for the circuit is shown in Fig. 19-18.

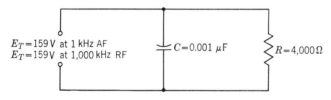

FIGURE 19-18
A "low-pass" filter.

1   For the 1-kHz audio frequency,

a

$$X_C = \frac{159,000}{f \times C} = \frac{159,000}{10^3 \times 1 \times 10^{-3}} \qquad (17\text{-}6)$$

$$X_C = \frac{159,000}{1} = 159,000 \ \Omega \qquad Ans.$$

Find the branch currents. Since

$$E_T = E_R = E_C = 159 \ \text{V} \qquad (4\text{-}1)$$

$$E_R = I_R \times R \qquad\qquad E_C = I_C \times X_C$$

$$159 = I_R \times 4,000 \qquad\qquad 159 = I_C \times 159,000$$

$$I_R = \frac{159}{4,000} = 0.04 \ \text{A} \qquad I_C = \frac{159}{159,000} = 0.001 \ \text{A}$$

b Find the total current.

$$I_T^2 = I_R^2 + I_C^2 = 0.04^2 + 0.001^2 \qquad (19\text{-}3)$$

$$= 0.0016 + 0.000001$$

$$I_T^2 = 0.001601$$

$$I_T = \sqrt{0.001601} = 0.04 \text{ A} \qquad Ans.$$

c Find the percent of the total current in the resistor.

$$\text{Percent} = \frac{I_R}{I_T} \times 100 = \frac{0.04}{0.04} \times 100 = 100\% \qquad Ans.$$

That is, practically 100 percent of the 1-kHz audio frequency passes through the resistor.

2 For the 1,000-kHz radio frequency: Since 1,000 kHz is 1,000 times as large as the audio frequency of 1 kHz, the X_C at 1,000 kHz will be equal to 1/1,000 of the X_C at 1 kHz. Therefore,

$$a \qquad\qquad X_C = \frac{159{,}000}{1{,}000} = 159 \ \Omega \qquad Ans.$$

Find the branch currents. Since

$$E_T = E_R = E_C = 159 \text{ V} \qquad (4\text{-}1)$$

$$E_R = I_R \times R \qquad\qquad E_C = I_C \times X_C$$

$$159 = I_R \times 4{,}000 \qquad\qquad 159 = I_C \times 159$$

$$I_R = \frac{159}{4{,}000} = 0.04 \text{ A} \qquad I_C = \frac{159}{159} = 1 \text{ A}$$

b Find the total current.

$$I_T^2 = I_R^2 + I_C^2 = 0.04^2 + 1^2 \qquad (19\text{-}3)$$

$$= 0.0016 + 1$$

$$I_T^2 = 1.0016$$

$$I_T = \sqrt{1.0016} = 1.001 \text{ A} \qquad Ans.$$

c Find the percent of the total current in the resistor.

$$\text{Percent} = \frac{I_R}{I_T} \times 100 = \frac{0.04}{1.001} \times 100 = 4\% \qquad Ans.$$

That is, only 4 percent of the 1,000-kHz current passes through the resistor. The circuit is evidently a good low-pass circuit. Practically all the low 1-kHz current goes through the resistor, but very little of the high 1,000-kHz current gets through. The majority of the 1,000-kHz RF current finds an easy path through the low reactance of the capacitor at this high frequency.

PROBLEMS

1. An 8-Ω resistor and a 15-Ω capacitive reactance are in parallel across a 120-V 60-Hz ac line. Find (*a*) the total current, (*b*) the

impedance, (c) the phase angle, and (d) the power drawn by the circuit.

2. A 26.5-Ω resistor and a 3-μF capacitor are in parallel across a 106-V 1-kHz ac source. Find (a) the total current, (b) the impedance, (c) the phase angle, and (d) the power drawn.

3. Repeat Prob. 1 for a 120-Ω resistor and a 60-Ω capacitive reactance.

4. An 8,000-Ω emitter resistor in parallel with a 4-μF capacitor in a 500-Hz circuit is shown in Fig. 19-19. If the voltage drop across the combination is 8 V, find (a) the total current and (b) the impedance of the combination.

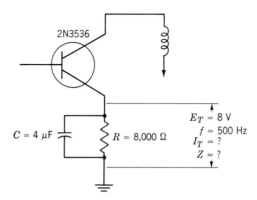

$E_T = 8$ V
$f = 500$ Hz
$I_T = ?$
$Z = ?$

$C = 4 \mu F$ $R = 8,000 \Omega$

2N3536

FIGURE 19-19

5. The 40-Ω cathode resistor for a 6DS5 tube is bypassed with a 5-μF capacitor. Find the total current flowing if the voltage across the capacitor is 10.6 V at 1.5 kHz.

6. In Fig. 19-20a, find the percent of the total AF current that passes through the resistor. Find the percent of the total RF current that passes through the resistor. On the basis of these answers, may the circuit be classified as a low-pass circuit?

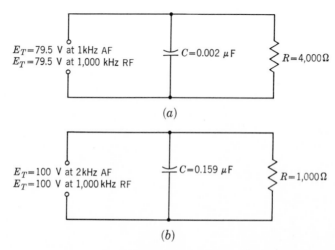

$E_T = 79.5$ V at 1kHz AF
$E_T = 79.5$ V at 1,000 kHz RF

$C = 0.002 \mu F$ $R = 4,000 \Omega$

(a)

$E_T = 100$ V at 2kHz AF
$E_T = 100$ V at 1,000 kHz RF

$C = 0.159 \mu F$ $R = 1,000 \Omega$

(b)

FIGURE 19-20

7. Repeat Prob. 6 for the circuit shown in Fig. 19-20*b*.
8. In a grid-leak circuit, $C = 250$ pF and $R = 1$ MΩ. If a 5-kHz AF signal causes a voltage drop of 0.6 V, find (*a*) the total current and (*b*) the impedance of the combination.
9. The grid-to-cathode capacity of 10 pF which is formed in the grid circuit of an amplifier is in parallel with the 1-MΩ grid resistor. If the signal voltage is 10 V at 318 kHz, find the current that will flow.

JOB 19-4 RESISTANCE, INDUCTANCE, AND CAPACITANCE IN PARALLEL. THE EQUIVALENT SERIES CIRCUIT.

Figure 19-23 shows a 30-Ω resistor, a 40-Ω inductive reactance, and a 60-Ω capacitive reactance connected in parallel across a 120-V 60-Hz ac line. $I_R = 4$ A, $I_L = 3$ A, and $I_C = 2$ A. The total current drawn by the circuit may be found by adding the currents in each branch. However, since the currents are not in phase, they must be added vectorially. The phase relations in the circuit are shown in Fig. 19-21*a*. The constant voltage is used as the reference line. The current in the resistor I_R is in phase with the voltage. The current in the capacitor I_C *leads* the voltage by 90°. The current in the inductance I_L *lags* the voltage by 90°. Since I_L and I_C are exactly 180° out of phase and acting in exactly *opposite* directions, the current I_C is denoted by a minus sign.

Addition of phasors. When there are three phasors, it is best to add only two at a time. To add the phasor I_C to I_L, place the tail of I_C on the head of I_L and draw it in its original length and direction, which will be straight *up* as shown in Fig. 19-21*b*. Since these phasors are acting in *opposite* directions, their *sum* is actually the *difference* between the phasors

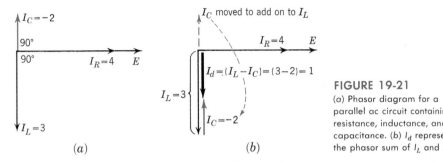

FIGURE 19-21
(a) Phasor diagram for a parallel ac circuit containing resistance, inductance, and capacitance. (b) I_d represents the phasor sum of I_L and I_C.

as indicated by I_d. That is, the addition of I_C to I_L is really found by $I_d = I_L - I_C$. After this addition, the phasor diagram looks like Fig. 19-22*a*. Notice that the effect of the capacitor current has disappeared. The 3 A of coil current has exactly balanced the 2 A of capacitor current and has left an excess of 1 A of coil current. This 1 A of coil current must now be added to the 4 A of resistance current. In Fig. 19-22b, the total current I_T is obtained by adding the phasor I_d to the phasor I_R. Place the tail of I_d on the head of I_R, and draw it in the proper direction. If I_C were larger than I_L, the phasor I_d would have an *upward* direction. The dis-

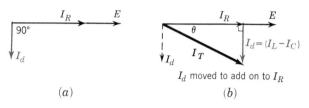

FIGURE 19-22

(a) I_d represents the result of adding I_C to I_L. (b) I_T represents the phasor sum of $I_R + I_C + I_L$.

tance from the origin of the phasors to the head of the last phasor is the sum of the phasors. In this instance, the phasor I_T represents the sum of the phasors $I_R + I_L + I_C$. The angle θ is the angle by which the total current *lags* the voltage. If I_C were larger than I_L, the total current would *lead* the voltage by this angle. By applying the pythagorean theorem to Fig. 19-22b, we obtain

FORMULA

$$I_T{}^2 = I_R{}^2 + (I_L - I_C)^2 \qquad \boxed{19\text{-}4}$$

By Ohm's law,

$$E_T = I_T \times Z \qquad (18\text{-}9)$$

By trigonometry,

$$\cos \theta = \frac{a}{h}$$

$$\cos \theta = \frac{I_R}{I_T} \qquad (19\text{-}2)$$

The power is still given by

$$W = E \times I \times \cos \theta \qquad (18\text{-}3)$$

EXAMPLE 19-8   A 30-Ω resistor, a 40-Ω inductive reactance, and a 60-Ω capacitive reactance are connected in parallel across a 120-V 60-Hz ac line. Find (a) the total current, (b) the impedance, (c) the phase angle, and (d) the power drawn by the circuit.

SOLUTION
The diagram for the circuit is shown in Fig. 19-23.

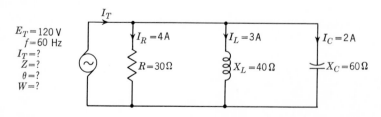

FIGURE 19-23

An ac parallel circuit containing resistance, inductance, and capacitance.

a Find the branch currents. Since

$$E_T = E_1 = E_2 = 120 \text{ V} \qquad (4\text{-}1)$$

$$E_R = I_R \times R \qquad\qquad E_L = I_L \times X_L$$

$$120 = I_R \times 30 \qquad\qquad 120 = I_L \times 40$$

$$I_R = \frac{120}{30} = 4 \text{ A} \qquad I_L = \frac{120}{40} = 3 \text{ A}$$

$$E_C = I_C \times X_C \qquad (17\text{-}7)$$

$$120 = I_C \times 60$$

$$I_C = \frac{120}{60} = 2 \text{ A} \qquad Ans.$$

Find the total current.

$$I_T^2 = I_R^2 + (I_L - I_C)^2 \qquad (19\text{-}4)$$

$$= 4^2 + (3 - 2)^2 = 4^2 + 1^2$$

$$= 16 + 1$$

$$I_T^2 = 17$$

$$I_T = \sqrt{17} = 4.12 \text{ A} \qquad Ans.$$

b
$$E_T = I_T \times Z \qquad (18\text{-}9)$$

$$120 = 4.12 \times Z$$

$$Z = \frac{120}{4.12} = 29.1 \ \Omega \qquad Ans.$$

c
$$\cos \theta = \frac{I_R}{I_T} = \frac{4}{4.12} = 0.9708 \qquad (19\text{-}2)$$

$$\theta = 14° \qquad Ans.$$

d
$$W = E \times I \times \cos \theta = 120 \times 4.12 \times \cos 14° \qquad (18\text{-}3)$$

$$= 120 \times 4.12 \times 0.971$$

$$W = 480 \text{ W} \qquad Ans.$$

In the parallel circuit, the total current of 4.12 A lags the total voltage by 14°.

EXAMPLE 19-9   In the circuit shown in Fig. 19-24, find (*a*) the impedance, (*b*) the phase angle, and (*c*) the equivalent series circuit.

SOLUTION
a Find the reactances.

$$X_L = 6.28fL = 6.28 \times 10 \times 10^3 \times 100 \times 10^{-3}$$

$$X_L = 6,280 \ \Omega$$

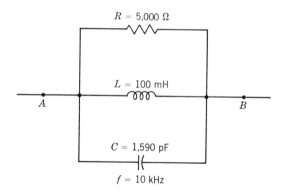

FIGURE 19-24

$$X_C = \frac{159,000}{f \times C} = \frac{159,000}{10 \times 10^3 \times 1590 \times 10^{-6}} = 10,000 \ \Omega$$

Find the branch currents. If the voltage is unknown, it may be assumed to be any value. For ease in calculation, it should be equal to, or greater than, the largest impedance. Assume $E_{AB} = 10,000$ V. Since

$$E_{AB} = E_R = E_L = E_C$$

$$E_R = I_R \times R \qquad\qquad E_L = I_L \times X_L$$

$$10,000 = I_R \times 5,000 \qquad 10,000 = I_L \times 6,280$$

$$I_R = 2 \ A \qquad\qquad I_L = 1.59 \ A$$

$$E_C = I_C \times X_C$$

$$10,000 = I_C \times 10,000$$

$$I_C = 1 \ A$$

Find the total current.

$$I_T{}^2 = I_R{}^2 + (I_L - I_C)^2 \tag{19-4}$$

$$I_T{}^2 = 2^2 + (1.59 - 1)^2$$

$$= 4 + 0.348$$

$$I_T{}^2 = 4.348$$

$$I_T = \sqrt{4.348} = 2.08 \ A$$

Find the impedance.

$$E_T = I_T \times Z \tag{18-9}$$

$$10,000 = 2.08 \times Z$$

$$Z = 4,800 \ \Omega \qquad Ans.$$

b Find the phase angle.

$$\cos \theta = \frac{I_R}{I_T} = \frac{2}{2.08} \tag{19-2}$$

$$\cos \theta = 0.9615$$

$$\theta = 16° \text{ lagging} \quad Ans.$$

c   Find the equivalent series circuit.

The impedance from *A* to *B* is 4,800 Ω with the current lagging the voltage by 16°. If the circuit between *A* and *B* had been a *series circuit,* then the 4,800 Ω of impedance would have been formed from an impedance triangle as shown in Fig. 19-25, containing resistance and inductance only because of the *lagging* current of 16°.

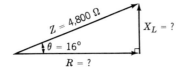

FIGURE 19-25
R and X_L in series are equivalent to the parallel impedance of 4,800 Ω.

1   Find the equivalent series resistance. In Fig. 19-25,

$$\cos 16° = \frac{R}{4,800} \tag{14-3}$$

$$R = 4,800 \times \cos 16°$$

$$R = 4,800 \times 0.9615 = 4,615 \ \Omega \quad Ans.$$

2   Find the equivalent inductance. In Fig. 19-25,

$$\sin 16° = \frac{X_L}{4,800}$$

$$X_L = 4,800 \times \sin 16°$$

$$X_L = 4,800 \times 0.2756 = 1,323 \ \Omega$$

Also, $$X_L = 6.28 fL \tag{16-1}$$

$$1,323 = 6.28 \times 10 \times 10^3 \times L$$

$$L = 0.021 \ \text{H}$$

$$L = 21 \ \text{mH} \quad Ans.$$

Therefore, the equivalent series circuit consists of a resistance of 4,615 Ω in series with an inductance of 21 mH. This circuit would produce the same load as the original parallel circuit.

PROBLEMS

1.   Find the series equivalent circuit for the circuit shown in Fig. 19-17 for Example 19-6.
2.   Find the series equivalent circuit for the circuit shown in Fig. 19-13 for Example 19-4.
3.   Find the series equivalent circuit for the circuit shown in Fig. 19-23 for Example 19-8.

4. A 24-Ω resistor, a 6-Ω inductive reactance, and a 15-Ω capacitive reactance are in parallel across a 120-V 60-Hz line. Find (a) the total current, (b) the impedance, (c) the phase angle, (d) the power drawn by the circuit, and (e) the series equivalent circuit.

5. Repeat Prob. 4 for a 30-Ω resistor, a 60-Ω inductive reactance, and a 40-Ω capacitive reactance across the same line in parallel.

6. A 50-Ω resistor, a 0.02-H coil, and a 3-μF capacitor are connected in parallel across a 100-V 1-kHz ac source. Find (a) the reactance of the coil and capacitor, (b) the current drawn by each branch, (c) the total current, (d) the impedance, (e) the phase angle, (f) the power drawn by the circuit, and (g) the series equivalent circuit.

7. Repeat Prob. 6 for a 2,200-Ω resistor, a 20-H coil, and a 0.8-μF capacitor in parallel across a 220-V 60-Hz ac line.

8. In a circuit similar to that shown in Fig. 19-24, $R = 1,590\ \Omega$, $L = 0.16$ H, and $C = 0.1\ \mu$F. Find the series equivalent circuit.

JOB 19-5   RESOLUTION OF PHASORS

Up to this point we have been considering only circuits which contained only "pure" inductances and capacitances. Actually, such pure components do not exist. There is always some resistance in every coil or capacitor. This resistance must be taken into account whenever the resistance is an appreciable value as compared with the reactance of the component. In addition, most motor loads may be considered to be a series combination of resistance and inductance or resistance and capacitance. For example, an *induction motor* may be considered to be a series combination of resistance and inductance in which the current *lags* behind the impressed voltage. A *synchronous motor* may be considered to be a series combination of resistance and capacitance in which the current *leads* the impressed voltage. The amount of lead or lag depends on the relative amounts of resistance in series with the inductance or capacitance.

These leading and lagging currents will not be out of phase by exactly 90° but may be out of phase by *any* angle. For example, the current in branch *A* of a parallel circuit may *lead* the total voltage by 30° and the current in branch *B* may *lag* the total voltage by 50°. The phasor diagram for this condition is shown in Fig. 19-26.

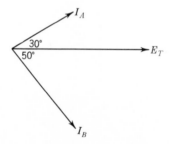

FIGURE 19-26
Leading and lagging branch currents in a parallel circuit.

The total current will still be the *phasor* sum of I_A and I_B. However, the pythagorean theorem may not be used because the angle between the phasors is no longer 90°. The phasor addition may be accomplished if we first resolve each phasor into its component parts which *are* 90° out of phase. Consider the phasor V in Fig. 19-27.

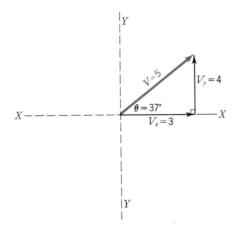

FIGURE 19-27

A phasor (or vector) V may be resolved into its horizontal component V_x and its vertical component V_y.

By the pythagorean theorem, V is the phasor sum of V_x and V_y.

$$V^2 = V_x^2 + V_y^2 \qquad\qquad (18\text{-}4)$$
$$V^2 = 3^2 + 4^2 = 9 + 16 = 25$$
$$V = \sqrt{25} = 5$$

When the process is reversed, a phasor V may be *resolved* into its two components whose phasor sum will be equal to the original phasor. These components are always at right angles to each other.

V_x is called the horizontal or x component of V.
V_y is called the vertical or y component of V.

The value of each component depends on the value of the total phasor and on the angle θ between the phasor and the X axis. The relationships between the components and the phasor are determined by the basic definitions of the sine and cosine of angle θ. For example, in Fig. 19-27,

$$\sin \theta = \frac{V_y}{V} \qquad \text{and} \qquad \cos \theta = \frac{V_x}{V}$$

Cross-multiplying each equation yields the

FORMULAS

$$V_y = V \sin \theta \qquad\qquad \boxed{19\text{-}5}$$

$$V_x = V \cos \theta \qquad\qquad \boxed{19\text{-}6}$$

The rectangular components V_x and V_y of the phasor V in Fig. 19-27 may now be found.

$$V_y = V \sin \theta \qquad\qquad V_x = V \cos \theta$$
$$V_y = 5 \times \sin 37° \qquad\quad V_x = 5 \times \cos 37°$$
$$V_y = 5 \times 0.6018 = 3 \qquad V_x = 5 \times 0.7986 = 4$$

EXAMPLE 19-10   A 10-lb force acts up and to the right at an angle of 30° with the horizontal. Find its horizontal and vertical components.

SOLUTION
The diagram for the problem is shown in Fig. 19-28.

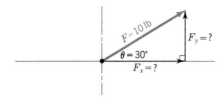

FIGURE 19-28

$$F_y = F \sin \theta \qquad (19\text{-}5) \qquad F_x = F \cos \theta \qquad\qquad (19\text{-}6)$$
$$F_y = 10 \sin 30° \qquad\qquad\quad F_x = 10 \cos 30°$$
$$F_y = 10(0.5000) \qquad\qquad\quad F_x = 10(0.8660)$$
$$F_y = 5 \text{ lb} \quad Ans. \qquad\qquad\quad F_x = 8.66 \text{ lb} \quad Ans.$$

EXAMPLE 19-11   A sled is being pulled with a force of 50 lb which is exerted through a rope held at an angle of 20° with the ground as shown in Fig. 19-29. How much of this force is useful in moving the sled horizontally?

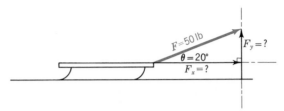

FIGURE 19-29

SOLUTION
Only the horizontal component F_x is useful in moving the sled horizontally.

$$F_x = F \cos \theta \qquad\qquad\qquad\qquad\qquad (19\text{-}6)$$
$$F_x = 50 \cos 20°$$
$$F_x = 50(0.9397) = 47 \text{ lb} \qquad Ans.$$

EXAMPLE 19-12   A window pole is used to pull down a window. If the force exerted through the pole is 30 lb at an angle of 72° with the horizontal, find the useful vertical component.

SOLUTION
The diagram for the problem is shown in Fig. 19-30.

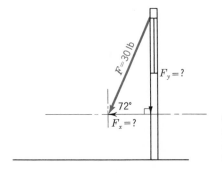

FIGURE 19-30
Only the vertical component of the force is effective in opening the window.

$$F_y = F \sin \theta \qquad\qquad\qquad (19\text{-}5)$$

$$F_y = 30 \sin 72°$$

$$F_y = 30(0.9511) = -28.5 \text{ lb} \qquad Ans.$$

Note: The minus sign in the answer is used to indicate that the force is acting *downward.* The direction in which a component acts is indicated by either a plus (+) or a minus (−) sign. These signs are the same as those used to locate points on a graph.

V_x components acting to the *right* are (+).
V_x components acting to the *left* are (−).
V_y components acting *upward* are (+).
V_y components acting *downward* are (−).

EXAMPLE 19-13   A current of 20 A in one branch of an ac circuit leads the total voltage by 40°. Find its "in-phase" current and its "reactive" current.

SOLUTION
The phasor diagram is shown in Fig. 19-31a.

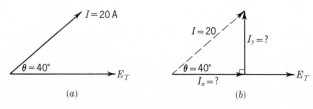

FIGURE 19-31
(a) Phasor diagram for a leading current. (b) The current *I* is resolved into its components I_x and I_y.

1   Resolve the current into its components I_x and I_y as shown in Fig. 19-31b.

I_x is the in-phase current, since it acts in the same direction as the total voltage E_T.

I_y is the reactive current, since it leads the total voltage E_T by 90°.

2 Find each component.

$$I_x = I \cos \theta \qquad (19\text{-}6) \qquad I_y = I \sin \theta \qquad (19\text{-}5)$$

$$I_x = 20 \cos 40° \qquad\qquad I_y = 20 \sin 40°$$

$$I_x = 20(0.766) = 15.32 \text{ A} \qquad I_y = 20(0.6428) = 12.86 \text{ A}$$

EXAMPLE 19-14   A current of 10 A supplying an induction motor lags the voltage by 53°. Find the in-phase and reactive currents.

SOLUTION
The phasor diagram is shown in Fig. 19-32a.

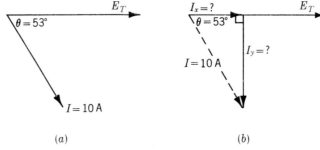

FIGURE 19-32
(a) Phasor diagram for a lagging current. (b) The current I is resolved into its components I_x and I_y.

1 Resolve the current into its in-phase component I_x and its reactive component I_y as shown in Fig. 19-32b.

2 Find each component.

$$I_x = I \cos \theta \qquad (19\text{-}6) \qquad I_y = I \sin \theta \qquad (19\text{-}5)$$

$$I_x = 10 \cos 53° \qquad\qquad I_y = 10 \sin 53°$$

$$I_x = 10(0.6018) = 6 \text{ A} \qquad I_y = 10(0.7986) = -8 \text{ A}$$

PROBLEMS

Find the in-phase current I_x and the reactive current I_y for each of the following currents.

PROBLEM	I, A	θ
1	20	30° leading
2	10	35° leading
3	20	60° lagging
4	10	55° lagging
5	26	42° leading
6	1.8	23° leading
7	0.1	50° lagging
8	4.5	19° lagging
9	14	25° leading
10	31	28° lagging

JOB 19-6   PARALLEL-SERIES AC CIRCUITS

The current in any branch of an operating ac circuit is never exactly 90° out of phase with the voltage. There is always some resistance in series with the capacitance or inductance which reduces the phase angle from 90° to almost any angle. These "out-of-phase" currents must be added by phasor addition to get the total current.

Addition of "out-of-phase" currents. Let us try to find the total current in a parallel circuit if the current in branch A leads the voltage by 30° and the current in branch B leads the voltage by 60°.

SOLUTION

The phasor diagram for the conditions stated is shown in Fig. 19-33a.

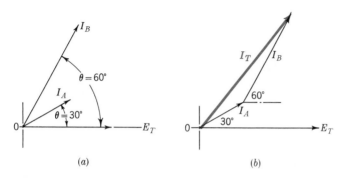

(a)   (b)

FIGURE 19-33
(a) Phasor diagram showing I_A leading the voltage by 30° and I_B leading the voltage by 60°. (b) I_T represents the phasor sum of I_A and I_B.

The total current is obtained by adding current I_B to current I_A *vectorially*. Place the tail of I_B on to the head of I_A and draw it in its original direction and length as shown in Fig. 19-33b. The distance from the origin of the phasors to the head of the final phasor is the sum of the phasors, or I_T.

Figure 19-33b may be redrawn as shown in Fig. 19-34 to show the x and y components of each current.

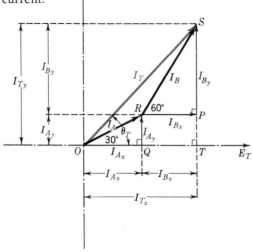

FIGURE 19-34
I_A and I_B have been resolved into their in-phase and reactive components. Their algebraic sums I_{T_x} and I_{T_y} are the components of the total current I_T.

I_{A_x} and I_{B_x} are the in-phase components of I_A and I_B.
I_{A_y} and I_{B_y} are the reactive components of I_A and I_B.
I_{T_x} is the algebraic sum of all the x components.
I_{T_y} is the algebraic sum of all the y components.

FORMULAS

$$I_{T_x} = I_{A_x} + I_{B_x} \qquad \boxed{19\text{-}7}$$

$$I_{T_y} = I_{A_y} + I_{B_y} \qquad \boxed{19\text{-}8}$$

By applying the pythagorean theorem to triangle OTS in Fig. 19-34, we obtain the

FORMULA

$$I_T{}^2 = (I_{T_x})^2 + (I_{T_y})^2 \qquad \boxed{19\text{-}9}$$

and by trigonometry,

$$\cos \theta_T = \frac{I_{T_x}}{I_T} \qquad \boxed{19\text{-}10}$$

In actual practice, the resolution triangles ORQ and RSP are drawn on the same constant-voltage base and added as shown in the following example. This method eliminates the problem of complicated phasor diagrams resulting from combinations of leading and lagging phasors.

EXAMPLE 19-15 In a parallel circuit, a current of 10 A in branch A leads the total voltage by 30°. A current of 20 A in branch B leads the total voltage by 37°. Find (*a*) the total current and (*b*) the angle by which the total current leads the total voltage.

SOLUTION

a

1   Draw the phasor diagram for the branch currents on the same voltage base as shown in Fig. 19-35*a*.

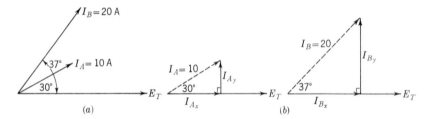

(a)   (b)

FIGURE 19-35
(a) Two leading currents in a parallel circuit. (b) Resolution of each current into its in-phase and reactive components.

2   Resolve the current in each branch into its components as shown in Fig. 19-35*b*. Calculate the components.

For branch A:

$$I_{A_x} = I_A \cos \theta \qquad (19\text{-}6)$$
$$= 10 \cos 30° = 10(0.866) = 8.66 \text{ A}$$

$$I_{A_y} = I_A \sin \theta \qquad (19\text{-}5)$$
$$= 10 \sin 30° = 10(0.5000) = 5 \text{ A}$$

For branch B:

$$I_{B_x} = I_B \cos \theta \qquad (19\text{-}6)$$
$$= 20 \cos 37° = 20(0.7986) = 16 \text{ A}$$

$$I_{B_y} = I_B \sin \theta \qquad (19\text{-}5)$$
$$= 20 \sin 37° = 20(0.6018) = 12 \text{ A}$$

3   Draw all the components on the same voltage base as shown in Fig. 19-36a. The total in-phase current I_{T_x} and the total reactive current I_{T_y} may now be found.

$$I_{T_x} = I_{A_x} + I_{B_x} \qquad (19\text{-}7)$$
$$= 8.66 + 16 = 24.66 \text{ A}$$

$$I_{T_y} = I_{A_y} + I_{B_y} \qquad (19\text{-}8)$$
$$= 5 + 12 = 17 \text{ A}$$

4   Draw these phasors as shown in Fig. 19-36b.

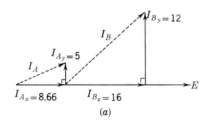

(a)

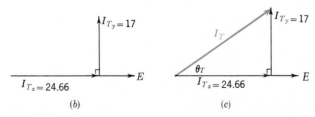

(b)   (c)

FIGURE 19-36
(a) The components of all the branch currents drawn on the same voltage base. (b) $I_{T_x} = I_{A_x} + I_{B_x}$ and $I_{T_y} = I_{A_y} + I_{B_y}$. (c) I_T represents the phasor sum of I_{T_x} and I_{T_y}.

5   Draw the phasor diagram for the total current by adding I_{T_x} and I_{T_y} vectorially as shown in Fig. 19-36c.

Find I_T.

$$(I_T)^2 = (I_{T_x})^2 + (I_{T_y})^2 \qquad (19\text{-}9)$$

$$= (24.66)^2 + (17)^2$$
$$= 608 + 289 = 897$$
$$I_T = \sqrt{897} = 30 \text{ A leading} \qquad Ans.$$

b Find the phase angle.

$$\cos \theta_T = \frac{I_{T_x}}{I_T} \qquad\qquad (19\text{-}10)$$

$$\cos \theta_T = \frac{24.66}{30} = 0.822$$

$$\theta_T = 35° \text{ leading} \qquad Ans.$$

EXAMPLE 19-16 An induction motor of 5 Ω impedance draws a current lagging by 26°. It is in parallel with a synchronous motor of 12 Ω impedance which draws a current leading by 37°. If the applied voltage is 120 V at 60 Hz, find (*a*) the current drawn by each motor, (*b*) the total current drawn, (*c*) the impedance, (*d*) the phase angle, and (*e*) the power drawn by the circuit.

SOLUTION
The diagram for the circuit is shown in Fig. 19-37.

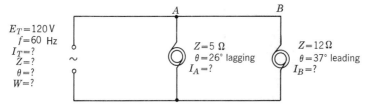

FIGURE 19-37

a Find the current in each branch. Since

$$E_T = E_A = E_B = 120 \text{ V} \qquad\qquad (4\text{-}1)$$

$$E_A = I_A \times Z_A \qquad\qquad E_B = I_B \times Z_B$$

$$120 = I_A \times 5 \qquad\qquad 120 = I_B \times 12$$

$$I_A = \frac{120}{5} = 24 \text{ A lagging} \qquad I_B = \frac{120}{12} = 10 \text{ A leading}$$

b The total current is found by adding the currents in the two branches. However, they are out of phase and must be added vectorially.

1 Draw the phasor diagram for the branch currents on the same voltage base as shown in Fig. 19-38*a*.
2 Resolve the current in each branch into its components as shown in Fig. 19-38*b*. Calculate the components.

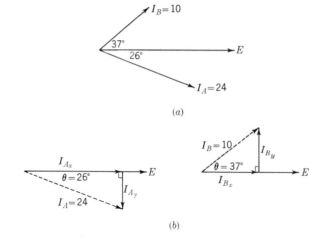

(a)

(b)

FIGURE 19-38

(a) Leading and lagging currents in a parallel circuit. (b) Resolution of each current into its in-phase and reactive components.

For branch A:

$$I_{A_x} = I_A \cos \theta \qquad (19\text{-}6)$$
$$= 24 \cos 26° = 24(0.9) = 21.6 \text{ A}$$

$$I_{A_y} = I_A \sin \theta \qquad (19\text{-}5)$$
$$= 24 \sin 26° = 24(0.44) = -10.56 \text{ A}$$

The minus sign in I_{A_y} indicates a lagging reactive current.

For branch B:

$$I_{B_x} = I_B \cos \theta \qquad (19\text{-}6)$$
$$= 10 \cos 37° = 10(0.8) = 8 \text{ A}$$

$$I_{B_y} = I_B \sin \theta \qquad (19\text{-}5)$$
$$= 10 \sin 37° = 10(0.6) = 6 \text{ A}$$

3   Draw all the components on the same voltage base as shown in Fig. 19-39a. The total in-phase current I_{T_x} and the total reactive current I_{T_y} may now be found.

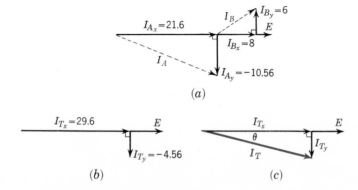

(a)

(b)

(c)

FIGURE 19-39

(a) The components of all the branch currents drawn on the same voltage base. (b) $I_{T_x} = I_{A_x} + I_{B_x}$ and $I_{T_y} = I_{A_y} + I_{B_y}$. (c) I_T represents the phasor sum of I_{T_x} and I_{T_y}.

$$I_{T_x} = I_{A_x} + I_{B_x} \qquad (19\text{-}7)$$

$$= 21.6 + 8 = 29.6 \text{ A}$$

$$I_{T_y} = I_{A_y} + I_{B_y} \qquad (19\text{-}8)$$

$$= -10.56 + 6 = -4.56 \text{ A}$$

The minus sign indicates a lagging reactive current.

4   Draw these phasors as shown in Fig. 19-39b.

5   Draw the phasor diagram for the total current by adding I_{T_x} and I_{T_y} vectorially as shown in Fig. 19-39c. Find I_T.

$$(I_T)^2 = (I_{T_x})^2 + (I_{T_y})^2 \qquad (19\text{-}9)$$

$$= (29.6)^2 + (-4.56)^2$$

$$= 876.2 + 20.8 = 897$$

$$I_T = \sqrt{897} = 30 \text{ A lagging} \qquad Ans.$$

c   Find the impedance of the circuit.

$$E_T = I_T \times Z \qquad (18\text{-}9)$$

$$120 = 30 \times Z$$

$$Z = \frac{120}{30} = 4 \ \Omega \qquad Ans.$$

d   Find the phase angle.

$$\cos \theta_T = \frac{I_{T_x}}{I_T} \qquad (19\text{-}10)$$

$$\cos \theta_T = \frac{29.6}{30} = 0.986$$

$$\theta_T = 10° \text{ lagging} \qquad Ans.$$

e   Find the power consumed.

$$W = E \times I \times \cos \theta = 120 \times 30 \times \cos 10° \qquad (18\text{-}3)$$

$$W = 120 \times 30 \times 0.986 = 3{,}546 \text{ W} \qquad Ans.$$

From this last example we can determine the procedure to follow in solving parallel-series ac circuits:

1   Find (a) the reactance, (b) the impedance, (c) the current, and (d) the phase angle for each branch of the parallel circuit.

2   Draw the phasor diagram for the branch currents on the same voltage base.

3   Resolve the current in each branch into its components.

$$I_y = I \times \sin \theta \qquad (19\text{-}5)$$

$$I_x = I \times \cos \theta \qquad (19\text{-}6)$$

Note: y components of lagging currents are negative (−). y components of leading currents are positive (+).

4   Find the total in-phase current I_{T_x} and the total reactive current I_{T_y}.

$$I_{T_x} = I_{A_x} + I_{B_x} \qquad (19\text{-}7)$$

$$I_{T_y} = I_{A_y} + I_{B_y} \qquad (19\text{-}8)$$

5   Find the total current.

$$I_T{}^2 = (I_{T_x})^2 + (I_{T_y})^2 \qquad (19\text{-}9)$$

6   Find the impedance.

$$E_T = I_T \times Z \qquad (18\text{-}9)$$

7   Find the phase angle.

$$\cos \theta_T = \frac{I_{T_x}}{I_T} \qquad (19\text{-}10)$$

8   Find the total power.

$$W = E \times I \times \cos \theta \qquad (18\text{-}3)$$

EXAMPLE 19-17   An induction motor of 6 Ω resistance and 8 Ω inductive reactance is in parallel with a synchronous motor of 8 Ω resistance and 15 Ω capacitive reactance and a third parallel branch of 15 Ω
resistance. Find (a) the total current drawn from a 150-V 60-Hz source,
(b) the total impedance, (c) the phase angle, and (d) the power drawn by
the circuit.

SOLUTION
The diagram for the circuit is shown in Fig. 19-40.

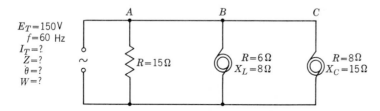

FIGURE 19-40

a

1   Find the series impedance, current, and phase angle for each branch.

For branch A:

$$Z = R = 15 \ \Omega$$

$$I_A = \frac{E}{R} = \frac{150}{15} = 10 \ \text{A} \qquad (2\text{-}1)$$

$$\cos \theta = \frac{R}{Z} = \frac{15}{15} = 1 \qquad (18\text{-}8)$$

Therefore, $\theta = 0°$

The current is *in phase* with the voltage.

For branch B:

$$Z = \sqrt{R^2 + X_L{}^2} = \sqrt{6^2 + 8^2} = \sqrt{36 + 64} = \sqrt{100} = 10 \ \Omega$$

$$I_B = \frac{E}{Z} = \frac{150}{10} = 15 \ A \qquad\qquad (16\text{-}6)$$

$$\cos \theta = \frac{R}{Z} = \frac{6}{10} = 0.6000 \qquad\qquad (18\text{-}8)$$

Therefore, $\theta = 53°$

The current *lags* the voltage by $53°$.

For branch C:

$$Z = \sqrt{R^2 + X_C{}^2} = \sqrt{8^2 + 15^2} = \sqrt{64 + 225} = \sqrt{289} = 17 \ \Omega$$

$$I_C = \frac{E}{Z} = \frac{150}{17} = 8.8 \ A \qquad\qquad (17\text{-}7)$$

$$\cos \theta = \frac{R}{Z} = \frac{8}{17} = 0.4706 \qquad\qquad (18\text{-}8)$$

Therefore, $\theta = 62°$

The current *leads* the voltage by $62°$.

2 Draw the phasor diagram for the branch currents on the same voltage base as shown in Fig. 19-41a.

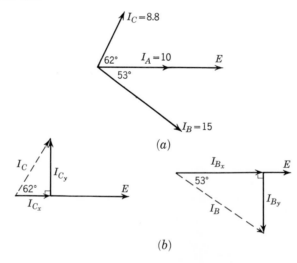

FIGURE 19-41
(a) Leading and lagging currents in a parallel circuit. (b) Resolution of each current into its in-phase and reactive components.

3 Resolve the current in each branch into its components as shown in Fig. 19-41b. Calculate the components.

For branch A:

$$I_{A_x} = I_A \times \cos \theta = 10 \times \cos 0° = 10 \times 1 = 10 \ A \qquad (19\text{-}6)$$

$$I_{A_y} = I_A \times \sin \theta = 10 \times \sin 0° = 10 \times 0 = 0 \ A \qquad (19\text{-}5)$$

For branch B:

$$I_{B_x} = I_B \times \cos\theta = 15 \times \cos 53° = 15 \times 0.6 = 9 \text{ A} \qquad (19\text{-}6)$$

$$I_{B_y} = I_B \times \sin\theta = 15 \times \sin 53° = 15 \times 0.8 = -12 \text{ A} \qquad (19\text{-}5)$$

Note: The minus sign in I_{B_y} indicates a lagging reactive component.

For branch C:

$$I_{C_x} = I_C \times \cos\theta = 8.8 \times \cos 62° = 8.8 \times 0.470 = 4.14 \text{ A} \qquad (19\text{-}6)$$

$$I_{C_y} = I_C \times \sin\theta = 8.8 \times \sin 62° = 8.8 \times .88 = 7.74 \text{ A} \qquad (19\text{-}5)$$

4   Draw all the components on the same voltage base as shown in Fig. 19-42a. The total in-phase current I_{T_x} and the total reactive current I_{T_y} may now be found.

$$I_{T_x} = I_{A_x} + I_{B_x} + I_{C_x} \qquad (19\text{-}7)$$

$$= 10 + 9 + 4.14 = 23.14 \text{ A}$$

$$I_{T_y} = I_{A_y} + I_{B_y} + I_{C_y} \qquad (19\text{-}8)$$

$$= 0 + (-12) + 7.74 = -4.26 \text{ A}$$

Note: The minus sign in I_{T_y} indicates a lagging reactive component.

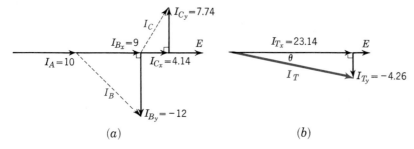

(a) The components of all the branch currents drawn on the same voltage base. (b) I_T represents the phasor sum of I_{T_x} and I_{T_y}.

FIGURE 19-42

5   Draw the phasor diagram for the total current by adding I_{T_x} and I_{T_y} vectorially as shown in Fig. 19-42b. Notice that I_{T_y} is drawn downward because I_{T_y} is negative. Find I_T.

$$I_T{}^2 = (I_{T_x})^2 + (I_{T_y})^2 \qquad (19\text{-}9)$$

$$= (23.14)^2 + (-4.26)^2$$

$$= 535.5 + 18.1 = 553.6$$

$$I_T = \sqrt{533.6} = 23.5 \text{ A lagging} \qquad \textit{Ans.}$$

b Find the impedance.

$$E_T = I_T \times Z \qquad (18\text{-}9)$$

$$150 = 23.5 \times Z$$

$$Z = \frac{150}{23.5} = 6.38 \text{ } \Omega \qquad \textit{Ans.}$$

c Find the phase angle.

$$\cos \theta_T = \frac{I_{T_x}}{I_T} \qquad (19\text{-}10)$$

$$\cos \theta_T = \frac{23.14}{23.5} = 0.9847$$

Therefore, $\qquad\qquad \theta_T = 10°$ lagging $\qquad$ *Ans.*

d Find the power drawn by the circuit.

$$W = E \times I \times \cos \theta = 150 \times 23.5 \times \cos 10° \qquad (18\text{-}3)$$

$$W = 150 \times 23.5 \times 0.985 = 3{,}472 \text{ W} \qquad Ans.$$

The total current of 23.5 A *lags* the total voltage of 150 V by 10°.

EXAMPLE 19-18 For the circuit shown in Fig. 19-43, find (*a*) the total current, (*b*) the total impedance, (*c*) the phase angle, and (*d*) the power drawn by the circuit.

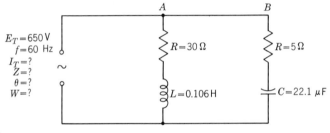

$E_T = 650$ V
$f = 60$ Hz
$I_T = ?$
$Z = ?$
$\theta = ?$
$W = ?$

$R = 30\,\Omega$

$L = 0.106$ H

$R = 5\,\Omega$

$C = 22.1\ \mu$F

FIGURE 19-43

SOLUTION

a

1 Find the reactance, series impedance, current, and phase angle for each branch.

For branch *A*:

$$X_L = 6.28 f L = 6.28 \times 60 \times 0.106 = 40\ \Omega \qquad (16\text{-}1)$$

$$Z = \sqrt{R^2 + X_L^2} = \sqrt{30^2 + 40^2} \qquad (16\text{-}4)$$

$$= \sqrt{900 + 1{,}600}$$

$$Z = \sqrt{2{,}500} = 50\ \Omega$$

$$I_A = \frac{E}{Z} = \frac{650}{50} = 13\text{ A} \qquad (16\text{-}6)$$

$$\cos \theta = \frac{R}{Z} = \frac{30}{50} = 0.6000 \qquad (18\text{-}8)$$

Therefore, $\qquad\qquad\qquad \theta = 53°$

The current of 13 A lags the total voltage by 53°.

For branch B:

$$X_C = \frac{159{,}000}{f \times C} = \frac{159{,}000}{60 \times 22.1} = 12 \ \Omega \qquad (17\text{-}6)$$

$$Z = \sqrt{R^2 + X_C{}^2} = \sqrt{5^2 + 12^2} \qquad (17\text{-}8)$$

$$= \sqrt{25 + 144}$$

$$Z = \sqrt{169} = 13 \ \Omega$$

$$I_B = \frac{E}{Z} = \frac{650}{13} = 50 \ \text{A} \qquad (17\text{-}7)$$

$$\cos \theta = \frac{R}{Z} = \frac{5}{13} = 0.3846 \qquad (18\text{-}8)$$

Therefore, $\qquad\qquad\qquad \theta = 67°$

The current of 50 A leads the total voltage by $67°$.

2 Draw the phasor diagram for the branch currents on the same voltage base as shown in Fig. 19-44a.

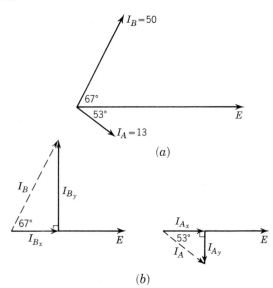

(a)

(b)

FIGURE 19-44

(a) Leading and lagging currents in a parallel circuit. (b) Resolution of each current into its in-phase and reactive components.

3 Resolve the current in each branch into its components as shown in Fig. 19-44b. Calculate the components.

For branch A:

$$I_{A_x} = I_A \times \cos \theta = 13 \times \cos 53° = 13 \times 0.6 = 7.8 \ \text{A} \qquad (19\text{-}6)$$

$$I_{A_y} = I_A \times \sin \theta = 13 \times \sin 53° = 13 \times 0.8 = -10.4 \ \text{A} \qquad (19\text{-}5)$$

For branch B:

$$I_{B_x} = I_B \times \cos \theta = 50 \times \cos 67° = 50 \times 0.385 = 19.25 \ \text{A} \qquad (19\text{-}6)$$

$$I_{B_y} = I_B \times \sin \theta = 50 \times \sin 67° = 50 \times 0.92 = 46 \ \text{A} \qquad (19\text{-}5)$$

4   Draw all the components on the same voltage base as shown in Fig. 19-45a. The total in-phase current I_{T_x} and the total reactive current I_{T_y} may now be found.

$$I_{T_x} = I_{A_x} + I_{B_x} = 7.8 + 19.25 = 27.05 \text{ A} \qquad (19\text{-}7)$$

$$I_{T_y} = I_{A_y} + I_{B_y} = -10.4 + 46 = 35.6 \text{ A} \qquad (19\text{-}8)$$

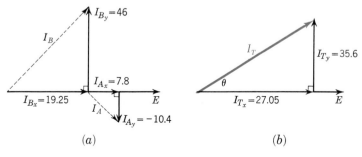

(a)   (b)

FIGURE 19-45
(a) The components of all the branch currents drawn on the same voltage base. (b) I_T represents the phasor sum of I_{T_x} and I_{T_y}.

5   Draw the phasor diagram for the total current by adding I_{T_x} and I_{T_y} vectorially as shown in Fig. 19-45b. Notice that I_{T_y} is drawn *upward* because I_{T_y} is positive. Find I_T.

$$I_T{}^2 = (I_{T_x})^2 + (I_{T_y})^2 \qquad (19\text{-}9)$$

$$= (27.05)^2 + (35.6)^2$$

$$= 729 + 1,267 = 1,996$$

$$I_T = \sqrt{1,996} = 44.6 \text{ A leading} \qquad Ans.$$

b Find the impedance.

$$E_T = I_T \times Z \qquad (18\text{-}9)$$

$$650 = 44.6 \times Z$$

$$Z = \frac{650}{44.6} = 14.6 \ \Omega \qquad Ans.$$

c Find the phase angle.

$$\cos \theta_T = \frac{I_{T_x}}{I_T} \qquad (19\text{-}10)$$

$$\cos \theta_T = \frac{27.05}{44.6} = 0.605$$

Therefore, $\theta_T = 53° \text{ leading} \qquad Ans.$

d Find the power drawn by the circuit.

$$W = E \times I \times \cos \theta = 650 \times 44.6 \times \cos 53° \qquad (18\text{-}3)$$

$$W = 650 \times 44.6 \times 0.605 = 17,540 \text{ W} \qquad Ans.$$

The total current of 44.6 A *leads* the total voltage of 650 V by 53°.

PROBLEMS

Find (*a*) the total current, (*b*) the impedance, (*c*) the phase angle, and (*d*) the power drawn by each circuit shown in Fig. 19-46.

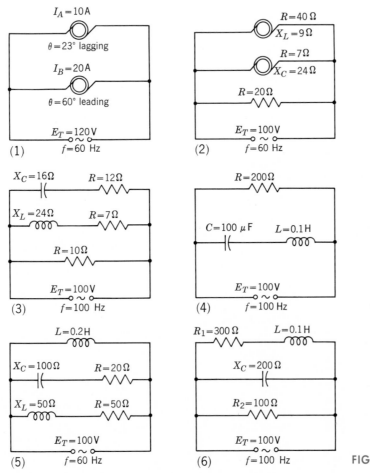

FIGURE 19-46

JOB 19-7 SERIES-PARALLEL AC CIRCUITS

EXAMPLE 19-19   Solve the circuit shown in Fig. 19-47 for (*a*) the equivalent series impedance, (*b*) the total current, (*c*) the phase angle, and (*d*) the power drawn by the circuit.

SOLUTION

1 The parallel branches *A, B,* and *C* are solved in the same way that we solved the branches in Example 19-18.

   a Find the reactance, series impedance, current, and phase angle for each branch. Since the voltage across the section from *D* to *E* is unknown, a voltage may be assumed.

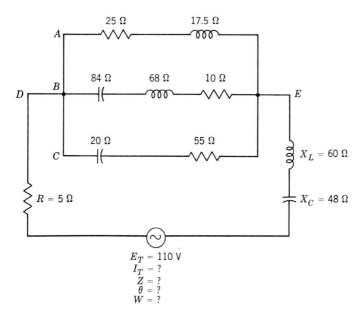

$E_T = 110\text{ V}$
$I_T = ?$
$Z = ?$
$\theta = ?$
$W = ?$

FIGURE 19-47

A series-parallel ac circuit.

b Draw the phasor diagram for the branch currents on the same voltage base.

c Resolve the current in each branch into its in-phase and reactive components.

d Draw all the components on the same voltage base. Find the total in-phase current I_{T_x} and the total reactive current I_{T_y}.

e Find the total current for the parallel branches by adding I_{T_x} and I_{T_y} vectorially.

f Find the parallel impedance.

g Find the phase angle for the parallel circuit.

2 The impedance found in step *f* above must now be resolved into its equivalent series resistance and reactance.

3 These are now combined with the other series resistances and reactances to get the total series impedance.

4 The phase angle, total current, and power are found as in any series circuit.

1 *a* Find the series impedance, current, and phase angle for each branch. Assume 100 V across *DE*.

For branch *A*:

$$Z = \sqrt{R^2 + X_L{}^2} = \sqrt{(25)^2 + (17.5)^2}$$

$$Z = \sqrt{625 + 306} = 30.5 \ \Omega$$

$$I_A = \frac{E}{Z} = \frac{100}{30.5} = 3.28 \text{ A}$$

$$\cos \theta = \frac{R}{Z} = \frac{25}{30.5} = 0.8197$$

$$\theta = 35° \text{ lagging.}$$

For branch B:

$$Z = \sqrt{R^2 + (X_C - X_L)^2} = \sqrt{(10)^2 + (84 - 68)^2}$$
$$= \sqrt{(10)^2 + (16)^2}$$
$$Z = \sqrt{100 + 256} = 18.9 \ \Omega$$

$$I_B = \frac{E}{Z} = \frac{100}{18.9} = 5.30 \ \text{A}$$

$$\cos \theta = \frac{R}{Z} = \frac{10}{18.9} = 0.5291$$

$$\theta = 58° \ \text{leading.}$$

For branch C:

$$Z = \sqrt{R^2 + X_C^2} = \sqrt{(55)^2 + (20)^2}$$
$$Z = \sqrt{3,025 + 400} = 58.5 \ \Omega$$

$$I_C = \frac{E}{Z} = \frac{100}{58.5} = 1.71 \ \text{A}$$

$$\cos \theta = \frac{R}{Z} = \frac{55}{58.5} = 0.9400$$

$$\theta = 20° \ \text{leading.}$$

b Draw the phasor diagram for the branch currents on the same voltage base as shown in Fig. 19-48*a*.

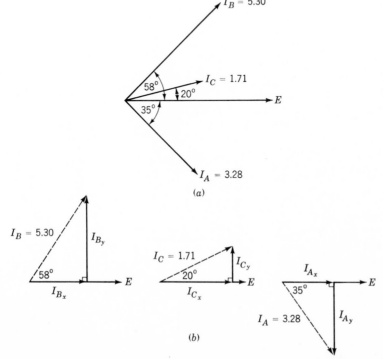

(a)

(b)

FIGURE 19-48

(a) Leading and lagging currents in a parallel circuit. (b) Resolution of each current into its in-phase and reactive components.

c Resolve the current in each branch into its components as shown in Fig. 19-48*b*. Calculate the components.

For branch *A*:

$$I_{A_x} = I_A \times \cos\theta = 3.28 \times \cos 35° = 3.28 \times 0.819 = 2.68 \text{ A}$$

$$I_{A_y} = I_A \times \sin\theta = 3.28 \times \sin 35° = 3.28 \times 0.574 = -1.88 \text{ A}$$

For branch *B*:

$$I_{B_x} = I_B \times \cos\theta = 5.30 \times \cos 58° = 5.30 \times 0.53 = 2.82 \text{ A}$$

$$I_{B_y} = I_B \times \sin\theta = 5.30 \times \sin 58° = 5.30 \times 0.848 = 4.49 \text{ A}$$

For branch *C*:

$$I_{C_x} = I_C \times \cos\theta = 1.71 \times \cos 20° = 1.71 \times 0.94 = 1.61 \text{ A}$$

$$I_{C_y} = I_C \times \sin\theta = 1.71 \times \sin 20° = 1.71 \times 0.342 = 0.59 \text{ A}$$

d Draw all the components on the same voltage base as shown in Fig. 19-49*a*. The total in-phase current I_{T_x} and the total reactive current I_{T_y} may now be found.

$$I_{T_x} = I_{A_x} + I_{B_x} + I_{C_x} = 2.68 + 2.82 + 1.61 = 7.11 \text{ A}$$

$$I_{T_y} = I_{B_y} + I_{C_y} - I_{A_y} = 4.49 + 0.59 - 1.88 = 3.20 \text{ A}$$

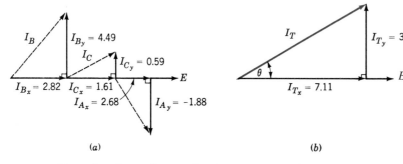

(a)   (b)

FIGURE 19-49
(a) The components of all the branch currents drawn on the same voltage base. (b) I_T represents the phasor sum of I_{T_x} and I_{T_y}.

e Draw the phasor diagram for the total current by adding I_{T_x} and I_{T_y} vectorially as shown in Fig. 19-49*b*. Notice that I_{T_y} is drawn *upward* because the total of all the *y* components is positive. Find I_T.

$$I_T{}^2 = (I_{T_x})^2 + (I_{T_y})^2$$

$$= (7.11)^2 + (3.20)^2$$

$$= 50.6 + 10.2$$

$$= 60.8$$

$$I_T = \sqrt{60.8} = 7.8 \text{ A} = I_{DE}$$

f Find the parallel impedance.

$$Z_{DE} = \frac{E_{DE}}{I_{DE}} = \frac{100}{7.8} = 12.8 \text{ }\Omega$$

g Find the phase angle for the parallel circuit between D and E.

$$\cos \theta = \frac{I_{T_x}}{I_T} = \frac{7.11}{7.8} = 0.9115$$

$$\theta = 24° \text{ leading.}$$

The total parallel impedance $= 12.8 \ \Omega$ at $24°$ leading.

2 The equivalent series impedance is made of the resistive and reactive components into which this parallel impedance must be resolved.

$$Z_x = R = Z \times \cos \theta$$

$$R = 12.8 \times \cos 24° = 12.8 \times 0.914$$

$$R = 11.7 \ \Omega \qquad Ans.$$

$$Z_y = X_C = Z \times \sin \theta \qquad (X_C \text{ because of the } leading \text{ current})$$

$$X_C = 12.8 \times \sin 24° = 12.8 \times 0.407$$

$$X_C = 5.26 \ \Omega \qquad Ans.$$

3 Find the total series impedance. The components of Z_{DE} are now combined with the other parts of the series circuit as shown in Fig. 19-50.

$$R_T = 5 + 11.7 = 16.7 \ \Omega$$

$$X_C = 5.26 + 48 = 53.26 \ \Omega$$

$$X_L = 60 \ \Omega$$

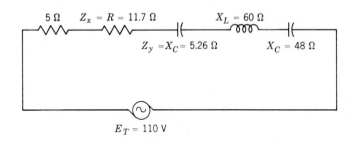

FIGURE 19-50
The components of Z_{DE} are parts of the equivalent series circuit.

$$Z = \sqrt{R^2 + (X_L - X_C)^2}$$

$$= \sqrt{(16.7)^2 + (60.0 - 53.26)^2}$$

$$= \sqrt{(16.7)^2 + (6.74)^2}$$

$$= \sqrt{279 + 45.5} = \sqrt{324.5}$$

$$Z = 18 \ \Omega \qquad Ans.$$

4 Find the total series current.

$$I_T = \frac{E_T}{Z} = \frac{110}{18} = 6.11 \text{ A} \qquad Ans.$$

5 Find the phase angle.

$$\cos \theta = \frac{R}{Z} = \frac{16.7}{18} = 0.926$$

$$\theta = 22° \text{ lagging.}$$

The total series current of 6.11 A lags the total voltage of 110 V by 22°.
  6 Find the power.

$$W = E \times I \times \cos \theta = 110 \times 6.11 \times \cos 22°$$

$$= 110 \times 6.11 \times 0.926$$

$$W = 622 \text{ W} \quad \textit{Ans.}$$

PROBLEMS

Solve each of the circuits shown in Fig. 19-51 for (*a*) the equivalent series impedance, (*b*) the total current, (*c*) the phase angle, and (*d*) the power drawn by the circuit.

JOB 19-8 PARALLEL RESONANCE

In a series circuit, it is possible to adjust the values of a coil and a capacitor so that their reactances will be equal for a definite frequency. The frequency at which the inductive and capacitive reactances are equal is the resonant frequency. Since the actions of the reactances are directly opposed to each other, the total reactance is zero and the impedance of the circuit becomes just the resistance of the circuit. Under these conditions, the current in the circuit will be a maximum.
  Now let us arrange the coil and capacitor in *parallel* as shown in Fig. 19-52.

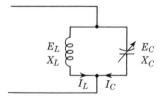

FIGURE 19-52
A parallel-resonant circuit.

At the resonant frequency,

$$E_L = E_C \qquad\qquad (4\text{-}1)$$

$$X_L = X_C \qquad\qquad (18\text{-}16)$$

By dividing Eq. (4-1) by Eq. (18-16),

$$\frac{E_L}{X_L} = \frac{E_C}{X_C}$$

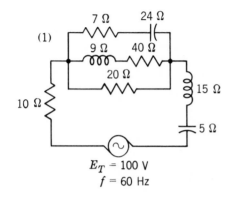

(1)

7 Ω 24 Ω
9 Ω 40 Ω
20 Ω
15 Ω
5 Ω
10 Ω

E_T = 100 V
f = 60 Hz

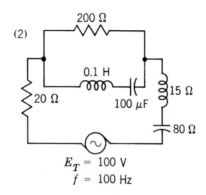

(2)

200 Ω
0.1 H
100 μF
15 Ω
20 Ω
80 Ω

E_T = 100 V
f = 100 Hz

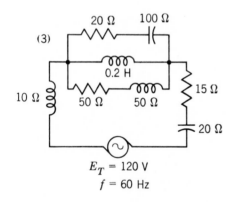

(3)

20 Ω 100 Ω
0.2 H
50 Ω 50 Ω
15 Ω
20 Ω
10 Ω

E_T = 120 V
f = 60 Hz

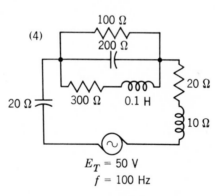

(4)

100 Ω
200 Ω
300 Ω 0.1 H
20 Ω
20 Ω
10 Ω

E_T = 50 V
f = 100 Hz

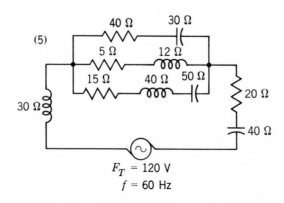

(5)

40 Ω 30 Ω
5 Ω 12 Ω
15 Ω 40 Ω 50 Ω
20 Ω
40 Ω
30 Ω

F_T = 120 V
f = 60 Hz

FIGURE 19-51

or
$$I_L = I_C \qquad \boxed{19\text{-}11}$$

Since the currents are exactly opposed to each other, the total current is equal to $I_L - I_C$ or practically zero. At the resonant frequency, then, since the total current is very nearly equal to zero, the impedance of the circuit to currents at that frequency will be very large. At any other frequency, since X_L is not equal to X_C, the currents will no longer be equal. The sum of the unequal currents may be quite large, which indicates a low impedance. To summarize, a parallel-resonant circuit will offer a very large impedance to currents at the resonant frequency and a low impedance to currents at all other frequencies.

Uses. Just as a series-resonant circuit is able to *accept* currents at the resonant frequency and reject all others, a parallel-resonant circuit is able to *reject* currents at the resonant frequency and accept all others. This makes it possible to reject or "trap" a wave of a definite frequency in antenna and filter circuits. It is also a convenient method for obtaining the high impedance required in the primary of coupling transformers.

Resonant frequency. The formula for the resonant frequency of a parallel circuit is the same as that for a series circuit.

$$f = \frac{159}{\sqrt{L \times C}} \qquad \boxed{18\text{-}18}$$

where f = frequency, kHz
$\quad L$ = inductance, μH
$\quad C$ = capacitance, μF

EXAMPLE 19-20   A 200-μH coil and a 50-pF capacitor are connected in parallel to form a "wave trap" in an antenna. What is the resonant frequency that the circuit will reject?

SOLUTION
Given: $L = 200 \ \mu H$ Find: $f = ?$
$\qquad C = 50 \text{ pF} = 50 \times 10^{-6} \ \mu F$

$$f = \frac{159}{\sqrt{L \times C}} \qquad (18\text{-}18)$$

$$= \frac{159}{\sqrt{200 \times 50 \times 10^{-6}}}$$

$$= \frac{159}{\sqrt{10^4 \times 10^{-6}}} = \frac{159}{\sqrt{10^{-2}}} = \frac{159}{10^{-1}}$$

$$f = 159 \times 10 = 1{,}590 \text{ kHz} \qquad Ans.$$

FINDING THE INDUCTANCE OR CAPACITANCE NEEDED TO PRODUCE RESONANCE

EXAMPLE 19-21   A 0.1-mH coil and a variable capacitor are connected in parallel to form the primary of an IF transformer as shown in Fig. 19-53. If the circuit is to be resonant to 456 kHz, what must be the value of the capacitor?

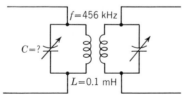

FIGURE 19-53

SOLUTION

1   Change 0.1 mH into 100 μH.
2   Find the required capacitance.

$$C = \frac{25{,}300}{f^2 \times L} \qquad\qquad (18\text{-}20)$$

$$= \frac{25{,}300}{(456)^2 \times 100}$$

$$C = \frac{25{,}300}{207{,}900 \times 100} = 0.0012 \ \mu F \qquad Ans.$$

PROBLEMS

1.   Find the resonant frequency of a wave trap using a 45-pF capacitor and a 20-μH inductance.
2.   Find the resonant frequency of a band-stop filter made of a 160-μH coil and a 40-pF capacitor in parallel.
3.   The inductance of a parallel-resonant circuit used as a wave trap in an antenna circuit is 100 μH. What must be the value of the parallel capacitance in order to reject an 800-kHz wave?
4.   The capacitor of a high-impedance primary of a transformer tuned to 460 kHz is 100 pF. What is the value of the inductance?
5.   The tank circuit of an oscillator contains a coil of 320 μH. What is the value of the capacitance at the resonant frequency of 1,000 kHz?
6.   The tank circuit of an impedance-coupled AF amplifier circuit uses an inductance of 10 H. Find the value of the capacitance necessary to produce resonance at (*a*) 500 Hz and (*b*) 1 kHz.
7.   What is the inductance of the coil in a 23.4-MHz trap of a video IF amplifier which uses a capacitor of 50 pF?
8.   The Zenith model 14A9C29 color TV uses an absorption-type wave trap in the second picture IF circuit. If the trap capacitance

is 56 pF and it is resonant to 19.75 MHz, what is the value of the inductance?

9. An IF coil in a superheterodyne receiver resonates at a frequency of 455 kHz. Find the inductance of the coil if the capacitor is valued at 50 pF.

10. A wave trap in the plate circuit of an IF stage is to resonate at 27.25 MHz. Find the capacity needed to produce resonance with a coil valued at 0.85 μH.

JOB 19-9 REVIEW OF PARALLEL AC CIRCUITS

In a purely resistive circuit:

$$E_T = E_1 = E_2 = E_3 \qquad \boxed{4\text{-}1}$$

$$E_T = I_T \times R_T \qquad \boxed{3\text{-}7}$$

$$I_T = I_1 + I_2 + I_3 \qquad \boxed{4\text{-}2}$$

$$W = E \times I \times \underline{\hspace{1.5cm}} \qquad \boxed{18\text{-}3} \qquad \cos\ \theta$$

The total current is __(in/out of)__ phase with the total voltage.   in

In a purely inductive circuit:

$$E_T = E_1 = E_2 = E_3 \qquad \boxed{4\text{-}1}$$

$$E_T = I_T \times \underline{\hspace{1.5cm}} \qquad \boxed{18\text{-}9} \qquad Z$$

$$I_T = I_1 + I_2 + I_3 \qquad \boxed{4\text{-}2}$$

$$W = E \times I \times \cos\theta \qquad \boxed{18\text{-}3}$$

The total current __(leads/lags)__ the total voltage by 90°.   lags

In a purely capacitive circuit:

$$E_T = E_1 = E_2 = E_3 \qquad \boxed{4\text{-}1}$$

$$E_T = I_T \times Z \qquad \boxed{18\text{-}9}$$

$$I_T = I_1 + I_2 + I_3 \qquad \boxed{4\text{-}2}$$

$$W = E \times I \times \cos\theta \qquad \boxed{18\text{-}3}$$

The total current __(leads/lags)__ the total voltage by 90°.   leads

In an ac parallel circuit of resistance and inductance:

$$I_T^2 = I_R^2 + \underline{\hspace{1.5cm}} \qquad \boxed{19\text{-}1} \qquad I_L^2$$

$$E_T = I_T \times Z \qquad \boxed{18\text{-}9}$$

$$\cos\theta = \frac{I_R}{?} \qquad \boxed{19\text{-}2}$$

$$I_T$$

$$W = E \times I \times \underline{\hspace{2cm}} \qquad \boxed{18\text{-}3}$$

cos θ
lags

The total current __(leads/lags)__ the total voltage by angle θ.

In an ac parallel circuit of resistance and capacitance:

$$I_T^2 = I_R^2 + \underline{\hspace{2cm}} \qquad \boxed{19\text{-}3}$$

I_C^2

$$E_T = I_T \times \underline{\hspace{2cm}} \qquad \boxed{18\text{-}9}$$

Z

$$\cos \theta = \frac{?}{I_T} \qquad \boxed{19\text{-}2} \quad \boxed{18\text{-}3}$$

I_R

$$W = E \times I \times \cos \theta$$

The total current __(leads/lags)__ the total voltage by angle θ.

leads

In an ac parallel circuit of resistance, inductance, and capacitance:

$$I_T^2 = I_R^2 + (I_L - ?)^2 \qquad \boxed{19\text{-}4}$$

I_C

$$E_T = I_T \times Z \qquad \boxed{18\text{-}9}$$

$$\cos \theta = \frac{I_R}{I_T} \qquad \boxed{19\text{-}2}$$

$$W = E \times I \times \cos \theta \qquad \boxed{18\text{-}3}$$

The total current will lead or lag the total voltage, depending on the values of I_L and I_C. If I_L is larger than I_C, the current will __(lead/lag)__ the voltage. If I_L is smaller than I_C, the current will __(lead/lag)__ the voltage. The angle of lead or lag is given by the angle θ.

lag
lead

PARALLEL-SERIES AC CIRCUITS

1   Find the reactance, the impedance, the current, and the phase angle for each branch of the parallel circuit.

2   Draw the phasor diagram for the branch currents on the same voltage base.

3   Resolve the curret in each branch into its components.

$$I_y = I \times \underline{\hspace{2cm}} \qquad \boxed{19\text{-}5}$$

sin θ

$$I_x = I \times \underline{\hspace{2cm}} \qquad \boxed{19\text{-}6}$$

cos θ

(y components of lagging currents are negative.)

4   Find the total in-phase and total reactive currents.

$$I_{T_x} = I_{A_x} + I_{B_x} \qquad \boxed{19\text{-}7}$$

$$I_{T_y} = I_{A_y} + \underline{\hspace{2cm}} \qquad \boxed{19\text{-}8}$$

I_{B_y}

5   Find the total current.

$$I_T^2 = (I_{T_x})^2 + \underline{\hspace{2cm}} \qquad \boxed{19\text{-}9}$$

$(I_{T_y})^2$

6   Find the impedance.

$$E_T = I_T \times Z \qquad \boxed{18\text{-}9}$$

7   Find the phase angle.

$$\cos \theta_T = \frac{?}{I_T}$$ $\boxed{\text{19-10}}$ I_{T_x}

8   Find the total power.

$$W = E \times I \times \cos \theta$$ $\boxed{\text{18-3}}$

SERIES-PARALLEL AC CIRCUITS

1   For the parallel branches: Repeat steps 1 through 7 for parallel-series circuits.

2   Resolve the parallel impedance found in step 6 above into its equivalent series resistance and reactance.

3   Combine these with the other resistances and reactances to get the total series impedance.

4   The total current, phase angle, and power are found as in any series circuit.

Parallel resonance. A parallel resonant circuit will offer a very large impedance to currents at the resonant frequency and a low impedance to currents at all other frequencies.

$$f = \frac{159}{\sqrt{L \times C}}$$ $\boxed{\text{18-18}}$

where L = inductance, measured in _____ μH
       C = capacitance, measured in _____ μF
       f = frequency, measured in _____   kHz

FINDING THE INDUCTANCE OR CAPACITANCE NEEDED TO PRODUCE A RESONANT CIRCUIT

$$L = \frac{25,300}{f^2 \times ?}$$ $\boxed{\text{18-19}}$ C

$$C = \frac{25,300}{f^2 \times L}$$ $\boxed{\text{18-20}}$

where L, C, and f are measured in the same units as called for in formula (18-18).

PROBLEMS

1. Two capacitors of 500 and 750 Ω reactance, respectively, are connected in parallel across a 25-V 25-Hz ac source. Find (a) the total current, (b) the impedance, and (c) the power drawn by the circuit.

2. A 0.01-H coil and a 5,000-Ω resistor are connected in parallel to form a filter circuit. Find the percent of the total current passing through the resistor for (a) a 1-kHz AF frequency and (b) a 1,000-kHz RF frequency. (c) Is this filter a high-pass or a low-pass filter?

3. A 200-Ω resistor and a 0.1-H coil are connected in parallel across a 100-V 1-kHz ac source. Find (a) the current in each branch, (b) the total current, (c) the impedance of the circuit, (d) the phase angle, and (e) the power drawn by the circuit.

4. A 500-Ω resistor in an emitter circuit similar to Fig. 19-19 is by-passed with a 5-μF capacitor. If a 1-kHz frequency causes a voltage drop of 10 V across the resistor, find (a) the current in each branch, (b) the total current, and (c) the impedance of the combination.

5. A 3,000-Ω resistor, a 1,200-Ω inductive reactance, and an 800-Ω capacitive reactance are connected in parallel across a 240-V line. Find (a) the total current, (b) the impedance, (c) the phase angle, and (d) the power drawn by the circuit.

6. A 0.5-μF capacitor, a 1-H coil, and a 2,000-Ω resistor are connected in parallel across a 220-V 60-Hz ac line. Find (a) the total current, (b) the impedance, (c) the phase angle, and (d) the power drawn by the circuit.

7. In a circuit similar to that used for Prob. 1 in Fig. 19-46, $I_A = 8$ A with $\theta = 30°$ lagging, $I_B = 15$ A with $\theta = 60°$ leading, and $E_T = 120$ V at 60 Hz. Find (a) the total current, (b) the impedance, (c) the phase angle, and (d) the power drawn by the circuit.

8. In a circuit similar to that used for Prob. 6 in Fig. 19-46, $R_1 = 100\Omega$, $L = 0.2$ H, $X_C = 500$ Ω, $R_2 = 200$ Ω, $E_T = 100$ V, and $f = 100$ Hz. Find (a) the total current, (b) the impedance, (c) the phase angle, and (d) the power drawn by the circuit.

9. A 0.001-μF capacitor and a coil are connected in parallel to form the primary of an IF transformer similar to that shown in Fig. 19-53. What must be the inductance of the coil in order for the circuit to be resonant to a frequency of 460 kHz?

10. The collector circuit of the 2SC563 mixer transistor in the Emer-

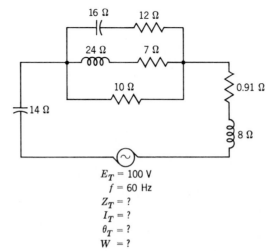

$E_T = 100$ V
$f = 60$ Hz
$Z_T = ?$
$I_T = ?$
$\theta_T = ?$
$W = ?$

FIGURE 19-54

son model 984 television receiver contains a 1-μH coil in parallel with a capacitance and resonant to 21.25 MHz. What is the capacitance?

11. Solve the circuit shown in Fig. 19-54 for (*a*) the equivalent series impedance, (*b*) the total current, (*c*) the phase angle, and (*d*) the power drawn by the circuit.

TEST—PARALLEL AC CIRCUITS

1. Two coils of 20 and 48 Ω reactance, respectively, are connected in parallel across a 120-V 60-Hz ac line. Find (*a*) the total current, (*b*) the impedance, and (*c*) the power drawn by the circuit.

2. A 0.1-μF capacitor, a 0.005-H coil, and a 1,000-Ω resistor are connected in parallel across a 100-V 10-kHz ac source. Find (*a*) the reactance of the coil and the capacitor, (*b*) the current drawn by each branch, (*c*) the total current, (*d*) the impedance, (*e*) the phase angle, and (*f*) the power drawn by the circuit.

3. In a circuit similar to that used for Prob. 1 in Fig. 19-46, $I_A = 6$ A with $\theta = 60°$ leading, $I_B = 10$ A with $\theta = 45°$ lagging, and $E_T = 120$ V at 60 Hz. Find (*a*) the total current, (*b*) the impedance, (*c*) the phase angle, and (*d*) the power drawn by the circuit.

4. The inductance of a high-impedance primary of a transformer is 1,000 μH. What is the value of capacitance needed to produce resonance to 460 kHz?

20

ALTERNATING-CURRENT POWER

JOB 20-1 POWER AND POWER FACTOR

The power in any electrical circuit is obtained by multiplying the voltage by the current flowing at that time. In a dc circuit, the unchanging voltage E is multiplied by the unchanging current I to give the power P. The formula for this was given in Job 6-1 as $P = E \times I$. In an ac circuit, the voltage and current are constantly changing. The power at any instant of time is obtained by multiplying the instantaneous voltage by the instantaneous current.

$$P_i = e \times i \qquad \boxed{20\text{-}1}$$

Power in a resistive circuit. In a purely resistive circuit, each instantaneous current occurs at the same time as the instantaneous voltage which produced it. Since the worth of all the instantaneous values is the effective value, the power in a resistive circuit is found by multiplying the effective voltage by the effective current.

$$P = E \times I \qquad (6\text{-}1)$$

Power in a reactive circuit. In an inductive circuit, the current will lag behind the voltage by some angle θ as shown in Fig. 20-1a. The power in this circuit will *not* be equal to the product of the voltage by the current, since they do not act at the same time. The actual power is equal to the voltage multiplied by *only that portion of the line current which is in phase with the voltage.* In Fig. 20-1b, OE represents the line voltage. OA represents the total line current as measured by an ammeter. This total line current may be resolved into its two component parts: OB, a component in phase with the voltage (the effective current), and BA, a component 90° out of phase with the voltage (the reactive current). By multiplying each of the current phasors of Fig. 20-1b by the line voltage, we can obtain a phasor diagram for the power in an *inductive* circuit

649

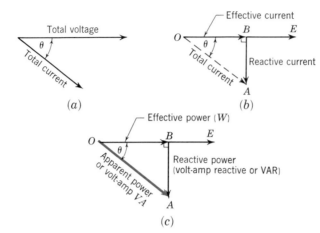

FIGURE 20-1

(a) Current lags behind the voltage in an inductive circuit. (b) Resolution of the total current into its effective and reactive components. (c) Phasor diagram of the power.

as shown in Fig. 20-1c. *OA* represents the *apparent power* as measured by a voltmeter and an ammeter.

FORMULA

$$VA = E \times I \qquad \boxed{20\text{-}2}$$

where VA = apparent power, VA

E = voltage, V

I = current, A

Take particular notice that this apparent power is measured in volt-amperes, *not* watts. *OB* represents the *effective power* as measured by a wattmeter *W*. *BA* represents the *reactive power* or var power.

The phasor diagram of Fig. 20-1c indicates that the apparent power is made of two component parts—the effective power and the reactive power. The apparent power may be likened to the power delivered to a flywheel. The *portion* of the apparent power which is delivered to the shaft to operate some device is similar to the effective power. The *portion* of the apparent power which is delivered by the flywheel *back* to the engine to keep it running is similar to the reactive power. The reactive power does no work itself. In an inductive electrical circuit it represents the power stored in the magnetic field (similar to the flywheel) and then returned to the line as the field collapses. This power merely moves back and forth between the coil and the line. In Fig. 20-1c,

$$\cos \theta = \frac{W}{VA} \qquad \boxed{20\text{-}3}$$

By cross multiplication,

$$W = VA \times \cos \theta \qquad \boxed{20\text{-}4}$$

Solving for *VA,*

$$VA = \frac{W}{\cos \theta}$$

$$\boxed{20\text{-}5}$$

where VA = apparent power, VA

W = effective power, W

θ = phase angle of the circuit, degrees

Power factor. The ratio of the effective power as read by a watt-meter W to the apparent power VA is called the *power factor* (PF).

FORMULA

$$PF = \frac{W}{VA}$$

$$\boxed{20\text{-}6}$$

By comparing formulas (20-3) and (20-6), we can see that the power factor is equal to the cosine of angle θ.

FORMULA

$$PF = \cos \theta$$

$$\boxed{20\text{-}7}$$

By substituting PF for $\cos \theta$ in formulas (20-3) to (20-5), we obtain

FORMULAS

$$PF = \frac{W}{VA}$$

$$\boxed{20\text{-}6}$$

$$W = VA \times PF$$

$$\boxed{20\text{-}8}$$

$$VA = \frac{W}{PF}$$

$$\boxed{20\text{-}9}$$

The power factor may be expressed as a decimal or as a percent. For example, a PF of 0.8 may be written as 80 percent. In this sense, the PF describes the *portion* of the voltampere input which is actually effective in operating the device. Thus, an 80 percent PF means that the device uses only 80 percent of the voltampere input in order to operate.

Power in a capacitive circuit. An identical set of relationships exists in a capacitive circuit, except that the apparent power VA will *lead* the effective power W by an angle θ.

EXAMPLE 20-1   Find the power factor of a washing-machine motor if it draws 5 A and 440 W from a 110-V 60-Hz line.

SOLUTION

Given: $I = 5$ A   Find: PF = ?

$E = 110$ V

$W = 440$ W

$f = 60$ Hz

$$PF = \frac{W}{VA} = \frac{440}{110 \times 5} = \frac{440}{550} = 0.8 = 80\% \qquad Ans. \quad (20\text{-}6)$$

EXAMPLE 20-2   A capacitor-type motor operating at a 70 percent PF draws 10 A from a 110-V ac line. Find (*a*) the apparent power and (*b*) the effective power.

SOLUTION

Given: PF = 70% = 0.70   Find: VA = ?

$I = 10$ A W = ?

$E = 110$ V

a. $VA = E \times I = 10 \times 110 = 1,100$ VA   *Ans.*   (20-2)

b. $W = VA \times PF = 1,100 \times 0.70 = 770$ W   *Ans.*   (20-8)

EXAMPLE 20-3   A capacitor-type motor draws 750 W at a power factor of 75 percent. Find the voltamperes of apparent power drawn by the motor.

SOLUTION

Given: $W = 750$ W   Find: VA = ?

PF = 75% = 0.75

$$VA = \frac{W}{PF} = \frac{750}{0.75} = 1,000 \text{ VA} \qquad Ans. \qquad (20\text{-}9)$$

EXAMPLE 20-4   An impedance coil of 3 Ω resistance and 4 Ω inductive reactance is connected across a 24-V 60-Hz ac source. Find (*a*) the PF, (*b*) the current drawn, and (*c*) the effective power consumed by the coil.

SOLUTION

Given: $R = 3$ Ω   Find: PF = ?

$X_L = 4$ Ω I = ?

$E = 24$ V W = ?

$f = 60$ Hz

a   Find the impedance.

$$Z = \sqrt{R^2 + X_L^2} = \sqrt{3^2 + 4^2} = \sqrt{9 + 16} = \sqrt{25} = 5 \text{ Ω}$$

Find the PF. Since

$$\cos \theta = \frac{R}{Z} \qquad (18\text{-}8)$$

and
$$\cos \theta = \text{PF} \qquad (20\text{-}7)$$

we obtain the

FORMULA

$$\text{PF} = \frac{R}{Z} \qquad \boxed{20\text{-}10}$$

where **PF** = power factor of the circuit
    R = resistance of circuit, Ω
    Z = impedance of circuit, Ω

Therefore,

$$\text{PF} = \frac{R}{Z} = \frac{3}{5} = 0.60 = 60\% \qquad Ans.$$

b Find the current drawn.

$$I = \frac{E}{Z} = \frac{24}{5} = 4.8 \text{ A} \qquad Ans. \qquad (18\text{-}9)$$

c Find the effective power. Since

$$W = VA \times \text{PF} \qquad (20\text{-}8)$$

and
$$VA = E \times I \qquad (20\text{-}2)$$

By substituting $E \times I$ for VA in formula (20-8), we obtain the

FORMULA

$$W = E \times I \times \text{PF} \qquad \boxed{20\text{-}11}$$

where **W** = effective power, W
    E = effective voltage, V
    I = effective current, A
  PF = power factor

Therefore,

$$W = E \times I \times \text{PF} \qquad (20\text{-}11)$$
$$W = 24 \times 4.8 \times 0.6$$
$$W = 69 \text{ W} \qquad Ans.$$

EXAMPLE 20-5 An induction motor operating at 80 percent PF draws 1,056 W from a 110-V ac line. Find the current.

SOLUTION

Given: PF = 80%   Find: $I = ?$

W = 1,056 W

E = 110 V

$$W = E \times I \times \text{PF} \qquad\qquad (20\text{-}11)$$

$$1,056 = 110 \times I \times 0.8$$

$$1,056 = 88 \times I$$

$$I = \frac{1,056}{88} = 12 \text{ A} \qquad Ans.$$

PROBLEMS

1. Find the power factor of a refrigerator motor if it draws 288 W and 3 A from a 120-V 60-Hz line.

2. Find the effective power used by a capacitor-type jigsaw motor operating at a power factor of 75 percent if it draws 4 A at 120 V.

3. The lights and motors in a shop draw 16 kW of power. The power factor of the entire load is 80 percent. Find the voltamperes of power delivered to the shop.

4. A capacitance of 5 Ω resistance and 12 Ω reactance is connected across a 117-V 60-Hz ac line. Find the power factor and the effective power.

5. A motor operating at 90 percent PF draws 270 W from a 120-V line. Find the current drawn.

6. Find the PF of a motor in an air-conditioning unit if it draws 500 W and 5 A from a 120-V line.

7. An industrial load draws 15 A from a 230-V line at a PF of 85 percent. Find the voltamperes of apparent power and the effective power taken from the line.

8. A 40-V emf at 1 kHz is impressed across a loudspeaker of 5,000 Ω resistance and 1.5 H inductance. Find (a) the impedance, (b) the PF, (c) the current drawn, and (d) the effective power drawn by the speaker.

9. A 10-hp motor operates at an efficiency of 80 percent and a PF of 90 percent. Find the voltamperes of apparent power delivered to the motor. *Hint:* Find the watt input to the motor by the efficiency formula (10-2).

10. An inductive load operating at a phase angle of 53° draws 1,200 W from a 120-V line. Find the current taken.

11. Find the current drawn from a 230-V line by a motor if it uses 6 kW of power at a PF of 0.65.

12. A 120-V 2-hp motor operates at an efficiency of 80 percent. Find the power input to the motor. If the current drawn by the motor is 20 A, find the PF.

JOB 20-2 TOTAL POWER DRAWN BY COMBINATIONS OF REACTIVE LOADS

As we learned in Job 6-2, the total power in a circuit may be found by adding the power taken by the individual parts. If the power drawn by one branch is not in phase with the power drawn by another branch, however, the addition of the power must be made by *phasor addition*. This will be done, as in Job 19-5, by resolving the power into its components and adding the components.

Resolving the apparent power into its components. In Fig. 20-1c,

$$\sin \theta = \frac{\text{var power}}{VA} \quad \text{and} \quad \cos \theta = \frac{W}{VA}$$

Cross-multiplying each equation yields the

FORMULAS

$$\text{var power} = VA \times \sin \theta \qquad \boxed{20\text{-}12}$$

$$W = VA \times \cos \theta \qquad \boxed{20\text{-}4}$$

or

$$W = VA \times \text{PF} \qquad \boxed{20\text{-}8}$$

Also, using the tangent function, we obtain the

FORMULA

$$\tan \theta = \frac{\text{var power}}{W} \qquad \boxed{20\text{-}13}$$

Applying the pythagorean theorem, we obtain the

FORMULA

$$(VA)^2 = W^2 + (\text{var } P)^2 \qquad \boxed{20\text{-}14}$$

Combinations of devices of different power factors

EXAMPLE 20-6   Find (*a*) the total effective power, (*b*) the total apparent power, (*c*) the total PF, and (*d*) the total current of the combination shown in Fig. 20-2.

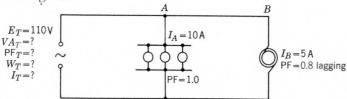

$$E_T = 110\text{V}$$
$$VA_T = ?$$
$$PF_T = ?$$
$$W_T = ?$$
$$I_T = ?$$

$I_A = 10\text{A}$

$\text{PF} = 1.0$

$I_B = 5\text{A}$
$\text{PF} = 0.8 \text{ lagging}$

FIGURE 20-2

SOLUTION

When the power in one branch is not in phase with the power in another branch, the apparent powers must be resolved into their components and the components added as shown below.

a   Find the total effective power.

1   Find the apparent power VA, the effective power W, the phase angle θ, and the var power (var P) for each load.

For branch A:

$$VA_A = I_A \times E_A = 110 \times 10 = 1{,}100 \text{ VA} \qquad (20\text{-}2)$$

$$W_A = VA_A \times PF_A = 1{,}100 \times 1 = 1{,}100 \text{ W} \qquad (20\text{-}8)$$

Since

$$PF_A = \cos\theta = 1.0, \ \theta = 0° \qquad (20\text{-}7)$$

$$\text{var } P_A = VA_A \times \sin\theta \qquad (20\text{-}12)$$

$$= 1{,}100 \times \sin 0°$$

$$= 1{,}100 \times 0$$

$$\text{var } P_A = 0 \text{ var}$$

For branch B:

$$VA_B = I_B \times E_B = 5 \times 110 = 550 \text{ VA} \qquad (20\text{-}2)$$

$$W_B = VA_B \times PF_B = 550 \times 0.8 = 440 \text{ W} \qquad (20\text{-}8)$$

Since

$$PF_B = \cos\theta = 0.8, \ \theta = 37° \ \textit{lagging} \qquad (20\text{-}7)$$

$$\text{var } P_B = VA_B \times \sin\theta \qquad (20\text{-}12)$$

$$= 550 \times \sin 37°$$

$$= 550 \times 0.6$$

$$\text{var } P_B = -330 \text{ var}$$

2   Draw the phasor diagram for the apparent powers on the same voltage base as shown in Fig. 20-3*a*.

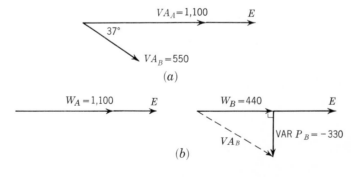

(a)

(b)

FIGURE 20-3

(a) VA_A and VA_B are not in phase, since they act at different power factors. (b) Resolution of each apparent power into its effective and reactive components.

3 Resolve the power in each branch into its components as shown in Fig. 20-3*b*.

4 Draw all the components on the same voltage base as shown in Fig. 20-4*a*. The total effective power W_T and the total reactive power var P_T may now be found by the

FORMULAS

$$W_T = W_A + W_B \qquad \boxed{20\text{-}15}$$

$$\text{var } P_T = \text{var } P_A + \text{var } P_B \qquad \boxed{20\text{-}16}$$

$$W_T = W_A + W_B = 1{,}100 + 440 = 1{,}540 \text{ W} \qquad (20\text{-}15)$$

$$\text{var } P_T = \text{var } P_A + \text{var } P_B = 0 + (-330) = -330 \text{ var } (20\text{-}16)$$

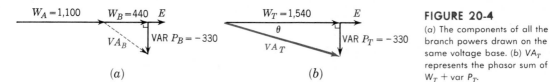

(a)   (b)

FIGURE 20-4

(a) The components of all the branch powers drawn on the same voltage base. (b) VA_T represents the phasor sum of W_T + var P_T.

b Find the total apparent power. Draw the phasor diagram for the total power by adding W_T and var P_T vectorially as shown in Fig. 20-4*b*. Notice that var P_T is drawn *downward* because var P_T is negative.

Applying the pythagorean theorem, we obtain the

FORMULAS

$$VA_T{}^2 = W_T{}^2 + \text{var } P_T{}^2 \qquad \boxed{20\text{-}17}$$

$$\text{PF}_T = \frac{W_T}{P_T} \qquad \boxed{20\text{-}18}$$

Find VA_T

$$VA_T{}^2 = W_T{}^2 + \text{var } P_T{}^2 \qquad (20\text{-}17)$$

$$= (1{,}540)^2 + (-330)^2$$

$$= 237 \times 10^4 + 11 \times 10^4$$

$$= 248 \times 10^4$$

$$VA_T = \sqrt{248 \times 10^4} = 1{,}575 \text{ VA} \qquad Ans.$$

c Find the total PF.

$$\text{PF}_T = \frac{W_T}{P_T} = \frac{1{,}540}{1{,}575} = 0.977 = 97.7\% \ lagging \qquad Ans. \quad (20\text{-}18)$$

d Find the total current.

$$VA_T = E_T \times I_T \qquad\qquad (20\text{-}2)$$

$$1{,}575 = I_T \times 110$$

$$I_T = \frac{1{,}575}{110} = 14.3 \text{ A} \qquad Ans.$$

Alternate solution. The phase angle and the apparent power may be found by applying the tangent formula to the right triangle shown in Fig. 20-4*b*. This solution is simpler, since it does not involve the labor of squaring numbers and finding the square root of the sum.

FORMULAS

$$\tan \theta_T = \frac{\text{var } P_T}{W_T} \qquad\qquad \boxed{20\text{-}19}$$

$$VA_T = \frac{W_T}{PF_T} \qquad\qquad \boxed{20\text{-}20}$$

a Find the phase angle in Fig. 20-4*b*.

$$\tan \theta_T = \frac{\text{var } P_T}{W_T} = \frac{330}{1{,}540} = 0.214; \text{ therefore } \theta = 12° \text{ (20-19)}$$

$$PF = \cos \theta = \cos 12° = 0.978 = 97.8\% \text{ lagging} \qquad Ans. \quad (20\text{-}7)$$

b Find the total apparent power.

$$VA_T = \frac{W_T}{PF_T} = \frac{1{,}540}{\cos 12°} = \frac{1{,}540}{0.978} = 1{,}574 \text{ VA} \qquad Ans. \, (20\text{-}20)$$

EXAMPLE 20-7 Find (*a*) the total effective power, (*b*) the total power factor, and (*c*) the total apparent power for the circuit shown in Fig. 20-5.

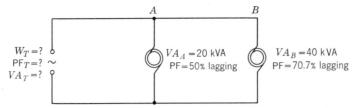

FIGURE 20-5

SOLUTION

a

1 Find the effective power and the var power for each load.

For load *A*:

$$PF = \cos \theta = 0.500; \quad \text{therefore } \theta = 60° \qquad\qquad (20\text{-}7)$$

$$W_A = VA_A \times PF_A = 20 \times 0.5 = 10 \text{ kW} \qquad\qquad (20\text{-}8)$$

$$\text{var } P_A = VA_A \times \sin \theta = 20 \times \sin 60° = 20 \times 0.866 = -17.32 \text{ kvar}$$

For load B:

$$\text{PF} = \cos \theta = 0.707; \quad \text{therefore } \theta = 45° \qquad (20\text{-}7)$$

$$W_B = VA_B \times \text{PF}_B = 40 \times 0.707 = 28.28 \text{ kW} \qquad (20\text{-}8)$$

$$\text{var } P_B = VA_B \times \sin \theta = 40 \times \sin 45° = 40 \times 0.707 = -28.28 \text{ kvar}$$

2 Draw the phasor diagram for the apparent powers on the same voltage base as shown in Fig. 20-6a.

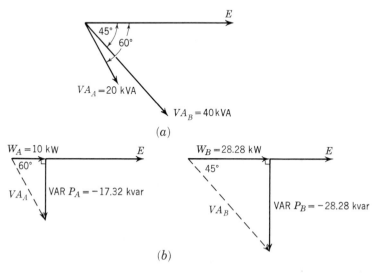

(a)

(b)

FIGURE 20-6

(a) VA_A and VA_B are not in phase, since they act at different power factors. (b) Resolution of each apparent power into its effective and reactive components.

3 Resolve the power in each branch into its components as shown in Fig. 20-6b.

4 Draw all the components on the same voltage base as shown in Fig. 20-7a. The total effective power W_T and the total reactive power var P_T may now be found.

$$W_T = W_A + W_B = 10 + 28.28 = 38.28 \text{ kW} \qquad Ans. \qquad (20\text{-}15)$$

$$\text{var } P_T = \text{var } P_A + \text{var } P_B = (-17.32) + (-28.28) = -45.6 \text{ kvar}$$

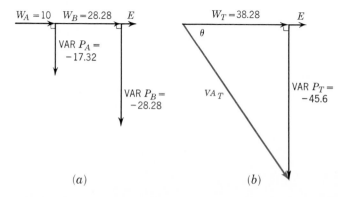

(a)

(b)

FIGURE 20-7

(a) The components of all the branch powers drawn on the same voltage base. (b) VA_T represents the phasor sum of $W_T +$ var P_T.

b Find the total power factor by adding W_T and var P_T vectorially as shown in Fig. 20-7b.

$$\tan \theta_T = \frac{\text{var } P_T}{W_T} = \frac{-45.6}{38.28} = -1.191; \quad \text{therefore } \theta = 50° \qquad (20\text{-}19)$$

$$\text{PF} = \cos \theta = \cos 50° = 0.643 = 64.3\% \ lagging \qquad Ans. \qquad (20\text{-}7)$$

c　Find the total apparent power.

$$VA_T = \frac{W_T}{\text{PF}_T} = \frac{38.28}{\cos 50°} = \frac{38.28}{0.643} = 59.5 \text{ kVA} \qquad Ans. (20\text{-}20)$$

EXAMPLE 20-8　An inductive load taking 10 A and 2,000 W from a 220-V line is in parallel with a motor taking 1,400 W at a PF of 50 percent lagging. Find (a) the total effective power, (b) the total PF, (c) the total apparent power, and (d) the total current drawn by the circuit.

SOLUTION
The diagram for the circuit is shown in Fig. 20-8.

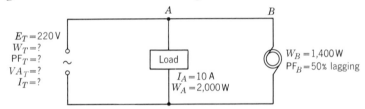

$E_T = 220 \text{ V}$
$W_T = ?$
$\text{PF}_T = ?$
$VA_T = ?$
$I_T = ?$

$I_A = 10 \text{ A}$
$W_A = 2,000 \text{ W}$

$W_B = 1,400 \text{ W}$
$\text{PF}_B = 50\% \text{ lagging}$

FIGURE 20-8

a

1　Find the apparent power, the effective power, the phase angle, and the var power for each load.

For load A:

$$VA_A = I_A \times E_A = 10 \times 220 = 2,200 \text{ VA} \qquad (20\text{-}2)$$

$$W_A = 2,000 \text{ W}$$

$$\cos \theta = \frac{W}{VA} = \frac{2,000}{2,200} = 0.909; \quad \text{therefore } \theta = 25° \ lagging \qquad (20\text{-}3)$$

$$\text{var } P_A = VA_A \times \sin \theta = 2,200 \times \sin 25° = 2,200 \times 0.423 = -931 \text{ var}$$

For load B:

$$W_B = 1,400 \text{ W}$$

$$VA_B = \frac{W}{\text{PF}} = \frac{1,400}{0.5} = 2,800 \text{ VA} \qquad (20\text{-}9)$$

$$\text{PF}_B = \cos \theta = 0.500; \quad \text{therefore } \theta = 60° \qquad (20\text{-}7)$$

$$\text{var } P_B = VA_B \times \sin \theta \qquad (20\text{-}12)$$

$$= 2,800 \times \sin 60°$$

$$= 2,800 \times 0.866$$

$$\text{var } P_B = -2,425 \text{ var}$$

2 Find the total effective and reactive power.

$$W_T = W_A + W_B = 2{,}000 + 1{,}400 = 3{,}400 \text{ W} \qquad Ans.$$

$$\text{var } P_T = \text{var } P_A + \text{var } P_B = (-931) + (-2{,}425) = -3{,}356 \text{ vars}$$

b Find the phase angle and the PF.

$$\tan \theta_T = \frac{\text{var } P_T}{W_T} = \frac{3{,}356}{3{,}400} = 0.987; \qquad \text{therefore } \theta = 45° \qquad (20\text{-}19)$$

$$PF = \cos \theta = \cos 45° = 0.707 = 70.7\% \text{ } lagging \qquad Ans. \quad (20\text{-}7)$$

c Find the total apparent power.

$$VA_T = \frac{W_T}{PF_T} = \frac{3{,}400}{0.707} = 4{,}809 \text{ VA} \qquad Ans. \qquad (20\text{-}20)$$

d Find the total current.

$$I_T = \frac{VA_T}{E_T} = \frac{4{,}809}{220} = 21.8 \text{ A} \qquad Ans. \qquad (20\text{-}2)$$

SUMMARY

Total power drawn by combinations of reactive loads

1 Find the apparent power for each load using any of the following formulas.

$$VA = E \times I \qquad (20\text{-}2)$$

or

$$VA = \frac{W}{PF} \qquad (20\text{-}9)$$

or

$$VA = \frac{W}{\cos \theta} \qquad (20\text{-}5)$$

2 Find the effective and reactive power for each load.

$$W = VA \times PF \qquad (20\text{-}8)$$

or

$$W = VA \times \cos \theta \qquad (20\text{-}4)$$

and

$$\text{var } P = VA \times \sin \theta \qquad (20\text{-}12)$$

Note: If the PF or the phase angle is not given, it may be found by either of the following formulas:

$$PF = \frac{W}{VA} \qquad (20\text{-}6)$$

$$\cos \theta = \frac{W}{VA} \qquad (20\text{-}3)$$

3 Find the total effective power.

$$W_T = W_A + W_B \qquad (20\text{-}15)$$

4   Find the total reactive power.

$$\text{var } P_T = \text{var } P_A + \text{var } P_B \qquad (20\text{-}16)$$

5   Find the phase angle θ.

$$\tan \theta_T = \frac{\text{var } P_T}{W_T} \qquad (20\text{-}19)$$

6   Find the total PF.

$$\text{PF} = \cos \theta \qquad (20\text{-}7)$$

7   Find the total apparent power.

$$VA_T = \frac{W_T}{\text{PF}_T} \qquad (20\text{-}20)$$

8   Find the total current drawn, using any of the following formulas.

$$VA_T = E_T \times I_T \qquad (20\text{-}2)$$

$$W_T = E_T \times I_T \times \cos \theta_T \qquad \boxed{20\text{-}21}$$

$$W_T = E_T \times I_T \times \text{PF}_T \qquad \boxed{20\text{-}22}$$

PROBLEMS

1. A refrigerator motor drawing 6 A at 80 percent PF leading is in parallel with a washing-machine motor drawing 8 A at 80 percent PF leading from a 110-V line. Find (a) the total effective power, (b) the total PF, (c) the total apparent power, and (d) the total current drawn.

2. Motor A draws 10 A and 800 W from a 110-V 60-Hz ac line. Motor B draws 6 A and 480 W from the same line in parallel. Find (a) the PF of each motor, (b) the total effective power, (c) the total PF, (d) the total apparent power, and (e) the total current drawn.

3. A purely resistive lamp load (PF = 1) drawing 8 A from a 110-V 60-Hz line is in parallel with an induction motor taking 10 A at 70 percent PF. Find (a) the total effective power, (b) the total PF, (c) the total apparent power, and (d) the total current drawn.

4. A lamp bank (PF = 1) drawing 1,200 W from a 110-V 60-Hz line is in parallel with an induction motor taking 8 A at a power factor of 90 percent. Find (a) the total effective power, (b) the total PF, (c) the total apparent power, and (d) the total current.

5. Find (a) the total effective power, (b) the total PF, and (c) the total apparent power for the circuit shown in Fig. 20-9.

6. A 2-kW lamp load is in parallel with a motor operating at a PF of 60 percent lagging and drawing 3 kW from a 110-V 60-Hz line. Find parts (a) to (d) indicated in Prob. 4.

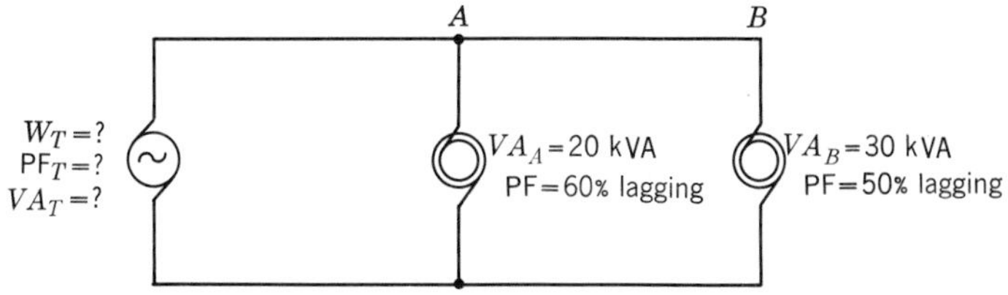

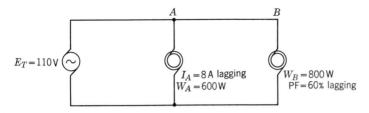

FIGURE 20-9

7. Repeat Prob. 4 for the following circuit: A motor drawing 5 kW at 80 percent PF lagging is in parallel with a second motor drawing 8 kW at 70 percent PF lagging from a 220-V line.

8. Repeat Prob. 4 for the circuit shown in Fig. 20-10.

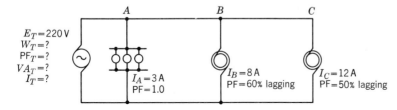

FIGURE 20-10

9. A 2-kW lamp load, a 70-kVA motor operating at a PF of 60 percent lagging and a 40-kVA motor operating at a PF of 70 percent lagging are connected in parallel. Find (*a*) the total effective power, (*b*) the total PF, and (*c*) the total apparent power.

10. Repeat Prob. 4 for the circuit shown in Fig. 20-11.

FIGURE 20-11

JOB 20-3 POWER DRAWN BY COMBINATIONS OF RESISTIVE, INDUCTIVE, AND CAPACITIVE LOADS

Power in capacitive loads. When the current is out of phase with the voltage, only that portion of the current which is in phase with the voltage is useful in producing usable power.

In an inductive circuit, the current lags behind the voltage, but in a capacitive circuit, the current leads the voltage. In such a circuit, the phasor diagrams will be very similar to those of an inductive circuit, except that now the current will be a *leading* current and a *leading* power. All the formulas developed for the inductive circuits in the last job will also apply to a capacitive circuit. The only difference is that the reactive power will *lead* in a capacitive circuit.

EXAMPLE 20-9   A lamp bank drawing 1 kW of power is in parallel with a synchronous motor drawing 2 kW at a leading PF of 80 percent from a 220-V 60-Hz ac line. Find (*a*) the total effective power, (*b*) the total PF, (*c*) the total apparent power, and (*d*) the total current drawn.

SOLUTION

The diagram of the circuit is shown in Fig. 20-12.

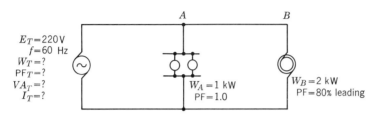

$E_T = 220$ V
$f = 60$ Hz
$W_T = ?$
$PF_T = ?$
$VA_T = ?$
$I_T = ?$

A B

$W_A = 1$ kW
$PF = 1.0$

$W_B = 2$ kW
$PF = 80\%$ leading

FIGURE 20-12

1   Find the apparent power, the effective power, the phase angle, and the var power for each load.

For load *A*:

$W_A = 1$ kW $= 1{,}000$ W   (given)

$$VA_A = \frac{W_A}{PF} = \frac{1{,}000}{1} = 1{,}000 \text{ VA} \qquad (20\text{-}9)$$

$$PF = \cos \theta = 1.0; \quad \text{therefore } \theta = 0° \qquad (20\text{-}7)$$

var $P_A = VA_A \times \sin \theta = 1{,}000 \times \sin 0° = 1{,}000 \times 0 = 0$ var   (20-12)

For load *B*:

$W_B = 2$ kW $= 2{,}000$ W   (given)

$$VA_B = \frac{W_A}{PF} = \frac{2{,}000}{0.8} = 2{,}500 \text{ VA} \qquad (20\text{-}9)$$

$$PF = \cos \theta = 0.8; \quad \text{therefore } \theta = 37° \text{ \textit{leading}} \qquad (20\text{-}7)$$

var $P_B = VA_B \times \sin \theta = 2{,}500 \times \sin 37° = 2{,}500 \times 0.6 = 1{,}500$ var

2   Find the total effective and reactive power.

$$W_T = W_A + W_B = 1{,}000 + 2{,}000 = 3{,}000 \text{ W}$$

$$\text{var } P_T = \text{var } P_A + \text{var } P_B = 0 + 1{,}500 = 1{,}500 \text{ var} \qquad (20\text{-}16)$$

b   Find the phase angle and the PF.

$$\tan \theta_T = \frac{\text{var } P_T}{W_T} = \frac{1{,}500}{3{,}000} = 0.5; \quad \text{therefore } \theta = 27° \quad (20\text{-}19)$$

$$PF_T = \cos \theta = \cos 27° = 89.1\% \text{ \textit{leading}} \qquad (20\text{-}7)$$

c   Find the total apparent power.

$$VA_T = \frac{W_T}{PF_T} = \frac{3,000}{0.891} = 3,367 \text{ VA} \qquad Ans. \qquad (20\text{-}20)$$

d   Find the total current drawn.

$$I_T = \frac{VA_T}{E_T} = \frac{3,367}{220} = 15.3 \text{ A} \qquad Ans. \qquad (20\text{-}2)$$

EXAMPLE 20-10   A 10-kVA induction motor operating at 85 percent lagging PF and a 5-kVA synchronous motor operating at 68.2 percent leading PF are connected in parallel across a 220-V 60-Hz ac line.
Find (*a*) the total effective power, (*b*) the total PF, (*c*) the total apparent
power, and (*d*) the total current drawn.

SOLUTION
The diagram for the circuit is shown in Fig. 20-13.

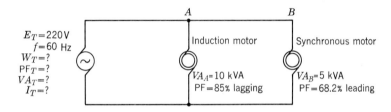

E_T=220V
f=60 Hz
W_T=?
PF_T=?
VA_T=?
I_T=?

A   Induction motor VA_A=10 kVA   PF=85% lagging

B   Synchronous motor VA_B=5 kVA   PF=68.2% leading

FIGURE 20-13

a

1   Find the apparent power, the effective power, the phase angle, and the
var power for each load.

For the induction motor *A*:

$$VA_A = 10 \text{ kVA} \qquad \text{(given)}$$

$$W_A = VA_A \times PF_A = 10 \times 0.85 = 8.5 \text{ kW} \qquad (20\text{-}8)$$

$$PF_A = \cos \theta = 0.85; \qquad \text{therefore } \theta = 32° \qquad (20\text{-}7)$$

$$\text{var } P_A = VA_A \times \sin \theta = 10 \times \sin 32° = 10 \times 0.53 \qquad (20\text{-}12)$$

$$\text{var } P_A = -5.3 \text{ kvar } \textit{lagging}$$

For the synchronous motor *B*:

$$VA_B = 5 \text{ kVA} \qquad \text{(given)}$$

$$W_B = VA_B \times PF_B = 5 \times 0.682 = 3.41 \text{ kW} \qquad (20\text{-}8)$$

$$PF_A = \cos \theta = 0.682; \qquad \text{therefore } \theta = 47° \qquad (20\text{-}7)$$

$$\text{var } P_B = VA_B \times \sin \theta = 5 \times \sin 47° = 5 \times 0.73 = 3.65 \text{ kvar } \textit{leading}$$

2   Draw the phasor diagram for the apparent powers on the same voltage
base as shown in Fig. 20-14*a*.

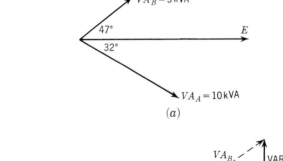

$VA_B = 5\,kVA$

$47°$ E

$32°$

$VA_A = 10\,kVA$

(a)

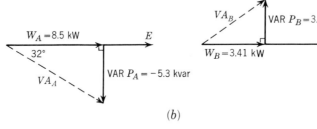

$W_A = 8.5\,kW$ E

$32°$

VA_A

VAR $P_A = -5.3\,kvar$

VA_B VAR $P_B = 3.65\,kvar$

E

$W_B = 3.41\,kW$

(b)

FIGURE 20-14

(a) Leading and lagging apparent powers. (b) Resolution of each power into its effective and reactive components.

3   Resolve the power in each branch into its components as shown in Fig. 20-14*b*.

4   Draw all the components on the same voltage base as shown in Fig. 20-15*a*. The total effective power W_T and the total reactive power var P_T may now be found.

$$W_T = W_A + W_B = 8.5 + 3.41 = 11.91\,kW \qquad Ans. \qquad (20\text{-}15)$$

var P_T = var P_A + var P_B = $(-5.3) + 3.65 = -1.65$ kvar *lagging*

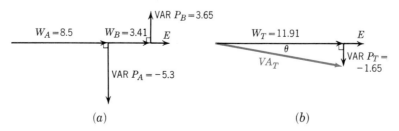

VAR $P_B = 3.65$

$W_A = 8.5$ $W_B = 3.41$ E

VAR $P_A = -5.3$

(a)

$W_T = 11.91$ E

θ

VA_T

VAR $P_T = -1.65$

(b)

FIGURE 20-15

(a) The components of all the branch powers drawn on the same voltage base. (b) VA_T represents the phasor sum of W_T + var P_T.

b   Find the total PF by adding W_T and var P_T vectorially as shown in Fig. 20-15*b*.

$$\tan \theta_T = \frac{\text{var } P_T}{W_T} = \frac{-1.65}{11.91} = 0.1385; \qquad \text{therefore } \theta = 8° \qquad (20\text{-}19)$$

$$PF = \cos \theta = \cos 8° = 0.99 = 99\% \ lagging \qquad (20\text{-}7)$$

c   Find the total apparent power.

$$VA_T = \frac{W_T}{PF_T} = \frac{11.91}{0.99} = 12.03\,kVA = 12{,}030\,VA \qquad Ans.$$

d Find the total current drawn.

$$I_T = \frac{VA_T}{E_T} = \frac{12,030}{220} = 54.7 \text{ A } \textit{lagging} \qquad Ans. \qquad (20\text{-}2)$$

EXAMPLE 20-11 A synchronous motor drawing 10 A at 60 percent leading PF from a 110-V line is in parallel with an induction motor drawing 1 kW at 80 percent PF lagging. Find (*a*) the total effective power, (*b*) the total PF, (*c*) the total apparent power, and (*d*) the total current drawn.

SOLUTION
The diagram for the circuit is shown in Fig. 20-16.

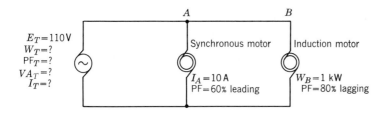

FIGURE 20-16

a
1   Find the apparent power, the effective power, the phase angle, and the var power for each load.

For the synchronous motor *A*:

$$VA_A = I_A \times E_A = 10 \times 110 = 1,100 \text{ VA} \qquad (20\text{-}2)$$

$$W_A = VA_A \times PF_A = 1,100 \times 0.6 = 660 \text{ W} \qquad (20\text{-}8)$$

$$PF_A = \cos\theta = 0.600; \quad \text{therefore } \theta = 53° \qquad (20\text{-}7)$$

$$\text{var } P_A = VA_A \times \sin\theta = 1,100 \times \sin 53° = 1,100 \times 0.8 \qquad (20\text{-}12)$$

$$\text{var } P_A = 880 \text{ var } \textit{leading}$$

For the induction motor *B*:

$$W_B = 1 \text{ kW} = 1,000 \text{ W} \qquad \text{(given)}$$

$$VA_B = \frac{W_B}{PF_B} = \frac{1,000}{0.8} = 1,250 \text{ VA} \qquad (20\text{-}9)$$

$$PF_B = \cos\theta = 0.800; \quad \text{therefore } \theta = 37° \qquad (20\text{-}7)$$

$$\text{var } P_B = VA_B \times \sin\theta = 1,250 \times \sin 37° = 1,250 \times 0.6 \quad (20\text{-}12)$$

$$\text{var } P_B = -750 \text{ var } \textit{lagging}$$

2   Find the total effective and reactive power.

$$W_T = W_A + W_B = 660 + 1,000 = 1,660 \text{ W} \qquad Ans.$$

$$\text{var } P_T = \text{var } P_A + \text{var } P_B = (+880) + (-750) = 130 \text{ var } \textit{leading}$$

b Find the phase angle and the PF.

$$\tan \theta_T = \frac{\text{var } P_T}{W_T} = \frac{130}{1,660} = 0.078; \qquad \text{therefore } \theta = 4° \qquad (20\text{-}19)$$

$$PF_T = \cos \theta = \cos 4° = 0.998 = 99.8\% \; \textit{leading} \qquad \textit{Ans.}$$

c Find the total apparent power.

$$VA_T = \frac{W_T}{PF_T} = \frac{1,660}{0.998} = 1,663 \text{ VA} \qquad \textit{Ans.} \qquad (20\text{-}20)$$

d Find the total current drawn.

$$I_T = \frac{VA_T}{E_T} = \frac{1,663}{110} = 15.1 \text{ A } \textit{leading} \qquad \textit{Ans.} \qquad (20\text{-}2)$$

PROBLEMS

1. An induction motor drawing 400 VA at 80 percent lagging PF is in parallel with a synchronous motor drawing 700 VA at 90 percent leading PF. Find (*a*) the total effective power, (*b*) the total PF, and (*c*) the total apparent power.

2. Repeat Prob. 1 for a circuit containing an induction motor that draws 100 kVA at a PF of 85 percent in parallel with a capacitive load that draws 80 kVA at a PF of 70 percent.

3. A capacitive load drawing 20 A at 70 percent PF from a 120-V 60-Hz line is in parallel with an induction motor drawing 4 kW at 70 percent PF. Find (*a*) the total effective power, (*b*) the total PF, (*c*) the total apparent power, and (*d*) the total current drawn.

4. Repeat Prob. 3 for a circuit containing a 60 percent PF induction motor drawing 1 kW in parallel with a synchronous motor rated at 120 V, 15 A, and 70 percent PF.

5. Find the total PF of a parallel combination of a 5-kW lamp load, a 10-kW inductive load (PF = 80 percent), and an 8-kW capacitive load (PF = 90 percent).

6. Find (*a*) the total effective power, (*b*) the total PF, (*c*) the total apparent power, and (*d*) the total current drawn by the circuit shown in Fig. 20-17.

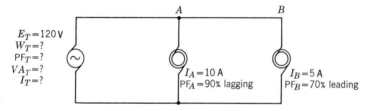

$E_T = 120 \text{ V}$
$W_T = ?$
$PF_T = ?$
$VA_T = ?$
$I_T = ?$

$I_A = 10 \text{ A}$
$PF_A = 90\% \text{ lagging}$

$I_B = 5 \text{ A}$
$PF_B = 70\% \text{ leading}$

FIGURE 20-17

7. Repeat Prob. 6 for the circuit shown in Fig. 20-18.

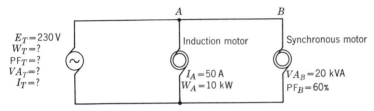

FIGURE 20-18

8. An induction motor draws 20 A at a PF of 80 percent from a 120-V line. What is the total PF of the circuit if (*a*) a lamp load drawing 15 A is connected in parallel and (*b*) a capacitive load drawing 5 A at a PF of 60 percent leading is connected in parallel?

9. Repeat Prob. 6 for a circuit containing an induction motor taking 4 A at 80 percent PF lagging, a synchronous motor taking 8 A at 50 percent PF leading, and a lamp load taking 6 A at 100 percent PF, all connected in parallel across a 120-V line.

10. Repeat Prob. 6 for a circuit containing a 100-W inductive load at a PF of 80 percent, a 600-W capacitive load at a PF of 60 percent, and an induction motor drawing 1 kW at a PF of 90 percent, all connected in parallel across a 120-V line.

JOB 20-4 POWER-FACTOR CORRECTION

Consider the three circuits shown in Fig. 20-19. Each circuit draws the same effective power, but at decreasing PFs.

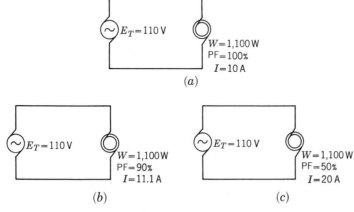

(*a*)

(*b*) (*c*)

FIGURE 20-19
In order to produce a constant effective power, the current must increase as the power factor decreases.

For the circuit of Fig. 20-19*a*:

$$W = E \times I \times \text{PF} \qquad (20\text{-}11)$$

$$1{,}100 = 110 \times I \times 1$$

$$I = \frac{1{,}100}{110} = 10 \text{ A}$$

For the circuit of Fig. 20-19*b*:

$$W = E \times I \times PF \qquad (20\text{-}11)$$

$$1{,}100 = 110 \times I \times 0.9$$

$$1{,}100 = 99 \times I$$

$$I = \frac{1{,}100}{99} = 11.1 \text{ A}$$

For the circuit of Fig. 20-19*c*:

$$W = E \times I \times PF \qquad (20\text{-}11)$$

$$1{,}100 = 110 \times I \times 0.5$$

$$1{,}100 = 55 \times I$$

$$I = \frac{1{,}100}{55} = 20 \text{ A}$$

By an investigation of the amount of current drawn in each of the circuits, we can see that as the PF decreases, more and more current must be supplied in order to produce the same effective power. Now, regardless of the current that is drawn to provide this 1,100 W of effective power, the consumer pays for only 1,100 W. Therefore, if the power company is forced to send 20 instead of 10 A to provide 1,100 W of power, it must provide heavier wires to carry the larger current. This is expensive. In addition, the larger the current, the greater the power lost in the transmission lines. For these reasons, the power company demands an extra premium payment if the PF falls below a certain value for a particular installation.

A low PF is generally due to the large consumption of power by underloaded induction motors which take a lagging current. In order to correct this low PF and raise it to the required value, synchronous motors, or capacitors which take a *leading* current, are placed in parallel with the inductive load. When synchronous motors are used, the required correction is accomplished by varying the PF of the synchronous motor by adjusting the excitation of its field.

EXAMPLE 20-12   An induction motor takes 15-kVA at 220 V and 80 percent lagging PF. What must be the PF of a 10-kVA synchronous motor connected in parallel in order to raise the total PF to 100 percent, or unity?

SOLUTION

Given: $VA = 15$ kVA ⎫

     $PF = 80\%$ *lagging* ⎬ induction motor

     $E = 220$ V ⎭

     $VA = 10$ kVA synchronous motor

Find: To get a PF $= 1$,

     PF of synchro-

     nous motor $= ?$

1   Find the var P of the induction motor.

Since

$$PF = \cos \theta = 0.8, \quad \theta = 37° \qquad (20\text{-}7)$$

$$\text{var } P = VA \times \sin \theta \qquad (20\text{-}12)$$

$$\text{var } P = 15 \times \sin 37° = 15 \times 0.6 = -9 \text{ kvar } \textit{lagging}$$

The phasor diagram for the induction motor is shown in Fig. 20-20a.

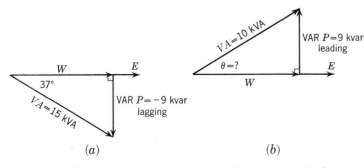

FIGURE 20-20
(a) Phasor diagram for the induction motor. (b) Phasor diagram for the synchronous motor.

2   To adjust the PF to unity means that $\cos \theta = 1.0$. At unity PF, if $\cos \theta = 1.0$, θ will equal 0°. When the phase angle is 0°,

$$\text{var } P = VA \times \sin \theta \qquad (20\text{-}12)$$

$$\text{var } P = VA \times \sin 0°$$

$$\text{var } P = VA \times 0 = 0 \text{ var}$$

Thus, to adjust a circuit to unity PF, all that is required is to make the total reactive power equal to 0 var. Since we already have 9 kvar *lagging* in the circuit, we must bring this down to zero by adding 9 kvar *leading*. This *leading* reactive power must come from the synchronous motor. The phasor diagram for the synchronous motor must be as shown in Fig. 20-20b. We can find the phase angle for the synchronous motor from this diagram.

3   $$\sin \theta = \frac{\text{var } P}{VA}$$

FORMULA

$$\sin \theta = \frac{\text{var } P \text{ of the induction motor}}{VA \text{ of the synchronous motor}} \qquad \boxed{20\text{-}23}$$

$$\sin \theta = \frac{9}{10} = 0.9000$$

$$\theta = 64°$$

4   Find the PF of the synchronous motor.

$$PF = \cos \theta = \cos 64° \qquad (20\text{-}7)$$

$$= 0.438$$

$$PF = 43.8\% \qquad \textit{Ans.}$$

EXAMPLE 20-13   A 220-V 50-A induction motor draws 10 kW of power. An 8-kVA synchronous motor is placed in parallel with it in order to adjust the PF to unity. What must be the PF of the synchronous motor?

SOLUTION

Given: $E = 220$ V $\left.\right\}$ induction motor
         $I = 50$ A
         $W = 10$ kW
         $VA = 8$ kVA   synchronous motor

Find: To get a PF $= 1.0$,
      PF of synchronous
      motor $= ?$

1   Find the var P of the induction motor.

$$VA = I \times E = 50 \times 220 = 11,000 \text{ VA} = 11 \text{ kVA}$$

Since

$$\cos \theta = \frac{W}{VA} \qquad (20\text{-}3)$$

$$\cos \theta = \frac{10}{11} = 0.909$$

$$\theta = 25°$$

$$\text{var } P = VA \times \sin \theta = 11 \times \sin 25° \qquad (20\text{-}12)$$

$$\text{var } P = 11 \times 0.423 = -4.65 \text{ kvar } \textit{lagging}$$

2   Draw the phasor diagram for the induction motor as shown in Fig. 20-21a. To adjust the PF of the circuit to unity, the phasor diagram for the synchronous motor must be a *leading* power as shown in Fig. 20-21b.

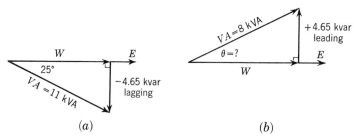

(a)   (b)

FIGURE 20-21
(a) Phasor diagram for the induction motor. (b) Phasor diagram for the synchronous motor.

3   Find the phase angle for the synchronous motor.

$$\sin \theta = \frac{\text{var } P}{VA} = \frac{4.65}{8} = 0.581$$

$$\theta = 36°$$

4   Find the PF of the synchronous motor.

$$PF = \cos \theta = \cos 36° = 0.809 = 80.9\% \qquad \textit{Ans.} \qquad (20\text{-}7)$$

Note: If only the effective power W of the synchronous motor is given, find angle θ for the synchronous motor by using the

FORMULA

$$\tan \theta = \frac{\text{lagging var } P}{W \text{ of the synchronous motor}} \qquad \boxed{20\text{-}24}$$

Then $$PF = \cos \theta \qquad (20\text{-}7)$$

EXAMPLE 20-14   An induction motor takes 6.4 kW at 80 percent PF from a 220-V 60-Hz line. Find (*a*) the apparent power, (*b*) the lagging PF, and (*c*) the capacity of a capacitor connected across the motor terminals in order to raise the PF to unity.

SOLUTION
Given: $W = 6.4$ kW   Find: $VA = ?$
   $PF = 80\%$ *lagging* $PF = ?$
   $E = 220$ V $C = ?$ to make $PF_T = 1.0$
   $f = 60$ Hz

a   Find the apparent power of the induction motor.

$$VA = \frac{W}{PF} = \frac{6.4}{0.8} = 8 \text{ kVA} \qquad (20\text{-}9)$$

b $$PF = \cos \theta = 0.800 \qquad (20\text{-}7)$$

$$\theta = 37°$$

c

1   Find the var P of the induction motor.

$$\text{var } P = VA \times \sin \theta = 8 \times \sin 37° \qquad (20\text{-}12)$$

$$\text{var } P = 8 \times 0.6 = -4.8 \text{ kvar } \textit{lagging}$$

2   In a "pure" capacitor, the current leads the voltage by 90°. Therefore, the $PF = \cos 90° = 0$. The var P will equal

$$\text{var } P = VA \times \sin \theta \qquad (20\text{-}12)$$

$$\text{var } P = VA \times \sin 90°$$

$$\text{var } P = VA \times 1$$

or $$\text{var } P = VA$$

Thus, to balance any lagging var P such as the 4.8 kvar in this problem, it is necessary only to insert a capacitor taking 4.8 kVA of apparent power, since *all* the apparent power in a pure capacitor acts as a *leading* var P in direct opposition to the lagging var P already in the circuit.

3   To find the capacity of this capacitor:

Find the current drawn by the capacitor at the rated voltage. Since 4.8 kVA = 4,800 VA,

$$VA = I \times E \qquad (20\text{-}2)$$

$$4{,}800 = I \times 220$$

$$I = \frac{4{,}800}{220} = 21.8 \text{ A}$$

Find the reactance of the capacitor.

$$E_C = I_C \times X_C \qquad (17\text{-}7)$$

$$220 = 21.8 \times X_C$$

$$X_C = \frac{220}{21.8} = 10.1 \ \Omega$$

Find the capacitance at 60 Hz to produce this reactance of 10.1 Ω.

$$X_C = \frac{159{,}000}{f \times C} \qquad (17\text{-}6)$$

$$10.1 = \frac{159{,}000}{60 \times C}$$

$$60 \times 10.1 \times C = 159{,}000$$

$$606 \times C = 159{,}000$$

$$C = \frac{159{,}000}{606} = 262 \ \mu\text{F} \qquad Ans.$$

EXAMPLE 20-15 When operating at full load, an induction motor draws 800 W and 4 A from a 220-V 60-Hz line. Find (a) the PF of the motor, (b) the lagging reactive power, (c) the apparent power drawn by a capacitor in order to raise the PF to unity, (d) the current drawn by this capacitor, (e) the reactance of the capacitor, and (f) the capacitance of this capacitor.

SOLUTION

Given: $W = 800$ W   Find: PF = ?
       $I = 4$ A   var P = ?
       $E = 220$ V   VA of capacitor = ?
       $f = 60$ Hz I_C = ?
                              X_C = ?
                              C = ?

a   Find the PF of the motor.

1                 $VA = E \times I = 220 \times 4 = 880 \text{ VA}$ (20-2)

2             $\cos \theta = \dfrac{W}{VA} = \dfrac{800}{880} = 0.909$ Ans.   (20-3)

$$\theta = 25°$$

b   Find the lagging reactive power.

$$\text{var } P = VA \times \sin \theta = 880 \times \sin 25° \qquad (20\text{-}12)$$

$$\text{var } P = 880 \times 0.423 = -372 \text{ var } \textit{lagging} \qquad \textit{Ans.}$$

c In order to raise the PF to unity, the capacitor must provide 372 var of reactive power leading. Since the apparent power in a capacitor is equal to the var P, 372 VA of capacitor power will exactly balance the lagging var P.

d Find the current drawn by this capacitor.

$$VA = I \times E \qquad\qquad (20\text{-}2)$$

$$372 = I \times 220$$

$$I = \frac{372}{220} = 1.69 \text{ A} \qquad \textit{Ans.}$$

e Find the reactance of the capacitor.

$$E_C = I_C \times X_C \qquad\qquad (17\text{-}7)$$

$$220 = 1.69 \times X_C$$

$$X_C = \frac{220}{1.69} = 130 \text{ }\Omega \qquad \textit{Ans.}$$

f Find the capacitance of the capacitor.

$$X_C = \frac{159,000}{f \times C} \qquad\qquad (17\text{-}6)$$

$$131.2 = \frac{159,000}{60 \times C}$$

$$131.2 \times 60 \times C = 159,000$$

$$C = \frac{159,000}{7872} = 20.2 \text{ }\mu\text{F} \qquad \textit{Ans.}$$

PROBLEMS

1. A 440-V line delivers 15-kVA to a load at 75 percent PF lagging. To what PF should a 10-kVA synchronous motor be adjusted in order to raise the PF to unity when connected in parallel?

2. A 220-V line delivers 10 kVA to a load at 80 percent PF lagging. What must be the PF of an 8-kW synchronous motor in parallel in order to raise the PF to unity?

3. A 220-V 20-A induction motor draws 3 kW of power. A 4-kVA synchronous motor is placed in parallel to adjust the PF to unity. What must be the PF of the synchronous motor?

4. A bank of motors draws 20 kW at 75 percent PF lagging from a 440-V 60-Hz line. What must be the capacity of a static capacitor connected across the motor terminals if it is to raise the total PF to 1.0?

5. A motor draws 1,500 W and 7.5 A from a 220-V 60-Hz line. What must be the capacity of a capacitor in parallel which will raise the total PF to unity?

6. A 4-hp motor operates at an efficiency of 85 percent and a PF of 80 percent lagging when connected across a 120-V 60-Hz line. Find the capacity of the capacitor needed to raise the total PF to 100 percent. *Hint:* Find the kilowatt input to the motor and proceed as before.

7. An inductive load draws 5 kW at 60 percent PF from a 220-V 60-Hz line. Find the kilovoltampere rating of the capacitor needed to raise the total PF to 100 percent.

8. *a.* A 30-kW motor operates at 80 percent PF lagging. In parallel with it is a 50-kW motor which operates at 90 percent PF lagging. Find (1) the total effective power, (2) the total PF, and (3) the total apparent power.

   b. Find the PF adjustment which must be made on a 20-kW synchronous motor in parallel with the motors in (*a*) in order to raise the PF of the circuit to unity.

JOB 20-5   REVIEW OF AC POWER

The apparent power VA is the product of the voltage and the current used by a circuit as measured by ac meters.

The effective power W is the actual power used by the circuit as measured by a wattmeter.

The power factor (PF) of a circuit is the ratio of the effective power to the apparent power. It may be expressed as a decimal or as a percent. The PF is also equal to the cosine of the phase angle of the circuit.

$$PF = \cos \theta \qquad \boxed{20\text{-}7}$$

The relations among VA, W, and PF are given by

$$PF = \frac{W}{VA} \qquad \boxed{20\text{-}6} \qquad \text{or} \qquad \cos \theta = \frac{W}{VA} \qquad \boxed{20\text{-}3}$$

$$W = VA \times PF \qquad \boxed{20\text{-}8} \qquad \text{or} \qquad W = VA \times \cos \theta \qquad \boxed{20\text{-}4}$$

$$VA = \frac{W}{PF} \qquad \boxed{20\text{-}9} \qquad \text{or} \qquad VA = \frac{W}{\cos \theta} \qquad \boxed{20\text{-}5}$$

The apparent power may be resolved into its components—the effective power W and the reactive power *var*—by the following formulas:

$$W = VA \times \cos \theta \qquad \boxed{20\text{-}4}$$

$$var \ P = VA \times \sin \theta \qquad \boxed{20\text{-}12}$$

The procedure for solving problems involving resistive, inductive, and capacitive loads is as follows:

1 For each load, find

  a The apparent power, using the formula

$$VA = E \times I$$ 20-2

  or $$VA = \frac{W}{PF}$$ 20-9

  or $$VA = \frac{W}{\cos \theta}$$ 20-5

  b The effective power, using the formula

$$W = VA \times PF$$ 20-8

  or $$W = VA \times \cos \theta$$ 20-4

  c The phase angle, using the formula

$$\cos \theta = \frac{W}{VA}$$ 20-3

  or $$\cos \theta = PF$$ 20-7

  d The var power.

$$var\ P = VA \times \sin \theta$$ 20-12

2 Find the total effective power.

$$W_T = W_A + W_B$$ 20-15

3 Find the total reactive power.

$$var\ P_T = var\ P_A + var\ P_B$$ 20-16

4 Find the phase angle for the entire circuit by adding W_T and var P_T vectorially. In the triangle thus formed,

$$\tan \theta_T = \frac{var\ P_T}{W_T}$$ 20-19

5 Find the total pf.

$$PF_T = \cos \theta_T$$ 20-7

6 Find the total apparent power.

$$VA_T = \frac{W_T}{PF_T}$$ 20-20

7 Find the total current drawn, using the formula

$$VA_T = I_T \times E_T$$ 20-2

  or $$W_T = E_T \times I_T \times \cos \theta_T$$ 20-21

  or $$W_T = E_T \times I_T \times PF_T$$ 20-22

POWER-FACTOR CORRECTION

  1 By synchronous motors:

a Find the var *P* of the induction motor given.

b For correction to unity PF, the leading var *P* of the synchronous motor must equal the lagging var *P* of the induction motor. Therefore, for the synchronous motor,

$$\sin \theta = \frac{\text{var } P \text{ of the induction motor}}{VA \text{ of the synchronous motor}} \qquad \boxed{20\text{-}23}$$

or

$$\tan \theta = \frac{\text{lagging var } P}{W \text{ of the synchronous motor}} \qquad \boxed{20\text{-}24}$$

from either of which the value of angle θ may be obtained.

c The PF of the synchronous motor is

$$PF = \cos \theta \qquad \boxed{20\text{-}7}$$

2 By static capacitors:

a Find the var *P* of the induction motor given.

b Set this var *P* equal to the apparent power *VA* drawn by the capacitor, since the apparent power of a capacitor is equal to its var *P*.

c Solve for *I* in the formula

$$VA = I \times E \qquad \boxed{20\text{-}2}$$

d Find the reactance of the capacitor.

$$E_C = I_C \times X_C \qquad \boxed{17\text{-}7}$$

e Find the capacitance at the given frequency.

$$X_C = \frac{159{,}000}{f \times C} \qquad \boxed{17\text{-}6}$$

PROBLEMS

1. A coil of 7 Ω resistance and 24 Ω reactance is connected across a 120-V 60-Hz line. Find the PF and the current drawn.

2. A 2-hp motor operates at a PF of 80 percent and an efficiency of 90 percent. Find (*a*) the watt input to the motor and (*b*) the apparent power delivered to the motor.

3. A motor drawing 10 A at 90 percent PF lagging is in parallel with another motor drawing 8 A at 90 percent PF lagging from a 120-V line. Find (*a*) the total effective power, (*b*) the total PF, (*c*) the total apparent power, and (*d*) the total current drawn.

4. A purely resistive lamp load drawing 20 A from a 220-V 60-Hz line is in parallel with a capacitive motor taking 8 A at 34.2 percent PF. Find (*a*) W_T, (*b*) PF_T, (*c*) VA_T, and (*d*) I_T.

5. A 1-kW lamp load, a 20-kVA induction motor operating at a PF of 70 percent, and a 15 kVA motor operating at a PF of 50 percent lagging are connected in parallel. Find (*a*) W_T, (*b*) PF_T, and (*c*) VA_T.

6. An induction motor drawing 250 VA at 70 percent PF is in parallel with a synchronous motor drawing 400 VA at 60 percent PF.

Find (*a*) the total effective power, (*b*) the total PF, and (*c*) the total apparent power.

7. An induction motor drawing 10 A at 80 percent PF is in parallel with a capacitive load drawing 1 kW at 90 percent PF from a 117-V 60-Hz line. Find (*a*) the total effective power, (*b*) the total PF, (*c*) the total apparent power, and (*d*) the total current drawn.

8. A lamp bank drawing 10 A, a synchronous motor drawing 8 A at 75 percent PF, and an induction motor drawing 5 A at 80 percent PF are all connected in parallel across a 230-V 60-Hz line. Find (*a*) the total apparent power and (*b*) the total current drawn.

9. A 120-V 20-A induction motor draws 2 kW of power. A 1.5-kVA synchronous motor is placed in parallel with it to adjust the PF to unity. What is the PF of the synchronous motor?

10. An induction motor draws 1 kW from a 110-V 60-Hz line at a PF of 70 percent. Find (*a*) the apparent power, (*b*) the lagging var power, and (*c*) the capacitance needed in parallel to raise the total PF to 1.0.

TEST—AC POWER

1. A purely resistive lamp load drawing 10 A from a 230-V 60-Hz ac line is in parallel with a 10-kVA induction motor operating at a PF of 60 percent lagging and with a synchronous motor drawing 6 kW at a PF of 77 percent leading. Find (*a*) the total effective power, (*b*) the total PF, (*c*) the total apparent power, and (*d*) the total current drawn.

2. An induction motor draws 3 kW from a 120-V 60-Hz ac line at a PF of 82 percent. Find (*a*) the apparent power, (*b*) the lagging var power, and (*c*) the capacitance needed in parallel to raise the total PF to unity.

COLOR CODES

FINDING THE VALUE OF FIXED RESISTORS

Instead of the number of ohms of resistance being stamped on carbon-type resistors, the resistors are colored according to a definite system approved by the EIA (Electronics Industries Association). Each color represents a number according to the plan in Table A-1.

TABLE A-1

COLOR	NUMBER	COLOR	NUMBER
Black	0	Green	5
Brown	1	Blue	6
Red	2	Violet	7
Orange	3	Gray	8
Yellow	4	White	9

Gold—multiply by 0.1.
Silver—multiply by 0.01.

The value of the resistor is obtained by reading the colors according to the following systems.

The three-band system. The first band represents the first number in the value. The second band represents the second number. The third band represents the number of zeros to be added after the first two numbers. If the third band is gold or silver, multiply the value indicated by the first two bands by 0.1 or 0.01, respectively, as indicated above.

EXAMPLE A-1   Find the resistance of a resistor marked red, violet, yellow as shown in Fig. A-1.

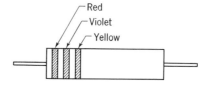

FIGURE A-1
The resistance value is indicated by three bands of color read in order from left to right.

SOLUTION

First band	Second band	Third band
Red	Violet	Yellow
2	7	0000

Resistance = 270,000 Ω   *Ans.*

EXAMPLE A-2   A resistor is marked yellow, orange, black. What is its resistance?

SOLUTION

First band	Second band	Third band
Yellow	Orange	Black
4	3	No zeros

Resistance = 43 Ω   *Ans.*

EXAMPLE A-3   A resistor is marked green, blue, gold. What is its resistance?

SOLUTION

First band	Second band	Third band
Green	Blue	Gold
5	6	Multiply by 0.1

The first two bands indicate a value of 56 Ω. Therefore,

$$56 \times 0.1 = 5.6 \ \Omega \quad Ans.$$

The body-tip-dot system. The colors must be read in the following order: body, tip, and dot. The body color represents the first number, the right-hand tip represents the second number, and the center dot represents the number of zeros to be added after the first two numbers. If the dot is gold or silver, multiply the value indicated by the first two numbers by 0.1 or 0.01, respectively.

EXAMPLE A-4   What is the resistance of the resistor shown in Fig. A-2?

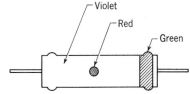

FIGURE A-2
The resistance value is indicated by the colors in the order: body, right-end tip, and center dot.

SOLUTION

Body	Tip	Dot
Violet	Green	Red
7	5	00

Resistance = 7,500 Ω   *Ans.*

EXAMPLE A-5   A resistor has a brown body, a blue right end, and an orange dot in the center. What is its resistance?

SOLUTION

Body	Tip	Dot
Brown	Blue	Orange
1	6	000

Resistance = 16,000 Ω   *Ans.*

EXAMPLE A-6   A resistor has a gray body, a red right end, and a silver dot in the center. What is its resistance?

SOLUTION

Body	Tip	Dot
Gray	Red	Silver
8	2	Multiply by 0.01

The first two colors indicate a value of 82 Ω. Therefore,

$$82 \times 0.01 = 0.82 \ \Omega \qquad Ans.$$

EXAMPLE A-7   A mechanic needs a 510,000-Ω resistor. What combination of colors in the body-tip-dot system is needed?

SOLUTION

The first digit is a 5, indicating green.
The second digit is a 1, indicating brown.
The four zeros that remain indicate yellow.

Therefore, the resistor will be color-coded as follows:

Body, green; right-end tip, brown; dot, yellow   *Ans.*

EXAMPLE A-8   What color combination is needed to indicate a 6.8-Ω resistor in the three band system?

SOLUTION

The first digit is a 6, indicating blue.
The second digit is an 8, indicating gray.

To obtain the number 6.8 from the number 68 it is necessary to multiply 68 by 0.1, which indicates gold. Therefore, the resistor will be color-coded as follows:

First band, blue   second band, gray   third band, gold   *Ans.*

Tolerance markings. A fourth band of color in the band system or a color on the left-hand side of the resistor in the body-tip-dot system is used to indicate how accurately the part is made to conform to the indicated markings. Gold means that the value is not more than 5 percent away from the indicated value. Silver indicates a tolerance of 10 percent, and black a tolerance of 20 percent. If the tolerance is not indicated by a color, it is assumed to be 20 percent.

PROBLEMS

What value of resistance is indicated by each of the following color combinations?

1.	Brown, black, yellow	2.	Red, yellow, red
3.	Gray, red, orange	4.	Green, brown, red
5.	Violet, green, black	6.	Red, black, green
7.	Yellow, violet, gold	8.	Brown, green, yellow
9.	Brown, red, gold	10.	Brown, red, red
11.	Brown, gray, green	12.	Orange, white, silver
13.	Blue, red, brown	14.	Brown, gray, brown
15.	White, brown, red	16.	Orange, orange, gold
17.	Yellow, violet, silver	18.	Yellow, green, silver
19.	Gray, red, black	20.	Green, blue, gold

What color combination is needed to indicate each of the following resistances?

21.	240,000 Ω	22.	430,000 Ω
23.	51 Ω	24.	150 Ω
25.	10,000,000 Ω	26.	5.6 Ω
27.	3,900 Ω	28.	0.47 Ω
29.	12 Ω	30.	750,000 Ω
31.	0.68 Ω	32.	1.2 Ω
33.	2.2 Ω	34.	100 Ω
35.	1.8 Ω	36.	1,000,000 Ω
37.	360 Ω	38.	6,200 Ω
39.	1.5 Ω	40.	1 Ω

FINDING THE VALUE OF FIXED CAPACITORS

Four different marking systems are used to indicate the value of the capacitance of molded capacitors. A series of colored dots shaped like arrows indicates the capacitance in units of micromicrofarads, or picofarads, as well as the working voltage, tolerance, and other characteristics of the capacitor. The meaning of the colors is shown in Table A-2.

TABLE A-2
COLOR CODE FOR MOLDED CAPACITORS

COLOR	NUMBER	TOLERANCE, %
Black	0	20
Brown	1	1
Red	2	2
Orange	3	3
Yellow	4	4
Green	5	5
Blue	6	6
Violet	7	7
Gray	8	8
White	9	9
Gold	....	5
Silver	....	10

The three-dot system. The capacitor must be positioned so that the arrows point to the right as shown in Fig. A-3a.

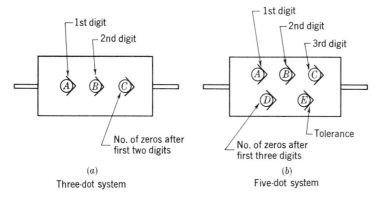

(a)
Three-dot system

(b)
Five-dot system

FIGURE A-3
Molded mica capacitor color codes. All capacitances are measured in micromicrofarads, or picofarads.

EXAMPLE A-9   A capacitor is color-coded as follows: The three dots reading from left to right in the direction of the arrows are *A*, red; *B*, green; *C*, brown. Find the capacitance of the capacitor.

SOLUTION

A (red)	*B* (green)	*C* (brown)
2	5	1 zero

$$\text{Capacitance} = 250 \text{ pF} \quad Ans.$$

The five-dot system. The capacitor must be positioned so that the line of three dots is the top row and the two dots are in the bottom row as shown in Fig. A-3b.

EXAMPLE A-10   A capacitor is color-coded in the five-dot system as follows: The three top dots are *A*, brown; *B*, red; *C*, green. The two bottom dots are *D*, red; *E*, silver. Find the capacitance of the capacitor.

SOLUTION

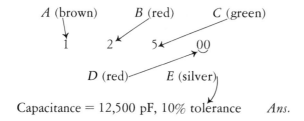

$$\text{Capacitance} = 12,500 \text{ pF, } 10\% \text{ tolerance} \quad Ans.$$

The six-dot system. The capacitor must be positioned so that the arrows point to the right as shown in Fig. A-4a. As noted, the voltage rating is always given in hundreds of volts. Close tolerances are indicated by the various colors as shown in Table A-2.

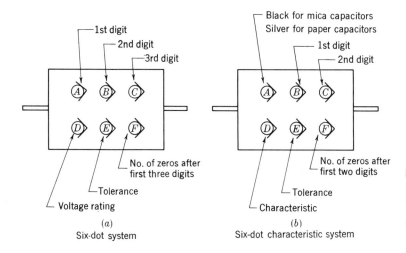

(a)
Six-dot system

(b)
Six-dot characteristic system

FIGURE A-4

Molded mica capacitor color codes. All capacitances are measured in picofarads. The voltage rating is measured in hundreds of volts.

EXAMPLE A-11   A capacitor is color-coded in the six-dot system as follows: The top row shows *A*, red; *B*, black; *C*, black. The bottom row shows *D*, violet; *E*, yellow; *F*, red. Find the rating of the capacitor.

SOLUTION

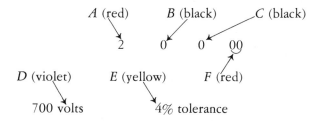

Capacitance = 20,000 pF, 700 volts, 4% tolerance   *Ans.*

The six-dot characteristic system. The capacitor must be positioned so that the arrows point to the right as shown in Fig. A-4*b*. The first dot in the top row, *A*, is used to indicate a mica capacitor (black dot) or a paper capacitor (silver dot). The lower left dot, *D*, is used to indicate certain characteristics which are relatively unimportant and is omitted from the following examples.

EXAMPLE A-12   A capacitor is color-coded in the six-dot system as follows: The top row shows *A*, black; *B*, gray; *C*, orange. The bottom row shows *E*, green; *F*, red. Find the rating of the capacitor.

SOLUTION

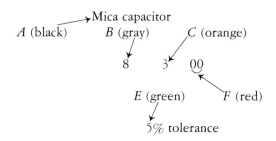

Capacitance = 8,300 pF, 5% tolerance   *Ans.*

PROBLEMS

What value of capacitance is indicated by each of the following color combinations in the three-dot and five-dot systems?

PROBLEM	*A*	*B*	*C*	*D*	*E*
1	Green	Brown	Black	. . . .	. . . .
2	Brown	Orange	Green	Black	Silver
3	Green	Blue	Black	Black	Red
4	Red	Violet	Red	. . . .	. . . .
5	Brown	Black	Orange	. . . .	. . . .
6	Red	Blue	Black	Red	Silver
7	Orange	Blue	Black	Black	Yellow
8	White	Brown	Red	. . . .	. . . .
9	Gray	Brown	Green	Black	Gray
10	Violet	Green	Black	. . . .	. . . .
11	Yellow	Green	Black	Orange	Gold
12	Brown	Gray	Green	Red	Silver
13	White	Brown	Brown	. . . .	. . . .
14	Orange	Orange	Brown	Black	Violet
15	Brown	Green	Yellow	Red	Black
16	Orange	White	Black	Black	Gold
17	Red	Green	Black	Red	Black
18	Blue	Red	Black	Black	Gold
19	Yellow	Orange	Black	. . . .	. . . .
20	Brown	Brown	Black	Red	Silver

Find the capacitance, working voltage, and tolerance indicated by each of the following color combinations in the six-dot systems.

PROBLEM	A	B	C	D	E	F
21	Red	Blue	Black	Yellow	Gray	Brown
22	White	Brown	Black	Green	Black	Orange
23	Silver	Brown	Gray	. . . .	Red	Black
24	Red	Violet	Black	Green	Green	Black
25	Silver	Orange	Blue	. . . .	Green	Black
26	Brown	Gray	Black	Brown	Violet	Brown
27	Black	Brown	Red	. . . .	Orange	Black
28	Black	Yellow	Violet	. . . .	Green	Black
29	Orange	Blue	Black	Green	Silver	Red
30	Silver	Orange	White	. . . .	Red	Black
31	Silver	Blue	Gray	. . . .	Green	Black
32	Green	Brown	Black	Green	Green	Black
33	Black	Red	Yellow	. . . .	Blue	Red
34	Yellow	Orange	Black	Green	Green	Brown
35	Red	Violet	Black	Brown	Silver	Black
36	Silver	Green	Blue	. . . .	Orange	Black
37	Gray	Red	Black	Green	Silver	Black
38	Brown	Green	Black	Green	Black	Red
39	Violet	Green	Black	Green	Black	Red
40	Yellow	Violet	Black	Red	Gold	Brown

BIBLIOGRAPHY

Cooke, Nelson M., and Herbert Adams: "Basic Mathematics for Electronics," 3d ed., McGraw-Hill Book Company, New York, 1970.

Dawes, Chester L.: "A Course in Electrical Engineering," Vols. I and II, 4th ed., McGraw-Hill Book Company, New York, 1952.

——: "Industrial Electricity," vol. I, 3d ed., 1956, and vol. II, 3d ed., 1960, McGraw-Hill Book Company, New York.

Fischer, Bernhard, and Herbert Jacobs: "Elements of Mathematics for Radio, Television and Electronics," The Macmillan Company, New York, 1954.

G.E. Transistor Manual, General Electric Company, 1964.

Hellman, Charles I.: "Elements of Radio," 3d ed., D. Van Nostrand Company, Inc., Princeton, N.J., 1956.

Helt, Scott: "Practical Television Engineering," rev. ed., Holt, Rinehart and Winston, Inc., New York, 1953.

Henney, Keith, and G. H. Richardson: "Principles of Radio," 6th ed., John Wiley & Sons, Inc., New York, 1952.

Latham, Donald C.: "Transistors and Integrated Circuits," J. B. Lippincott Company, Philadelphia, 1966.

Levine, Samuel: "Vocational and Technical Mathematics in Action," Hayden Book Company, Inc., New York, 1969.

Lemons, Wayne: "Learn Electronics Through Troubleshooting," Howard W. Sams & Co., Inc., Indianapolis, 1969.

Lister, Eugene C.: "Electric Circuits and Machines," 3d ed., McGraw-Hill Book Company, New York, 1960.

Marcus, Abraham: "Radio Servicing: Theory and Practice," 3d ed., Prentice-Hall, Inc., Englewood Cliffs, N.J., 1960.

Marcus, Abraham, and William Marcus: "Elements of Radio," 4th ed., Prentice-Hall, Inc., Englewood Cliffs, N.J., 1959.

Nadon, John M., and Bert J. Gelmine: "Industrial Electricity," 2d ed., D. Van Nostrand Company, Inc., Princeton, N.J., 1951.

"National Electrical Code for Electric Wiring and Apparatus," NBFU Pamphlet No. 70, National Board of Fire Underwriters, New York, 1968.

Navy Training Course, Navpers 10086-A, "Basic Electricity," Government Printing Office, Washington, D.C., 1960.

Navy Training Course, Navpers 10087, "Basic Electronics" Government Printing Office, Washington, D.C., 1955.

Navy Training Course, Navpers 93400A-1a, "Fundamentals of Electronics," Government Printing Office, Washington, D.C., 1965.

Navy Training Course, Navpers 93400-1b, "Fundamentals of Electronics," Government Printing Office, Washington, D.C., 1965.

Pike, Charles A.: "Transistor Funda-

mentals," vol. 2, Howard W. Sams & Co., Inc., Indianapolis, 1968.

Richter, H. P.: "Practical Electrical Wiring," 6th ed., McGraw-Hill Book Company, New York, 1960.

Schure, Alexander: "Basic Transistors," John F. Rider, Publisher, Inc., New York, 1961.

Sears, Francis Weston: "Electricity and Magnetism," Addison-Wesley Publishing Company, Inc., Reading, Mass., 1951.

Siskind, Charles S.: "Electricity—Direct and Alternating Current," 2d ed., McGraw-Hill Book Company, New York, 1955.

Slurzberg, Morris, and William Osterheld: "Essentials of Radio-Electronics," 2d ed., McGraw-Hill Book Company, New York, 1961.

Tepper, Marvin: "Basic Radio," John F. Rider, Publisher, Inc., New York, 1961.

Timbie, William H.: "Elements of Electricity," 4th ed., John Wiley & Sons, Inc., New York, 1952.

Timbie, William H.: "Basic Electricity for Communications," 2d ed. revised by Francis J. Ricker, John Wiley & Sons, Inc., New York, 1958.

Van Valkenburgh, Nooger and Neville, Inc.: "Basic Electricity," John F. Rider, Publisher, Inc., New York, 1954.

Veatch, Henry C.: "Transistor Circuit Action," McGraw-Hill Book Company, New York, 1968.

ANSWERS TO PROBLEMS

Job 2−1: Page 13
1. $25\frac{1}{2}$ ft
2. $3\frac{3}{4}$ hp
3. 90 V
4. 7 Ω
5. 68 cents
6. 228 kWh
7. $37\frac{1}{2}$ h
8. $94\frac{1}{2}$ W
9. 36 lb
10. 20 ft 3 in
11. 8
12. 8
13. 66
14. $\frac{1}{6}$
15. $\frac{1}{50}$
16. $\frac{1}{2}$
17. $\frac{3}{32}$
18. $2\frac{1}{2}$
19. $45\frac{1}{3}$
20. 16

Job 2−2: Page 16
1. $\frac{1}{2}$
3. $\frac{1}{4}$
5. $\frac{3}{4}$
7. $\frac{1}{4}$
9. $\frac{1}{3}$
11. $\frac{3}{100}$
13. $\frac{3}{8}$
15. $\frac{7}{16}$
17. $\frac{1}{3}$
19. $\frac{3}{5}$
21. $\frac{2}{1}$
23. $\frac{49}{1}$
25. $\frac{2}{5}$

Job 2−2: Page 17
1. $\frac{9}{4}$
3. $\frac{20}{9}$
5. $\frac{13}{10}$
7. $\frac{25}{6}$
9. $\frac{37}{8}$
11. $\frac{10}{3}$

Job 2−2: Page 18
1. $1\frac{3}{4}$
3. $4\frac{1}{3}$

5. $3\frac{3}{4}$
7. $1\frac{3}{5}$
9. $3\frac{3}{10}$
11. 10
13. $9\frac{2}{3}$
15. 16
17. $3\frac{3}{5}$
19. 12
21. 7
23. $1\frac{7}{10}$
25. $5\frac{2}{9}$
27. 12
29. $12\frac{1}{4}$

Job 2−2: Page 19
1. 4
3. $\frac{3}{10}$
5. $2\frac{1}{2}$
7. $\frac{1}{15}$
9. 6
11. $5\frac{1}{4}$ hp
13. 46 Ω
15. 2 oz
17. 21 cents
19. $\frac{15}{64}$ in
21. $\frac{1}{3}$
23. $\frac{5}{7}$
25. $\frac{12}{25}$
27. $\frac{1}{10}$
29. $\frac{21}{40}$
31. $\frac{1}{8}$

Job 2−2: Page 21
1. $\frac{2}{3}$
3. $9\frac{1}{2}$
5. $\frac{1}{3}$
7. 5
9. $\frac{2}{3}$
11. $4\frac{1}{2}$ V
13. (a) $25\frac{1}{2}$ in
    (b) 51 in
    (c) 153 ft
15. $1\frac{3}{10}$ min
17. $2\frac{17}{20}$ lb
19. $21\frac{3}{4}$ Ω
21. 43 man-hr
23. $73\frac{1}{2}$ in

Test on Fractions: Page 23
1. (a) $\frac{5}{8}$
   (b) $\frac{2}{5}$
   (c) $\frac{5}{16}$
   (d) $\frac{2}{3}$
   (e) $\frac{1}{25}$
2. (a) $\frac{11}{8}$
   (b) $\frac{13}{4}$
   (c) $\frac{11}{2}$
   (d) $\frac{27}{10}$
   (e) $\frac{13}{3}$
3. (a) $2\frac{1}{4}$
   (b) $7\frac{2}{3}$
   (c) $3\frac{4}{5}$
   (d) $8\frac{2}{5}$
   (e) $7\frac{5}{8}$
4. (a) 88
   (b) $5\frac{1}{2}$
   (c) 25
   (d) 7
5. (a) $\frac{27}{32}$
   (b) $\frac{1}{2}$
   (c) $14\frac{5}{8}$
   (d) $\frac{243}{512}$

Job 2−3: Page 26
1. 110 V
3. 120 V
5. 55.8 V
7. 117 V
9. 44 V
11. 150 V
13. No! 0.27 V used.
15. 104.9 V
17. 32 V
19. 18.75 V
21. 0.05 V
23. 1.2 V

Job 2−4: Page 28
1. 5.55 A
2. 122.8 V
3. 0.01525 μF
4. 0.0378 in
5. 0.35 A
6. 2.6 V
7. 1.185 in

8. 65.75 V
9. $0.23
10. 0.004 Ω
11. 12.55
12. 3.75
13. 0.4 A
14. (a) Four and three tenths
    (b) Three hundred and fifty-
        nine thousandths
    (c) Forty-one hundredths
15. 0.015
16. (a) 0.25
    (b) 0.571
    (c) 0.625
    (d) 0.0625
17. 6.24
18. 1.1, 0.30, 0.050, 0.0070
19. 0.05
20. 2.25

Job 2−5: Page 31 (Top)
 1. 0.7
 3. 0.114
 5. 0.06
 7. 0.018
 9. 0.11
11. 0.013
13. 0.045
15. 0.6
17. 0.4, 0.16, 0.007
19. 0.8, 0.06, 0.040
21. 0.5, 0.18, 0.051
23. 0.4, 0.236, 0.1228
25. 0.19, 0.08, 0.004
27. 0.14, 0.02, 0.004

Job 2−5: Page 31 (Bottom)
 1. 2.3
 3. 3.144
 5. 2.025
 7. 2.020
 9. 1.002
11. 9.145

Job 2−5: Page 34
 1. 0.25
 3. 0.625
 5. 0.4
 7. 0.15
 9. 0.875
11. 0.444
13. 0.094
15. 0.625
17. 0.02
19. 0.192

Job 2−5: Page 36
 1. 13.492
 3. 22.832
 5. 11.967
 7. 45.46 V
 9. 0.4375 in
11. 2.2525 in
13. 0.0315 A
15. 2.400 in

Job 2−5: Page 37
 1. 0.23
 3. 0.34
 5. 7.56
 7. 0.317
 9. 2.92
11. 5.9
13. 2.39
15. 0.262
17. 2.62
19. 0.515
21. (a) 0.304
    (b) 1.106
    (c) 0.39
    (d) 5.75
    (e) 1.98
23. 0.914
25. 6.41
27. 9.55 Ω
29. 131.4 V

Job 2−5: Page 39
 1. 0.41
 3. 0.463
 5. 30.31
 7. 0.221
 9. 0.0186
11. 4.77
13. 4.55 A
15. 0.694 in
17. 67.5 V
19. 0.275 in
21. 4.112 in
23. 56.52 Ω
25. 0.0288 in

Job 2−5: Page 42
 1. 13
 3. 161
 5. 4.7
 7. 786
 9. 2.32
11. 200 ft
13. 60.7
15. 0.025 in

Job 2−5: Page 44
 1. 0.7
 3. 0.01
 5. 0.05
 7. 0.09
 9. 1.575
11. 0.45
13. 0.016
15. 0.817
17. 1.104
19. 0.196

Test on Decimals: Page 44
 1. 13.848
 2. 94.983
 3. (a) 0.2, 0.05, 0.0035
    (b) 0.62, 0.063, 0.0061
 4. 28.932
 5. 6.141
 6. 0.429
 7. 0.667
 8. 0.5012
 9. 13.2
10. 1.65

Job 2−6: Page 45
 1. 0.6 A
 2. 300 Ω
 3. 111 V
 4. 4 A
 5. $\text{kW} = \dfrac{I \times E}{1,000}$
 6. 2 A
 7. 25 Ω
 8. 0.125 A
 9. 11 A
10. 100 V

Job 2−7: Page 49
 1. $P = IE$
 3. $\text{Eff} = \dfrac{P_o}{P_i}$
 5. $X_c = \dfrac{159,000}{fC}$
 7. $D = 1.414s$
 9. $d = D - 2h$
11. $A = \frac{1}{2}BH$
13. $P = 2L + 2W$
15. $I_m = I - I_s$
17. $R_s = \dfrac{R_m}{N - 1}$

Job 2–7: Page 50

1. The number of watts of power consumed by a circuit is equal to the voltage across the circuit multiplied by the current through the circuit.
3. The wavelength of a radio wave equals 300,000 divided by the frequency in kilohertz.
5. The resistance of a wire is equal to the product of the specific resistance and the length divided by the area of the wire.

Job 2–7: Page 53

1. 135 sq ft
3. 10 A
5. 0.866 in
7. 140.4 Ω
9. 1.338 in
11. 20 Ω
13. $\frac{1}{4}$ A
15. 68°
17. 60 lb
19. 72.6 Ω

Job 2–8: Page 60

1. 5
3. 6
5. 9
7. $13\frac{2}{3}$
9. 5.85
11. 40
13. 400
15. 200
17. 800
19. 390
21. $\frac{1}{16}$

Job 2–8: Page 61

1. 2 Ω
3. 13 Ω
5. $1\frac{1}{2}$ A
7. 20 A
9. 5,000 Ω
11. 0.133 Ω
13. 1,200 Ω
15. 2.25 A
17. 3.67 A
19. 0.0015 Ω
21. 1.76 Ω
23. 0.002 A
25. 21.43 Ω
27. 0.06 A

Job 2–9: Page 65

1. 110 V
3. Yes
5. 18 V
7. 24 V
9. 5 A
11. 0.005 Ω
13. 12,000 Ω
15. 17.3 V
17. 0.03 A
19. 20 A
21. 0.0081 A
23. 4 Ω, 0.8 Ω
25. 300,000,000 Ω

Test—Ohm's Law: Page 67

1. 115 V
2. 0.0183 A
3. 22 Ω
4. 25.5 V
5. 1.48 A
6. 8 Ω
7. 120 V
8. 28 A
9. 36 V
10. 250,000 Ω

Job 3–1: Page 73

1. (a) 24 V
   (b) 0.2 A
   (c) 120 Ω
3. (a) 42.9 V
   (b) 0.3 A
   (c) 143 Ω

Job 3–2: Page 78

1. (a) 4 A
   (b) 74 V
   (c) 18.5 Ω
3. (a) Dash = 2.5 Ω, tail = 5 Ω
   (b) 7.5 Ω
   (c) 0.8 A
5. 0.0088 A
7. (a) 4.31 V
   (b) 7.7 V
   (c) 12.01 V

Test on Ohm's Law in Series Circuits: Page 79

1. (a) $E_T = 97$ V
   (b) $I_T = 0.15$ A
   (c) $R_T = 647$ Ω
2. (a) 4 A
   (b) 115 V
   (c) 28.75 Ω

3. $E_{AB} = 12$ V
4. (a) 0.5 A
   (b) 90 V
   (c) 180 Ω
5. (a) $I_{AB} = I_2 = 0.00002$ A
   (b) $E_2 = 8$ V
       $E_{AB} = 10$ V
   (c) $R_1 = 100,000$ Ω
       $R_{AB} = 500,000$ Ω

Job 3–3: Page 84

1. 550 V
3. 4.8 V
5. 0.012 A
7. (a) 0.0006 A
   (b) 50,000 Ω
   (c) 30 V
9. (a) 204 V
   (b) 4 A
   (c) 51 Ω

Job 3–4: Page 88

1. 54 V
3. 6 V
5. (a) 45, 75, 150 V
   (b) 270 V
   (c) 18,000 Ω
7. (a) 1.2 A
   (b) 132 V
   (c) 110 Ω
9. $E_T = 32$ V
   $I_T = 0.4$ A
   $I_1 = I_2 = I_3 = 0.4$ A
   $R_1 = 20$ Ω
   $R_2 = 25$ Ω
   $R_3 = 35$ Ω

Test on Series Circuits: Page 89

1. 6 V
2. (a) 0.3 A
   (b) 117 V
   (c) 390 Ω
3. (a) $I_T = 1.5$ A
   (b) $E_T = 150$ V
   (c) $R_T = 100$ Ω
4. $I_T = I_1 = I_2 = I_3 = \frac{2}{3}$ A
   $R_1 = 45$ Ω
   $R_2 = 90$ Ω
   $R_3 = 30$ Ω
   $E_T = 110$ V
5. 150 V

Job 3–5: Page 90

1. 29
2. 26

3. 1.1 A
4. 17.4
5. 7
6. 45
7. 12
8. 3
9. 25 Ω
10. $103\frac{1}{3}$ Ω

Job 3-6: Page 95
1. 6
3. 70
5. 52
7. 25
9. 7.3
11. 28.2
13. $5\frac{1}{4}$
15. 6.1
17. 56.1
19. 120
21. 73
23. 0.00008
25. 1.45

Job 3-6: Page 98
1. 17
3. 22
5. 5
7. 12.5
9. 79
11. $10\frac{3}{4}$
13. $15\frac{1}{4}$
15. 80
17. 0.099
19. $21.83
21. 172
23. 17.05
25. 109

Job 3-6: Page 102
1. 11
3. 6
5. 10
7. 12
9. 8
11. 1.54
13. 10
15. 11.5
17. 0.021
19. 11.48
21. $1\frac{1}{2}$
23. 180
25. 30
27. 76.5
29. 0.00025

Job 3-7: Page 107
1. 25 Ω
3. 8 Ω
5. 84 Ω
7. 4 Ω
9. 90 Ω
11. 202 V
13. $I_{max} = 11$ A,
$I_{min} = 2$ A
15. 0.025 Ω

Job 3-8: Page 110
1. $I_T = I_1 = I_3 = 2$ A
$E_T = 110$ V
$R_T = 55$ Ω
$R_1 = 12$ Ω
$E_2 = 60$ V
$E_3 = 26$ V
3. 12 Ω
5. 28 Ω, 2.67 A, 74.8 V
7. (a) 2.2 A
(b) 10 Ω
9. 30 Ω
11. $R_E = 200$ Ω
$V_{CC} = 34$ V

Test on Series Circuits: Page 111
1. $R_1 = 8$ Ω, $I_1 = 2$ A
$E_2 = 60$ V, $I_3 = 2$ A
$R_3 = 22$ Ω, $E_T = 120$ V
$I_T = 2$ A, $R_T = 60$ Ω
2. $I_1 = I_2 = I_3 = \frac{1}{2}$ A
$R_2 = 100$ Ω
$E_3 = 38$ V
$E_T = 118$ V
$I_T = \frac{1}{2}$ A
$R_T = 236$ Ω
3. $R_1 = 125$ Ω
$I_2 = I_3 = 0.4$ A
$E_2 = 20$ V
$R_2 = 50$ Ω
$R_3 = 100$ Ω
$I_T = 0.4$ A
$R_T = 275$ Ω
4. 32 Ω
5. 50 Ω

Job 4-1: Page 117
1. (a) 5 A
(b) $E_1 = E_2 = E_3 = 110$V
(c) 22 Ω
3. 4 A
5. 30 lamps; 20 lamps
7. 9.1 A; yes
9. 9.5 A, 1.26 Ω

Job 4-2: Page 122
1. (a) 18 V
(b) $I_1 = 6$ A, $I_2 = 3$ A, $I_T = 9$ A
(c) 2 Ω
3. 2 A, 6 A; $I_T = 12$ A
5. (a) $E_T = E_1 = E_2 = E_3 = 114$ V
(b) $I_2 = 6$, $I_3 = 2$, $I_T = 20$ A
(c) $R_1 = 9.5$ Ω
$R_T = 5.7$ Ω
7. (a) 30 Ω for 3 lamps;
15 Ω for fourth lamp.
(b) 0.25 A
(c) $1\frac{1}{2}$ V
(d) 6 Ω
9. $I_T = 1.05$ A
$E_T = 6.8$ V
$R_T = 6.47$ Ω

Job 4-3: Page 123
1. $\frac{17}{24}$ hp
2. $\frac{1}{6}$
3. $\frac{9}{64}$ in
4. $\frac{15}{32}$ in
5. $22\frac{7}{8}$ lb
6. $\frac{19}{30}$
7. $1\frac{13}{16}$
8. $2\frac{11}{24}$
9. $1\frac{11}{18}$
10. $1\frac{27}{28}$
11. $2\frac{1}{8}$
12. $4\frac{15}{16}$
13. $4\frac{1}{4}$
14. $2\frac{11}{16}$
15. $\frac{1}{60}$

Job 4-4: Page 127
1. $1\frac{3}{8}$
3. $1\frac{11}{24}$
5. $\frac{1}{6}$
7. $\frac{2}{5}$
9. $\frac{1}{120}$
11. $\frac{57}{64}$
13. $\frac{3}{20}$
15. $1\frac{11}{32}$
17. $15\frac{7}{16}$
19. $\frac{15}{16}$
21. $\frac{11}{600}$ mhos
23. $7\frac{3}{16}$ in

Job 4-5: Page 131
1. $\frac{1}{2}$
3. $\frac{3}{8}$
5. $\frac{5}{16}$
7. $\frac{1}{12}$
9. $\frac{1}{6}$

11. $^1/_{12}$
13. $^1/_{80}$
15. $^1/_{500}$
17. $4^3/_4$
19. $7^1/_3$
21. $5^7/_{16}$
23. $^1/_{300}$
25. $76^3/_4$ ft
27. $1^7/_8$ in

Job 4–6: Page 133
1. 1,800
2. $62^1/_2$
3. 2 A
4. 843 Ω
5. 6 V

Job 4–7: Page 136
1. 24
3. 12
5. 1
7. 2
9. 8
11. 6,750
13. 54
15. 4,000
17. 30
19. 93.97

Job 4–7: Page 139
1. 2
3. 4
5. $3^1/_3$
7. 15
9. 15
11. 1.2
13. 10
15. $3^1/_2$
17. 7.8
19. 315
21. 120 turns
23. $33^1/_3$
25. 60 Ω
27. 500 lb
29. 1.02 Ω

Job 4–7: Page 141
1. 6
3. 80
5. 51
7. 27
9. 25
11. 10
13. 1.44
15. $5^1/_3$

17. 0.1
19. 1.84

Job 4–8: Page 144
1. 1.5 Ω
3. 21 Ω
5. 13.6 Ω
7. 2 Ω
9. 62.5 Ω
11. 462 Ω
13. 900 Ω
15. 400 Ω

Job 4–8: Page 146
1. 50 Ω
3. 0.75 Ω
5. (a) 7.33 Ω
   (b) 15 A

Job 4–8: Page 147
1. 20 Ω
3. 23.7 Ω
5. 7,143 Ω
7. 3.53 Ω
9. 28.6 Ω

Job 4–9: Page 148
1. 40 V
3. 4.8 V
5. 14.4 V
7. 14.4 V
9. 17.1 V

Job 4–10: Page 153
1. $I_1 = I_2 = 4$ A
   (The current in a circuit
   divides equally between
   equal parallel branches.)
3. (a) 42 Ω
   (b) 12.6 V
   (c) 0.15 A
   (d) 0.15 A
5. $I_G = 0.008$ A
   $I_s = 0.192$ A
7. 12 A, 8 A, 6 A
9. 0.071 A
11. $I_1 = 0.0006$ A
    $I_2 = 0.0024$ A

Job 4–11: Page 156
1. (a) 5.75 A
   (b) 110 V
   (c) 19.1 Ω
3. $I_T = 47$ A
   $R_T = 9.36$ Ω
   $E_1 = E_2 = E_3 = 440$ V

$I_2 = 22$ A
$R_1 = 44$ Ω
$R_3 = 29.3$ Ω
5. 26.7 Ω
7. (a) 10 Ω
   (b) 8 Ω
   (d) Series
   (e) 18 Ω
   (f) 20 A
9. 600 Ω
11. 85.7 Ω
13. (a) 2,550 Ω
    (b) 102 V
15. (a) 10.5 Ω
    (b) 12.6 V
    (c) 0.6 A
    (d) 0.6 A

Test on Parallel Circuits: Page 158
1. (a) 120 V
   (b) 8 A
   (c) 15 Ω
2. 4,800 Ω
3. (a) 1.5
   (b) 2
4. 12 V
5. $I_5 = 7.5$ A
   $I_{15} = 2.5$ A

Job 5–2: Page 163
1. $R_T = 24$ Ω
   $I_T = 5$ A
   $I_1 = I_2 = 3$ A
   $I_3 = 2$ A
   $E_1 = 30$ V
   $E_2 = 90$ V
   $E_3 = 120$ V
3. $R_T = 6$ Ω
   $I_T = 2$ A
5. (a) 12,000 Ω
   (b) 0.03 A
   (c) 360 V
   (d) 0.012 A
   (e) 0.018 A
   (f) 54 V
   (g) 306 V
7. 8 Ω

Job 5–3: Page 176
1. $I_T = 10$ A
   $I_1 = 10$ A
   $I_2 = 7.5$ A
   $I_3 = 2.5$ A
   $R_T = 13$ Ω
   $E_1 = 100$ V

$E_2 = 30$ V
$E_3 = 30$ V
3. (a) $I_2 = 0.003$ A
  (b) $E_2 = 3$ V
  (c) $E_L = 14.4$ V
  (d) $I_L = 0.0012$ A
5. 0.5 A
7. (a) 6,640 Ω
  (b) 0.0015 A
  (c) 3 V
9. $R_T = 30$ Ω
11. (a) 14 k
  (b) 6 k

Test on Combination Circuits:
Page 179
1. (a) 24 Ω
  (b) 74 Ω
  (c) 0.5 A
  (d) $I_1 = 0.5$ A
    $E_1 = 25$ V
    $E_2 = E_3 = 12$ V
    $I_2 = 0.3$ A
    $I_3 = 0.2$ A
2. (a) $R_A = 80$ Ω
    $E_A = 120$ V
    $R_B = 48$ Ω
    $E_B = 120$ V
  (b) $I_A = 1.5$ A
    $I_B = 2.5$ A
  (c) 4 A
  (d) 30 Ω
  (e) For the 50-Ω:
    $I = 1.5$ A
    $E = 75$ V
    For the 30-Ω:
    $I = 1.5$ A
    $E = 45$ V
    For the 20-Ω:
    $I = 2.5$ A
    $E = 50$ V
    For the 28-Ω:
    $I = 2.5$ A
    $E = 70$ V
3. 53.05 Ω
4. 284,300 Ω
5. (a) $R_T = 50$ Ω
  (b) $I_T = 2$ A
  (c) $I_1 = 2$ A
    $I_2 = I_3 = I_4 = 1.33$ A
    $I_5 = 0.67$ A
    $I_6 = 2$ A
  (d) $E_1 = 28$ V
    $E_2 = 4$ V
    $E_3 = 8$ V

$E_4 = 20$ V
$E_5 = 32$ V
$E_6 = 40$ V

Job 5-4: Page 184
1. $E_l = 2.4$ V
  $E_L = 114.6$ V
3. 0.25 Ω
5. 6.048 V, No. 14
7. 113.3 V

Job 5-5: Page 189
1. (a) $E_1 = 15.2$ V
    $E_2 = 4.8$ V
  (b) 101.8 V
  (c) 97 V
3. $E_A = 112$ V
  $E_B = 109.6$ V
5. $E_G = 126.4$ V
  $E_B = 111.1$ V
7. 125.8 V
9. $E_{M_1} = 109$ V
  $E_{M_2} = 110$ V

Test on Distribution Systems:
Page 191
1. (a) 119.2 V
  (b) 113.2 V
2. (a) 120.4 V
  (b) 116 V
3. (a) 127.5 V
  (b) 112.8 V
4. (a) 113.2 V
  (b) 117.2 V

Job 6-1: Page 195
1. 480 W
3. 22 W
5. 374 W
7. 110 W
9. 0.06 W
11. 40 W
13. 900 W
15. 1 W
17. 2,508 W
19. 6.6 W

Job 6-2: Page 198
1. 11.2 W
3. Yes. (0.135 W developed)
5. 0.382 W
7. 1,930 W
9. (a) 10 A
  (b) $P_1 = 640$ W
    $P_2 = 960$ W
    $P_3 = 160$ W
    $P_4 = 240$ W

  (c) $P_T = 2,000$ W

Job 6-3: Page 199
1. 5 A
3. 50 A
5. 1.2 W
7. 0.5 A
9. 5.45 A
11. 20 A
13. 1.23 A

Job 6-4: Page 201
1. 720 W
3. 6.25 W, 13 W
5. 0.006 W
7. 3,361 W
9. 661 W
11. 0.055 W
13. (a) 60 Ω
  (b) 2 A
  (c) 240 W
15. (a) 100 Ω
  (b) 2 A
  (c) 400 W

Test on Power: Page 203
1. 495 W
2. 1,560 W
3. 118 V
4. 550 W
5. 360 W

Job 6-5: Page 203
1. 200
2. 360
3. 20 V
4. 65 Ω
5. 0.0000005 F

Job 6-6: Page 205
1. 3,600 cir mils
3. 268.8 in^3
5. 254.34
7. 0.45 A
9. 21.6 hp
11. 9.77

Job 6-7: Page 208
1. 480 W
3. 132.3 W
5. 6.5 W
7. 6.36 A; 16.2 W
9. 11.1 W; 28.9 W

Job 6-8: Page 209
1. 8
2. 13
3. 4.2

4. 59
5. 112
6. 7.6
7. 3.74
8. 23.8
9. 276.5
10. 5.48
11. 0.807
12. 932.6

Job 6-9: Page 216
1. 59
3. 3.9
5. 137
7. 6.32
9. 8.06

Job 6-10: Page 218
1. 10 A
3. 3,333 Ω
5. 0.14 A
7. 6,050 Ω
9. 1.6 A
11. 110 V
13. 38.7 A
15. 6.3 V

Job 6-11: Page 220
1. 660 W
3. 550 W
5. 43.2 W
7. 6.25 V
9. (a) $R_T = 16.8$ Ω
   (b) $P_T = 6.05$ W
11. 12.3 W
13. 90 Ω
15. $I_l = 20$ A
      $E_L = 110$ V
      $P_L = 2,200$ W
      No. = 44 lamps
17. (a) 116.5 V
    (b) 112.5 W
    (c) 46.75 W
    (d) 757.25 W

Test on Power: Page 222
1. 10 A
2. 10 W
3. 242 W
4. 0.224 A
5. 2,500 Ω

Job 7-1: Page 224
1. $8x$
3. $6R$
5. $12x$
7. $5x$

9. $4.4R$
11. $3.5x$
13. $5/6\ T$
15. $9R$
17. $7.5x$
19. $4.5x$
21. $6.6R$
23. $2^7/8x$
25. $3x$
27. $1.12x$

Job 7-2: Page 226
1. $10R + 7I$
3. $2x + 9$
5. $6R + 8$
7. $3R + 60$
9. $6x + 5y$
11. $0.9I + 1.9R$
13. $8I_1 + 10I_2$
15. $4x + 5y + 10$
17. $1.2I_2 + 2$
19. $2.4 + 3.4I$
21. $6I + 55$
23. $0.45R + 25$
25. $19I_3 + 3I_2$

Job 7-3: Page 233
1. 7
3. 5
5. 5
7. 5
9. 12
11. 5
13. $5^1/3$
15. 200
17. 30
19. 70
21. 5
23. 0.8
25. 5
27. 2
29. $24^1/2$
31. 7
33. 3
35. 6
37. 6
39. $1/4$
41. 0.7
43. $6^2/3$
45. $10^4/5$
47. 2
49. 40
51. 6 in, 3 in, 12 in
53. $A = 13, B = 0.4, C = 21.6$
55. $A = 32, B = 16, C = 8$
57. 24

59. 1.25 in

Job 7-4: Page 238
1. 10
3. 30
5. 16
7. 15
9. 10
11. 13.2
13. 3
15. 28
17. 12
19. 14 ft

Test on Equations: Page 239
1. 24
2. 22
3. $1/5$
4. 48
5. 200
6. 20
7. 9
8. 3
9. 7
10. 20
11. 4
12. 30
13. 4.4
14. 0.7
15. 9
16. $1/2$
17. 15
18. 10
19. 3
20. 8

Job 7-5: Page 240
1. $-\$3$
3. $+23°$
5. $+2$db
7. -10 mph
9. -5 blocks
11. -4 V

Job 7-5: Page 242
1. $+12$
3. $+6$
5. -17
7. $+7$
9. -17
11. -14
13. $+16$
15. -52
17. $+1.9$
19. $+1/4$
21. $-5/6$
23. $-5^{11}/16$

25. +3
27. +7
29. −25
31. +0.5
33. −2.9
35. (a) 0 V
   (b) −4 V
   (c) −7 V
   (d) −8 V

Job 7–6: Page 244
1. $-2x + 7$
3. $-4I_1 - 2I_2$
5. $-2x - 4y$
7. $-3x - 7$
9. $-20 - 2x$

Job 7–7: Page 245 (Multiplication)
1. +18
3. −8
5. +30
7. $+18R$
9. $-10R$
11. $+10R$
13. 0
15. −104
17. $-85R$
19. $-144R$
21. −6
23. $-2.4I$
25. $-3R$
27. −14.72
29. $-5.1R$

Job 7–7: Page 245 (Division)
1. +4
3. −4
5. +12
7. $-6R$
9. $-\frac{1}{2}$
11. $+\frac{1}{2}$
13. 0
15. −7
17. $-7\frac{1}{2}$
19. −3
21. $+3\frac{1}{5}$
23. +130
25. −2
27. −3.2
29. −62.5

Job 7–8: Page 247
1. $6 - 8x$
3. $-3x + 12$
5. $3x - 5$
7. $6I - 24$
9. $1 - 2R$

11. $29 - 3x$
13. $20 + 2I_1 + 2I_2$
15. $7R - 12$
17. $5 - 2R$
19. $3I_1 + I_2 - 24$

Job 7–9: Page 250
1. 2
3. 9
5. 4
7. 10
9. 5
11. 7
13. $\frac{1}{3}$
15. 5
17. 4
19. 9
21. 7
23. 8
25. 5
27. $\frac{1}{3}$
29. 2.1

Job 7–10: Page 252
1. −8
3. −5
5. $-\frac{1}{2}$
7. −8
9. +7
11. −4
13. −1
15. −5
17. −11
19. −3
21. −2
23. −7

Test—Combining Terms and Solving Equations: Page 253
1. $7x + 2y + 4$
2. $-R - 11$
3. $10x - 24$
4. −4
5. +6
6. +10
7. +30
8. +6
9. −300
10. $-6\frac{2}{3}$

Job 7–11: Page 255
1. 1
3. −2
5. 2
7. −3
9. 3
11. −1

13. 3
15. −4
17. 7
19. 4
21. −21
23. $\frac{1}{2}$
25. 3
27. $5\frac{1}{2}$
29. 1.1
31. 25
33. 48 Ω
35. 650 W
37. 0.98

Job 7–12: Page 258
1. 2
3. 40
5. 30
7. 8
9. 7
11. 6
13. 300
15. 10
17. 2
19. $17\frac{1}{7}$
21. 108

Test—Equations with Parentheses and Fractions: Page 259
1. 12
2. 8
3. $-2\frac{1}{5}$
4. −5
5. 9
6. 5
7. 1
8. 6
9. 12
10. −6

Job 7–13: Page 265
1. $x = 3, y = 2$
3. $x = 5, y = 2$
5. $I_1 = 6, I_2 = 2$
7. $E = 7, R = 2$
9. $I = 7, E = -2$
11. $a = 1, b = -3$
13. $x = 5, y = 1$
15. $a = 6, b = 10$
17. $I_2 = 7, I_3 = -3$
19. $I_2 = 5, I_3 = 2$

Job 7–14: Page 271
1. $x = 5, y = 3$
3. $x = 5, y = 2$
5. $x = 2, y = 7$
7. $x = 5, y = 3$

9. $x = 1, y = 4$
11. $x = 1, y = 4$

Job 7-15: Test—Algebraic
Equations: Page 273
1. -10
2. -30
3. 2
4. $x = 4, y = -2$
5. $I_1 = -3, I_2 = 4$

Job 8-3: Page 283
1. (a) $I_T = 4$ A
 (b) $E_2 = 20$ V
 $E_4 = 12$ V
3. (a) $I_T = 2.4$ A
 (b) $E_2 = 14.4$ V
 $E_3 = 9.6$ V
 $E_5 = 12$ V
5. (a) $I_T = 3$ A
 (b) $E_2 = 12$ V
 $E_4 = 15$ V
 $E_6 = 6$ V
7. 8.43 A

Job 8-4: Page 289
1. $E_T = E_1 = E_2 = E_3 = 90$ V
 $I_T = 15$ A
 $I_2 = 4.5$ A
 $I_3 = 1.5$ A
 $R_2 = 20$ Ω
3. $E_T = E_1 = E_2 = E_3 = 300$ V
 $I_T = 20$ A
 $I_2 = 2.5$ A
 $I_3 = 7.5$ A
 $R_2 = 120$ Ω
5. $E_T = 108$ V
 $R_3 = 6$ Ω
7. $I_1 = 1.95$ A
 $I_2 = 0.65$ A
 $E_T = 7.80$ V
9. (a) $I_{16} = 6$ A
 $I_{48} = 2$ A
 $I_{24} = 4$ A
 (b) $E_G = 96$ V

11. $I_1 = \dfrac{R_2}{R_1 + R_2} \times I_T$

Job 8-5: Page 303
Set No. 1
1. $x = 2$ A, $y = 3$ A, $z = 5$ A
3. $x = 3$ A, $y = 2$ A, $z = 1$ A
5. $v = 12$ A, $w = 3$ A, $x = 5$ A,
 $y = 10$ A, $z = 2$ A, $E_T = 104$ V
7. $x = 12$ A, $y = 4$ A, $z = 8$ A

Job 8-5: Page 305
Set No. 2
1. $x = 4$ A, $y = 2$ A, $z = 6$ A
3. $x = 1$ A, $y = 0.5$ A, $z = 0.5$ A
5. $v = 6$ A, $w = 5$ A, $x = 3$ A,
 $y = 8$ A, $E_T = 170$ V, $z = 2$ A
7. $x = 7$ A, $y = 3$ A, $z = 4$ A

Job 8-5: Page 305
Set No. 3
1. $x = 0.5$ A, $y = 1.5$ A, $z = 2$ A
3. $x = 0.8$ A, $y = 0.6$ A, $z = 0.2$ A
5. $v = 1$ A, $w = 2.5$ A, $x = 0.5$ A,
 $y = 3$ A, $z = 2$ A, $E_T = 26$ V
7. $x = 5.5$ A, $y = 2$ A, $z = 3.5$ A

Job 8-6: Page 308
9. 223.5 W

Job 8-6: Test—Kirchhoff's Laws:
Page 308
1. (a) $I_T = 1.1$ A
 (b) $E_2 = 11$ V
 $E_3 = 33$ V
 $E_5 = 22$ V
2. $E_T = 60$ V
 $R_3 = 30$ Ω
3. $x = 7$ A, $y = 4$ A, $z = 3$ A
4. $w = 3$ A, $x = 2$ A, $y = 3$ A,
 $z = 1$ A
5. $x = 0.8$ A, $y = 1$ A, $z = 0.2$ A

Job 8-7: Page 315
1. $R_a = R_b = R_c = 20$ Ω
3. $R_a = 6$ Ω
 $R_b = 4$ Ω
 $R_c = 2.4$ Ω
5. $R_{AD} = 3.67$ Ω
7. $R_{AD} = 10.95$ Ω
9. (a) $R_T = 5$ Ω
 (b) $v = 5$ A, $w = 5$ A, $x = 4.5$ A,
 $y = 5.5$ A, $z = 0.5$ A
 (c) $E_T = 50$ V
11. (a) $R_T = 12.67$ Ω
 (b) $v = 4$ A, $w = 6$ A,
 $x = 7.87$ A, $y = 2.13$ A,
 $z = 1.87$ A
 (c) $E_T = 126.7$ V

Job 8-8: Page 327
1. $I_L = 1$ A
 $E_L = 10$ V
3. $I_L = 12$ A
 $E_L = 4.32$ V
5. $I_L = 0.2$ A
 $E_L = 4.6$ V
7. $I_5 = 3$ A

$E_5 = 18$ V
9. $I_L = 0.0025$ A
 $E_L = 25$ V

Job 8-9: Test—Delta Circuits and
Thevenin's Theorem: Page 329
1. $v = 4$ A, $w = 6$ A, $x = 4.8$ A,
 $y = 5.2$ A, $z = 1.2$ A, $E_T = 360$ V
2. (a) $z = 5$ A
 (b) $E_7 = 10$ V

Job 9-1: Page 331
1. 7.2
3. $3,090$
5. $3,700$
7. 0.6
9. $2,700$
11. 0.078
13. $15,400$
15. 1
17. 80
19. $234,000$

Job 9-1: Page 332
1. 65
3. 880
5. 0.06
7. 0.835
9. 0.6538
11. 0.0045
13. 0.0085
15. 0.0286
17. 0.00002

Job 9-1: Page 333
1. 25
3. 0.15
5. 6.25
7. 0.0025
9. 0.00754

Job 9-1: Page 334
1. $1,920$
3. 850
5. $7,200$
7. 0.000045
9. $88,000,000$
11. $3,000$
13. $3,000,000$
15. 0.0006

Job 9-1: Page 335
1. 6×10^3
3. 1.5×10^5
5. 2.35×10^5
7. 4.96×10^3
9. 9.8×10^2
11. 1.25×10

13. 4.82×10
15. 8.8×10^8
17. 3.83×10^4
19. 1.75×10^6
21. 4.83×10^5

Job 9-1: Page 336
1. 6×10^{-3}
3. 3.5×10^{-3}
5. 4.56×10^{-1}
7. 7.85
9. 9.65×10^{-2}
11. 5×10^{-1}
13. 8.15×10^{-3}
15. 7.25×10
17. 6×10^{-1}
19. 3.6×10^{-2}

Job 9-1: Page 338
1. 5
3. 6,400,000 or 6.4×10^6
5. 30,000 or 3×10^4
7. 120
9. 0.03
11. 5×10^{-7}
13. 960
15. 628,000 or 6.28×10^5

Job 9-1: Page 339
1. 10^5
3. 120
5. 0.0002
7. 2×10^{-7}
9. 8
11. 5×10^{-3}
13. (a) 53 Ω
    (b) 63 Ω
    (c) 3.18 Ω

Test—Powers of Ten: Page 340
1. 1.4×10^5
2. 1.75×10^6
3. 8.45×10^{-2}
4. 3.5×10^{-2}
5. 9.6×10^{-6}
6. 7×10^{-2}
7. 0.34
8. 12,000 or 12×10^3
9. 0.0064
10. 0.00078 or 7.8×10^{-4}
11. 10,700 or 10.7×10^3
12. 4×10^6
13. 120
14. 6
15. 10^6
16. 100
17. 16

18. 0.4
19. 50
20. 8×10^4

Job 9-2: Page 343
1. 0.225 A
3. 3,500,000 Ω
5. 550,000 Hz
7. 0.07 MΩ
9. 65 mA
11. 0.075 V
13. 0.006 A
15. 0.0039 A
17. 5,000 pF
19. 1,000,000 Hz
21. 8 mV
23. 60 pF
25. 0.00000015 F
27. 8 kW
29. 4 μA

Job 9-3: Page 344
1. 0.2 mA
3. 0.02 Ω
5. 10 V
7. 215,000 Ω or 215 kΩ
9. 800 Ω
11. 7,500 Ω or 7.5 kΩ
13. 81 W
15. 6 V

Test—Electronic Units of Measurement: Page 345
1. 0.05 MΩ
2. 770,000 Hz
3. 0.1 V
4. 0.0037 A
5. 0.0004 μF
6. 50 μA
7. 25×10^{-10} F
8. 80 mV
9. 0.006 A
10. 2,500,000 Ω
11. 2 V
12. 1 μA
13. 833 Ω
14. 80 Ω
15. 6 V
16. 30 V
17. 2,500 Ω
18. 4 μA
19. 0.00035 μF
20. 525 kΩ

Job 9-4: Page 353
1. (a) $I_{RL} = 1.44$ mA
   (b) $E_{RL} = 7.2$ V

   (c) $V_C = -2.8$ V
3. (a) $I_C = 0.25$ mA
   (b) $I_E = 0.25$ mA
   (c) $E_{RL} = 10$ V
   (d) $V_C = -3$ V
   (e) $E_{RE} = 0.5$ V
   (f) $V_{CE} = 2.5$ V

Job 9-5: Page 356
1. (a) $I_C = 1$ mA
   (b) $E_{RL} = 1$ V
   (c) $V_C = -9$ V
3. (a) $I_E = 3.67$ mA
   (b) $V_E = -0.73$ V
   (c) $I_C = 3.63$ mA
   (d) $E_{RL} = 3.63$ V
   (e) $V_C = -4.37$ V

Job 9-6: Page 360
1. 3 Ω
3. 0.051 Ω
5. 0.747 Ω
7. 0.21 Ω

Job 9-7: Page 361
1. 15 mA
3. 40.4 mA
5. 70.7 A

Job 9-8: Page 365
1. (a) 290,000 Ω
   (b) 168 V
3. (a) 2,995 Ω
   (b) 21.6 V
5. (a) 17,000 Ω
   (b) 51,000 Ω
7. (a) 45,000 Ω
   (b) 95,000 Ω
   (c) 145,000 Ω

Job 9-9: Page 367
1. 0.182 Ω
3. 60.6 mA
5. 1,500 Ω
7. (a) 2,250 Ω
   (b) 12.8 V
9. 0.56 Ω

Test on Meters: Page 368
1. 0.86 Ω
2. 32.5 mA
3. (a) 15 V
   (b) 333 Ω per V
   (c) 25,000 Ω
4. (a) 9,000 Ω
   (b) 58 V
5. (a) 175,000 Ω

(*b*) 108 V

Job 9-10: Page 372
1. $R_1 = 50,000 \ \Omega$
   $R_2 = 7,143 \ \Omega$
   $R_3 = 20,000 \ \Omega$
3. $R_1 = 10,000 \ \Omega$
   $R_2 = 3,333 \ \Omega$
   $R_3 = 1,111 \ \Omega$
5. $R_1 = 10,000 \ \Omega$
   $R_2 = 7,143 \ \Omega$
   $R_3 = 12,500 \ \Omega$

Job 9-11: Page 377
1. $1,250 \ \Omega$
3. $11.1 \ \Omega$
5. $E_k = 33.3$ V
   $E_x = 66.7$ V
7. (*a*) $E_1 = 25.6$ V
   (*b*) $E_2 = 58.1$ V
   (*c*) $E_3 = 116.3$ V
9. 130 V
11. 0.1 V

Job 9-12: Page 380
1. $843 \ \Omega$
3. $6.04 \ \Omega$
5. $1,289 \ \Omega$
7. $465 \ \Omega$
9. $0.16 \ \Omega$

Test on Voltage Dividers and Resistance Measurement: Page 380
1. $R_3 = 7,353 \ \Omega$
   $R_2 = 10,714 \ \Omega$
   $R_1 = 50,000 \ \Omega$
2. 70 V
3. $400 \ \Omega$
4. 90 V
5. $1,480 \ \Omega$

Job 9-13: Page 385
1. $R_1 = 12 \ \Omega, R_2 = 3.75 \ \Omega$
3. $R_1 = 5 \ \Omega, R_2 = 5.45 \ \Omega$
5. $R_1 = 36 \ \Omega, R_2 = 40 \ \Omega$
7. $R_1 = 20 \ \Omega, R_2 = 400 \ \Omega$
9. $R_1 = 75 \ \Omega, R_2 = 33.3 \ \Omega$

Job 9-13: Page 388
1. $R_1 = R_3 = 20 \ \Omega$
   $R_2 = 80 \ \Omega$
3. $R_1 = R_3 = 20 \ \Omega$
   $R_2 = 80 \ \Omega$
5. $R_1 = R_3 = 7.14 \ \Omega$
   $R_2 = 3.43 \ \Omega$
7. $R_1 = R_3 = 77.7 \ \Omega$
   $R_2 = 25.3 \ \Omega$

Test on Attenuator Circuits: Page 388
1. $R_1 = 45.6 \ \Omega, R_2 = 2.53 \ \Omega$
2. $R_1 = R_3 = 5 \ \Omega, R_2 = 20 \ \Omega$
3. $R_1 = 600 \ \Omega, R_2 = 266.7 \ \Omega$
4. $R_1 = R_3 = 66.7 \ \Omega,$
   $R_2 = 266.7 \ \Omega$

Job 10-1: Page 389
1. $100 \ \Omega$
2. 0.765 lb
3. 17.25 A
4. No
5. 70.5 V
6. 90 percent
7. 93.3 percent
8. 57.6 W
9. 117.6 V
10. $81.25
11. $79.62
12. 25 percent
13. $3.33
14. 12.8 oz
15. 90 percent

Job 10-2: Page 390
1. 0.38
3. 0.06
5. 0.04
7. 0.036
9. 1.25
11. 0.167
13. 0.625
15. 0.125
17. 0.0225
19. 0.0425

Job 10-2: Page 391
1. 50 percent
3. 20 percent
5. 145 percent
7. 100 percent
9. $62\frac{1}{2}$ percent
11. 22.2 percent
13. 70 percent
15. $5\frac{1}{2}$ percent

Job 10-2: Page 392
1. 25 percent
3. 40 percent
5. $62\frac{1}{2}$ percent
7. 30 percent
9. 50 percent
11. 65 percent
13. $66\frac{2}{3}$ percent
15. 45.4 percent
17. $33\frac{1}{3}$ percent

19. 22.2 percent

Job 10-2: Page 393
1. 33
3. $7.50
5. $37.50
7. 17.25 A
9. 116.7 V
11. 5
13. 7.5 W
15. $19.18

Job 10-2: Page 395
1. 25 percent
3. 40 percent
5. 2 percent
7. 150 percent
9. $33\frac{1}{3}$ percent
11. $12\frac{1}{2}$ percent
13. 40 percent
15. 2.4 percent
17. 20 percent
19. 5 percent

Job 10-2: Page 396
1. 20
3. 40
5. 2,000
7. $82
9. 15 A

Job 10-2: Page 397
1. (*a*) 0.62
   (*b*) 0.03
   (*c*) 0.056
   (*d*) 0.008
   (*e*) 1.16
   (*f*) 0.045
   (*g*) 0.0625
3. (*a*) 75 percent
   (*b*) 60 percent
   (*c*) 42.9 percent
   (*d*) 30 percent
   (*e*) 23.1 percent
   (*f*) $16\frac{2}{3}$ percent
   (*g*) 46.1 percent
5. $90
7. 40 percent
9. $48.75
11. 20.8 percent
13. 1.5 percent
15. 48
17. $30, $110, $5.72
19. 0.9 W = 1 W

Test on Percent: Page 398
1. (*a*) 375 percent

(b) 68 percent
(c) 0.7 percent
(d) 150 percent
2. (a) 0.015
(b) 0.08
(c) 0.35
(d) 0.375
3. $21.25, $63.75
4. 95 percent
5. 155.6 V

Job 10-3: Page 399
1. 6,500 W
3. 2.3 kW
5. 50 W
7. ³⁄₄ kW
9. 1.69 kW
11. 0.094 kW
13. 5.33 hp
15. 13¹⁄₃ hp

Job 10-4: Page 401
1. 83¹⁄₃ percent
3. 60 percent
5. 96 percent
7. 88.9 percent
9. 91.3 percent
11. 80.2 percent; 19.8 percent

Job 10-5: Page 404
1. 3.6 hp
3. 0.587 hp
5. 4,508 W
7. 2,647 W
9. 2,200 W, 3.26 hp
11. 220 V

Job 10-6: Page 405
1. (a) 0.5 kW
(b) ²⁄₃ hp
(c) 1,500 W
(d) 1,125 W
(e) 13.3 hp
(f) 7.5 kW
3. 91.4 percent
5. 0.62 hp
7. 0.625 kW

Test on Conversion Factors and Efficiency: Page 406
1. (a) 0.7 kW
(b) 1,313 W
(c) 4.8 hp
(d) 6 kW
2. 83.3 percent
3. 2.64 hp

4. 2.2 kW
5. 7.66 A

Job 11-1: Page 408
1. 18 hp-hr
3. 18 hp-hr
5. 2.4 kW-hr
7. 2,618 watthr
9. 0.64 kWhr

Job 11-2: Page 410
1. $1.50
3. $0.18
5. $1.08
7. $0.07
9. $0.34

Job 11-2: Page 411
1. $0.04
3. $0.08
5. $0.14
7. $.81; about one-tenth of the battery cost

Job 11-2: Page 412
1. 0.2 kWhr, $0.01
3. $0.25
5. $0.19

Job 11-3: Page 413
1. 3.75 hp-hr
3. 0.85 kWhr
5. $1.12
7. $0.42
9. $0.15

Test on Cost of Energy: Page 413
1. 3¹⁄₃ kWhr
2. $0.11
3. $0.26
4. $0.11

Job 12-1: Page 414
1. 2:5
2. 4:1
3. 9:1
4. 10:11
5. 3:4
6. 0.007 Ω
7. $8.75
8. 45 oz
9. 15 V
10. 104 Ω
11. $\dfrac{R_1}{R_2} = \dfrac{I_2}{I_1}$
12. 2 V

Job 12-2: Page 418
1. 1:4
3. 2:3
5. 2:1
7. 4:1
9. (a) 3:2
(b) 2:3
11. 1:4
13. 1:4
15. 83.3 percent
17. 171
19. 40
21. 10
23. 1:48
25. (a) 2 V
(b) 1.7 percent
(c) 98.3 percent

Job 12-2: Page 422
1. 2,750 lb
3. 4¹⁄₂ hr
5. 71.4 ft³
7. 1,000 Ω
9. 45 V

Job 12-2: Page 425
1. 5 in
3. 66.7
5. 500
7. 0.08 A
9. 0.93 Ω
11. 0.25 A

Job 12-3: Page 426
1. (a) 1:3
(b) 1:6
(c) 1:10
(d) 5:8
(e) 3:4
3. 36
5. 72
7. 0.6 A
9. 110 V

Test on Ratio and Proportion: Page 427
1. (a) 10:3
(b) 1:4
(c) 1:2
(d) 1:5
(e) 8:1
2. (a) 3:5
(b) 4:5, or 80 percent
(c) 35:36
(d) 1:100
3. 500 turns

4. 140 Ω

Job 12-4: Page 430
1. No. 21, 0.0285 in
3. No. 2, 250 mils
5. No. 6, 162 mils
7. 64.08 mils, 0.0641 in
9. No. 18, 0.0403 in

Job 12-4: Page 431
1. 0.010 in, 100 cir mils
3. 0.064 in, 64 mils
5. 32 mils, 1,024 cir mils
7. 0.0872 in, 7,604 cir mils
9. 0.173 in, 173 mils

Job 12-5: Page 433
1. 19.6 Ω
3. 12.5 Ω

Job 12-6: Page 434
1. 3.68 Ω
3. 4.06 Ω
5. 1.205 Ω, 5 A
7. 32.82 Ω, 3.35 A
9. 33.7 Ω, 6.74 V

Job 12-7: Page 436
1. 52.5 Ω
3. 508 Ω
5. 12.86 Ω

Job 12-8: Page 438
1. 0.104 Ω
3. 0.0062 Ω
5. 4.46 Ω, 24.6 A, 2.71 kW
7. (a) 0.145 A
   (b) 0.87 W
9. 0.2 V

Job 12-9: Page 440
1. 1.7 Ω
3. 96.1 ft
5. 3 ft
7. 370 ft
9. Nichrome

Job 12-10: Page 442
1. 9.4 mils
3. 6.93 mils
5. 32.2 mils
7. No. 17

Job 12-11: Page 443
1. (a) 25 mils, No. 22
   (b) 102 mils, No. 10
   (c) 125 mils, No. 8
   (d) 128 mils, No. 8

3. 44.9 Ω
5. 1.4 Ω
7. 3.07 ft

Test on Resistance of Wires: Page 444
1. 23 Ω
2. (a) 23.6 Ω
   (b) 0.42 A
   (c) 4.2 W
3. 1.67 ft
4. 91.2 mils, 0.0912 in

Job 13-1: Page 447
1. 50 A
3. No. 6
5. 31.4 V
7. 0.00025 Ω per ft
9. No. 3

Job 13-2: Page 449
1. No. 6
3. No. 4
5. No. 1

Job 13-3: Page 453
1. No. 4
3. No. 0
5. No. 3
7. No. 8
9. (a) 5,250 W
   (b) 250 W
   (c) 44 A
   (d) 5.7 V
   (e) No. 1
11. 450 ft

Job 13-4: Page 455
1. 40 A
3. No. 3
5. No. 14
7. No. 8
9. No. 1
11. No. 12

Test on Size of Wiring: Page 455
1. (a) 40 A
   (b) No. 8
   (c) No. 6
   (d) 80.8 mils
2. No. 14
3. No. 4
4. No. 00

Job 14-1: Page 462
1. sin = 0.2462
   cos = 0.9692

   tan = 0.2540
3. sin = 0.3243
   cos = 0.9459
   tan = 0.3428
5. sin = 0.8823
   cos = 0.4706
   tan = 1.8750

Job 14-2: Page 465 (Top)
1. 18°
3. 80°
5. 30°
7. 30°
9. 60°

Job 14-2: Page 465 (Bottom)
1. 15°
3. 58°
5. 65°
7. 16°
9. 46°

Job 14-3: Page 467

	∠A	∠B
1.	53°	37°
3.	30°	60°
5.	55°	35°
7.	51°	39°
9.	11°	79°

11. 67°, 113°
13. 3°
15. 58°

Job 14-4: Page 472
1. 10 in, 30°
3. 89.4 ft, 40°
5. 151 Ω, 60°
7. 940.4 ft, 62°
9. 123 Ω, 75°
11. 87.7 ft, 82.4 ft
13. 3.54 in
15. 27.2 ft
17. $I_x = 12.69$ A, $I_y = 5.92$ A
19. $X_C = 728$ Ω

Job 14-5: Page 474
1. 0.5878
3. 2.6051
5. 0.9063
7. 65°
9. 11°
11. 17°
13. 73°
15. 37°
17. 71°
19. 58°

21. 930 W
23. 38.5
25. 833 Ω
27. 2,828 W
29. 236 V
31. 81°, 99°
33. 3°
35. 1.72 in
37. 23°
39. 233.3 Ω

Test on Trigonometry: Page 475
1. (*a*) 48°
   (*b*) 42°
   (*c*) 71°
2. $B = 64°$; $A = 26°$
3. 64.3
4. 16.1
5. 60
6. 112.7 ft
7. 26.6 ft
8. 61°
9. 2,309
10. 1,155 Ω

Job 15−1: Page 482
1. (*a*) 0.54 A
   (*b*) 0.63 A
   (*c*) 0.66 A
   (*d*) 0.72 A
   (*e*) 0.79 A
   (*f*) 0.87 A
   (*g*) 0.99 A
5. Max eff = 80 percent; 50 hp

Job 15−3: Page 495
1. 10,000 meters
3. 126.4 V
5. 17°
7. 43.3 A
9. (*a*) 30°
   (*b*) 37°
   (*c*) 60°

Job 15−4: Page 499

	MAX	EFF	INSTANT
1.	——	24.7	17.5
3.	622	——	476
5.	——	109.6	77.5
7.	155.5	——	140.9
9.	35	24.7	——
11.	——	70.7	26°

13. 17.3 V
15. (*a*) 10.6 A
    (*b*) 900 W

Test on AC Waves: Page 500
1. Graph
2. $E = 212$ V
   $e = 150$ V
3. Max = 70.7 mA
   $i = 61.2$ mA
4. Max = 129.4 V
   $E = 91.5$ V
5. 56°; $E = 141.4$ V

Job 16−2: Page 506
1. (*a*) 439.6 Ω
   (*b*) 8,792 Ω
3. (*a*) 7,536 Ω
   (*b*) 0.02 A
5. 37.7 Ω
7. 5 H
9. 62,800 Ω
11. 2,864 Ω
13. 2.7 mH
15. 255 μH

Job 16−3: Page 508
1. 10^{10}
3. 9×10^6
5. 10^{10}
7. 64×10^6
9. 121×10^4
11. 625×10^{-10}

Job 16−3: Page 510
1. 10^4
3. $4 \times 10^2 = 400$
5. $4 \times 10^2 = 400$
7. 0.005
9. 60
11. $6.32 \times 10^2 = 632$
13. 4
15. $2 \times 10^2 = 200$
17. $1.732 \times 10^3 = 1,732$

Job 16−4: Page 513
1. 4
3. 31.4
5. (*a*) 10
   (*b*) 1,000 Ω
7. (*a*) 9,420 Ω
   (*b*) 10,664 Ω
   (*c*) 3.8 mA
9. (*a*) 314 Ω
   (*b*) 330 Ω
11. 0.7 mA

Job 16−5: Page 515
1. 3.18 H
3. 0.796 H
5. 0.51 H

Job 16−6: Page 516
1. (*a*) 125.6 Ω
   (*b*) 1,256 Ω
   (*c*) 12,560 Ω
   (*d*) 125,600 Ω
3. 3,140 Ω
5. 60
7. 30 Ω
9. 0.61 H

Test on Coils: Page 517
1. 37,680 Ω, 0.3 mA
2. 192 Ω
3. 157,000 Ω
4. 6.36 H
5. 1.59 H

Job 16−7: Page 520
1. 360 V
3. (*a*) 48:1
   (*b*) 48:1
5. 600 turns
7. 6,000 V
9. 1.5 V
11. 300 turns
13. 240 V
15. (*a*) 2 turns
    (*b*) 5¼ turns
    (*c*) 500 turns

Job 16−8: Page 524
1. 2 A
3. (*a*) 0.16 A
   (*b*) 19.2 W
5. (*a*) 0.136 A
   (*b*) 7.5 V
7. (*a*) 0.086 A
   (*b*) 9.45 W
9. (*a*) 5 A
   (*b*) 1,500 V
11. 511 A

Job 16−9: Page 526
1. 87.5 percent
3. (*a*) 180 W
   (*b*) 168 W
   (*c*) 93.3 percent
5. 80 percent
7. (*a*) 10,417 W
   (*b*) 5.21 A
9. (*a*) 77 W
   (*b*) 88 V

Job 16−10: Page 530
1. 20:1
3. 4:1
5. 1:5
7. 12,100 Ω

9. 41.8 : 1 or 42:1 (approx)
11. 31.6 : 1 or 32:1 (approx)
13. 2.9 : 1 or 3:1 (approx)
15. 28,800 Ω

Job 16−11: Page 532
1. (a) 176 turns
   (b) 8:1
3. 1,750 turns
5. (a) 100 turns
   (b) 22.7 turns
7. (a) 1.25 A
   (b) 150 W
9. (a) 0.063 A
   (b) 7.56 W
11. 93.3 percent
13. 12.5 : 1
15. (a) 240 V
   (b) 12 A
   (c) 40 mA
   (d) 2,880 W

Test on Transformers: Page 533
1. 13 turns
2. (a) 1.33 A
   (b) 18 V
3. (a) 200 W
   (b) 1.67 A
4. 3.16 : 1
5. 50,000 Ω

Job 17−2: Page 538
1. 373 pF
3. 5,065 pF
5. 30,085 pF
7. 150 pF

Job 17−3: Page 542
1. 1.333 μF
3. 19 pF
5. 31 to 162 pF
7. 3 μF

Job 17−4: Page 546
1. (a) 17,667 Ω
   (b) 5,300 Ω
   (c) 662 Ω
3. 0.19 A
5. 400 pF; 3,975 Ω
7. 1.67 μF
9. (a) 15.9 Ω
   (b) 3.18 Ω
   (c) 0.795 Ω
11. 13,250 Ω
13. 0.00133 μF
15. 0.5 A
17. 0.75 Ω
19. 60.2 μF

Job 17−5: Page 548
1. 41 Ω
3. 15,900 Ω (the resistance may be neglected)
5. 10,500 Ω

Job 17−6: Page 550
1. 2.65 μF
3. 2.94 μF
5. 10 μF

Job 17−7: Page 551
1. 0.0497 μF
3. 1.6 μF
5. 187 pF
7. (a) 26.5 Ω
   (b) 0.053 Ω
9. 44.7 Ω
11. 0.318 μF

Test on Capacitance: Page 552
1. 0.001 μF
2. 2.18 μF
3. 640 Ω
4. 1.59 μF
5. 830 pF

Job 18−1: Page 556
1. 60 Ω
3. 0.222 A
5. 150 Ω, 96 W
7. 0.4 A, 44 W
9. 600 W

Job 18−1: Page 559
1. 1 A
3. 25.12 V
5. 3,000 Ω, 7.96 H

Job 18−1: Page 562
1. (a) 2.25 A
   (b) 0 W
3. 124 Ω
5. 39.75 Ω, 0.1 A
7. 0.25 mA
9. 100 Ω, 0.00159 μF

Job 18−2: Page 565
1. 10
3. 16
5. 26.5
7. 4.5
9. 144.2 ft
11. 7.62 ft
13. 46 ft
15. 32 in

Job 18−3: Page 572
1. (a) 13 Ω

(b) 8 A
(c) $E_R = 40$ V
   $E_L = 96$ V
(d) 67°
(e) 321 W
3. 0.92 A, 74°
5. (a) 150 Ω
   (b) 170 Ω
   (c) 85 V
7. 1.5 μA
9. 4.5 A
11. 3,770 Ω, 0.01 A
13. 28.6 H
15. $X_L = 7.5$ Ω; 43°

Job 18−4: Page 577
1. (a) 17 Ω
   (b) 7 A
   (c) $E_R = 56$ V
   $E_C = 105$ V
   (d) 62°
   (e) 392 W
3. (a) 141 Ω
   (b) 0.8 A
   (c) $E_R = 80$ V
   $E_C = 80$ V
   (d) 45°
   (e) 64 W
5. 159,000 Ω, 18,800 Ω
7. (a) 500 Ω
   (b) 400 Ω
   (c) 6.63 μF
9. 113 Hz

Job 18−5: Page 584
1. (a) 65 Ω
   (b) 2 A
   (c) $E_R = 32$ V
   $E_L = 166$ V
   $E_C = 40$ V
   (d) 76°
   (e) 64 W
3. (a) $X_L = 6,280$ Ω
   $X_C = 3,180$ Ω
   (b) 5,060 Ω
   (c) 0.025 A
   (d) 37°
   (e) 2.47 W
5. 0.7 V
7. 1.5 A
9. 271 Ω

Job 18−6: Page 588
1. (a) 795 kHz
   (b) 50 Ω
3. (a) 2 kHz
   (b) 502 Ω

(c) 502 Ω
(d) 12 Ω
(e) 0.5 A
(f) 251 V
5. 1,988 kHz
7. 1,988 kHz
9. 1,590 kHz

Job 18-7: Page 592
1. 84.3 μH
3. 0.506 H
5. 35.1 μF
7. 72 μH
9. 2.53 mH

Job 18-8: Page 594
1. 180 V
3. 5.3 H
5. (a) 6,360 Ω
   (b) 7.9 mA
   (c) $E_R = 7.9$ V
       $E_L = 49.6$ V
   (d) 81°
   (e) 0.06 W
7. (a) 41.2 Ω
   (b) 4,790 Ω
9. 71.3 kHz

Test on Series AC Circuits: Page 595
1. (a) 17,000 Ω
   (b) 7 mA
   (c) 28°
2. (a) 3,723 Ω
   (b) 0.027 A
   (c) $E_R = 54$ V
       $E_L = 84.8$ V
   (d) 58°
   (e) 1.45 W
3. (a) 552 Ω
   (b) 0.025 A
   (c) 25°
4. 1,590 kHz
5. 0.01 H

Job 19-1: Page 602
1. (a) 14.4 A
   (b) 8.33 Ω
   (c) 1,728 W
3. (a) 1.5 A
   (b) 66.7 Ω
   (c) 0 W
5. 0.11 A, 1,636 Ω; 0 W
7. (a) 0.159 A, 0.064 A
   (b) 0.223 A
   (c) 538 Ω
   (d) 0 W

Job 19-2: Page 607
1. (a) 13 A
   (b) 9.23 Ω
   (c) 67°
   (d) 601 W
3. (a) 2.15 A
   (b) 46.5 Ω
   (c) 22°
   (d) 200 W
5. 70 percent, 100 percent; Yes, but not a good filter, since it also passes low frequencies.

Job 19-3: Page 611
1. (a) 17 A
   (b) 7.06 Ω
   (c) 28°
   (d) 1,799 W
3. (a) 2.23 A
   (b) 53.9 Ω
   (c) 63°
   (d) 120 W
5. 0.566 A
7. 44.8 percent AF, 0.05 percent RF; Yes, but not a good one.
9. 200 μA

Job 19-4: Page 617
1. $R = 7.2$ Ω; $C = 276$ μF
3. $R = 28.2$ Ω; $L = 16$ mH
5. (a) 4.12 A
   (b) 29.1 Ω
   (c) 14° leading
   (d) 480 W
   (e) $R = 28.2$ Ω; $C = 376$ μF
7. (a) $X_L = 7,536$ Ω
       $X_C = 3,312$ Ω
   (b) $I_L = 0.029$ A
       $I_C = 0.066$ A
       $I_R = 0.1$ A
   (c) 0.106 A
   (d) 2,075 Ω
   (e) 19° leading
   (f) 22 W
   (g) $R = 1,963$ Ω; $C = 3.9$ μF

Job 19-5: Page 622
1. $I_x = 17.32$ A
   $I_y = 10$ A
3. $I_x = 10$ A
   $I_y = -17.32$ A
5. $I_x = 19.32$ A
   $I_y = 17.4$ A
7. $I_x = 64.3$ mA
   $I_y = -76.6$ mA
9. $I_x = 12.69$ A
   $I_y = 5.92$ A

Job 19-6: Page 635
1. (a) 23.4 A
   (b) 5.13 Ω
   (c) 35° leading
   (d) 2,305 W
3. (a) 14.1 A
   (b) 7.09 Ω
   (c) 0°
   (d) 1,410 W
5. (a) 1.8 A
   (b) 55.5 Ω
   (c) 48° lagging
   (d) 120 W

Job 19-7: Page 640
1. (a) $Z = 21.1$ Ω
   (b) $I_T = 4.74$ A
   (c) $\theta = 17°$ lagging
   (d) $P = 454$ W
3. (a) $Z = 60.7$ Ω
   (b) $L_T = 1.98$ A
   (c) $\theta = 31°$ lagging
   (d) $P = 204$ W
5. (a) $Z = 30.9$ Ω
   (b) $I_T = 3.9$ A
   (c) $\theta = 12°$ leading
   (d) $P = 457$ W

Job 19-8: Page 643
1. 5,300 kHz
3. 400 pF
5. 80 pF
7. 0.92 μH
9. 2.45 mH

Job 19-9: Page 646
1. (a) 0.083 A
   (b) 301 Ω
   (c) 0 W
3. (a) $I_R = 0.5$ A
       $I_L = 0.16$ A
   (b) $I_T = 0.52$ A
   (c) 192 Ω
   (d) 16°
   (e) 50 W
5. (a) 128 mA
   (b) 1,875 Ω
   (c) 51°
   (d) 19.2 W
7. (a) 17.1 A
   (b) 7 Ω
   (c) 31° leading
   (d) 1,756 W
9. 120 μH
11. (a) 10 Ω
    (b) $I_T = 10$ A
    (c) 37° leading

(d) 800 W

**Test on Parallel AC Circuits:
Page 648**
1. (a) 8.5 A
   (b) 14.1 Ω
   (c) 0 W
2. (a) $X_L = 314$ Ω
   $X_C = 159$ Ω
   (b) $I_R = 0.1$ A
   $I_L = 0.318$ A
   $I_C = 0.629$ A
   (c) 0.327 A
   (d) 306 Ω
   (e) 72°
   (f) 10 W
3. (a) 10.3 A
   (b) 11.7 Ω
   (c) 12° lagging
   (d) 1,208 W
4. 119 pF

Job 20–1: Page 654
1. 80 percent
3. 20,000 volt-amp
5. 2.5 A
7. 3,450 volt-amp, 2,933 W
9. 10,417 volt-amp
11. 40 A

Job 20–2: Page 662
1. (a) 1,232 W
   (b) 80 percent leading
   (c) 1,540 volt-amp
   (d) 14 A
3. (a) 1,650 W
   (b) 89.9 percent
   (c) 1,835 volt-amp
   (d) 16.7 A
5. (a) 27 kW
   (b) 54.5 percent
   (c) 49.5 kV-amp
7. (a) 13 kW
   (b) 73.1 percent
   (c) 17.8 kV-amp
   (d) 80.9 A
9. (a) 72 kW
   (b) 64.3 percent

(c) 112 kV-amp

Job 20–3: Page 668
1. (a) 950 W
   (b) 99.8 percent
   (c) 952 volt-amp
3. (a) 5,680 W
   (b) 92.1 percent
   (c) 6,167 volt-amp
   (d) 51.4 A
5. 98.8 percent
7. (a) 22 kW
   (b) 90.6 percent
   (c) 24.28 kV-amp
   (d) 105.6 A
9. (a) 1,584 W
   (b) 94.6 percent
   (c) 1,674 volt-amp
   (d) 13.95 A

Job 20–4: Page 675
1. 17.4 percent
3. 58.8 percent
5. 38 μF
7. 6.67 kV-amp

Job 20–5: Page 678
1. 28 percent, 4.8 A
3. (a) 1,944 W
   (b) 90 percent
   (c) 2,160 volt-amp
   (d) 18 A
5. (a) 22.5 kW
   (b) 62.9 percent
   (c) 35.8 kV-amp
7. (a) 1,936 W
   (b) 99.5 percent
   (c) 1,946 volt-amp
   (d) 16.6 A
9. 45.4 percent

Test on AC Power: Page 679
1. (a) 14.3 kW
   (b) 97.8 percent
   (c) 14.6 kV-amp
   (d) 63.5 A
2. (a) 3,659 volt-amp
   (b) 2,100 var

(c) 386 μF

**Answers to Odd-numbered
Appendix Problems: Page 682**
1. 100,000 Ω
3. 82,000 Ω
5. 75 Ω
7. 4.7 Ω
9. 1.2 Ω
11. 1,800,000 Ω
13. 620 Ω
15. 9,100 Ω
17. 0.47 Ω
19. 82 Ω
21. Red, yellow, yellow
23. Green, brown, black
25. Brown, black, blue
27. Orange, white, red
29. Brown, red, black
31. Blue, gray, silver
33. Red, red, gold
35. Brown, gray, gold
37. Orange, blue, brown
39. Brown, green, gold

Page 686
1. 51 pF
3. 560 pF, 2 percent
5. 10,000 pF
7. 360 pF, 4 percent
9. 815 pF, 8 percent
11. 450,000 pF, 5 percent
13. 910 pF
15. 15,400 pF, 20 percent
17. 25,000 pF, 20 percent
19. 43 pF
21. 2,600 pF, 8 percent, 400 V
23. 18 pF, 2 percent
25. 36 pF, 5 percent
27. 12 pF, 3 percent
29. 36,000 pF, 10 percent, 500 V
31. 68 pF, 5 percent
33. 2,400 pF, 6 percent
35. 270 pF, 10 percent, 100 V
37. 820 pF, 10 percent, 500 V
39. 75,000 pF, 20 percent, 500 V

INDEX

SYMBOLS AND ABBREVIATIONS

Term	Symbol	Abbreviation	Term	Symbol	Abbreviation
Alternating current		ac	Microfarad	C	μF
Ampere (unit of current)	I	A	Micromicrofarad	C	pF
Milliampere		mA	Picofarad	C	pF
Microampere		μa	Foot		ft
American Wire Gage		AWG	Frequency	f	freq
Apparent power	VA	va	Audio		AF
Angle	$\angle$		Intermediate		IF
Area	A		High		HF
Circular mils		cirmils	Low		LF
Square inches		sq. in.	Radio		RF
Base	B		Resonant		f
Candlepower		cp	Grid	G	
Capacitance	C		Ground		gnd
Collector	C		Henry (unit of	L	H
Constant	K		inductance)		
Continuous wave		cw	Millihenry	L	mH
Cosine		cos	Microhenry	L	μH
Coulomb	Q		Hertz		Hz
Current	I		High pass		h·p
Average value	I_{av}		Horsepower		hp
Change in current	ΔI		Horsepower-hour		hp-h
Effective value	I		Hour	T	h
Instantaneous current	i		Impedance	Z	
Maximum value	I_{max}		Inch		in
Cycles			Inductance	L	
Cycles per second		Hz	Kilo (1,000)		k
Kilocycles per second		kHz	Low pass		l-p
Megacycles per second		MHz	Maximum		max
Decibel		db	Mega (1,000,000)		M
Delta (Greek letter)	Δ		Micro (one-millionth)		μ
Diameter	D, d	diam	Micromicro (one millionth		
Degree	$°$	deg	of a millionth)		p
Diode	D		Milli (one-thousandth)		m
Direct current		dc	Minimum		min
Efficiency		Eff	Ohm (unit of resistance)	R	Ω
Electromotive force	E	emf	Pi (Greek letter)	π	
Emitter	E		Pico		p
Energy	W		Phase angle (theta)	Θ	
Farad (unit of	C	F	Power	P	
capacitance)			Apparent power	VA	